Seal of Henry VII (1485–1509)

Seal of Charles I (1625–1649)

Seal of Queen Anne (1702–1714)

All courtesy New York Public Library

THE
ENGLISH

A HISTORY OF
POLITICS AND SOCIETY
TO 1760

Norman F. Cantor

SIMON AND SCHUSTER

NEW YORK

To Howard and Judy

Contents

Illustrations

There are two sections of illustrations. The first section (covering the period between 950 and 1470) follows page 96. The second section (covering the period between 1470 and 1760) follows page 320.

Preface

I HAVE tried in this book to present to the general reader an understanding of the course of English political and social history from about 450 A.D. to the middle of the eighteenth century. I have sought not to provide a conventional narrative of events but instead to impart a sense of the political and legal experience of the English people in the context of economic and intellectual change. I have tried to explain what institutions meant in the daily life of society and I have also attempted to give the reader an impression of the leading personalities of English history.

This volume is concerned with English politics and society in the pre-industrial world. A subsequent volume will be devoted to England since the industrial revolution.

There are two fundamental assumptions running through this book that condition its form and direction. The first is a commitment to the principles of liberalism and a corollary belief that the historian has both a right and a duty to make moral judgments and, as Lord Acton said, "never to debase the moral currency." The second is the belief that to a very considerable extent history is an imaginative construction of the past by historians; consequently I have devoted much attention to the various schools of interpretation of English history, and to the debates among historians on critical problems.

This book is an attempt at a work of synthesis, and I hope that I have made clear in the following pages how much I owe to the labor and insight of other scholars.

In the writing of this book, I have drawn heavily upon a course of lectures on English constitutional history that I gave at Columbia University in 1963–64. I wish to acknowledge the extensive assistance given me by my former graduate student, Miss Barbara M. Delman, in the work of turning these lectures into expository prose. Miss Delman also did most of the work involved in selecting the illustrations.

Another former graduate student of mine, Mr. Martin Baron, now an instructor at Columbia University, read parts of the manuscript and gave me valuable criticism. Mr. Michael S. Werthman and Mr. Eli Zabar, also my former students, helped me in the later stages of work on the manuscript. I wish to acknowledge the assistance of several people in the typing of various drafts of the book. These are: Miss Prudence Costa, Miss Carol Berkin, Miss Kathleen Bolster, Mrs. Audrey Neck, and Miss Michele Smith. During the four years that were devoted to this book, my wife's encouragement and assistance were instrumental in achieving the completion of the work.

My friends Herman Ausubel, Eugene Black, Sidney A. Burrell, and Leonard Levy were consulted at various times by me during the writing of this book and I have benefited greatly from their profound knowledge of English history. But I wish to emphasize that I am alone responsible for any error, either in fact or inference, that may be found in this book.

In the writing of this book, I was greatly helped by generous grants from the Columbia University Social Science Research Council and from Brandeis University.

Chapter Eight, part IV, was originally published, in slightly condensed form, in the March 1966 issue of the *Political Science Quarterly*.

N.F.C.

March, 1967
Lexington, Mass.

CHAPTER ONE

INTRODUCTION:
THE SHAPE OF
ENGLISH HISTORY

I. *The Use of English History*

FORTY YEARS AGO, when the sun never set on the British empire, the value of English history appeared self-evident. Great Britain still seemed to be the greatest military and economic power in the world, and it was necessary for all educated men to be acquainted with the course of English history. These propositions are no longer easily tenable, with the virtual extinction of the British empire and the decline of England to a second- or third-rate power in terms of military and economic potential. It now seems clear that English hegemony in Europe and the world was a brief and transient thing and that far from being determined by long-range historical laws, as the English themselves and American Anglophiles used to think, it was due to a single cause: the Industrial Revolution—as a result of a happy combination of economic circumstances—occurred in England a half century or so before any other country. Now that many other states with far greater population and resources have experienced the industrialization and urbanization which took place in England in the latter part of the eighteenth century, the English have lost their leadership in the world to others.

Therefore if we wish to be realistic about the utility and purpose of studying the history of England, we can no longer justify it in terms of English dominance in the contemporary world. We have to ask what is there distinctive and unique about the English contribution to civilization: in what area of human endeavor does England's greatness lie? As we have seen, it does not consist of any distinctive achievement in economic enterprises because the economic development of England, though very interesting, is in retrospect far from being singular or unique. Unless one has a peculiar taste for Sir Edward Elgar or Gilbert and Sullivan, the English greatness certainly does not lie in musical accomplishment. The English have produced two or three outstanding scientists and two or three brilliant philosophers, but in these areas the Germans, the French, and the Americans have probably excelled to a greater degree. In belletristic literature, particularly in poetry, the English contribution has been second to none, but while the historian ought to take into account this singular success and try to relate it to social change, he had best leave the history of English literature to critics and literary scholars.

It becomes evident that the English achievement is in politics and law. The English developed the common law, which stands beside Roman law as one of the two great legal systems of the Western world, and this common law, in modified form, is operative today throughout the English-speaking world. It is also the legal system which in the opinion of many has been more protective of the rights of the individual and more conducive to the flourishing of human dignity and freedom than any other. In the area of politics and government the English record is equally astonishing in retrospect. It is generally recognized that of all the European peoples, the English achieved the greatest success in the creation and working of political institutions which foster social peace and national welfare. It was the English who created through parliamentary government the liberal representative institutions which, for better or worse, have been emulated throughout the civilized world during the past hundred years. It is also generally assumed that at least since the middle of the nineteenth century the English have shown more respect for the civil rights of the individual than has any other country, and they have to a degree probably unparalleled elsewhere maintained in political life the spirit of moral decency and fair play.

Even without a personal commitment to those ideals of liberalism which were largely an English invention, it would have to be admitted that on strictly pragmatic grounds the English must be considered the most successful political society in world history. No other country has had such a remarkable degree of continuity in the history of its political institutions. Except for the second half of the eleventh century there was no case of a radical interruption of political development because of the invasion of an alien conqueror. And except for the seventeenth-century aberrations and revolutions, the consequences of which have long been absorbed into a common social consensus, England never suffered violent internal upheaval. This is not to say that there were not several other moments of great crisis and controversy in England, for there were several other eras when the common consensus was on the verge of breakdown, and disintegration and revolution threatened, but somehow the English managed to avert those long series of debilitating upheavals which mark the histories of other European countries. It is especially remarkable that alone among the important peoples of the Western world, in the nineteenth century the English did not experience a civil war or revolution. Only in England among the great states of Western Europe in this century do we find that the agonizing effects of the First World War and the Great Depression did not result in the triumph of totalitarianism, as was the case in Germany, Italy, and Spain, or in the collapse of the moral bases of government, as occurred in France.

The primary purpose of studying English history is therefore to account for the distinctive character of English political life. It is obvious that the history of English government has to be considered within the context of social, economic, and intellectual change, which provided the dimensions within which the English political experience operated. It is also obvious that the study of English history demands consideration of England's place in Europe and in the world. But the theme that gives value and meaning to the study of English history must in all eras be the ways in which this peculiar island people developed their governmental and legal institutions and ideas.

It must be stated at the outset that although Victorian historians of England sometimes attributed the national political success to an innate racial genius, this view can no longer be sustained in terms of either modern anthropological knowledge or what we know to be the extremely mixed ethnic composition of the English people, at least after the middle of the eleventh century. Ethnically the English came to be a mixture of German, Scandinavian, Celtic, and French peoples, and yet the political history of Germany, Scandinavia, France, and the Celtic lands is markedly different in several important ways from that of England.

It can be said that the geographical-topographical nature of England should be regarded as a much more significant conditioning factor in the development of English institutions than any doubtful racial stereotype. As an island, England was saved from that continual series of invading armies which so disrupted the development of government and society in Germany and Italy. There can be no doubt that the English Channel played an important role in preserving the remarkable continuity of English political and legal institutions, and this is true not only of the medieval period but also of the twentieth century. The German Wehrmacht found it as difficult to cross the channel in 1940 as did the armies of medieval French kings or the forces of Napoleon Bonaparte. In a relatively small country with a population in the Middle Ages and in the sixteenth and seventeenth century never more than a third of that of France, the royal government in England before the Industrial Revolution was never as frustrated by a primitive communications network as were the central governments in France and Germany, in controlling local and provincial society. The remarkably early centralization of government and law in England was also facilitated by the relative absence of divisive internal geographical barriers. There were strong regional differences in England at all times, and to some degree these still persist, but the English king and his ministers never faced the tremendous degree of regionalism which made the north and the south of France, and the east and west of Germany, into distinctive cultures and societies.

Thus, it is easy to elucidate geographical and topographical factors which strongly contributed to continuity and centralization of political life in England. Yet these factors were no more than a conditioning framework and they cannot be held to have *determined* the course of English history in any precise way. The making of English government and law is a human and not a geographical story. It was the result of human decisions, conflicts, and traditions over many centuries and no pre-existing deterministic factor, whether ethnic or geographical, can be said to have produced the kind of political and legal organization which came to exist in modern England. At many points along the road the English could have gone in a different political direction. In the thirteenth and seventeenth centuries, despotism of the continental type seemed an immediate prospect in England, and at several moments in the eighteenth, nineteenth, and twentieth centuries cataclysmic upheaval and not continuity was anticipated by many well-informed Englishmen. History is concerned with men, not blood types or mountains, and the history of English government is a story of a series of choices which the leaders of English society made at critical moments between the fifth and twentieth centuries to live according to a certain group of institutions and ideas.

II. The Interpretation of Medieval English History

As EARLY AS the fifteenth century, educated Englishmen were accounting for their country's prosperity by favorably comparing English political and legal institutions with those of the less fortunate French and Germans. An English chief justice of the mid-fifteenth century, Sir John Fortescue, in fact, worked out a whole treatise on political theory using this theme. He asserted that the nature of the English constitution was a limited monarchy in which the consent of the people, that is, the important groups in society, had to be taken into account by the king and the royal government. In contrast, Fortescue maintained, the French and the Germans suffered from the oppressive effects of despotism, which was suitable in his eyes for French and German peasants but not for English gentlemen. The outlines of this historiographical theme were earlier adumbrated, in the middle of the thirteenth century, by a very well-informed monastic historian named Matthew Paris, who wrote an extremely detailed account of the struggles between the king and the barons in his day. He saw in these conflicts more than squabbles over land and money; he emphasized that they were the product of conflicting theories of kingship and authority, and he strongly favored the baronial party because he believed that this group wished to make the king in some way responsible to the community of the country.

This interpretation of medieval English history remained popular until the sixteenth century when it almost disappeared during an era of unusually effective and popular royal government. Thus, William Shakespeare in his play about King John never mentions the Magna Carta of 1215, although throughout the thirteenth and fourteenth centuries the importance of this document had already been celebrated.

The historiographical themes delineated by Fortescue and Matthew Paris were revived and extensively developed in the early seventeenth century during the long struggle over the right of parliament and the judiciary to limit the king's authority. Sir Edward Coke, first a chief justice and, after his removal from office by the king, a leader of the House of Commons, played the most important role in establishing an interpretation of the history of medieval England as a struggle between despotism on the one side and monarchy limited by parliament and the rule of law on the other. By carefully picking his precedents from the fourteenth and fifteenth centuries, when English kings were particularly weak and incompetent, Coke argued that the English constitution had been fundamentally established by Magna Carta which in his reading assured the rule of law, trial by jury, and the responsibility of royal authority to a national parliament. Learned partisans of the king or parliament hotly debated the validity of this thesis and in so doing at least agreed that the history of medieval English government and law had immediate relevance to the contemporary world in which they lived. These debates also had the effect of inducing more dispassionate scholars to collect and study the surviving records of medieval English government and law. As a result the English came to value and preserve their medieval records whereas a great part of the documents of government in medieval France and Germany disappeared during the seventeenth and eighteenth centuries. Out of these studies came some distinguished works of scholarship, at least one of which, *The History of the Exchequer* by Thomas Madox, is still very much worth reading.

The knowledge and interpretation of medieval England did not advance during the eighteenth century. During the first fifty or sixty years of the century, political life was so placid and unreflective that there seemed little need to reconsider contemporary government in an historical perspective, and when in the last four decades of the century great political conflicts arose, they were usually debated in philosophical rather than historical terms, as was characteristic of the Enlightenment mind. The best historical mind of eighteenth-century England, Edward Gibbon, briefly considered devoting his great talents to English history but finally decided that the subject did not present a theme of sufficient grandeur. It was left for the Victorian historian to provide definitive interpretations of the history of medieval England.

The second half of the nineteenth century was a great age of historical writing in every West European country, and particularly in the field of the history of government. In every Western country the established interpretation of the national past against which twentieth-century historical revisionists, if they may be so called, have had to contend in recent decades, was the creation of the last three or four decades of the nineteenth century. The reasons for this peculiar historiographical phenomenon are not hard to perceive. In the heyday of nationalism there was a need for historians in every Western country to inquire into the national past, demonstrating the origins of the distinctive institutions of each national state and the processes of national integration. The beneficence of such developments was assumed; it remained only to reveal their course; and the earlier the emergence of national unity and consciousness was revealed, the better, for national pride desired the prescriptive rights of antiquity on its side. The task of these national historians was frequently eased by the extensive publication of documentary sources; these publications were usually financed by governments.

Nineteenth-century historians had the time and leisure to produce large tomes of historical synthesis based on great erudition which brought historical scholarship to the service of popular feeling and governmental policy. By the beginning of the twentieth century these tomes adorned the shelves of every good library, had become textbooks in the universities and seemed to provide for the students of the national past not only all that they knew but also all they needed to know. Against these nineteenth-century interpretations, based as they were on vast learning, broad and humane synthesis, and popular nationalist feelings, which are not yet altogether outmoded, the development of revised and novel interpretations in the twentieth century has been a slow, painful, and confusing process. Too often have critics been deluded by the blatant nationalistic prejudices of the established interpretation into overlooking the learning and reflection which went into its composition and into assuming that the preconceptions of a later era can automatically serve as the foundation of a new historiographical view.

The interpretation of the history of medieval English government and law which was worked out in Victorian England followed these general tendencies. The nucleus of the interpretation remained that conflict between despotism and royal authority on the one side and the rule of law and the responsibility of the king to Parliament on the other, which as we have seen was already known to writers in the medieval period and in the seventeenth century. This view of the English past had been upheld, in an unreflective way, by the aristocratic leaders of the Whig party during the eighteenth and early nineteenth centuries. It was enthusiastically embraced by the middle class Victorian liberals who allied themselves with the Whigs, and one of these liberal politicians, Thomas Macaulay, made it the operative assumption upon which his great *History of England from the Accession of James the Second* rested. Macaulay's view of the late seventeenth-century King James II as a revolutionary tyrant who was upsetting the balance of English constitutional monarchy and going against the previous course of English history, and his appraisal of the Whig aristocrats who opposed James as national patriots, had to depend on the assumption that Sir Edward Coke's interpretation of medieval English political history was fundamentally correct.

Macaulay's Whig-liberal interpretation of English history was immensely popular but as yet no scholar had appeared to justify in a detailed work of scholarship his underlying assumptions about the nature of the medieval English constitution. Given the fact that Macaulay had demonstrated to the satisfaction of all educated men that the Whig aristocracy of the late seventeenth century had upheld the liberal nature of the medieval constitution against the despotic machinations of James II, the question remained: How did this enlightened national system of government and law come into existence in the first place? At the same time, nineteenth-century scholars, even before Darwin, were entranced with the idea of organic growth. They firmly believed that institutions had identifiable origins out of which logically and inevitably there was a natural growth. What, then, was the original acorn out of which the grand tree of English liberty sprouted? The answers to these pressing questions were provided in the 1870's in the *Constitutional History of England to 1485*, a three-volume work by William Stubbs, an Anglican clergyman who became an Oxford professor of history and was eventually rewarded for his historical services to the nation by appointment as Bishop of Oxford.

Stubbs's *Constitutional History* is one of the greatest works of nineteenth-century historiography, combining a majestic erudition with a clear presentation of a general interpretation. Stubbs believed that the nature of political institutions is essentially organic, growing from generation to generation. There *is* an identifiable constitution growing from its beginning in Anglo-Saxon England between the fifth and eleventh centuries. From this beginning the development of the constitution can be traced through the medieval period and, by implication, to the present, the great era of Victorian freedom. The essential nature of English constitutionalism is the idea that the government is responsible to the governed and that a higher law overrides royal authority. The personnel changes, particular institutions appear, flourish, and are altered, but the idea of the constitution remains the same, whether in the Anglo-Saxon period or the Victorian era. Stubbs discovers the origins of the constitution in pristine Germanic society, whose institutions were brought to England by the Anglo-Saxon invasion in the fifth century. This philo-Germanism may seem repugnant or absurd in the mid-twentieth century but it was an ingrained fetish of the Victorian mind. We should recall that German culture was very popular among the English ruling classes until shortly before the First World War. From the society of the German forest described by the Roman historian Tacitus, then, the seed of liberal institutions is carried to England. Law resides not in the king but in the folk, and the king is merely an executive of this folk law. Here already is the operative principle of the common law. From this point, the rule of law and the will of the folk have only to be worked out through effective national institutions for the English constitution to emerge full-blown. Stubbs believed that a national unity and a sort of national consciousness had come to exist in England by the end of the twelfth century so that the baronial rebellions against the crown in the thirteenth century were inspired by high constitutional and political ideals, as the thirteenth-century monk Matthew Paris had maintained. Stubbs went on to show that the distinctive institutions of English limited monarchy made their appearance with the emergence of Parliament in the thirteenth century. He claimed that this thirteenth-century Parliament was a representative assembly of three estates to which the middle class of town and country was summoned to give consent to royal legislation, thereby laying the foundations for a distinctive and powerful House of Commons by 1300. He concluded by viewing the history of the fourteenth and fifteenth centuries as centered on the struggle to preserve this constitutional system which in embryo was already modern parliamentary government and the rule of law. Throughout his great work Stubbs emphasized that these dramatic developments on the national scale were closely integrated with, and in part modeled on, the structure of local government, so that the community of the realm, expressed institutionally in Parliament, finds its origin to an appreciable degree in the community of the county court which dates from the early Anglo-Saxon period.

By Victorian standards, Stubbs was a high Tory, a very conservative man, and not an enlightened middle class liberal like Macaulay, and it is therefore doubly significant that his interpretation of the course of medieval English history should fit in so well with the liberal outlook and should provide the necessary scholarly superstructure for the edifice of the liberal interpretation of English history which had been building up since the seventeenth century. In Stubbs's day there was a broad consensus in English historiography and it must be said that although his work has been attacked, sometimes savagely, on particular important points, it remains the most holistic and synthetic interpretation of English history to 1485 that has ever been made. As late as 1948 it was placed by the history faculty of Cambridge University in a special canonical category for students of medieval constitutional history, a category in which no other modern book was found worthy to belong. A recent textbook on medieval English constitutional history by one of the ablest American historians of medieval institutions, Bryce Lyon, draws heavily on Stubbs, whose "insights into constitutional history," Professor Lyon believes, "will never be superseded."

The undermining of Stubbs's interpretation was inaugurated in the 1880's by Frederic William Maitland, who was professor of English law at Cambridge. Maitland was one of the leading minds among that great late nineteenth-century generation of English liberal intellectuals who were especially associated with Cambridge University's critical and scientific spirit and whose heirs in the early twentieth century were known as the Bloomsbury group. After failing to win a competition for a fellowship in political theory at Cambridge, Maitland became a conveyancer, or expert on the law of real property. Then, partly under the inspiration and guidance of Paul Vinogradoff, a Russian scholar who had been appointed to the chair of legal history at Oxford, Maitland turned to the definitive study of the origins of the common law. He was finally rewarded for his work in this field with a professorship at his alma mater. Maitland's *The History of English Law before the Time of Edward 1* was officially written in collaboration with Sir Frederick Pollock, a leading light of the English bar. But Pollock, after having written a few introductory pages, seems to have realized that his collaborator was an authentic genius; he withdrew, and these two volumes, which are among the few eminent scholarly works that are universally cherished on both scholarly and literary grounds, are Maitland's great monument.

Maitland had the fullest respect for Stubbs, and he never explicitly contradicted any of Stubbs's interpretations, although his personal letters indicate that Maitland was acutely aware that he was developing a new understanding of medieval institutions. Writing before self-conscious revisionist history was invented, Maitland managed to raise by implication some fundamental objections to the established view of English history which Stubbs's work had done so much to buttress. It is ironic that although Maitland, unlike Stubbs, was a committed middle-class liberal, the effect of his work was to call into question some of the fundamental assumptions of the liberal historical interpretation. He does this by avoiding the organic view of the origins of the common law as determined by some mythical acorn planted in the German forest. As seen by Maitland, the whole Anglo-Saxon period is much less important in the making of the common law than the work of English monarchy in the twelfth and thirteenth centuries and certain crucial decisions on the use of the jury made by royal judges in the thirteenth century. The development of medieval English law is regarded by Maitland not as the fulfillment of the will of the folk but rather as a series of clever pragmatic moves on the part of the royal government in the two centuries that followed the Norman conquest of 1066. Stubbs sees the development of medieval English institutions as essentially the fulfillment of an overriding popular idea of the constitution. Maitland agrees with Stubbs that the common law is an indigenous creation and owes little or nothing to continental Roman law. But for Maitland the English legal system emerges slowly and painfully out of a series of *ad hoc* steps worked out by astute royal officials and judges to suit the interests of the king. Thus the course of medieval English history as seen by Maitland is far less inevitable and deterministic, and much more accidental. From reading Maitland's brilliant pages we come away with the impression that things could indeed have worked out very differently, though he is very happy of course that they happened the way they eventually did. We also come away with the impression that if there is such a thing as an English constitution, it has its origins in effective royal authority and administration. In another one of his works, Maitland is at pains to show that Stubbs misinterpreted the nature of the thirteenth-century parliament; it was not a popular representative legislature but merely a special kind of royal court. Thus modern English liberal institutions have their beginnings in the authoritarian inclinations and *ad hoc* experimentation of medieval English kings and royal officials.

Maitland's work indicated that the understanding of the development of medieval English government and law could best be achieved through detailed study of various kinds of royal administration. Most historians of medieval England who have worked in the past half century have taken this conclusion as their basic assumption, and scholars such as T. F. Tout and G. O. Sayles have further elucidated how royal government and law actually operated in medieval England. The tendency of their work has been to confirm Maitland's appraisal of the authoritarian disposition of medieval English government and the pragmatic way in which institutions came into existence to suit the interests of the king rather than an overriding idea of the rule of law or will of the community. On the other hand, in pursuing this interpretation it is not easy to come out with any synthesis which relates to the subsequent pattern of English history, nor even one which brings the myriad of details about medieval administration and law into a meaningful sequential thesis. Some very able scholars, such as J. E. A. Jolliffe, B. Wilkinson, J. G. Edwards, and Helen Cam, have tried to expound a neo-Stubbsian view which maintains the outlines of Stubbs's liberal interpretation while taking account of the criticisms made by Maitland and his disciples. But no general works of sufficient erudition and subtlety have yet appeared to gain wide approval and to establish a new consensus.

The most illuminating and imaginative studies of medieval England have since 1940 come more from scholars interested in ecclesiastical and intellectual development or in the course of economic change than from those concerned with strictly political and legal history. The works of M. D. Knowles and R. W. Southern have so enriched our understanding of medieval church culture, and a lively group of economic historians led by M. M. Postan has so intensified our knowledge of medieval agriculture and commerce, that the functioning of administration and law can now be put in the context of how medieval men understood themselves and the world and how they made a living. In this perspective the problems of government and social control in the medieval world become more real and meaningful to us.

CHAPTER TWO

THE EMERGENCE OF
ENGLAND
from the first century B.C.
to 1066 A.D.

I. *Caesar, Arthur, and Beowulf*

THROUGH FOUR CENTURIES, from the middle of the first century to the second quarter of the fifth century A.D., Britain was a province of the Roman Empire. The Roman influence on the political, social, and religious life of France was profound. But the Roman legacy in Britain was a negligible one, and of no account in the subsequent development of government and society in the British Isles. This seems to be a remarkable paradox, until we realize that the Roman conquest of Britain was never more than a military action. The Roman legions crossed the channel in 55-54 B.C. and attacked the native Celtic population originally to suit the vanity of Julius Caesar. Once firmly established there in 43 A.D., the Romans proceeded to build cities, particularly London, as military and governmental centers, and also excellent roads to facilitate their infantry marches, and walls in the North to keep out the marauding Scots. But Britain remained a distant frontier region to the Roman emperors, and the extent of colonization by immigrants from Italy, aside from military people, was very small. The native British population learned Christianity from their conquerors in the fourth century A.D. and they were protected from Scottish and Irish invasion and also from the Germanic pirates who tried to enter the country from across the North Sea. But the British never imbibed the industrial and commercial arts of urbanized life; the cities remained the isolated enclaves of the Roman conquerors. The British do not seem even to have learned very much about the techniques of Roman agriculture, and in the fifth century they were still partially a pastoral people. At the same time, protected by the Roman legions, they lost their military skills, in which they had not been very proficient in the first place. Therefore, about 425 A.D., when the attacks of German invaders from beyond the Rhine and the Danube upon Italy and Gaul forced the withdrawal of the Roman legions from Britain to defend the Eternal City itself, the British were unable to make use of their new freedom. They could not prevent the penetration of the eastern river estuaries of the country by the North Sea pirates whom the Romans had easily repulsed during the previous hundred years.

It was a strange country that these invaders found. It had excellent roads which continued to be the basis of the English road network until the eighteenth century, and at least one impressive city, now largely a ghost town, but very little in the way of commerce or industry. About half of the country was covered with thick and often impenetrable forests and near the east coast there were vast swampy areas which for the most part remained undrained until the seventeenth century. Britain was by and large a cold wet land with only a large, roughly triangular area in the south-central part of the country readily suitable for agriculture. Surrounding this interior triangle were either forests, swamps, or hills which at best could support a pastoral or hunting and fishing economy. Thus the invaders did not find a great prize in their new land, although it compared favorably enough with the swamplands of the Low Countries whence most of them came. But then, neither did the British receive a great prize with the arrival of the Anglo-Saxon invaders.

It is with these invasions of the fifth century that the history of English government and society begins. The native British were either enslaved or pushed westward into the hills of Cornwall and the mountains of Wales or driven for safety across the English Channel to Brittany in northern France. A people so enslaved and destroyed could teach their conquerors nothing, not even the rudiments of the Christian religion, and the invaders were to remain heathens until the end of the sixth century, in many areas as much as a century later. The British were unable to communicate to their conquerors the Roman tradition of law and government and the idea that the state is a public corporation distinct from the person of the ruler; indeed it is doubtful that during the long centuries of Roman rule the British had themselves absorbed these traditions and ideas.

Who were these invaders and what were their institutions and ideals? It has long been recognized that these are important questions for the subsequent course of English political history, although since we no longer firmly believe in the Victorian organic view of institutions, the questions do not perhaps have the overriding importance they presented to nineteenth-century historians like William Stubbs. Actually the surviving documentary information for the earliest English society is extremely meager. A contemporary British monk named Gildas purported to write an account of the Anglo-Saxon invasion but what he has to say is not of much use to us, particularly if we are interested in institutions. As clergymen are wont to do, particularly in the Middle Ages, he uses history as a vehicle for a sermon against the wickedness of the British for whose sins the conquest was deemed to be the punishment. This makes for a dull sermon and bad history. The eighth-century heroic poem *Beowulf*, an early epic, is very informative about the life of the warrior class which we find out consists mostly of heavy drinking, fighting, and boasting. It also tells us that the pervading ideal of this society is loyalty—the allegiance of a man to his lord. Historians have tended to assume that the Christian allusions in the poem are a superficial overlay and that the work as written down is derived from an oral tradition which goes back to the fifth century. *Beowulf* has thus been used by many scholars, and most perceptively by H. M. Chadwick, to provide an account of the organization and ideals of earliest English society, but recent literary criticism has suggested that the poem is in fact a conscious Christian allegory and that Beowulf himself is a kind of Christ figure. If this interpretation is correct, what the poem gains in literary interest it tends to lose in historical value, at least as far as the fifth century is concerned.

It has been traditional for historians of Anglo-Saxon society to make extensive use of the *Germania* of the Roman historian Tacitus which was written in 98 A.D. Because many of the institutions described by Tacitus reappear in later accounts and legal documents the work has a generally circumstantial appearance. But there is no doubt that the *Germania* was inspired by problems in contemporary Roman society and the work as a whole was probably intended to be an ironic reverse mirror-image of Roman society at the end of the first century A.D. It therefore may be regarded as one of the earliest examples of utopian literature, and we are justified in our skeptical attitude when Tacitus expounds the pure morality of the Germanic peoples and expatiates upon the chastity of the Germanic *Hausfrau*.

The most valuable source for earlier Anglo-Saxon history is the *dooms* or laws, which are the most extensive collection of Germanic laws in any European society. They show no influence of Roman thought beyond a few traces inevitably imbedded in the collections by the Latin-speaking churchmen who wrote them down, beginning in the last decade of the sixth century. The dooms, which provide us with our most accurate, detailed, and fascinating picture of the political and social life of early England, were definitively edited in the first two decades of the twentieth century by the great German scholar Felix Liebermann.

New information about Anglo-Saxon England has become available in the last four decades through archaeological evidence. The most famous archaeological find of artifacts from the early Anglo-Saxon period was the Sutton-Hoo ship burial discovered in 1939; it provided the almost total remains of a ship burial of a seventh-century Anglo-Saxon king off the east coast of England together with all his prized stores and jewelry. Such a ship burial is in fact described in the opening lines of *Beowulf*. The results of a great mass of archaeological investigation have been carefully summarized in R. H. Hodgkin's *History of the Anglo-Saxons*.

The most extensive narrative source for the early history of England is the work of the early eighth-century monastic historian Bede, *The Ecclesiastical History of the English People*. He made extensive use of oral traditions about the Anglo-Saxon invasion and, while some of the stories he recounts seem farfetched, anthropological science has taught us to respect the historical substratum in the oral historical traditions of primitive people. It is Bede who tells us that the invasions began when a British prince invited a band of German pirates from across the North Sea to assist him in his wars with other native princes. The invited mercenaries liked the country enough to send back home for reinforcements and the invasions were underway. It is also Bede who provides the information that there were three Germanic peoples who invaded England, the Angles, the Saxons, and the Jutes. Historians have been unable to further identify the Jutes except for the plausible hypothesis that they were a very small tribe which settled in Kent and were then absorbed into the larger Germanic peoples. We must remember that Bede was very much a Christian scholar for whom it was natural and necessary that everything, including invaders, come in threes.

It seems unlikely in any case that the invaders had any consciousness of belonging to a large nation like Angles or Saxons. The way in which the invasion was carried out undermined the pristine tribal structures. The invaders came over from the Low Countries and probably in some instances directly from Denmark in small groups—in a dozen or so boats at a time under the command of a warrior chieftain. These small groups in their long open boats slowly pushed westward up the river estuaries of eastern England. Gradually, as the Germans established settlements and enslaved or drove back the British, several groups, from whatever tribe they may originally have stemmed, coalesced into one large "folk" under the leadership of a great warrior king, the "booty-giver" and "ring-giver" described by *Beowulf*. Such a folk would in the course of time come to rule an area contiguous with the extent of the later English county, or perhaps two or three counties.

The coalescence of the pirate warbands into a folk and the emergence of warrior kings was in part made necessary by the stiff, although ultimately futile, resistance put up by the British princes, particularly in the wealthy agricultural triangle of midland England. Such princes could only be overcome by relatively large armies in more or less pitched battles. It was not until the early sixth century that the last British resistance was overcome by the German war leaders and the whole country south of the Scottish frontier and east of the Welsh mountains was under the sway of a number of the Anglo-Saxon folks. It was during this period of bitter British resistance in the late fifth century that the historical Arthur, the last hero of Christian Britain, performed those valiant deeds which were celebrated and romanticized by his descendants in Wales down the long cold centuries until after about 1130 they were taken up into the corpus of European literature.

Bede tells us that in the sixth century the Anglo-Saxon kingdoms were seven in number but this is again a sacred figure in Christian thought. Actually, during the three centuries following the Anglo-Saxon invasion, the number of separate little kingdoms fluctuated widely as one powerful folk defeated and absorbed its neighbors and then in turn was overcome by a newly ascendant kingdom. In the sixth century the Kentish king in the southeast was particularly important; in the seventh century the kings of Northumbria were famed for their prowess; and in the eighth century the king of Mercia in the rich agricultural midland established a temporary hegemony. Finally in the ninth century new Danish invaders destroyed all the Anglo-Saxon kingdoms except that of Wessex in the southwest, and henceforth the king of Wessex was by default pre-eminent in English society. In the tenth century the kings of Wessex established their suzerainty over the Danelaw, the northeastern half of the country, and at least in a formal sense, created a united realm of England.

Some of the early Anglo-Saxon kings held the title of *Bretwalda,* implying a kind of superking over a few less powerful rulers, and this title confirms our impression of the unstable and transient nature of the early Anglo-Saxon kingdoms. One king would conquer others, and after this great warlord passed from the scene, his folk would come under the hegemony of some new Bretwalda renowned for his dragon-slaying and booty-giving.

II. *Kinship and Community*

MAITLAND TELLS US that it is naïve to suppose that the further back we go in history the simpler institutions become. People in early societies may be simpler in their motivation, but society is actually more complex precisely because these primitive people cannot define and organize things clearly. In a primitive society like England after the Anglo-Saxon invasion the simplicity which comes from rationalized order is lacking. Instead there is confusion and disorganization, violence and conflict, and this society presents to the modern mind a murky pattern that resists facile explanation. To overcome the confusions of primitive society men need to have a distinct and decisive authority. This was certainly lacking in early Anglo-Saxon England and was scarcely even prevalent when the last Anglo-Saxon king fell at the Battle of Hastings in 1066.

The lack of a decisive authority and any idea of sovereignty are immediately evident when we look at the Anglo-Saxon dooms. Unlike the code of Roman law, which was definitively put together in the reign of the sixth-century Byzantine emperor Justinian, the Anglo-Saxon law collections are not codes. They are in no way systematic or comprehensive or based on abstract political and moral synthesis. The Anglo-Saxon law was fundamentally oral and customary; it resided in the bosom of the folk and in the memories of the wise old men of the community. The only laws written down are those that refer to difficult points at issue or situations that are unusual, such as the peace problems created by the appearance of a new group in society. If we could interview an Anglo-Saxon doomsman, he would say that the written laws represent not more than half of the customs of the community. Like an iceberg, a great part of Anglo-Saxon law lurks beneath the surface.

The law to the Anglo-Saxon mind is thus a pre-existing substance, and its confusion and contradictions are sanctified by antiquity. The concept of legislation is totally lacking and the good law is the old law. Even when an enterprising and intelligent king under the guidance of churchmen actually creates new laws he must always do this by asserting that he is merely making clear and confirming the good old law. The law, like an English fog, is always there, covering the way of life of the community, and this customary way of life cannot be abrogated or even substantially altered by any overruling authority.

These Anglo-Saxon notions about law are directly opposite to the Roman idea of jurisprudence. The Romans believed that law resides in the will of the emperor, who as the public corporate embodiment of the state has the authority to proclaim whatever law he deems to be in accordance with the moral law of nature. Insofar as the Anglo-Saxons could even comprehend such a proposition they found it fundamentally wrong and socially dangerous, and for long centuries there was great hostility in England to any Romanist ideas of sovereignty. When in 1399 King Richard II was understood to say that law resided in his own mouth, he was held to have enunciated a very un-English fancy for which, among other reasons, he had to be done away with.

The Germanic idea of law which strongly conditions the whole political outlook of Anglo-Saxon England thus fundamentally inhibited the emergence of an idea of sovereignty. The Anglo-Saxons could not conceive of the state as a public body separate from the various leaders of society. They could only conceive of loyalty to a person or a social group and they never attained that level of political thinking which conceives of all men and women in the country of whatever social rank as being equally subordinate to the public authority of a sovereign ruler. There are many historians who would say that such an idea did not clearly appear in England until the seventeenth century, although the course of institutional change after the Norman Conquest of 1066 slowly began to force the sentient members of society toward this kind of political understanding. The total lack of an idea of sovereignty in the Anglo-Saxon period precluded the overcoming of personal and group loyalties that were always prevalent in the Germanic world, as they probably are in all primitive societies. These loyalties continued to conflict with and interact upon one another throughout the six centuries of Anglo-Saxon history, producing the confused complexity and disorder which is the most fundamental characteristic of English government and society before the Norman Conquest. Before the nominal unification of England under one ruler from the house of Wessex in the tenth century, the confusion and disorder were further enhanced by variations in the strength of competing loyalties between region and region and kingdom and kingdom. Even after the nominal unification of the country, during the tenth and first half of the eleventh centuries, because monarchy lacked the authority to overrule other customary social allegiances and obligations, the conflict and competition of loyalties was never transcended.

Among the variety of demands for allegiance placed upon Anglo-Saxon society, five generic loyalties predominate: the kin or family, the community or folk, various kinds of lordship, the church, and finally kingship or the central government. In the Anglo-Saxon period these five loyalties exist side by side, overlap in the obligations and responsibilities they place upon the members of society, intensely compete with one another, and vary in the degree of loyalty which they are accorded by society from century to century and sometimes from region to region. The history of subsequent medieval government may be said to be the attempt to discriminate among the authorities of family, community, lordship, church, and kingship, and to arrive at something approaching an overriding central power and a vague idea of sovereignty within the realm.

The form of social cohesion which was most clearly comprehensible to the Anglo-Saxon mind was kinship or the family bond. In their eager search for political and legal institutions which looked forward to the modern state, historians have tended to underrate the overwhelming impact of kinship and the family unit in the early centuries of English society. Even after other loyalties emerged to compete with the kinship bond, the family always remained the most immediate unit of medieval life; this is why the death of kings and the disintegration of political order were of so little concern to medieval people. It is hard for us to remember this fundamental social fact when the modern state has absorbed so many family functions and when the death of a president may have a greater impact on a man's life than the death of his father.

The Anglo-Saxon family unit was large and all-embracing, and in return for the protection and sustenance kinship provided, the individual was heavily obligated to it. Distant cousins to the seventh degree were all part of the same kin and children in the medieval world were thought of as merely small people who were involved in all aspects of family life as soon as they were weaned. For males the obligation to the family was primarily to fight, either to protect against an enemy or to gain revenge for a wrong inflicted upon a member of the kin. The duty of females to the kin was to provide sustenance for the fighters, primarily by bringing them enough to eat and drink, and to spawn a new generation of warriors.

The blood feud in Anglo-Saxon society was as central to social life as employment and taxes are today. The Middle Ages have been called the Age of Faith. This term can be justified, but more obviously the medieval period, in fact the whole era before the seventeenth century, should be called an age of violence. The one aspect of medieval life that all of us would find unbearable was the constant prevalence of violent death. And this, as anyone knows who has read Shakespeare, is still largely true of English life at the end of the sixteenth century. In the Anglo-Saxon world it was considered normal and just to kill a man in an open and fair fight. Manslaughter was no crime; murder, or socially condemned manslaughter, only took place when a man was killed by stealth and did not have the opportunity to defend himself. In earliest Anglo-Saxon society, it was only the aggrieved kin of a man killed in an open fight who sought retribution upon the slayer. And it was only the threat of having to deal with a powerful family that could discourage the prospect of manslaughter. So savage were these people—even after their nominal conversion to Christianity in the seventh century—and so frequent were violent robberies and wild drunken brawls, that this threat seems to have been remarkably ineffectual. Everyday life was so conditioned by mayhem that the blood feud was continually in operation. Furthermore the blood feud had a tendency to be self-perpetuating; revenge once taken by an aggrieved kin upon a slayer would call forth a new blood feud by the family of the man upon whom revenge had been taken, and such feuds could involve hundreds of people and could persist in the most brutal fashion for several decades. There is one famous case of a blood feud which broke out between two prominent Anglo-Saxon noble families in the 1050's and which was still being waged twenty years later, even after the Norman Conquest had greatly reduced the wealth and power of the families. God, king, lord, and folk could easily be forgotten and all the energy and intelligence of an Anglo-Saxon family organized simply for the purpose of inflicting manslaughter. This kind of conduct was as self-evident to the Anglo-Saxon as service to the state is to twentieth-century people.

In a society whose mores allowed for unrestrained violence, strong family cohesion was both sensible and necessary, but the resolving of manslaughter through the kin's exercise of its right of blood feud in itself presented social problems of increasing importance. A man with a hundred male kin could easily find himself involved in an interminable number of blood feuds, to the point where he had no time for anything else. Furthermore as the Anglo-Saxons settled down in their new land and became organized in various kingdoms, the unchecked operation of the blood feud was found to be socially enervating and politically dangerous. The families within a given kingdom could be so dedicated to slaughtering one another that the king lacked a sufficient number of able warriors to lead against the neighboring kingdom. In addition the blood feud worked well only in cases of open manslaughter; where murder or robbery had been done by stealth the aggrieved family faced the problem of determining the victim upon whom they should take their vengeance, and the danger was always prevalent that they might take vengeance on the wrong person, usually someone whom they disliked in any case or who was known to be physically weak or who lacked powerful kinsmen. It therefore became more and more evident that an alternative to blood feud vengeance had to be worked out and a legal process had to be discovered for determining those guilty of secret crimes. This required an authority wider in jurisdiction and more powerful than even the kin, and upon this social necessity the authority of the folk or community court was founded.

In the very beginnings of English society, there appears to have been a widespread sense of belonging to a large community or folk, which embraced several or even a great many distinct groups of kin. This sense of community did not extend, after the invasion of the fifth century, to the pristine Angle and Saxon nations. It extended only to the small kingdoms which emerged all over the country in the later fifth and sixth centuries. The men of Wessex, Kent, Northumbria, Mercia, etc., or at least those of the leading warrior class, had in each case some consciousness of their membership in a community of the folk. The obligations which this membership imposed upon them were such as to preserve the identity of the folk and to establish the necessary prerequisites of its common welfare. From the seventh century on, the dooms tell us that loyalty to the folk requires that all of its members repair bridges, maintain roads, and serve in the *fyrd*, the folk army; these obligations comprise the so-called three-fold necessity. In the tenth and eleventh centuries during periods of Scandinavian invasion, the king obtained general assent to the proposition that all members of the community must pay a *geld* or national tax to support the army or buy off the Danish invaders.

Beyond these basic responsibilities, loyalty to the folk, at least from the late sixth century, required participation in a court which provided a legal process whose function was to abrogate or prevent the operation of the socially debilitating blood feud. The folk *moot* or community court, according to the dooms, overrules the immediate loyalty which all men owe to their families and provides a legal jurisdiction which takes in a greater or smaller area, but always one which is beyond that of a single kin. By the eighth century the folk moot is coming to be differentiated into two kinds of community courts involving in the first case an area of local jurisdiction comprising one or more villages, roughly the size of the modern American township, and a much broader jurisdiction involving the whole kingdom, or an area contiguous with one of the sub-kingdoms ruled by a great Bretwalda. The smaller area of folk moot jurisdiction comes to be called the hundred and the larger one the shire: the word shire simply means a share or division; no historian has succeeded in explaining the precise etymology of the term hundred. But it is clear that from the beginning these words respectively signify concentric local and county community court jurisdiction. The foundation of both the hundred and the shire was a communal feeling, broader than the kin, that allowed the court to function and to govern animosities among families. How far back before 500 A.D. the community court came into existence is uncertain, but it seems probable that the communal feeling had less to do with race, tribe, and tradition than it did with social necessity. The leading men in a given locality, whether it was one or two villages or a

35

much larger unit, felt compelled to come together and put a stop to indiscriminate fighting by setting up a court with a definite legal process providing alternatives to the pristine blood feud.

Whether it was the hundred or the shire court, the leading men of the community presided and arrived at decisions by a kind of consensus or sense of the meeting. These leaders of the court may be called dooms-men or elders or wisemen but in all cases they were inevitably the men of greater substance and influence whose task was to work out and perpetu-ate legal processes in accordance with customary law. In the case of the hundred court the elders of the court could be ordinary peasants; in the case of the shire court they would always be the great warlords in the community. The first task of the folk moot was to build upon the old Germanic tradition that the blood feud could be abrogated in return for monetary compensation, the *Wergeld* (literally, man-money), to the dead man's kin. The kin were not required to take the wergeld and waive their right of revenge; it was the first obligation of the court to urge them to accept it. It was their second task to prepare lists of wergelds for every possible kind of violence, from the loss of a toenail, to the killing of a slave, to the killing of a nobleman or king (the king's wergeld was placed so high that no man, no matter how many cattle he owned, could afford to pay it). It is not surprising, therefore, to find that the earlier dooms consist for the most part of lists of wergelds. We can see in such lists how the authority of the community is struggling to assert itself against the primordial rights of the blood feud.

The additional task of the folk moot was to inhibit the exercise of family vengeance by discovering who was guilty of murder and robbery by stealth. The criminal, once convicted, would be hung on the spot, his chattels confiscated, and the blood feud made unnecessary. This deter-mination of guilt was no easy task in an illiterate society which, in con-trast with people subject to Roman law, had no concept of the nature of evidence and no process for the rational interrogation of witnesses. The Anglo-Saxon solution was the invocation of divine aid in determination of the verdict, through two kinds of process, the ordeal and compurga-tion.

The ordeal provided a process which was heavily weighted against the defendant. In the ordeal of hot iron, the defendant was required to put his hand on a piece of red hot metal; his hand was then bound up and if on the third day the wound was found to be festering, the defendant was promptly hung. This was probably merciful since he was likely to die an even nastier death from blood poisoning. In the ordeal of cold water, a special favorite in England where there were so many streams and ponds, the defendant was bound hand and foot and thrown into the water. If he sank he was innocent and if he floated he was guilty, on the premise that water, being a holy element, would not receive a guilty man. The defendant thus had a choice between probable death by drowning and certain death by hanging. It was the function of the court to decide on which method of proof would be used, and if the defendant was required to "make his law" by ordeal, how severe the test should be. Thus in the ordeal by hot water in which the defendant had to retrieve a stone from the bottom of a boiling cauldron, the court could prescribe a single, twofold, or threefold ordeal depending on whether the depth of the water was up to the wrist, elbow, or shoulder.

The ordeals appear at first sight to be hideously irrational, and no one would claim that they represent a highly sophisticated form of judicial process. Yet they were used in English trials until the thirteenth century, and there was an element of rationality in these savage procedures. Part of this rationality was provided by the church which initially found them extremely repugnant and which only came to accept them because they were so fundamental in Anglo-Saxon life. Before being put to the ordeal the defendant had to swear on the Bible or holy relics that he was innocent, while the priest enjoined him to confess his guilt, if such were the case, rather be damned in the next world as well as hung in this. We assume that this ecclesiastical brainwashing induced some guilty people to break down and confess, in order to avoid mortal sin and thus gain the privilege of purgatory. The other element of rationality in the ordeal was provided by the folk court itself. Only those defendants were put to the ordeal who were either commonly suspected of guilt or were of the lower social strata. An important lord or a prominent churchman was never subjected to an ordeal. It was a process almost exclusively designed for those who were peasants or who were "ill-famed," which to the medieval mind with its strong class biases, meant almost the same thing. Those who are horrified by this deep social prejudice might reflect on the kinds of people who have suffered capital punishment in the United States, noting the overwhelming proportion of Negroes and poor people. In this respect we have remained true to the traditions of Anglo-Saxon law.

The wealthy and the prominent had the privilege of compurgation in "making their law" against indictments in the folk court. This method also called for divine intercession, but in a much less dangerous and arduous manner. The defendant swore to his innocence and he then provided oath-helpers, whose importance was weighted according to their wergelds, to swear not that the defendant was innocent but only that his oath was "clean," that is, that the defendant was a man of good repute. The function of the court was only to decide on who should have the privilege of compurgation and how weighty the oath-helpers had to be. Beyond this, a rich man who was oblivious to the heavenly perils of perjury and who had powerful relatives and friends of like dispositions could commit murder and robbery with legal impunity. He might be dealt with by the kin of the victim, but the court would not convict him. Thus Anglo-Saxon process tended to provide one procedure for the rich and the powerful and another for the poor and unknown. This class bias in somewhat less flagrant forms was to have a long history in English law and has not entirely ended at the present time.

In a society which had no police officials or prisons, the apprehension of criminals and the bringing of accused persons before the court became the responsibility of the members of the hundred. Loyalty to the folk required the performance of a kind of communal police action. When a murder or robbery was seen it was the obligation of any bystander who had witnessed the crime to set up a "hue and cry." He and others within earshot of his shouts were supposed to pursue the criminal to the borders of the hundred where the hue and cry and pursuit were supposed to be taken up by members of the neighboring community. Since there were no prisons in which to incarcerate apprehended criminals for trial, and since this was a society which was constantly threatened by famine and could therefore not conceive of maintaining criminals at public expense, it was the custom to hang on the spot criminals thus caught red-handed and apprehended by community pursuit.

It is obvious that this kind of popular police action was not very effective and that the forests of medieval England were full of outlaws. This is one reason why the Anglo-Saxon mind was so suspicious of strangers; a stranger who proceeded along the highway without blowing a horn was assumed, and reasonably so, to be a fugitive criminal who could be shot down on sight. The church made police action even more difficult by its generous, but somewhat misguided, promulgation of the right of sanctuary by which someone fleeing from the hue and cry could not be taken from a church where he sought refuge. The outraged community was forced to wait until he was starved out or turned over to them by the cleric who had presumably consulted divine authority on the guilt or innocence of the refugee. It is apparent that the effectiveness of sanctuary depended on the degree of zeal of the churchman and the notoriety of the fleeing criminal, and that in many a rural community the right of sanctuary was violated with impunity by the hundred.

Given these extremely slipshod police actions, once the basic jurisdictions and procedures of the hundred and the shire courts had been established, the leaders of the community would want to make more effective and rational the means of producing the defendant and also the actual procedure in criminal suits. The dooms reveal these developments during the last two centuries of Anglo-Saxon society. The basic irrationality and class bias in procedure was never superseded and the chaotic nature of police action was never meliorated in a fundamental way, because society lacked the intelligence necessary for thoroughgoing political evolution and because the kings never considered it their actual function to provide justice but merely to advocate it. The responsibility for law remained with the community. All that the king would or could do was to provide injunctive guidelines for communal legal action ("self-government at the king's command," one historian has called this with unintentional humor) and claim a share of the fines and forfeitures obtained by the folk moot. Given these severe limitations in judicial institutions and ideas, the later Anglo-Saxon period is nevertheless marked by certain improvements in the legal functioning of the community, and these improvements superimposed some rational form on a process that was fundamentally irrational.

The king in the tenth and early eleventh centuries enjoined the hundred court to divide all of its members into groups of ten. The participants in each corporate "tithing" were to be responsible for each other before the court, making sure they kept the peace and bringing any member of the tithing who was ill-famed to the meeting of the hundred. The necessity for the organization of this extremely small and local communal group indicates the inability of the community of the hundred to deal adequately with the maintenance of the peace and the bringing of criminals before the court. Even then, the tithing did not work very well. The later dooms are constantly ordering the hundred court to make sure that all are placed within these new peace groups; this indicates that many in later Anglo-Saxon society failed to find a place in a tithing, because they were too poor or too notorious to be considered responsible members of this kind of legal community.

It was the intention in the tenth century to improve the effectiveness not only of police action but also of the operation of legal process itself. An attempt was made to preclude the constant resort to perjury in proof by compurgation by providing that the court itself set up panels of trustworthy witnesses whose testimony would be sought as to the cleanness of oath of defendants. This in effect is asking court-impaneled groups of reliable members of society to certify the veracity and general reputation of a defendant. This novel procedure is getting close to the principle of the jury system as we know it; the decision on innocence or guilt lies with well-informed representatives of the community. Even closer to the modern jury principle and in fact already the institution of the grand jury full-blown are the "twelve leading thegns" of the shire who are instructed in the dooms of King Ethelred, circa 1000 A.D., to declare before the court those who are known to be guilty of crime. In effect this constitutes a communal indictment, in which the whole folk, speaking through its most responsible leaders, summons those who are ill-famed before it. Such a communal indictment was presumably intended as a supplement to the individual accusations made by aggrieved kin and particular plaintiffs. It may be assumed that the institution of the communal indictment represents dissatisfaction with prejudiced and perjured accusations made before the court with the intention of subjecting the unpopular or the ill-connected to the terror of the ordeal. The institution of the twelve leading thegns was a great advance in the rationality of legal procedure and fundamentally it is equivalent to the grand jury of indictment or presentment which comes to be used continuously in England from the 1160's on. Can the origins of the grand jury therefore be said to lie in Anglo-Saxon procedure? Historians have had to give a negative answer to this question because there is no evidence of the use of this institution after the end of the reign of Ethelred in 1016, and no indication that the kings and jurists of England after the Norman Conquest knew of this experiment and used it as a precedent. The fact that the jury after the Norman Conquest appears only in civil suits, in imitation of French practice, and that it does again not operate in criminal procedure until the later twelfth century indicates that the Anglo-Saxon jury was a noble but short-lived and abortive experiment. Without a monarchy which took as its function the effective operation of legal institutions, and without a royal judiciary to supervise the procedure of the community court, the Anglo-Saxon grand jury seems to have been abandoned as quickly as it appeared. The community court believed their function was not to provide justice but rather to stop the blood feuds, and the rational ideas of justice implicit in the grand jury were beyond the ken of the leaders of the folk moot.

The Anglo-Saxon community was thus unable to overcome the limitations set by its origins as a group designed to bring the leaders of various kin together in order to limit violence and establish a modicum of peace. And yet some historians have said that in the folk courts lies the root or germ of all English freedom. Is there any validity in this Victorian conviction? Only in a very special way (but a real and important one) can this question be answered affirmatively.

The maintenance and operation of the law was the obligation of the community in Anglo-Saxon society. The law operated in a realm which transcended the kin. Kings decreed the meeting of the folk court and set guidelines for its operation, but the knowledge and working of legal procedure was primarily the responsibility of the doomsmen and not of the king or his officials. Prominent lords and churchmen certainly dominated the meetings of the shire court, but the decisions arrived at were, in principle, the communal consensus of the folk. Thus law became entrenched as a matter of communal decision and operation and the shire and hundred courts became institutionalized as the primary corporate judicial agencies in England. Although in the century after 1066 the royal government and the central judiciary came to control the operation of the community court, the Anglo-Saxon tradition of the ultimate judicial responsibility of the community was perpetuated.

III. *The Dimensions of Anglo-Saxon Lordship*

ANGLO-SAXON SOCIETY reflected the general nature of social structure in medieval Europe in that it tended toward organization along hierarchic lines. Even in the earliest dooms it is apparent that there are certain men, sometimes called "lords," who have more wealth and power than other people in the folk, and the rest of society is somehow dependent on the leadership of these lords. Medieval churchmen took it as self-evident that society, like the church itself, should be organized hierarchically, from the slaves at the bottom of the social order to lords, kings, and ultimately God at the head of it. They justified this exploitative social system on functional grounds. They viewed society as an organism in which each member had a certain function. A tenth-century Anglo-Saxon monk tells us that there are three functional orders in society: those who work, those who pray, and those who fight. It was the assumption among literate and thinking people that the fighters along with those who prayed should govern society and should be supported by the large mass of laborers. This social theory, which goes back at least as far as Plato's *Republic*, was confirmed for churchmen by the actual workings of the society in which they lived. The original warrior class became transformed into a lordly elite who assumed unto themselves an increasing amount of wealth and power, and by at least the tenth century the great majority of people in the Anglo-Saxon world became dependent on this ruling group in one way or another.

The dimensions of Anglo-Saxon lordship are not easy to define because they varied appreciably from century to century and from region to region. An error commonly made in describing Anglo-Saxon society is the disregard of this chronological and regional variation. This results in the establishment of abstract categories which falsifies the distinct variation in forms of lordship and ignores the divergent sources which contributed to the making of this elite group. It is also a serious mistake to be entrapped by labels like "Anglo-Saxon feudalism." As Maitland said, feudalism was introduced into England in the seventeenth century; it was a term coined by lawyers and political theorists; medieval people employed no such term. Even the word *feudum*, or knight's fee, from which the generic term feudalism is derived, is a word known only after the Norman Conquest. Therefore, while some historians have engaged in vigorous debate about the nature of Anglo-Saxon feudalism, this can only be a semantic exercise which multiplies abstraction and violates the real nature of Anglo-Saxon social organization.

It is clear that after 1066 there was a vigorous reorganization of the upper strata of English society. The Norman Conquest resulted in the creation of a strictly organized social hierarchy in accordance with principles established by French practice and the theories of clever churchmen, professional administrators, and well-informed lawyers. But this rationally organized social hierarchy did not exist in Anglo-Saxon England. Both the nature of lordship before the Norman Conquest and the way in which it came into existence was incoherent, imprecise, and confused.

It is certain that by the tenth century lordship is very much in evidence in the Anglo-Saxon world. There are lords who have a great deal of wealth, legal authority, and political power, although the precise degree varies markedly from region to region and even from one lord to the next. Nevertheless by 950, the lords are the main operative force in Anglo-Saxon society without whom kings cannot govern nor the community operate its legal system. It is by no means certain how and when these lords came into existence and by what kinds of social change they became so indispensable to government and law. It was a common nineteenth-century (originally seventeenth-century) assumption that Anglo-Saxon history began with a free people who voluntarily followed a few great war leaders but who were innocent of lordship in the later sense. This view was based on now-exploded theories about pristine democratic Germanic communities of free and happy peasants. As far as it is possible to tell from the scanty sources, it is clear that there was a degree of social hierarchy in the earliest Anglo-Saxon society. At the bottom of the social scale was a class of slaves whose numbers greatly increased as the defeated British were subjugated. In the middle of the social scale there was indeed a very large group of peasants equally free before the law but varying considerably in the extent of their wealth and influence. At the top of the social scale was the king, his relatives, and—what is of great importance in the context of the present discussion—the king's *gesiths*, or companions. The latter were the great warriors of the folk who lived in the king's hall, feasted nightly on his largess, and went out with him to slay dragons and Celts. The success of the invasions assured that the king would reward his companions with booty and land and that they would rapidly become a superior caste of magnates, exercising leadership over the other free members of the community.

From the sixth to the ninth centuries this relatively simple social structure underwent a steady polarization so that the wealth and power of the upper strata increased whereas many of the hitherto main body of free peasantry were pushed down into varying degrees of dependence upon the lord, including that of involuntary servitude. There is nothing surprising about this social polarization of Anglo-Saxon England. Precisely the same kind of social change took place in France during the sixth and seventh centuries after Roman Gaul was settled by invading Germanic tribes. What is remarkable is that the extent and effect of social polarization varied markedly between the geographic regions of England. In the central agricultural triangle of Mercia and Wessex, the degree of polarization was most extreme. In order to maintain and insure a constant force of laborers in the farming midlands, a very substantial proportion of the original free peasantry was pushed down into a servile class of manorial villeins. Here it was that the classic medieval manor came to flourish from at least the eighth century. This system of agrarian economy was one which was marked by an involuntary serfdom of peasants absolutely bound to the land, and forced to provide labor services and rents to the lord who owned the land on which their villages existed. The lord provided open fields which the peasant community divided into strips for their own sustenance agriculture, and he was also supposed to grant them those rights of pasturage in his meadows and forests which to the manorial villein often meant the difference between survival and starvation. The lord, or more usually his steward, presided at the manorial court and held the power of life and death over this absolutely dependent peasantry. The manorial community would also contain a group of economically marginal landless peasants, perpetually facing the spectre of starvation, and before 1066 some personal slaves of the lord who had no rights at all against their masters.

In Anglo-Saxon England and for two centuries after the Norman Conquest, at least half of the rural peasantry eked out their bitter and hopeless lives in this draconic and severely exploitative economic and social situation. It is true that after the seventh century more and more of them came to enjoy the comforts of religion and the promise of a heavenly reward. But the happy English peasantry dancing around a maypole on the village greensward is something that existed only in the minds of nineteenth-century romantic writers. On the other hand, it must be emphasized that before 1066 even in the midlands not all peasants were serfs, and that outside the agricultural triangle of midland England, manorialism was often not economically feasible; it was a social system which could only work well in farming districts. In the east and north of England, and the West Country approaching the Welsh frontier, the land was not arable and the perpetuation over the centuries of pastoral and hunting and fishing economies preserved in these regions a substantial mass of free peasantry, long after the villeins of the midland had "bowed their necks" as the Anglo-Saxons said, to the aggressive landlords.

Again, it would be a mistake to romanticize the life of the peasantry in these outer regions of the country. The relatively high degree of legal freedom which was perpetuated there did not preclude a looser political and economic dependency on the magnates of these areas, and the freedom which ordinary men continued to enjoy there was partly vitiated by the poverty of the countryside and the constant threat of famine. Many an Anglo-Saxon serf in Mercia was far better off than a free man of the North Country. Nevertheless, the perpetuation of legal freedom in the outer regions had the effect of preserving a much looser and more open social organization, marked by the leadership of tribal chieftains and a few great warlords, which had been the original pattern of English social organization in the fifth century. In the long run this meant that the men of the north, east, and west, although poor and backward, had a much greater sense of the value of legal and political freedom than the subjugated villeins of the midlands.

It is therefore not surprising to find that throughout the medieval period and even in the sixteenth and seventeenth centuries, rebellions always begin in the outer regions of the kingdom and that the area which is always under the firmest control of the royal government is the manorial district of the midlands. From the eleventh century through the fourteenth and fifteenth centuries, and even down to the reign of Elizabeth I, and the Civil War of the mid-seventeenth century, the rebels against centralizing authority are always the men of East Anglia or the North Country, or from the Welsh frontier. This is partly explained by the patriarchal authority and traditional separatism of the frontier magnates, but it can also be attributed to the tradition of legal and political freedom among the ordinary populace of these areas. The Peasants' Revolt of the late fourteenth century begins in East Anglia and from the same area, some of which had been swampy land and economically unsuitable for manorial serfdom, also came the radical Puritanism of the seventeenth century. In this way the regional differentiation in the social structure of the Anglo-Saxon world was perpetuated in subsequent English social developments and the struggle between authority and freedom over the centuries was conditioned by underlying geo-social factors.

In accounting for the steady growth of the central importance of lordship in Anglo-Saxon society during the five centuries which followed the Anglo-Saxon invasion, it is possible to discern four causes for this profound cultural and political change, in addition to the consequences of the manorial form of agriculture. These causes are: first, a need to find a substitute for socially inadequate kinship bonds; second, the need for making decisions and asserting leadership in the loosely organized folk; third, the direct delegation of authority and landed wealth from the king; and fourth, the impact of the hierarchical theory of the church.

Lordship, which came by the tenth century to permeate the entire structure of Anglo-Saxon society, thus drew its power from the four other loyalties operating within it. And in this fourfold genesis of lordship we can also discern the fourfold nature of the authority held by the lord.

Although it may appear paradoxical, it can be seen that lordship emerged from the context of kinship itself. Though some historians have posited kinship and lordship as fundamentally opposite forms of social organization, the two are ultimately similar in kind. The idea that lordship represents a rupture of blood ties and the dissolving of the family bond was initially presented by Tacitus and more recently by H. M. Chadwick, who in a brilliant book conceived of a transitional "heroic age" marked by the warrior's shifting allegiance from his family to his lord. There is much to recommend this view but the shift can be seen as a more natural and less dialectical one. In the kinship bond a man followed a leader in his own family, perhaps his father, or brother, or uncle. An organic relationship between kinship and lordship was posited by the great social historian of the Middle Ages, Marc Bloch, who suggested that the lord was essentially a father-substitute. In the community which can no longer organize itself effectively along blood lines, either because the kin are too numerous, large, and disorganized to limit the effects of the blood feud or because the kin have already been decimated by incessant violence, the lord replaces the headman of the family or several disintegrating families. This is a very convincing theory and it makes sense in a simple human way. A man's devotion and loyalty to his lord is exactly the kind of feeling we expect to find in a family context. This emotional attitude is evoked not simply because the lord provides a lot of booty and drink. In *Beowulf* it is very clear that the lordless man is a doomed man who will suffer not only because he will cease to obtain booty and the dragon's gold, but also because he is morally culpable. Beowulf is the leader of a group of men who are bound together not because of blood but through common interest and desire; they are a new kind of family. Beowulf is a patriarchal figure who provides not only leadership in war but also moral comfort and emotional sustenance. In a society which in many ways was still tribal, the lord came to take the place of the father and enjoyed the personal-emotional loyalty which had hitherto been accorded to the leader of the kin.

The second cause and basis of lordship is empirical; it is the remedy for institutional impotence in response to the need for what we now call decision-making. By and large nineteenth-century historians were right in saying that at the beginning Anglo-Saxon society was largely comprised of free men, but they failed to see that these men had no institutions for making decisions and that therefore the medieval community could not operate in a democratic way. Since the Anglo-Saxons had no inkling of decision by majority vote and only a vague understanding of the concept of the corporate sense of the community, they were naturally forced to turn to the leadership of men of importance and stature, which in the beginning at least meant simply the outstanding warriors of the folk. The shire and the hundred courts, although their decisions were given in the name of the community, were really controlled by the most respected and powerful men who attended their meetings. There was no other way that decisions could be arrived at in the communities of Anglo-Saxon England. The elite group which made the decisions for the community naturally favored the strengthening of its own power and wealth in society. Even when the folk moots retained their free and corporate nature, and were not transformed into private courts under the direct control of a lord—which certainly occurred in the case of many hundred courts—the nature of Anglo-Saxon legal procedure was such as to bring the great majority of the free men in society into a loose dependency upon the few magistrates who made all the legal decisions. The legal authority of the folk moot enhanced rather than inhibited the growth of lordship in England. The vesting of judicial responsibility in the community of the shire, which to a substantial degree was a practice which survived even the Norman Conquest, had the effect of building up the leadership and influence in society of that handful of great landlords who inevitably dominated the procedure of the courts. This fundamental social and legal fact was to remain as characteristic of thirteenth- and even eighteenth-century England as it conditioned the simpler world of the tenth century.

Whenever powerful kings existed in Anglo-Saxon England who possessed large amounts of land and a degree of political and legal authority, however vague and ill-defined, it was inevitable that a certain kind of high lord should emerge, deriving his initial wealth and authority from the king's grant. This delegation of royal property and power to a new aristocracy originating as his servants was a common development in early medieval society whether in England, France, or Germany. In England this new kind of great lord makes his appearance particularly during the period of the consolidation of the realm under the House of Wessex from the late ninth to the middle of the eleventh century. In the ninth century we begin to hear about a lord called a *thegn*, a term which originally carried the connotation of administrative service to the king, in contrast with the earlier gesith, the happy warrior-companion of the early Anglo-Saxon rulers. By the end of the tenth century the word thegn has lost this original connotation of royal service and has become another synonym for lord. The dooms and other sources also tell us about a very responsible and influential representative of the king who rules a whole shire or even several of them; this official in the ninth century is called the *aldorman* and by the year 1000 he is known as the *earl*. At the time of the Norman Conquest the earl is very much the ruler of the shire or shires, but his official responsibility to the king has become vague and ill-defined, and the term is beginning to take on its later connotation of a particularly high and wealthy nobleman.

These subtle semantic changes indicate the transition, common to all early medieval kingdoms, by which the king's favorite, designated as his local or provincial representative, becomes a territorial lord of enormous power and prestige who ignores the king's authority with impunity. The men designated as the king's local officials, and enriched with royal land, identify themselves rapidly with the interests of the community they are assigned to govern. They turn themselves into territorial lords and transform the king's generous grant into an hereditary patrimony. This process is facilitated not only by the wildly fluctuating degree of royal authority, as a personally weak king succeeds an energetic and able one, but also by the terms of the original royal grant. In order to reward a particular favorite or support a provincial official who has unusually onerous responsibilities, the king would grant away not only the income from the royal property that he delegates but also all the royal legal and administrative authority over the land. This grant of immunity from royal control and taxation, transforming the granted estates into private jurisdictions (called in the Anglo-Saxon period *sac and soc*), was usually given with the understanding that this ultimate privilege was conditional upon satisfactory service to the king. But so centrifugal and local are the inclinations of medieval society, and so quickly does the earl become the regional leader of the folk, that the land and privileges can only be regained by costly and often ruinous wars. This creation of a new territorial aristocracy through the usurpation of delegated power and wealth was as characteristic of later Anglo-Saxon England as it had been of France in the ninth century.

The fourth basis of lordship in Anglo-Saxon society was the church's hierarchic conception of the world. The increasing prevalence of the bonds of lordship in the tenth and eleventh centuries only served to confirm the ideal nature of a social order which churchmen in England, as elsewhere, learned from their study of the writings of the Church Fathers. That certain men should in civil society control nearly all the wealth and power was as self-evident a proposition to the Anglo-Saxon ecclesiastics as the hierarchic organization of the church itself. This assumption induced the church to give religious and moral sanction to the bonds of lordship. In the ninth and tenth centuries the loyalty which men owed to their lord was given additional force by the development of an oath of fealty, modeled on continental precedents. Men were required to swear inviolable oaths of allegiance to their lord "loving what he loves and shunning what he shuns," with the result that disloyalty was penalized by divine as well as by secular punishment. The justice of the hierarchic organization of society was further proclaimed in the sermons of bishops and priests. In these ways the increasing polarization of society was affirmed as a necessary and holy thing, bringing the world closer to the perfect divine prototype.

During the last 150 years of the Anglo-Saxon era, the operation of law and government becomes increasingly dependent on lordship, which had such powerful factors contributing to its proliferation and entrenchment. The later dooms require that all members of society find a place not only in a corporate tithing but also under a lord, and a lordless man, by 1066, is potentially an outlaw in the eyes of the folk. As early as the time of King Alfred, at the end of the ninth century, the plotting of a lord's death is made a crime equivalent to the plotting of the king's murder. And the oath of fealty, which in the tenth century all men are supposed to swear to the king, uses the same wording as the ordinary oath of fealty to a lord, so that it became impossible to make a clear distinction between loyalty to the king and loyalty to one's immediate lord. With a lack of generic discrimination between loyalty to the king and loyalty to the lord, the great majority of men in later Anglo-Saxon society fulfilled the obligations of their oath of fealty to that master whose exercise of power was strongest and most immediate. In 1066 it was very hard for most people in England to distinguish between the authority of the king and that of the great earls.

It must be concluded that, whatever the wishful thinking of seventeenth-century and Victorian writers about the free Anglo-Saxon society, in 1066 Englishmen were under the rule of lords almost as completely as they were to be a half-century later. What then can be said to be the fundamental differences between Anglo-Saxon and Anglo-Norman lordship? The answer lies along two lines. In the first place, although Anglo-Saxon England was an hierarchic society, the hierarchy was a loose and in many ways confused one, whereas after 1066 the social structure was purposefully organized on an extremely coherent and rational basis by an aggressive and highly intelligent central government. The most obvious instance of this is that by the twelfth century, the royal lawyers and administrators had established an absolute legal dividing line in society between the free and the unfree. Before 1066 this distinction had not been carefully defined and there were a great many people in society of whom it would be difficult to say whether or not they were free men. Nor did this seem to be a very important question in the folk moots; it is only after the Norman Conquest that the establishment of one's status as a *liber homo* (freeman) was the primary qualification for pleading a case in the shire courts. In Anglo-Saxon England there was a mass of peasantry who acknowledged that an important local landowner was their lord, but it is not clear whether this acknowledgment was voluntary or involuntary. After 1066 this matter is no longer questionable; all the peasants, at least in agricultural regions, were dependent hereditary serfs.

The second distinction between Anglo-Saxon and Anglo-Norman lordship rises out of the relative backwardness of pre-Conquest England in military technology. Since the eighth century a profound military change, which had far-reaching social consequences, had been underway in France. The tribal army of the whole folk-in-arms was replaced by a professional army of armored cavalry—the feudal knights. The Anglo-Saxons, however, never learned to fight on horseback and the army which came down to Hastings in 1066 to engage the Norman cavalry was still the fyrd, the folk-in-arms. The English warlords rode horses, but they made the fatal mistake of dismounting to fight.

The emergence of the professional cavalrymen in France had a profound effect on the bonds of loyalty and lordship. The men of the lord became *vassals* whose oath of allegiance implied, and was often specifically made to include, military service. And in return the lord rewarded his vassals with estates (*fiefs*) by which they could support themselves and meet the heavy costs of armor and cavalry equipment. Therefore in France a new kind of specific feudal contract has emerged by the eleventh century, in which the oath of fealty signifies military service and the acceptance of a vassal's homage by a lord was frequently understood to imply the promise of a fief.

In later Anglo-Saxon England there were lords, soldiers, and lucrative estates for the granting, but these elements never congealed into the feudal contract prevalent across the channel and in England after 1066. Occasionally in the first half of the eleventh century we find a group of professional soldiers who, except for their propensity to dismount before battle, resemble the French chevaliers. One such group was that of the *housecarles*, a royal bodyguard introduced by the Danish king Canute, who ruled England from 1016 to 1035. Another such body of professional *cnihts* was under the authority of a wealthy early eleventh-century bishop. These professional soldiers received grants of land, but close scrutiny reveals that they did not fight because of a feudal contract binding them to military service in return for grants of land, but rather as part of their fundamental social obligation to join the fyrd and fulfill their duties as members of the folk.

It is an intriguing thought that later Anglo-Saxon lordship resembled the social structure of medieval France in its earlier ill-defined form, before the latter became congealed and rationalized along feudal lines. Given another century of autonomous development, it is possible that England would have experienced a similar revolution in military technology which would have produced a relatively precise feudal contract, as had occurred in France. Anglo-Saxon society was not to have this opportunity, and this is partly attributable to the qualities of Anglo-Saxon lordship itself. The warrior class in England was archaic in its military technology and this archaism was a privilege which the French chevaliers did not allow them to enjoy for long. Secondly, the regional powers of the great earls, the fundamental lack of distinction between loyalty to the king and loyalty to the local lords, and the generally imprecise, inchoate, and confused nature of social organization inhibited the development of a powerful central government which could have withstood the French invasion.

IV. Church and Kingship

THE OBLIGATIONS of loyalty in Anglo-Saxon society were primarily and most immediately directed to kinship, community, and lordship. But there were two other institutions, namely church and kingship, which in rather different ways, and in a less consistent manner, commanded the allegiance of all groups in society. Men ordinarily lived out their lives within the framework of family, folk, and lord, but in addition to this traditional framework of social cohesion, Anglo-Saxon people were heavily conscious of the demands placed upon them by churchmen and monarchs. While the obligations of kinship, community, and lordship were based upon immemorial custom and immediate practical necessity, the obligations of loyalty to church and king were also founded upon additional sanctions of a religious and moral nature. If these sanctions could be made effective, the result would be a high degree of social melioration and political centralization, for church and kingship, which worked in close alliance, possessed between them the greater part of the literate intelligence and capacity for rational decision-making in this society. During the tenth and first half of the eleventh centuries, across the channel in Normandy and also in the German Empire, the cooperation of church and kingship produced unified states with centralized governments of great power and efficiency. In comparison the working together of Anglo-Saxon monarchy and church resulted in rather more modest achievements. Therefore the most important question with regard to English church and kingship before 1066 is to account for their failure to achieve a centralized state in spite of the personal excellence, in terms of both religious devotion and literate intelligence, on the part of many churchmen, and the high degree of consciousness of their role as divinely appointed leaders of society on the part of the kings.

The English church was founded by the papacy. This was true of none of the other territorial or national churches of Europe, and this peculiar fact was to condition the Roman attitude toward England at least until the end of the eleventh century. Even at the beginning of the sixteenth century the English king and church were supposed to pay an impost called Peter's Pence to Rome, in recognition of the papal service of

Christianizing England, and occasionally this nominal tax actually resulted in the dispatch of a modest sum to the papal *curia*.

In the latter part of the sixth century the conversion of England was inaugurated by Irish missionaries who crossed the Irish Sea to bring the faith to the northern part of the country. Because the Celtic church was currently at odds with Rome on several significant issues, Pope Gregory I the Great hastened to make England a province of the Roman church. He dispatched a Benedictine monk named Augustine, a man of rather timid temperament and obtuse intelligence, together with a few companions to the court of King Ethelbert of Kent. Ethelbert was chosen to receive the gospel because his wife, a French princess, was already Christian, but this fortuitous choice turned out to be a good one because Ethelbert was an important and influential king. His acceptance of Christianity encouraged his gesiths to receive baptism and the Roman missionaries began to radiate north and west from the Kentish kingdom and succeeded in converting the southern half of England by the middle of the seventh century. Ethelbert's fortress town of Canterbury (literally, Kent Town) naturally became the primary seat of the English church, although in the late eleventh and twelfth centuries and again in the early sixteenth century, the proud bishops of York and London abortively contested the primacy in the realm of a bishopric which had been thus established by chance in the quiet southeastern corner of the realm.

By the middle of the seventh century, the Roman missionaries had come into direct conflict with the Irish churchmen working in the north of England, and for a decade or two the question of whether England would belong to the Roman or Celtic church, or would suffer a religious partition, was a real one. Finally at the Synod of Whitby in 664 the overwhelming majority of English ecclesiastics opted to accept the authority of the Roman pope and the Celtic missionaries withdrew from the country. It was almost inevitable, given the traditional hegemony of the See of Peter and the superior resources of the papacy, that this choice should be made. The somewhat independent Irish conversion of northern England had as its legacy the creation of a separate ecclesiastical province under the Archbishop of York, although Canterbury asserted its primacy over the whole country.

The decision at Whitby was fortunate for the English church in that it immediately resulted in the papal appointment as Archbishop of Canterbury of an eminent scholar from Asia Minor, Theodore of Tarsus, who made Canterbury a great center of learning and scholarship in the late seventh century. At the same time a northern thegn who had become a Benedictine monk and taken the name of Benedict Biscop founded at Jarrow in Yorkshire another flourishing center of ecclesiastical study. By 700 the monastic and episcopal schools in England were turning out learned and zealous monks who had a profound impact on the continental church in the eighth century. It was an English missionary, Willibrord, who began the conversion of the Low Countries, the original homeland of most of the English folk. More famous was St. Boniface (to use the Latin name he was given by the Pope) who became the apostle of Germany, the founder of Christian civilization east of the Rhine, and who provided the leadership in reinvigorating the eighth-century French church and bringing it in close contact with Rome. The most learned Christian scholar of the early eighth century was Bede, a monk at Jarrow, and another Yorkshire churchman, Alcuin, was brought to France by Charlemagne in the last decade of the eighth century to serve as his chief assistant in ecclesiastical and educational matters. Not again until the early fourteenth century would Englishmen play such a leading role in the intellectual life of Europe.

The Irish church was exclusively monastic, and something of a Celtic tradition can be seen in the tendency of the English church in the eighth century to have nearly all its most zealous and learned members in the ranks of the Benedictine monastic order. The ordinary secular clergy, the bishops and priests, were as a group decidedly inferior to the regular clergy of the Benedictine order, and this fact in part explains why the English church had such a profound impact on the continent but played a decidedly less important role in the shaping of English government and society. Large numbers of the most devoted and learned eighth-century English monks went off to the continent when summoned by their compatriot St. Boniface, and this heavy loss of literate and intelligent manpower was a severe drain on the resources of an undeveloped and largely illiterate society. While providing indispensable aid to the French kings in the eighth century, the English churchmen did little to improve the effective working of monarchy in their own country. And while St. Boniface and his disciples earned the eternal gratitude of the Roman church in effecting the conversion of what is today western Germany, the great mass of Englishmen remained only formally baptized and their fundamental outlook on life was still enshrouded by superstition and heathenism. It is a harsh but nevertheless true judgment that the most vital group in the eighth-century English church gained their great missionary successes at the expense of turning their backs on the needs of government and society at home. Nor is this a judgment which is entirely dependent on hindsight and the values of the modern rather than the medieval world. At the end of his great *Ecclesiastical History of the English People,* completed in the early 730's, Bede comments on the growing instability and violence in English life and the beginnings of a decline in the high intellectual level of the English church. These developments were at least in part the result of the over-commitment of English monks to their continental missions and the failure in large part of the English church to overcome the deep-rooted inadequacies of Germanic kingship.

Although some historians begin their accounts of early English society with an analysis of the institution of Germanic kingship, it is always realistic in the Anglo-Saxon world to begin at the most local level, with kinship and community, since in this society the more general an authority is, the weaker it is likely to be. We must emphasize again that communications were incredibly bad, that the lives of nearly all men revolved around their neighborhood pigsties, and that the king, although theoretically wielding what we would regard as the widest and most universal authority, did not really signify very much in the day-to-day lives of his people. But he was there, and he must have done something. In the fifth and sixth centuries he mostly fought and drank. The king was a great chieftain who was different from the other warlords because there was something special about his family, something sacred about their blue blood. The royal family was descended from Woden, and kingship was something that belonged to the royal family irrevocably and endowed them with a vaguely charismatic authority. The most throne-worthy (that is, toughest) member of the blue-blooded family would be chosen king by the other chiefs. This Germanic idea of throne-worthiness and election by the folk as against primogeniture lingered on in England throughout the medieval period. It operated in 871 in the selection of King Alfred, who was intended for a clerical career until the early deaths of his brothers left him the only surviving male adult in the house of Wessex. It also was in effect in 1199 when King John was chosen by the magnates over his nephew because of his superior military skill, which did not however fulfill expectations. The notion of throne-worthiness was resurrected in intentionally obscure ways in the fourteenth century to justify the deposition of kings by magnates and Parliament.

The earliest Anglo-Saxon king, then, was a particularly uncouth warrior who sat around with his companions in a big hall and got drunk on mead or else fought and parceled out booty. There was nothing glorious about this kind of king and there was not meant to be. The arrival of Roman missionaries at the end of the sixth century offered possibilities for fundamental changes in the ideals and image of kingship. The churchmen had come trailing clouds of Roman glory behind them. They began to propound very general ideas of what the king as a public leader should do for his realm: he should protect the church—always the first requirement—and he should establish peace, improve the law, and generally oversee the welfare of his people. The clergy thought of kingship in terms of the prototype they found in patristic literature. A king was a Christian Roman emperor, like Constantine or Theodosius, who wielded absolute authority, fostered justice, and of course protected and enriched the church.

Did this rhetorical tinsel have any significance in the seventh and eighth centuries? It was one thing for St. Augustine to tell Ethelbert that he should be a king like Constantine and for the flattered chieftain to agree that this was a fine idea, and another for this rhetorical exchange to have any positive impact on government and society. There *was* a limited impact of Christian ideology on Anglo-Saxon kingship during the seventh and eighth centuries. We know that kings did issue collections of dooms at the encouragement of churchmen who wanted the protection of the law through inclusion in the wergeld lists, and it was in fact the clerics, the only literate members of society, who wrote down these collections. But the king did more than assign a wergeld to the churchmen; he clarified other parts of the law, and this may be seen as fulfilling the obligations which the church imposed upon him to further peace in society. When the kings decreed that the folk court should meet, we can believe they were not moved only by the fines they would collect but by Christian idealism as well, for the meeting of the community court provided the only way to limit the blood feud.

It was also at least partly under ecclesiastical inspiration that the king took more and more people under his *mundbyrd*, his personal protection. In Germanic society all lords had their *mundbyrd* and included a variety of people and places dear to them within its scope: their families, their retainers and soldiers, their drinking halls and fortresses. But the English kings, once converted, were impelled to take all the churchmen in their realm into their mundbyrd. This was not a casual obligation because the churchmen had a tendency to wander off into the forests and anarchic border country. As soon as the king brought the church under his protection he had a much wider area to be concerned with; he had drawn a line of obligation for himself that might easily include monasteries a hundred miles away from his big drinking hall.

The king having once fundamentally altered the scope of the mund-byrd by bringing the church within it, it was natural that he should go on expanding it so that by the eleventh century the circle of his protective responsibilities has slowly expanded to include, in theory, just about everyone in the whole realm except for the no-man's land in the wild frontier region. The king's mundbyrd had become the king's *frith*, or peace. All the while the churchmen encouraged this expansion of royal responsibility by their enunciation of Roman ideals of the monarch as a public official responsible for the welfare of the whole society. This does not mean, however, that the king was able to comprehend the glorious Roman tradition which the churchmen unreflectively repeated in their political jargon. The difference between the king as a personal authority, commanding loyalty because of his personal prowess and energy, and the idea of a king as the holder of a public authority of the corporate state was an extremely difficult one for the medieval mind to formulate and to grasp, because Germanic thought had no understanding of the king other than in the former aspect. The idea of the king as a public corporation, the king as the crown, will begin to flash out fitfully in the twelfth and thirteenth centuries, but there is no comprehension of it before 1066. What does happen is that by the eleventh century, under ecclesiastical influence, the personal responsibility of the king has become so extensive that it literally becomes too much for him to handle and therefore potentially begins to be more than personal. But the Anglo-Saxons are unable to define the way in which the institution of monarchy has transcended the personal quality of the king.

What the church did for kingship in the seventh and eighth centuries was therefore to make the king accept certain obligations which moved him beyond the circle of his own kin and warriors, and this in a sense was a great step forward. But otherwise the learned ecclesiastics of this period, so enthused with missionary zeal for work on the continent, failed fundamentally to improve the extremely meager institutional and intellectual bases of Germanic monarchy. The churchmen did not provide a permanent group of royal officials to carry out the literate work of government: aside from the dooms there are extremely few documentary records of English monarchy before the tenth century. Nor did the churchmen before 800 succeed in formulating liturgical ceremonies that would raise the king above the warrior class and provide new moral and religious strength for royal power. At the end of the eighth century kings were still primarily Germanic warlords, the country was still divided into several small kingdoms, and the church had still failed to put its learning and intelligence to the effective service of Germanic kingship.

The effect of the Scandinavian invasions which began in the last decade of the eighth century and continued for almost a hundred years, was cataclysmic for the Anglo-Saxon church and kingship alike. Driven by the pressure of overpopulation on a meager food supply and by obscure tribal feuds in Norway and Denmark, the Vikings took to their longboats and, like their Germanic kinsmen three centuries before, assaulted the east coast of England, beginning in Yorkshire and pressing steadily southwestward. Aside from confirming the tendency of the social structure of eastern England away from manorialism and in the direction of a large mass of free peasants, the Vikings had nothing to offer to the development of government and society in England. The Scandinavians at this time were a savage, heathen, and violent people with a notable propensity for drowning their kings in wells when they had no further use for them. Contrary to the wishful thinking of some fervent modern partisans of the Vikings, there is no contemporary evidence that allows us to view the ninth-century Scandinavians as having political and social institutions other than those employed by their German kinsmen when they invaded England in the fifth century.

The numbers of the invaders were not great in comparison with the size of the native population and aside from a few loan-words which entered into the terminology of politics and law (for example, *wapentake* for hundred) they left no tradition behind them. But the immediate consequence of their onslaught was a catastrophe for English churchmen and kings. The great centers of learning in Yorkshire, including Jarrow, were obliterated, and monastery after monastery was sacked by these savages as they moved invincibly forward to conquer all of England. By 870 only the kingdom of Wessex in the southwest remained unconquered, and it was only by the closest of margins and the most desperate measures that Alfred, the scholarly king of Wessex, finally fought the Danes to a draw and made them accept a truce which divided the country between the Danelaw in the northeast and Wessex in the southwest.

In the tenth century, Alfred's descendants established a loose suze-rainty over the Danelaw and brought the whole of England under the house of Wessex. But the cost of the century and a half of almost in-cessant warfare was tremendous. The English church which before the Scandinavian invasions had been the most learned and zealous in Eu-rope was by the early tenth century impoverished and backward, its librar-ies scattered, its great centers of learning destroyed, and the quality of its churchmen markedly inferior in learning and zeal in comparison with the now-flourishing monastic centers in the Low Countries and the Rhineland, which had originally been founded, in many instances, by Englishmen of the eighth century.

In the mid-tenth century under the leadership of the Archbishop of Canterbury, St. Dunstan, the reconstruction of the English church was inaugurated by drawing upon royal assistance and the intellectual re-sources of the great centers of monastic learning in the Low Countries and northern France. St. Dunstan himself studied in one of these cen-ters. The result of this work was the partial rebuilding of the English church to the level which it had attained in the eighth century. Monas-teries were refurbished, new libraries gathered together, and a new gen-eration of churchmen was educated for pastoral work. But before 1066 the English church never regained the intellectual distinction and zeal it had enjoyed before the Viking invasions, and in the first half of the eleventh century England could claim only one of the less flourishing territorial branches of the Latin church.

There were three fundamental defects in the work of the later Anglo-Saxon church. In the first place, the English ecclesiastics were out of touch with Rome and after about 1050 when a great reform movement was launched by the papal *curia*, this provincialism made the English bishops and abbots appear particularly backward and incompetent in the eyes of the Roman cardinalate. Secondly, in the tenth and early eleventh centuries the English church was singularly lacking in either eminent scholars or strong leaders. St. Dunstan was a devoted archbishop but withal a man of mediocre quality who merely imitated the policies of the churchmen he knew across the channel, and with no particular flair or ingenuity. The later Anglo-Saxon church produced one scholar of some quality, a learned abbot named Ælfric, but the content of his writings was conservative and rather old-fashioned in comparison with the bril-liant philosophers and canon lawyers who in the early eleventh century were inaugurating a great intellectual upheaval on the continent. It was a severe limitation for Ælfric and other late Anglo-Saxon scholars that they were so thoroughly bilingual and that much of their best work, usually in the form of sermons, was published in the vernacular. While this contributed to the perpetuation of English as a literary language, it prevented Ælfric from gaining any reputation as a theologian and social theorist among continental scholars. It was not, in fact, until the nineteenth century that the superior qualities of his mind were recognized.

A final defect of later Anglo-Saxon churchmen arises out of their characteristic interest in personal piety and in homiletic work. This had the salutary effect of making them worthy pastors of their communities but it resulted in a kind of Christian devotion which was intensely personal and markedly nonintellectual. While the churchmen of France and Germany were achieving distinction as either great public figures and ecclesiastical statesmen, or as pioneers in new forms of clerical thought, particularly in rational theology and canon law, the English ecclesiastics were renowned mostly for their sanctity. Therefore a phenomenal number of later Anglo-Saxon churchmen were, in consequence of their inspiring impact on popular piety, elevated to the community of saints, but not one of them played an important role in shaping the development of government and society.

The English kings of the tenth and early eleventh centuries were as singularly lacking in strong personalities as the ranks of the churchmen, and this lack in part accounts for the general weakness of later Anglo-Saxon kingship. Whatever might be the administrative skill or the degree of sophistication in ideology of early medieval monarchy, the power of kings was still dependent most of all on the image they presented to the people as warlords and strong personalities. And although the later Anglo-Saxon kings were rather a sincere and well-intentioned lot, and two of them were even saints, their personal qualities were such as to instill little fear among the lords and gain no fervent loyalty from the population as a whole. Ethelstan (924-939) completed the nominal unification of the country and exhibited considerable skill in the improvement of the institutions of the royal administration, and Edgar (959-975) was renowned for his loyalty to the church and his support of Dunstan's efforts at ecclesiastical recovery. But neither of these rulers achieved any significant success in the creation of an effective centralized government which could reverse the steady advance of the political and social power of the great earls. The long reign (from 978 to 1016) of Ethelred the Redeless (that is, the ill-counseled or incompetent) was distinguished by the steady enfeeblement of royal authority, culminating in the easy conquest of his kingdom by the great Danish ruler Canute (1016-1035).

It is an illuminating comment on the quality of the later Anglo-Saxon kings that the most effective of them by far was a Scandinavian. Canute tried to provide for English monarchy the same kind of institutional framework which had worked well for the new centralized governments in Normandy and the German empire. He created a professional army in the royal service, brought church and kingship closer together in a mutually beneficial alliance by appointing to bishoprics and abbacies clerics who had served in his government and who were politically rather than spiritually minded, and tried to establish some sort of entente with the Roman curia. All aspects of this program were to be repeated in the work of the Anglo-Norman monarchy in the late eleventh century, but Canute's efforts did not survive his death. The ensuing civil war in Denmark and the weakness of his sons who succeeded him in England extinguished both his line and his reform program, and left the way open for the English earls in 1042 to ferret out of a Norman monastery and place on the throne a saintly descendant of the house of Wessex.

The twenty-four years of Edward the Confessor's reign (1042-1066) were a disaster for English monarchy; if there was one thing worse for medieval government than a saint on the throne, it was a saint who lived too long. During Edward's reign there was a constant squabbling among the great earls for the spoils of royal authority and property and additional conflicts between Norman churchmen whom Edward promoted to office in England and the jealous but unenlightened English clergy. The great northern earl Godwin walked off with most of the spoils and even succeeded in driving out the Norman-French Archbishop of Canterbury in favor of his own obscure candidate. This scandal scarcely improved the already dark image of the English church held by the reforming papacy.

Edward the Confessor, although married, was thoroughly celibate and not even a medieval saint could produce an heir under these circumstances. Consequently when Edward died in 1066 Harold Godwinson was able to fulfill his father's policy of making off with the power and wealth of the monarchy by forcing the other earls to elect him as king. Harold appears in some respects as a strong and attractive personality but he was unfortunate in having to meet the attack of the greatest ruler of eleventh-century Europe, and this last of the Anglo-Saxon kings was cut down at the Battle of Hastings before he could do anything to overcome the long record of incompetence and weakness on the part of his predecessors on the English throne.

In spite of this general failure of later Anglo-Saxon kingship, there were two areas in which these kings made some contribution to the strengthening of monarchy, and William the Conqueror took full advantage of these achievements. The first of these was the improvement in the ideological foundation of kingship through the institution of royal anointment by the Archbishop of Canterbury at the time of coronation. Through anointment with the same consecrated oil by which a bishop was elevated to his office, the religious sanction of kingship and the idea of the king as ruler by the grace of God was emphasized. The ceremony and doctrine of royal anointment were introduced by King Edgar and St. Dunstan in 973. It was part of a new coronation ceremony in which, before the sacring, the Archbishop made the king swear to protect the church and pursue justice, and asked the assembled leaders of the folk, that is, the lords, to affirm their acceptance of the royal candidate. Thereby the church made succession to the throne dependent on community approval and ecclesiastical acceptance and at the same time proclaimed the king, as a result of his holy anointment, the holder of a sacred office. This coronation ceremony and its corollary doctrine of theocratic monarchy was readily perpetuated by William the Conqueror and his sons, and in fact the Anglo-Saxon coronation order in 973 has continued, with only minor revisions and additions, through all succeeding reigns down to and including that of Elizabeth II. It by no means originated with Edgar and Dunstan, but was imported wholesale, including most of the actual terminology of the ceremony, from France.

The proclaiming of the English king as the Lord's anointed was designed not only to strengthen the alliance between church and monarchy but also to increase royal authority in the country through the addition of a clearcut religious sanction. It is likely that the earls and great lords who witnessed the ceremony were suitably impressed and that it at least discouraged them from thoughts of assassinating the king, for he now had a priestly status. But the Anglo-Saxon lords were not famous for the luminous quality of their intellect. Their attention span was probably not greater than that of a six-year-old child in the modern world, and once they returned to their shires the high-flown terminology and glorious ceremony of the coronation order were easily forgotten. They were in no way dissuaded from usurping the power and wealth of the anointed king.

The second contribution of later Anglo-Saxon kingship to the subsequent development of royal government in England was on the administrative side. In the tenth and early eleventh centuries there were some institutional innovations in the working of the king's government which were taken up and improved upon after the Norman Conquest. From the reign of Ethelstan the kings had a chancery, or secretariat, in which royal clerks drafted certain documents according to prescribed forms, dispatched them to interested parties, and took pains to keep records. There were two kinds of documents issued by the late Anglo-Saxon chancery. The first of these, the charter or land deed, was by no means unique but was used by all the royal governments of Europe and by many of the great lords of the realm. In the later Anglo-Saxon period some property is being deeded as *bookland*, that is, by book or charter, as well as in the more usual form of *folkland*, or oral custom. The strong tendency toward oral procedure in Germanic law is reflected in the fact that the pre-Conquest charters appear to have been testamentary rather than dispositary in nature, that is, they merely witnessed the oral deeding of land, and the document itself did not effect the transfer. Another indication of the somewhat archaic attitude of the Anglo-Saxons toward written records was the practice of the chancery to depart from prescribed and definite forms in their drafting of royal charters. The medieval charter had five parts: the salutation, the harangue or statement of the reasons for the grant, the careful description of the land and privileges being granted, the curse put on those who violated the terms of the grant and invaded the property, and finally the witness list, to which the grantor and grantee, and the interested parties witnessing the transaction, subscribed their testamentary seals. It was characteristic of the Anglo-Saxon chancery to be rather careless about the inclusion of the harangue and to use certain curses which have a markedly individual rather than formal tone. The royal clerks before 1066 also were inclined to lengthen or shorten the witness list in accordance with the amount of empty parchment that was available when they reached the bottom of the charter, with the result that some impressively long witness lists on royal charters are fraudulent. These charming eccentricities of the Anglo-Saxon chancery are characteristic of a group of administrative amateurs, and sharply distinguish the royal clerks of Edward the Confessor's day from the self-conscious professionals who drafted the documents of the Anglo-Norman monarchy.

On the other hand the chancery clerks of the tenth and early eleventh centuries were remarkably ingenious in developing a new kind of royal document which is not to be found on the continent. This was the royal *writ* which, in contrast with the long elaborate charter, was a small piece of parchment addressed to a royal official or dependent requiring him to perform some task for the king. It is not easy to judge from the hundred or so Anglo-Saxon writs that have survived how extensively the chancery made use of this new institution. But in any case, the communication of royal policy to the local community could only have had frustrating results. The shire reeve (or sheriff) who was supposed to be the king's local representative came increasingly after 900 under the domination of the real holders of regional power, the earls. Without the control exercised by a strong central authority in command of a professional royal army, the sheriff could ignore the royal writs with impunity, and the earls treat these orders with contempt. The Anglo-Saxon chancery clerks had thus conceived of a system of royal control over the local communities which they were impotent to put into successful operation. After 1066 the royal writ became the sinews of the English administrative and legal system. The writ became not only the means of communicating the royal will in political and administrative matters, but also the documentary agency in the growth of a centralized legal system. The Norman kings then had to take hold of this procedure and develop it effectively, but the first writs were issued by the incompetent kings of the tenth century.

The later Anglo-Saxon chancery made great strides in improving the literate work of government, but the royal treasury was, at the same time, remarkable for its failure to organize the wealth of the country in the interests of royal power. Later Anglo-Saxon England was by medieval standards a heavily populated and rich country. The population of England in 1066 was close to a million; at the end of the sixteenth century the population had risen only threefold and in 1700 there were still only about five million people in England. In 1066, at least eighty percent of these million people lived in the southern half of the country. Furthermore, at least ninety-five percent of the population lived on the land. At the time of the Norman Conquest, there was a flourishing cross-Channel and North Sea trade, but the urban population was still very small. London, the largest city in the realm, may have had fifteen thousand people; York's population was somewhere around nine thousand;

Norwich probably had seven thousand inhabitants, and Lincoln's population was probably equal to this number. But all the other boroughs had fewer than five thousand inhabitants, and it is questionable whether we can term these other boroughs truly urban centers in any sociological sense. In view of the paucity of burgesses in later Anglo-Saxon England, the intensive quality of settlement in the agricultural regions of the southern half of the country becomes readily apparent. It is probable that in many areas of rural England the density of population was the same in the mid-eleventh and the mid-eighteenth centuries.

Yet the later Anglo-Saxon kings failed dismally in their attempts to control the resources of this rich land in their own interests. Their only effort at taxation was the *Danegeld,* which was a payment demanded once every ten or twenty years from the whole folk, beginning in the reign of Ethelred, to allow the king to fight or buy off the Danes. This tax produced very high returns and (in view of its national character) it looks forward beyond the feudal period to the thirteenth century. But otherwise the Anglo-Saxon kings had no taxation system, not even a customs levy. The king in 1066 still lived off his own estates. Each royal manor was assigned as a "farm of one night," or more, and the king and his entourage moved from one royal estate to another, spending one or more days there and eating up the produce like a plague of locusts. Anglo-Saxon government never developed any sanction for taxation beyond the occasional Danegeld levy. And when the money came in from the Danegeld or from the royal share of fines in the community courts, the royal treasury kept no record of it. Although the coinage itself was remarkably good in the quality of the type faces and the purity of the silver content, the royal treasury developed no accounting machinery, and even in the time of Edward the Confessor the proceeds from the Danegeld were simply heaped in a strongbox under the king's bed.

The inadequacies of Anglo-Saxon administration are partly explained by the fact that all the kings and not only the luckless Ethelred were ill-counseled. The churchmen who worked for the kings in the tenth and first half of the eleventh centuries were too limited in their education and too narrow in their experience to be able to inform the king on the radical steps that he had to take in order to overcome the centrifugal tendencies of lordship and establish an effective centralized government. The English churchmen, unlike their counterparts in France, knew very little of military life and the problems involved in raising and leading a professional army. Nor were they trained in the traditions of Roman law and canon law which, in the eleventh century, were already part of the education of some of the great continental ecclesiastics. Therefore they had no standard against which they could measure the irrational and outmoded procedures to which the community courts were still devoted. The king's *witan* (literally, counsel of wise men), which nineteenth-century historians regarded as a kind of Anglo-Saxon parliament filled with armored Gladstones, was certainly no help to the king. It was an occasional assembly of great lords brought together to witness royal charters and to listen, usually in vain, to the royal appeals for harmony and support. In the reign of Edward the Confessor, the meetings of the witan seem to have been primarily devoted to petty quarrels between the king and Earl Godwin. Wherever an effective royal government emerged in the tenth and eleventh centuries in Europe, the king was always surrounded by aggressive churchmen learned in law and experienced in administration and war, and by a few lords who for one reason or another were willing to give the king loyal and invaluable advice on the practical steps by which he might use the military and financial resources of the landed magnates for his own ends. The Anglo-Saxon kings lacked counselors of this type.

Later Anglo-Saxon royal administration, ingeniously experimental in some respects, but fantastically primitive in others, and hopelessly incompetent in general, characterizes the fundamental nature of government and law in this society as a whole. The king ordered the community courts to meet and obtained a share of the fines from the folk moot, but the law continued to be the possession of the communities who remained loyal to the customary irrational legal procedures. The communities in turn came under the domination of great lords whose ambitions did not extend beyond the expansion of their patrimonies. The churchmen celebrated the glories of theocratic monarchy but they were unable to show the king how he might effectually establish his authority in the realm.

Anglo-Saxon England has always proved attractive to scholars and lay students of English history. This is not merely due to an obsession with origins, national or institutional; it is indeed possible to find in this world fragmentary evidence of the political and social ideas and institutions of later eras. Yet this fragmentary quality was a fatal deficiency of English government and society before 1066. The loyalties which were given to kin, community, lord, church, and king conflicted with each other, and in the end canceled each other out so that this wealthy society, with considerable intellectual resources, achieved neither a centralized and effective government nor a rational legal procedure. At bottom the government of Anglo-Saxon England is government of the absurd.

CHAPTER THREE

RATIONALIZATION AND
CENTRALIZATION
from 1066 to 1135

I. The Conquerors

WITH THE EXCEPTION of the problem of the origins of the Civil War in the seventeenth century, the impact of the Norman Conquest on English government and society has been the subject providing the most persistent debate in English historiography. This concern with the evaluation of the significance of the Norman Conquest is justified because the interpretation of the course of English history for the century and a half following 1066 is largely dependent on the view taken of the institutions and ideas which the French conquerors contributed to English political and legal development.

Norman Frenchmen writing in either England or Normandy in the generation after 1066 were the first historians of the Conquest. The most perceptive of these was a Norman monk resident in England named William of Malmesbury. It is not unnatural that these writers should have viewed the Conquest with great satisfaction since they were members of the new conquering elite, nor, since they were churchmen, is it surprising that they interpreted the triumph of William the Conqueror in ecclesiastical and sacred terms. These earliest accounts of the Norman Conquest inaugurated what may be called the liberation theory—the idea that English government was rescued from disorder and ineptitude by the importation of superior Norman institutions, and that the English church had been saved from decrepitude and isolation by a devout King William who served the interests of the papacy and the Catholic church.

Early in the twelfth century the decisiveness of the break between pre- and post-conquest England was played down and a somewhat new interpretation established a thread of continuity in both governmental and ecclesiastical matters. This change was partly induced by a more favorable attitude toward Anglo-Saxon culture prevalent among the royal clerks and partly by the process of merging of the Norman and English races. Significantly the most skilled spokesman for this new interpretation was the monastic historian Orderic Vital, who was half English and half Norman by birth. Orderic depicted William as the natural successor to Edward the Confessor, who emerged as the ideal anointed king, and several Norman monks resident in England found favorable things to note in the English monastic tradition. At the same time, the Anglo-Saxon Chronicle, which had been prepared in various monasteries since the time of King Alfred, was continued into the twelfth century by surviving English monks. The authors of the Chronicle, who may be regarded as spokesmen for the defeated side, found the Norman kings fearsome but capable. Behind the tone of awe and terror that suffuses the later sections of the Chronicle, we can see that the English monks realized that royal government had become remarkably more effective after 1066.

To the polemicists of the first half of the seventeenth century, the Norman Conquest was an historiographical problem of great importance because their political and social theories were dependent on their interpretation of the nature of the Norman Conquest. Modern critics have called this seventeenth-century interpretation the "Norman myth." This view was mainly the creation of revolutionary left-wing writers who maintained that England was a happy democratic country before the Norman nobility crushed her helpless people. These radicals thereupon felt justified in calling upon the English finally to rise up and throw off the oppressive Norman yoke, whose living embodiment was paradoxically a king of Scottish provenance.

In somewhat attenuated form, the "Norman myth" was still popular among nineteenth-century historians. The Victorian scholar E. A. Freeman, whose five-volume *History of the Norman Conquest* is still the most complete account of these great events, postulated that before 1066 the English were governed by a constitutional system involving the consent of the people and he explicitly portrayed Earl Godwin as an eleventh-century Gladstone. The implication in this view is that the autocratic rule introduced by the Normans was so severe that two hundred years had to pass after the conquest before the English tradition of government by consent was again vindicated through the emergence of parliament. By and large this is also the view of William Stubbs, who saw in the survival of the shire courts after 1066 the institutional means of perpetuating, even in the age of autocratic Norman feudalism, the Anglo-Saxon principle that law resided in the community.

The Norman myth suffered its first great deflation in the work of F. W. Maitland, who was far less inclined than previous historians to find the origins of English constitutionalism in pre-conquest England. By viewing the jury as French in origin, and by attributing to the Anglo-Norman monarchy the creative work in the formation of the common law, Maitland inaugurated a general devaluation of Anglo-Saxon institutions and an historiographical trend toward regarding the Norman Conquest as the best thing that happened to medieval England. This new interpretation was given definitive form in the first two decades of the twentieth century by H. W. C. Davis, an Oxford professor who made the first systematic study of the government and administration of William the Conqueror, and by C. H. Haskins, an American scholar whose *Norman Institutions*, published in 1918, is still the authoritative work on the subject. As seen by Davis and Haskins, the Norman Conquest was not the invasion of a peaceful and happy land devoted to liberal institutions by alien autocrats; rather, the events of 1066 constituted the rescue of a declining and disintegrating society by political leaders of great genius. The Norman Conquest made England part of Europe and saved it from being absorbed into the barren Scandinavian world and from turning into another Iceland. Here again is the liberation thesis, but now England is viewed as being liberated not so much for the church as for Western civilization. This Normanist interpretation, as it may be called, considers Anglo-Saxon government hopelessly feeble and pre-Conquest culture insignificant; it emphasizes the impact of French higher culture in transforming English civilization and makes all the important political and legal institutions of late eleventh- and twelfth-century England the result of the Anglo-Norman monarchy. For Haskins, who was a highly influential man of affairs as well as a great scholar, the Normans were eleventh-century "supermen," geniuses at the art of government who took feudal institutions which had been agencies of decentralization and reshaped them into powerful centralizing institutions. Under feudal guise the Normans applied rationality and organizational skill to the problems of medieval government for the first time. Therefore the beginnings of the modern bureaucratic state are to be found in late eleventh-century England.

Until about 1940 the Normanist interpretation, stated so forcefully by Haskins and Davis, was unchallenged. But in the last twenty-five years English historiography has begun to slide back to the "Norman myth" of the seventeenth century. No great work of scholarship has appeared to give the "Norman myth" any new definitive form, but in studies made by some learned and reputable historians—R. R. Darlington, D. C. Douglas, G. O. Sayles, Frank Barlow, and the American student of military institutions, C. W. Hollister—there has been a noticeable decline in enthusiasm for Norman genius. The Normans are now depicted as uncouth soldiers who were very lucky to conquer a people as civilized as the English. We are told that it was the clever, literate English who taught their alien masters how to govern. It is claimed that the most effective instruments of Anglo-Norman government—the ideology of sacred kingship, the community courts, the writ, and national taxation—were taken over from the Anglo-Saxons. Some writers have even been able to find the feudal contract in the reign of Edward the Confessor, although they have not yet succeeded in showing that the pre-conquest nobility fought on horseback. This neo-Victorian enthusiasm has had the salutary effect of forcing scholars of the Norman Conquest to re-examine the whole problem of late eleventh-century government and to define its nature through a careful and critical study of the contemporary sources. We know it is not enough to deify the Normans as supermen; we actually have to explain what William the Conqueror and his assistants were trying to do, why they tried to do these things, and how successful they were. This critical re-examination of Anglo-Norman government is still underway and there are some problems which have not yet achieved definitive solutions.

Not the least of the problems connected with Norman history is the explanation of how and why the Duke of Normandy should in 1066 have had the most centralized and rational government in western Europe. The first eight decades of the Duchy of Normandy, after its founding in 911, give no promise of this remarkable achievement. The Normans were Scandinavian pirates who descended upon the French Carolingian Empire at the end of the ninth century. Their number was not great, probably not more than twenty percent of the population they came to rule. These marauders, led by a wild chieftain called Rollo, established their hegemony in the diocese of Rouen, which was not a particularly fertile or wealthy part of France. Rollo and his warlords accepted Christianity, but this nominal conversion did not lessen their inclination to perpetual blood feuds. Rollo and his successors became the nominal vassals of the kings in Paris, but in fact ruled independently.

Until the last decade of the tenth century, these Scandinavian warriors fought among themselves in a particularly bloody and anarchic fashion. Then, beginning with the reign of Duke Richard I in 990 there was a marked change as the ducal government became devoted to peace and centralization of authority in its hands. Although our sources of information are meager and confused, it appears that this new phase in the history of Norman society was inaugurated under the influence of highly intelligent and ambitious churchmen who came into the duchy, usually at the urging of the duke, from Flanders, the Rhineland, and northern Italy. Particularly in the Rhineland and northern Italy the great bishops and abbots were in very close alliance with the German emperor, to the mutual benefit of both monarchy and church. In the four decades following the beginning of the reign of Duke Richard I in 990, a similar alliance was effected in the Norman duchy. During this period there was a conscious attempt to bring intelligent and literate men into Normandy. The dukes had a progressive vision and at least a vague idea that somehow good government was bound up with literacy and therefore inevitably with the church. At first the churchmen whom the duke invited to become the abbots of monasteries and to found new ones under his auspices were reluctant to come, such was the reputation of the duchy as a remote and violent place. Learned churchmen experienced in the problems of royal government were only attracted by generous offers of large endowments for the ecclesiastical institutions they would preside over, and after the year 1000 these offers brought into the duchy several ecclesiastics of very great ability. These men founded centers of learning and piety, and they were also able to advise the duke on how to establish peace in his duchy and control over the savage nobility. The churchmen also did all the literate work of government.

The most visible symbol of the great changes taking place in Normandy after the year 1000 was the erection of several magnificent stone churches in what historians of architecture call the Romanesque style. It is unlikely that before the year 1000 there was a single stone building in the whole duchy beyond a few unimpressive fortresses, but now some of the greatest churches of eleventh-century Europe begin to rise on the Norman plains. To build a great stone church in the early eleventh century required someone who was well trained in geometry, and it also called for the effective organization of labor, which meant in practice guilds of stonemasons. The building of the Norman churches could not therefore have been achieved without skilled planning, and the kind of intelligent organization that was effective in architecture could be equally successful in governmental decision-making. Rationality, order, control, the efficient use of resources—these tools will now be turned upon problems of political and social organization. And again the minds of churchmen will direct great enterprises. The duke is their great protector and patron; the stronger the duke is the more influential and wealthy will the bishops and abbots become; so the duke commands their unquestioned loyalty. The duke will consult his clerical advisors on how to transform the disordered heroic society dominated by the Scandinavian warlords into a centralized political and legal unit, and the duke will use the ecclesiastics in executing the program they urge him to adopt. In this way is begun the great transformation of Norman institutions which by 1066 will make the duke the most envied and feared man in Europe.

For a century after 990 the dukes of Normandy were unusually intelligent, ambitious, and energetic when measured against the usual medieval rulers. The churchmen who assisted the dukes were also, as a group, remarkably superior in learning and in their sensitivity to the problems of political life. The monks who came to Normandy from the Rhineland and northern Italy had in many instances received the benefit of study in the new schools of Roman and canon law which made their appearance in these regions in the early eleventh century. While some of these churchmen were renowned for piety and for their theological knowledge, they generally did not allow themselves to be distracted by spiritual interests from the need to establish an ordered and peaceful society. Beyond these superior qualities of the elite group in Norman society, the rise of ducal power can be explained in terms of the peculiar social framework of the duchy. The traditions of the previous Carolingian government had been largely obscured by the Scandinavian invasions; the Norman lords had been interested only in the pursuit of the primordial blood feuds and had never developed any sense of community; therefore once the duke and the churchmen allied to achieve a centralized authority, the other forms of loyalty in this society were unable to withstand the impact of the intelligence and energy of the new elite group. In Normandy, more easily than anywhere else in western Europe, ecclesiastical recollection of the beneficent authority of the Christian Roman emperors could be realized in practice. But in an intensely rural and de-urbanized society where the nexus of feudal institutions had already begun to crystallize in the previous Carolingian era, it was obvious that the rise of ducal power would have to be attained through manipulation and reconstitution of these feudal institutions. In this way, in the first three decades of the eleventh century the duke and his clerical allies arrived at their singular policy of achieving centralized authority through the medium of a reconstituted feudalism.

The most difficult task for the early eleventh-century dukes was to destroy the power of the great lords, the descendants of Rollo's companions, and to turn themselves from tribal chieftains into autocratic rulers who commanded absolute loyalty and strict service from their vassals. The transformation of Scandinavian tribalism into a tightly controlled feudal order was difficult to achieve; this was still a very simple and inchoate society, so that sheer force was the most effective tool in political centralization and the duke had to become personally more powerful than other lords. This end was attained in the first three decades of the eleventh century by drawing the greater part of the duke's army from ecclesiastical estates. Knights were enfeoffed on church lands, and the bishops and abbots became the vassals of the duke. By 1035 three hundred well-equipped and well-trained cavalrymen were in this way settled on ecclesiastical land and the duke's ecclesiastical vassals placed this new army at his disposal for beating down the independent lay nobility. The duke himself could probably draw between sixty and a hundred knights from his own estates so that he could put into the field an armored force which was very large by medieval standards.

By the 1020's the second stage of Norman feudalization was under way, in which the duke was forcing strict vows of homage upon the lay nobility of Normandy, rewarding those who were willing to give him the loyalty and service he demanded, and systematically destroying the old families who resisted him. By this process a new aristocracy began to emerge in the duchy, strictly subservient to the duke's authority. The only interruption in this carefully calculated and extremely rational reorganization of feudal institutions occurred in 1035 when Duke Robert the Magnificent in a fit of piety went on a pilgrimage to Jerusalem and died before he could return. His heir was a minor who had furthermore been born before his parents' marriage, and the Norman aristocracy decided to avail themselves of this opportunity to head off the centralization of the government. Their rebellion was assisted in Paris by the king of the new Capetian dynasty, who, although he had been placed on the throne with the assistance of the Norman duke, now feared the consequences of the emergence of this new state on the very borders of the Île-de-France. It was the loyalty of the churchmen which saved the duchy for Duke William II the Bastard (1035-1087) better known by his later and more glorious appellation of William the Conqueror. The knights drawn from ecclesiastical land held off the armies of the Norman nobility and the French king until, in the late 1040's, William reached his majority and gained the first of his many triumphs. He expelled the French king and completed the work of his predecessors in subjugating the lay nobility.

With the advice of churchmen such as the monastic scholar Lanfranc, who had begun his career as a lawyer in his native northern Italy, William made Norman feudalism a political and social system which transcended the original nature of feudal institutions, fundamentally inclined to decentralization. He arrived at a governmental structure which placed all authority in his own hands. The feudal hierarchy became a political and social pyramid with the duke at the pinnacle. The leaders of the lay and ecclesiastical nobility held their lands from the duke by feudal contract and their sub-vassals in turn had to take an oath of loyalty to the duke which in case of conflict pre-empted any obligation they had to their immediate overlord. It was this liege-lordship which made all free members of society directly subject to the duke's authority and which precluded the situation that existed in other feudal states by which the sub-vassals were loyal only to their immediate lords and passed out from under the authority of the central government.

In addition every churchman and layman knew precisely how many knights he owed in military service to the duke in return for holding his fief; in Normandy the knight-service owed was distributed in multiples of five roughly in accordance with the value of the vassal's holdings. Each of the duke's tenants-in-chief knew that if he defaulted in giving the service owed he would be held to account in the duke's court, and that if he were found guilty by his peers he would have to forfeit his land and with it the status in society which he and his family enjoyed. Similarly, no lord could build a castle or engage in a private feud without the duke's license on pain of forfeiture. The duke's local representative, called the viscount, operated as an effective regional agency of the central power, supervising the administration of the duke's demesne, keeping watch on the local nobility, and returning to the duke's treasury the income which accrued from various incidents of feudal taxation. All the great vassals of the duke were required to attend meetings of his court in order to be informed of his policy and to participate in the trials of those magnates who had violated their oaths of allegiance.

William the Bastard presided at councils of the Norman church and exercised as close a control over the bishops and abbots as over the lay nobility. In order to enter into their offices, the bishops and abbots alike had to be invested with the symbols of their office by the duke himself, and this allowed William in effect to designate the candidate to be elected as bishop by the cathedral clergy and as abbot by the monastic community. William was inclined to appoint his own relatives to the episcopacy and the monastic clerks who had served in his own chancery to head the greater abbeys. In addition, William the Bastard enthusiastically supported the church's program of the Peace of God, by which the lay and ecclesiastical magnates were supposed to form themselves into peace organizations to prevent and exclude the endemic violence characteristic of feudal society. The Peace of God movement was more effective in Normandy than anywhere else in Europe because William made himself its president in his duchy. Once he had established a tightly organized political and social system with himself in complete control of the feudal hierarchy, he had everything to gain from the promulgation of peace and the prohibition, or at least drastic limitation, of private feuds. By the 1060's a Norman lord who rebelled against the duke found himself facing the overwhelming military superiority of the duke's army, condemnation in the duke's court by the subordinated vassals, forfeiture of his patrimony, and in addition, excommunication by the church.

By 1060 William the Bastard controlled a massive military machine in the form of a highly trained feudal host of a thousand knights which because of the strictness of feudal contract in Normandy could actually be called out and put into the field. Although Normandy was by no means a very wealthy land, the duke had so organized his resources that at least west of the Rhine he was the most formidable military power of the middle of the century. But now he had another problem—he had to provide a war for his military aristocracy. The highly skilled Norman knights were not supposed to fight each other but they had no function in life other than a military one, and consequently William had to find an opportunity abroad for his massive armored power. The Norman lords, although beaten down, had no great love for the ducal family. Dissatisfaction and insurrection were always just beneath the surface. The pressure on the duke's government to appease the military ambitions of the lay nobility was increased by the steady population rise among the Norman aristocracy which meant a frustrating shortage of land for the younger sons of the prolific lords. In the early eleventh century there was a steady stream of emigrants from the duchy to Sicily and southern Italy, where the younger sons of Norman nobility, landless, restless, and unhappy, could carve out new estates for themselves. To a government capable of rational planning, this emigration of some of the best soldiers in Europe seemed an unfortunate waste of the duke's resources. It was far more prudent to use the duke's military machine in an organized conquest of new territory which could both satisfy the bellicose energies and insatiable greed of the Norman nobility and also increase William's wealth, authority, and reputation. Thus, because of the very nature of the warrior society William the Bastard and his predecessors had created, the duke after 1060 could not be satisfied with what he had achieved; he had to become William the Conqueror.

But where could he lead an army? He could not march on Paris because the Capetian king, although lazy and ineffective, held his authority as an anointed ruler with the church's sanction, and in any case the other proud dukes and counts of France would never stand by idly and watch William depose the French king. Though William could easily have captured Paris it was most unlikely that he could have held it for long. It was also risky to attack the neighboring Count of Flanders. He, too, was a feudatory of no mean ability, and besides, the count controlled a cluster of rich industrial towns whose formidable walls offered very difficult siege problems for eleventh-century military technology. William could have successfully invaded the Duchy of Brittany but it was a savage frontier area which offered little in the way of wealth and insuperable problems of government. The geo-political situation therefore made it inevitable that William should turn to England. Of course, England was also a risky choice; it was a wealthy and thickly settled country whose population was at least five times greater than that of Normandy in 1066. The Battle of Hastings thus represents a classic case of a confrontation between an old, feeble monarchy unable to control the resources of a large and wealthy country and a new ferocious military aristocracy under the command of an extremely able leader who was forced by social circumstances to expand his territory. The clash between China and Japan is a close modern parallel.

It is probable that in the early 1060's William persuaded Edward the Confessor, who was surrounded by Norman churchmen at his court and who before he came to the English throne had lived for some years in a Norman monastery, to recognize him as his successor. As Edward's second cousin, William had a slim claim to the throne and by the rules of inheritance at least a better claim than that of Harold Godwinson, who was in no way related to the house of Wessex. But inheritance was by no means the only basis of succession to the throne in the eleventh century. There was still an elective principle in the English monarchy which became the foundation of Harold's succession to the throne after Edward died. Harold also asserted that Edward had promised him the throne. In any case, since Edward was likely to promise anyone anything, William needed an additional sanction to justify his invasion of England and his seizure of the English crown.

In the mid-eleventh century the church still controlled all the moral prerogatives in European society, and William looked to the church to provide an additional sanction. It so happened that since 1048 a vigorous papacy dominated by a group of zealous cardinals led by Hildebrand, the head of the papal administration, had been attempting to build up effective Roman leadership in the Latin church. On the one hand, the arbitrary way in which Earl Godwin had expelled the Norman Archbishop of Canterbury and illegally installed his own man without reference to Rome had deeply offended the reforming papacy; on the other hand, William had taken pains to establish a highly favorable reputation at Rome. Among other acts, he had put himself at the head of the Peace of God league and he had gained a reputation as a generous patron of monasteries. So when the prospect offered itself that William would invade England to claim his birthright, Hildebrand was happy to support him because the cardinal thought that the Duke of Normandy would reform the English church along the lines advocated in Rome. The papal sanction helped to make up for William's lack of election by the English folk and it helped him to recruit additional contingents of mercenaries from Flanders and Brittany to supplement his feudal army. A banner sent by the Pope to William was carried ashore at Hastings and therefore the invasion of England was in a way a holy war—a crusade to reform the

English church and free it from the corrupting influence of the English earls. The papal support which William received was of great importance in his ultimate victory; it partly accounts for the way in which opposition to him melted away once Harold was dead, and the ease with which William got the surviving English lords to elect him as their king.

The transporting of William's army across the channel was an enormously difficult task and it is the highest tribute to the organizational skill of William's government that it could carry out a cross-channel invasion which defied the ingenuity of military powers even in the nineteenth and twentieth centuries. The duke had to land on the English shore about fifteen hundred knights and their horses and perhaps an additional three or four hundred infantrymen, mostly used as bowmen. Anglo-Saxon apologists maintain that if Harold Godwinson had been waiting on the shore William could not have made a successful landing. When William landed, Harold was up in the north repulsing yet another invasion of England by a Scandinavian king, this time a king of Norway. Harold gained a tremendous victory over the Norwegians, but then he had to turn around and march his army 250 miles to the south coast to fight again. We can be sure that his troops were exhausted, and many of them were undoubtedly drunk by the time the king arrived at Hastings. Furthermore, many of the Anglo-Saxon lords and their dependents had simply gone home; medieval nobility were reluctant to risk their lives in an organized battle more than once a year. If these lords had known what kind of man William the Bastard was and what the cataclysmic nature of his conquest would be, they would have undoubtedly chosen to fight at Hastings.

We do not know the size of Harold's army. He possibly had more soldiers than William but they were all infantrymen and many were ill-equipped and ill-trained peasants who had been summoned to the national fyrd. Harold's army fought well and in the beginning they had the advantage of the terrain. But partly because of William's clever strategy and partly because of the good fortune that always favors the strong— Harold was killed by an arrow through his eye, proof that the Anglo-Saxon open-face helmet was in fact obsolete—the English defense collapsed after a day of bitter conflict. The Battle of Hastings, which is dramatically portrayed for us in the Bayeux tapestry made in the circle of William's queen a few years after 1066, was an extremely bloody affair by medieval standards. Perhaps half of the Anglo-Saxon lords fell at the battle and the rest soon lost their lands, since William claimed the whole of England as his private demesne. William dashed to London and had himself anointed and crowned as the legitimate heir of Edward the Confessor.

A wealthy but disorganized kingdom had been conquered by a ferocious, greedy, military aristocracy led by an intelligent ruler capable of rational planning in government as well as in warfare. The Norman aristocracy and the other French mercenaries who had joined the expedition as freebooters eagerly awaited the distribution of the spoils of conquest while William the Conqueror and his clerical advisors set about trying to impose on English society a centralized political and legal system modeled on that which prevailed in Normandy. It was a question in 1066 as to whether the Norman settlement could strike a viable balance between aristocratic ambition and royal centralization and rationalization.

II. *The Norman Settlement*

Ix 1066 England was *terra regis*, the king's land. William the Conqueror owned the whole country and he had the opportunity for systematic political and social planning on a scale that only appears again in the eighteenth and nineteenth centuries when Englishmen seized control of vast overseas territories. Several distinguished scholars have established for us the structure of government and the form of social organization that William imposed on England during his long reign (1066-1087). F. W. Maitland's pioneering study *Domesday Book and Beyond* is still a work of the highest importance. F. M. Stenton and D. C. Douglas have made careful analyses of the nature of Anglo-Norman feudalism and have also written definitive biographies of the Conqueror. V. H. Galbraith has illuminated some important aspects of Anglo-Norman administration and R. Lennard has thoroughly studied the organization of rural society in the late eleventh century. These scholars have availed themselves of a great variety and volume of sources which have come down to us from the Anglo-Norman period. The contemporary monastic historians were very well-informed on the course of political development because many of the monastic communities to which they belonged were under the patronage of the royal family, and in any case the great monasteries served as the hotels of late eleventh-century England at which kings and lords would stop over on their travels and impart reliable information to the religious brethren. It was also the custom of the Anglo-Norman chancery to send copies of important documents to the great monasteries for preservation. A large number of royal writs and charters from the reigns of William the Conqueror and his sons have come down to us and allow us to make judgments on most of the important aspects of royal administration. Most significant of all for the social historian is the extremely detailed and systematic record of the land holding and wealth of England put together by the royal clerks at the end of the Conqueror's reign, in two volumes known as Domesday Book. There is nothing like this inquiry, which attempted to enumerate every estate, town, church, cow, pig, and fish pond in the kingdom, in the history of any other medieval European government. It allows the historian to be more certain in describing the social structure of England in 1087 than he can be in analyzing English society in the nineteenth century. It is possible to work out the social geography of England in the 1080's and arrive at a clear and reliable picture of its topology and demography. This in fact has been done in H. C. Darby's *Domesday Geography of England*.

There is extensive and convincing evidence that when William the Conqueror died in 1087, English government and society had assumed the shape it was to have for the next hundred years, and during the following two centuries this political and social framework was only modified in some important ways but never essentially changed. It is easy, then, for the historian to delineate the institutional nexus and governmental and legal system of Anglo-Norman England. What is much more difficult and interesting—and it is by no means a problem which historians have definitively resolved—is the process of William's settlement. What we need to know is the dynamic of political and social organization in the reign of William the Conqueror—how institutions were experimented with, weighed, modified, and either carried further or abandoned. To understand the nature of English government and society in the reign of William I, we need to know not only the shape that political and social life eventually assumed after two decades, but also how and why this institutionalization was effected.

The political and social framework of England in 1087 was the consequence of the interaction of two distinct elements: rationality and force.

The former is centered in the royal government and the latter in the way of life of the nobility. These elements are not always contradictory; they often work together and complement each other, but to an important degree they are incompatible. The institutions of Anglo-Norman England are the result neither entirely of rational decision-making nor of aristocratic traditions and ambitions, but rather of their confluence and in some ways of their conflict. In addition to these two elements, it must be emphasized that rationality and force operated within the context of the resources, technological and educational, of late eleventh-century England, and the potentiality and limitations of these resources, particularly with regard to the communications network, also served to shape the institutional framework which finally emerged.

More than any previous medieval European government, Anglo-Norman government was rational. Thus historians who yearn to pinpoint the origins of the modern state can with some justification say it is being born here. Although we cannot yet find the concept of sovereignty which is a necessity in the modern world, the administrative methods and characteristic attitudes of the central government in modern society can be glimpsed in late eleventh-century England. This is the first planned society since the Roman Empire. A very small group of aggressive and highly intelligent men, most of them well-educated, are in control of the royal administration. There are many technological checks and restrictions upon what they can do; the mindless pressures of aristocratic society always lie heavily upon them, but within these limits they plan with a degree of intensity that has seldom been matched in human history. They are given a magnificent opportunity by the cataclysmic nature of the Norman Conquest. Since England in 1066 lay at the feet of the king, the royal government did not have to perpetuate Anglo-Saxon traditions which it did not find useful, but could evaluate them strictly on utilitarian grounds. Even the institutions of Norman feudalism could be scrutinized and readjusted before they were imported across the channel.

In his own person William the Conqueror combined the two strands of Anglo-Norman government and society; he was the most feared warrior in the country and in fact in all of Europe, and yet he could understand and appreciate ideas, and he actively directed his government's rational decision-making. Most medieval kings quickly became bored with administrative detail, and only fighting and hunting could sustain their interest for any length of time. William spent perhaps half his reign in warfare but it was always war which would bring him some advantage. William was also devoted to the hunt, but he organized his recreation as efficiently as he did everything else, setting aside vast forest preserves for himself and his family and never letting his hounds and hawks and stags distract him from the problems of government. By the standards of his age William was devout, but his religiosity was of a kind to strengthen rather than inhibit his political ambitions. He firmly believed in an hierarchic universe, knew that he stood as high as any man in it, and was confident that he had been placed on the English throne to rule by God's will. He endowed monasteries and showed formal respect to the Pope, but it never occurred to him that the resources of the church could not be used extensively for the purposes of enhancing his own power.

William was not a tolerant man; all contemporary accounts tell us that his wrath was terrible and the surviving Anglo-Saxon monks shook under their cowls when the royal entourage approached. The king was not known for generosity. Almost immediately after Hastings he dispossessed all the Anglo-Saxon lords of any consequence and we assume that many of them, if they could not find employment as mercenaries, were driven into the ignominy of serfdom. The king ruthlessly hunted down a handful of Anglo-Saxon thegns who unwisely chose to flee to the East Anglian swamps and tried to resist his army. When the frontier lords of the north gave William trouble, he laid waste vast stretches of Yorkshire so that for a generation it was a desolate land. Not even blood ties counted for much with William the Conqueror. When his half-brother Bishop Odo of Bayeux, whom he had made Earl of Kent, proved obstreperous, he dispossessed him and let him rot in prison for several years. Such severity was rare among medieval kings, who were recklessly inclined to forgive in the conduct of their relatives what they would not tolerate from any other members of the great aristocracy.

The day-to-day operation of William's government was in the hands of a small group of administrators, less than twenty at any given time. Historians have chosen to call this administrative corps the Small Council of the King, to distinguish it from the feudal Great Council, the full *curia regis* (king's court), which was a meeting of all the great magnates of England summoned at least three times a year. It has become conventional to say that the members of the Small Council regarded themselves as the permanent nucleus of the *curia regis*, carrying on the work of government between the occasional meetings of the full *curia regis*. It is unlikely, however, that these intelligent and ambitious administrators looked upon themselves as a sub-committee of the assembly of the feudal magnates whose violence and patrimonial ambitions they were constantly trying to inhibit and control in the king's interest. The royal administrators held their sanction not from the structure of feudal society but from the king's will. They were *his* men and their loyalty to royal authority was unlimited and undivided. These administrators operated the chancery, drafted charters, sent out writs, prepared the business of the full *curia regis*, advised the king on ecclesiastical appointments, investigated laws, and though they had no clear idea of the nature of legislation, drafted proposals for legal reforms. They supervised the work of the king's chief agents in the counties, whom they addressed usually as sheriff, but occasionally by the Norman title of viscount. The king's servants also concerned themselves with the administration of the royal demesne and with the management of the other sources of royal income. They worried about which Anglo-Saxon traditions to preserve and improve and which it was best to forget entirely; they helped the king work out the plan for the feudalization of England; and they conceived and executed the great Domesday investigation which was far beyond the resources of any other medieval government before the middle of the thirteenth century. William the Conqueror's government was thus the responsibility of a small bureaucratic elite, talented and intensely loyal men working to the utmost limits of their energies and intellectual resources.

The men who comprised the central administration in William's reign appear at first sight to be a group varied in their background. But closer examination reveals a common characteristic beyond the fact that they were all Frenchmen, either from Normandy or from neighboring territories. In the king's service are a few unlettered laymen who witness royal charter after royal charter and are obviously close advisors of the Conqueror and constantly at the center of affairs. Such men are Norman lords of substantial wealth and status, but they are not from the great aristocracy. The churchmen who do the literate work of government, indispensable to this rationalized bureaucracy, are of two kinds. Some are regular clergy on permanent leave from their monastic communities; this kind of Benedictine monk had been the most important servant of central authority in Normandy and in fact in all the West European kingdoms since the ninth century. But another type of royal clerk makes his appearance in the administration of William the Conqueror: secular clerics who come from the ranks of the worldly-wise cathedral clergy of northern France. These men are the products of the new cathedral schools sponsored by learned and illustrious bishops at Chartres, Laon, and Paris. These cathedral schools will develop in the twelfth century into the great universities of northern Europe and the university graduates produced by this educational revolution, which is already beginning in the late eleventh century, will become the bureaucrats and lawyers of both church and state in the high Middle Ages.

Whether products of monastic or cathedral schools, William the Conqueror's clerks are men whose ambitions match their learning. They are skilled Latinists; they can draft a charter and work up a coronation ceremony and if need be they can even write a poem about the glories of kingship. Some historians think these poems are full of profound symbolism but the ability to turn out a decent verse was just one of the useful skills that talented churchmen would learn at school, and to the king's clerks the liturgical celebration of anointed kingship would be just another one of their daily tasks, somewhat more challenging, but not much more important than the drafting of a particularly complicated royal charter. For these royal clerks, service to the king was a good career and one which was likely to bring the reward of appointment to a lucrative bishopric or abbacy after several years of service.

Whether they were middling nobility or cathedral clergy or Benedictine monks, William the Conqueror's administrators have in common a fundamental characteristic: in varying degrees they are men alienated from the traditions of medieval society. The laymen who served the king were lords who lacked a great patrimony, either because their families were not very wealthy to begin with or because they were younger sons of the fertile aristocratic families. Service to the king was a way of rising in the world, of being rewarded by the occasional grant of a fief from the royal demesne, and of gaining power among the magnates of the shire, which such men ordinarily would not have achieved by royal appointment as sheriffs of the king. These unlettered lay servants of Anglo-Norman monarchy are from the feudal hierarchy, but to a considerable degree they have become alienated from its customary way of life and they have found a new attitude and a new calling in royal service. Although illiterate, they have in royal service learned to be disciplined and to make rational decisions.

To a much greater and more constant degree, the royal clerks are alienated from feudal society and even by and large from the church which has educated them. The provenance of royal clerks is always the lesser ranks of the nobility or the younger sons of the aristocracy for whom a comfortable life was chosen by their families in dispatching them to ecclesiastical institutions for education and training in the priesthood. But these itinerant monks and cathedral clerks find their careers not in the traditional service to bishop or Pope but rather in the royal administration. They have come to serve another master, and if they are ever concerned that this conflicts with their clerical profession, they can always justify it on the grounds that the king is anointed of the Lord and himself therefore the holder of high priestly dignity. The churchmen who served William the Conqueror rarely if ever worried about the potential conflict between loyalty to the king and their clerical status. They have found a place in society for their unusual talents which not only in some ways elevates them to a position of authority over the greatest magnates in the realm, but also allows them to impose upon society the peace and order inculcated by the teachings of the church.

William's friend and chief advisor, Lanfranc, whom the king recruited from his Norman monastery to become Archbishop of Canterbury, was one of these new men who had tried many things before he found his role as organizer and ruler of a whole society. Lanfranc had been a lawyer in northern Italy, a distinguished theologian in Norman France, and finally the most eminent monastic scholar in William the Bastard's duchy. As Archbishop of Canterbury he placed all his learning and fine intelligence in the service of the king, helping the Conqueror plan his new society and reorganizing the resources of the church in England for the same end. This brilliant, hard, and shrewd man showed no generosity for the surviving Anglo-Saxon bishops and abbots, who seemed to inhabit a slower, more mystical world than the one he chose to live in. Although the Norman higher clergy were not noted for their celibacy and in fact spawned a vast tribe of clerical bastards, Lanfranc accused the English clerics of immorality and perversion and succeeded in deposing all of them, except for one lonely bishop who was protected by the incorruptible odor of sanctity. From northern France Lanfranc brought a whole new generation of clerics, whose outlook resembled his own, to occupy the high offices in the English church. When vacancies again appeared in the ranks of bishops and abbots in the 1080's, they were used to reward the royal clerks for their invaluable services to the king.

If the clerics and laymen who administered the central government of William the Conqueror represent the element of rationality in the Norman settlement, the large army of French lords and knights that crushed the Anglo-Saxon fyrd represents the element of irrationality and force. The ambiguities of Anglo-Norman government arise from the conflict between rationality and irrationality, between careful centralized planning and centrifugal baronial interests, between the authoritarian attitudes of the king's administrators and the particularist and selfish inclinations of the nobility. Within this complex framework, the royal officials had to strain all the resources at their command in order to effect a settlement which would leave in the king's hands the greater share of power and wealth. The natural inclinations of the royal officials were undoubtedly to concede as little as possible to the Norman lords who after 1066 were clamoring for lands and privileges in England. It was impossible, however, to rule the country outside the network of a feudal hierarchy. The royal officials, even including the sheriffs working in the counties, were very few in number and could not constitute themselves as an authoritarian bureaucracy which retained all power and wealth in its own hands. Power and wealth had to be shared with the conquering army, and not only because of the barons' insistence that they be given a large share of the spoils of war as a reward for their services to the king. England was a conquered hostile country and for some years Anglo-Saxon partisans held out in the East Anglian swamps. In addition, the Scottish and Welsh frontiers had to be defended, and for at least a decade after 1066 the possibility of another Scandinavian invasion remained a real threat. Hence William, even if he had been able to, could not afford to send most of his French vassals and mercenaries back across the channel. Therefore, a settlement had to be worked out by the royal government which, while meeting the minimum demands of the barons, kept enough power and wealth in the king's hands to allow him to control the feudal hierarchy effectively and to provide the institutional basis for subsequent enlargement of royal authority. The royal officials were successful in achieving this goal but not without strain and conflict between their own planning and the baronial ambitions. The tension between king and barons that pervades Anglo-Norman England reflects this fundamental precarious balance between the rationality of the central government and the unthinking force of the great aristocracy.

Historians used to believe that the feudalization of England, involving the distribution of great estates or "honors" to the high nobility and the consequent sub-infeudation of the vassals of these great barons, occurred very rapidly after 1066. This was the thesis propounded by the Edwardian scholar J. H. Round, but in the 1930's the work of F. M. Stenton and D. C. Douglas revealed conclusively that the feudalization of England was a much slower and more complex process. From what we know of the attitude of the royal officials, we would suspect this *a priori*, because they would not have surrendered wealth and privileges to the aristocracy *en masse* before assuring themselves of the means of control over the feudal hierarchy. From the study of the documentary records of Anglo-Norman feudalism we know that at the end of William's reign at least half the French knights were still landless. They were supported directly as household knights of either the king or the great aristocracy. It is furthermore evident that the process of feudalization moved along lines of coherent and rational planning in at least three distinct stages. As was the case in Normandy in the early eleventh century, the feudalization of church land appears to have been carried out first so that the king had a strong nucleus of knights from ecclesiastical lands before he ventured to settle the lay barons on their fiefs. The effort of the royal government, very soon after Hastings, to impose homage and knight service upon the bishops and abbots may have accelerated the tendency to get rid of the Anglo-Saxon higher clergy; it was necessary to have French ecclesiastics in office who were experienced in the control of feudal armies and the rendering of knight service to the king. By the middle of the twelfth century there were about five thousand knights in England, all of whom were technically, at least, members of the king's feudal host. Of these probably a quarter came from church lands. These statistics allow us to gauge how important it was for William to impose feudal obligations on the bishops and abbots before attempting to satisfy the lay nobility. The enfeoffment of ecclesiastical land stopped in England in the year 1080; we may assume that four or five years previously the feudalization of the church had reached a point where William could begin to deal with the great barons who had accompanied him to England.

It would be wrong to picture all of the French lay aristocracy in the reign of William the Conqueror as thugs and savages. We have seen that a small group of barons were sufficiently intelligent and disciplined to work for the king either in the central government or as sheriffs. Furthermore, under the impact of Christian ideals and the pacifying effect of centralized monarchy, a slow transformation was underway among the great barons, from savagery to chivalry, or at least from their pristine condition as violent men to the more or less responsible leaders of society which they will become by 1200. William's eldest son was in fact one of the first of the European aristocracy to be influenced by the new sentimentality and romantic idealism which went to make up the chivalric code. But by and large the Norman aristocracy which gained the victory at Hastings were still undisciplined and violent men. The only things they want are power and wealth of a rather obvious kind for themselves and their families, in the form of great estates, and the only thing they understand is force. The coronation ceremony which enshrouds the Norman duke with the charisma of Anglo-Saxon kingship means nothing to them nor do they see themselves as part of a national community. They understand that receiving estates from the king implies service on their part under the terms of feudal contract, and these services will often be onerous, but otherwise they have no conception of any other kind of relationship or responsibility to the king or the country. The great barons want land—this is the aim of their whole life—and if they do not get it they will be sullen and rebellious. Even when they receive their great honors, they will be inclined to rebellion whenever the opportunity presents itself, not because they are fighting for any ideal, but precisely because these violent men cannot see the king in any capacity other than the one set down in the feudal contract.

In the distribution of lands and privileges the frontier regions had to be given special consideration. The Anglo-Norman kings (and in fact all kings until the later thirteenth century) were much more interested in expanding their territories in France than on the Scottish and Welsh frontiers. Given the difference in the economic conditions of France on the one hand and Scotland and Wales on the other, and the opportunity for conquest across the channel until the rise of a powerful French monarchy at the end of the twelfth century, this was the most sensible thing to do. It does, however, show a total lack in the Norman period of a nationalist conception of the king as the potential ruler of all Britain. The king shared, in this sense, the outlook of the feudal aristocracy and like them he was interested in gaining whatever territory offered the best return. In fact the problem through the eleventh and twelfth centuries was not to expand the frontiers of the English kingdom as much as it was to keep out the Celtic marauders. This was particularly true of the northern part of the country where there was as yet no difference between the society of Scotland, characterized by anarchic tribalism, and that of thinly populated and economically backward Yorkshire.

William's solution to the frontier problem was the setting up of vast

county palatinates along the northern and western borders. To the palatine lords of these regions he granted away not only huge feudal domains
but also full rights of legal and political private jurisdiction so that the
lords of the border areas, or *marches,* as they were called, were in effect
given the same patrimonial and tribal authority as the Welsh and Scottish enemies they faced. The principle was that the marcher lords should
have special privileges enjoyed by no other vassals of the king in return
for their arduous task of keeping out the Celtic marauding bands. As
long as the king himself was not interested in advancing the borders of
his realm to the north and west, and did not wish to commit the limited
resources of his government to defending the distant frontiers, this was
the only feasible solution. But the marcher lords with their county palat-
inate jurisdiction were bound to gain a loyalty from the population they
ruled of a kind much more intensive than the other vassals of the king
enjoyed, and they were therefore to be tempted, more constantly than
the inland barons, to rebellion against the crown. William the Conqueror himself experienced the particularism and disloyalty of the northern marcher lords and through the subsequent course of the history of
medieval English government, until the frontier regions were finally incorporated under the direct control of the central government in the
sixteenth century, the rebellion of these great aristocrats on the borders
of the kingdom was to be an ever-recurring danger. It is indicative of the
high degree of rationality involved in the Norman settlement that the
Conqueror attempted to guard against this inevitable situation by making the Bishop of Durham the greatest of the marcher lords in the north,
on the principle that as a churchman the bishop would uphold royal
authority in Yorkshire. But even this wise provision proved of limited
value, for the leader of the baronial rebellion that broke out a year after
William's death, and had to be put down with accustomed Norman
ferocity, was the episcopal count palatine of the north.

There is a world of difference between the necessarily lavish grants to
the marcher lords and the strictly controlled enfeoffment of the Conqueror's companions in the rest of the country. Only the most reliable
and the most influential of the French barons were granted feudal estates before 1087 so that when William died one fourth of the landed
wealth of England still belonged to the royal demesne. By the end of the
reign of the last of William's sons, Henry I, in 1135, the king still retained between ten and fifteen percent of the arable part of the country
in his own hands; by 1200 the royal demesne had further shrunk to about

five percent of the landed wealth of England. When the Conqueror enfeoffed the great aristocrats, he took care to split his honor among two or more counties so that away from the frontier regions no vassal of the king held such an extensive block of territory that he could set himself up as a patrimonial leader of a whole shire. In any given county at least three or four great families would have to share the wealth and influence among them, and there would always be a large group of middling landowners to provide a balance to the great barons in the shire court. Nothing more vividly illustrates the rationality of William's government than this splitting up and distribution of great honors among several counties so that the patrimonial and particularist inclinations of the king's vassals would be inhibited from the first by the special nature of the feudal settlement.

Beyond this fundamental policy, the royal government sought to control the feudal hierarchy through imposition upon the tenants-in-chief of the king of exactly the same kind of feudal contract which prevailed in Normandy. In Anglo-Norman feudalism we again find knight service owed by the king's vassals precisely set down in units of five, the total amount of knight service taking into account the income that the land yielded and the grantee's personal relations with the king. Private war among the lords and their knights, and the building of castles without royal license, were prohibited. Not only the king's immediate tenants-in-chief but all their sub-vassals had to take an oath of liege or prime lordship to the Conqueror. One chronicler in fact tells us that in the year before he died, William summoned all the knights of England before him on the Salisbury Plain and had them take an oath of fealty to him as their liege lord, an oath which overruled the bond of homage and fealty between one of the great aristocrats, who held directly of the king, and his own vassals. The royal court established the principle that violation of any of these provisions of the feudal contract involved a "felony." No word was as dreaded as this one by the great barons, for conviction of felony in the royal court by a trial of their peers meant a sentence of forfeiture of all their lands and privileges and with it the extinction of all the hopes and ambitions of a baronial family.

William rewarded some members of his household with lands granted on serjeantry tenure, for which service as grooms or cooks sufficed; and occasionally he would bestow an estate on an abbey or bishopric requiring only frankalmoign or free-alms tenure—that is, service at the altar, singing masses for the souls of the royal family. But the lands granted on these nonfeudal tenures were few and far between. Nearly all the estates which William and his sons granted for the use of others were by feudal tenure, involving strictly defined knight service, and this included most of the land held by churchmen. There was nothing generous about the Anglo-Norman monarchy; if land were to be given to others from the royal demesne it was to be subject to the principles of feudal law, which meant that the recipient had only *seisin* or possessory use of the land, and could claim no *ius in re*, absolute property rights to it. This meant not only that the land returned to the king's hands on felonious violation of the feudal contract, and also "escheated" or reverted to the royal overlord if the grantee's family died out, but also that the fief returned specific benefits to the king. Service in the feudal host of the king's vassals and their sub-vassals was the most obvious return, but the royal officials found in the institutions of the feudal contract several sources of revenue. Feudalism meant for them not only a military but even more constantly a taxation system.

The first of these feudal sources of royal revenue was *relief*, a kind of inheritance tax falling on the families of the king's tenants-in-chief. When one of the king's vassals died, his honor reverted to the king's hands because in theory a fief was a loan of land for one life only and hence technically not inheritable. The potential heir had to "relieve" the fief from the royal grasp through payment of a sum which varied according to the wealth of the baron and the favorable or unfavorable attitude of the king to the particular family. An amount equal to a year's revenue from the estates to be inherited was considered severe but not unusual. The institution of relief provided a way in which the crown could punish obstreperous aristocratic families who had just managed to avoid overstepping the line which would bring upon them a sentence of felony. It was particularly useful in impoverishing the heirs of rebellious marcher lords. Given the fact that life expectancy for the lay nobility in late eleventh century England was not more than thirty-five years of age—such was the calamitous impact of disease and violence—the royal government could reasonably expect to collect relief from every tenant-in-chief's family at least once a decade. Thus the feudal incident of relief provided a quite regular way of siphoning off the wealth of great baronial families into the royal treasury.

A feudal tax of potentially even greater severity was *wardship*. When one of the king's vassals died leaving a minor as his heir, or when the male line died out and the estates passed either to the widow or an unmarried daughter, the king became the guardian of these dependents and the royal clerks looked forward to substantial gains for the royal treasury. Until the vassal's minor son became of age or until the king would give permission for the widow or heiress of the vassal to marry a royally approved member of the baronial class, the royal officials administered the estates of these king's wards. It was a matter of great controversy as to how much of the revenue of the lands in wardship should go to the king, but it was customary for the royal treasury to take all the income beyond a pittance generously left for the wards to maintain themselves and their families. Furthermore, the Anglo-Norman administrators had a habit of removing everything from the estate they could carry away. Feudal law justified the taking of a ward's lands into the king's hands on the ground that the king had to be compensated for his loss of military service when a fief had descended to a minor or a woman.

Wardship, like relief, was a feudal prerogative which could be used for political as well as financial ends. A long royal wardship over a minor heir or a woman belonging to a troublesome aristocratic family would invariably impoverish the patrimony and keep the family quiet for several years. Next to the word felony, wardship was the most hated term known to a medieval baron, and as often as they tried to find ways of limiting the effectiveness of this institution, as strenuously did the king insist on his privilege of serving as the guardian of aristocratic dependents. The institution of feudal wardship in fact persisted in England until 1660, when it was finally abolished by parliamentary statute.

Even when an inherited fief could be relieved from the king's hands and the rightful heir receive royal assent to enter into the estates and privileges of his father, he had to do homage and swear fealty to the king in the traditional manner. To assure himself of enjoyment of his predecessor's wealth and privileges, it would be beneficial to obtain a new charter from the king so that the royal officials could not later bring into question the extent of the vassal's holdings and whatever rights of private jurisdiction he held over those who lived within the boundaries of his honor. The issuing of new charters was again a steady source of royal income; to this aggressive and intelligent government no privilege was given without payment. A final source of income to the king from his feudal prerogatives was the three regular feudal "aids." When a lord knighted his eldest son and heir, married off his eldest daughter, or was captured and held for ransom, he had an arbitrary right to gifts of money from all his vassals. Furthermore, when the lord needed money at some crucial moment, such as the occasion of a war, he could ask his vassals to consent to a freely given gift to him, called a "gracious aid." The feudal aids were to become of prime importance in the history of thirteenth-century royal taxation but the Anglo-Norman kings used this institution sparingly as a source of income. The Conqueror and his sons demanded lavish gifts for the knighting and marrying of their eldest children, but they were not so feckless as to be captured and held for ransom. Nor did they make much use of the "gracious aid," because the consent required would give their barons an opportunity to extract compensatory privileges from the king.

There was however an additional way of obtaining money from the king's feudal lordship, and this involved the substitution of a money payment for actual knight service. This practice again graphically illustrates the rationality and common sense of William the Conqueror's government. There was of course something splendid about a feudal army, and medieval kings even in the fourteenth or fifteenth centuries loved to ride along at the head of their lords and knights with banners waving. It was a glorious spectacle but William already knew that it was costly and inefficient. The Norman ruler who had at his command the greatest feudal army in Christendom was never captivated by the glamour of leading the feudal host and he early recognized the relative inefficiency of feudalism as a military system. The king spent almost half his reign fighting on the continent against the other great dukes and counts of northern France and he soon saw that the problem of transporting the English feudal host across the channel was an acutely difficult and costly one. Furthermore, even if he had managed to ferry his whole army across the channel, he could not rely on it to fight effectively. Feudal law required only forty days' service a year. This meant adequate length of service when the feudal host fought on their home territory, for medieval armies (and in fact just about all armies until the French Revolution) only took to the field when the weather was good, from May to October. But the task of transporting the knights across the channel consumed several days of their service and in addition changes in military technology in the late eleventh century, especially in France, were increasing the length of the campaign. The defense was catching up with the offense after several hundred years, as the crafty bourgeois threw up thick walls around their towns. A retreating feudal army simply withdrew into one of these fortresses, making long sieges necessary. It was frustrating for the Anglo-Norman king, campaigning on the continent, to watch his army dissolve after forty days' service just when a siege appeared to be successful. Yet another defect of feudalism was the requirement that the king's vassals bring to the feudal host a designated number of knights who were supposed to be fully trained and well-equipped. Obviously it was to the baron's financial advantage not to expend his family's resources to provide a full complement of superior knights which the king then put to his own use. Several of the king's barons tried to get by with inferior grades of knights, resulting in bitter quarrels between the king and his tenants-in-chief. A famous scandal occurred in 1095 when the king accused the Archbishop of Canterbury of felony on the ground that the good prelate had sent to the feudal host not standard French knights but some obscure English thegns who had been presumably vegetating as peasants on the Canterbury estates.

It was to avoid these inherent defects in the feudal military system, as J. O. Prestwich has shown, that William determined to make extensive use of mercenaries for his continental wars. He allowed his barons to make a money payment instead of bringing their sub-vassals to the feudal army. This payment, after 1100 called *scutage* or "shield money," was set at a certain number of marks per knight's fee. A mark was equal to two thirds of a pound, and in the twelfth century scutage was usually two marks per fee. The personal service of several of the barons was required by the king in order that he might have generals for his continental army, but the less valorous of his tenants-in-chief he also allowed to remain at home on payment of fines. It is paradoxical but highly significant that the same Norman ruler who fully realized the military potential of the feudal contract and consequently achieved the great victory of 1066, soon perceived the limitations of the knight's service and proceeded to surpass it with a new kind of military system. William the Conqueror, with the rationality characteristic of his government, was the first European ruler to appreciate the superior value of mercenaries. For his continental wars he inaugurated the military system that was universal by the middle of the thirteenth century and which dominated European warfare until the revival of national armies during the French Revolution. The introduction of scutage not only increased the financial resources of the monarchy and increased the king's military prowess; it also had a profound impact on English landed society. By the end of the eleventh century only a minority of the sub-vassals were ever summoned to continental wars, with the result that these knights lost their original military efficiency, and to a degree their function as armored units of the royal army. They remained at home, managing their estates, participating in the affairs of the shire court, and were slowly transformed into the country gentlemen of later English history.

The institutional framework of Anglo-Norman feudalism was the consequence of the necessity to bestow great landed wealth and privileges on the leading members of the lay aristocracy, coupled with the government's inflexible determination to keep these magnates firmly under control and to force them to pay dearly for the grants they received from the king. The same tension is found in the political and legal institutions of Anglo-Norman England. The royal officials had to rule through the cooperation of the magnates, and to a degree with their consent to royal policies, but at the same time this situation was a matter of necessity and does not detract from the fundamentally authoritarian inclination of the king and his chief officials. There was no authoritarian state in England during the Anglo-Norman period, but not because the king and his men shrank from the very idea; on the contrary the vision of an hierarchic order of society and the knowledge of Roman and canon law among Lanfranc and the other clerical ministers of the king made them sympathetic to a despotic political system such as had existed in the Christian Roman Empire of the fourth and fifth centuries. Most of the king's chief advisors were clerics and their learning inclined them to a political theory which viewed the king as the Lord's anointed, holding supreme office in society by the grace of God and responsible only to divine authority and certainly not to the feudal magnates. The trouble which the royal clerics took to perpetuate the Anglo-Saxon coronation order, with its view of the king as both king and priest, and to celebrate the sacredness of kingship in elaborate royal liturgies indicates that these men saw no earthly limitations on the power of government and the authority of the crown. The last thing we must envision the royal clerics being interested in was the perpetuation of the Germanic ideal that law resided in the folk; they had no real concern for the legislative power of the community. To the extent that Germanic ideas of law survived in England after 1066, or that the king's government operated with the consent of the magnates as the leaders of society, this was the result not of the ideology of the royal clerics but rather of the technological and social limitations imposed upon eleventh-century government. However much the royal clerics might have wanted to control everything from the center, to root out the vestiges of Anglo-Saxon law, and to replace it with the legal sovereignty of the king, given the realities of

The Anglo-Saxon king as war leader, from an
illustrated manuscript circa 1000

Anglo-Saxon king and his Witan, from an illustrated Old Testament
manuscript, 11th century

Anglo-Saxon justice: whipping and branding

The embarkation of the Norman Army. Duke William is
leading the horsemen to the ships.

Norman atrocities: the burning of a hut in Hastings

Both from The Bayeux Tapestry, *ed. by Sir Frank Stenton, published by Phaidon Press*

EARLY ROYAL WRITS

OPPOSITE

Writ of Edward the Confessor (1042–1066) to Westminster Abbey.

Writ of William the Conqueror (1066–1087) to the citizens of London, confirming their privileges. The writ is in Old English.

Part of a page from Domesday Book, 1086 (see opposite page, bottom). The top part of the right-hand column reads (in translation from the Latin text):

SURREY   THE LAND OF GILBERT SON OF RICHER

xxiiii. Gilbert son of Richer
de Aigle holds WITLEY. Earl Godwin held it. Then it was assessed for 20 hides, now for 12 hides. There is land for 16 ploughs. In demesne are 2 ploughs; and there are
37 villeins and 3 cottars
with 13 ploughs. A church there and 3 acres of meadow. Wood [with pannage] for
30 pigs.
In the time of King Edward and afterwards, it was worth 15 pounds; now 16 pounds.
IN BRIXTON HUNDRED

LAND OF GEOFFREY DE MANDEVILLE

xxv. Geoffrey de Mandeville holds CLAPHAM. Turbern held it
from King Edward. Then it was assessed for 10 hides, now for 3 hides. There is land for 7 ploughs. In demesne is one plough, and there are 8 villeins and 3 bordars with 5
ploughs.
There are 5 acres of meadow. In the time of King Edward it was worth 10 pounds; afterwards, the like; now, 7 pounds 10 shillings.
The men say that Geoffrey has this Manor unjustly because it does not belong to the
land of Asgar.
What Geoffrey gave in alms out of this Manor is worth 20 shillings.

IN WALLINGTON HUNDRED

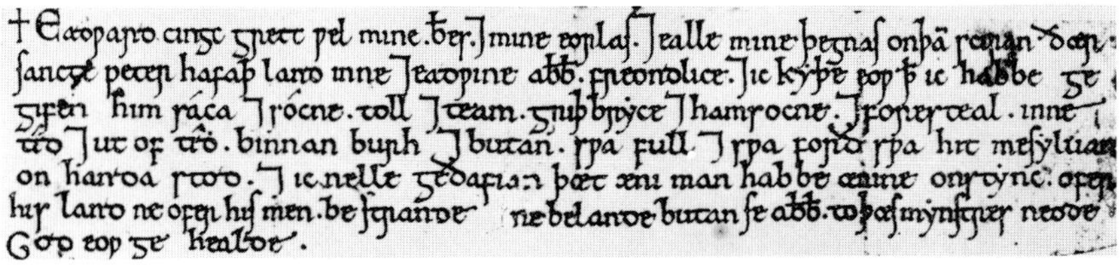

Both Clarendon Press, Oxford

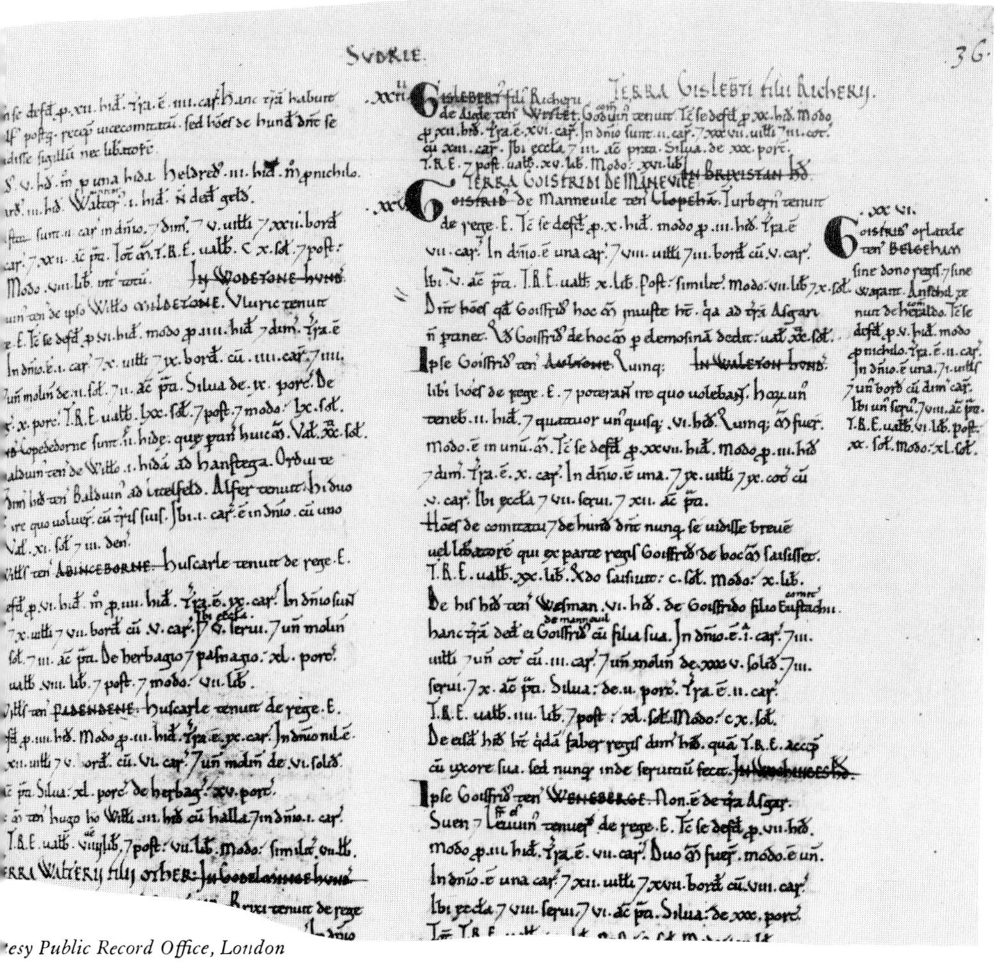

[cour]tesy Public Record Office, London

Anointing of Edward the Confessor (1042–1066)

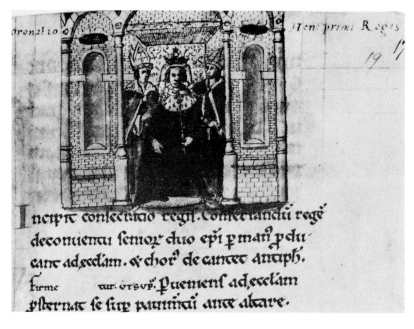

Coronation of Henry I (1100–1135)

SEALS OF MEDIEVAL ENGLISH KINGS

William the Conqueror
(1066–1087)

Henry II (1154–1189)

Richard I (1189–1199)

John (1199–1216)

Oldest surviving common law writ, 1190, summoning jurors to Westminster

Trial by battle in the reign of Henry III (1216–1272). This sketch was made on an assize roll which records the judicial combat between Walter Bloweberme and Hamo le Stare. Walter was a confessed thief who was pardoned on condition that he accuse and defeat his fellow criminals. Walter accordingly made an appeal against Hamo and defeated him. As Maitland tells us, "Hamo's consequent fate is depicted in the background."

Salisbury Cathedral,
finest example of English Gothic

Norman Castle at Dover

Edward I's castle at Carnarvon, Wales

All courtesy British Travel Association

TURNING POINTS IN MEDIEVAL ENGLISH HISTORY
AS DEPICTED IN A FOURTEENTH-CENTURY MANUSCRIPT

Archbishop Thomas Becket debating with Henry II, 1164

Edward I confirming Magna Carta, 1297

Both courtesy British Museum, London

Richard II (1377–1399) delivered to the citizens of London by his cousin, Henry Bolingbroke, soon to be Henry IV. From a fifteenth-century manuscript. (Richard is wearing the long cloak and looks depressed.)

Seal of Henry IV (1399–1413)

COURT OF COMMON PLEAS IN THE FIFTEENTH CENTURY

In the top row are seven judges; below are the officials of the court. The long-haired, bare-legged defendant stands at the bar in the custody of the tipstaff (constable). The illustration, as well as those on the following three pages, is from a law treatise of the time of Henry VI (1422–1461). This leaf was the beginning of the table of contents.

COURT OF KING'S BENCH IN THE FIFTEENTH CENTURY

The judges are at the top; below them are the king's coroner and attorney. Standing on the table are the ushers, one of whom (at left) is administering the oath to the jury. The prisoner is at the bar in chains, and in the foreground other prisoners are guarded by tipstaffs, or constables.

COURT OF EXCHEQUER IN THE FIFTEENTH CENTURY

The judges are seated at the top; at the table clerks and officers of the court are counting coins. In the foreground are the prisoners.

COURT OF CHANCERY IN THE FIFTEENTH CENTURY

The two central figures in the top row are the judges, one of whom is tonsured. Around the table are clerks. At the lower right of the table is the sealer, who is pressing down the matrix of the Great Seal with a roller. On the table in front of him are the sealed writs. Standing at the bar are three sergeants, who can be identified by their coifs.

King Edward IV (1461–1483)

political life, they could not as intelligent and experienced administrators ever hope to implement these ultimate ideals.

The two fundamental limitations on the authoritarian ideology and ambitions of the Anglo-Norman government (aside from the obvious need to work, to some degree, with baronial consent) were first, the primitive communications network characteristic of an underdeveloped society, and second, the limited number of educated personnel available for royal service in late eleventh-century Europe. The problems presented by a primitive communications network were endemic in Europe until the Industrial Revolution and probably had more to do with inhibiting the achievement of fully authoritarian and totalitarian forms of government than all the political theory ever written. A government which lacked rapid postal systems and the telegraph and telephone and other ways of communicating its orders to its local agents, and which also had no rapid and thoroughly effective mass media for communication available to it was severely hampered in effecting its authority, no matter how despotic and socially irresponsible the attitudes of the royal officials. This is almost as true of the French Bourbon monarchy of the eighteenth century as of the government of William the Conqueror. Since it took several days to carry a message to the hinterlands of the kingdom and much longer to get the feedback which would allow the royal officials to know the impact of its orders, we can say that the nature of the communications network placed a perpetual limitation upon the ambitions of even the most energetic king and the most aggressive and ambitious royal ministries. Nevertheless it is a cliché of history that an authoritarian political system did develop in France in the late twelfth and thirteenth centuries—authoritarian in the sense that the king and the central administration ruled by royal will and without the need for gaining the consent of the great magnates of the kingdom, let alone representatives of less wealthy groups in society. No medieval king ever had a better opportunity to establish such an authoritarian system than William the Conqueror, who held the political power and landed wealth of the whole realm in his hands in 1066 and did not have to bow to any principle of either Germanic or feudal law that was contrary to his interests.

We cannot account for the fundamental differences between the Anglo-Norman and later French monarchies by saying that the French administrators of the thirteenth century were inspired by authoritarian principles of Roman law, because Archbishop Lanfranc, the chief minis-

97

ter of William the Conqueror, had himself begun his long career as a master of the Roman law, and several other royal clerics had been well-educated in the Roman canonical tradition of legal absolutism. Why then could William the Conqueror's government not achieve what the Capetian monarchy effected 150 years later, even though the ideology for both groups of royal officials was substantially the same and the communications network did not substantially improve between 1066 and 1200? The answer must lie in the failure of the European educational system before the end of the twelfth century to meet the personnel requirements of an authoritarian government. No matter how enlightened and efficient the central bureaucracy of William the Conqueror, it could not muster enough literate local agents to carry out its orders. What few literate men were available, and also interested in and capable of administrative and legal work, barely met the requirements of the central government in the late eleventh century. It was not until about 1200 that the new universities began to turn out generation after generation of trained lawyers who were the ideal men to serve as provincial bureaucrats. These university graduates became the local representatives of the French monarchy. The Capetian kings of the thirteenth century were the first European rulers to benefit fully from the educational revolution of the twelfth century and thereby to create an authoritarian system of government which developed along very different lines than the English one. But the shortage of literate and effective personnel to rule the shires forced the Anglo-Norman monarchy, against its fundamental instincts, to rely for local government on the cooperation of the barons, the powerful landed men who dominated county society.

The chancery clerks of William the Conqueror held assumptions about the nature of government which were derived from hierarchic theories which have long since passed out of the view of government officials in English-speaking countries. But the operative ideals of Anglo-Norman government would be easily comprehensible to civil servants in London today—they wanted to serve society by increasing the power and wealth of the crown. In achieving this end they would gain substantial personal reward. Certain modern notions, particularly that it is the function of government to war against poverty, were alien to them; they had enough difficulties without worrying about the poor in obscure villages or in urban communities. The function of royal government was to maintain and improve the law, preserve peace in the realm, and collect sufficient taxes to enable the king to withstand any invader. It was not until the late sixteenth century that English royal government accepted any additional functions, and since until the nineteenth century all that the king did for the poor was to tell local agencies to take care of them, it can be said that the obligations of royal officials did not change substantially from the Norman Conquest until the reign of Queen Victoria. The real problem which William the Conqueror's government faced was not the definition of its duties but rather how to carry them out, and this as we have seen was a very difficult matter in view of the limitations of the communications network and the dearth of reliable and trained personnel.

It will be illuminating to provide a hypothetical example of the most critical problem encountered by the royal government in the Anglo-Norman period. This problem, which arose out of the difficulties of controlling the work of the local agents of the king in the face of an inadequate communications network and the dearth of bureaucratic personnel, was to remain the most persistent dilemma of royal administration before the sixteenth century. Let us suppose that the sheriff responsible for collecting the royal taxes in Lincolnshire has not been heard from by the king's clerks in London for half a year. A writ goes out from the chancery to the sheriff of Lincolnshire instructing him to come to Westminster three days after Michaelmas to give an account of the royal farms, that is, the income in his county from the royal demesne, the profits of justice, the feudal incidents, and other sources of royal revenue. The messenger who delivers the writ after an arduous journey taking two or three weeks reports to the chancery clerks that the sheriff is indeed alive and that he received the writ. But Michaelmas comes and goes and no sheriff appears, and another writ has to be sent out to the hinterlands from London. This time the sheriff does reply—he is ill and cannot possibly travel. In the spring another writ is sent out demanding the sheriff's presence at the treasury a week after Easter. The sheriff replies again that he cannot come because he is still ill, or that he is urgently engaged in county business, or even that in a burst of piety he has taken the cross and is planning to set out for Jerusalem on a pilgrimage or crusade. It is customary in English law that anyone summoned to the royal court can excuse himself three times before he forfeits his case, and since three months' grace after each excuse is the minimal allowance, at least a year will go by and the Lincolnshire taxes will be no closer to receipt by the treasury. What sanction has the royal government against a scoundrel like this? Ultimately only the use of force. The king will send out an army which will besiege the castle where the sheriff has taken refuge and eventually the delinquent sheriff will be dragged to Westminster and in a trial in the king's court he will be declared felonious. But from the first summons to the sheriff to give account of his farms until the final judgment in the king's court almost two years will have elapsed during which the breakdown of royal control in the county of Lincolnshire will be increasingly evident. After two years a new sheriff will be appointed and his first project will be to collect all the back taxes in the county. His will be a hard and unenviable assignment, and a very substantial part of royal revenue from the county will have been lost forever. The Anglo-Norman sheriffs were feudal lords of middling status and the king will regain some of his lost revenue from the property of the felonious official. But it is unlikely that the royal treasury will recoup the greater part of its losses.

How can the government cope with such a situation, which is constantly threatening, and keep the sheriffs in every county in line? This is where the king with a terrible reputation, such as that enjoyed by William the Conqueror, has a great advantage. No matter how intelligent and industrious the royal clerks, medieval government will only work well if the king is renowned to be a formidable warrior. The royal government will maintain its control over its county agents when the sheriff is afraid of the king's wrath. The sheriff will regularly perform his duties and collect the income from his farms and remit it to the treasury if he knows that the king, sooner or later, will bring him to justice if he fails to carry out the king's orders. The nature of the administrative system was such that the central government would only discover after several months, in most instances, that its county agents had fallen down on the job. Ultimately it is the threat of the devastating penalty of forfeiture which keeps the sheriffs at work, and for this threat to be effective the king must have a great reputation as a severe master and invincible warrior.

In the context of the communications and bureaucratic system the government has a similar and somewhat more difficult problem maintaining its control over the great barons of the realm. The government needs an information agency, it needs to publish its orders in an unequivocal way, and to make known the king's will on many particular matters of great importance. How can it do this in an illiterate, technologically backward society? The most obvious and least expensive way is to bring the leaders of society before the king; the great meeting of the *curia regis,* the king's court, was engineered to serve this function. Every great baron, under feudal law, has a right to summon his vassals to give him advice, to listen to his plans and orders, and to render judgment on their peers. As the greatest feudal lord in the whole kingdom William the Conqueror had the right to summon his own tenants-in-chief, the leading magnates of England, before him at Westminster, and he made use of this right at least three times a year. These meetings of the *curia regis* were an indispensable institution of Anglo-Norman government and the chief medium of communication between the central administration and the leaders of the feudal hierarchy. We must not assume that the barons, except for a few gossips and social butterflies, were eager to attend these meetings. It was expensive and dangerous to travel up from the counties to London. While the baron was away attending the *curia regis,* an enemy might invade his estates or at least steal some cows and kill a few of the baron's peasants. The Anglo-Norman magnates also learned very quickly that when the king summoned them to the *curia regis* he did not just have in mind chatting about the weather and the harvests or even just expatiating on the glory of anointed kingship; he wanted something very tangible, service and money and lawful judgment. The king did not summon his vassals because he respected feudal law, as some historians have suggested, but because he wanted to make known his will to the leaders of society. Feudal law happily gave William and his successors a sanction for demanding the presence at Westminster of the greatest lay and ecclesiastical lords, and they would be fined if they refused to appear and ultimately subject to condemnation for felony if they persisted in this refusal.

Thus at least three times every year about a hundred of the most important men in this intensely hierarchical society will appear before the king and his chief officials. The barons are dressed in armor or splendid ecclesiastical robes; it is an impressive assembly which illustrates the king's position as liege lord of the realm. No other eleventh-century European ruler could have gathered such a group together as a matter of course. But the formal aspect of the *curia regis* is only its most obvious function; the king and his ministers have been carefully preparing for the important business which will be transacted at these meetings. Usually the king himself will not speak on these items of government business; the chancellor or in the case of William the Conqueror, his chief advisor, Archbishop Lanfranc of Canterbury, will address the magnates in the king's name while the king, wearing his crown to emphasize his

majesty, will sit on a throne and glare at the barons. If the king is going
to war, his vassals have to be informed and generally their assent will be
requested, for they have to provide the knight service owed to the king
or else pay scutage in compensation. Scutage and the feudal incidents
belong to the king by right and he does not need the barons' consent,
but if the magnates are not told in advance what the royal government is
going to do it will be hard to collect the money. It is assumed that the
information and instructions given to the feudal leaders of society will
filter down to the others so that the sub-vassals and the cathedral clerks
will come to know soon after the meeting of the *curia regis* the details of
royal policy insofar as it affects them.

After each harangue by the chancellor or archbishop explaining why
the king is taking money from the magnates, the barons stand around
and talk it over. There is a great deal of noise and confusion and the
conclave sometimes continues for several days. The king's spokesmen
steer the conversation into the right channels so that assent will be
forthcoming. They nearly always get the barons' consent to royal policy;
the crucial question is how enthusiastic the magnates are about the royal
project that has been presented to them; reluctant consent foreshadows
later trouble, for once the baron has returned to his county, in the
bosom of his family and retainers and away from the terrible visage of
the king, he is much more likely to be recalcitrant and resistant to the
attempts of the royal officials to get money from him. If the barons
should refuse a royal request at a meeting of the *curia regis*, then the
king if he is shrewd, and the officials if they are careful and intelligent,
will know that they are in deep trouble and that a great feudal rebellion
is in the offing. It hardly needs to be said that such outright refusal of
assent to royal will never occurred in the reign of William the Conqueror, and only once in the reign of his successor, but grudging and
halfhearted consent on the part of the barons to some royal program was
not rare even in the Anglo-Norman period. When this occurred the government had a difficult decision: to abandon the venture or to proceed
in the face of inevitable baronial recalcitrance. It was characteristic of
the aggressive and self-confident Anglo-Norman royal government that it
should proceed to try to implement policies that were visibly unpopular
among the barons who attended the *curia regis*, but it was also in line
with the shrewd and rational outlook of these kings and officials that
they did not push so hard to get what they wanted that the barons were
driven to contemplating the prospect of a united rebellion against their

royal liege lord. Some later medieval English kings and their ministers would not be so wise, or so fortunate.

In addition to its functions as an information agency and the institutional means of obtaining consent to royal policies, the *curia regis* also provided the time and place for great judicial trials involving men and issues too grand for settlement in the shire court. At the *curia regis* the king would accuse rebellious vassals of felony or two royal tenants-in-chief would engage in a plea involving the right to possession of some great estate. Feudal law dictated that such pleas could be decided only in the king's court, for only at these assemblies of the leaders of feudal society would the barons be present in sufficient number to enjoy the right of trial by their peers, or social equals. We have a detailed record of the process of one of these trials in the Anglo-Norman *curia regis*. It occurred in 1088, the year after the death of William the Conqueror, although the account in the form that it has come down to us seems to have been written down some fifteen years later. Nevertheless this account graphically illustrates the ways in which pleas were held in the *curia regis* in the late eleventh century. The Bishop of Durham, a very arrogant Frenchman who was a frontier lord holding an enormous marcher fief, was charged with rebellion against the king, and his vast feudal estates were therefore liable to forfeiture on conviction of felony. The king appeared and stood glowering while Archbishop Lanfranc spoke for him. The charge was felonious betrayal, treason against the king, and the bishop's peers were asked to convict him so that a sentence of forfeiture might be made. The bishop, who was palpably guilty of the charge, defended himself by means of a legal ploy. He challenged the jurisdiction of the feudal court, claiming that as a bishop he should be tried in ecclesiastical court; although he had never been known for his devotion to Rome the Bishop of Durham now insisted that he had a right to appeal to the Pope. Lanfranc's rejoinder was that the bishop was being charged in his capacity of a royal vassal and that this was a secular matter to be decided in the *curia regis*. Then the assembled barons discussed the case and, as might be expected with men who lacked the insight into legal and ecclesiastical subtleties, it was necessary for Archbishop Lanfranc to make his points several times before even the brightest of the barons clearly comprehended the issue. Finally, after what must have been several hours of debate, a consensus was reached and the bishop was sent from the room while the final decision was made. He was summoned back to hear the inevitable verdict that he was guilty of felony and that he was to be punished by forfeiture of all his land and expulsion from the kingdom.

This kind of trial by peers in the *curia regis* was a privilege jealously guarded by the king's vassals. To be able to plead one's suit at the great meeting of the *curia regis* was a demonstration of one's superior status in society and at the same time a baron was liable to gain a more sympathetic hearing from the other magnates of the realm than he would at the shire court. Nevertheless it is probable that the Anglo-Norman barons did not view their participation in these lawsuits in the *curia regis* as an unmixed blessing. They would be required to render judgment which involved the king's wealth and property, and to decide against the king, as occasionally happened, involved a certain risk for every great baronial family was sooner or later vulnerable to relief and wardship. And even the vehement expression of opinion against a great earl who was involved in a plea in the *curia regis* might eventually bring reprisal.

The regular meetings of the great council of the barons as the full *curia regis* constituted an institution fundamental to the operations of royal government and law in the Anglo-Norman period and in fact for the subsequent four centuries of English history. For six to eight weeks a year the leaders of rural society were in the king's presence, they were addressed by the king's officials, they were made aware of what was going on in the realm, and they were made parties to the formulation of royal policy. The royal government could not have worked without such assemblies. But this system did have its drawbacks and defects, principally two in nature. In the first place the barons were given too close a view of the mysteries of government, and by being brought together so often the great magnates were slowly welded into a community, or at least given a consciousness of themselves as a cohesive group. The full effect of this development was not clearly evident until the thirteenth century by which time the barons had achieved a common feeling of solidarity against the crown and identified themselves with the "community of the realm." But even by the 1120's, as a consequence of a half-century of joint participation in the *curia regis*, the great feudal lords are beginning to coalesce into a distinct political group whose influence is due not only to their wealth and patrimonial status in the counties but also to their belief that they can understand the workings of government and law as well, if not better, than the royal officials. Ultimately what the continual meetings of the full *curia regis* achieved was the removal of the veil of mystery from royal government. The baronage by the end of the eleventh century could see who was actually engaged in the day-to-day work of royal administration and like the modern corporation executives who discover that there are professors in Washington, the magnates were scarcely awed by a bunch of royal clerks. If the king's government could be carried on by a handful of churchmen with the assistance of a few middling landholders, it must be an easy task, they decided. The meetings of the *curia regis* made the English barons too familiar with government; to them the royal bureaucrats were not faceless men; they knew that most of the royal officials were simply ambitious Frenchmen of modest family background who had university degrees. It is significant that in France, where there was no national assembly of the aristocracy until the first decade of the fourteenth century, the royal government found it much easier to surround itself with an aura of majesty. Because in England the king from the time of William the Conqueror found it necessary to rule to a considerable degree with the consent and cooperation of the magnates, this was bound sooner or later to induce the aristocracy to attempt some kind of control over the royal administration. This did not occur in the reign of William the Conqueror, so preeminent was he among the great magnates of his country, and it did not become a crucial issue until after 1200. But already in the second and third decades of the twelfth century the great barons are complaining that the king is trying to rule them and limit their rights and privileges by means of a bureaucracy of obscure men "raised from the dust," and henceforth a large part of the energies of the royal administration will be devoted to the relations between the king and an aristocratic group growing more or less steadily in self-consciousness and a sense of corporate identity.

The other weakness of trying to implement the royal policy through the periodic meeting of the *curia regis* is a more obvious one. When the great barons returned to their honors they would assume their usual role as leaders of county society and surrounded by their families and vassals they would try to forget about their obligations to the king, which they had readily recognized in the royal presence. Therefore it falls upon the permanent group of royal officials, which some historians have arbitrarily called the small *curia regis*, to remind the magnates of their obligations and to keep the pressure upon county society to fulfill its responsibilities to its liege lord the king. The royal officials, who are responsible for the operation of the king's chancery and treasury, will still in the reign of William the Conqueror occasionally follow the king in his peregrinations around the country, but most of the time they will be hard at work at the center of government, at Westminster where the chancery clerks are resident, or at Winchester where the royal treasury is kept. And although the chancery and treasury officials may sometimes accompany the king as he moves around within England, they will not follow him to the continent where as Duke of Normandy he spends half his reign. When William was out of the country his chief advisor Archbishop Lanfranc in effect acted as regent and the ordinary workings of royal government were not interrupted. This perpetuation of royal government without the king's presence reveals that the idea is slowly emerging that monarchy is some majestic force which operates above and beyond the king's personality, although it will not be until the early twelfth century that there is any clear conceptualization of this fundamental constitutional theory and not until the thirteenth century will the idea of the crown as an impersonal corporate entity loom large in the consciousness of the English ruling elite.

To maintain control over county society between periodic meetings of the full *curia regis*, the royal officials needed a reliable means of communication with the leaders of rural society and a local agent to carry out their will. The means of communication was found in the royal writs with which the Anglo-Saxon kings had experimented. The pre-conquest kings could not exploit the potentiality of the writs which their chancery clerks had invented because there was scarcely anyone outside of the royal family who was willing to follow their orders. In the Anglo-Norman period the writs became the sinews of the administrative system, the most effective way aside from the meetings of the full *curia regis* of making the king's will known. The writ was not just sent hopefully into outer darkness; it gave a command or made known a royal policy which the recipient was required to fulfill. To refuse to carry out the order in a royal writ, or to fail to give a reply when one was demanded was technically felonious, a crime for which a man was answerable to the king.

The writs of the Anglo-Norman period fall into two categories. One kind of writ is a sort of royal proclamation of some major clarification of law or improvement in government: the king announces that he is introducing trial by combat as a method of proof for the benefit of the French aristocracy or that he is separating the secular and ecclesiastical courts. These general writs are addressed to the magnates in every county; they are read in every shire court, and copies are deposited in the archives of all the larger monasteries in the realm. The sheriff, the bishop, and the great magnates of the county could understand the meaning of these writ-proclamations and explain their contents to the other landlords who attended the meetings of shire courts.

The greater number of Anglo-Norman royal writs are not these grandiose general proclamations but rather short messages, terse and precise, imparting particular information. There is no rhetoric in these writs; they come right out and order someone to do something, usually connected with peace, taxation, or unusual kinds of legal procedure. The sheriff was the most common recipient of these short writs sent out by the Anglo-Norman chancery, for this official became the prime local agent of royal government in the Anglo-Norman period. There were times in pre-conquest England when the sheriff had functioned in the same way, as the word shire-reeve implies, but in the reign of Edward the Confessor the sheriff's role as the king's representative in the rural communities had become a nominal one. The later Anglo-Saxon sheriff was unable to contend with the great authority of the earls who by the 1040's had come to dominate the county court. In the reign of William the Conqueror the power of the sheriff rose with the authority of the king he served. In the eyes of the royal officials the sheriff should have the power and responsibility of the Norman viscount, and this is indicated by their occasional reference to the sheriff as a *vicomte*. He was a middling landowner of substantial wealth and influence in the county which he served but he derived his power not from his personal status but from his position as the king's agent. The great magnates of Anglo-Norman England had to obey the sheriff when he came armed with a royal writ directing him to collect taxes or institute some legal process, or else they were answerable for a charge of felony in the *curia regis*.

The use of the writ to communicate royal will to the counties and the employment of the sheriff to carry out the commands embodied in the writs, enabled the royal officials to institute a novel melioration of the judicial procedure of the county courts. The traditional methods of proof involving ordeals and compurgations were allowed to stand with the addition of trial by battle as a form of ordeal suited to the way of life of the feudal magnates. But in civil suits involving land tenure, the royal government added a new and more rational way of making judgment. This was effected by way of importing from Normandy the institution of the sworn inquest of twelve lawful men, resident in the neighborhood where the disputed land lay, who were required to make recognition of whether the plaintiff or the defendant actually had right to seisin of the land. The sworn recognitors, who because of their oath (*iuramentum*) to attest the true facts of a case eventually came to be called the jury, were required to go out and literally "view the land," walking around its circumference to make sure that they had clearly in mind what was under dispute, and then come before the county court and attest the true facts involved in the plea. The inquest or jury of recognition made no decision; this was still the province of the leaders of the community assembled in the shire court. But once the jury had attested its knowledge of the truth the court could only accept their recognition as the sole basis for its judgment. The operation of the Anglo-Norman inquest in this sense already follows the pattern of the use of the jury in later English common law procedure, as we know it to the present day. The jury even today technically does not make judgment, which is the province of the court; it only recognizes the truth of the plea, and the court accepts the view of the jurymen as the basis for its formal judgment.

The thesis that it was William the Conqueror and his clerks who introduced the institution of the jury in civil suits into England from Normandy, a thesis originally propounded by the great German legal historian Heinrich Brunner and confirmed by Maitland, has recently been challenged. R. C. van Caenegem has discovered what looks like the use of a jury of recognition in a plea involving the abbott of Ramsey Abbey a dozen years before the Norman Conquest. Largely on the basis of this single instance—which is, by the way, known to us by post-conquest or very confused accounts—he has speculated that there were two elements in the late eleventh-century jury: a popular element, the practice of the shire courts continuing from the Anglo-Saxon period, and a royal element, the king's confirmation of pre-conquest practice on the model of the Norman inquest. For two reasons it is hard to agree with this brilliant hypothesis, which is based on one doubtful instance of the pre-conquest use of the jury. In the first place there were several Norman-French clerks at the court of Edward the Confessor and this pre-conquest cross-channel influence may explain the singular use of the jury of recognition in 1054, if such it was. Even more important, the cast of mind of both the royal officials and the feudal magnates in the reign of William the Conqueror was such as not to be interested in occasional Anglo-Saxon experiments. They would not have been interested enough to discover a singular instance of pre-conquest improvement of judicial process in civil suits when they had ready to hand in Normandy such a procedure which could be introduced full-blown into England for the settlement of lawsuits involving feudal landholders.

Every aspect of the jury in the reign of William the Conqueror reveals that it was a royal institution. The jury of recognition was established on an *ad hoc* basis by a writ issued from the royal chancery directing the sheriff and the other prominent men of the county to make use of this procedural innovation. The jury of recognition was available only to leading members of the feudal class who gained this special privilege either because the king was particularly interested in their welfare—which was certainly the case in the Conqueror's reign with a bishop and an abbot whose landed privileges were confirmed by inquest procedure—or because the inquest was instituted after a heavy payment to the king. A fundamental change in jury procedure will occur in the second half of the twelfth century when the inquests are instituted as a matter of course to settle the plea of any plaintiff from among the whole class of free men who is willing to pay a set fee to the chancery. In the 1160's and 1170's the impaneling of a jury by a royal writ becomes a routine procedure and the chancery in issuing the writ merely follows a prescribed form which has been prepared in advance. But in the reign of William the Conqueror the inquest in a civil suit was an *ad hoc* procedure involving a royal writ specially drafted to suit the occasion, and it was still an unusual and experimental judicial process and in no sense a routine matter. We misunderstand the nature of William the Conqueror's government and the problems his clerks had to resolve if we see the writ impaneling an inquest as other than a carefully considered measure coming out of the circle of royal officials who are concerned with the irrationality of traditional Germanic law and who are trying to bring into England a Norman institution which will improve that procedure, particularly in lawsuits of great moment involving the feudal magnates.

The same spirit of preserving the basic institutions of Anglo-Saxon law while trying to improve its procedure, and adapting it to the new political and social situation of the Norman settlement, inspired other judicial clarifications and amendments stemming from William the Conqueror's government. In general it can be said that the king and his clerks had no particular commitment to Germanic law because it postulated a political and social system which differed from, and at times contradicted the authoritarian inclinations of the monarchy and the severely hierarchical organization of feudal society. Only insofar as Anglo-Saxon judicial institutions could be utilized within this authoritarian and feudal framework and could be made serviceable to maintain peace in the country were they worthy of perpetuation. Therefore when William proclaimed that "all should keep and hold the law of King Edward the Confessor" with the addition of certain amendments made by him for the common benefit of the realm, the king was not only emphasizing the legitimacy of his accession as King Edward's successor but also his government's pragmatic attitude to Anglo-Saxon legal institutions which would be retained as long as they fitted in with the centralizing and rationalizing proclivities of his rule.

It was found useful not only to retain the shire and hundred court as judicial communities but also the general principle that it was the function of the local communities to maintain peace within their jurisdictions. The Anglo-Saxon tithing was continued in the Anglo-Norman institution of the *frankpledge*, by which the free men in the local communities were grouped in units of ten and were mutually held responsible for maintenance of peace. Over the next two centuries the preservation of peace in the villages of England will be heavily dependent on this frankpledge system and the king's justices will be enjoined to make sure that all members of the hundred court are organized in these basic peace and judicial units of ten men. Later Anglo-Saxon law had already decided that all men should place themselves under lords who would be responsible for producing the criminals among their dependents before the community court. The entrenchment of lordship with the introduction of a comprehensive feudal hierarchy in William the Conqueror's reign made the use of lordship as a peace institution all the more feasible, and hence the king stipulated that lords should be required to apprehend the murderers among their dependents or else pay a heavy fine to the king. But if both the frankpledge system and lordship should fail as peace and police institutions and the criminal still not be brought before the community court, then the entire hundred in which the homicide was committed had to bear a common responsibility and pay the *murdrum* fine to the royal treasury. As special protection for the French conquerors the king enjoined that whenever a homicide occurred, the local community must immediately determine whether the victim was a Frenchman or an Englishman; in the former case the severity of the crime and the immediate need to find the slayer was obviously greater. A hundred which failed to make this "presentment of Englishry" in the case of every homicide within its jurisdiction was susceptible to payment of a fine to the king. It is characteristic of both the conservatism and greed of English government in the twelfth century that royal justices would continue a century and more after the conquest to fine a hundred court for failure to carry out presentments of Englishry long after the distinction between conquering Frenchmen and vanquished Englishmen had been eradicated and forgotten.

The principle under which the Anglo-Norman judicial system operated was that crime must result in the paying of a fine by someone to the king for violation of royal peace, and if responsibility could not be made to fall on the culprit's lord or the frankpledge unit to which the criminal belonged, then the whole community of the hundred must compensate the king for this transgression of the peace and security he has proclaimed for his whole realm. It is in many ways a draconic system, for the king places upon the communities of the country a very large share of the burden for upholding the peace system which he has decreed. This system will make men wary of their neighbors and eager to get rid of any troublemakers in their midst. But if the king has a great reputation for venting his wrath upon any community which cannot apprehend and produce in court the disturbers of the peace—and the Conqueror and his sons certainly had this kind of reputation—then it will be as effective a peace system as can be achieved in an underdeveloped society plagued by bad communications and a dearth of bureaucratic personnel. This system vividly illustrates how William the Conqueror's government could make a reasonable and effective political and judicial organization out of extremely localized and fundamentally primitive sets of institutions.

The administration of the royal treasury in William the Conqueror's reign was marked by the same general characteristic, which we have found in the government's organization of judicial institutions, of preserving and at the same time improving a pre-conquest system. There is some evidence that William retained in his service for some years after 1066 an official called the treasurer who had served Edward the Confessor. This was not because the king and his French officials admired English perspicacity, as some historians have quaintly imagined, but simply because the new government had thoroughly to acquaint itself with the financial resources of the monarchy. William obtained a large share of his income from his demesne, as Edward the Confessor had done, but instead of the king and his family's traveling around the country eating up the produce on the royal estates, the sheriff brought the income from the royal demesne in specie to the treasury. We do not know in detail the workings of the Anglo-Norman treasury before 1100. But it is certain that William the Conqueror's treasury had some kind of accounting division, because it took the trouble to "blanch" or assay the coins that the sheriffs brought in payment of their farms, in order to establish that the specie was "white money," that is, that the silver content of the coins was equal to their face value. Like the Anglo-Saxon kings, the Anglo-Norman rulers obtained a share of the fines in the law courts, but as we have seen, they took steps to introduce novel ways by which the whole community of the hundred could be amerced if no malefactor could be found. In general there was a great increase in the judicial revenue of the king during the Anglo-Norman period because of the royal sheriff's leading role in the county courts, which during the later Anglo-Saxon period had been under the domination of the great earls. We have seen that after 1066 a completely new source of royal revenue derived from feudal incidents, particularly reliefs and wardships, and also from the compensation (called scutage after 1100) paid by the royal tenants-in-chief when they availed themselves of the option of not sending their contingents of knights to the royal feudal host.

But even the revenue gained from all these resources did not satisfy the king and his treasurers. The king's greed, augmented by the need to find as much money as possible to hire mercenaries for continental wars, was insatiable. What in fact most impressed well-informed contemporaries on the continent when they commented on the Anglo-Norman monarchy was the vast income of William the Conqueror and his sons. An early twelfth-century clerical minister of the King of France referred to the English ruler as "that rich man, that marvelous buyer and collector of knights." Under these conditions, it was not to be expected that William and his advisors would allow to lapse any form of income which the later Anglo-Saxon kings enjoyed, and this included the Danegeld which had been a tax paid by the whole English folk to preserve the country from Scandinavian invasions. Therefore, although there was no sanction for such a national impost in the new feudal world, William and his sons several times levied the geld upon the lands of the magnates. The barons resisted paying the geld because there was no sanction in their relationship to the king as their liege lord for such a tax, and the income which the royal officials extracted from the reluctant magnates was always disappointing and far less than the huge sums which Edward the Confessor had obtained from this kind of levy.

It was characteristic of Anglo-Norman government that the king, having perceived a possible additional source of income from the geld, should elect to proceed with this clearly unpopular policy, hoping to get his way eventually in the face of baronial opposition, and at the same time it was characteristic of William that he should not push the issue to the point that the barons found the geld to be a major source of grievance against their liege lord. To the royal clerks it appeared that the disappointing return from the Danegeld could be improved upon if the treasury had at its disposal a complete assessment of the landed and movable wealth of all the landlords in the kingdom. It was therefore to put together a geld-book or general tax assessment, as Maitland suggested, that the investigations which resulted in the two volumes we know as Domesday Book were originally launched. However, as V. H. Galbraith has shown, it seems likely that the royal officials decided to obtain a record of wealth and privileges which in some instances went beyond the needs of a tax assessment, in order to have a complete record of land tenure in England going back to the reign of Edward the Confessor. This was made necessary by the large number of disputes about seisin of land among the great magnates in the latter part of the Conqueror's reign, which in many cases were settled by the impaneling of juries of recognition. It seems to have occurred to the chancery officials that many lawsuits could be obviated by one series of systematic inquests throughout the whole realm whose results would be summarized in one or two volumes and kept at hand for reference by the royal administrators. In attempting to increase the income from the geld by assessing all the properties and revenue of the barons and to preclude the appointment of *ad hoc* juries of recognition, the royal clerks were engaging in overintellectualized planning that turned out to be naïve and utopian on both counts. But this hope of resolving some of the most difficult financial and judicial problems of the government through the carrying out of one grand national inquest illustrates to the highest degree the attitude of William the Conqueror's government. No other medieval monarchy will conceive of anything in the least approximating Domesday Book until the thirteenth century and no other investigation of wealth and privileges in a medieval society will be effected with anything approaching the thoroughness of the Domesday inquest which was inaugurated in 1086.

All the important political and judicial institutions of Anglo-Norman England were utilized in the making of the Domesday inquest, from the central administration down to the sheriffs in the counties, the hundred courts, and the juries of recognition in every vill in England. The juries were required to testify under oath as to who held the land, how much of it was in the lord's demesne, how much of it was the peasants' plough-land, how many peasants lived in the manor (or in the case of a town, how many burgesses), what the legal status of the various peasants was, and "how much woods, how much meadow, how many pastures, how many mills, how many fish ponds, how much has been added or taken away, how much it was worth altogether, and how much now." Further-more, the jurors had to give all this information "three times over, namely in the time of King Edward, when King William gave it out, and how it is now." The royal treasury was especially interested in the final question put to the jurors: "Whether more can be had from the land than is being had." In each county of England the returns were listed hundred by hundred with the names of the jurors appended. The coun-try was divided up into some four or five regions and the returns from the shires were sent to the king's commissioners responsible for each region, and by these regional officials the county returns were further or-ganized and summarized. Finally, the regional returns were sent to the chancery which reduced the information they received to a summary form suitable for inscribing in two large folio volumes. It appears that when William the Conqueror died, this final stage of the Domesday inquest was not quite completed and the royal officials working on the ultimate version of Domesday Book suspended their work and never re-sumed it. This ironic fact illustrates how heavily William the Conquer-or's officials depended on the king's leadership and energy in carrying out their plans.

A final judgment on the nature of the Norman settlement which em-phasizes the rational planning undertaken by the king and his assistants and the high degree of political and judicial centralization which was achieved, ought not on the other hand to underrate the power which was left in baronial hands. This was not only the consequence of the great wealth and military prowess of the magnates but was also due to the legal control and influence which they exercised. The frontier lords and some other privileged magnates were given extensive rights of pri-vate jurisdiction so that no sheriff could enter their lands and no royal writ could be served upon their dependents without their permission. In addition every tenant-in-chief of the king had his own feudal *curia* in which he presided at trials involving disputes between himself and one of his vassals or between two of his own vassals. Under these conditions of feudal law it is obvious that a large number of lawsuits of greatest moment to the members of the feudal hierarchy did not come within the immediate jurisdiction of the royal court.

There was yet another and more subtle way in which the magnates exercised great influence and authority in the judicial life of the realm. The men who dominated the procedure of the shire court, along with the sheriff, were the chief lay and ecclesiastical magnates who held land in the county. Under the provisions of feudal law society was absolutely dichotomized; the upper level consisted of those who enjoyed the status of a *liber homo*, a free man who was a member of the feudal hierarchy, stretching from the great earl at the top down to the humblest sub-vassal or *vavasour*; on the lower level were the unfree, the servile peasant class excluded from the ranks of the military aristocracy. The French church-men who served the king were in fact among the strongest advocates of this rational simplification of the class structure in contrast with the im-precision and confusion of Anglo-Saxon society. In the reign of William the Conqueror the shire court came to be the judicial preserve of the feudal class and only a *liber homo* could be a suitor there. This impor-tant judicial change had two effects. On the one hand it strengthened the corporate nature of the shire court, giving its members a stronger sense of community as they were now to a greater degree than before 1066 homogeneous in their social background. This increase of the com-munity consciousness of the shire will have profound constitutional sig-nificance in the twelfth century. The second and more immediate effect of making the county court the preserve of the *liber homo* is the enhanc-ing of the judicial influence of the great barons. For in one way or another all the free men of the shire are the dependents of a very small group of the greater magnates of the shire, and therefore the legal process of the shire court, even though it meets under the presidency of the sheriff and may make use of juries of recognition impaneled by royal writ, will be heavily conditioned by the attitudes and ambitions of the great barons of the county who are the tenants-in-chief of the king.

In eleventh-century society, even more than in our own, judicial power meant political authority. Therefore the extensive baronial rights of pri-vate jurisdiction, the important business which fell within the purview of baronial courts, and the inevitable domination by the great barons of a more firmly crystallized community of the shire, all contributed to a situation in which the whole system of centralized government painfully built up by William and his clerical advisors could potentially be undermined and torn to pieces by the separatism and patrimonial ambitions of great feudal lords. Fortunately, the two sons of William the Conqueror who succeeded him were rulers whose energy, military skill, and authoritarian inclinations were equal to their father's. Therefore we shall see that especially after the second decade of the twelfth century the royal government will try to extend its legal jurisdiction over some of the areas of law which the circumstances of feudal privilege had under the terms of William the Conqueror's settlement necessarily left in baronial hands.

III. The Church and the World

I T WAS A COMMON PRACTICE among ecclesiastical thinkers in the eleventh century, in England as elsewhere, to use interchangeably the words *ecclesia* and *mundus*, the church and the world. This usage reflected the common assumption that as a result of the Christianization of European society in the early Middle Ages the church and the world had become identical and synonymous entities. In a society in which kings were anointed with the same oil with which bishops were consecrated and churchmen played leading roles in royal government and in the structure of the feudal hierarchy, this identification of *ecclesia* and *mundus* seemed to be a proposition whose truth was self-evident. But beginning in the 1050's a group of brilliant and energetic cardinals at Rome led by Cardinal Hildebrand critically examined the implications of this identification of the church and the world. They concluded that the ideal of a Christian society involved a new right order in which churchmen would be freed from the authority of kings and secular magnates and that all the rulers of western Europe should be subject to the universal authority of the Pope as a vicar of Christ on earth. During the pontificate of Hildebrand as Pope Gregory VII (1073-1085) this revolutionary Christian ideal led to a long-drawn-out and bitter conflict between the papacy and the German emperors who regarded the Roman view of church-state relations as destructive to the foundations of the government and society which they ruled. The issue which particularly fomented conflict between Pope and emperor was the papal claim that the imperial investiture of bishops and abbots with the symbols of their office was in fact investiture by a layman and therefore contrary to canon law.

While Hildebrand always regarded the German emperor as the enemy of Christian right order in the world, he had great expectations that Duke William the Bastard of Normandy would be a faithful servant of Rome, and hence he had arranged for William to have the privilege of invading England under the papal banner. The church-state system which William the Conqueror and his learned assistant Archbishop Lanfranc of Canterbury created in England did in fact more closely approximate Roman ideals than the ecclesiastical system of the pre-Conquest period. William separated the ecclesiastical from the secular courts, in accordance with the papal demands for "freedom" of the English church from secular control. Archbishop Lanfranc worked assiduously to introduce French monastic learning in England, to improve the intellectual and moral level of the secular clergy throughout the realm, to establish the effective supremacy of the Roman-founded See of Canterbury over the whole British episcopate, and to make continental canon law widely known among the English clergy.

After a decade of William's reign it became evident to Pope Gregory, however, that he had seriously misunderstood the Norman ruler's attitude in church-state relations. The Norman settlement, considered as a whole, actually strengthened royal authority over the church in England. The Conqueror was not loath to buttress his position by perpetuating the traditions of theocratic monarchy which had dominated political thought in the late Old English period. He took over the Anglo-Saxon coronation order and anointment by which kings were thought to assume priestly powers and a sacred right to interfere in the life of the church. Thereby William and the royal clerks were able to justify the king's investiture of bishops and abbots, for under the doctrine of theocratic monarchy the king was not a layman and investiture could not be condemned by canon law. The continued use of what Pope Gregory had condemned as lay investiture and the requirement that bishops and abbots make their feudal homage to the king before entering into the properties associated with their offices, gave the king absolute control over the appointment of the leading ecclesiastics of the realm, and he proceeded to fill up these offices with royal clerks who had demonstrated their inflexible loyalty to him. In general, William's rapid feudalization of church lands and the bringing of the episcopate and the abbots within the feudal order which he established in England had the effect of increasing royal control over the church and of perpetuating the identification of the church and the world along the lines which had been condemned by the reforming papacy.

Even on the local level, that of appointment of priests to parish churches, secular control over the church was continued and stiffened in the two decades after 1066. Gregory and his Roman colleagues had found particularly heinous the proprietary church system by which it was assumed that a lord who owned the land upon which an ecclesiastical structure was built had the right to appoint the churchman holding office within the building, whether he was a bishop or a parish priest. The Norman settlement not only continued but actually further entrenched this proprietary church system in the life of English society. Under the institution of the *advowson* the king's court held that the landlords of England had the right to appoint the priests for whatever churches they provided the landed endowment from whose income the priest drew his living. As the greatest landlord in the realm the king retained in his own hand hundreds of advowsons, or appointments of clerics to their livings (without which they could not assume their offices), and the royal clerks were as assiduous in maintaining the royal advowsons as they were in preserving any other part of the king's property and privileges. From the time of the Norman Conquest, the institution of the advowson became so firmly fixed in the life of the English church and society that it exists in the Church of England to the present day; about a fifth of the parish priests of the Church of England still owe their appointments to laymen who have effective rights of lordship over local churches.

Lanfranc's view of the function of the church in English society strongly contradicted several of the ideals held by Gregory VII and the Roman *curia*. The Archbishop believed that churchmen should be learned and have good incomes, but he thought that the English church should serve the interests of the king and be completely subject to royal control in all matters save enunciation of dogma. While the lay and ecclesiastical courts were separated from each other and for the first time "Courts Christian," as they were called, were established in England under the presidency of bishops, the function of these ecclesiastical courts in the Anglo-Norman period was limited to the trivialities of church administration which could not in any way affect the interests or the wealth of the king. The Conqueror's general writ setting up the Courts Christian did not specify their function, and in practice the ecclesiastical courts could only deal with the relatively insignificant matters which the king's court allowed to come within their jurisdiction. Any plea affecting church property or which concerned the relations between the king and a churchman or between a lay magnate and the church still came under the purview of royal justice. William prohibited the bishops and abbots from excommunicating any of his barons or officials or impleading them in the ecclesiastical courts without his permission. Furthermore, the king's leave was required to recognize a Pope—a provision of great importance at a time when the German emperor had set up his own candidate as an anti-Pope against the reforming Roman *curia*. The Norman settlement also provided that no churchman was to receive a papal letter without royal permission, which effectively precluded Gregory from communicating personally with English churchmen in order to command them to pursue his revolutionary policies in church-state matters. Finally, the king took it upon himself to sponsor and supervise councils of the English church, just as he had presided at ecclesiastical synods in Normandy. These meetings of the English bishops and abbots could be summoned only under royal mandate and no one was allowed to propose legislation at these councils without royal permission. It appears that the background and outlook of the Anglo-Norman ecclesiastics before 1087 was such that they were deaf to the revolutionary program proclaimed in Rome, but in any case all the churchmen were so completely under royal domination that Pope Gregory found no opportunities for introducing his program into England.

In view of the Anglo-Norman church-state system which had taken shape by the 1070's it is not surprising that Pope Gregory indicated his deep disappointment with his Norman protégé and some regret for having helped William the Bastard become the most powerful anointed king in Christendom. Yet because of the papacy's commitment to its already seemingly interminable war with the German emperor, Gregory had to move cautiously against the Anglo-Norman monarchy. The Pope could not afford the extravagant steps of excommunication and deposition he had taken against the German emperor. Instead, Gregory repeatedly summoned Archbishop Lanfranc to Rome for conferences on the condition of the church and did go so far as to suggest that William owed him an oath of fealty because the Norman ruler had conquered England under the papal banner. In these attempts to assert his authority over the English king and primate, the Pope was frustrated at every turn. William repeatedly refused the papal command for fealty and Lanfranc not only rejected Gregory's repeated summonses to Rome, but even wavered in his allegiance to the reforming Pope by initiating secret negotiations with the imperial anti-Pope. Therefore when William the Conqueror died in 1087, to be followed two years later by his great friend Archbishop Lanfranc, the Gregorian reform movement had not penetrated among the Anglo-Norman clergy, and the English bishops were still accustomed to look at the king as the source of all advancement and, for most of their guidance in church affairs as well.

The unanimity which prevailed in England on the nature of the church-state system broke down in the reign of the Conqueror's son and successor, William II Rufus (1087-1100). William was survived by four legitimate children, three sons and a daughter. The daughter, who was as tough as the Conqueror himself, he had married off to the Count of Blois, a small but strategically important French principality bordering on Normandy. His eldest son Robert Curthose (Short-Pants), whose devotion to the chivalric ideal of generosity and whose general incompetence as a ruler made him a man very different from his father, he designated as Duke of Normandy in his will. The Conqueror made his second son, William Rufus, king of England. Apparently the Conqueror did not believe that either Robert or Rufus was capable of the tremendous task of governing both England and Normandy, and this judgment of his children was a very shrewd one. Robert's easygoing manner and relaxation of his father's ruthless control over the Norman feudatories almost immediately got him into trouble, and his only way out of the disastrous consequences of his feckless rule was to take the cross in the First Crusade of 1095 and depart for the Holy Land. William Rufus was a caricature of his father in the opposite direction. His harsh and irresponsible pursuit of all feudal prerogatives of the crown and his imprudent if not illegal manipulation of feudal law so as to increase substantially royal taxation of the church gained for him not only fear and awe among the lay and ecclesiastical magnates, but also dissatisfaction and bitterness which contrasts strongly with the consensus and harmony that William the Conqueror's government had instilled among the great lords and bishops. The perverse side of William II's character did not enhance his popularity with the leaders of society. Rufus was the only king in all of English history who never married; his flagrant homosexuality and his propensity to fill up his entourage with long-haired foppish friends of dubious background was, to say the least, deeply disturbing to the churchmen who had so loyally served the monarchy in his father's reign. In addition, William Rufus exhibited a marked sympathy toward the Jewish merchants whom his father had brought over from France and allowed to settle in London and other important towns in considerable numbers. No one was more likely to arouse the indignation of an eleventh-century churchman than a homosexual who liked Jews, particularly at the time when the preaching associated with the First Crusade was increasing both Christian sensibility and church-sponsored anti-Semitism. William the Conqueror had a third son, Henry, whom he had apparently intended for the church because he saw to it that this youngest son, as was traditional in aristocratic families, received a modicum of education. In his will the Conqueror bequeathed to Henry a small cash legacy and his best wishes. But the young prince, who, it turned out, most resembled his father among all the king's children, was satisfied with neither this bequest nor the limited prospects of an ecclesiastical career. By William the Conqueror's will, Robert and Rufus were to succeed each other in England or Normandy when one of them died, but young Henry decided to await this prospect with the intention of making a different arrangement.

William the Conqueror's settlement had brought the church in England completely within the feudal order, and the bishops and abbots were therefore subject to the various kinds of feudal taxation. Rufus exploited the feudal capacities of the ecclesiastical magnates in ways which were not without precedents from his father's reign, but which taken together denote a new severity and arbitrary attitude on the part of the king. Rufus intentionally kept bishoprics and abbacies vacant for several years and refused to appoint new men to these offices in order that he might keep the property which belonged to these ecclesiastical institutions in royal wardship and divert the wealth of the bishops and abbots into his treasury. In at least one instance William II went so far as to demand a relief from the vassals of a vacant bishopric, an ingenious confusion of feudal and ecclesiastical law which indicates the new tone of extremism that marked his government.

The See of Canterbury itself was kept vacant for four years after the death of Lanfranc, and a successor was appointed only when Rufus thought he was on his deathbed and was urged by the bishops to select a new archbishop in order to save his soul from damnation. His choice fell upon Lanfranc's disciple, the venerable Italian-Norman abbot St. Anselm, who was renowned as both a holy man and as the greatest theologian and philosopher in Christendom. The king did not expect that a man of such angelic and learned inclinations would give him any trouble. But like many an intellectual promoted to high administrative office, Archbishop Anselm turned out to be surprisingly tough-minded in defending the wealth of his See against the depredations of the royal treasury. What was even more disturbing to the king and also alarming to Anselm's episcopal colleagues, most of whom were former royal clerks, the new archbishop also indicated his sympathy with the Gregorian reform program. This produced a tremendous row between the king and the primate of the English church which contrasted sharply with the consensus on church-state relations in the previous reign. It is significant that the lay magnates showed greater personal sympathy to the saintly scholar than did the great bishops because they welcomed any attempt to limit the expansion of royal authority, even for such misguided reasons. But in the final showdown between the king and archbishop in 1095, neither Anselm's episcopal colleagues nor the magnates would give him any substantial assistance and Anselm left the country for Rome in order to appeal personally to Pope Urban II for support. Gregory VII would have taken full advantage of this conflict between the two most eminent leaders of English society, but Urban was conducting papal policy along quite other lines. He was at heart a conservative who did not wish to carry out the revolutionary Gregorian program in the face of the bitter opposition from European kings, and the famous First Crusade of 1095 which Urban proclaimed was in fact one of the expedients he used to re-establish peace between church and state in Europe. In return for recognition as legitimate Pope by the English king, Urban refused to give Anselm any effective aid in his conflict with Rufus, and the archbishop, weary and disillusioned, quietly retreated into exile in France and devoted himself to completing one of the greatest works of medieval theology.

The situation of both English monarchy and church changed radically in 1100. Rufus was killed in what was reported to be a hunting accident, but there is circumstantial evidence that Henry, who was in the hunting party, participated in a plot to assassinate his brother, for as soon as Rufus lay dead he acted with remarkable speed and effectiveness to make himself king and subsequently he rewarded the magnate who had fired the fatal arrow at the king. Assassination of medieval kings was extremely rare because their anointment protected them from personal violence in the same way that priests were shielded by their consecration. It is, however, significant that the three medieval English kings who died miserable and violent deaths—Rufus in 1100 and Edward II and Richard II in the fourteenth century—were all notorious homosexuals, and it may be assumed that such was the antipathy of the medieval mind toward this kind of perversity that homosexuality may have been the only sin which was deemed sufficiently mortal to wash the balm from an anointed king.

Henry dashed from the royal forest where Rufus lay dead to Winchester where he seized the royal treasury and together with a handful of bishops, royal clerks, and a few friends among the lay nobility, took over the government and had himself crowned and anointed. Archbishop Anselm of Canterbury, who by tradition had the privilege of royal crowning and anointment, was too far away to be summoned back in this urgent situation. Henry had to act very fast, especially because his elder brother, Duke Robert of Normandy, in his usual feckless way, was dawdling somewhere in the Mediterranean on his way back from the crusades, and Henry had to gain the throne before Robert could appear and claim his inheritance in accordance with the Conqueror's will. To pacify the lay and ecclesiastical magnates, Henry issued a charter of privileges at the time of his coronation, promising to preserve the good old law of Edward the Confessor—which had come to be regarded in a vague way as a sort of fundamental law of the realm—and to keep the church in England "free." More specifically, Henry's coronation charter promised not to keep bishoprics and abbacies vacant for long periods and not to abuse the feudal prerogatives of relief and wardship. Over the course of his long reign (1100-1135) Henry kept these promises only to the extent that his government acted in the rational and careful manner which had characterized the monarchy in his father's reign and avoided the reckless and arbitrary conduct for which Rufus had been notorious. The king promised to reward with suitable ecclesiastical preferment the bishops and royal clerks who rushed through his coronation, and these promises were kept to the full. Henry tried to meet part way Anselm's sympathies with the Gregorian ideals by changing the coronation ceremony so that he was consecrated with the less sacramental catechumen oil and not the highly sacramental oil used in espicopal ordination; this signified that he was willing to acknowledge that his priestly identity was of a lower order than that enjoyed by the bishops.

Immediately after his coronation, Henry summoned Anselm back to England and treated him in a most respectful and deferential manner. It turned out that the king badly needed the archbishop's assistance in effecting a marriage with a certain Lady Matilda who was the grandniece of Edward the Confessor. The clever royal clerks, troubled by Henry's poor claim to the throne through his own family relationship, decided that it would be advisable for the king to marry a descendant of the house of Wessex. The French churchmen who had previously disdained Old English culture and who probably allowed many priceless Anglo-Saxon illuminated manuscripts to be destroyed, now affected a great enthusiasm for native English monasticism, and there was a flurry of publication of Latin versions of Anglo-Saxon saints' lives. The culmination of this consciously neo-Saxon policy of the royal circle in the early years of Henry's reign was the brilliantly fomented myth of the "green tree" of English kingship. Edward the Confessor was claimed to have prophesied the eventual uniting of the Norman and Anglo-Saxon ruling families so as to produce a new flourishing royal family tree. But Henry was prevented from fulfilling King Edward's purported prophecy by the embarrassing fact that his betrothed had been living in a nunnery for several years. Archbishop Anselm, who took a liking to this handsome and energetic young man, decided that Matilda had never actually taken the veil and could therefore become Queen of England. Henry's marriage was the final step in his securing of the throne and he had no difficulty in expelling his brother from England when the tardy crusader finally showed up to claim his inheritance. By 1105 in fact, Henry was invading Normandy in order to reunite the duchy and the English realm under his rule, as had prevailed in his father's day.

Archbishop Anselm was reluctant to disturb the renewed harmony between the church and the monarchy by pressing the issue on lay investiture, but a new Pope in Rome, Paschal II, turned out to be a devoted disciple of Gregory VII, and by 1103 a controversy between the Pope and the English king of potentially the gravest consequences was under way. The disheartened archbishop, now overruled by a radical Pope as he had formerly been betrayed by a conservative one, again left the country for a French exile, and the king and the royal clerks prepared for a fundamental and long-drawn-out struggle on church-state relations such as had plagued and ultimately ruined the German empire. Among the steps taken by the royal government to meet the arguments of the papacy was the publication of an extensive polemical literature defending the king's control over the church as being justified on the ground that monarchy was a sacred and theocratic office. The chief works of royal propaganda were several eloquent and learned treatises, anonymous in authorship but stemming from the circle of Archbishop Gerard of York, who had been a royal clerk from William the Conqueror's days, and as the Bishop of Hereford had been the leader of the episcopal group which put Henry on the throne in 1100. Harking back to Anglo-Saxon tradition, the "Anonymous of York" tractates affirmed the sacred nature of kingship and thereby attempted to validate royal investiture of ecclesiastics.

The English royal government had the intellectual resources for a great polemical conflict with the papacy over the nature of a right order in Christian society, but Henry's heart was not in this kind of ideological struggle. He knew that the administrative, legal, and financial resources of the monarchy were sufficient to retain control over the bishops and abbots even without investiture and by the Concordat of London of 1107 he succeeded in bringing the investiture controversy with the papacy to an end. Paschal II was willing to accept a compromise because except for St. Anselm and his disciples among the English monks, the Pope could find no party in the English church willing to support the implementation of Gregorian doctrines in England, and also because the Pope wished (in vain, it turned out) to obtain Henry's support for a crusade against Constantinople. The Concordat of London, which opened the way for Anselm's return to England and a complete reconciliation between him and the king before the archbishop's death two years later, embodied a compromise whose fundamental principle came out of the practice of the *curia regis*. Just as at the trial for felony of the Bishop of Durham in 1088 Lanfranc had made a distinction between the feudal and spiritual capacities of the great churchmen, so now the Concordat of London provided that the king should give up investiture of churchmen but should retain the right to have the feudal homage of the bishops and abbots before they could enter into their offices. In this way royal control over the appointment of the higher clergy was maintained inviolate while the king surrendered his claim that his anointment gave him such a sacrosanct character that he had the authority to invest the bishops and abbots. Paschal II had intended that the Concordat of London should only be a temporary settlement but with a decline of the Gregorian revolutionary ideals in the papal *curia* in the second decade of Henry's reign, the king's authority was not to be challenged again by the papacy. Within a few years of the Concordat of London, the king had completely restored royal control over the composition and life of the English church and he commanded the loyalty and intellectual, military, and financial resources of the bishops and abbots as fully as his father had done.

The English investiture controversy was an ephemeral event in comparison with the cataclysmic impact of a similar conflict between the Pope and the German emperor. But Henry's dispute with Rome did influence the development of English government in the twelfth century because it forced the king to reconsider the kind of personnel he used in his administration, and it encouraged him toward the employment of bureaucrats whose cast of mind was decidedly more secular than that of the clerks hitherto employed by the Anglo-Norman monarchy. The investiture controversy taught Henry that monastic assistants were unreliable and vulnerable to ideological considerations that ran against the current of the extension of royal power. Henry's initial hope for the revival of the good old days of the Conqueror, when his father's chief assistant was an eminent monastic scholar, had proved vain. Whatever support the Gregorian reform movement had in England came from Anselm and his monastic disciples. And from without Henry had to withstand the attack that the Italian monk Pope Paschal II had launched against the foundation of the Anglo-Norman church-state system. Consequently, in the second and third decades of his reign Henry turned more and more to the exclusive use of secular clerks, graduates of the French cathedral schools, for his literate bureaucratic personnel. Those men are only ecclesiastics in the sense that they are graduates of the new cathedral schools and have inevitably taken orders in the church. They are in effect university graduates of modest social background eager to find jobs and to rise in the world through royal service. The age of the monastic servant of medieval monarchy is over, at least as far as England is concerned; now the literate work of English government through the twelfth and thirteenth centuries will be accomplished by these astute university graduates, fanatically loyal to the cause of expanding royal authority. William the Conqueror had already made some use of this new kind of personnel; by the 1120's the monastic clerks have disappeared from royal government and the secular clerks alone, with the help of a few nonliterate middling lords have, by Henry's choice, become the royal administrators.

The ablest of these new men was an obscure French cleric whom Henry I discovered on one of his trips to Normandy, appointed to serve in his chancery, and eventually elevated to the wealthy bishopric of

Salisbury. Roger of Salisbury was the head of the royal administration in the last decade of Henry's reign and he was the founder of the first great English bureaucratic family. His bastard sons Nigel and Alexander were sent to the new universities in France for education and then given the bishoprics of Ely and Lincoln respectively. Nigel of Ely was the head of the royal treasury in the 1130's and his son Richard was to be the great English treasurer of the reign of Henry II. No one in either their time or since has ever confused Roger and his sons and grandsons with the saints of the church, but they deserve to be ranked among the great statesmen of English history. Twelfth-century royal administrators were extremely well paid out of the king's household funds, and in addition, as was the case with Roger and his family, they enjoyed the vast income of wealthy bishoprics. These secular-clerical servants of the king lived in a grand style but they did not spend their money only on elaborate private establishments. Alexander of Lincoln was a patron of litterateurs; among the writers he supported was an obscure Welsh clergyman named Geoffrey of Monmouth, whose *History of the Kings of Britain*, published in England in 1136, inaugurated the great Arthurian romantic cycle in medieval literature and was undoubtedly the greatest English literary achievement between *Beowulf* and the fourteenth century. There is a boldness, grandeur, and self-confidence in the style of royal government in the last half of Henry I's reign which goes along with the outlook and manner of life of Roger of Salisbury, his sons, and the other secular clerks in the royal administration.

In the last twenty-five years of his reign, Henry I had both a general and a particular reason for improving the judicial and financial institutions of central government. In general he wanted to continue along the lines of rational planning which his father's reign had inaugurated. The king and his officials wanted to tighten up and improve the communications system of royal administration so that it could exercise more firm control over the communities of the shire and diminish the extent of the legal jurisdiction which the Conqueror had found necessary to leave in baronial hands. Similarly Henry I aimed to draw more extensively upon the wealth of the country in order to have the resources for increasing royal power. William had established a remarkable governmental system, striking an effective balance between rationality and force; through institutional improvement Henry made the Anglo-Norman monarchy function at peak efficiency and, even more successfully than his father, circumscribed the violent and patrimonial inclinations of the feudal magnates within the framework of a centralized judicial and financial system.

The particular reason why Henry was eager to improve the operation of his government was that after he conquered Normandy from his brother Robert, as a result of his great victory at the Battle of Tinchebrai in 1106, the king divided his time and energy between England and the duchy. Therefore, as G. O. Sayles and H. G. Richardson have emphasized, he needed a government which could operate as smoothly when he was across the channel as when he was personally able to supervise the work of his chancery and treasury officials. Whether the king is in or outside the country, there is a growing tendency in Henry's reign for the royal administrators to act as a self-sufficient bureaucracy serving the king's interests, sending out writs in his name, operating under his mandate, and for considerable periods, working without Henry's personal leadership. In the late 1120's Roger of Salisbury is given a new administrative title of justiciar with the duty of acting as the king's regent when Henry is in Normandy and also of presiding over the bureaucracy even when the king is in the realm. At various times in the twelfth century, the royal official who supervises the general operation of the king's government will bear the title of justiciar; at other times it will be the chancellor who holds this ultimate responsibility.

Out of these administrative practices there is slowly emerging in the latter part of Henry's reign a sense of the distinction between the king as a person and the king as an office and idea for which service is performed, regardless of whatever the king in his natural body happens to be doing at the moment, or wherever he might be. This growing sense of the distinction between the political and natural body of the king is reflected in the use of the phrase "the pleas of the crown" which turns up in the records of Henry's government in the 1130's. When royal judges are commissioned not merely to maintain the king's peace but also to hear the pleas of the crown, we can perceive the appearance of a new understanding of the nature of government carrying us far from the undefined confusion of Germanic thought to the dawn of constitutional thinking that presages the modern state.

This realization that the royal government is to some degree a mysterious entity above and beyond the personal qualities and inclinations of the king encouraged Henry I's bureaucrats to further refine and improve their legal and administrative institutions. There is some evidence that in the second decade of Henry I's reign an ambitious experiment was made in the operation of the judicial system. The king's government attempted to establish resident royal justices in every shire to take up the slack in the communications network. The royal clerks wanted the shire courts to work continuously as royal courts with a justice learned in the law resident in every county in the realm and constantly presiding over the communities of the county in legal matters. But the system of royal resident justices—which was used successfully by the French monarchy from the end of the twelfth century and which became the foundation of French provincial administration—was inoperable in England in the reign of Henry I. There were simply not enough justices to go around among the counties of England. A resident royal justice had to be loyal, aggressive, literate, and learned in the law. About thirty such men were required for a system of resident lower justices and Henry had perhaps only ten from among his clerks who were available for this kind of work. The dearth of educated men in the early twelfth century who could be employed as royal bureaucrats was a fundamental factor in shaping royal institutions.

Another problem which made the system of resident justices inoperable was that the judges were far from sure of the precise content of royal law. The royal justices were faced with a bewildering conflict of legal traditions; no one knew whether royal law was basically Germanic, feudal, or Roman, and if it was to draw upon all three sources known to the royal judges, what the definitive structure of the resulting legal syncretism ought to be. There have survived from Henry's reign at least two unfinished and fundamentally abortive attempts at legal codification— books that bear the titles *The Laws of Henry I* and the *Quadripartitus* (The Four-Part Law Book). These law codes reveal that the royal clerks thought that by making use of a heavy overlay of Roman law they could solve the problem of diversity and conflict of laws. *The Laws of Henry I* and *Quadripartitus* began boldly with quotations from the Justinian Code proclaiming the king as the source from whose will law radiates through the whole kingdom. But this concept of legal absolutism fundamentally contradicted the Germanic tradition, which had been perpetuated through the preservation of shire courts in the reign of William the Conqueror, that law resided in the community and could not be arbitrarily changed by royal will. Furthermore, Roman law was blatantly antifeudal: instead of the notion of contract it propounded the idea that the community had irrevocably surrendered its legislative powers to royal authority. Henry I's legal experts could not find their way toward resolving these basic conflicts, and therefore when they attempted to incorporate feudal and Germanic law under a superstructure of Roman judicial theory, the results were eclectic in the most confused way and unusable as a judicial system. It is intriguing to note that the French royal lawyers in the thirteenth century did manage to achieve this Roman dominance over feudal and customary law in the form of a usable synthesis which the officials of Henry I could not effect in the second decade of the twelfth century. The rise of French absolutism in the thirteenth century took place along institutional lines which remarkably coincide with Henry I's unsuccessful and discarded experiments.

The royal government, finding it impossible to implement the system of resident royal justices and the codification of prevailing legal traditions within a Roman framework, turned in the last two decades of Henry's reign toward less radical but ultimately more effective kinds of judicial melioration. Instead of resident justices in each county of the realm, the government made use of circuit panels of itinerant justices, called justices in eyre, who were dispatched from the central court to preside over the shire courts. The advantage of these panels of itinerant justices was that only one member had to be literate, and the other justices could be middling landholders experienced in service to the king. A panel of justices in eyre would preside at meetings of three or four shire courts in succession, staying in each county for two or three weeks and attending to all the pleas of the crown. In this way, all the judicial business of the shire courts which the king believed came within the jurisdiction of royal law would be satisfactorily decided by his own justices presiding at the shire court three times a year for a period of a couple of weeks in each case. By making the shire court a branch of the central royal court through the presidency of these justices in eyre, the number of appeals to the central *curia regis* could be reduced and issues that previously would drag on for several months could be settled very quickly. The sheriff who had presided at meetings of the shire court would now become the adjutant to the itinerant justices by making the necessary preparations for their appearance in his county, and the sheriff was by 1130 given an assistant for this work, "the keeper of the pleas of the crown." In the thirteenth century this official would be called the coroner.

Since the Norman Conquest the community courts had been royal courts in the sense that the king's representative in the county, the sheriff, presided over their meetings; but now the introduction of the system of itinerant justices greatly enhanced the royal character of the shire court. For these justices in eyre came from the *curia regis*, and their interest was in following those procedures and confirming those points of law, from the welter of feudal and Germanic traditions, that accorded with the aims and assumptions of the king and central administration. In following this judicial policy, the itinerant justices in the half-century after 1120 will slowly and pragmatically create a uniformity of legal procedures and principles for use in all the shire courts of the realm. Thus the "common law," the law which runs in all the royal courts whether at Westminster or in the shires, will slowly be crystallized by the day-to-day work of the itinerant justices. As the royal judges move through the counties, they will have a broad and in fact national vision; they will be continually faced by the necessity for decision on which of many feudal and Anglo-Saxon customs they ought to retain and which it would be more convenient and reasonable to ignore. If the judges encounter local peculiarities or novel judicial complexities of a baffling nature they will hold the plea over, and when they get back to the *curia regis*, they will confer with the other royal justices coming in from other circuits. Then and there they decide what can be accepted by royal law. Thus out of the experience of several decades of hearing of pleas of the crown, the judges will hammer out a new common law that runs in the whole realm. The judges will recognize a very great part of feudal tradition, they will incorporate some of Germanic tradition, and they will take an apt phrase or adapt a useful principle from the Roman law in which the clerics among the royal justices will have been trained. But the ultimate shape of the common law in the twelfth century will rise above these constituents and will take on a life of its own as a distinct judicial system which has been tested by expediency and convenience in many years of judicial practice.

In retrospect it can be said that it was fortunate Henry I lacked the personnel to implement the resident system of justices. This system would have led to fractionalism and provincialism, the perpetuation of the custom of each county which could have been overcome only by an arbitrary overlay of Roman law imposed by the central government. In essence, this is the pattern of legal development in twelfth- and thirteenth-century France. But the English royal government in the reign of Henry I, because it had to use itinerant justices, inaugurated the crystallization of a uniform common law for the whole realm by the pragmatic refinement of feudal, Germanic, and Roman traditions into an independent and distinctive legal system which had emerged by the thirteenth century as the only alternative in Europe to the full-scale reception of Roman law. And because the full reception of Roman law came trailing clouds of judicial and political absolutism behind it, it is of the greatest significance for subsequent English constitutional development that Henry I's government was forced to undertake its makeshift judicial experimentation.

The creation of the system of itinerant justices and the heightening of the royal character of the shire court was inevitably concomitant in the latter part of Henry I's reign with a policy of expanding the jurisdiction of the county courts as against the private and feudal jurisdictions of the great barons. While in 1135 the legal authority of the great magnates was still very extensive and still constituted a potential threat to the political and legal unification of the realm, we can see Henry I's ministers inaugurating the movement toward drawing cases out of baronial courts and into the county courts under royal control, which is to be fulfilled in the legal revolution effected by Henry II in the 1160's and 1170's. A dispute over land tenure between a great baron and one of his vassals or a plea between vassals of the same baron was allowed by Henry I to remain within the scope of the baron's court. Henry I and his officials found no sanction for contravening this judicial legacy of the Norman feudal settlement. But one of Henry I's general writs declared that in the case of a plea "between vassals of two [different] lords let the plea be tried in the county court." *The Laws of Henry I* further stipulate— and we assume that this provision was effectively implemented and was not merely wishful thinking on the part of a royal clerk—that jurisdiction in all capital cases involving members of the feudal hierarchy belongs to the king and therefore is the business of either the shire court or, in the case of a great magnate, one of the three annual meetings of the full *curia regis*. It is apparent that Henry I's government aimed within the limitations of feudal law to bring as many cases as possible involving the sub-vassals, the middling and lesser landholders, into the royal court as a way of reinforcing the crown's direct relationship with the lower rungs of the feudal hierarchy and of undermining the great magnates' control over their knights. We shall find that these practices become a major policy of the English monarchy in the second half of the twelfth century.

The expansion of the royal judicial system not only implemented the authoritarian attitude of the king and his ministers; it inevitably in-

creased royal revenue. By and large Henry I did not devise novel sources
of royal income; his government perpetuated the taxation policy of William the Conqueror, deriving royal income from the law courts, the royal
demesne, the feudal prerogatives of the crown, and the occasional and
still unsatisfactory Danegelds. The vicious and scandalous manipulation
of relief and wardship which Rufus had practiced was in large part
avoided but the government generally pushed hard upon its tax resources
in the face of increasing baronial complaint. The only novel tax of
Henry's reign was the use of the feudal gracious aid, a tax taken from the
tenants-in-chief of the king with their consent. The gracious aid which
in the reign of Henry I was cautiously solicited from the magnates
through the shire courts, county by county, will, beginning in the first
decade of the thirteenth century, be taken with the consent of the great
council of the barons and will eventually become the basis of a new
nonfeudal national system of taxation.

The fundamental characteristic of Henry I's taxation policy was not in
the development of new taxes but rather in the increasing of royal income through improved accounting and recording procedures at the
king's treasury. This again is a form of improvement of the communications network. All sorts of people owe the crown money and the government has to keep up with them and press hard upon delinquents. In a
society where there is great resistance to paying taxes, where it is hard
to maintain information on people's whereabouts and even to know
whether they are dead or alive, the government must keep very detailed
and accurate accounts. This is the area where the Anglo-Norman treasury had hitherto been deficient and where there was an extremely important change in the second or third decade of Henry's reign. The innovation was made possible by the educational revolution taking place in
France. The French universities were in the process of absorbing the
new mathematics from the Arab world, and a royal clerk who had
studied at Laon contributed to the royal treasury a new accounting system and the most advanced computer of the twelfth century, namely the
abacus. In consequence, by the 1120's there had been established an
accounting division of the royal treasury which came to be known as the
exchequer, because when the abacus computation method was laid out
on a huge tablecloth at the treasury, for reckoning in units of ten, it
resembled in appearance a checkerboard.

The exchequer was divided into an upper and lower division. The
"barons" or officials of the upper exchequer were a judicial body acting

as a branch of the *curia regis* with power to issue writs and demand the fulfillment of financial obligations to the crown. The lower exchequer consisted of a group of clerks who assayed the money that was brought in, decided to what degree the coins delivered were blanched or white money, recorded the tax returns on a roll, and finally issued receipts, in the form of wooden tallies, to the sheriffs and others who had fulfilled their financial obligations to the crown. Only one of the exchequer rolls, which came to be called "the pipe rolls," has survived from the reign of Henry I. This pipe roll of 1130 shows the exchequer already firmly established; twice a year the sheriffs appear before the barons and deliver the receipts from their farms. And large numbers of magnates and gentlemen who also owe obligations of various kinds to the crown likewise are summoned before the barons to play the costly checker game with the royal clerks until they finally satisfy the treasury officials, hear the sweet words "he is quit," and are given their tallies.

The pipe rolls of the English exchequer, for which we have a complete series beginning in 1154, are the historians' gold mine. Next to Domesday Book they are the most revealing records of the rise of centralized royal government; the French monarchy produced nothing like them until the thirteenth century and the medieval German government nothing at all that resembled these extremely detailed records of the medieval English treasury. The pipe rolls refer to many royal institutions of which we would otherwise know little or nothing. In the twelfth century as in the twentieth, people who deal with money get down to the important things of political, legal, and social life. The pipe rolls provide evidence of how twelfth-century government and society really functioned in a detailed and specific manner that is beyond the scope of the most eloquent tractates on the glories of kingship.

The pipe roll of 1130 shows the centralizing and rational spirit of Anglo-Norman government in day-to-day operations. The sheriffs render account of their farms; the returns from the circuit of the itinerant justices are recorded; the king's income from vacant bishoprics is noted; the fines levied for trespass of royal forests are set down; great barons appear to satisfy the demands of relief and wardship. In reading these financial records we can understand how heavily the judicial, financial, and administrative structure of royal government pressed upon the great magnates and circumscribed their lives at every turn. The pipe rolls allow us to understand the bitter feelings which lay behind the complaints of the barons, in the later years of Henry I, that the king had raised from the dust obscure men like the justiciar Roger of Salisbury to arbitrary authority over them. As long as a king with Henry's ambition, energy, and authoritarian inclinations sat on the throne, the magnates had no recourse against the steady expansion of power and wealth of royal government. Their only chance for escape from the pressure which the crown constantly exerted upon them lay in the fundamental fact that no matter how rational and bureaucratic this government might be, or how firm the consciousness of the royal officials that they served a crown which rose above and beyond the natural body of the king, the effectiveness of royal government still ultimately depended on the king's personal qualities. The government was still very much the king's, whatever might be the elaboration of royal institutions and the sophistication of the royal bureaucracy: upon this crucial issue turned the whole subsequent history of English government over the next six centuries.

Even while in Henry's later years the effectiveness of royal judicial and financial institutions constantly increased, the king, the royal officials, and above all the barons knew that there was a fatal flaw in the Anglo-Norman monarchy which darkened the future of royal government and sooner or later would give the forces of baronial particularism their opportunity. Henry's only legitimate son was drowned crossing the channel and this left only his daughter Matilda to inherit the English throne. By feudal law a woman could inherit a fief, provided she married, but it was a question of whether the inheritance of a kingdom followed the same rule as the descent of landed property. It was not however so much her sex as her character that made Matilda unsuitable as the heiress of the Anglo-Norman monarchy. She was a selfish, narrow-minded, waspish lady who had for a time been the wife of the German emperor. Even after she was widowed and came back to England, Matilda put on airs and acted in a mean and domineering manner which incensed the aristocracy and encouraged thoughts of baronial vengeance when the old king should finally die. Henry, who was fully conscious of this situation, made the magnates swear fealty to Matilda as the heiress to the crown, but this did not head off the rebellion against the power of the Anglo-Norman monarchy which followed the death of Henry I in 1135.

CHAPTER FOUR

THE MAKING OF ANGEVIN KINGSHIP

from 1135 to 1189

I. The Triumph of Henry Plantagenet

THE THREE BASES of medieval monarchy were the personality of the king, the ideology of kingship, and royal administrative institutions. However deep the consciousness of the separation between the crown and the king, royal government was always heavily dependent on the king's personality, and without an intelligent and energetic monarch on the throne the effectiveness of royal administration and law was bound to be diminished. On the other hand, a king of great qualities could have a profound impact on the expansion of royal authority. This was the case in England during the reign of Henry II Plantagenet, from 1154 to 1189. Of all the kings of medieval England after William the Conqueror, Henry II, the offspring of the second marriage of Matilda, daughter of Henry I, and the Count of Anjou, most fully possessed those qualities that contributed to the success of medieval monarchy.

Henry of Anjou was a handsome stocky redhead who came to the throne in full possession of his extraordinary energy and intelligence. According to a description of the king given by one of his courtiers, he was in every way "a strong, bold, active man" with a tremendous physique and "lofty intelligence." He commanded that physical prowess and skill in war which the magnates admired and he exhibited, too, those courtly, gentlemanly aristocratic qualities which were also coming to be recognized as necessary in a leader of society. At the same time, in the words of the same writer, there was "no one keener in council and of more fluent eloquence." Henry II was as skilled in the arts of peace as he was in war and the hunt; he actively collaborated with the royal clerks in developing new legal and administrative institutions, and he enjoyed the fervent admiration and loyalty of the educated men in the bureaucracy. Henry was a passionate and loyal friend and at the same time an implacable enemy of anyone rash enough to stand in his way. His almost unqualified success in war and government, his unflagging zeal in pursuing the expansion of royal power, the ease with which he gained control over a vast empire, and his extremely impressive personal appearance made him, in the eyes of contemporaries, a ruler of superhuman qualities. Never again, at least not before the sixteenth century, would the genetic lottery of royal succession place upon the English throne a king of such quality. His reign was bound to have a profound effect on the development of English government and society.

The greatest obstacles that Henry Plantagenet had to overcome in his long lifetime were those involved in gaining the English throne itself. The rebellion of the magnates against the centralizing authority of the Anglo-Norman monarchy, which Henry I had anticipated before his death, was not long in coming. In 1138, three years after the death of Henry I, a new claimant to the English crown made his appearance in the realm to contest with the unfortunate Matilda the right to the English throne. This claimant was Stephen of Blois, the son of William the Conqueror's daughter, a man of high ideals and generous disposition, but uncertain in judgment and mediocre as a soldier. This chivalric French aristocrat provided an ideal opportunity for many of the great magnates; they gathered to his support and elected him king with every expectation that he lacked the strength and energy to perpetuate those centralizing and rationalizing tendencies of the Anglo-Norman monarchy which they had come to fear and hate. The late 1130's and 1140's were therefore marked in England by a civil war for the crown between Queen Matilda and King Stephen, a desultory and confusing conflict in which neither party had the resources necessary for victory. First Stephen, then Matilda would gain control of London and temporarily be in the ascendant, only to find their baronial supporters shifting to the other side and their authority teetering toward collapse. Put simply, the great magnates played each claimant to the throne off against the other; they blackmailed Stephen and Matilda for yet more privileges of private jurisdiction and grants of fiefs from the royal demesne, and gleefully observed the steady erosion of royal authority as both the legal and financial system of the crown fell into confusion and disarray. The most famous instance of this baronial policy of self-aggrandizement at the expense of the claimants to the crown was the rise in power and influence of Geoffrey de Mandeville, who, playing the game of extortion and usurpation for all it was worth, momentarily ended up as an earl with vast estates and the holder of the shrievalties of several counties.

The barons of the north, always inclined to particularism and rebellion, were notably successful in enhancing their landed and privileged possessions during this civil war between Stephen and Matilda. The 1130's and 1140's were the first great age of the settlement and economic development of northern England, under the leadership of the great patrimonial lords of the North Country. They were assisted in their advancement to political and economic importance by the appearance of the new Cistercian monastic order which sought to establish its houses in frontier areas so that the monks might pursue their puritanical spiritual exercises beyond the temptations of organized manorialism and urban wealth. It is no accident that several of the most important lords engaged in undermining the authority of the crown in the 1140's were also the leading benefactors of the new Cistercian order. By acting as the patrons of the new monasteries of these "white monks" in Yorkshire, they opened up for settlement and economic exploitation their vast, almost unpopulated northern demesnes at the same time that they weakened royal authority by seeing to it that the war between Stephen and Matilda came to no solution. The Cistercian monks, the vanguard of a new puritanical popular piety that was sweeping through western Europe, gave spiritual comfort to the robber barons of the north; by accepting the patronage of these great magnates and by expressing their gratitude through the singing of masses for the souls of their benefactors, the Cistercians gave an aura of legitimacy and even of sanctity to the centrifugal depredations of the marcher lords. The monastic frontiersmen also contributed in a more material way to the power of the northern magnates. By engaging in the extensive cultivation of sheep-raising, whose woollen product was exported with great profit to meet the needs of the new manufacturing centers in Flanders, the Cistercians showed the northern barons how Yorkshire could at last become a viable economic area. One other group greatly benefited from the war between Stephen and Matilda; the bishops, like the barons, made full use of the weakening of central authority to gain privileges and a new measure of independence from the crown.

The two decades following Henry I's death in 1135 were termed "the Anarchy" by Victorian historians. It was only an anarchy in comparison with the strong framework of centralized royal government which both preceded and followed this interlude of baronial usurpation of royal power and assertion of feudal autonomy. In comparison with the framework of royal government operative at the same time in France and Germany, the condition of royal administration and law between 1135 and 1154 was not particularly anarchic. As best they could, considering that it was not clear who was the rightful holder of the throne, the royal judges, chancery clerks, and exchequer officials continued their work, although they were constantly frustrated by the extravagant concessions which Stephen and Matilda felt compelled to make to the demands of baronial greed. Nevertheless it was clear by the early 1150's that even the powerful legacy of Anglo-Norman centralization could not survive much longer in the face of the civil war. Fortunately the anarchy was brought to an end when Henry Plantagenet, gaining the throne in 1154, began a far-reaching recovery of royal power and reconstruction of royal institutions.

The anarchy was brought to an end and the civil war over the throne was resolved for three reasons. In the first place, the middling and lesser feudal lords, the "knights" as they were coming to be called, finally understood after a decade of confused conflict that they themselves had nothing to gain from the growth in the power and privileges of the great magnates whose vassals they were. On the contrary, the steady erosion of royal justice placed the knightly class more firmly under the jurisdiction of the baronial courts and made them more vulnerable to the arbitrary decisions and ruthless ambitions of the earls and other great magnates. By the end of the 1140's the sub-vassals were looking back to the reign of Henry I as a golden age when they enjoyed the protection of the royal justices in eyre in the shire courts, and they welcomed the reconstitution of royal authority. When this division of interests between the great barons and their sub-vassals became evident, it was no longer as easy for the magnates to use their feudal armies for the purpose of meddling in the conflict over the throne, and the way was open for a solution to the succession crisis.

The death of the unpopular Queen Matilda and the reversion of her claim to the throne to her son by the Count of Anjou, Henry Plantagenet, also facilitated the ending of the civil war. Not only was Henry an immensely more attractive figure in the eyes of the landed classes than his peevish mother, but he was increasingly a dominant power in the ranks of the great French aristocracy. Henry inherited from his father not only Anjou, but also Normandy, which the Count had subdued on behalf of his son. Through his marriage to Duchess Eleanor of Aquitaine, Henry made himself the ruler of this wealthy part of southwestern France, so that by the early 1150's he held a vast collection of principalities stretching from the borders of Flanders to the Pyrenees. It was clear that sooner or later a king as mediocre in war as Stephen was would succumb to the vast military resources which Henry commanded. But a decisive conflict was made unnecessary when Stephen's only son and heir died prematurely in 1153. The heartbroken chivalric ruler made a peace with Henry by which Stephen was to have the throne for his lifetime and the Angevin claimant was to become king when Stephen died. With his accustomed generosity Stephen passed from the scene the following year and Henry Plantagenet, first of the Angevin line and grandson of Henry I, began his long and momentous reign in 1154.

Henry II's heavy involvement with the affairs of his French principalities did not prevent him from undertaking a systematic reconstruction of royal government and law. He aimed to recover the authority of the crown as it had existed in the reign of his grandfather, Henry I, and building upon Anglo-Norman institutions to go on from there toward subordinating even more fully all groups in society to royal power and jurisdiction. Henry was literate, and well-informed on the ideology of kingship. If one of his courtiers exaggerates when he says that Henry always had a book in his hand when he was not holding a weapon, it is at least certain that from his reading and his clerical ministers the king drew a full knowledge of the traditions of theocratic kingship. These ideological influences united with the natural authoritarian inclination always exhibited by men of his intelligence and energy to fasten in his mind a view of kingship that we can only call absolutist and despotic. Henry never doubted that he ruled with God's grace and that ultimately he was responsible to no other earthly authority. For him there was no question of the end to which his government should be devoted: as far as the political and social framework allowed, to centralize all power in his own hands, to make the crown supreme over all groups in society, and so to draw upon the resources of the country as to bring into the royal treasury a steadily increasing share of the wealth of England. Henry surrounded himself with an extremely able group of royal officials, the most important of whom were graduates of the French universities, and he worked with them year after year to achieve his authoritarian aims. The king and his ministers sought to undo the consequences of the civil war by taking away from the barons their usurpation of royal law and administration and reducing even beyond the level of 1135 the wealth and privileges of the great magnates. The king wanted to reinvigorate the royal chancery and exchequer and refine the administrative and financial institutions of the crown. He wished to bring the church back under full royal control by recovering the king's authority over the epis-copacy and making the higher ecclesiastics completely dependent on royal will. He aimed to continue the construction of a judicial system of common law in the whole realm in ways which would virtually destroy the legal jurisdiction of the baronial courts and which would bring be-fore the royal justices all important civil and criminal pleas involving the members of the landed classes. Anyone, whether a baron or a bishop, who was so foolish or shortsighted as to oppose these policies would have to be destroyed and taken out of the way in as ruthless and efficient a manner as possible. On the other hand, those who actively assisted the king in achieving the rise of the Angevin monarchy were to be gener-ously rewarded.

What made it possible for Henry to achieve his aims during the first two decades of his reign, one of the most remarkable eras in the his-tory of European government, was not only his own superior qualities and the intelligence and zeal of his officials but also the legacy of the civil war itself. The two decades of conflict over the throne and the resulting decentralization and reversal of the course of Anglo-Norman govern-ment had exhibited for all to see the reckless and selfish proclivities of the great magnates. For all but a handful of aristocratic families, the peace and welfare of society had been shown to depend on the effective functioning of royal legal and administrative institutions. In 1154, and for the next two decades, there was a widespread and profound disposi-tion among the great majority of both the lay and ecclesiastical magnates to allow the king and his administrators to do whatever they thought necessary to restore and expand the authority of the crown. Under these conditions no king in the 1160's and 1170's with any degree of intelli-gence and energy could have failed to recover much of the ground which the monarchy had lost between 1135 and 1154. It is the mark of Henry Plantagenet's genius that he went far beyond this minimum achievement, and by skillfully playing upon the interests of society, he constructed a judicial and administrative system which came as close to absolutism as was possible without entirely abandoning the political and social framework inherited from the Norman settlement.

II. The Interests of Twelfth-Century Society

O F ALL PERIODS of English history the second half of the twelfth century is probably the easiest for the historian to study. All the important sources have been published, including the magnificent pipe rolls, and they are voluminous enough for the historian to answer all reasonable questions and to speculate fruitfully on the nature of life in Angevin England without having to cope with almost illegible manuscripts and dreary and uncomfortable archives, which becomes the lot of the historian interested in the period after 1200. Fortunately too, in recent years we have had some very perceptive studies of government and society in Angevin England, particularly by the American scholar Sidney Painter and the English historian J. E. Jolliffe. H. G. Richardson's and G. O. Sayles's The Governance of Medieval England, although marred by an unnecessary polemic against Bishop Stubbs, is also a work of great value. These studies, taken together with Maitland's magisterial explication of the development of the common law, let us see with accuracy and clarity what was happening in twelfth-century England and enable us to discuss with assurance the realities of Angevin institutional development within the framework of the social structure.

If we were to ask a literate man in Henry II's reign what the pattern of society was, he would still expound the traditional ecclesiastical view. There are, he would say, three social orders: men who work, men who fight, and men who pray. As we can see from the major work on political philosophy written in Henry II's reign, John of Salisbury's Policraticus, the theory of society was still the Platonic conception that society was an organism in which each member had special functions within the whole. Although the traditional threefold view of society was still by and large true, it excluded two groups that actually did serve important functions. The first of these was the townsmen, the burghers who, as both internal and foreign trade increased, grew in both numbers and wealth. Medieval theorists never in fact clearly decided what part the bourgeoisie played in society and what their function was or ought to be. (Not until the seventeenth century and not fully until the nineteenth century will there be a social theory that satisfactorily integrates the bourgeoisie into the body politic.) Nor did these traditional theories account for the administrators and courtiers—the king's hard-working officials as well as his more decorative flunkeys. In Henry II's reign these men constituted a small but very distinctive group, and although the bureaucrats and courtiers emerged from the clerical and baronial classes, by the 1170's we can no longer designate such men as either churchmen or nobility; they have an ethos and way of life which is peculiarly their own. Even John of Salisbury, who came to England fresh from several years' service at the papal court and who developed his political theory within the framework of the church's traditional hierarchic view of the world, remarked with indignation that the royal bureaucrats and courtiers held attitudes which did not conform to the traditional outlook of the customary three orders in the body politic. Another flaw in the threefold functional medieval view of society was its blindness to variety and heterogeneity within each social group. Among churchmen and nobles there existed a tremendous range which was reflected in their incomes, mores, ambitions, and interests.

In the reign of Henry II at least ninety-five percent of the population of England still lived on the land. Perhaps three fourths of these people were peasants whose standard of living was improving due to general prosperity and inflation and demand for their services as laborers. Their diet was improving, hence their numbers and longevity were slowly but steadily increasing. But their way of life was still uniformly harsh and dull, and they had no impact or influence on the important decision-making within English society. The great majority of the peasantry were still in 1200 manorial serfs, and were therefore excluded by reason of their unfree status from the purview of royal justice. In the closing decades of the century, the manumission of serfs was just beginning; but even this change only transformed peasants from legally subservient laborers to economically dependent renters and wage-workers and in no way made them part of the political nation, the groups who decided the destiny of society.

The most important element in twelfth-century society was the baronial or landed classes, and these landholders were to remain the dominant group in the English political nation until the nineteenth century. We can say that in the twelfth century the elusive entity often recklessly labeled "the urban middle class" did indeed rise, but this meant only that several of its members became rich. In 1200 there was still doubt as to the free status in the eyes of the common law of even the wealthiest burghers and they played no part in government, administration, or law outside the walls of their overcrowded cities. In the twelfth century the interests of society taken as a whole still meant the interests of the landed classes. In the great battles over English liberty which begin in the early thirteenth century, the liberties defended and defined and exalted are the liberties of the landed classes. Their property, or their way of holding it, or the privileges that belong to them as a group, are the rights that are fought over and protected in the thirteenth and fourteenth centuries and even by and large in the seventeenth and eighteenth centuries.

In the twelfth century a fundamental change is taking place in the life of the English landed classes considered as a whole: they are experiencing a social polarization more rapid and extensive than in any other part of western Europe. By the 1160's the landed classes have come to form two very distinct groups that will be perpetuated down into the nineteenth century. The first of these groups is the high nobility—magnates, great barons, aristocrats, nobles, lords, or whatever other term may be used. They are men who hold vast estates, who dominate at least one and often several county courts, who are specially summoned by the king's writ to the meeting of his *curia regis*, and who will become in the fourteenth century *the* peers of the realm and the members of the House of Lords. Such men form the top slice of the upper strata of this still generally hierarchic society; in the reign of Henry II less than a hundred families belong to this aristocratic group. Although the number of these families is small, their power and influence is enormous. In terms of wealth and power they are at the pinnacle of society and they know it. More and more the great baronial families are developing a rigid self-consciousness, a deep sense of their own superiority. They know that there is something special about themselves, something about the way they do things, and this superior quality is perpetuated through their "blue blood." The chivalric code and the romantic ideals associated with it, which were given increased emphasis in England by Henry II's queen,

Eleanor of Aquitaine, were used by the great barons to fashion a new aristocratic ethos. Their distinctive quality no longer consists in wealth and power, for the bourgeoisie sometimes have as much wealth, and the royal administrators, at least in practice, more power. But what the great barons have is nobility—a greatness of soul, a grand manner of conduct, an inherited superior nature which no other group in society can legitimately claim. Therefore the great baronial families are becoming more and more loath to intermarry with others outside their small group. The barons by the middle of Henry II's reign have advanced far beyond the outlook of the freebooting companions of William the Conqueror from whom they are usually descended. They have become a tightly knit, self-perpetuating aristocratic caste who look with contempt on the other members of landed society and with fear and hostility upon the royal bureaucrats.

The other group which has distinctively emerged as a result of the process of social polarization is that of the middling and lesser landholders who, because they were at least in origin the sub-vassals of the great magnates, are called in the twelfth and thirteenth centuries "the knights," and who will from the sixteenth century be referred to as the gentlemen or "the gentry." It is anachronistic but historically sound to call such people gentry in the twelfth century. The name did not exist but the people are the same; the characteristics of this social group, the great majority of the landlords of England, will really not change very much over the next five centuries. The families of knightly gentry possess not vast estates, but still substantial property, at least enough so that they can live off the income from landed wealth. Although a Marxist writer would be quick to slap an exploitative label on them, it would be quite correct to say that in addition to all the hard work they put in managing their farms or sheep runs, they are supported by peasant labor —their legally dependent serfs in the reign of Henry II, their often legally free but nevertheless economically dependent tenants in the thirteenth century. The knights are substantial people in their counties and of great importance in the shire court, and in the hundred courts they are supreme. We might call them the local peer group, for they set the tone and standards of behavior in the neighborhood community. The knights in the twelfth century have no national prominence and in the reign of Henry II they are never summoned to the *curia regis* to counsel the king; no one ever consults them about taxes, war, or legislation, and it is still assumed that the great magnates can consent to royal proposals on their behalf, nor does the privilege of having lawsuits tried by peers in the full *curia regis* extend to them. The knights are the lesser nobility, men—not one of whom as yet has any real weight or significance as an individual—who together constitute a class that will be the single most important group in the history of county government and society until the nineteenth century.

Already in the reign of Henry II the gentry have assumed the burden of local government and administration which will be their peculiar possession until the rise of the welfare state in the second half of the nineteenth century. The knights are the men who make the shire courts work as legal and administrative agencies of the crown. Certainly the sheriff is essential for summoning and operating the shire court. The king's itinerant justices who establish the framework of the common law and the aura of royal authority, are also indispensable, and of course one or more lay and ecclesiastical magnates should be present at the meetings of the shire court to exude power and rank. But the recognitors, the jurymen, and most of the suitors are the knights. Without the time and intelligence they devoted to civil and criminal pleas, the judicial procedure of the common law would have been inoperable. Furthermore, Henry II's government imposed upon the gentry the extremely difficult and thankless work of assessing and collecting royal taxes, so that without the administrative labors of the knights the structure of royal finances would also collapse. More than the great nobles, the knightly families are those which dominate the ordinary day-to-day political and social life of the county community. The great lords are frequently not present; they spread themselves thin; the nobles are off somewhere in other castles, other counties, or at court or at war. But these lesser men never leave the county; they are always on the land and always involved in the legal and administrative work of the shire court, and by virtue of their constant presence and extremely important labors, the more wealthy and energetic knightly families are becoming in the reign of Henry II the persistent leaders of county society.

There is no point, however, in romanticizing the gentry and in attributing to them intellectual and spiritual qualities which they rarely if ever possessed. There is nothing remarkable about either their brains or their education. They are earthy men, smelling of the fields, involved in the diurnal tasks of rural life—the growing of corn (grain) in the agricultural Midlands for the English market, the producing of wool in the North Country for the looms of Flanders, and as always, piracy and thievery on the frontiers and along the coastline. By 1200, perhaps five percent of the gentry are literate, by 1300 perhaps fifty percent. But even when they can read a royal writ, we would still have to call the knights unlettered. The gentry are not interested in, nor are they capable of, great thoughts and ideas. Family, farm, county—these are the things they really care about—and, above all, the law: they have a passionate involvement with the law, and not in any rarefied or abstract sense. It is not the theory of a rule of law or a higher justice, but a kind of mundane, intensely particular, intellectually unexciting law that is instrumental to their way of life; it is the law of real property, its writs and forms of action growing out of feudal traditions as recast and modernized in response to social change by the king and the royal justices. Since the knights care about accumulating property, holding onto it and preserving it for posterity, since their landholding and not blue blood or royal or ecclesiastical office determines by and large their status in society, the gentry are extremely sensitive to the details of the land law, and they constantly find that they need recourse to the royal courts to gain or preserve their chief source of wealth and status. The knights therefore become almost morbidly interested in the details of the common law, and any gentleman of substance very rapidly becomes experienced and knowledgeable about the workings of the courts. Consequently they make excellent jurymen and they become indispensable to the busy, overworked itinerant justices. There are men of knightly provenance in Henry II's reign who become royal judges, and after 1300 the English legal profession will be staffed exclusively by men drawn from the knightly class. But even in the second half of the twelfth century there are many knights who never journey farther from their estates than the county seat, who are fully "law-worthy." Such men know the law intimately, and like the damp air of rural England, it penetrates into their bones until they come to identify their whole way of life with the legal process of the county courts.

The knights in the reign of Henry II were eager to assume the heavy burden of judicial and administrative work in the counties because the opportunity to serve the crown was a recognition of their social status and the proof that a gentry family had arrived. To be influential in county society a man had to be active on juries and participate in the thankless tasks of tax assessment and collection. In the twelfth century— and indeed for the next six hundred years—a gentleman who is active in the judicial and administrative life of the county will win a position of leadership among the other landed families. He will be able to arrange good marriages for his children, he is more likely to receive favorable decisions in lawsuits, he may be rewarded for long and faithful service to the crown by appointment to minor county offices which offer some financial reward, and for those who are most distinguished there is the possibility of eventual appointment as sheriff. In the thirteenth century and thereafter local good works will be the way a knight becomes so prominent in the county court that he can be chosen as a representative of the shire at the peculiar meetings of the *curia regis* called parliaments. The great majority of knights, however, who faithfully served the crown with little or no remuneration, did not emerge from anonymity and obscurity; they simply assumed their tasks as a reflection of their social status and undertook them gladly.

Henry II was a king as authoritarian in his attitude as anyone who sat on the English throne before the sixteenth century. But the heavy reliance of his government upon the knights to carry out the work of local administration and law meant that he had to rule with the cooperation of the gentry. The decision made by the king and his administrators to govern in this way was fundamental for the subsequent course of English history. Until the nineteenth century, royal government, law, and administration can work only through an alliance between the central authority and the gentry out in the shires. When the king and the knights of the shire are in accord, this system of government works well and with a phenomenal economy. Its cheapness—particularly in comparison with the heavy costs of royal administration in France, where the king's local agents are well-paid bureaucrats—is truly amazing. And since the English system was by and large based not on force but on the consent or at least the willing assent of county society, it could be a very effective approach to tying in the communities of the county with the central royal officials. But this administrative system was obviously one not without severe risks and hazards. Without the gentry the royal government has no arms; if the knights are disgruntled and recalcitrant, the king's ministers will have a hard time carrying out their plans.

For the century after the accession of Henry II, England hummed with good feeling between the crown and the knights. There were two reasons for this mutual harmony and complacency. In the first place, the twelfth and earlier thirteenth centuries formed an era of unprecedented prosperity for the English rural economy. The demographic curve was rising rapidly and there was also a growing export market to the continent. Capitalist agriculture expanded and flourished to satisfy the needs of population growth. Sheep-raising, in which the gentry were heavily involved, yielded huge profits as the booming wool industry of Flanders devoured the fine wool produced on the wet slopes of English hills. In medieval Europe as in twentieth-century United States, when people are rich governments can get away with murder. Even when, during the reign of Henry II and his sons, the knights were dubious about some things the royal officials were doing, they did not protest loudly or for very long.

The impact of prosperity was reinforced by the legal revolution which Henry II's government effected, whereby the gentry were able to plead most of the cases involving their land tenures in royal rather than baronial courts. We can readily imagine what the transference of cases from baronial to royal courts meant to a middling knight. A property dispute that formerly had been adjudicated under the personal supervision of a great magnate in his own court would now come to the shire court meeting under the presidency of a panel of royal itinerant justices. The decision would be based on the facts and merits of the plea as determined by an inquest of gentlemen, and there was more than a sporting chance that justice would be done. It is doubtful that Henry II, the most eminent lord among the high French aristocracy, was particularly anxious to befriend the gentry, but he found it a happy coincidence that his government's destruction of baronial privilege simultaneously served the interests of the class of knights whose services were so valuable to the crown. To the knights of the shire the king was a distant, awesome, incomprehensible, and mysterious force. They had no cause to consider the ultimate implications of Angevin kingship as long as royal justice secured what they really cared about, their lands, and allowed them to crawl out from under the traditional feudal authority of the great barons.

When a magnate no longer has legal jurisdiction over his vassals the feudal bond is shattered, and even though an earl may still be the biggest lion at the county court, much of his traditional way of asserting authority in society has evaporated. This fundamental change, which is evident by the later decades of Henry II's reign, does not mean that the power and wealth of the nobility have collapsed. It does mean that baronial control over society is less sure and formal; aristocratic leadership can no longer rely on legal authority and institutionalized feudal structure. The supremacy in society of the high nobility must, from the later years of Henry II, rest on less direct and necessarily more desperate and insidious means of social persuasion. Coercion and threats, open bribery, and blackmail of prominent knightly families are the tools that an earl will have to use, and no doubt many did in the late twelfth century, but at every turn the even more ruthless and powerful Angevin government blocked their way. It is only when the king and his officials begin to falter in the thirteenth century, and even more when they make mistake after mistake in the fourteenth and fifteenth centuries, that the barons will be able to reassert the leadership in county life which they enjoyed when Henry Plantagenet was crowned. Meanwhile, the later twelfth and earlier thirteenth centuries were the halcyon days for the medieval English gentry; they flourished economically and politically and were freed from the limitations of the feudal hierarchy because their interests coincided with the aims of Angevin monarchy.

Although betrayed and undermined by political and social change, the great magnates are still of prime importance in English society in the second half of the twelfth century. It was one of the most common and grossest errors of the late nineteenth- and early twentieth-century historians to emphasize the decline of the feudal aristocracy without the reservation that the high nobility continued to hold tremendous wealth and influence in society. It is one of the fundamental facts of English history (and of European history in general) that the aristocracy, however temporarily depressed or dilapidated, remained at the center of political and social life until the twentieth century. The history of the English aristocracy is a dialectical or cyclical one in which there are strongly ascending and descending phases, but there is a minimum line of power, wealth, and influence below which the aristocracy cannot fall because of their vast estates and because, at any rate until the second half of the nineteenth century, it was universally acknowledged that the great nobles were the natural leaders of society at least in war, if not also in peace. Therefore historians who are inclined to kill off the aristocracy too early are always faced with the embarrassing fact of the revival of their prominence a few decades later. The most critical question is not whether the great barons had political and social influence, because in view of their enormous landed wealth and their supposed military genius they were bound to be at the center of things, but rather why in some periods, such as the reign of Henry II, their leadership in society is visibly slipping.

In almost every conceivable way the monarchy in the later decades of the twelfth century was crimping the freewheeling style of aristocratic life. Spurred on by Queen Eleanor, a vivacious Frenchwoman, the royal circle was setting a wickedly fast pace and a glittering high style, and many of the great magnates ruined themselves trying to keep up with the new fashions. In addition to being spendthrifts, the great nobles showed little acumen in managing their vast estates, and before they were quite conscious of their improvident course, many aristocratic families were heavily in debt. Intelligence and concentration were required to supervise the vast honors of the great nobles and although the aristocrats could fight and ride and sing and dance with great dash, very few of them had either the ability or the inclination for agrarian economy. Therefore they turned over their landholding to stewards or estate managers, and these were men who, when they were not ineffective, were inevitably crooked. It did not help matters that the great aristocrats were so often away from their honors, finding outlets for their peculiar talents in the tournament war games or the grand parades which operated under the guise of crusades.

Aristocratic power and influence were also undermined by royal law and administration in the later twelfth century. The escape of the gentry from baronial jurisdiction damaged both the pride and the authority of the magnates, and made them unhappy and resentful. Furthermore it became increasingly evident that the royal government was purposely setting out to ruin specific aristocratic families who were either over-mighty or obstreperous. Barons found it more and more unpleasant to live in the Angevin world, for the king had at hand several tools for their ruination. He could make relief excessively high, he could seize their lands in wardship and exhaust the resources of the honor, and he could frustrate them cruelly in the royal courts. By the end of the 1170's a royal writ was required to inaugurate a lawsuit concerning any property of substantial value, as for instance to recover an estate which some arrogant knight had seized from a great lord's steward. It was necessary even for an earl to obtain a writ to get redress under these circumstances, unless he wished to take the risk of using force, thus disturbing the king's peace and facing the charge of felony before the royal justices, who would be only too eager to find a pretext for a heavy fine or even the dreaded sentence of forfeiture. So even a great earl would have to request a writ out of chancery and a hard-faced clerk would tell the lord or his agent to come back next week; next week turned out to be Michaelmas and the chancery was closed.

The variations on this kind of game were endless and were used extensively by the Angevin officials when they were trying to ruin a great family. Anyone who has ever tangled with a bureaucracy knows that it is a game where all the advantages are on one side, and the magnates of England in the reign of Henry II, many of them descendants of William the Conqueror's companions, had the privilege of being the first in medieval society to discover this hard fact. The barons were amazed to discover that the rules of the bureaucratic game were rather more complex than those used in tournaments. The royal officials had found many ways of tampering with due process, or as it was called then, "the law of the land." It was not very hard for the chancery clerks and royal justices to exhaust and even destroy a baronial family by meshing it in an inextricable nexus of pleas; the royal courts would entertain writ after writ designed to undermine the property and status of the family while the chancery would never get around to issuing the writs which the baron needed to institute his own plea. In a myriad of ways the great aristocrat would find himself convicted by the royal justices and declared to be "in the king's mercy." By the end of the reign of Henry II royal mercy had become as dreaded a term as felony to the great families of the realm. For the king was of course not merciful, and once you were in his mercy he was reluctant to let you out until he had squeezed you to death in his loving embrace. The inexorable arithmetic of the exchequer rolls tells us that by 1200 perhaps half the baronial families of England had been at least once in the king's mercy.

Angevin government was therefore not beneficent as far as the barons were concerned; on the contrary, it was mean, ruthless, and arbitrary. Naturally the nobles began to be paranoid, and the feeling became widespread among the aristocracy that the royal government was out to get them. And more and more the Angevin monarchy was indeed out to get them, to seize their estates, to bring them to heel, to crush them. It is wrong to think that as the gentry became more secure in the late twelfth century the barons inevitably fell. But the aristocracy did not need great intelligence to realize that the foundations of their wealth and influence were being steadily eroded by the concerted action of royal bureaucrats. By the later years of the twelfth century they knew they were in trouble and their bitterness and resentment grew incessantly. At the same time, with the spread of literacy and the growing impact of the new chivalric aristocratic ethos, the magnates were becoming more conscious of themselves as the elite group in society. Their attendance at the king's court and council allowed them to see firsthand the process of decision-making in the royal government, and it can be assumed that they will not yield forever to the arbitrary acts of the royal clerks and lawyers whom the nobility despised as social inferiors. What is amazing is that the great barons submitted as long as they did to Angevin monarchy, that they did not really try to break out until twenty-five years after the death of Henry II, and then they were only emboldened to engage in rebellion—and even then less than half of them—when Angevin kingship had been discredited by catastrophic military defeats in France.

During the twelfth century in northern Italy and southern France the great aristocracy moved into *palazzos* in the flourishing towns of these regions and began to cultivate a consciously urban style of life. Nothing like this happened in England where only a summons to the *curia regis* would induce a baron to show his face in London. Both the aristocracy and the knights remained doggedly rural classes in England and chose to play no part in urban society. The burgesses in England were completely cut off from the power elite of rural society and were in no way accepted during the twelfth century as part of the political nation. Whereas in Flanders and the Rhineland and particularly southern France and northern Italy the high bourgeoisie came during the twelfth century to obtain considerable influence on the course of political change, in England they remained a politically and legally underprivileged group which was unable to translate its possession of capital into membership in the political community.

The political backwardness of the twelfth-century English burgesses was partly the result of the fact that they were such a small portion of the total population. After the Norman Conquest, there was a steady increase in cross-Channel trade, but the impact of this commercial enterprise on urban growth was largely confined to London. By 1200, London's population may have totaled forty thousand people, which made it a metropolis by medieval standards and one of the three or four largest cities in Christendom. London's preeminence in English urban life was not to be challenged until the end of the eighteenth century.

Historians have devoted more effort to the hoary problem of the origins of English towns than to the more significant issue of the actual nature of twelfth-century urban life. Maitland inaugurated the debate by contending that Anglo-Saxon towns began as military centers, as the word *burh* (fortress) implies. In the 1930's a great controversy raged between the English historian James Tait and the American scholar Carl Stephenson on the question of the origin of the medieval English town. Stephenson, who was a disciple of the influential and persuasive

Belgian economic historian Henri Pirenne, subscribed to what is called
the "mercantile theory." He did not fundamentally disagree with Maitland's "garrison theory" on Anglo-Saxon boroughs; rather, in accordance
with Pirenne's interpretation, he defined a town as a commercial center,
and claimed to find very little in the way of this kind of town before
1066. English urbanism, in Stephenson's view, substantially begins with
the Norman Conquest. Tait's careful research indicated that before
1066 there was both a garrison and a mercantile character to several
English boroughs. In retrospect this debate, like so many historical controversies, seems to have turned more on a matter of definition than a
real issue. If a royal or episcopal administrative and military center con-
sisting of a castle or a cathedral and a few houses surrounded by a wall
can be regarded as a town, then the garrison theory is correct; but if one
is thinking of genuine urbanism involving substantial numbers of burgesses engaged in commerce and industry, then there is much merit in
the Stephenson-Pirenne thesis. The great weakness of the latter view was
its dogmatic insistence that towns had to originate as centers of international commerce; this would be plausible for the larger centers like
London, York, and (in the thirteenth century) Bristol, but does not
make much sense for the small inland towns like Oxford or Lincoln.
There are many small cities in England whose main street, to the
present day, is called the Corn Market, which indicates that the medieval merchants who lived there were primarily engaged in the grain
trade and other kinds of local commerce. All medieval English cities did
in fact have as their center either a royal, aristocratic, or ecclesiastical
"garrison," that is, either a castle or a cathedral. The difference in the
nature of the city depended on the size of the mercantile and industrial
element. At various times between the tenth and the twelfth centuries, a
group of merchants and industrial craftsmen came to live within or under the walls of a castle or cathedral for protection against the violence of
rural society. Eventually, if the town flourished so that suburbs were necessary outside these walls, yet another wall would have to be built in fifty
or a hundred years. Thus it can be said, in general, that the English
towns, like most of those in northern Europe, grew slowly in concentric
circles around a central garrison. Those towns which flourished as commercial centers, particularly London, came by the twelfth century to take
on distinctively urban characteristics, but the great majority of English
cities, even by 1200, were still dominated by the original castle or
cathedral.

During the twelfth century the population of London grew steadily, and the great merchants acquired from their role as middlemen in the woollen export trade to Flanders what was, for this rural and underdeveloped society, large amounts of capital. Such accumulations did not gain for the high bourgeoisie either social acceptance by the landed classes or a place in the political nation; they only made more pressing the question of who would be able to extort money from the burgesses. The twelfth-century bourgeois, even the great merchants, were unattractive persons who led grubby lives. Although many of them were literate enough to do accounts, they were basically vulgar people smelling of the warehouse and the shop. They came from the lower ranks of the gentry, from the peasantry, or from among the bastards of the cathedral clergy, and even their possession of capital did not free them from the contempt of the landed classes. When they acquired great wealth, the London merchants built large stone houses and took to wearing ermine cloaks and garish rings on their fingers, thereby carrying a substantial part of their capital around with themselves. The twelfth-century English burgesses were very far indeed from the elegant urban aristocracy of Renaissance Italy and the austere businessmen of nineteenth- and twentieth-century England. The merchants' only escape from immediate involvement in trade and industrial production was an emotional and puritanical religion, to which they were driven by the guilt feelings engendered by the church's denunciation of capitalist endeavor as sinful usury.

The high bourgeois of London and other mercantile centers were constantly frustrated by the dismaying fact that the king and the barons and the whole hierarchy of landed society were interested not in the rational intelligence they demonstrated as successful entrepreneurs, but rather in their capital. During the "anarchy" from 1135 to 1154, both of the contending parties constantly aimed to capture London, but it was not the political support of the burgesses they sought, merely their fat purses. On the continent there was a great struggle over who would get the burgesses' money; sometimes it was the bishop, sometimes the count, and in a few places in northern Italy and the Rhineland the bourgeoisie achieved a high degree of political autonomy and managed to hold onto their money themselves. But the circumstances of the Norman settlement had predetermined that in England it would be the king who would have the privilege of blackmailing the burgesses and draining a substantial share of their capital into the royal treasury. It was clearly and unequivocally established by common law that all the important towns were on the royal demesne, and that therefore the legal status of the burgesses was equivalent to that of peasants living on the royal manors. This meant that if the burgesses wished to set up a town government and to attain the communal right of administering urban affairs free from the interference of the sheriffs and the itinerant justices they had to obtain a royal charter, which was granted only reluctantly and in return for heavy payments to the king. It was only in 1191 that the high bourgeois of London were granted a satisfactory charter of communal privileges, vesting administration and law within the city in the hands of the great merchants who controlled the guilds. The outlook of the high bourgeoisie was as autocratic and hierarchic as the social ideas of landed society. The great merchants wanted the privilege of self-government not only because they wanted to be free from the interference of royal sheriffs and justices and to set up law courts which could deal with the problems of commercial law, but also because they wished to exercise tight control over the lesser members of urban society. They wanted to organize commerce within the framework of exclusive merchant guilds, or trading corporations, which would prevent interlopers and reduce competition. Similarly they aimed at the tight organization of industrial production in craft guilds which would fix prices and wages, set the standard for the goods produced, and exclude free competition. The royal grant of communal charters in the Angevin period allowed the high bourgeoisie to achieve their aims but only at the cost of tremendous payments to the royal treasury.

The granting of communal rights in administration and law to the towns did not free the burgesses from the subservient status they were accorded by the royal government, through inclusion in the royal demesne. Their legal status remained a cloudy one, and although a merchant might possess enormous capital which made him one of the richest men in the kingdom, he was not accorded the status of a *liber homo*, and technically the royal justices could regard him as equivalent to an unfree serf who was outside the protection of the common law. Because the burgesses obtained the right to hold their own courts, the legal effect of this clouded judicial status was not as severe as it might have been, but the political and social implications were maddening to the great burgesses who could never become part of the social elite and the political nation as long as they did not achieve the full status of free men in the eyes of the common law.

The more immediate effect of the semi-free legal status of the burgesses was that the king could impose upon them, as upon the peasants on the royal manors, a *tallage,* or arbitrary tax. The judicial traditions of manorial society allowed the lord to tax his peasants at will and the great merchants of London found themselves subject to similar tallages by the king. This meant that the royal treasury could steadily drain off from the great merchants a substantial share of their capital. Whenever the exchequer in the Angevin period felt compelled to increase royal income, the king would announce a tallage upon burgesses. This allowed the sheriff to go from house to house assessing the merchants' property and income and demanding a tenth or some other arbitrary fraction for the royal treasury. The burgesses were usually eager to avoid this humiliation by compounding for a lump sum from each town which they would give to the king as an "aid" in order to avoid the servile implications of the hated word tallage. But the king and his ministers ignored the subterfuge which the burgesses used to soothe their feelings and continued to protect jealousy the king's power to tallage all the important towns in the realm. As far as the royal officials were concerned, the burgesses were outcasts from the social order who were important only because they represented a steady source of royal income. Under these conditions it is not surprising that the high burgesses of London should by 1200 begin to think and talk about what government was and ought to be, and to apply their rational intelligence to theorizing about the nature of kingship, but nobody was interested in these bourgeois speculations. The Angevin monarchy had the townsmen in a subservient position which made extortion by the exchequer easy. At the very end of the twelfth century some of the disaffected barons were beginning to take an interest in the burgesses, but only because they thought that bourgeois money might be useful in a baronial struggle against the crown. Neither the king nor the leaders of landed society during the Angevin period really imagined that the burgesses belonged to the community of the realm— they were merely the commoners of London, vulgar people more akin to peasants than gentlemen, who could pay handsomely for their liberties.

A special group among the twelfth-century English burgesses were the Jews, whose activity and status were a grotesque caricature of the general life of the high bourgeoisie in England. On the one hand some Jewish burghers, who had been brought over in substantial numbers from northern France by William the Conqueror and his sons, made vast fortunes out of usury. By the end of the twelfth century a very substantial number of the great monasteries and barons were heavily in debt to

Jewish moneylenders. But on the other hand, these Jewish capitalists had no status in society whatsoever, not even the difficult and dubious one enjoyed by their Christian competitors. The Jews were outside the framework of the common law and they existed in England only under the personal protection of the king. The Jews were in effect slaves of the crown, placed in the body politic as social parasites to extract money from the landed classes through usury and in turn subject to merciless extortion by the royal treasury. A separate branch of the exchequer was set up to deal with the income derived in one way or another from the Jews, and this income was substantial; perhaps ten percent of the income of the crown in the Angevin period was funneled through the exchequer of the Jews. The Jewish capitalists were completely subject to arbitrary royal taxation, and in order to make sure that they continued to have capital which could be extorted by the royal officials, the crown enforced their recovery of debts from the lay and ecclesiastical nobility. Occasionally the exchequer would allow a churchman or baron to default on his debts to his Jewish creditors in return for the payment of a lump sum to the exchequer. Either way, the king would enjoy the profits of Jewish capitalism. The position of the Jews in twelfth-century England was extremely anomalous and precarious; some of the Jewish usurers were among the richest men in the kingdom but they were protected from violence at the hands of their debtors only by the grace of the king. In the later decades of the century even royal favor was not very effective in protecting the Jews from massacre. Fanatical anti-Semitism was a leading aspect of the rise of intensive popular piety in twelfth-century England. The anti-Jewish blood libels, which pictured the Jews as engaging in the ritual murder of Christian children, originated in Lincoln and York in the 1160's and 1170's, and along with the other twelfth-century English contribution to popular culture, the Arthurian romances, were disseminated eastward into France and Germany to become a fundamental ingredient of medieval piety. Subject to pogroms carried out by followers of such leaders of popular devotion as St. Hugh of Lincoln, and always prey to default and violence by their debtors among the social elite, the Jews in later Angevin England became even more dependent on royal will as the only defense against general massacre. The increasing deterioration of the Jewish position in medieval society could only be looked upon with eager expectation by the king and his ministers, for it promised to augment income to the exchequer of the Jews.

The emergence of the anti-Jewish blood libels was only the most volatile consequence of the intense seriousness with which Christian theology and ritual were regarded by all groups in twelfth-century English society. The Benedictine order continued to grow in numbers and to receive lucrative endowments from the members of landed society who were convinced that the monks' prayers on their behalf were the shortest way to heaven. The new Cistercian order of white monks proliferated its communities with astonishing speed, particularly in northern England. The increasing availability of literate churchmen made possible the spread of the parish system throughout the country so that the humblest peasant in a manorial village had, by 1200, the benefits of the Christian sacraments, albeit they were usually administered by a parish priest who was only semi-educated and who himself usually came from the ranks of the peasants. The cathedral clerks participated in the generally flourishing condition of the church in England and many of them lived very well on their "prebends" or clerical endowments. What was generally lacking in the twelfth-century English church, however, was idealistic leadership which could direct the vast wealth and popular enthusiasm which churchmen enjoyed to some common end.

The twelfth-century papacy after the period of Gregorian reform was in the hands of skillful but politically minded canon lawyers who avoided any policy which would arouse the enmity of the enormously powerful English kings, particularly at a time when the Pope was embroiled in Italian politics in conflicts with the German emperor. This meant that the Angevin king had a free hand in appointing trusted royal clerks to the bishoprics and important abbacies, and that the English church was firmly under royal control, placing its enormous financial and intellectual resources at the service of Angevin monarchy. Nearly all the archbishops and bishops of later twelfth-century England were professional careerists who served the interests of monarchy far more zealously and astutely than they did the Holy Spirit. As a result, great opportunities were missed to use the resources of the church to the advantage of Christian piety and thought. The Benedictine communities during the reign of Henry II lost the importance in scholarship and art which they had in 1100, and the quality of their learning and zeal slowly deteriorated. We have an intimate picture of Abbot Samson of Bury St. Edmunds, one of the largest and wealthiest of the Benedictine communities in the reign of Henry II, written by his secretary Jocelyn of Brakelond. In Jocelyn's description, Abbot Samson emerges as a hard-working administrator engaged in the diurnal business of a great ecclesiastical corporation, but almost totally blind to both piety and learning. By the end of the reign of Henry II this attitude can be said to be characteristic of the English Benedictine order as a whole. The Cistercians, from whom great things were expected as leaders of Christian devotion and who did produce in the mid-twelfth-century Abbot Ailred of Rievaulx, one of the most important leaders of twelfth-century European piety, had by the end of the century been corrupted by the unexpected wealth they obtained from the production of wool and the settlement of the originally barren frontier lands on which they had founded their communities. The Cistercians were simple and naïve men who on the whole disdained learning; they were overwhelmed by the advance of civilization into Yorkshire and by their unexpected prosperity. By 1200 the Cistercian abbots were actively engaged in usury, and the popular image of the white brothers changed from that of puritan saints to that of a particularly greedy and selfish species of hypocritical monks. Although for a time in the early twelfth century the English church gave promise of great achievement in theology and philosophy, by the end of the century the English centers of scholarship were markedly inferior to the great university which was developing in Paris. From about 1140 there was a group of scholars at Oxford, but all twelfth-century English churchmen who received renown as theologians or philosophers were products of the French universities, and some of the best of them remained to teach at Paris or went on to service in the Roman *curia*. One of these in fact, Nicholas Breakspear, became in the middle years of the century Pope Adrian IV, the only Englishman ever to sit on the papal throne.

The decisive moment for the twelfth-century English church, after the ending of the investiture controversy in 1107, came during the late 1160's. It was decisive not only for the shape of the English church but also for the growth of royal power during the reign of Henry II. After the conflict of the 1160's the English church was to have no leadership directing its material and intellectual resources to a common end, and the church was removed as an independent force which could place a limitation on the growth of royal authority. It is a tribute to Henry Plantagenet's political acumen that from the beginning of his reign he clearly perceived the importance of firmly establishing his control over the great ecclesiastics and of preventing the church from acting as a corporate entity to block the expansion of royal domination over society. During the civil wars of the 1140's several of the bishops had taken advantage of the breakdown of royal control to act in an independent manner, to support the dissemination of Roman-inspired canon law in England and to establish close relations with the papacy. Henry regarded these acts as an alarming reversal of the trend of church-state relationships in the Anglo-Norman period, and he determined from the first to bring the churchmen back under the monolithic sway of royal majesty. He soon found a brilliant and ambitious young cleric, who was serving as the secretary of the Archbishop of Canterbury, to become his chancellor and impose the royal will on the bishops and abbots as well as on the leaders of lay society. This man was Thomas Becket, the son of an impecunious Norman knight who had been forced to go into trade and had become a wealthy London merchant. Becket's father was determined that his pre-cocious son should escape the political and legal limitations of bourgeois life, a feat only possible—and even then not often—through ascent in the ecclesiastical hierarchy. Thomas was sent to be educated in theology and canon law in the schools of northern France and after his return to England passed quickly from the service of the Archbishop of Canterbury to the office of royal chancellor.

Henry II had found a servant worthy of himself. Driven by a deep sense of inferiority stemming from the stigma of his bourgeois prove-nance, Becket worked assiduously to undo the consequences of the civil wars and to regain for the monarchy the legal and financial resources it had possessed at the death of Henry I, including the royal control over the resources of the church. As chancellor, Becket appeared to be an enormously energetic and skillful administrator, completely lacking any scruples which would deter him from destroying any baron or bishop who stood in the way of the unlimited expansion of royal authority. Like many brilliant and sensitive men who are disappointed in their fathers, he achieved a sense of personal satisfaction in completely identifying himself with an authoritarian institution and serving a strong man who exhibited all the qualities which his father had lacked. Becket lived os-tentatiously and seemed to delight in making enemies among the lay and ecclesiastical magnates who were powerless to take vengeance upon the king's favorite and chief minister. When the dotard Archbishop of Can-terbury finally died, Becket seemed to Henry to be the ideal man to assume the primacy of the English church and to further enhance royal control over ecclesiastical wealth and learning. But Becket only reluc-tantly, and after Henry's repeated insistence, accepted the see of Canterbury. He realized that his devotion to the Angevin monarchy had been the result of a need to identify himself with an authoritarian institution and was not based upon any firm royalist conviction.

Becket's choice of John of Salisbury as his secretary immediately revealed that as archbishop he would not be the willing tool of royal authority. John of Salisbury was one of those English churchmen who became leading lights of the new University of Paris and then went on to service in the papal *curia*. In 1159, after John's return to England, he published his *Policraticus*, a long treatise which attempted to resolve the painful conflict between papal hierarchical theories—which viewed monarchy as the servant of the church—and the realities of the English situation in which churchmen were at best the dumb and often the willing agents of royal authority. For a thinker steeped in papal theory, John was remarkably liberal in his view of the function of the state in the Christian body politic. Along with the traditional hierarchic doctrine John ambiguously concedes that the end of the state is the perception of truth and the rewarding of virtue, with the implication that when the state pursues moral ends it has a sanction in and of itself. John's modification of hierarchic doctrine would have infuriated Pope Gregory VII; it is the earliest example of the shift from a pessimistic to an optimistic view of the state, which was to be a fundamental theme of political thought for the next hundred and fifty years. The king and the royal clerks, however, did not appreciate John's agonizing attempt to strike a balance between traditional theory and the fact of the new central role of the state in Christian society which he had discovered on his return to England. There was still too much in John's work which had Gregorian overtones. He emphasized the traditional distinction between king and tyrant and speculated on the possibilities of justifiable tyrannicide. Furthermore, the *Policraticus* included a bitter and circumstantial account of the irresponsible attitudes and corrupt tendencies of the Angevin justices and administrators. Yet this was the man whom Becket had chosen to be the secretary and confidant of the Archbishop of Canterbury.

A conflict between Henry II and Thomas Becket was not long in coming, and furthermore it was of such a fundamental and irreconcilable nature that it brought forward the whole question of whether there was to be any limitation at all on the power of the Angevin monarchy. Becket went back beyond the moderate views of John of Salisbury to the intransigent Gregorian position that the church, as the body of Christ, was outside the jurisdiction of royal law and administration. The English episcopacy, led by the learned and clever Bishop Gilbert Foliot of London, who had coveted the Archbishophric of Canterbury for himself, and who had long detested Becket as a bourgeois *arriviste*, could in no way accept this radical doctrine which struck at the foundations of English government and society. Even the Pope, a wily canon lawyer engaged in an exhausting struggle with the German emperor, was embarrassed by the raising of these fundamental ideological issues and sought to avoid any action on his part which would offend the English king. But Becket had now submerged his personal frustrations in service to the Heavenly City as he had formerly achieved satisfaction by devotion to royal authority, and—finding support in the more speculative provisions of the canon law—he pursued a reckless course which could only bring him into open conflict with the king and his episcopal colleagues. Not even John of Salisbury's cautionary warning could stay Becket from the perilous role he now chose to play as the antagonist of the Angevin monarchy.

The specific issue which the king and archbishop chose as the ground of battle was the question of "criminous clerks," that is whether clergymen accused of felonies were to be tried before the royal justices or, claiming benefit of clergy, were to have the privilege of defending themselves in the inevitably more lenient episcopal courts Christian. It was a very fundamental issue, not because the English clergy were involved in a crime wave—although since so many of the parish priests were semiliterate peasants there were many of dubious character in clerical orders —but because it raised the whole question of whether the king was to exercise legal sovereignty in the realm or recognize the church as a separate judicial entity. Becket soon found himself at a great disadvantage. Gilbert Foliot produced a learned and subtle treatise on the divinely ordained foundations of royal majesty, and the king, acting with his accustomed dispatch and thoroughness, summoned a great assembly of ecclesiastical and lay magnates in 1164 at the royal manor of Clarendon. Faced with Henry's wrath and indignation and his episcopal colleagues' contempt, Becket lost his nerve and assented to the Constitutions of Clarendon, which reaffirmed royal control over the church "as it was in the time of our grandfather," Henry I. Among the chapters of the Constitutions of Clarendon was the provision that criminous clerks were to be impleaded in the royal courts. Soon after the meeting at Clarendon, Becket repudiated his assent as given under duress; he fled to the continent to seek the protection of the French Capetian king, archenemy of the Angevin dynasty, and appealed to the Pope for assistance. It soon became clear to Becket that he stood quite alone, and he retreated more and more into an inner world of fantasy and devotion, in which he saw himself as the only witness in Europe to the true Christian faith, which, in a sense, perhaps he was. From France he continued his quarrel with the king, who had become in his eyes a satanic symbol, and thundered useless excommunications against his episcopal colleagues. More and more martyrdom seemed to Becket's increasingly disordered mind the only fit ending of the struggle for the souls of mankind in which he now thought himself involved, and he returned to Canterbury in 1170 prepared to meet his saintly destiny which was so far beyond his grubby bourgeois beginnings. As every student of modern drama knows, the exasperated king in a careless moment called upon his courtiers to rid him of this intransigent troublemaker, and four young bloods among the courtiers took Henry at his word and slaughtered the archbishop, as he stood facing his murderers, and fully expecting martyrdom, before the altar of Canterbury cathedral.

Thomas Becket was far more useful after his death than during his stormy episcopal career, to both Canterbury and Rome. The archbishop's secretaries rushed into publication with biographies of the martyr designed to portray him as an heroic leader of the church. The cult of St. Thomas the Martyr rapidly gained the enthusiastic devotion of lay society and was celebrated as far away as Iceland. Between the thirteenth and sixteenth centuries the church of Canterbury gained substantial additional income as the center of English pilgrimage. The astute and politically minded Pope, who had never been one of Becket's more fervent admirers, was quick to take advantage of the archbishop's martyrdom to extract important concessions from Henry in return for absolving the king from his part in Becket's death. Henry had to recognize the peculiar institution of benefit of clergy as part of the common law, and this practice lasted until the Reformation of the sixteenth century. If a man, indicted in a royal court, could prove that he was a member of the clergy, the case was transferred to the jurisdiction of the courts Christian. In practice, however, the royal judges frequently ignored the judicial benefit of clergy and proceeded to try the defendant and hang him before he could obtain an episcopal letter proving his clerical status.

The most important concession which Henry made to Rome was not, however, benefit of clergy, but rather the king's recognition that all English churchmen could have freedom of final appeal to the papal court in ecclesiastical disputes, including cases of disputed election of bishops and abbots. The Constitutions of Clarendon had restored the king's supreme authority over ecclesiastical elections and disputes. The Constitutions had provided that elections should be held in the king's own chapel and by royal assent, and that the bishop-elect should perform homage and fealty to the king before consecration; thereby the royal control over the election of higher churchmen was fully regained. Furthermore, the Constitutions had stipulated that in the case of a dispute over ecclesiastical matters the king should be the final court of appeal, and that the issue should not proceed further, that is, to Rome, without royal assent. As a result of Becket's martyrdom Henry had to allow the papal *curia* to serve as a final court of appeal for the English church. Since among the matters that could now be taken to Rome was a disputed election of a bishop or an abbot, a way was opened up for the Pope to overrule the king's candidate for appointment to high ecclesiastical office in England, provided that a group of cathedral clergymen and monks were sufficiently bold and obstreperous to flout the king's will and appeal to Rome. This was the first instance of the penetration of some form of effective papal jurisdiction into the life of the English church. The fact that it took the assassination of an Archbishop of Canterbury to effect this change indicates the monolithic nature of royal control over the English church since the time of William the Conqueror. Henry's concessions provided the entering wedge for papal influences in English ecclesiastical organization, but the twelfth-century papacy was too overawed by Angevin power and too slow and lackadaisical to take advantage of the new framework of Anglo-papal relations.

In the three decades after Becket's death, royal power in England suffered not at all from the dramatic events of 1170. The Constitutions of Clarendon had confirmed the fundamental condition of church-state relations in the Anglo-Norman period in that it decreed that all the higher clergy "have their possessions of the king as baronies and are answerable for them to the king's justices and ministers." As before, the bishops and abbots continued to fulfill their feudal obligations to the crown, and regalian right of wardship of ecclesiastical estates during episcopal and abbatial vacancies remained a lucrative source of royal income. Before 1200 the English higher clergy singularly lacked an outstanding spiritual leader who might question the king's use of the material and intellectual resources of the church. On the contrary, as a result of the free hand which the papacy continued to give the king in ecclesiastical appointments, several of the bishops were, as in the reign of Henry I, former royal administrators and justices, and not a few continued their service to the king while they held episcopal office. Thus Henry Plantagenet's aim, from the very beginning of his reign, to recover what the Constitutions of Clarendon called "the customs and liberties and rights of his ancestors" with regard to the church was almost wholly achieved, in spite of the momentary setback following Becket's martyrdom. The fundamental reason that the king could fully implement his ecclesiastical policy was the absence among the English clergy of any leader who regarded the church as a distinct and separate community in English society. Becket alone, for whatever motive, had a different view of the church's place in society, and the king, Becket's episcopal colleagues, and even the papacy saw to it that the archbishop was frustrated at every turn and offered martyrdom as his only recourse.

III. "The Glory of Regal Majesty"

THE WELL-EDUCATED and worldly-wise clerics and the astute and politically experienced knights who served Henry Plantagenet as his chief ministers were profoundly convinced that their master was a great man, a ruler who possessed what we would call charismatic qualities. Working very closely with the king, when he was not abroad taking care of his vast continental domain, they were constantly impressed by what Richard Fitzneal (or Fitznigel), the royal treasurer for three decades, called "the glory of regal majesty." The success of Henry II's government was inseparably founded on the qualities of his personality. He had all the attributes the high baronage admired, and for a long time they were so taken by his aristocratic virtues that they were unable to credit what the king was doing to undermine their political and legal influence in the realm. Henry was handsome, physically powerful, adored by women, and he just happened to be the richest king in Christendom. The magnates could readily appreciate these aristocratic attributes; what they failed to grasp, at least during the first half of his reign, was that the king was seriously involved in government in a thoroughly professional way. Henry understood the niceties of administration and the intricacies of legal process, but he saw government and law basically as nothing else than tools to enhance the power which had been given him by divine grace. As much as the king had, he always wanted more; this was why government had to be made more effective on the local as well as the central level, why the institutions of the common law had to be worked out and amplified. Henry II was not, as the Victorian historians wistfully believed, founding the constitution or preserving the rule of law; he was looking out for himself.

The only person in the Angevin realm who was a match for Henry Plantagenet was his queen. Eleanor of Aquitaine was a very vivacious and highly intelligent and literate southern French lady who had not been happy with her weak and stodgy first husband, Louis VII of France. After their divorce, Henry chased her, caught her, married her, bedded her, spawned several children by her, and lived to regret that he had made Eleanor his wife. He enjoyed having the vast and wealthy duchy of Aquitaine which came to him as his wife's dowry, but Eleanor showed herself to be increasingly independent and tough-minded, and she made her husband's later years miserable by encouraging their sons to rebel against the aging king. Nevertheless Eleanor was a superior kind of queen. She dazzled the English barons and in fact she paralyzed them. It was inconceivable to rebel against a king who had a fancy wife like Eleanor.

Largely under Eleanor's influence, the Angevin court became something besides an administrative and legal center. For the first time, it became to some degree "courtly," in the French manner, a place where literature and music and a highly stylized, refined, and expensive way of life were cultivated. For the first time in English history, we can perceive a small group of men at the royal court who are not hard-working administrators or justices, but rather, professional courtiers. They are the retainers or hangers-on of the king and queen and they seek reward from regal majesty not for political or legal service but because they are talented, creative in art and literature, clever and amusing people who ornament the royal entourage. The courtiers are what was called in the twelfth century "frivolous" men, that is, learned and clever litterateurs and scholars who never quite got responsible jobs or achieved positions of power. In an age when there was as yet still no plethora of university graduates and when literacy was still a quality highly coveted, it was remarkable to find royal retainers who year after year hung around the court surviving on occasional handouts from the king and queen and who yet were never deemed trustworthy enough by the king to receive important office in church or state. The courtiers of Henry II's time were all bright men with some signal glaring fault. There was Gerald of Wales, an extremely clever and knowledgeable man, but he told too many indiscreet anecdotes about life at court or engaged in long and boring disquisitions on life in the Celtic fringe. For twenty years Gerald sought a Welsh bishopric from the king, and for twenty years the king found convenient excuses for turning him down. Another courtier cleric, Gerald's friend Walter Map, was also very bright and a skilled Latinist but he ruined his career by choosing to write sharp exposés about what was going on at court. Then there was the learned Peter of Blois, an expert on theories of kingship, who kept up an interminable correspondence with French clergymen, another thing one did not do if one wanted to gain the king's trust.

Although the function of these talented but feckless people was essentially ornamental, they did play a significant role in the framework of the Angevin monarchy. No great baron, however wealthy, had men like this around him; the emergence of a group of professional courtiers who surrounded the king helped to emphasize the difference between the Angevin ruler and the great lords, to illustrate that Henry II enjoyed a more exalted status than that of being merely the head of the feudal hierarchy. Even more important, the courtiers contributed a great deal to the characteristic style and outlook of Angevin government. These very bright people like Peter of Blois and Walter Map were eloquent, at times strident, about the glories of monarchy. They served as the ideologues of Angevin kingship, they spoke to its self-consciousness and unceasing confidence, and, in a more menacing way, they pandered to its ruthless temper; they were forever urging the king on, encouraging him to be more irresponsible and arbitrary, probably because they thought that was what Henry wanted to hear. And it is likely that at least in his later years, Henry began to believe what the courtier poems proclaimed, that he was like a Roman emperor, that he was glorious and majestic and omnipotent. When in the later years of Henry II's reign there seems to be a growing tone of recklessness and an incipient lack of caution and balance in the ways of the Angevin monarchy, we can see that the frivolities of Eleanor of Aquitaine's courtiers have influenced the king and his chief ministers.

The men who really administered Angevin government and shaped its policies were not these ideologues. Henry II's chief ministers consisted of the same kind of bureaucratic personnel who had dominated the royal administration and judiciary in the latter part of Henry I's reign. Most prominent among these, and indispensable to the king, were English graduates of the flourishing French universities. From about 1140 there was a school situated at an oxenford on a tributary of the Thames, but it was not until after 1200 that the University of Oxford began to compete with Paris as a center of higher education. The clerical servants of Angevin monarchy were a group of men impressive both for their skill in administration and law and for their ability to apply their learning to the needs of royal service. Richard Fitzneal, the head of the exchequer, and eventually as a reward for his service to the crown also Bishop of London, was a scion of the great administrative family founded by Roger of Salisbury; he is the author of the *Dialogue of the Exchequer*, the first administrative treatise produced in medieval Europe. This delightful book, intended to instruct novices serving in the royal treasury, was written in the lively dialogue form popular in the twelfth-century French schools. In the *Dialogue* a senior official of the exchequer instructs the new man on everything he has to know about the administrative department in which he is employed: its history, its personnel, and its techniques. Above all the senior official impresses upon the novice the spirit prevailing among the royal officials. They serve a master whose power is derived from God, and even if the kings obtain wealth "not by some established legal right, but sometimes . . . from their own arbitrary acts, nevertheless their actions ought not to be discussed or condemned by their subjects." It is not the privilege or duty of the royal officials to judge the origin or manner of the king's acquisition of wealth but rather as diligently and as carefully as possible to collect and manage the royal revenues. Money is necessary, says Richard Fitzneal, not only in time of war but also in time of peace. The security of the "state of the realm" depends upon the king's wealth. Thereby the mundane work of the exchequer officials contributes to the glory of illustrious King Henry, "greatest of earthly princes." The *Dialogue of the Exchequer* eloquently epitomizes the assumptions and attitudes of the Angevin administrators and justices: aggressive, self-confident, rational, pragmatic, and at the same time severely authoritarian. Such an outlook was ideal for the men who were engaged in the task of expanding royal authority. As a group these men believed that the only recognizable sanctions were reasons of state; their only goal was the increase of royal wealth and power and these fundamentals were assumed, they were not matters of strenuous theorizing or controversy. No English king had more amenable or congenial servants.

During the reign of Henry II the exchequer revived and pressed hard upon the sources of royal wealth which had been already well exploited in Henry I's reign: feudal aids, reliefs, wardships, and tallages. The king's right to take scutage in compensation for not demanding service in the feudal host of the contingents of knights owed by the tenants-in-chief seemed to Henry II's government a source of income which could well be expanded. Consequently scutage was taken much more frequently than in the Anglo-Norman period. The monarchy also made a strenuous effort to increase the number of knights per tenant-in-chief upon which scutage could be assessed. In 1166 the government conducted a great inquest into knight's fees in order to discover how many additional knights were actually settled on the estates of a tenant-in-chief—"the new enfeoffment"—beyond the original "old enfeoffment" of the Norman period. The returns from this inquest, the Cartae Baronum, revealed a very substantial new enfeoffment on many of the great baronial honors. The magnates bitterly resisted the government's attempt to assess scutage on the new enfeoffment. In accordance with the pragmatic outlook of the Angevin monarchy a compromise was worked out; in general the barons were conceded the theoretical point that scutage was to be levied only on the old assessment but in compensation for the loss of additional service to the king the magnates had to pay heavy fines to the exchequer when they themselves did not accompany their liege lord on his many continental expeditions.

The most substantial increase in royal revenue in Henry II's reign came from the enormous expansion of "the pleas that belong to the crown of the lord king." Yet the benefit to royal finance was only one motive behind the Angevin legal revolution. The other motives were political, the expansion of royal authority at the expense of baronial power and specifically judicial, the rationalization of legal process in both criminal and civil pleas. In the mid-1160's the king and his ministers faced a critical moment of decision, and we are told that they worked far into the night on institutional changes in common law. The king's political principles were absolutist in nature; he believed that he was responsible only to God and to no earthly community. The royal officials were authoritarian in inclination, and they had received training in Roman law in the French schools which provided them with both an absolutist political doctrine and a rational and effective legal procedure hallowed by antiquity. Yet there had survived from the reign of Henry I the nucleus of an alternative legal system in the form of the common law which had been worked out by Henry I's justices. The common law as it came down from the Norman period was in the eyes of Henry II and his ministers far from being an ideal judicial system and in many ways compared unfavorably with Roman law. Common law criminal procedure was markedly irrational since it relied on the ordeal as a method of proof whereas Roman law provided for a thorough inquisition by a panel of learned judges who had full authority to decide the case in accordance with abstract principles of justice. In civil matters involving property disputes, as compared with criminal pleas, the common law at the beginning of Henry II's reign had moved closer toward judicial rationalism because it provided for the summoning of a jury of recognition to attest the facts of the plea. But the summoning of such inquests was still an occasional, *ad hoc,* and unusual process; it had not been integrated into the formal and customary operation of the judicial system. Furthermore, most of the pleas involving landholding between any party save the king and his immediate tenants-in-chief still came under the jurisdiction of baronial courts which were devoted to the aristocratic ordeal of trial by combat, and where in any case a knight was often not likely to receive justice in a lawsuit against his lord. Even the jury of recognition, which was the most rational institution in the common law process derived from the Anglo-Norman period, could not be endorsed without reservations by men trained in the Roman legal tradition. For the jury system made the justices in effect only the chairmen of the court and placed the effective decision in the hands of representatives of the community. This enhancement of the judicial responsibility of the community directly conflicted with Roman absolutism.

The contradictory political implications of Roman and common law were even more apparent in the area of legislation. The Justinian Code dogmatically proclaimed royal authority as a sovereign legislator which could and should make new law in order to bring the judicial code into conformity with abstract justice enshrined in the law of nature. The common law had no idea of justice but sought only the maintenance of peace and order in society. Furthermore, and even more crucial, following Germanic and feudal tradition, it had no concept of either legislation or of royal authority to make law by the king's will. Law consisted of the customs of the groups in society, the collective liberties and privileges, however irrational or unjust in the abstract, of various classes. The only kind of lawmaking which the common law provided for was the declaring or clarifying of these customs and privileges by the king and the leaders of the community acting together. Thus the political implications of the common law, however authoritarian or arbitrary royal justices might be in practice, was in the direction of affirming the king's responsibility to a judicial entity which was outside and beyond his will, and of recognizing the king's need to obtain communal consent before declaring the law.

It was a moment of greatest importance for the subsequent history of English government and society that Henry II and his ministers chose to perpetuate and to amplify and improve the common law rather than to jettison the imperfect judicial framework inherited from Henry I's reign and impose the Roman judicial system upon England. The reception of the Roman law was inaugurated in France in the early thirteenth century and even in Germany in the later thirteenth and fourteenth centuries, so that by the end of the medieval period all of continental Europe had come under the sway of Roman judicial institutions with their authoritarian political implications. The Angevin monarchy chose a different path and ultimately this was to open up the prospect of a different political tradition in England. But Henry II and his ministers, given their absolutist attitude, would have been appalled if they had known this long-range consequence of their critical decision. Roman law was useful to them in a minor way by helping to clarify certain confusions heretofore existing in the common law. Thus the Justinian Code taught Henry II's judicial experts that there was an absolute distinction between criminal and civil pleas. But both the process and the assumptions of common law remained fundamentally untouched by continental influence. On the contrary, the legal revolution implemented in the 1160's and 1170's built upon the nucleus of the judicial traditions of the Anglo-Norman period so as to expand greatly the jurisdiction of the royal courts and significantly to improve the rational character of common law procedure. Henry II and his judges in fact believed that they could achieve the same absolutist and rational end as that provided by Roman law by reconstructing and amplifying the native English legal system. It was highly convenient to do so and involved much less of an upheaval than would be caused by full-scale reception of Roman law. If Henry I had succeeded in implementing his original idea of establishing a resident justice in each county of England it would have been far easier for Henry II to introduce Roman judicial process. A resident justice working full time in the county would have inevitably operated somewhat in the manner of a Roman inquisitor judge, and the full Roman process could then have been introduced in the reign of Henry II—as it was in France after 1200—without any critical rupture in legal development. But the system of itinerant justices which Henry I had been forced to employ had in fact preserved, and in some ways heightened, the judicial responsibility of the community so that an attempt made by the Angevin monarchy to impose the Roman judge-centered court upon the shires would inevitably have caused judicial confusion and would have put the magnates and the knights on their guard against the authoritarian political tendencies of the royal government. The prospect of judicial upheaval and political debate did not appeal to Henry II, particularly when so much of his time was taken up with his vast continental domain, and he therefore wanted judicial melioration in England to be as quick and as easy as possible.

The development of common law institutions rather than the reception of Roman law in England also appealed to Henry II because the English system could be operated far more cheaply. Since the amplification of common law procedure meant yet greater reliance on the representatives of the community, judicial reform could be carried out without any great cost to the royal government. The extension of the use of the jury, which the Angevin monarchy now decided upon, allowed the king to avoid the expense which Roman law demanded in its requirement that all the important work of the court be carried out by panels of learned inquisitor-judges. The income from the expansion of royal justice would in fact be highly profitable to the crown. Thus the Angevin government arrived at its momentous judicial decision for both reasons of expediency and profit. And if the expansion of the jury system was an institutional innovation which was bound to be favored by the gentry who would staff the juries and would find their participation in the process of the common law enhanced, thereby stiffening their grateful loyalty to the crown, this was a happy coincidence, although it was certainly not an important reason for the nature of the legal revolution which was effected in the 1160's and 1170's.

The dimensions of the changes in criminal process to which the king and his ministers were inclined is already indicated in one of the chapters of the Constitutions of Clarendon of 1164. One of the defects of the ecclesiastical courts in the eyes of the royal officials and justices was the relative ease with which a false appeal or accusation against a layman could be made in the bishop's court and the opportunity for collusion between an ecclesiastical judge and the accuser. Therefore one of the chapters of the Constitutions of Clarendon provided that laymen should not be accused in the presence of a bishop "except for known and lawful accusers and witnesses." If such reliable and esteemed accusers could not be found, then the community acting through a jury of twelve lawful men from the neighborhood or vill shall under oath before the bishop "set forth the truth in the matter according to their own knowledge." Underlying this provision of the Constitutions of Clarendon is the government's suspicion of the good faith of many who bring appeals or personal accusations in criminal suits. The way around these prejudiced and false accusations is to require that the appellors be men of substance and good reputation, or, even better, that the community in which the crime was said to have taken place choose a corporate jury who will present before the court an indictment on behalf of the community, against the reputed criminal. In 1164 this procedure was only required for ecclesiastical courts. It was, however, such a rational improvement over the old individual accusation that in 1166 by the Assize of Clarendon and again in 1176 by the Assize of Northampton, this new judicial process was extended to the royal court, constituting a fundamental change in common law criminal procedure.

What the Assize of Clarendon and the Assize of Northampton did was to establish the jury of presentment or indictment, the grand jury as it will be known by the end of the thirteenth century, as the prime method of inaugurating a criminal plea. At every meeting of the shire court under the presidency of the lord king's itinerant justices, juries representing "the community of the county and the lawful knights of the countryside" will present to the justices a list of reputed felons who are to be tried at the meeting of the shire court. Before the court meets, the sheriff will see to it that a jury of twelve men is constituted in every hundred, preferably of the knightly class, and a jury of four men in every vill in the hundred, who after consulting together will appear before the king's justices, and after being put on oath to tell the truth they will declare "whether in their hundred or in their vill there is any man publicly accused or known as a robber or murderer or thief." The principle under which the grand jury operated is that panels of reliable and upstanding gentlemen are to be the legal representatives of their community and that they are to inform the justices not who is guilty—for that is to be determined by whatever method of proof is available—but rather who is "ill-famed" in the community for felonious acts. Thereby the Angevin common law procedure perpetuates the Anglo-Saxon idea that it is the opinion of one's neighbor's, one's *fama* or reputation in the community, which is fundamental in judicial-criminal procedure.

Henry II's ministers and justices still cannot bring themselves to let the community decide on guilt or innocence. Those indicted by the jury of presentment are required to "make their law," that is, go to the ordeal in the traditional manner of proof. But the Angevin king and his ministers are doubtful of the rationality of the ordeal and can no longer let it stand as the inviolate method of proof. Anyone who makes his law and is cleared of the ordeal, if he has been publicly ill-famed by the testimony of the grand jury of his hundred, shall in spite of his proof of innocence by divine signification, abjure the realm within forty days. The only alternative for these people who have lost their legal status in society as a result of decision by the grand jury is to take to the woods and become outlaws, in which case they will, as medieval men said, "wear the horns of a stag" and be hunted down like animals. Thus the new form of inaugurating criminal suits in the 1160's and 1170's is a great victory for rationalism over superstition: the king's government professes its belief that the testimony of the neighborhood should ultimately overrule even providential signs. Those defendants who, having been accused by the jury of presentment are then convicted by the ordeal, are to be hanged and their chattels forfeited to the king. The Assize of Northampton, reverting to a dubious humanitarian expedient tried in the reign of William the Conqueror and designed to salve the conscience of the many clerics among the royal justices, provided for maiming instead of hanging. But this meant only the substitution of an agonizing slow death from gangrene and the Angevin court rolls show us that in practice the royal justices immediately abandoned this unworkable experiment and resorted to the stout oak trees of England for the punishing of convicted felons.

In the Assizes of Clarendon and Northampton the government of Henry II aimed not only at the rationalization but also at the nationalization of criminal law in England. In every county the same procedure was to be followed and the juries of knights were to appear from every hundred to make their presentment before the itinerant justices. No one was allowed to plead the privileges of private jurisdiction as an excuse for abstaining from service on the grand jury and attendance at the shire court to make the criminal presentments. Throughout the kingdom all felons were to be subject to the same method of trial, and the king was to have jurisdiction over them and forfeiture of their chattels to the crown. In addition to the rationalization and nationalization of criminal law, the institution of the grand jury signified a great increase in the legal responsibility of the communities of the shire, which in effect meant the indispensable involvement of the gentry in criminal law procedure. Not only did the knights staff the juries of the hundreds and speak as the voice of these local communities before the itinerant justices; they also represented the shire court as a whole in judicial process. The Assize of Clarendon provided that "if the justices are not soon to come into the county where felons were seized" after they had been ill-famed by a jury of the hundred, two lawful men could go along with the sheriff before the justices who were presiding over the county court in a neighboring shire, and "bringing the record of the county of the hundred in which the felons were apprehended," speak for the whole county court. This in effect meant that the whole county court could choose two upstanding knights to represent it in a criminal plea before the king's justices who were presiding over a different county court. Not only the community of the hundred but the community of the shire itself was in this way required by the Assize of Clarendon to depute lawful men who would be its judicial representatives under oath. Many historians have seen this representation in Angevin common law procedure as the most important background to representation of the knights of the shire before the king in Parliament in the second half of the thirteenth century. Judicial representation provided the experience for later political representation.

The word "assize" in its original meaning signified a setting down, establishment, or declaration of law. The Assizes of Clarendon and Northampton were the laws set down at meetings held at these places. Although the content of the Assizes of Clarendon and Northampton had been carefully drafted by the king, his ministers, and justices, the legislative format employed was strictly in accordance with the tradition of Germanic and feudal law: the king setting down and declaring the law with the consent of the community. Therefore the king summoned meetings of the full *curia regis* and obtained consent to the promulgation of these assizes. Thus the Assize of Clarendon contains a prologue in which it is stated that the assize is "made by King Henry with the assent of the archbishops, bishops, abbots, earls, and barons of all England." The use of the traditional legislative procedure not only avoided disputes about the nature of the king's legislative power but it also more easily communicated the details of the legal revolution to landed society through the magnates who were present at Clarendon and Northampton.

There is, however, another meaning of the word "assize" in the reign of Henry II which in fact becomes the usual and common understanding of the term in later decades and centuries, down to the present day. By the 1170's it is said that the king's justices in their court are "holding the assizes," that is, they are presiding over certain judicial procedures in civil pleas in the shire courts arising out of disputes about seisin, or the holding of property. These new procedures in civil matters were promulgated in the Assizes of Clarendon and Northampton in addition to the inauguration of the jury of presentment. Thus the word "assize" comes to be transposed during the Angevin period, from its original meaning of a collection of laws set down by the king with the assent of the community, to certain specific processes in civil matters which have been inaugurated by the authority of the assizes. The assizes are judicial institutions established by the legal promulgations called assizes.

There is a detailed discussion of the new civil assizes in the treatise on *The Laws and Customs of England* written in the later years of Henry II's reign and ascribed to Ranulf Glanville, who was a justice in eyre for many years and then justiciar in the 1180's. Glanville was a layman, one of the middling landowners who worked along with the brilliant clerics in Henry II's government. We are not sure whether he was literate, or at least literate enough to write this treatise. It may have been written by his nephew Hubert Walter, an astute and learned royal clerk who was later rewarded for his services to the Angevin monarchy by appointment as Archbishop of Canterbury. It is entirely conceivable that the treatise was written jointly by Glanville and Hubert, drawing upon Glanville's judicial experience and Hubert's more theoretical knowledge.

Glanville, as this treatise is always called, makes two fundamental points about the common law. In the first place, common law is royal law; it consists of the procedure and principles employed in the pleas that belong to the crown. Secondly, the common law on the side of civil pleas is writ law. To inaugurate a suit in a civil matter in the royal court the plaintiff must, on payment of a fee and the provision of surety that the plea is brought in good faith, obtain a writ issued by the royal chancery. There are two fundamental characteristics of these writs. First of all, there are several of them, and the plaintiff must choose the writ which will inaugurate an action designed to deal most directly and fully with his complaint. Secondly, the writs now are to be not *ad hoc* and special but formal writs of course. The chancery has devised formularies for these writs designed to inaugurate the civil suit; the king and his ministers do not, as was the case in the Anglo-Norman period, decide on the merit of each request for the issuing of a judicial writ, but rather the writ will be granted to any gentleman who can pay the fee and provide the necessary surety.

The judicial processes in civil suits inaugurated by the formal writs of course are called the assizes because, as we have seen, most of these procedures were promulgated in the Assizes of Clarendon and Northampton, although one of them, the assize *utrum,* which provided a way of determining the nature of the tenure by which an ecclesiastic held his land, was already provided for in the Constitutions of Clarendon of 1164. The distinguishing feature of the assizes as processes in civil or property disputes was their use of the jury of recognition to give testimony before the itinerant justices in such a way that the jury's statement in effect settled the question at hand. Henry II's assizes therefore constituted a great enlargement and formalization of the Anglo-Norman *ad hoc* and infrequent use of the jury of recognition.

As Glanville tells us, the civil assizes were divided into two kinds, the petty assizes and the grand assize. The petty assizes were so called because they dealt only with possession and not with ultimate title to property. They were designed to give seisin to that party in the dispute who was known by his neighbors to have recently enjoyed possession of a tenement, or was the legitimate heir of the most recent possessor. The petty assizes were not designed to deal with the further question of whether the recent possessor was legitimately holding the land on the basis of ultimate title. Thus the assize of *novel disseisin* was inaugurated by a writ from the king to the sheriff which would result in a jury of recognition's viewing the land and declaring whether the plaintiff claiming to be recently dispossessed was in fact the recent possessor, in which case he could legitimately repossess the tenement. The assize of *mort d'ancestor* was designed to have the jury recognize whether the plaintiff was the nearest surviving heir of the recently deceased and whether the decedent was indeed in possession on the day that he died, and if the jury answered affirmatively in both cases then the plaintiff could enter into possession of the tenement under dispute. The assize of *darrein presentment* required the jury to decide who had the last right of advowson or appointment of the cleric to a certain church and its affiliated property, in which case the most recent nominator to the benefice was presumed to again have the right of presentment. The assize *utrum* had the jury recognize whether a certain tenement was held by lay fee or church fee; in the former case the regular incidents of feudal tenure were owed to the vassal's lord; in the latter, only free alms or the service at the altar. All the petty or possessory assizes were therefore designed to have a jury of recognition give testimony which would determine the court's decision on the most common disputes over possession of property which were constantly arising in the life of landed society.

The petty assizes were a great boon to the lesser magnates and the knights. It was the smaller landholders, those of the gentry class, who were the most susceptible to dispossession by violence. Redress was not easy to obtain if their only recourse was to plead their cause in the court of their baronial lords. The four possessory assizes established by Henry II made it possible for the gentry now to have almost immediate recourse to royal justice which would restore them to the possession of their tenements against the machinations of their immediate overlords. Furthermore, the real decision as to the facts of the case would lie with a jury of men drawn from the knightly class, so that the vassal of a great lord would not be placed in the disadvantageous position of having his complaint negated simply by the word of an aristocrat of great wealth and influence. The petty assizes therefore undermined the legal jurisdiction of the baronial courts and gave security of tenure to the gentry at the same time as they expanded the province of royal justice to include most of the disputes which were important in the life of landed society.

The grand assize was intended to settle questions of ultimate property right, or title, as distinct from recent possession. Both the petty and the grand assizes, as A. W. Simpson has pointed out in his excellent *Introduction to the History of English Land Law*, dealt with different aspects of the same question, namely that of seisin, the holding of a landed tenement. The petty assizes were concerned with seisin on immediate grounds, recent possession; the grand assize was designed to determine the ultimate right of seisin, or long-range title to property. "This legal institution emanates from perfect equity," says Glanville. Since the Anglo-Norman period it had been the custom to determine property rights by trial by combat, but this was obviously disadvantageous to the knights. The parties to the dispute were allowed to choose "champions," or representatives who fought on their behalf, and it is obvious that a great baron could afford to hire a better fighter than a small landholder. The rational spirit of Angevin law required that an alternative to trial by combat in property disputes be found. Hence Henry II and his justices developed the grand assize by which a jury of recognition could be impaneled to witness the facts of the case as an alternative to proof by combat. The jury in the grand assize was asked not who was the recent possessor but who had "the greater right" to the land—a question much more complex and far-reaching in its implications.

Because it was concerned with ultimate title, in practice the grand assize offered far greater difficulty and was much less used than the petty assizes. A jury of lawful men of the neighborhood knew who was the recent possessor but if the question of ultimate title went back more than a couple of decades, they were not likely to be able to reach a conclusion as to ultimate property right in the land. Undoubtedly the king and his justices were fully aware of this situation. They knew in several instances that whoever was sitting on a given tenement at the beginning of Henry's reign was very likely to remain in seisin of the tenement even though this landholder, or his father or grandfather, may have been an unlawful usurper at some time before 1154. In the myriad of disputes about landholding, which was the staff of life for the baronial and knightly classes, the government knew that very rarely could rightful seisin be established for a time previous to the beginning of the Angevin monarchy. The government was prepared to make this hostage to fortune and in effect to create a new starting point in the law of English property. Whatever family had seisin in 1154 was usually going to have its possession confirmed by the juries of recognition in the petty assizes and was in effect, except in the most unusual circumstances, to acquire a title to the tenement, regardless of the way in which the family originally gained its possession. At least after the inauguration of the petty assizes in the 1160's no one could gain seisin of land without due process of common law. Therefore in practice the petty assizes were much more useful than the grand assize in establishing a legal basis for the holding of property in England. The royal justices of the thirteenth century in fact recognized this situation; they decided that anyone who could show that he held a tenement or a privilege going back to 1189 could claim that he was a holder by legal warrant. The effect of the changes in civil law made in Henry II's reign was therefore to give a legal sanction and effective title to whoever could establish that his family was sitting on the land in recent times.

Henry II's government developed several writs of course in addition to those which were designed to institute the petty and grand assizes, and after 1189 new writs proliferated with every passing decade. But there were two writs established in the 1160's and 1170's which were especially significant since they were designed to remove civil cases from baronial to royal courts, and they therefore originated processes which had far-reaching political as well as legal implications. The first of these was the *writ of right*, or writ in default of justice. A plaintiff who felt that he had not received justice in his plea at the court of his lord could, after the trial in the baronial court, appeal to the king, who would direct the lord to do justice to his vassal on pain of having the sheriff act so as to bring the case into a royal court. The writ of right was therefore an indirect way of bringing a case from a baronial to a royal court, the plea becoming actionable before the royal justices on complaint of default of justice only after the suit had already been held in the baronial court. In view of the king's position as liege lord and his obligation to maintain justice in relations among all members of the feudal hierarchy, it was impossible for the magnates to deny the legal basis of the writ of right no matter how unpalatable they found the prospect of the royal court acting as an appeal court to overrule baronial decisions.

A much more direct way of transferring cases from the baronial to royal courts was the writ *præcipe*, by which the king told the sheriff to command a lord to do justice to a plaintiff even before the end of a trial in a baronial court, on pain of having the case immediately brought before the royal justices. The writ *præcipe* therefore immediately stopped a plea in a baronial court and transferred it to royal jurisdiction before a decision could be rendered in the baronial court. It was not based on the legislative consent of the community, as were the possessory assizes, nor was it a writ in default of justice, but it simply stemmed from a decision by the king and his ministers that a suit in a baronial court could not proceed and that the plea should be held before the king's justices. This was the most arbitrary and authoritarian of the new judicial procedures devised by the Angevin government and had no sanction in feudal law. It was the only aspect of the legal revolution of the 1160's and 1170's which the great magnates could claim had no judicial validity. After 1200 the aristocracy would demand the abolition of the writ *præcipe* on the grounds that it arbitrarily "deprived a free man of his court." It is indicative of the general power and influence and popularity of Henry II's rule that it took so long for the baronage to make an effective protest against this authoritarian procedure.

During the last two decades of the twelfth century it became evident even to the knights, who had found *præcipe* and the writ of right and the possessory assizes so beneficial to their interests, that the primary motive behind the Angevin legal revolution was not the furtherance of the welfare of the gentry or even the remarkable improvement in the rational quality of common law procedure. The goal of Angevin monarchy was simple and, as it was more and more realized in practice, awesome and increasingly terrifying to landed society: the unlimited expansion of royal wealth and power. The expansion of royal legal jurisdiction and the improvement of the procedure of the shire courts as agencies of royal justice became the vehicle for attaining this goal. Beginning in the later years of Henry II, the royal itinerant justices sent to preside at the shire courts were given commissions of "general eyre" which imposed upon them a great variety of important political and administrative as well as judicial functions. The meeting of the shire courts under the presidency of the justices in eyre became the prime means by which the Angevin monarchy imposed its will on county society, and the usual way in which the king and his ministers communicated their program to the aristocracy and the knights and made demands upon them in a face-to-face confrontation.

The coming of the Angevin justices in eyre to a county town was a terrifying experience for all members of the community of the shire. It was a supremely serious moment when not only all felonious malefactors but also everyone who owed some obligation to the king would be called to account. We are not surprised to learn under these circumstances that whole villages in the more outlying and violent regions like Cornwall took to the woods when they heard that the king's justices were about to descend upon them. The entry of the justices in eyre to a county town at the end of the twelfth century was appropriate to the seriousness of their tasks. With a flourish of trumpets and a waving of royal banners, accompanied by the sheriff and the keeper of the pleas (coroner) of the shire, and followed by an armed bodyguard, the justices would ride through the main streets of the town, which was jammed to overflowing with magnates and knights who had been summoned from every corner of the shire. With grand juries of twelve men from every hundred and four from every vill, with all the juries of recognition and principals who had been summoned in cases of petty and grand assizes, with the felons who had been apprehended on oath of the indicting juries, required or forced to be in attendance, the population of the county town, on these court days, swelled to several times greater than the normal numbers of the native burgesses. There was no room either in the inns or the jails.

After the panel of justices, between three and six in number with at least one cleric as the chief of the panel, had suitably refreshed themselves, the business of the court commenced. The articles of the general eyre in the king's commission were read, and the justices went through a long list of administrative and financial matters of interest to the crown before turning to the strictly judicial proceedings. All matters affecting the royal demesne and the king's position as liege lord were dealt with, including such questions as feudal escheats to the crown, wardships to which the king was entitled, royal advowsons, the debts owed to Jews, feudal aids owed to the king, and tallages of the burgesses. Then the criminal and civil pleas were entertained. The judges were extremely busy and hardpressed men who could stay only a week or two in the county before they had to move on to another shire or back to Westminster. They did not have time to concern themselves deeply with the question of whether justice was being done to an accused criminal in any particular instance, and this was especially true if the accused had little wealth or status in society. The judges were eager to have the indictments of the grand juries, to proceed immediately to the ordeal, and then either to hang the defendant and direct the sheriff to seize his chattels for the crown, or to banish a defendant who had been cleared "by the water" but who was nevertheless ill-famed in his community. Similarly in civil suits the judges wanted the jurors to recognize the precise points asked of them in the assize writs: whether the plaintiff was indeed unlawfully and without judgment disseised of his tenement, whether the land under dispute is or is not held by feudal or frankalmoign tenure, whether the plaintiff is indeed the legitimate heir of the recent possessor of the tenement.

The common law was devoted to formal pleading partly because of the heavy schedule under which the judges operated and partly, no doubt, because of Germanic tradition; the judges wanted no long discussions in court. In criminal suits, there was to be a formal appeal by an individual accuser or a formal indictment by the grand jury; then the defendant was to make his formal denial and go to the ordeal. In civil suits, the plaintiff made his complaint; the defendant, his formal denial of the truths of the complaint; the jury of recognition, thrust before the court by the sheriff, made its precise recognition of the true facts, and the justices rendered immediate judgment. As we read the court rolls of the Angevin period, we feel that the judges wanted no trial, whether civil or criminal, to take more than five minutes, and most of them did not, proceeding in the most formal and austere manner. The Angevin justices always seemed to have foremost in their minds the pressure of the king's business in the next county and the warm fire and good dinner waiting for them back at the inn. Nothing irritated the justices more than juries that failed to give presentments or recognitions when they were asked to; this slowed up the regular and quick procedure of the court, and inevitably the justices would punish the community by raising embarrassing questions about whether everybody in the hundred was in frankpledge or whether Englishry had been presented, resulting in the amercement of the community.

Although the common law was, by the fourteenth century—and is even today—notorious for the slowness of its procedures, compared with Roman law process, this was not the case in the last two decades of the twelfth century. The Roman judges would be slowed up by having to study carefully written briefs presented by plaintiffs and defendants and by having to make a careful inquisition themselves on the facts of each case. It was undoubtedly an attractive prospect to the Angevin king and his justices that they did not have to take these pains. All the pleading was oral, and the common law judges had to make no preparation before the trial began. The hard work of investigation had furthermore been done for them by the juries of presentment and recognition. Between lunch and dinner the justices could therefore run through literally dozens of civil and criminal pleas and return to Westminster after a couple of months on the road with the satisfaction that they could inform the king they had cleared up all the lawsuits in no less than five counties. Under Roman law procedure, the equivalent number of trials would have occupied five panels of learned inquisitor-judges for perhaps a whole year. It is no wonder that Glanville was proud of the accomplishments of Angevin law; it was extremely effective judicially, in a somewhat rough way, and was at the same time a gold mine for the crown.

It was to the advantage of Angevin monarchy to retain the simple and rapid judicial procedures put into effect by the legal revolution of the 1160's and 1170's. But almost immediately common law procedure began to develop in directions which made it more complex, slower, and also more attentive to the precise details of the case. There were three lines along which this qualification of the juducial procedure of the 1170's took place. The first of these was the allowance of delays in civil procedure. English law had always been reluctant to deprive a free man of his tenement when he was not present in court, although it had never been reluctant in a criminal plea to condemn an indicted defendant as an outlaw if he did not appear to plead his case. The grand assize, as described by Glanville, from the beginning allowed a party in a property dispute three *essoins* or excused absences before the party was deemed to have forfeited his suit. Thus in the grand assize three court sessions could go by before the plea involving title to land was actually tried before the justices. The principle of the essoin was by the thirteenth century also applied to the possessory assizes, and this inevitably slowed the procedure in all civil pleas.

The second line of development from the judicial process of the 1170's not only interrupted the initially impetuous pace of Angevin procedure but also greatly enhanced the degree of justice rendered in both criminal and civil suits. This was the consequence of the introduction of the *exceptio* (exception) to the formal pleading, the inauguration of what was called "special pleading" in common law. Instead of the regular and starkly simple process of indictment or complaint, formal denial, and then proof and judgment, the defendant in both a criminal and civil case took exception to, or made a special plea against, the indictment or complaint. A common form of special plea in civil suits was a denial of the appropriateness of the writ under which the assize had been instituted; thereby the defendant hoped to throw the case out of court before the jury could be asked by the justices to attest the facts of the case. Special pleading in criminal cases usually arose when the case was inaugurated by a personal appeal or accusation. Instead of making a formal denial the defendant would claim that the accusation was invalid because it had been brought *de odio et atia,* out of spite and hatred. By 1200 we find that defendants subject to personal appeal are paying for a writ *de odio et atia* which allows the court to have the grand jury attest the validity of the personal appeal. If the grand jury found that the accusation was indeed malicious then the justices would stop the plea and amerce the false accuser, but if the jury confirmed the genuineness of the accusation, the regular procedure in a criminal plea would be followed. By the second decade of the thirteenth century the special plea *de odio et atia* had developed into part of the formal procedure of the court; all personal accusations had to be confirmed by grand jury indictment.

It is obvious that the development of the special pleading meant that the court was taking greater pains to assess the detailed evidence in lawsuits at the expense of slowing down the speed of the common law process. The development of the *exceptio* in common law also expanded the judicial functions of the inquest in civil procedures. Because of a special plea, a jury of recognition might be asked by the justices to give their opinion not on the issue for which the inquest was originally impaneled but on some new question arising in the course of the lawsuit itself. This development medieval lawyers called "turning an inquest into a jury." It marked an important advance toward the modern jury system because in this instance the jury is not asked to give its corporate opinion on a matter which they have decided *before* the court meets, but rather to confer *during* the lawsuit and render their decisive statement on the point at issue. It is likely that the Angevin judges were initially not happy about the *exceptio* which interrupted the formal pleading. But the questions raised by these special pleas about the validity of the indictment or complaint were so patently crucial that the judges could not refuse to consider them. In any case the *exceptio* was a well-known institution in Roman law and the learned cleric who inevitably presided as the chief justice of the panel of justices in eyre was bound to sympathize with the introduction of this procedure into common law and perhaps indeed to encourage it.

The third development from the legal system of the 1170's was the emergence of distinct permanent central courts at Westminster. The *curia regis,* as the high court for trials involving the tenants-in-chief of the king, had of course existed since 1066 as a central royal court. What is new in the last two decades of the twelfth century is the projection from the *curia regis* of central courts presided over by panels of the king's justices who would hear important and difficult suits even when the full *curia regis* was not in session. The pleas in the full *curia regis* came to be confined mainly to trials of the king's tenants-in-chief on charges of treason or other felonies; such nobles would have to be tried in an assembly of the great magnates of the realm in order that they might have "trial by peers," that is trial by their social equals, which would be impossible in the shire court. By 1200 the royal government is in process of institutionalizing three permanent central courts as adjuncts of the *curia regis:* exchequer; *coram rege* ("in the king's presence"), later known as the king's bench; and *de banco* (the bench), later known as common pleas. The upper branch of the exchequer had always had judicial functions in the sense that the barons or officers of the exchequer could sit in judgment and impose fines on tax delinquents. But in the later years of Henry II the exchequer becomes more distinctly and consciously a tax court. The king's bench was in general concerned with pleas between the king and his subjects, while common pleas was the court for civil suits between subjects of the king involving either property too great in value or points of law too difficult to be settled by the quick and simple assize procedure in the shire courts.

Exchequer, king's bench, common pleas, and the panels of itinerant justices all drew upon the same small group of royal judges. A royal legist who served as a justice in eyre was also bound on his return to Westminster to sit on the bench in one of the three central courts, and in the Angevin era this same justice could serve in all four legal justicial capacities during a period of a few months. Because of the duplication of personnel in the king's bench, common pleas, exchequer, and shire courts, a panel of justices in assize who found a particularly weighty or difficult case before them in the county would frequently reserve the case for one of the central courts. On return to Westminster they would confer with their colleagues coming in from other eyres and then render a decision from the bench at Westminster. This practice had the effect of continuing that amplification of the common law by judicial decision which had already begun in the reign of Henry I. It also reduced both the speed and finality of assize procedure in the shire court. The more important or unusual lawsuits were either referred to the courts at Westminster or impleaded there in the first instance. This rationalization of common law process was somewhat vitiated by failure to define absolutely the lines demarcating the jurisdiction of each of the three central courts. For example, cases are impleaded in common pleas which by definition we would expect to come up in king's bench or exchequer, or cases which would seem pertinent to common pleas appear in one or the other of these two courts. Since there was a great overlapping of the personnel of the bench in the three courts, it is not surprising that the royal justices who were sitting in the exchequer court, for example, should immediately decide a case rather than hold it over for later judgment in the more proper jurisdiction. Initially this easy and pragmatic attitude to legal jurisdiction contributed to the speed of common law procedure, but by the middle of the thirteenth century it was more a factor conducive to judicial confusion. In general, the development of the common law after the 1170's was such that the price which the English judicial system paid for increased sophistication and attention to the precise details of the lawsuits was the emergence of jurisdictional confusion and a concomitant tolerance by the judges for the flagrantly dilatory tactics of the suitors.

The increasing complexity of legal procedure and jurisdiction in the last two decades of the twelfth century arising from the use of essoins, special pleadings, and the development of the new central courts at Westminster, contributed to the emergence of a legal profession. As early as the time of Henry I, wealthy men had employed professional pleaders to speak for them in court. Under the formal pleading of common law, it was necessary to adhere to the precise terminology of the prescribed judicial formularies or suffer the loss of one's plea, and therefore experts in pleading, who were not liable to fall into error, became useful to great men involved in lawsuits. When it became necessary in the Angevin period for parties in a civil lawsuit to choose alternatives between an increasing variety of writs, pleas, and courts, wealthy men found it expedient to have not only professional pleaders but also legal experts who could advise them on what route to follow through the proliferating judicial forest of the common law. Roman law provided the example of attorneys who were given full proctorial powers to conduct cases on behalf of their clients, and a small group of professional attorneys makes its appearance in England in the later years of Henry II's reign. These attorneys are either clerics or laymen who have gained great experience from the royal courts. Glanville himself acted as an attorney for a wealthy client on at least one occasion. In common law procedure until the late seventeenth century, an attorney could only plead in court, on behalf of his client, in civil suits. In criminal pleas the defendant himself had to reply to the indictment. But it is clear from the court records that at least by the thirteenth century wealthy men under criminal indictment often sought the advice of attorneys.

The Angevin legal profession, like everything else connected with law and government in Henry II's reign, operated only with the sufferance of the crown. The attorneys were completely dependent upon the grace and favor of the judiciary. They were merely assistants to the royal courts who facilitated legal procedure. Before the end of the Angevin period the English legal profession had not achieved an independent status with rights and privileges and a corporate identity of its own.

The Angevin legal revolution constitutes, after the codification of the Roman law in the sixth-century Justinian Code, the most magnificent chapter in the history of medieval jurisprudence. Alongside the administrative and financial system which Henry II inherited from the Anglo-Norman monarchy and then expanded and improved, the king and his ministers had created a distinctly new legal system in Western civilization. It was a legal system which was national in scope, central in organization, and fundamentally rational in procedure. It was also aggressively authoritarian in spirit. Although the king and his justices did not commit themselves to any clear idea of sovereignty or absolutism, they made the Angevin judicial system work so that nothing could withstand the king or his writ, no group or great person in society. As far as the political implications of the common law were concerned, by the last decade of Henry II's reign it might as well have been Roman law. All justice in the realm among free men that was of any significance belonged to the king; Henry was indeed like a Roman emperor without Roman law and Roman political theory.

The English legal system now operated as an engine of despotism alongside the exchequer to ruin the great baronial families. On the one side the magnates were subject to an incessantly heavy taxation and the exchequer could ruin any obstreperous baronial family by the malicious use of reliefs and wardship. On the other side, the barons found them-

selves driven down through a maze of legal procedures to certain ruin.
Once the grand framework of the common law had been erected, the
king's justices could tamper with the process they themselves had created so as to deny the equal protection of the law of the land to any
family or community they wished to bring low. When the securing of
the property and status of landed society depended on the functioning
of the common law of the land, the denial of due process to a particular
lord or aristocratic family meant that they would lose their seisin and go
under. It was no longer necessary for the king to use force to destroy
anyone who stood in his way. A writ of *novel seisin* denied or even long
delayed, the use of *præcipe* against a baronial jurisdiction, pressure
brought by the justices upon assize juries—these legal niceties were now
sufficient to achieve on behalf of royal authority what had once taken
great armies and tremendous battles.

But an opening had been left in the framework of Angevin absolutism. The whole legal system ultimately rested not on the king's will but
on the legislative consent of the leaders of society and on the acquiescence and cooperation of the knightly class in law and administration.
Angevin kingship was a legal and administrative system that could be
used for authoritarian ends, but it was lacking a theory of absolutism and
a judicial and legislative sanction for despotism. The legal revolution of
the 1160's and 1170's had allowed to stand the idea that law resides in
the community and can only be altered through the collaboration of the
king and community. The expansion of the jury system had in fact
greatly increased the judicial responsibility and legal self-consciousness of
county society. The form of procedure in common law was, in a more
subtle way, an additional factor that worked against judicial absolutism.
As it crystallized in Henry II's reign, common law became committed
to what legal theorists call the "adversary system" of judicial procedure.
Whereas in Roman law that came to dominate on the Continent, the
judges took the leading role in directing the course of the trial, the
bench in common law acted as impartial arbitrators, as it were, enforcing
the rules and handing down the judgment, while allowing the contending
parties—plaintiff and defendant in civil suits, community and defendant
in criminal pleas—to struggle judicially against each other. This adversary
system placed the judges in an elevated position and served to entrench
the belief that the actual trial was a function of communal, popular institutions. This impression was enhanced by the itinerant judges' peculiar position as social aliens in the shire, momentary (although neces-

sary) interlopers in the ordinary life of county society. These fundamental facts were almost lost sight of in the heyday of Angevin power
in Henry II's reign. But authoritarian men had for reasons of expediency
left room for an anti-authoritarian principle to be asserted later against
the absolutist system they had sought to create.

CHAPTER FIVE

THE BEGINNINGS OF CONSTITUTIONALISM

from 1189 to 1307

I. *The Constitutional Significance of Magna Carta*

INSTITUTIONS and ideologies notwithstanding, medieval government was the king's government; with a weak or stupid king at its head it was bound to function poorly. Henry II was a remarkable man, undoubtedly the greatest of all medieval English kings. But his two sons who followed him on the English throne, Richard I the Lionhearted (1189-1199) and John (1199-1216), exhibited only one or the other of their father's qualities, and even then only to a limited degree. Richard had the reputation as the greatest chivalric warrior in Christendom, which made him personally popular with the nobility, but he was inept in government and law. It is probably fortunate for English royal power that he spent nearly all his reign in overseas crusading ventures and left the government in the capable hands of his father's bureaucrats. John, on the other hand, was something of an administrative genius and made some important contributions to the technique of royal administration. He was, however, a paranoiac who suspected treachery everywhere and flagrantly abused the processes of the common law in order to vent his hatred against certain noble families whom he suspected of treason. Eventually these families were driven to become rebels as the only way of saving themselves from ruin. He was furthermore susceptible to manic-depressive tendencies, at times exhibiting frenetic energy and then, particularly at crucial moments when his presence was required on the battlefield, becoming totally incapable of action.

The third weakness of John's personality, his lecherous proclivities, inaugurated the chain of events which brought about his crushing defeat by the Capetian monarchy. He took as his queen the daughter of a minor French count, whose father had already betrothed her to another obscure feudatory. The enraged lord, whose intended had been stolen from him in violation of contemporary custom by the English king, appealed to Philip Augustus, the king of France. Since John was technically the vassal of the king of France for Normandy, Anjou, and Aquitaine, Philip Augustus was the mutual overlord of both parties to the dispute. John was in one of his deep funks, and he refused to answer the summons to the French court. He was declared a contumacious vassal by Philip Augustus' court in 1204 and held to have forfeited Normandy and Anjou to the French crown. Had John quickly put his army into the field, he would likely have prevented Philip from seizing Normandy and Anjou. But John did nothing—did not even give instruction to his captains in Normandy. Thus the original homeland of the English kings fell to the Capetian monarch with scarcely a blow being struck.

The loss of Normandy was a disaster not only for the Angevin family but also for many of the English nobility who had fiefs across the channel. They henceforth had to confine their interests to England, and they necessarily became more and more concerned with John's use of royal legal and financial institutions. Any medieval king who was defeated on the battlefield was bound to lose the respect of his people and find his authority challenged at home. John was simply employing in a more relentless and severe manner the institutions of royal power which had developed in his father's day. But his complete lack of an attractive and imposing personality removed from the English political situation the factor which had previously compensated for the stringency of Angevin institutions.

John's second defeat came at the hands of the brilliant and effective church leader, Pope Innocent III, who in the first decade of the thirteenth century was reasserting papal leadership in European society. The papacy had always been extremely wary of becoming involved in a struggle with the English king, but Innocent pressed such a contest and won a complete victory. The quarrel between the Pope and King John arose over a disputed election to the See of Canterbury which, in accordance with new provisions of canon law and the agreement made between Henry II and the papacy, was appealed to Rome. Innocent rejected the candidates offered him and appointed instead Stephen Langton, an Englishman who had been a theologian at Paris and was at that time a cardinal in the Roman curia. John regarded this as a gross violation of the traditional royal authority over the English church; he furthermore regarded Langton as a papal agent, and he refused to recognize the archbishop-elect and forbade him to enter England. A bitter conflict ensued in which both Pope and king used extreme measures. Innocent placed England under an interdict, which suspended church services, and John seized a great part of the landed wealth of the English church. Finally Innocent encouraged Philip Augustus to prepare for the invasion of England under the papal banner, and John, terrified that he would lose England to his great enemy as he had lost most of his continental possessions, abnegated himself before the Pope. He not only accepted Langton as archbishop, but he became the Pope's vassal and made England the fief of the papacy. John's homage to Innocent was a further blow to the prestige of the English crown. But the king's eagerness to become the Pope's vassal was partly motivated by a plan to secure papal assistance in the event of a baronial rebellion.

In 1214 John suffered his second great humiliation and defeat at the hands of his archenemy Philip Augustus of France. He had allied himself with his relative, Otto IV of Germany, to foment a two-front attack on the Capetian kingdom. Otto was supposed to come down from Germany through Flanders by a route which would become familiar to German armies in the nineteenth and twentieth centuries, while John pushed upward from Poitou to complete a great pincers movement. John won some initial successes, but he was overcome by one of his periodic fits of depression. He stood idly by while Philip deployed most of the French army against Otto and inflicted a crushing defeat on the German emperor at Bouvines.

This second military disaster was the signal for the crystallization of baronial revolt against Angevin power in England. John had for a long time been using the prerogatives of the crown, such as relief, wardship, and scutage, in an unusually severe manner in order to increase royal income from taxation. John's government was very hard-pressed; the king had a growing administration, and he was engaged in far-flung diplomatic and military ventures, and with the general introduction of heavy-plate armor and other improvements in military technology, the costs of warfare were steadily increasing. The baronial leaders did not, however, sympathize with John's predicament; they did not want to be subjected to very heavy taxation for the support of a king who was a failure on the battlefield, who had lost them their lands in Normandy, and who furthermore had corrupted the law courts in order to obtain judgments against baronial families which John suspected, in many cases on little or no grounds, of disloyalty. The king had furthermore been defeated and humiliated by the Pope, and he had entered into a position of vassalage to the papacy, which was a flagrant turnabout in Anglo-papal relations as they had existed since the time of William the Conqueror.

The majority of the great barons, led by members of certain northern families who had particularly suffered from arbitrary procedures in the royal courts, prepared the first real rebellion against the royal liege lord in England since the Norman invasion. The baronial movement appears to have been given defined and conscious aims by the Archbishop of Canterbury, Stephen Langton, who, far from being the papal sycophant that had been expected, turned out to be a man of strong and independent opinion. Ignoring the fact that John was the Pope's vassal, Stephen aligned the English church alongside the lay magnates in what was a little later to be called the community of the English realm. It appears to have been Stephen who suggested to the barons that they stipulate their grievances in the form of a "great charter," which they forced the king to approve and seal in 1215. Stephen took as a precedent for Magna Carta the coronation charter of promises made to the English church and people by Henry I in 1100. Magna Carta contained a long list of baronial rights and privileges which the king promised not to infringe. It was, of course, a document which was biased in favor of the interests of the baronial class, but it was a class which claimed, and on the whole had the right, to speak for the "whole people of England."

The form of Magna Carta, which contemporary writers tell us was consciously modeled after Henry I's coronation charter, is similar to earlier charters of liberties and privileges. It begins with the usual salutation and closes with the traditional sanction clause which sets out how the king may be forced to maintain its provisions. At the very end comes the witness list and seals. In spite of the flowery Victorian illustrations we are all familiar with, John did not write his name on the parchment—the way to testify to a medieval document was by seal, not signature. Magna Carta is not a particularly well-drafted document; the body of the charter is an unsystematic array of sixty-three clauses arranged in no very coherent or logical order. Perhaps practitioners of the new criticism might elicit some subtle Spenserian kind of internal order, but it would be more realistic simply to accept Magna Carta as a rather hastily drafted and disorganized document.

At first the barons met with a cleric—one contemporary chronicler tells us it was Archbishop Stephen Langton, a plausible and appealing candidate. We cannot be sure, though Stephen was exactly the kind of man who would have been there. To this churchman, whoever he was, the barons must have poured out their grievances, while a clerk feverishly wrote them all down in a rather helter-skelter way. This initial session resulted in the Articles of the Barons, a first draft of which was shown to the king, who proceeded to strike out a good many articles that trespassed too far on his prerogative. After this, the barons went back to work and produced the Great Charter, which the king then affirmed. As a legal document Magna Carta of 1215 did not last very long. Claiming he had been forced to assent under duress, John repudiated it almost at once and appealed to Innocent III, whose vassal he was, to relieve him of his oath. The Pope, who had been trained in Roman law, could not take very seriously a controversy about something as ephemeral as the common law, and he was concerned that if the power of his vassal were curbed it would reflect badly on papal authority in England. John was allowed to repudiate his oath and thus, half a year after its beginning, Magna Carta seemed to be dead. At this point the barons invoked clause 61, declared *diffidatio* (feudal rebellion) against the king for violating his feudal promise, and brought in as their ally Prince Louis, the heir to the French throne.

Both sides were equally matched; only about half—if that many—of the barons fought against the king, some of them supported him, and John commanded all those mercenaries for whose pay he had been ruthlessly extracting money from the baronage. It is hard to speculate on how the war would have ended had John not died in 1216. The great earl, William Marshal (something of an elder statesman) and the few other lords who formed a regency during Henry III's minority, took two steps to pacify the realm. They managed to send Louis home to France by convincing him they really did not want to fight any more (they also paid him handsomely) and they reissued Magna Carta, which was once more a living legal document. The regents graciously indicated that the crown was prepared to accept the document as a whole; nevertheless certain clauses were struck out at the time of this reissue. When the regency was terminated and royal government was restored in 1225, Magna Carta was again reissued, but cut down now by a third from its original version. The most radical provisions, the strongest measures against the power of the crown, were eliminated. It was this 1225 version that became—and still is—the law in England. The first law inscribed on the statute roll at the end of the thirteenth century is Magna Carta.

Once enrolled as statute, Magna Carta had a real substance; it could be appealed to as the fundamental law of the realm. And though its provisions might be totally irrelevant to current issues, thirteenth- and fourteenth-century kings proved their benevolence and good intentions by confirming Magna Carta—it was a pledge to uphold "the law of the land," the due process of the common law, and an acknowledgment of the legislative importance of the community of the realm. The king's invocation of Magna Carta was an expression of general good will toward his subjects; the community's invocation of it, however, was invariably an expression of grievance and general dissatisfaction, the belief that the king was acting in some arbitrary manner. The cant phrases might change—the king would be accused of betraying the fundamental law, of subverting the liberties of freemen—but whatever the specific complaint might be, the king was sure to have broken Magna Carta. And his willingness to conform to Magna Carta was supposed to make everything all right once more.

In 1297 Edward I temporarily lulled the rebellious barons—who suspected he was bent on destroying the vestiges of their feudal prerogatives —when he confirmed Magna Carta. He was, of course, still trying to undo them, but he managed to soothe their feelings. And in the fourteenth century the confirmation of the charter signified royal recognition that the common law was fundamental to due process and that the legislative procedure rested upon the consent of the community of the realm, though it was never finely set out exactly what these things might be or how they worked. Disputes persisted and clashes between king and baronage did not slacken, but every invocation of Magna Carta was reconfirmation of a theory. Thus, even in the fourteenth century, there were —in a sense—two Magna Cartas, the haphazard documentary expression of specific baronial grievances and an exalted, though vaguely defined, theoretical manifesto.

To depose Richard II in 1399, Parliament cited (among every other reason they could dream up) his violation of Magna Carta. After such a lapse, the implication was that Richard could be murdered, which he was. But in the fifteenth century men were mostly worried about making government work at all, not in attacking and limiting its authority. When the common law is failing, when government is precariously balanced on the edge of chaos, the memory of Magna Carta is not very robust or significant. This was the situation for the first three quarters of the fifteenth century. And in the late fifteenth and sixteenth centuries a new judicial system developed as an adjunct of the royal prerogative. Though not defunct, the common law was no longer the exclusive procedure of the judicial system, nor was it particularly popular. Rather it was supplemented by a new kind of legal system vested solely in the crown. In times like this Magna Carta is simply not relevant, it is just another long and tedious statute. Shakespeare does not even bother to deal with it in his *King John*.

The seventeenth-century conflict between the crown and the common law, the judges, and Parliament, evoked Magna Carta's glorious renaissance. Sir Edward Coke rehabilitated it as the enshrinement of fundamental law and found in it all the rights of Englishmen, particularly the right to trial by jury and no taxation without representation, as well as all the other rights he needed to pit against the king's prerogative. Historians have treated Coke very severely, but what he read into Magna Carta and drew out of it was not completely farfetched. Magna Carta did establish the principle that the king must act in accordance with due process. Obviously Coke was anachronistic; we can say he was a bad historian, or ignorant, or meretricious when he ascribed to 1215 due process certain procedures that we know, and maybe he knew, could not have been there—full-blown trial by jury, for instance. But though Coke is fair game these days for the aggressive historian, he was basically right about the fundamental constitutional principle.

Coke's extravagant view of Magna Carta was the one that prevailed through the Victorian era, and by the end of the nineteenth century it had become a veiled and sacred document, shrouded in a haze of nobility and romance. Its invocation was a way to relieve arid oratory, a national means of satisfaction and self-applause. Magna Carta was the bastion of English liberty; it accounted for the wealth and virtue of the English people, the supremacy of the British navy, Queen Victoria and the Reform Act. The trouble was that no one bothered to read it until in the 1890's the Oxford legal scholar Edward Jenks began to dismantle the myth. The entire nineteenth-century view, he said, was ridiculous cant; Magna Carta was a baronial document, formulated by men who were selfish aristocrats, not enlightened patriots at all. The liberties were merely those of the great barons, and Magna Carta itself had very little to do with nineteenth century English liberalism. Scholars rallied to this new interpretation and, urged on by the revisionist atmosphere at the turn of the century, rushed to the other extreme.

The great age of historical revisionism has receded, but the Jenks disparaging view of Magna Carta is still fashionable; we are taught to look coolly and cynically at Magna Carta as a great statement of English liberty. It is hard to see, however, why we should expect the barons to have been interested in anything but their own privileges. The centuries-old inflated reputation of Magna Carta has no doubt been sufficiently punctured, but the selfishness of the barons need not rob it of all significance. In a sense, their unenlightened self-interest gives real force and vitality to Magna Carta; it means that Magna Carta was based on realities of power and politics and, in this context, it is pragmatic, successful and meaningful. It would really be disturbing if the magnates had been dreamy, altruistic do-gooders. Thus the barons at Runnymede belong squarely in the grand tradition of English liberty; they represent the deep-rooted concern with specific liberties and privileges and the equally traditional lack of interest in hazy, abstract theories of liberty. (This latter conception of liberty did not have any popularity until the seventeenth century.) It is exactly this circumscribed, specific, unromantic notion of liberty that distinguishes the English idea from the ambitious and comprehensive French and American natural rights conception. This is the basic idea, and it pervades English constitutional history. Liberty always means civil liberty, the liberty a man happens to have under the due process of the law, the liberty he is entitled to because of his status under the law. There is no implication of equality in political rights or in social status. There is liberty for barons, liberty for peasants; that they are quite different liberties is a fact of life, not a matter for theoretical debate. Liberty is equated with due process, but not (until the rise of modern democratic liberalism) with equality. The egalitarian conception first appears in the seventeenth century and again in the democratic movement of the late eighteenth and nineteenth century, but this has nothing to do with Magna Carta—though thinking often seemed to make it so—and it is a secondary theme in the history of English liberty.

Considering the central importance of Magna Carta in English history, it is odd that no scholar has yet produced a definitive book on the subject, that places the Great Charter in its immediate historical background and also explicates in detail the significance of each clause in the document. W. S. McKechnie's *Magna Carta*, although published a half-century ago, and too strongly under the debunking attitude of the day, is still the only detailed commentary. J. C. Holt, the author of a valuable study of the northern barons who led the rebellion against the king, has recently published a general study of Magna Carta. By taking into account modern scholarship, particularly the work of the American scholars Sidney Painter and S. K. Mitchell, Holt's study is much superior to McKechnie's as regards the historical context of Magna Carta—the social structure of early thirteenth-century England and the working of royal administration. But McKechnie's clause-by-clause explication of the text of the Charter still has not been superseded. Anyone who wishes to understand the constitutional and legal issues involved in the king's confrontation with the barons in 1215 should read J. E. A. Jolliffe's *Angevin Kingship*, although the book is highly technical in its presentation and difficult for the lay reader.

Perhaps the most fruitful and realistic way to treat Magna Carta is to analyze it first as a tax document. It is fairly clear that John's violations of law would not have led to insurrection if he had not been ignominiously defeated in battle, and if he had not tried to enforce certain financial policies which fell uncomfortably on all landowners. Certain families who had been specially persecuted by arbitrary violations of due process also quickened baronial discontent. Of 63 clauses, at least 24 deal with taxation—a looser reading of the text (the total of 24 is based on a strict interpretation) could easily expand this to 40. On one level, Magna Carta is a document concerned with royal financial policy and is a profound reaction to specific tax policies of John. Medieval taxation is only slightly less boring than modern taxation (it does, however, have the charm of distance), but we will have to consider it. Since we have all the necessary records after 1154 we can, fortunately, talk about medieval English taxation with a high degree of accuracy.

Inflation and the steadily rising costs of military technology made sure that John's government never had enough money. Heavy-plate armor, bigger horses, thicker walls—all these made war dearer than it had been. Government itself cost more; there were more and more salaried administrators whose wages seem lavish to us, accustomed to the idea that civil servants are ordained to live on subsistence wages. (Perhaps this explains why Angevin governments were staffed with the most talented men available.) John was supposed to rely on the ordinary sources of royal income to meet expenses. This included the income from the royal demesne, the law courts (where the expansion of the royal writ system was a boon) and feudal taxes. John's government managed the royal domain very well, and his judges conscientiously levied all the fines they could think of, no matter how irrelevant. Fines were imposed, for instance, for failure to present Englishry, even though no one could tell the difference between a dead Englishman and a dead Frenchman. No matter how efficiently run, however, there were absolute limits to what the demesne and the courts would yield. As far as the feudal taxes were concerned, the government had a good deal of latitude—there was much scope for maneuvering. And John's government took all the leeway it could; it consistently overstepped the bounds of personal and social propriety. Relief could be assessed in a punitive way—often it was three, four and even five times the annual income of the particular fief. Considering the death rate, a baronial family could expect to pay a relief every five to ten years. Thus excessively high relief was a neat way to keep a baronial family bankrupt and this *was* going beyond the limits—it was precisely the kind of violation of the "law of the land" that the barons had in mind when they drafted clause 39.

John's insanity gave Angevin toughness a peculiar color. John was really mean, and he delighted in his viciousness. He habitually sold off the widows and heiresses who were his wards to the highest bidder and he was ecstatic when he could get—and he did once get—20,000 pounds for an heiress. It specially amused John to marry his rich wards to obscure foreigners, to French mercenaries. This "disparaging" of the fair daughters of the English aristocracy was very offensive to the nobility, and the several provisions about relief and wardship in Magna Carta reflect their distaste. Wardship appears four different times. Clause 2, which deals with punitive relief, establishes relief at 100 pounds per baron. This clause was accepted in the 1225 reissue, and thereafter relief was fixed at this nominal sum. The enforcement of this rigid settlement was a heavy blow to the exchequer officials, who had counted on relief as a growth-potential tax. Though relief was eliminated, the English crown continued to be the guardian of aristocratic heirs and to marry off widows. It is interesting that the crown accepted limitations on the more general and dependable tax of relief, but stubbornly refused to give up wardship which, though it yielded an occasional bonanza, was too much of an intermittent matter to be much help to royal finances. (Wardship continued to be a source of royal income until 1660, when it was abolished by act of Parliament.) Thus Magna Carta effectively ended the excessive exploitation of the regular sources of crown income—sources which yielded John approximately 27,000 pounds per year.

John's government consequently had to turn to the extraordinary, irregular sources of royal revenue and attempt to increase taxation in this direction. These efforts were bound to be controversial and to foment political discontent. Scutage was the most obvious of these extraordinary sources of crown revenue that could possibly be augmented. Henry II's government had begun to think of scutage not as an integral part of the military system, but rather as a prime source of revenue. They also saw that the king's tenants had more tenants than they were paying for. Scutage was still based on the "old enfeoffment" of the Norman period. But in the twelfth century new manors had been carved out of old lands, new knights settled, land had been cleared, and it supported more men. The government was not getting any of this additional income; a vassal who had owed the service of 25 knights a half-century ago might now have 45 knights. With scutage at 2 marks per knight, the government—aside from what inflation was doing to the value of the mark—was losing 40 marks absolutely. This was exactly the kind of problem Henry II's administrators thought they knew how to solve. In 1166 they undertook a comprehensive investigation of knight's fees; they asked for returns from every baron stating how many knights he had, what was the old enfeoffment, what was the new one. The barons stiffly refused to pay any new scutage, and Henry II's government never did settle the issue. It was doubtful in law if the barons owed scutage on their new knights, and they could not be made to pay. They were willing to pay a lump fine, but would not acknowledge the principle.

John looked at scutage again, and decided there were other ways to squeeze it out of the recalcitrant magnates. First he raised scutage from two to three marks, which, he said, was justified by inflation. And he took it more often—eleven times in sixteen years, in the amount of 3,000 pounds per levy. This provoked bitter resistance. After eight or nine scutages the barons were furious. The most they could be expected to tolerate was scutage about every five years—that seemed reasonable for a fighting king. But John would demand scutage, call out the army, and then fail to fight. He had various explanations—the wind had changed, or the political situation was not quite ripe. Meanwhile, he was converting an incidental feudal revenue into an arbitrary annual tax. Clause 12 of Magna Carta, which states that "Scutage or aid shall be levied . . . only by the common counsel of our kingdom" is designed to cope with this problem. If the king has turned a feudal prerogative into a regular annual tax, it must have a sanction; it must be taken with consent. To the royal officials, this new sanction was an invasion of the king's feudal prerogative and they dodged the issue by reverting to Henry's II's practice of occasional composition. Although the 1225 reissue of Magna Carta rejected clause 12, John's government had been stopped from turning an old feudal levy into an annual tax.

Tallage, another sore point, was traditionally the way of blackmailing the bourgeoisie. Occupying an ambiguous region somewhere between the *liber homo* and the serf, the bourgeoisie had no clear status in law. And on the principle that—not being freemen—they were subject to arbitrary taxation like any serf on the royal domain, the townsmen were ruthlessly exploited. Tallage was the royal euphemism for extortion; the bourgeois euphemism for tallage was aid. "Aid" might seem to give the whole unpleasant business an aura of volition, but it deceived no one. The refusal of the crown to recognize their status as freemen kept the bourgeoisie anxious and frustrated. John tallaged them nine times in his sixteen-year reign, and gained an income of 2,500 to 5,000 pounds per levy. It was obvious that they were about to lose whatever insecure status they had; their consolidation in law with the peasantry— really an awful fate—seemed imminent. This explains that peculiar phrase in clause 12, which states that "aids" for the city of London shall be taken with consent. Tallage was one prerogative tax that Magna Carta did not arrest. Clause 12 was later rejected by the crown, but even in 1215, as far as the bourgeoisie were concerned, it was obviated by clause 25.

Clause 25, which allows the king to do what he wants on his own property, is the first statement of the principle later expressed as "the king shall live of his own." Magna Carta allows the king to tax as he pleases on the royal demesne. The barons thought this was a very good idea, but it was disastrous for the burgesses who did in fact live on the royal demesne. Clause 12 was, therefore, effectively nullified by clause 25. The former was a sop to the burgesses, but the latter really gives the king the right to tax them as much as he wants. And he does. Tallage increased in the thirteenth century and did not vanish until, at the end of the century, towns were brought under parliamentary taxation. And even then the higher rate they pay still reflects the old, inferior status in law.

Another clever scheme of John's hard-pressed government was carucage. This was a bright new name for the old Danegeld, and John tried to apply it once, when it yielded only 2,000 pounds. In the sense that carucage was levied on everyone's land, it was a national tax, and everyone refused to pay. This was exactly the sort of thing that finally caused the barons to balk—it was bad enough to sell widows and fair daughters, but for the king to tax their land was unacceptable. But he could still tax all their other property. Here 1207 was a great breakthrough, the turning point in the history of medieval taxation. In 1188 a crusading tax, the Saladin tithe, had been levied under the auspices of the church. Ten percent of all rents and movables was taken, and this was done under papal authority. This tax, levied through an extensive use of local officials and juries of recognition in every village, provided a huge income. In 1207 the crown went back to this idea and, on its own authority, levied a thirteenth. The sanction was the principle of gracious aid— the king could request freely granted aid in order to go to war. The magnates were summoned, as spokesmen of the community of the realm, to give consent for the whole country. Ostensibly they were being consulted in accordance with the Norman feudal principle, but what they consented to was, in effect, a national tax. As in 1188, the method of assessment was the jury of recognition and the unit of taxation was, significantly, not the barony, but the vill. And it was the most lucrative of all John's taxes, yielding 60,000 pounds. This tax served as the precedent, in Henry III's reign, for a new national tax which in turn became, in the reign of Edward I, parliamentary taxation.

As effectively as Magna Carta put an end to forms of feudal taxation, it also forced the king to expand nonfeudal taxation. Left with a dwindling feudal income, the crown from this point on groped its way toward a national tax. The one area of taxation that was left untouched by Magna Carta was to become, under Henry III and Edward I in the thirteenth century and Parliament in the fourteenth, the most important source of royal income.

Since it would be foolish to pretend that Magna Carta is merely a tax document, that is does not transcend the thirtenth-century context, and in order to evaluate it sensibly in its larger perspective, we might pose two questions. What do we mean by constitutional government, and how does Magna Carta contribute to it? Our answer to this first question will have to be arbitrary. There are all sorts of "constitutionalisms" including those of Louis XIV, Hitler, W. E. Gladstone and John Milton. But, as it specially pertains to English history, there are three requisite elements of constitutional government: viable government, sense of the community, rule of law.

The first requirement, which may sound fatuous, is government itself —a central government that effectively carries out the functions of law, peace and security. In short, government must be able to protect the realm; if it cannot do this it is no government. According to this definition, there was no constitutional government in England before 1066. Anglo-Saxon government was really government of the absurd, it was government by random organization, there was nothing rationalized about it. From the time of William the Conqueror until the end of Henry II's reign, viable government was established in England and, given the limitations forced upon it by problems of communications and baronial privilege, English government was very effective.

The second criterion of constitutional government is the sense of the community. Government must not consist of an alien group ruling in an arbitrary fashion. The king must realize that he is not absolute, he must see himself as a member of a corporate society, and the leaders of society must identify themselves as the community of the realm. In Henry II's reign we begin to get this kind of identification. At first it is an unformed and tentative feeling, but later in the twelfth century people will actually begin to talk about it; the new term "pleas of the crown" is an expression of it. The king begins to have an idea of office; there is a distinction between king and crown, between the king in his public and personal aspect. In his public capacity the king belongs to the community to which he is responsible. And early in the thirteenth century, the sense of being the "community of the realm" is impressed upon the magnates —they feel that they are more than a group of powerful, self-seeking individuals; now they see themselves as leaders of a corporate society to which they, too, have responsibilities.

The last criterion of constitutionalism is the responsibility of government to law. Government must respect the law; the machinery for changing it must not be an arbitrary procedure lodged exclusively in the king's hands. If fluctuation of the king's will can change law; if—like the emperor of the Justinian Code—he is the living law, then he is responsible to nothing but himself. In the tradition of English law, however, the king is responsible to a law over which he does not have ultimate authority. Though the law is not his, though he does not exert legislative sovereignty over it, he must maintain it, and must obtain the consent of the community in order to change it. In the great council of the Angevin monarchs the consent was more nominal than real. But there was, even here, service rendered to the principle that the king is not a living law, that he is somehow responsible to a will and a force outside himself. We cannot say that twelfth-century men carefully defined the relationship between king and law, or determined with any clarity how it was external to the king. Not until the seventeenth century will a clear definition be reached, and not until the eighteenth century will the idea be fully worked out in an institutional way.

In the reign of John these three constitutional elements were present: effective central government, sense of community, and the idea that the king is responsible to law which is external to him and not entirely under his control. This last idea is embodied in Magna Carta; it is the most important constitutional idea in the document, and it is postulated very clearly in two short and unequivocal clauses. Article 39, the due process clause, is the basis of English constitutionalism. "No freeman shall be captured or imprisoned . . . except by the lawful judgement of his peers and by the law of the land." The word to note here is "freeman." Serfs, who constituted about 40 percent of the population, are not under the protection of the law. All others, though, have the right of access to the law of the land—whatever it might be. Lawful judgment of peers in 1215 means the jury of presentment in criminal pleas, the jury of recognition in civil suits; for magnates it means trial at the king's court.

This article sets forth the idea that law is external to the king. Without this idea, clause 39 has no meaning; we know this is what the magnates were groping for. If the king has absolute control of the operation of the law, this clause is nonsense. Under John the royal judges were manipulating the legal system. The law of the land had been established by government with the consent of the community, but then the legal system had been treated by the Angevin king as his own creature; it had not been allowed to operate as something external to the king and his administration. Although the king and administrators operate the legal system, it is not theirs. This is a very hard concept to understand clearly and it will be very difficult to teach men to operate, without prejudice, something that is firmly in their hands. It will take five hundred years, but at least the idea is here. We could tell subsequent English history as the story of the institutional working out of clause 39 of Magna Carta, of the attempt to fulfill the theory that the legal system is not the king's, that the law of the land resides in the community.

"To no one will we sell, to no one will we deny or delay right or justice." Clause 40 postulates the same idea in these words; the clause was not designed to cancel the income from writs, but to put an end to practices of suspending cases for money, bribing judges, and other similar offenses. It sounds bold and sure, but for four hundred years clause 40 represents little more than wishful thinking. (The government of Elizabeth I was notorious for selling justice.) Again, however, the principle—without which reformers never get anywhere—is here.

There are some other clauses of legal significance. Clause 18 ratifies —with two interesting amendments—the assizes of Henry II, and perpetuates the system of royal courts. One amendment states that all assizes are to be held in the county of origin—cases are not to be moved. Here again is the idea of the community of the shire and trial by peers. To move a case is somehow to rupture its necessary link with the community. Even when a case is merely taken into the next county, the members of the jury—no longer on their home territory—are more susceptible to threat and subornation. Here is the notion that the best protection of the rights of Englishmen is to be found in the community, that a man will find justice in his own shire. The other amendment provides that the assizes shall be held more often and catch up with the backlog of pending cases. The gentry, who benefited from the assizes, were eager to keep and reinforce Henry II's legal changes. For cases against the great barons, the gentry needed the royal court, and they emphatically wanted to maintain the sitting of the common pleas in Westminster. By and large, as long as the king upholds the law of the land, the gentry will be satisfied.

Clause 34 abolishes *præcipe*, the writ which arbitrarily deprived a freeman of his own court. The power of baronial courts was broken by the competing jurisdiction of the assizes and by lifting cases directly out of them by royal command. There were two ways to accomplish the latter. By a writ of right a suitor who felt he had been wronged in the baronial court could appeal to the king and have his case retried. Here the royal court acted more or less as an appellate court. But there was another method—writ of *præcipe*—which achieved the same purpose in a more drastic and ferocious manner. By *præcipe*, a suit could be stopped while it was still in the baronial court; the barons were right when they claimed this was tampering with the feudal law. Though *præcipe* was eliminated, the writ of right was still very much alive and, though it was much slower, could be used for exactly the same purpose. (In the thirteenth century judges began to invent legal fictions, especially the writs of entry, by which a case that should have gone to a baronial court could be brought into the royal court.) Once the centralization of justice is under way, it cannot be stopped; except for the hundred or so great barons, everyone likes it. Clause 34 is the last great, but doomed, effort of the magnates to maintain the shreds of their private jurisdiction.

Clause 61 provides the sanction to ensure that the king upholds and maintains the charter. A committee of twenty-five barons is appointed to scrutinize the operations of the king's government. When a complaint is received they are to ask the king please to cease his bad practice, and upon his refusal may proclaim feudal rebellion and proceed to fight him until he once again agrees to maintain the due process of the law. This is, of course, an unwieldy method of exercising control over the king's government, a ridiculously cumbersome procedure for making sure that the king obeys the law of the land. Subsequent English history, from the thirteenth to the nineteenth century, is the story of how a satisfactory substitute for clause 61 was found, how a way to observe and control the king's government and make it responsive to the community of the realm was slowly worked out. But the idea is here; the problem after 1215 is one of institutional development, not of principle. It was a tremendously hard thing to achieve and a lasting solution was not to be found in the medieval period. Historians who say that the beginning of Parliament was a great step forward toward institutional control have a romanticized picture of what really happened in a thirteenth-century parliament, but this was to be a vast improvement over the committee of twenty-five.

II. Thirteenth-Century Culture, Society, and Government

OF ALL MEDIEVAL PERIODS, the thirteenth century is perhaps the most celebrated. It has been labeled "thirteenth, greatest of centuries," it has stood for an enviable synthesis, balance and harmony. There is no denying that there was a kind of golden aspect to thirteenth-century civilization, a rich, autumnal glow that historians find very attractive. The trouble is that after 1300 medieval civilization fell apart, a fact that might lead us to consider what were the underlying tensions and forces of decay in this smooth and harmonious age. On the continent as well as in England the golden age rapidly deteriorated into chaos. It is curious that no one has been able to explain this or answer the nagging question: Why does misery immediately issue from such a grand consensus in intellect, politics and law, from the great cultural achievements? There has been no clear answer, either for England or for European civilization.

The most interesting writing about the thirteenth century has been done by F. M. Powicke, who, during his Oxford career from 1925 to 1948 dominated medieval studies in England, was acclaimed, and finally knighted. Powicke was a learned, intelligent man and a very careful worker; his books tell us a great deal about what happened in the thirteenth century, but they do not illuminate this underlying problem. He never explains what was going on under the surface, what were the faults in this society that allowed such great problems to emerge after 1300. Powicke never escaped from the sunny view of the thirteenth century; his image was of a glorious, happy time in European civilization, one that has never been matched or surpassed. This is a warm and appealing view, but a superficial one. Powicke's two-volume account of the reign of Henry III (1216-1272), *King Henry III and the Lord Edward,* is a very detailed, accurate and meticulous work. But since Henry III was not a typical medieval ruler, it is not very valuable for general study—though it does tell us what Henry III and the great barons were really like. Powicke's volume on the thirteenth century in the Oxford History of England series devotes a tremendous amount of space to the wars in Wales and the incomprehensible disputes among Welsh warriors and lords. For readers who have a consuming passion for Welsh military history this must be splendid, but the emergence of Parliament receives only cursory treatment. The second half of this book provides a fine account of Edward I (1272-1307). Here we go in with the sun, come out with the gloom. Powicke does a very good job of telling us what happened, but he does not delve below the surface, we do not learn why such darkness came on so quickly.

One of the more controversial medievalists is G. O. Sayles who has probably the strongest mind of his generation of medieval political historians, although only late in his career has he achieved any fitting academic recognition. Sayles's work became more and more filled with polemic against the academic establishment. This is not necessarily detrimental to scholarship—it may, in fact, be salutary—but obsessive attacks on Stubbs are bound to lead to extremism too. It is exactly this lack of balance that spoils Sayles's most recent book. *The Governance of Medieval England*, written with his alter ego, H. G. Richardson, is a violent attack on Stubbs, a rather pathetic tilting at windmills; it is the equivalent of an American scholar's effort earnestly to set about refuting Bancroft point by point. Sayles's and Richardson's work on thirteenth-century Parliament is very good, but is also marred by excess of polemic. Sayles's most important contribution has been to edit the legal records of the court of king's bench. Here he successfully establishes that in the thirteenth century the common law had already begun to crumble, that in the reign of Edward I—the so-called English Justinian—the breakdown of law is apparent.

A valuable work is T. F. Tout's massive *Chapters in Administrative History*. Tout, who died in the 1930's, was a professor at Manchester; his early work was not particularly good, but he labored assiduously in the Public Record Office and produced these six volumes telling us how English government and administration actually operated in the thirteenth and fourteenth centuries, a study of enormous interest to historians and sociologists who are concerned with the development of bureaucracy. As it goes along, Tout's work gets better and better—for the thirteenth century, he was not yet sure of his methods and powers. One of Tout's students, Bertie Wilkinson, was for three decades a distinguished scholar at the University of Toronto. In his three-volume *Constitutional History of Medieval England*, which covers the period from Magna Carta to 1485, Wilkinson presents a neo-Stubbsian interpretation. Though critics have denounced Wilkinson's work as ridiculous Whiggery, what he says about the thirteenth century cannot be ignored; it is quite possible that thirteenth-century barons were Whigs. Though Wilkinson's books are full of echoes of the Victorian liberal myths, what makes them invaluable are the attempts at synthesis and the documents he publishes in excellent translation after every chapter.

The first thing to note, when we turn to the thirteenth-century sources, is that we have now reached the point where there is unpublished material. For any new research, one must go to the Public Record Office in London which is drafty and dusty, but where the people serve tea and are extremely nice. (It is perhaps an accurate image of contemporary Britain.) New kinds of documents—close rolls and patent rolls—appear in the reign of Henry III. Almost all government documents, except writs, appear in the letters close or patent. The letters close—("close" because they are folded up and sealed) are short letters directed to a government agent instructing him to do something. They are direct descendants of the little Anglo-Saxon writs and, like them, are *ad hoc*, specific and crisp. Letters patent, which take their form from the charter, are open, quite formal, and bear official seals. They were sent from the crown to a public official; they grant an office or issue general instructions that are often complicated and of long-range import. Between these two kinds of documents—and thousands of them are extant—we can know what was really going on; now we are able to understand just how decisions are made, or not made. (In the Norman and Angevin periods we knew what government did, but usually not why.) Now we can observe the day-to-day operations of government, we can see how problems are recognized, formulated and then solved, evaded or ignored. We can see what the grounds were for or against specific decisions and courses of action. In Latin, and very often in terrible handwriting, these documents do not inspire light browsing, but since the 1920's, Calendars—English summaries—have been issued. Some administrative records, however, still remain unpublished, and the legal records have barely been touched.

The thirteenth century is the last great age of the English chroniclers and we will miss them as we move on to the fourteenth. Their absence is, perhaps, one reason why historians are so confused about what was happening in the fourteenth and fifteenth centuries. After 1300 the monks are less energetic; they are no longer concerned or well-informed about public affairs. But before this they had been very busy writing contemporary history; they were alert and diligent; they made sure to interview whomever they could, to collect as much information as possible. The most famous thirteenth-century chronicler is Matthew Paris, who was lucky enough to live in St. Alban's, a monastery twenty miles north of London, smack on the high road to the north. Barons on their way to and from London would be entertained at St. Alban's—it was the last good inn before the city—and all the latest news and gossip would be picked up and written down by Matthew. His chronicle is rich and absorbing, but its reliability is questionable. Matthew Paris had very definite opinions; he was sympathetic to the baronial party, he believed in the responsibility of the king's government to the community—with the result that often historians see (they can hardly help it) thirteenth century problems and issues through the eyes of a baronial partisan. David Knowles has said that Matthew Paris is the first Whig, a kind of thirteenth-century Macaulay. And it is symptomatic that a monk should take the side of the baronial class; it is evidence of a new, often disquieting cross-current in thirteenth-century society.

Something else is new and interesting. The thirteenth century is the first era of English history where there is a genuine constitutional debate; not until the seventeenth will the nature of government and society be so vehemently debated by men of learning and affairs. There are other parallels between the thirteenth and seventeenth centuries. Both suffered tremendous upheaval, perhaps this is why historians of each seem to find it so hard to apprehend what really took place. In order to grasp what was happening to government and society, there are four fundamental and pervasive aspects of thirteenth-century life we must be aware of. There are aspects of social change, which account for much of the confusion and turbulence of thirteenth-century history; often elusive, they are, however, always present, and we will need to keep them in mind. They are the economic situation, war, education, and the friars.

The most prominent economic aspect of the thirteenth century was, until the 1280's and 1290's, runaway inflation. Universal prosperity meant that everyone was making money in the most obvious and flagrant ways. Even the peasants prospered; many were gaining legal manumission and legally, if not economically, they were becoming more or less free farmers. Capitalist agriculture was booming—grain sold for high prices in market towns all over England; this too was the period when the wool trade became the great staple of English commerce and industry. It is no exaggeration to say that everyone involved in it made money, and that everyone—lords, merchants, gentry, churchmen, the king—was involved in the wool trade. All members of landed society were concerned somehow with the raising of wool and shipping it from the eastern ports to Flanders.

But inflation and prosperity, by the second half of the century, were producing side effects that engendered severe economic and social problems. The demand for agricultural products motivated landlords to bring an ever greater amount of marginal land under cultivation and to mine the soil recklessly for quick profits. By the end of the century the rural entrepreneurs were faced with soil exhaustion and smaller yields. In addition, as in all times of inflation and prosperity, there was an enormous population boom in the mid-thirteenth century. This led to extensive overpopulation in the peasant villages and slowed down the pace of manumission, because with a surplus labor supply the landlords could afford to be severe in their treatment of the manorial serfs. Finally, in the last two decades of the century, the great boom came to an end: war on the continent interfered with wool export, a significant amount of land went completely out of cultivation, the population started to level off, and even before the Black Death of the 1340's, the demographic curve, that powerful and mysterious historical force, was already moving downward in England. These momentous economic changes, which have been elucidated by M. M. Postan's careful researches and brilliant insights, follow a boom-bust, prosperity-depression cycle that is characteristic of unregulated capitalist economies. Late in the thirteenth century the great aristocrats no longer toss their money around as if there were no tomorrow; the burgesses are not so quick to pile more furs on their backs, or rings on their fingers. And hard times persisted, with perhaps two cycles of recovery and relapse, until the middle of the fifteenth century.

In the last decades of the thirteenth century we rapidly pass from sun to darkness; there is a sudden shift, not only from prosperity to depression, but also from peace to war. Until the 1290's, the thirteenth was the century of the long peace; we shall not see another again until the nineteenth. From the Battle of Bouvines in 1214 (when John and the German emperor were defeated) until the 1290's, there was no important war. This is a factor of great significance; without war government is likely to have a much easier time. (That Henry III's government went bankrupt in peacetime strikingly proves its incompetence.) A long peace also means the atrophy of the military functions of the aristocracy. If they cannot fight, what else are they to do? To sing and dance and write poetry is all right for recreation and staving off boredom, but the only thing that really demands their concentration, the one thing the aristocrats do supremely well, is to fight. Without any fighting, they are restless, at loose ends. In the reign of Edward I (1272-1307) the situation begins to change. This king's highest ambition was the expansion of the frontiers of England. Edward was the first English king who was really interested in conquering the Celts. Certainly the marcher lords had already forced their way into Wales, had carved out a few estates in Ireland, but until Edward no English king has purposefully tried to establish a hegemony over Britain. And Edward did succeed in conquering Wales; he even—with much less success—became involved in Scotland. The 1290's, which happened to be the end of prosperity, also brought the great war with France, a clash between ambitious, headstrong kings who could draw—so they thought—on substantial resources. And they had a compelling motive, what we now call economic imperialism—the prize was control of Gascony, the wealthy wine-producing area, and of Flanders, the great European industrial center. The real issue was who would be the dominant power in northern Europe. Edward put forth a good deal of nationalistic propaganda, such as the claim that the French were bent on destroying the English people, but this was the real issue.

Once it started, the war never stopped for a century and a half. School children know it as the Hundred Years' War, but we could properly call it the 150 years' war—it dragged on from the 1290's until the middle of the fifteenth century, when both sides were exhausted and both England and France were in chaos. There were some peaks; from 1294 the war was waged intensively until 1303. After three decades of occasional conflict, Edward III revived the war in full force and it sputtered out in the 1370's. There was intermittent conflict in the last two decades of the fourteenth century, and then the full-scale war started up again in the second decade of the fifteenth century. At the conclusion of the long, wearisome conflict nothing very much had been accomplished. The war is, however, significant for two things. It was the first great European war, and it inaugurated that now familiar phenomenon, the war economy. All the resources of the crown will be organized and geared for the war effort, and the shift in government from a peace to a war economy means that its entire outlook and tone will change too.

The war with France was a good thing for one group of people—the aristocracy. Under the Angevins the baronage had been driven hard and, even in the thirteenth century, their future is still uncertain. For the simple reason that they were the generals, the French war brought them back on stage in a grand way; it revitalized them as a class. War gave the aristocracy license to raise what were, in effect, private armies—an earl would command a good-sized body of troops who were loyal directly to him. This will soon create tremendous problems; the powerful aristocracy will turn their strength against the king who provided their new life and force by ending the long peace.

The thirteenth century is the first great age of the English universities;

"university" then stood for Oxford and Cambridge—in some ways it still does. The famous founding of the university is very hard to pinpoint. Whenever the masters incorporated themselves, the university was at that moment in existence. This is what "universitas" (literally, "corporation") means. But though Oxford existed in the twelfth century, it did not flourish until the thirteenth. Then, for the first time, a lot of people are beginning to take English B.A.'s—although afterward they may still go to the continent to study something useful like Roman law. Cambridge in 1200 was still nothing but a bridge over the river Cam, but Oxford was becoming rather rowdy and distracting and, after a particularly violent town-gown riot, a hardy group of students and masters set off for the remote and undisturbed East Anglia swamps. There was, no doubt, enough peace and quiet there. In fact very little was heard of Cambridge until the sixteenth century when the new humanists and the preaching of a few radical Protestants put it on the map. But thirteenth-century Oxford was, along with Paris, one of the two greatest centers of thought and learning in Christendom. By the 1260's and 1270's the most brilliant and advanced thinkers in Europe were to be found at Oxford working on the frontiers of knowledge. What they were doing was nothing less than creating modern science. This stunning phase of exploration of mathematical propositions and experimentation in the natural sciences, is linked with the arrival of the Franciscans in England.

The appearance of the friars has not been sufficiently recognized as a critical event in thirteenth-century England. A new and radical wing had developed in the thirteenth-century church and a new outlook and technique was expressed in the mendicant orders. This idea—a great idea which, had it come a hundred years sooner, would have saved the Catholic church from decline and schism—was to combine piety and the world: to have men of piety working in the world. There were two new orders, the Dominicans—Order of Preachers—and the Franciscans—the Order of Friars Minor, or Little Brothers. The Dominicans were not very active in England; they were the leaders of the Inquisition, and thirteenth-century England was the only country in Western Europe that, having no heretics, had no Inquisition. In the fourteenth century, when heresy proliferated, the king's refusal to let the Inquisition into the country was of tremendous significance for subsequent English legal history. On the continent, secular law copied from the Roman law which the Inquisition used to such good effect; an Inquisition in England might well have influenced the procedure of the common law too. Though it is perilous and hard to speculate about negative influences, there is something very important here.

The Franciscan order exerted a profound influence on thirteenth-century English life, on the religious thinking of ordinary people, peasants and burgesses. To these people the Franciscans brought religion in terms of their understanding and in response to their needs. An appeal to the personal and emotional sources of religious life was bound to de-emphasize the hierocratic social functions of the church. Perhaps the seeds of English heresy were planted here, perhaps the Franciscan influence on experiential religion will flower in Lollardry and the radical heresies of the sixteenth century. There is a discernible continuity over the centuries of personal, puritanical, non-sacramental religion. And, as a result of Franciscan infiltration, the university produced two men of transcendent genius—the logician Duns Scotus, and the logician, metaphysician, politician *cum* child prodigy, William of Ockham. Ockham and Scotus were teaching at Oxford in Edward's reign. Anti-Thomist, and anti-papal as well (Ockham denounced the absolute authority of the Pope, appealed instead to church councils and even beyond that to individual conscience), their thinking had an important impact on the English church. Now its personnel would come out of Oxford tinged with radical ideas. Unfriendly to Rome, unenthusiastic about the old notions of hierarchy, they contributed to the slow building up of an English heretical movement. Some of these radical men will find work in royal government; they will not be great servants of the Pope; on the contrary, they will not hesitate to support the king against the Pope. And every decade, the growing strength of anti-clericalism and anti-papalism encourages intransigence on the part of royal officials. Radicals, extremists —these are exactly the kind of men the king needs. Some of the Franciscans end as political radicals. In the 1260's there will be an alliance between some of them and the baronial movement. The Franciscans do not like the Pope; the barons do not like the king; Henry III, who was closely allied with the Pope, is their common enemy. The most radical, extremely hostile attitude toward the royal power is expressed in a poem —"The Song of Lewes"—written by a Franciscan friar.

We can say that the friars acted as dissolvents of the structure of medieval society. They nourish budding radical movements, they support the king against the Pope but, as they also encourage the political radicalism of the barons against the king, they support and enhance the baronial view of the constitution. It is hard to work out this confused chain of cause and influence. There was a bubbling up of new ideas, ideas that undermined the hierocratic view of society. The friars offered a new view of the world, a new mode of life and of thought. These ideas will have subtle and various effects on the way people will act. The tenuous connections between thought and action are difficult to work out; often the connections cannot be made in an explicit way. But, as we try to make sense out of this shifting and puzzling century, we should keep in mind these four crucial factors: prosperity and depression; peace and war; the universities; the friars.

In the thirteenth century we can, for the first time, legitimately call the barons "aristocratic." Now their self-consciousness becomes highly developed; a class ethos, formally expressed in chivalry and courtly love, has been worked out and accepted. An aristocrat is not merely whoever happens to be a baron or a tough fighter or a great landowner. He has to have something more—the proper tone. He is superior in mind; he has an exalted soul; he is literate, knows how to act—the way one does things. To be an aristocrat means that one is attuned to a very special, rarefied way of life. And no one else has got it—this particular style, which somehow lurks in the blood of an aristocrat; this is his breeding. Thus his blood must remain pure—a notion that gives rise to a new code of gentility and of intellectual and social superiority. Not surprisingly, the aristocracy tends to see itself more and more as the "community of the realm," the natural leaders of society. If there is something superior about their minds and their blood, it is only right that they should rule. They are the most important group in society; they are its great oaks. What Burke said in the eighteenth century might equally apply to the thirteenth. Simon de Montfort is really not a very different kind of man than the Duke of Newcastle, or Burke's own Rockingham. The essence here is the style, the mode. Men who can kiss hands, and dance, and write poems, can run the government too. In the 1250's and 1260's they try. They assert their control over the government, and they fail completely. The Provisions of Oxford, which set up a permanent baronial council, were designed to make government and administration responsible to the aristocracy. But it does not work, and government lapses into chaos.

Over and over we will witness the same kind of failure. Certainly, the aristocrats are sophisticated; they are well educated, they have a wide, national vision. But they suffer from two fundamental defects. They can never agree among themselves for very long; jealousy breaks out almost at once, one earl always wants more than the next. By the very nature of his code of life, an aristocrat is never content to take second place. As soon as the king is defeated, aristocratic in-fighting and jockeying for position and power begins. Aristocratic government invariably means unstable government. The other weakness, which already appears in the 1250's, will show greatly during the next two hundred years. They are lazy—it is the defect of their quality. Men of this stamp cannot be expected to sit around the exchequer and worry about sheriffs who bring in two pounds instead of five pounds; they are too high-strung, of too fine a temperament. Very soon they become bored with the daily tasks of administration which are not, after all, specially elegant or dashing. The aristocrats are capable of drafting magnificent programs, but they will not take pains. Aristocratic governments do not fall so much as they disappear. During the summer, the hunting season, the dancing season, government fades away, only to reappear during the winter. In the fifteenth century this pattern lasted for sixty years—fighting and governing in the winter, country life in the summer. But for better or worse, beginning in the late thirteenth century, the aristocracy becomes very important in English life; their leadership in society is secure.

The gentry continued to thrive until the last two decades of the thirteenth century. They are entrenched in law and administration. There are two changes which enhance their legal and political importance and make them the most powerful group in society on the level of local— and perhaps even central—administration. In the thirteenth century an interesting official called the "keeper of the peace" appears (soon he will be known as the justice of the peace). Appointed initially to assist the sheriff, his function was to maintain order in society. By the fourteenth century he is the most important peace and law official in the county; he is recruited, and will be until the 1880's, from the most influential and respected gentry in the county. The J.P.'s will dominate the shire court; by the end of the fifteenth century they will have appropriated most of the functions of the sheriff. Their glorious history is only beginning in the thirteenth century, but we can already see them in the later years of Henry III's reign. The thirteenth century also saw a change in the legal profession, the decline of the clerical lawyer and the rise of the lay lawyer. Perhaps late in Henry's reign, certainly by the reign of Edward, this has happened. The last great ecclesiastical lawyer in English history is Henry de Bracton; after him they are all laymen from the gentry class. A corporate legal profession is formed; entry into it is tightly controlled—a lawyer must have certification, he must be called to the bar. All these formalities and restrictions emanate from one little place—the Inns of Court in London. Already established in Edward's reign, the Inns become the controlling body, they provide legal education, and they draw students and members almost exclusively from the ranks of the gentry. (The odd cases—sons of merchants, for instance—are quickly absorbed, and they too become gentlemen.)

Law no longer belongs to the church, but to the knightly class, the landed gentlemen of England. The Inns of Court are their university. As a rule the gentry do not send their sons to Oxford, unless they are meant to be theologians—something as rare then as it is now—or clerics. Even if they do not become lawyers, young gentlemen spend a year or so at the Inns; they learn land law, the basis of their way of life; then they go back to the county and manage their family estates. More and more the gentry learn to identify their way of life with the operations of the common law, an identification that—except for a short period in the fifteenth and sixteenth century—will remain strong until the reign of Queen Victoria. Thus the gentry tightens its hold on local administration. They will provide central administrators as well; many bureaucrats and all the justices will be gentry. A substantial proportion of the bureaucracy had always been lawyers, but where they had been recruited from the church, now they will be landed gentry from the Inns of Court. And, as the clerics had once done, the gentry will rise to be great ministers of the crown—by the fourteenth century this will be happening.

For the bourgeois, the thirteenth century was an era of terrible frustration. He was accumulating more and more money, but still had no political power. He could not find a way to breach the solid wall presented to him by king, church, aristocracy and gentry—none would give him any real power. The burgess is an outcast from society—a sociologist would be quick to label him alienated from the power elite. The only thing he could do was gain some recognition of his legal freedom. In the reign of Edward he finally gets what he wanted. By 1300 parliamentary taxation replaces tallage, and the burgess is summoned to Parliament. His rate of taxation is, of course, heavier than anyone else's, a survival of his inferior status. And he has no role in Parliament, he has no choice but to pay half again as much as the landed classes. Then, late in the thirteenth century, his real calamities begin. The grain market declines because of the depression, and the international war makes it harder than ever to ship wool. He still manages to do fairly well however; he gets along. The political instability of the fourteenth century effectively puts an end to his economic well-being. For about 140 years the towns of England were considerably less prosperous than they had been in the thirteenth century—not until the late fifteenth century will the bourgeoisie revive.

Ordinary churchmen were caught unhappily in the conflict between friars and the old clergy; between radical, experiential fervor and the old formal, sacramental religion; and in the bitter struggles among papacy, king and barons. Henry III was the ally and servant of the Pope. Neither barons nor churchmen could approve of this—it seemed to both that the king and the Pope were conspiring to "disadvantage" the English clergy. The king allowed the Pope to send Italian clerics to hold English offices —this was an outright offense, and a growing national sense inflamed hostility toward Rome. The churchmen naturally sought to ally themselves with a national force, whoever would stand for England against Rome, whoever would give them light and direction; the barons during Henry III's reign, with the king himself during Edward's. But the churchmen did not play these games to their gain. By the end of the thirteenth century they have lost their control over law and the law schools; thus their influence on society has significantly declined.

In the thirteenth century it is quite clear that the king is more than a personality—he is what Maitland has called a "corporation sole." The king has a dual quality; one existence in his own person, and another in the crown. Even if the king is incompetent or uninterested, government can function without him—the substance of his public authority lies in the crown, not his person. The idea that the king is a corporate body, that the crown is more than the strengths and frailties of one man, is a tremendous advance. This idea also leads to great problems, and later we will be faced with them. Nevertheless, government still means—until the eighteenth century it will mean—the king's government. (Historians are addicted to comparing the reigns of Henry III and Edward I—to Henry's disadvantage of course—and are fond of ascribing the comparative failure and success of the two monarchs to their personalities. Though it somewhat begs the question of how much success there really was in Edward's reign, there is substantial truth in the old cliché.)

Henry III perfectly illustrates the saying that nice guys finish last. He was really a sweet person. Badly treated by history, Henry probably deserved—much more than his wife's brother-in-law, Louis IX of France, who was a puritan rather than a saint—to be canonized. Henry was truly devout, he really loved the church, the Pope, and the sacraments. His taste in art was remarkably good; he built Westminster Abbey, a respectable monument. Henry was a very decent, cultivated man, but quite hopeless as a king. There is no denying that many of the troubles of his reign fall squarely on his shoulders. His difficulties began when he was still a gleam in his father's eye. John's pursuit of Isabella, an obscure French countess, led to his fight with Philip Augustus, brought on his military defeats and the loss of Normandy. Henry never managed to do much better. Coming to the throne at the age of nine, he had an overprotected childhood, and not a particularly high intelligence. In the next few centuries we will meet a lot of kings like this—sweet but stupid. (One of them, Henry VI, was also the product of an English king and a Frenchwoman.)

Henry's sense of the dignity of monarchy was either too archaic or too advanced; he thought of himself as an irresponsible king, as a monarch by divine right. The significance of Magna Carta eluded his comprehension; to the extent that he grasped the notion of consent, he thought it was a bad idea. Henry believed government belonged to him and that no one else, except perhaps the Pope, should control it. It was a respectable and sophisticated (though unoriginal) idea of kingship, but it was irrelevant to and out of touch with the English experience. After 1215 the barons will not let the king rule without consent—they will not submit to arbitrary means of taxation or other authoritarian procedures. Administrative organs like the exchequer must be responsible to them.

His supporters brought out the worst in Henry; they made him irresponsible. The French relatives encouraged his idea of government— what they wanted were soft jobs in it, and they urged Henry to rule without consent. The Pope, who was a Roman lawyer and an Italian as well, did not understand the problem at all. To him the baronial views were heretical, they shook and undermined the hierarchy—if this sort of thing were permitted, the next step would be for some fanatic to suggest that the Pope was responsible to his bishops. Urged on, Henry let himself be pushed into sharp conflict with the barons. The magnates, of course, were not unselfish; they wanted to get their hands on the royal treasury, to increase their power and status, and to oust the French relatives from their cozy sinecures. Ironically, the king's French brother-in-law, Simon de Montfort, who had inherited the great earldom of Leicester, became the leader of the dissident barons.

Henry's way of escaping from baronial pressure was to fall back on household government. Historians tell us that this was a very significant move, that for the next three or four centuries the household will remain an important and separate branch of government. Chancery and the exchequer, which grew out of the *curia regis*, are susceptible to the magnates. They are the parts of the royal administration that are most exposed to baronial scrutiny; the magnates can bring pressure to bear on these semi-public institutions. This was exactly what the king wanted to circumvent; the last thing he wished was to be accountable to the magnates in any way. Thus he turned to his household officials. He took obscure people, his personal servants, and gave them public power. Since they are still technically his household officials, it is much harder for the magnates to scrutinize and control them; it is a different matter than prying into the activities of the chancellor or the exchequer. It was hard for the great barons to cope with this move; suddenly government was the king's again—certainly the household, which was taking over more and more government functions—was the king's.

The chamber, that branch of the household concerned with the king's bedroom, became a treasury separate from the old exchequer. By issuing writs under the privy seal—to sheriffs, tax collectors—the king siphoned off money from the exchequer and directed it into the chamber. We will see many operations of this nature in the next four hundred years; in the sixteenth century the king will still be thinking them up. It is a shrewd and effective way to avoid public gaze and public accountability. But it is also a very messy system. In part, taxation is now carried out by an old agency, the exchequer, and in part by a new one. This means there will be much confusion and overlapping, and a great deal of chaos is inevitable. Where the Angevin kings strove for clarity and system, the *raison d'être* of this new method is ambiguity and mystery; it makes system impossible. In the late thirteenth and fourteenth centuries the growth of chamber administration is one of the causes of ever-increasing maladministration and inefficiency. The leaders of the community will also become more and more suspicious of the king, and they will spend much time and energy attempting to gain control of his household. They never succeed, even in the fifteenth century; rather the household and the royal council control Parliament. (This long story, elucidated by Tout, has been well summarized by S. B. Chrimes in his *Introduction to the Administrative History of England*.)

Thus the monarchy remains personal; but it tends even more to come into conflict with the barons, whose efforts to control the government are frustrated by the elusive nature of household administration. Henry was not clever enough to work chamber administration properly. He fell into debt, and only a meeting of the *curia regis* and grants of gracious aid could rescue him. A king who tries to run his government from his own bedchamber and kitchen can only succeed if he does not have to ask the barons for money. When he does, they will invariably demand to know what his cook and chamberlain have been doing. During the next three hundred years those kings (particularly in the late fifteenth and sixteenth century) who manage to work the system properly and skillfully hardly ever need Parliament. It is a game with very strict rules. A king who insists upon a personal administration must carry it all the way; he cannot play it both ways, he cannot insist on acting in his personal capacity as king, and when he is in difficulty suddenly emerge in his public capacity as crown. This is the fundamental aspect of all constitutional crises of the next two hundred years. Kings try to manage with household government, but they do not make it work; then in desperation they call upon landed society for assistance, at which point trouble ensues. (The tremendous trouble the seventeenth-century Stuarts got themselves into may be seen to represent, in a way, exactly this kind of constitutional problem.)

Henry fell into financial difficulties because he listened to the Pope. Rome's struggle with the German emperor had thrown the Pope into a panic. In the 1250's, terrified of being caught in a pincers movement, he was looking for a way to evict the German imperial family from southern Italy. The Pope's idea was to put Sicily on the block; whoever paid would presumably drive the Germans out in order to take possession. Henry was weak-minded enough to get involved; he gave the Pope a huge down payment, but when he failed to keep up with the installments, the Pope sold Sicily to France. Now Henry had neither money nor territory, and he had to turn to the barons. Once again he had been outsmarted by his brother-in-law, Louis IX. Louis was always one step ahead of Henry—in sanctity, in politics, even in war; he defeated Henry in battle in a pointless war that lasted a few weeks. Thus Henry lost Sicily, lost some of his land in France and, when he turned to the barons for help, he virtually lost his throne.

Under the leadership of Simon de Montfort, the barons insist that if the king wants money, what they want is reform, and the royal government was in effect put into commission. In accordance with the baronial reform plan, set down in the Provisions of Oxford of 1258, a committee of barons "on behalf of the whole community of the land" takes over the operation of the royal administration. Their prime aims are to make sure that law and taxation function, in their interest, and to prevent the king from using household officials as his personal agencies, free from scrutiny by the Great Council. All tax receipts, the Provisions of Oxford decree, shall come to exchequer "and not elsewhere."

The thirteenth-century aristocracy, with its grandiose self-esteem, has for the moment attained the fulfillment of its highest ambition—control over the resources of the crown. But the baronial party's hold on power is a tenuous one. First of all, there is rumbling from below. The upper stratum of the gentry is deeply suspicious of the baronial reform plan; it suspects law and administration will now serve the aristocracy, and perhaps be even less concerned with the welfare of the "knights" than were Henry III and his French relatives. And in what does the gentry's well-being consist? In legal protection of their landholding. They want assurances that Magna Carta's application of the due process of the common law to seisin will be specifically applied to them. In the Provisions of Westminster of 1259 the baronial party gives the gentry this assurance: "Without the king's writ, no one may henceforth distrain his free tenants to respond concerning their free tenements." The knights are satisfied; they can now rest assured that baronial government will not subvert their land tenures.

But the king could not be satisfied; he was restless and unhappy. The Pope and St. Louis told Henry that this was no way for a king to run his government and his other French relatives complained, too. In 1264 Henry went to war against Earl Simon and the baronial party and was beaten at the Battle of Lewes. The only reason the king survived at all was that the great earls fell to quarreling at their moment of triumph and many of the other barons drifted away from Westminster during the hunting season. Simon's hasty summoning of representatives of the knights and burgesses to a "parliamentum" could not counterbalance the effect of this disintegration of the baronial reforming group. Henry's able son Edward escaped from captivity, raised an army, and defeated and killed Simon de Montfort. Henry was declared in possession of royal power "without the impediment or contradition of anyone." Those barons and gentry who did not agree were declared disinherited—dispossessed of their property and status. A few hotheads did refuse to accept the reassertion of royal authority and took to the woods as outlaws, perhaps to be memorialized as Robin Hood and his Merry Men in popular legend.

Henry had regained control over the royal government, but there was no hiding the fact that his reign had been one disaster after another. But Edward I had learned one thing from it—to be tough and sneaky, to move fast, faster than the barons could follow, to play one group against another. Edward's entire reign was one great shell game. Until recently he has had a very good press, his reputation has been on a level with Henry II and William the Conqueror. In a sense Edward was a national king; when he went to war against France, he made strenuous efforts to advertise himself as the protector of the national welfare against Gallic malevolence. Although Edward proclaimed this role in Latin and French, he clearly did have some sense of the distinctive identity of the English people. Edward liked to think of himself as the leader of the whole national community—not only the lay and ecclesiastical barons, but also the knights of the shire, the bourgeoisie, even the lower clergy. He was indifferent to what remained of the old feudal system of land tenures, and in his statute of *Quia emptores*, he prohibited further subinfeudation, thereby accelerating the complex social and legal process that was bringing all landed society directly under the jurisdiction of the crown. Edward was intelligent, and he had glamour and stature. He had a great reputation as a crusader, and he began his reign in an aura of holiness and heroism. It was this aura that allowed Edward early in his reign to carry out a systematic inquest into the privileges and franchises of lords and towns, in which the royal investigators demanded to know by what warrant (*quo warranto*) barons or urban corporations exercised these powers. Of course, in many instances the royal warrant could not be produced, either because the charter had been lost or because the franchise was an illegal usurpation. The royal officials had a wonderful time either cutting down on baronial and urban franchises or eliciting substantial payments for new charters from the king.

For twenty years the king managed to maintain the glamour. Edward never thought about institutions, or precedents nor—until the last few years of his life when he saw that his son was incompetent—did he worry about what would happen after him. He played a grand game—for land, power, wealth, military repute; he cared about these things, but not at all about how he got them. What he did with Parliament was bound to establish a precedent; it inevitably turned an occasion into an institution, it created problems for his successors. Edward made Parliament so important that after him no king could rule without it. He also made concessions to the magnates when he had to in order to keep his game going, and again he did not worry about the consequences. He approved a vast reorganization of the land law—a change that suited the interests of the great barons, but he never reflected about its implications. Edward had a buoyant, energetic, optimistic temper, and he overstepped himself. It seemed that he could do anything—conquer Wales, invade Scotland—he thought he could take on the king of France as well. He should have worried about this plan; it took him in over his head and it cost him more money than he could afford to lose.

In the last years of his reign, government was in deep trouble, it had to resort to dangerous expedients for raising money—often to reckless, improvident schemes. The expulsion of the Jews from England in the 1290's was, in the middle run, silly; though the crown seized all their property at once, though for the moment Edward must have felt rich, he had killed the goose to get the egg. By 1303 Edward was so desperate for money that he stooped to calling together the wool merchants at York to grant him an increased customs tax. After demeaning himself, he did not even get the tax—by this time even the merchants knew that taxation had to come through Parliament, not individual communities.

In spite of his self-confidence and his many talents, Edward was not a good administrator; we can see that the problems that plagued government in the next 150 years were already there in his reign. Judges were corruptible, juries were bribed, the aristocracy dominated the assize courts, and to get justice in the courts a man needed a lord to maintain him. (Later this kind of "maintenance" will give rise to all sorts of evils, and it will become a sinister word.) Edward was careless, he let things get sloppy and run down. He had great force of character and dash, but he did not pay attention. The growth of household government was the nemesis of efficient administration; it provided unlimited opportunities for the king's servants to line their pockets (even bishops were doing it, and it was not very hard amid all the confusion), and the money trickled away. All these things will be very characteristic in the next century and a half, but they are already there during Edward's reign. Administration is not precise, accounting breaks down, corruption is the norm, and the common law is notorious for its injustice—this was Edward's legacy, along with Parliament, though Edward would have been surprised to learn this startling fact.

III. Parliament, the Common Law, and the Debate on the Nature of the Constitution

I T IS HARD TO ACCOUNT for the lengthy and fierce historiographical debate on the origins of Parliament—the documents we have seem too scanty and insufficiently obscure to support so many weighty arguments. According to the documents, the problem has no right to be so complicated. For the thirteenth century these consist almost exclusively of parliamentary writs. Historians have had to raise all their theories on the writs of summons which, though inadequate, are all we have to work with. Not until 1376 do we get a detailed but unofficial account of a debate in Parliament—we will not have a full official record until the nineteenth century.

The first important discussion of the history of medieval parliaments took place late in the sixteenth and in the early part of the seventeenth century when the claims that members of the House of Commons had always enjoyed certain privileges sent scholars scurrying to search for records. The debate on privileges continued for centuries; the raising of the issue in the reign of Elizabeth I had the salutary scholarly effect of saving the thirteenth-century writs from being eaten by rats in the Tower of London. In the 1820's a committee of the House of Lords undertook a detailed study to answer the question, "What is a peer?" and produced some very good scholarly work. Then came Stubbs, whose work on Parliament has been likened to the Book of Genesis in that it describes an act of creation that is no longer believed. Stubbs saw the Parliament of 1295 as a full-fledged national assembly; he believed it was a consequence of the rise of the middle class—that Victorian, but scarcely thirteenth-century, phenomenon. The new importance of knights and burgesses dictated their integration into what we now know as the power structure. For Stubbs the three estates of the realm existed right at the beginning—he could see them clearly in Simon de Montfort's summons of knights and burgesses in 1264 and 1265. Thirteenth-century Parliament was a national assembly of estates of the realm, in which the presence of the third estate was a reflection of their new national importance. Parliament, says Stubbs, was summoned primarily to assent to taxation and legislation. It is easy to criticize Stubbs, but in his massive, heavy-footed overstatements lies a great deal of truth.

Stubbs had worked entirely from writs. In his introduction to an edition of a newly discovered 1305 Parliament roll (published in 1893), Maitland gently but surely undermined Stubbs's sweeping interpretation. Maitland found that something called "Parliament" met before the knights and burgesses arrived and after they had gone as well: the commons did not appear to be a fundamental or necessary element of a "parliamentum." And he found that the 1305 Parliament was not asked to consent to any taxation—at this assembly it is hard to find a shadow of the economic influence of the middle class that so impressed Stubbs. The chief business of the knights and burgesses was, it seemed, to present petitions; assent to taxation or legislation was not the reason for their presence. They came to complain about corrupt juries and incompetent sheriffs, to request new bridges, to ask for all sorts of favors—but not to assert themselves as representatives of a new and powerful class. They are at Westminster primarily to ask the king to do something for them. Thus Maitland concludes that Parliament was simply a different name for the *curia regis*, that its key members—the men who make it go—are the same men who were important in the old *curia regis*: the king, the chancellor, the great lords. The knights and burgesses appear only as petitioners before the king's court; Parliament is fundamentally the old *curia regis*. The view of Parliament that Maitland propounded neatly coincides with a definition set down by Fleta, a legal writer in the early fourteenth century: "The king has his court in his council in his parliaments, there being present his prelates, earls, barons, magnates, and other skilled men, and there are terminated doubts concerning judgements, and new remedies are devised for new wrongs that have arisen, and justice is done to each one according to his deserts."

Maitland's interpretation, a marked departure from Victorian Whiggery, was, as usual, brilliantly set forth. The court theory was quickly taken up by C. H. McIlwain in *The High Court of Parliament*, published in 1910. He picked up where Maitland left off, and put forward the thesis that until the seventeenth century Parliament must be considered mainly in terms of its legal functions; that until then it was essentially a high court of judicature. Thus there were, by the early twentieth century, two divergent lines of thought on the problem: the Stubbsian vision of a legislative assembly and the Maitland theory, worked out in detail by McIlwain, that Parliament was a high court. In the 1930's and 40's, G. O. Sayles and H. G. Richardson further supported Maitland's interpretation in several highly learned and polemical studies.

But the 1930's also marked the appearance of a kind of neo-Stubbsian interpretation that maintains the bishop was basically right, but does concede that his work needs to be modified. Though the essential function of Parliament may have been to legislate, the knights and burgesses were petitioners too. J. G. Edwards, director of the Institute for Historical Research, pointed out (in a brilliant article published in 1938) that completely to embrace the high court theory is to overlook some important things in the writs, particularly one critical phrase that instructs the sheriff to summon two knights from every shire with full power (*plena potestas*) to represent their communities. Why should the knights have full powers of attorney unless they are supposed to assent to binding legislation? The king did not want them to come with full powers merely to hand in their petitions—it must be that he wanted them to consent, in his presence, to new taxes and to statutes. He needed to avoid the chance of any subsequent claims, when taxes were actually being collected, that the representatives had overstepped their authority. The knights were invested with full authority to speak for the county so that whatever they assented to would be law.

Another theory, one that seems very obvious now, says that Parliament functioned as a propaganda and information agency of the crown. This was put forth rather casually around the time of World War I by Georges Lefebvre, who later went on to become the great historian of the French Revolution. Lefebvre happened to be research assistant to Charles Petit-Dutaillis, who was in the midst of revising Stubbs. Although he had only looked at a few writs, it seemed quite clear to Lefebvre that the king's main purpose in summoning Parliament was to tell the country what he wanted to do, and that once everyone was assembled, taxes might as well be levied with consent. If the king wanted to go to war, or change the law, the knights and burgesses had to be informed sooner or later. Of course he could send out writs, but it was surer and more convenient to bring everyone together. Since the reign of William the Conqueror dissemination of information had always been one of the main functions of the *curia regis*. The king's council was always the hub of the communications network. Now, however, when the feudal hierarchy was no longer powerful enough to serve as a communications medium, the meeting of the magnates alone could be relied upon no longer. The king had to communicate directly with the gentry, now the real administrators of his realm—they are the men who have to know what the king is doing. Thus Parliament merely continued—in an extended and modified fashion—the old information and communications activities of the *curia regis*. More recently the Lefebvre thesis has been revived by J. R. Strayer of Princeton, and it is a very plausible and convincing idea. Of all the theories, this is probably the one that most closely approaches the way Edward's government actually thought about Parliament. It was a convenient way to announce policy. Edward never worried much about obtaining consent and approval for his policy decisions, if he could get away with it. His real concern was that everyone who mattered knew what the royal policy was and expedited it. As in many other constitutional developments in English history, expediency played a more direct role than theory in the origins and growth of Parliament.

A subsidiary theme in the prolix parliamentary controversy is the debate over the origins of representation. It is strange that this aspect should be secondary, since the evidence allows much more scope for genuine controversy and legitimate argument. Stubbs was the great proponent of the common law origin of representation. As early as the reign of Henry II, he said, representatives of one county were carrying legal records to judges in other counties, or even to Westminster. The sheriff chose two men to represent the county "to bring up the record" of the shire court in legal procedures; from this, it was no great leap for the sheriff to choose men to represent the county in political procedures. At this point the high court thesis can fruitfully be integrated with Stubbs's idea—there was little difference between representing the county before the king's bench or before the high court of Parliament. It is a logical transition, only a matter of degree, and it was an easy and natural development. Stubbs's theory has most recently been supported by Bertie Wilkinson, who traces it even further back—to the feudal idea of representation. The great barons had always spoken for their tenants—even in the eleventh century. But social change had made this particular variety of representation obsolete and ineffective. The rise of self-consciousness among the gentry and the wealth of the burgesses had vitiated aristocratic authority. The magnates could no longer speak for all the king's subjects, and the royal government, responding to this new social situation, summoned representatives from the new communities. There is something appealing in this idea, though it is rather tenuous.

There are also two quite radical themes that try to account for the development of the representative principle. One was put forward before World War I by Ernest Barker, who later gained great distinction as a political theorist. The idea of representation, he said, finds its genesis in the habits of the Dominican order which practiced representative government on a grand scale. Aware that they were the shock troops of the church, they rationally set out to draw upon all the talent they could muster, and once every year the friars sent representatives from all over Europe to an international meeting of the Dominican chapter general. If we had any satisfactory evidence of Dominican influence in thirteenth-century England we would have to take Barker's theory very seriously, but it happens that the Franciscans, not the Dominicans, were the important order of friars in England. In the 1260's astute Franciscans were serving as baronial advisors, and they particularly influenced the baronial leader Simon de Montfort. The Franciscans propagated many new ideas, but representation, which they did not practice, was not one of them. Barker's thesis, though readily disproved, did stimulate people to think about the origins of representation within the context of religious thought and intellectual life and to look more closely at the spread of Roman law ideas. Roman law as well as canon law clearly expressed the concept of attorneyship, and men like Bracton were very learned in both. Gaines Post at Princeton believes that this idea was assimilated by crown lawyers who, when they instructed the sheriffs to send representatives to Parliament, were simply propagating what they had learned from Roman law. It does seem possible that the Roman idea of attorneyship, coming to England through the clerical servants of the king, may have reinforced the practice of representation and sharpened its focus. But the most important breeding ground of English representation was the common law, and perhaps to some extent, the feudal hierarchy.

We can say that Parliament was a high court, an extension of the *curia regis*, but then we must also say that certain meetings of the *curia regis* were occasions for obtaining consent to taxation and legislation. A convenient opportunity was grasped—it was practical to bring the urban and rural representatives here, to consent as well as to present petitions. An old institution was infused with new life; no longer was it sufficient to secure the consent of the magnates alone. They could no longer speak with certainty for what was now the most important group in rural society, nor were they any longer responsible for carrying out royal policy at the county court. If we look closely we can see in these embryonic parliaments the overlapping of old and new functions. And we can see how pragmatic these meetings were, to what degree they were prompted by expediency. Parliament was not inevitable. Until 1300 taxation and legislation could have been accomplished by other methods.

In 1207 the consent of the magnates at the *curia regis* had sanctioned a thirteenth on income and movable property. It is no coincidence that the period of the emergence of Parliament is also the era of the rise of a new system of national taxation for which this tax in 1207 was the precedent. Parliamentary consent became the legal sanction for national taxation and in its pristine form of a gracious aid taken with consent of the magnates, the essence of parliamentary taxation already existed in 1207. The basic procedure was there—only the knights and burgesses had to be added in order to make it complete. The first move came in 1213 with the Oxfordshire assembly of knights summoned by the king. By then the king was already conscious of the importance of the gentry. John knew very well that a feudal rebellion was brewing and he hoped that by talking things over with the knights he might secure their support. But nothing came of this, and in the 1230's and 1240's gracious aid was obtained by Henry III with the consent of the magnates only. Then, in 1254, we are confronted with a cryptic, difficult document. While the king is in France, the regency, which has many vexing and urgent problems to cope with, calls together an odd sort of assembly that does include representatives of the shires as well as magnates. The legal and technical nature of this meeting is obscure, but the idea of county representation was clearly active in 1254. In 1264-65 we get the famous Oxford parliamentum of Simon de Montfort. The crown is in commission and the baronial government, desperately in need of money, calls a special meeting of the king's council to which both knights and burgesses are summoned. The barons are a revolutionary party acting against the crown, they want to implement great reforms. They must have money, but the lines of the feudal hierarchy are too weak to provide it. The new, insecure, barely legitimate government cannot count on the automatic support of the knights and burgesses—it must have their overt consent.

And Edward I, who was a very pragmatic man, took over this ready-made procedure. He used it in 1275 when he wanted to introduce a new national customs tax. The "great custom" was levied with the consent of the magnates, knights, and burgesses. After this the government began to worry; they realized that it was not necessary to bring the knights and burgesses together; it might instill a feeling of solidarity and identity among the various communities of the realm. This could be troublesome; it was clearly in the government's interest to keep them divided. Edward knew that the French king obtained consent through several separate meetings, that he avoided the dangerous practice of bringing everyone together. In the early 1280's and 1290's the English government tried similar methods. Hence 1282 saw the peculiar scheme called Kirkby's Quest—a royal official named Kirkby rode through all the shires getting consent from each community individually, but this took a ridiculously long time. Other plans were tried; separate meetings of magnates, knights and burgesses were introduced, as was the practice in France. But it was more expedient for the English crown to obtain consent from everyone at once. Any other procedure was painfully slow and cumbersome, and Edward was a greedy and impatient man. Thus after a hiatus of several years, Edward in 1295 went back to the comprehensive assembly; he even brought in representatives from the lower clergy (who after 1330 were to meet in a separate convocation).

The evolution of Parliament in Edward's reign is very clear. At the beginning taxation was imposed with consent in a full Parliament. Then Edward backed away. It was obvious that this kind of meeting was a potential hazard. But once Parliament had been used, he found all other methods of taxation inconvenient and unwieldly, so he went back to using the *curia regis* in its new function of national assembly. In his last years Edward became exceedingly wary; he began really to worry about the possibility that the crown would be forced to depend on this new procedure. So he again searched for other expedients. But it was too late; Parliament had been established, the precedent had been fixed. When in 1297 Edward tried to collect a tax to which the magnates had not consented, the barons indignantly claimed they were being "tallaged"— arbitrarily taxed like mean serfs on the royal demesne—and they made Edward confirm Magna Carta and the principle of due process and promise not to levy a tax without consent of the community of the realm. Edward's son and grandson would become even more dependent on this new institution of Parliament.

With the reign of Edward I, Maitland brought his great book to a close. By this time, he believed, the common law had assumed its definitive shape and form; by the end of the thirteenth century the lasting structure of courts and procedure had been evolved and fixed. Also, from the 1290's onward, the legal sources are so voluminous that just to absorb and digest them would require a whole lifetime. Only in outline, then, can we apprehend the subsequent history of English law.

The common law existed as a distinct legal system by the end of John's reign. Though it drew upon Germanic, Roman and feudal law, the English common law is not specifically any of these things. It is, rather, the royal law, it runs in the royal courts, the king administers it. It is whatever his justices have worked out. In many ways the common law is imperfectly defined, it is not codified; what the law is at any given time depends to a considerable degree on the judges and attorneys who operate it. The common law is a peculiar amalgam of three distinct kinds of legal systems—but these basic elements have been reshaped and transmuted. It is, however, possible, and useful too (so long as we recognize the special overriding royal character of the common law) to analyze it by examining what it borrowed and preserved from its diverse sources.

The common law perpetuated the Germanic conception of legislation, a negative idea expressed in a reluctance to accept the idea of positive legislation. In the thirteenth century men still believe they are declaring the law; they claim they are merely clarifying it. The tenacious idea that the law, a kind of omnipresent, fundamental substance, needs only to be declared and defined, dies very hard in England. (Its ghost still haunts the eighteenth century.) Some historians—T. F. T. Plucknett, for example—insist that a firm and viable idea of legislation existed by the end of Edward's reign, but this is a fragile and unsupported thesis. Not until the seventeenth century is the idea that legislation is the manufacturing of new law clearly formulated and grasped. This aversion to positive legislation is part of the vestigial notion that law resides in the community and that only with the consent of the community can it be declared and confirmed. There was universal agreement on this point; the only significant question in the thirteenth century was who constituted the community, who shall speak for it? Was it to be the king and his judges and the magnates? Did it also include the communities of the shire, and the boroughs? This was the single most important question—and it was not resolved; men did not think it out clearly. A royal justice at the end of Edward's reign did not for a moment believe that legislation had to take place with the consent of the barons and the shires in a parliamentum— this would be a shocking concept. Some legislation, a very great deal in fact, was accomplished without any representation from the shires. Toward the end of the reign, however, we can see a certain sensitivity on this point, and by the mid-fourteenth century it is commonly acknowledged that the best, the most legal and the least controversial—if not the only way—is through Parliament. Even in the sixteenth century men were not absolutely sure what legislation was, nor were they at all certain that the voice of the community necessarily spoke in Parliament. From the time of Edward I through the middle of the fourteenth century, however, it came to be understood that the nature of parliamentary statute was of the *highest* legality. Law placed on the statute roll was, in any controversy, the last and decisive word. Statue was the most binding kind of legal statement—it could not be a matter of dispute.

Through the royal justices of the twelfth and thirteenth centuries—clerics trained in Roman and canon law—the common law absorbed ideas borrowed from Roman law. After Edward's reign the clerical lawyers disappear; from then on the legal system is controlled by lay lawyers trained at the Inns of Court, and the qualified reception of Roman law ceases until the late fifteenth and sixteenth centuries. But, while the common law was being molded, Roman law ideas were current and influential. Civil law training inculcated a belief that the purpose of law is to obtain justice, that law aims to establish right in the kingdom. In the thirteenth century royal judges have strong feelings on this score, and in the late fifteenth century a concern for justice will stimulate the establishment of new kinds of courts. The conciliar courts of chancery and Star Chamber were then established to provide justice that was unobtainable through the common law courts.

The common law also borrowed from the Roman code its very clear distinction between civil and criminal law. It should not really have been a difficult distinction to make, but in early Germanic law the point was confused and obscure. Eventually people would have stumbled upon it —everyone did know that a criminal case was one you hung for—but Roman law did encourage them to build the distinction into the English system. The third idea taken from Roman law was the concept that the king has both a natural (personal) and a political (public) body, that the monarchy is a corporation. This idea also emerged from general legal-political developments of the late eleventh and twelfth centuries, but the strong corporate and communal sense that informs Roman law helped the judges to conceptualize it. And in the thirteenth century they did; the judges were able to perceive the monarchy as a crown corporation. The permanent influence of Roman law is a vexed question in English legal history and there has been much controversy about the extent of its "reception." We can say that although Roman law did not directly form any part of the common law, it did guide it along certain lines. An awareness of Roman law ideas sharpened the conceptual focus of the common law; thus a theoretical element was introduced that was entirely absent in Germanic law.

The feudal sources of the common law may be seen in their most undiluted form in the law of real property, which grew directly out of feudal laws concerning vassalage and inheritance. During the thirteenth century the feudal bonds of society lose their power (although the aristocracy retained its wealth and influence) and feudal ideas were revised and rearranged in accordance with the new social situation. Many aspects of feudal law were submerged, but the ideas of property survived and became the basis of English land law that was worked out in the thirteenth and fourteenth centuries. The law of property is fundamental to English political thinking; certain aspects of it, especially the concept of due process, impinge on general constitutional ideas in the most critical way. Maitland has remarked, provocatively, that the whole of English constitutional history is an appendix to the land laws.

Three elements—Germanic, Roman, and feudal law—are constituents of the common law which is, though, something more than any of them. The judges made of these elements a different blend; they revised and reshaped them to create a system that does not exactly resemble any of its components. The common law worked out its own peculiar processes and procedure in the courts. By the first decade of the thirteenth century these achievements are clearly evident. And they are lasting—we can still see them as fundamental to Anglo-American law.

The great changes of the thirteenth century were in criminal law procedure. On the whole, what happens in thirteenth-century civil law is evolutionary; we observe variety and complexity, most significantly in the development and frequent use of legal fictions, which allow more and new kinds of cases to come to court. Once in court the subject of the plea can be changed—this becomes extremely important in the land law. But this was a natural and predictable development out of what had already been established. What happened to criminal procedure during the thirteenth century was nothing less than a judicial revolution. In the thirteenth and fourteenth centuries, criminal pleas could be initiated in two ways: by appeal, a perpetuation of the Germanic process of personal accusation (X accuses Y of felony before the court), or by jury of presentment—the grand jury. Here the process is accusation by the community of the shire, through its representatives, before the king's justices. Gradually the appeal was absorbed by the indictment. All appeals were made subject to review and authorization by the grand jury—the shift probably took place in John's reign. The judges ask the grand jury to certify that a personal appeal has not been made simply out of spite or hatred; if the jury finds evidence of *odio et atia* the plea is stopped and the vindictive appellor is amerced. Only when the grand jury has decided a plea is plausible can they move on to consider the nature of proof.

In 1215 the church forbade clerical participation in the ordeal, thus making it impossible to continue the practice. Maitland has written a brilliant account of the next six or seven decades during which the English judges sought a method of proof to replace the ordeal. The instability of Henry III's reign meant that they were able to experiment—they were forced to rely on their own judgment and imagination. It is interesting to speculate on what might have happened if a king like Henry II had been on the throne—probably more Roman law procedures would have been introduced consciously. But without guidance or instruction, the judges went on with the grand jury. It already provided a viable method of indictment; now, as they searched for a method of proof, they kept it in mind and eventually they worked directly with it. At first, however, they tried to improve the other method they were familiar with —compurgation. They resurrected a tenth-century procedure, something called a "suit of witnesses"—really a panel of blue-ribbon compurgators whose testimony the court could trust. Effective enough in obviating widespread perjury, this technique was also ridiculously inconvenient. It was no casual matter to bring suits of witnesses from all over the county; it overwhelmed the little market town where the assizes were held— there was simply no room, not enough organization. Furthermore, the judges had to rely on the judgment of these blue-ribbon witnesses, respectable men of substance who were simply not cognizant of most of the cases they were asked about. The men who did know were bound to be the same unreliables who had made compurgation a system of legal perjury. So the attempt to work with one handy and familiar principle broke down and the judges were driven to the only other system they knew. Thus a jury was asked to bring in a verdict just as another jury had made an indictment. The judges got to this very haphazardly, and only after they had stumbled—sometimes in a simple-minded fashion—along a path of pragmatic experimentation.

At first the royal justices were not very confident about relying on the verdicts of men against God's word and, though Henry II's judges had been disillusioned and disgusted with the ordeal, Henry II's bench hesitated to give up the idea of compurgation. The first jury of verdict consisted of forty-eight men—twelve from each of the four points of the compass. But it was not very practical to summon forty-eight men to the county seat. Many of them are bound not to appear, and the royal judges are not patient men. Perhaps by the 1250's and 1260's—certainly by the 1270's—they have devised the petty jury: twelve men who decide the truth of an accusation made by the grand jury. This new procedure was astonishingly efficient. We have to assume that unless a defendant could take exception to his indictment by making a special plea, the proportion of petty jury convictions was extremely high. Both juries were selected from the same neighborhood people, and the grand jury indictment was usually decisive. This suits the judges. Even though the Roman law principles they are always enunciating tell them they should be seeking justice, they are mainly eager to settle cases, to seize the chattels of felons for the crown and move on to the next county. Royal justices did not lie awake at night wondering if justice was being done. They were not men known for their tender consciences. In the twelfth century they had relied on the voice of the community to a great extent—in the thirteenth century they took it all the way. There is nothing a royal judge likes less than a hung jury, nothing could be calculated to annoy him more effectively. In common law procedure a hung jury was a very bad thing, a waste of time. It meant that the case had to be carried over, and this involved a whole other set of problems. The defendant himself was the biggest. Jail breaks seem to have been an everyday occurrence in medieval England; obviously there was nothing hard about it. So the judges were pleased to get quick convictions—and their attitude encouraged the juries. They knew it was not good for their community if the royal judges were irritated. The royal justices could always make life complicated and expensive; a peevish judge was likely to bring up some archaic and embarrassing technicality—presentment of Englishry was a great favorite.

There was also a serious problem of defense in the common law. The defendant had, first of all, to agree to abide by the judgment of the petty jury—to put himself on the country. Here was a new procedure, a risky, untried method, and the defendant had the option of deciding whether he would submit to it. He knew, as everyone else did, that ninety-nine times out of a hundred the jury of verdict would not find contrary to the jury of presentment. No wonder defendants were not eagerly clamoring to come before the jury of verdict—trial by jury had not quite become a sacred constitutional right. But a defendant who refused to "put himself on the country" was a nuisance. If he could not be prevailed upon by sweet reason, he was subjected to *peine forte et dure*, a charming method of persuasion. Weights would be piled on top of his chest until he accepted jury trial or died. It was an infallible procedure. If he put himself on the country he was hanged—but he did have the privilege of choice. By the end of the thirteenth century the defendant is no longer asked his choice—he is automatically put on the country. In the course of eight or nine decades the judges bring about the greatest single change (in the method of proof, at any rate) that has ever taken place in English legal history. Thus the jury of verdict came to be a definitive part of common law procedure.

Another change in legal procedure appears in the second half of the thirteenth century, certainly by the reign of Edward I. This is the abandonment of the general eyre. The commission lists of 1194 tell us that the Angevin government ordered the itinerant justices to deal with everything concerning the crown—political and administrative matters as well as judicial cases. This interference was bitterly resented by landed society; royal judicial procedures were necessary to their way of life, but alert and continual investigation by judges into crown rights, into taxation, was more than they had bargained for. This sort of prying was objectionable, and was the source of much knightly dissatisfaction. The gentry were to some extent justified here. The judges were very busy men, they were overburdened with tasks, they were tough, and their decisions tended to be swift and arbitrary. Royal judges were never chosen for their kind and sympathetic temperaments, and even with more leisure and less pressure, they would not have coddled or appeased the gentry. The judges were not interested in subtleties or mitigating circumstances; they meant to secure for the king exactly as much as he could legally get, to see that no inch of property that might escheat to the crown remained in other hands. They were eager to discover and report to the king whatever might call for investigation. And though the gentry liked to bring their own cases into the royal court, they felt that the general eyre was not good for due process. Therefore in Edward's reign the judges are no longer given commissions of general eyre—they receive instead specific, restricted legal commissions. This may have had something to do with the fourteenth-century decline in the wealth and authority of the crown. Without constant and rigorous scrutiny the monarchy will lose fees and income; all kinds of revenue—taxes in particular—will slip through the royal fingers. But now administrative inquests can only be conducted on an *ad hoc* basis, and these irregular procedures demand more energy and ingenuity than fourteenth-century administrators could summon.

Pressure from landed society around 1300 was thus able to confine the commissions of itinerant judges to special judicial matters. Some of them are still used. There were three kinds of legal commissions. The first was to hear criminal pleas—the commission of jail delivery. This means exactly what it says—empty out the jails; do something about everyone found in jail; prisoners must not be allowed to languish in jail. This commendable urgency was not, however, prompted by feelings of humanity or justice—it was virtually impossible to keep prisoners in jail. To clean out the jails and send the prisoners either to freedom or to the gallows was an imperative of crown policy. The second commission, *nisi prius,* dealt with civil suits. At *nisi prius* all writs had to be returned, unless they had previously been dealt with; this is the commission to decide all pending civil cases. The third commission was called *oyer and terminer,* a phrase taken from legal French, a peculiar jargon that lingered on in England for an amazingly long time. This bastard language is often nothing but mumbo jumbo and always very hard to decipher. Perhaps this is one reason why legal history is so full of blank spots and murky patches. Oyer and terminer means to "hear and determine" all pleas of the crown—anything not covered under jail delivery or *nisi prius.* (In England the clerk of the court still opens the session by announcing oyer and terminer.)

Another thirteenth-century development was the growth and settlement of the central court system. King's Bench, common pleas, exchequer and—the highest court of all, Parliament—became more defined in their functions and, at the same time, much busier. Though no historian has worked this out in any detail, it is clear that toward the end of the thirteenth century more and more civil cases involving substantial amounts of property are falling into the central courts. Civil cases that dealt with more than modest sums will now come immediately within the purview of the central courts. These are often difficult suits; they involve legal complexities, provoke long, elaborate trials and demand skill and reflection on the part of the judges. It is only natural that they should come before a panel of judges at Westminster. In the reign of Edward I, the central judiciary also became more active in criminal pleas. King's bench could now exercise original jurisdiction over any case that involved breach of peace; it also served as the central court that could review, on a claim of erroneous judgment, any decision in the county courts.

From this tendency toward judicial centralization it was not hard to get to the idea that the way to obtain improvements in government and society was to make a parliamentary statute. Constant resort to statute was a favorite fourteenth-century way to solve all sorts of problems. Statutes were passed to build bridges, and statutes declared there should be no obstacles to navigation on the river Severn. This one appears about six times in the fourteenth century and demonstrates a rather touching belief in the efficacy of statute. There was a naïve faith in the magical properties of statute; men apparently were convinced that by saying something was law they made it so. Thus fourteenth-century and early fifteenth-century Parliaments indulged in orgies of legislation. Later fifteenth-century governments saw the futility of this and a severe disenchantment with statute followed. At this point we get the shift back to conciliar government, where decrees and proclamations of the king's council supplant statutes. But meanwhile there had been a medieval period when parliamentary legislation was important, when many things were registered on the statute roll. And the leaders of the House of Commons who claimed in the seventeenth century that the king could not do anything important without parliamentary consent, could cite the fourteenth-century statute roll as proof that the constitution was always like that. This was not a completely accurate claim, but it was quite true that, in contrast to the Anglo-Norman period and the late fifteenth and early sixteenth centuries, there was a time when statute had flourished. Thus a precedent was established—a precedent so solid that even the Tudors paid obeisance to this early period of intense legislation. When they wanted to do something of tremendous consequence—when they wanted to change religion or deny the authority of the Pope—they did it by parliamentary legislation. It is not clear that they had to do it this way, but an act of Parliament was unquestionably valid. It was a way of stamping absolute legal confirmation on the king's religious policy. The fourteenth-century parliamentary legislation set a precedent as well as a consciousness that statute was the soundest law. By endowing statute with the highest legality, the way was paved for the seventeenth-century claim that the king could do nothing without it.

The decline of the clerical legal profession and the rise of the lay lawyer had an important impact on the course of the common law in the fourteenth and fifteenth centuries. Men trained at the Inns of Court were not prepared to undertake codification or rationalization of the law. Nor were they interested. As practicing attorneys they rather liked the confusion and complexity that was already endemic in the common law. It had a built-in bias in favor of the interests of the legal profession and the profession, which controlled every aspect of the law—every judge and attorney came from the Inns—was not eager for change. New law can be made by parliamentary statute, and existing law may be clarified by judicial decision. Where the law is silent, the judges can sift the precedents, they can stipulate what the law is on a specific and confused point. But there is no codification of English law. Because most of the legal profession were now ignorant of Roman law ideas of systematization, or else despised them, law could change only through parliamentary statute or judicial decision. In the reign of Edward I we are aware of a passion to collect judicial records. These are the precedents judges must use and cite in making their decisions. Even Bracton amasses precedents and tries to write down decisions made by himself and his colleagues on the bench. In 1292 the Inns of Court begin to publish Year Books—text book compilations of important cases and decisions—which will enable the judges to determine what the law actually is. We must not glamorize this practice or overestimate what is only a feeble effort at organization. There will be much confusion, clarification will come with agonizing slowness and for centuries much decision-making in law will fall upon the judiciary by default.

The first full-blown theoretical debate on the nature of the constitution and the nature of kingship takes place in the thirteenth century. There had been constitutional conflicts in 1215, but later in the thirteenth century, particularly during the reign of Henry III, men are able to articulate, for the first time, what they believe. "What should be the office of the king?": this was the problem as well as the title of the most interesting treatise of the early thirteenth century. Written by someone in London, most probably by a cleric, possibly—though less likely—by a burgess, it reveals a great uneasiness about kingship. The author's double vision of the king leads to tension and uncertainty; it gives the work its anguished tone. The king is exalted, he is God's representative on earth, the leader of the folk, he is every man's liege lord. But at the same time the writer is racked by a concern that the king should be responsible to something or somebody—the law, the community—however these might be defined. This ambiguity lies at the heart of the debate. Everyone wanted to exalt kingship; men sincerely believed that the king's dignity and honor were and ought to be of the very highest. But what did this mean in relation to the community? Can the king—the lord king—govern without consent, or is he responsible to the community for the law by which he rules? These anxious questions signify a great advance in the verbalization of political issues; this is really a debate over what the sixteenth century will call "the king's two bodies"—his natural and political body, his personal and public capacities. Men of perception in the thirteenth century apprehended this problem, it beset them and worried them. They do not express it so neatly, but they are painfully aware of it, and they agonize over it. It is a very hard problem indeed.

In the thirteenth century the king was the vicar of God—this was not just pious cant or simple-minded sentiment. Intelligent and sophisticated men believed it; it was a deeply rooted and widely held emotional response to kingship. There was no other way to think about the king. Even when a weak unimpressive king like Henry III puts on the crown he evokes tremendous feeling. People respond positively toward him. It is still very much a hierarchic world and the king himself is the embodiment of hierarchic principle and power of the mightiest kind. The king is the closest thing to God that men can see and know in the world, and they have a profound attachment to him. This makes the other side of the picture even more difficult—what should one do when the king acts badly or meanly? The duty of the king is to uphold the crown. This was how some thirteenth-century writers stated it, and here they hit upon the notion that there is a distinction between Henry Plantagenet and the crown. It was a common enough assumption. Most of the people who were part of the political nation thought this way; they had a lively sense of the fundamental distinction. The king should uphold all things in the kingdom, including "the law of the land." But this idea was still hazy and inchoate; it was not of any use in formulating institutional decisions. It was exactly this unresolved double vision that led to so much tension and ambiguity. Men hail the majesty of the king but they also expect him to support the law and rule with the consent of the magnates. Men assume that the king and the crown are inseparable, but when his two aspects did not fit together, when the magnates were forced to wrest the effective authority of the crown from the hands of the king, it must have been a great emotional wrench. Actually to fight against the king was a tremendous shock and disillusionment. Though some great barons were always ready to fight, most people were just lost and bewildered at the prospect.

Another important treatise in the debate is the "Song of Lewes," a poem of great power, written by a Franciscan friar who supported Simon de Montfort. Though it ultimately sets forth the political philosophy of the baronial party, the poem begins with an exposition of the king's

point of view about his own servants. If the barons can have their own
stewards, why cannot the king have his own ministers? Why should he be
less free in the choice of his government than his vassals are in the choice
of their servants? To restrict his authority in this sphere is to disparage
him and the dignity of kingship. "The command of the king has the
force of law"—here the Justinian Code is quoted. What, then, is the
answer? The poet bids the baronial party speak. They are not hostile to
the royal honor, they protest at first. All they want is to magnify the royal
estate. (This is the obligatory statement—all men have to say they stand
for Christ and the king. Like democracy and motherhood, today, these
are the passwords; men who fail to utter them mark themselves as extremists. They cannot participate in the debate.) "We give first place to
universitas," the barons say, to community. The magnates are the guardians of the law; they are the ones to protect the kingdom against the
king, the crown against the weak and foolish man Henry Plantagenet.
We are more royal than the king, they proclaim. The community has a
voice in the matters that concern it—and here the barons show they too
know how to cite Roman law maxims. "What touches all should be
approved by all," they say. The realm is not the king's personal property;
if he misuses and damages the realm, the community must take it away
from him.

The highest thing in the realm is not the king, but the law; indeed
"law rules the royal dignity, for law is light and rules the world." And
law is the divine word itself—is it not written in the gospel that "By me
kings reign"? The "Song" goes on to say that "No king shall change that
established law, but shall find strength in it for his changing self." The
truly exalted king, then, is the one who rules according to law. This is
heady stuff. Liberty is equated with the law alone, the law of the land
which somehow can cause the king to transcend himself, to fulfill his
royal office in a way that brings him closer to God. The most kingly king
is the one who rules according to law, and "Whoever is truly king is truly
free." This is a high and subtle idea that perhaps could only have been
conceived by a Franciscan. It was an ideal of government, in fact, that
few men in the thirteenth century could even have apprehended—certainly not the rather slow Henry III or his cool and tough-minded son,
Edward I.

In his treatise *Concerning the Laws and Customs of England,* the
learned and much venerated royal judge Bracton tries to cope with the
problem of the king's responsibility to the law. But he does not really suc-

ceed. By lifting passages out of context, Bracton can be made to sound like a nineteenth-century liberal, but most of the time he walks an uneasy line between the view that the king is responsible to God and the view that he is responsible to the community. Bracton himself cannot quite decide which is correct. Certainly the king should be under God and the law—*rex non debet esse sub homines sed sub Deo et lege* ("the king ought not to be under men but under God and the law") was the memorable way Bracton stated it. Seventeenth-century polemicists were particularly devoted to this succinct phrase and we will see it cited over and over in later debates. It is indeed a splendid statement. But a couple of lines later Bracton also says that "no writ runs against the King." If the king wrongs you there is no legal sanction against him—one can only petition for mercy and redress. The king must maintain law; where there is no law there can by no king. Where, then, is the sanction? Bracton has a hard time finding any, because no action in law can lie against the king. He returns to this later. "There is no remedy against him by assize"; the king cannot be sued for violation of the law. Now Bracton sounds like an exponent of the divine right of kings—the monarch must be approached on one's knees. If the king behaves wrongly or contrary to law, God will be the judge, men can only be supplicants. This is no different from the divine right notions of the sixteenth century. In his heart Bracton believes finally that the king is responsible only to God. In case he wrongs you, you must beg for his mercy; if he does not listen, you must weep and pray that God will see fit to remove him quickly. There is no other redress. Though this is what Bracton really believes, he also knows that many people do not agree with him, that they are convinced the community of the realm has the right and duty to maintain the royal estate against the king himself. When the king destroys law he is destroying his own dignity—this is their reasoning and their justification.

This was about as far as the medieval constitutional debate progressed. The thirteenth century left it hanging on an unresolved note, but with a growing concern about what should be done when the king fails to maintain the law. It was argued that the king should be made responsible, that men can rebel in order to preserve the crown against the king. What they lacked, however, was any institutional control; the theory existed; at times it was even formulated with force and clarity. But there was no way to implement it.

This institutional weakness is fully apparent in the last decade of Edward I's reign. By the 1290's the king's glamorous image has evaporated, and the barons are weary and disillusioned by war and heavy taxation. In 1297 they refuse to serve overseas in the war with France over Flanders and they draft a protest document, *De tallagium non concedendo*, claiming they have been "too much worn down" with excessive and illegal taxes. The literal translation of the title of their manifesto, which is put in the form of a petition to the king, reads "Tallage must not be conceded," but an accurate free translation would be "No tax without representation." The barons want the king to promise that "no tallage or aid be levied by us or our heirs in our realm, without good will and assent of the archbishops, bishops, earls, barons, knights, burgesses and other freemen of our realm"—in other words no taxation without Parliament as it had been constituted in 1295. This concession the king refuses to make; government belongs to him, not the community of the realm. He makes a formal recognition to maintain the law of the land by confirming Magna Carta, and promises merely that henceforth he will only tax "by the common assent of the whole kingdom," leaving undefined the institutional form of such assent. Furthermore, Edward makes this concession "saving the right of our crown," a phrase that a contemporary chronicler tells us the barons rightly found "ambiguous." In 1305 Edward obtained from the pliant papacy absolution of his vow to observe even these limited and ambiguous concessions.

In the 150 years after Edward's death in 1307 the issues central to the crisis of 1297 would be raised again and again, without any clear decision as to the precise relationship between crown and community, and in the seventeenth century the constitutional debate would be pursued once more, only this time at last to be argued, and fought, to a conclusion. In the seventeenth century re-enactment of the thirteenth-century constitutional debate, the conflict finally took the form of war against the king in order to maintain the authority of king-in-Parliament. The theory of government enunciated by the House of Commons when it took up arms against the king in 1642 was substantially the same as that enunciated by the baronial party in the thirteenth century. For four hundred years after Edward I's reign there would be no fundamental change in constitutional ideas. The debate would be concerned with practical implementation of the doctrine of the king's two bodies, his personal and public capacities, with the institutional forms the idea ought to take.

There is, after all, only one classic issue at the core of all English political history—who shall operate the law, whom does the law benefit? It is not surprising that the course of events in the seventeenth century should look like a replay of those of the thirteenth. In each era violence is long brewing, and the clash is finally evoked by the ineptitude of the king and the pressure of a financial crisis. Each series of events is conditioned by questions of involvement in the European power struggle, and in each case a king at the end of his financial rope is forced to summon the community of the realm. Once called, of course, those who believe they represent the community demand control of the king's government. They, in turn, find themselves pressed by other groups in society: in the seventeenth century by the lesser gentry and radical democrats; in the thirteenth by the upper gentry who want the law to serve their interests as well as the barons'.

The central issue in both eras is the law. The thirteenth-century conflicts are set firmly in the feudal context; those of the seventeenth relate to the common law, which is then at its fullest bloom. The cry of the gentry in the thirteenth century was that free tenement shall be protected; they demanded that all cases concerning freehold must proceed by writ. The slogan "liberty and property" was simply seventeenth-century language for the very same principle.

CHAPTER SIX

THE WANING OF
THE MEDIEVAL ORDER
from 1307 to 1471

I. *The Disintegration of Society and Government*

THE FOURTEENTH and fifteenth centuries are the *terra incognita* of English history. We know less about the course of political and social change during these centuries than for any other era of English history after 1066. Victorian historians—following the suggestion of sixteenth-century writers—viewed the years from the death of Edward I in 1307 to the accession of Henry VII Tudor in 1485 as one period, distinguished by the decline and, at times, virtual collapse of royal power in the face of a resurgent aristocracy. The consensus among scholars today is that the resurgence of royal power began not in 1485 but in 1471 when the Yorkist king Edward IV finally overcame the opposing Lancastrian faction and secured control of the central government. Beyond this small adjustment in periodization, historians have not fundamentally altered the Victorian evaluation of the significance of the fourteenth and fifteenth centuries in English history.

It can be said at the outset that the period from 1307 to 1471 is a confusing time, if only because we know very little about what happened. The source materials for the study of the period are voluminous and, to a great extent, still unpublished. There are literally thousands of terribly hard-to-read manuscripts that scholars shrink from studying. They have good reasons. The English government bureaus and the law courts of the late Middle Ages were understaffed; there simply were not enough secretaries, and the handwriting of the overworked scribes is frequently close to being undecipherable. The documents themselves are more often than not written in a kind of legal French (which does not merit the designation of any known language) that has no obvious logic or grammar; nor is there any guide or handbook to it. Scholars are not eager to plunge into all this. And even if all the documents were Xeroxed, the fourteenth and fifteenth centuries would still be unattractive. We cannot call them the height of the Middle Ages, nor are they the beginning of the modern world. Like legal French itself, this is a kind of bastard age. Certainly it has been an historical stepchild. Few historians are drawn to it—no one wishes he had been born then and, except for a few fanatical genealogists, its appeal is very limited. It is even hard to know, amid all the disorder and confusion, what is important and should be studied. And it is unsurprising that no attempt to sketch a general portrait of this disturbed period has been entirely satisfactory. One great handicap is the inadequacy, beginning late in the thirteenth century, of the chroniclers. They are fewer, less energetic, duller, less reliable and informative—a weakness that in itself signifies the general decline of the monastic orders. There are simply no contemporary narratives on which to build a coherent structure. The fifteenth century is even more arid than the fourteenth. There is only Froissart, and he seems to have inhabited his own special dream world, where Freudian analysis is perhaps more appropriate than anything else.

From William Stubbs to the most recent historians of late medieval England, those scholars who try to give us a general view of the period have encountered insuperable difficulty in bringing the fourteenth and fifteenth centuries into clear focus. Nearly all seem to be overwhelmed and numbed by the complexity of events and vastness of the material. It even seems to be impossible to straighten out the incredibly involved genealogy of the contending Lancastrian and Yorkist royal houses. The third volume of Stubbs's *Constitutional History*, which deals with the period from 1307 to 1485, is in many ways a remarkable study, still very much worth reading, but it is the least appreciated part of his work. Stubbs found the kings of the period incompetent and the contending aristocratic factions viciously shortsighted. During these two centuries he sees England suffocating in a cloud of gloom and doom. But in his indomitably optimistic teleological manner, he can still discern institutional progress in the midst of personal failure and social disaster. Parliament—and in particular the House of Commons—became so centrally fixed in the process of government and law that even the despotically inclined Tudors could not do without it. Furthermore, Stubbs perceived a proto-modern constitutionalism under the Lancastrian monarchy of the fifteenth century—an ill-defined but nevertheless real sense of the need of royal government to be responsible to Parliament. Twentieth-century scholars like J. E. Neale have had a fine time attacking Stubbs for his anachronistic interpretation, while ignoring the caution with which the great bishop put forward his view of the Lancastrian constitution. Also, the deeper we look into late medieval thought, the less prepared are we to say that an idea of the sovereignty of Parliament was necessarily beyond the world view of fourteenth- and fifteenth-century men. Although Stubbs's delineation of the proto-constitutionalism of the late middle ages was strongly inspired by his organic, evolutionary view of institutional development, he may have been right on this specific point, although perhaps for the wrong reason. The idea of popular sovereignty may indeed have fitfully flashed out in the feverish atmosphere of the late medieval period. More difficult concepts, such as the law of falling bodies in physics, certainly did appear.

The best general history of late medieval England is A. R. Myers' volume in the Pelican series; it is a thoroughly competent and in many ways subtle account, but the limitation of space and perhaps the author's native caution make him shrink from dealing with the more difficult major problems of historical change. George Holmes's one-volume history of the period is more perceptive and bold on social change but not as valuable as Myers on political and legal institutions. The attempt at a synoptic view of the Lancastrians and Yorkists made by S. B. Chrimes (whose *English Constitutional Ideas in the Fifteenth Century* is an important, if rather old-fashioned study in political thought) succeeds at least in establishing that the glamorous phrase "Wars of the Roses" was invented by Sir Walter Scott.

The two pertinent books in the erratic Oxford series present a disconcerting contrast. May McKisack, who wrote on the fourteenth century, seemed to think she was supposed to produce a text for freshmen, while E. F. Jacob, writing on the fifteenth century, was apparently under the delusion that he was communing with the British Academy. Miss McKisack's book is lucid and illuminating, but tends to be simple-minded. She avoids many important problems, shies away from economics, is quite good on Parliament and law, but not on religion or intellectual life, which she neglects to place within their social context. Jacob's account simply sinks in a welter of names. We are given a parade of earls and dukes, each of whom is bound to have—at one time or another—three different titles. Since Jacob does not usually bother to differentiate them, the work has a kind of Proustian ambiguity—charming enough, but rather discouraging if we care about historical understanding. Bertie Wilkinson's writings on the fifteenth century are, as usual, Stubbs in modern dress. T. F. Tout's detailed studies of fourteenth-century royal administration are highly illuminating; they suffer only from his failure to consider the problems of late medieval English government in the context of the comparative history of European bureaucracy. If Tout had transcribed a few less household accounts and had spent a few hours reading Max Weber instead, his work would now seem more valuable.

K. B. McFarlane, of Oxford, possessed the keenest mind at work on late medieval England. His little book on John Wyclif tells us more in 250 pages about late-fourteenth-century thought, religion, and education than all the other ponderous works of Wyclif scholarship combined. But McFarlane suffered from reticence and an intense reluctance to share his knowledge and insights. He produced four or five great articles on fifteenth-century social politics, and the people who were lucky enough to hear them tell us that his Ford lectures, given several years ago at Oxford, were absolutely brilliant. But he did not see fit to publish them, and the rest of us must remain ignorant. A. R. Steel's sensitive biography of Richard II contains some psychological analysis, which the subject cries out for.

The hardest thing for an historian to do, it seems, is to believe that things really do change. A recent popular and widely applauded approach in English historiography has been to assume that life is static—this is known as Namierism. But this viewpoint is particularly wrong for the fourteenth and fifteenth centuries. For two hundred years there was chronic instability; change was vast, enveloping, and inescapable. Wherever we look are panic, brutality, violence in the streets. This is an upside-down world; a troubled, feverish world. Institutional historians who never look at what happens outside Parliament and the law courts are blinded by their narrow vision; within its limited compass things can appear unchanged, neat and calm (although even in these areas fundamental change was taking place). "The world is right wild," writes a gentleman of the mid-fifteenth century. Even the most superficial account of the history of great aristocrats is a record of conflict, treachery, killing, beheading, and murder—even the surface pattern is one of general and extended violence. And underneath this surface lies a general dissatisfaction and unhappiness, and a tremendous yearning. This is the great age of English mysticism—in fact the great age of European mysticism. We see it in the Low Countries and Germany and France as well. Often it takes mad and frenzied forms. People were sickened by the world they lived in; they tried desperately to escape from it. The extreme methods of escape that men resorted to tell us how unbearable they must have found their lives. The most illuminating book on the fourteenth century is Morton Bloomfield's study of *Piers Plowman*, which comes to grips with the prevailing apocalyptic feeling—the deep and haunting belief that the world is coming to an end. It must often have seemed that way. The world was shaken and disturbed—there was no aspect of life that offered peace or serenity. We can attempt to characterize these disturbances. They are all the things we noticed in the thirteenth century intensified. Then they were vague tensions and currents that remained underneath the smooth surface of society. No longer hidden, they burst through the surface, and now the disturbances—in economic, political, social and religious life—are obvious and shattering.

The catastrophic effects of the Black Death that swept away twenty to forty percent of the population of Europe, including England's, in the 1340's is well known. But the economic problems were already becoming apparent in the last quarter of the thirteenth century. The grave and general problems that bedeviled the medieval economy were first perceived by the German economic historian, W. Abel, who discovered widespread depopulation in Germany at the end of the thirteenth century. This investigation was taken up by the English scholar M. M. Postan who, while studying the estates of the Bishop of Winchester, had observed the same phenomenon in England. Postan concluded that the population decline set in late in the thirteenth and early in the fourteenth centuries and that the Black Death merely accelerated what was already a marked trend. We also know, from studying fourteenth- and fifteenth-century trade records, that there was an international depression at the same time. This meant a marked decline in the available labor supply, in the amount of land in cultivation, and in the volume of export trade.

For about two decades, which seems to be the average life-span of any historical interpretation, this view has prevailed, but now Postan's thesis of a late medieval depression has been questioned. Here and there, it is true, we can find a manor where Postan's conclusions do not obtain, but it is still hard to deny that critical and widespread economic problems existed. There is no way of evading the fact that the European economy was in serious trouble from the thirteenth century until the great upsurge of population in the eighteenth century and the onset of the Industrial Revolution. Because there was a period of great prosperity during the sixteenth century this dismal curve is often overlooked. But that boom, which was really very short-lived, was artificially induced by the flow of specie into Europe from the New World and enhanced by the opening of overseas trade and speculation. It seems, then, that for at least four centuries, from 1270 to 1700, there was only one period of prosperity—1500 to 1580.

This is not to say that some people did not become rich. Of course there was individual wealth, but the general economy remained stagnant. The single basic flaw in the European economy was that distribution was unable to keep pace with production. The resources, ingenuity and the techniques were available, but primitive methods of communications and transportation frustrated expansion and development. New products often could not reach markets, and new mass markets could not be established. Beginning in the fourteenth century, economic difficulties lead to complaints against the government—we can now begin to think about the interraction of economics and social politics.

Since the twelfth century the crown had demanded a great deal from people. Now royal government figures prominently in everyday life, it really counts. In the days of Edward the Confessor no one noticed it very much, it barely had any impact on life. But ever since William the Conqueror—particularly since Henry II—the crown was very much involved in the life of landed society. And now, when landed society is in trouble, its leaders make demands on government. Thus economic problems stimulated the political breakdown and led to political instability. The chronic economic dislocation of the late Middle Ages presented a tremendous challenge to royal government. There were problems which demanded intelligence, energy, wisdom and moderation—qualities with which the English kings and their administrators were skimpily endowed. These men of small talent had a much harder job than the kings of the late twelfth century—and they were infinitely less qualified. To make things even harder, people were excited and restless. They kept close watch on government; blunders would not go unnoticed—and the kings were always making mistakes.

Economic circumstances produced important changes in the structure of rural society. No one has carefully worked it out, but the drop in population is astounding. In the thirteenth century population had grown enormously—in 1300 there may have been more than three million people in England (as many as during the reign of Elizabeth I). But from 1290 to 1390 population fell by at least thirty percent—a decline for which the bubonic plague was not entirely responsible. These statistics, uncertain as they may be, are worrisome and problematic. Demography is still a mysterious science, and the causes of population decline are still obscure and usually inexplicable. We do know, however, how the population decline affected the landowning class.

In the late thirteenth century villages were overflowing with laborers, and this is why—in comparison with the continent—the manumission of serfs was retarded in England. The landlords were firmly in control. It was a buyer's market; the landlords could be tough and unmerciful—there was little the peasants could do to bargain for improved status. The severe labor shortage later in the fourteenth century put the peasant in a much stronger position, however, and this was the last stage in the manumission of serfs; it marked the end of villeinage in England. The serf is becoming a tenant farmer (from now on he will be known as a copyholder). This does not mean that the peasants thrived particularly. Their position was still precarious, and in the late fifteenth and early sixteenth centuries some of them were driven off the land. But they did succeed in escaping the traditional servile obligations of manorial life. Day laborers could now secure higher wages; tenants could obtain better terms. And now the landlords who faced an alert, aggressive peasantry tried to reverse this process—they resorted to parliamentary statute in an effort to control and curb the peasantry. One of the immediate causes of the 1381 peasant revolt was this attempt to freeze wages. But peasant activity could not be stopped. The huge and terrible explosion in 1381 set the king and government to shaking in their boots, and if the peasants had not happened to believe that Richard II was their savior, they might have indulged in wholesale landlord slaughter. (They did kill the Archbishop of Canterbury, who happened to be a notoriously exploitative landlord.) Suddenly, in the fourteenth and fifteenth centuries, the peasant is lifting his head and looking around. He is gaining consciousness— of his place in society, and of himself as a person.

It is a modern commonplace that social revolution never occurs until conditions have already improved to some extent, that people need to be aware of opportunities before they can even think to reach out to seize them. This is the phenomenon we call the revolution of rising expectations—and we can see it happening in the fourteenth century. An important transformation in rural social structure brought a new pressure to bear on the landlord class. We can assume that the smaller landlord was very hard pressed on all sides—from the population decline, from the decline in the market for his grain, and from an alert, intransigent and, at times, highly organized peasantry. And the gentry, who did not understand their predicament, who tried, often desperately, to cope with the new and bewildering economic circumstances, were to find war very attractive. Hard-pressed and frustrated knights, and their sons, were eager to run off and escape—to fight and pillage on the continent in the Hundred Years' War. One could still beat up peasants in France.

The fourteenth and fifteenth centuries also saw a further polarization in the baronial class. A few great lords are growing richer and richer; others, whose grandfathers were prosperous enough in the thirteenth century, are now struggling to keep up. But nothing stands in the way of the great lords—men who dominate and, sometimes literally own, whole counties. They operate on a bigger margin, and they continue to prosper in the face of spreading misery. About half of these people have royal blood, and they can compensate for hard times by pillaging the crown. Economic problems do not bother these men—in fact they probably benefit from them. By the last decade of the fourteenth century there are ten dukes and a dozen earls; they stand out as a separate caste. And, as members of that caste, they pursue a very special occupation. They fight for the crown and for control of the royal government. At any one time they comprise no more than twenty-five or thirty people, they can have everything in the world: wealth, intellect, learning, culture—anything money and position can secure is theirs. The only thing left was the crown itself, and more of the crown's property. Between 1370 and 1470 they fought for these things—the result was anarchy and utter chaos. The same thing was happening in France as well, where an unremitting struggle among the princes for control of the French crown was decimating the country. Great aristocratic conflict is a general aspect of later medieval European society. The most perceptive book on the subject is Johan Huizinga's *Waning of the Middle Ages*, which, although it is specifically concerned with the situation in the Low Countries, tells us, more than any supposedly relevant work does, what things were like in late medieval England.

All wealth and power was vested in a small, courtly group, whose way of life was meant to be a formal work of art. They lived in a dream world, where life becomes stylized choreography. The trouble is that they have a real impact on the world outside; because of the intricacies of their fantasy world, blood is shed. For them, however, it is all nothing but play—a self-conscious drama that they gracefully enact. This is how Huizinga describes the Burgundian court, and it was like this in fourteenth- and fifteenth-century England, too. These people, acting out their esthetic attitude toward life, are totally irresponsible. Every action is some kind of posture, the striking of an attitude. Everything is given a special ritual quality. Even executions are ritualized. It is hard to account for this. Perhaps it is symptomatic of the last, decadent stages of a civilization; certainly it is the result of a loss of vitality, the death of an ideal. Nothing is left but empty and meaningless form. If we believe that civilizations are organisms, this is the only possible explanation.

Everyone knows about chivalry, but no one has properly evaluated its social significance. The whole aristocratic ethos, with its concept of gentility, its knighthood, its tournaments, is more important than modern scholars generally think. The last, extravagant flowering of chivalry is, perhaps, a response to the emergence of the bourgeoisie. The aristocrats are not the only people who can have property now; other people have money and wealth, they can even fight. The aristocratic ethos, which first appeared in the twelfth century, now reaches its ultimate expression. The power and privileges of great lords depend on their qualities as superior people. Anyone can get money, but only aristocrats can be born right. More and more this becomes an inflexible ideology—a dogma. Nothing else matters to these men. Their ideology plays a crucial role in the peculiar conduct of the English and French nobility in the fourteenth and fifteenth centuries. The only thing they think about is their exclusive chivalric circle—the world was a hothouse where they cultivated their code. Everything else passes dimly before them. There are cities, industry, wealth, great thinkers, piety, devotion; but these things have no effect. It might have been amusing and harmless, like the petty courts of eighteenth-century Germany, except that these people also held real power. Chivalry is deadly. The welfare of states with vast economic and human resources was wrecked and torn to pieces by these great people at play. What they did in their fantasy world really did matter. Everything in society was employed in the pursuit of their fantasies, in their courtly ritual, in the great aristocratic tournament they made of life.

Under William the Conqueror and Henry II this could never have happened. These kings were too rational, too much in touch with reality. They were able to exploit the aristocratic code (Henry II was particularly skillful here), yet remain apart from it. But in the fourteenth and fifteenth centuries the monarchy itself is absorbed into the high aristocratic ethos. And kingship suffers. Kings no longer see themselves as separate or unique. With the possible exception of Richard II, who was anomalous in many ways and had to be deposed, all the kings succumbed. The aristocratic ethos takes over the king, the court, and the government. Finally the crown itself is seen as nothing but the grand prize in a courtly game. This is what the misnamed Wars of the Roses is all about. The idea of the dignity of the crown and the sense of the state, which had been vital in the thirteenth century, all but vanishes in the fourteenth and fifteenth centuries.

The English kings now endow their sons and brothers: they make them dukes and grant them vast holdings. Edward I initiated the practice, but with Edward III in the mid-fourteenth century it becomes really significant. The problems of kingship are now compounded; the endowment of princes and the creation of resplendent titles symbolized the blurring of the distinction between monarchy and aristocracy. By naming his second son duke of Lancaster, the king in effect makes the aristocracy royal. No longer is there much difference between the royal family and the great barons. The sense of distance, of cleavage, has gone. By 1370 the great barons are the royal family, the kings have been swallowed up by the courtly, aristocratic world. No longer can there be a struggle between the king—supported by his ministers, judges and administrators—and the great barons. This division had been fundamental in England from 1066 to 1307; it had served a healthy social purpose, and its disappearance in the fourteenth century was a disaster. Government was no longer able to rule the aristocracy. The force that the Anglo-Norman and Angevin monarchs countered and controlled now overwhelms the monarchy. Government itself is tossed about in accordance with the outcome of what are, in effect, feuds within the royal family. These conflicts will wreck government and tear apart society.

The intellectual and religious upheaval of fourteenth-century England contributed as much as economic and political change to the waning of the medieval order. Not again until the age of Newton will scholars at English universities play such a leading role in European thought. In the first quarter of the fourteenth century while the royal government is beginning to falter and the onset of the great depression is causing dismay and anguish in society, Oxford is the intellectual capital of Europe. It was the Oxford Franciscans Duns Scotus and William of Ockham who brought about a revolution in European thought. Duns Scotus was the greatest of medieval logicians; the tendency of his doctrine is very like the radical empiricism of that other Scottish genius, David Hume. William of Ockham went even further than Duns in separating the world of reason and the world of faith, thereby undermining the Thomist synthesis and exercising an enormous impact on late medieval thinking. Ockham argued that the mind can establish general propositions only about the world of nature but not about God, who can be known only intuitively, by direct religious experience. Ockham thereby encouraged scholars at Merton College, Oxford, to improve upon the scientific work of Robert Grosseteste and Roger Bacon and achieve significant breakthroughs toward establishing general laws in mechanics—the first great steps toward modern physics. Ockham also encouraged the proliferation of mysticism in fourteenth-century England. He himself became steadily more anti-orthodox in his thinking. First he claimed that a general council of the church can overrule the Pope and then that individual conscience was the only test of faith. Not surprisingly, Ockham was excommunicated by Rome, and died in exile at the court of the German emperor, where he occupied himself by turning out anti-papal pamphlets.

Radical as Ockham was, and as wide as his influence spread (Luther was to proclaim himself an Occamist), the arch-heretic of the fourteenth century was another distinguished Oxford professor, John Wyclif. Every idea that can be found in sixteenth-century radical Protestantism can also be found in Wyclif, who was teaching in the third quarter of the fourteenth century. Wyclif was fiercely anti-sacerdotal and anti-sacramental; he did not even believe in transubstantiation—an incredibly radical position at the time. Laymen, he said, had the right to seize the property of the church. It was this belief that enabled Wyclif to die peacefully in bed. Government in England was all in favor of seizing church property—there was already a long and respectable tradition of that—and John of Gaunt, Duke of Lancaster, who controlled the royal administration in the 1360's and 1370's, was not about to burn a man who preached such sound doctrine.

Wyclif evoked a tremendous popular response and found his most aggressive disciples in the heretical wandering preachers, the Lollards. In the fourteenth century the English church is losing control over popular piety. Though the secular clergy detested them, the Franciscans had salvaged the church's authority in the thirteenth century. But something had gone wrong with the Franciscan order; it split apart, and some of its members (Ockham among them) were branded by the Pope as heretics. The demand for teaching, truth, and divine light remained; to fill it there were only the popular preachers—friars, renegade friars, and the openly heretical Lollards. This was a spontaneous response to a deep and widespread need. The world made no sense; all around them men saw economic misery, political upheaval, the murder of kings. Someone was needed to explain and justify it. This accounts for the great upsurge of revivalism, of millennial, apocalyptic, puritanical religion. Inflammatory sermons were being preached all over England; an amazing number of them were written down and preserved. (Many have been published by the Early English Text Society, and they have been well studied by G. R. Owst.) Some of them strike notes we will hear again in the sixteenth and seventeenth century, and the question inevitably arises whether there was a continuity of puritanical, experiential religion; whether popular piety took root and remained important. The consensus of scholarship today is to see a direct continuity from fourteenth-century Lollardry to sixteenth-century radical Protestantism. In any case, fourteenth-century English piety tended to be contemptuous of the papacy, and it was sometimes openly heretical. Sometimes social democracy was preached— the idea that all men are equal before God. It was no coincidence that a leader of the Peasants' Revolt of 1381 was a Lollard. The peasants murdered the Archbishop of Canterbury not only because they hated landlords, but also because some of them were intensely anti-sarcerdotal as well.

Fourteenth-century England was the seedbed of European heresy; English heresy may even have given rise to the Hussite movement in central Europe, though this connection, plausible enough, is also very hazy. Early in the fifteenth century, the royal government became very frightened, and launched a full-scale inquisition which revealed, to their shock and amazement, that heresy was not just an aberration found among peasants. Gentlemen like Sir John Oldcastle—the model for Shakespeare's Sir John Falstaff—were deeply involved as well. We cannot yet be sure if Lollardry was destroyed, or merely forced underground. Nineteenth-century historians were sure there was a continuous Protestant stream in England from the fourteenth to the sixteenth century. This meant, of course, that the Reformation was not just an authoritarian scheme inspired by Henry VIII's lust. Recently this interpretation has been revived—and there may be a good deal of truth in it.

Religious upheaval in the fourteenth and fifteenth centuries is enmeshed with the other kinds of disturbance we have noted; in many ways it is a response to them. The lines of authority and leadership collapsed on all but the most local level. With a vacuum at the center, when the church, and government as well, were disintegrating, security could only be found under the protection of the local magnate. Only through maintenance and livery, by putting on the badge of the local duke and getting the magnate's support in the law court, could a man secure his person and his property. This is what we mean by bastard feudalism—a real retrogression to a primitive form of social organization. It was a natural response to what was virtually abdication by the traditional leaders of English society—the church and the king. The church suffered from special problems that made its leadership ineffective. No one was even sure who the Pope was. There was a Pope at Avignon and another one at Rome, and Englishmen rejected the authority of both. Kingship had special problems as well. An incredible array of incompetent men took their places on the English throne during this period.

First there was Edward II (1307-1327), the most repulsive king until George I. An unattractive homosexual, whose French wife took up with a Welsh lord after the king had revealed his affection for various unsavory courtiers, Edward was finally forced to abdicate and was then murdered by his queen and her lover. Edward III (1327-1377) was only slightly more appealing. Not very strong-minded, he was the sort of man who should have been given some wooden soldiers and locked up in a castle. Edward was very dim; he really loved the chivalric idea of warfare and adored to go marching off to battle in France with his pretty army behind him, pennants waving and trumpets blaring. Games enchanted him and he insisted on playing them. But they were very costly games. It cost 50,000 pounds just to mount one French expedition, and a parliamentary subsidy yielded 38,000 pounds. Thus every time Edward had the pleasure of riding at the head of his army it put him 12,000 pounds deeper in debt. Edward had to live on loans from Italian bankers—he even farmed the English customs to them, and finally he defaulted on his debts—not a very kingly thing to do. Edward did manage to win glorious battles, but they never seemed to mean anything. He did kill thousands of French peasants and once he captured the French king, who happened to be even less intelligent than Edward, a distinction of some kind. Edward's son, the romantic Black Prince, was a great national hero; he was indeed a magnificent warrior but also a vicious sadist. Finally, in the 1370's, Edward III lay slowly dying of venereal disease while his sons and grandsons squabbled over the crown.

Richard II (1377-1399), the Black Prince's son, who got it, did have some notion of what kingship was all about—the Shakespeare portrait of him is very accurate. His problem was that he had too many enemies—everyone seemed to line up against him. That Richard was a homosexual, and probably psychotic as well, did not help him to win friends. Richard lost his throne to his shrewd Lancastrian cousin, Henry Bolingbroke. Henry IV (1399-1413) was a mysterious king. Perhaps there is a good deal of the Renaissance monarch in him; a crafty, intelligent man, he might have been capable of reviving the monarchy while playing on and destroying the aristocracy. But he climbed onto the throne with the help of an aristocratic faction; hence he was obligated to them and, seated so unsteadily on the throne, he could never overcome the insecurity of his dubious title. Henry V (1413-1422) takes us back to Edward III. Shakespeare and Laurence Olivier were all wrong about Henry V. He happened to win the battle of Agincourt because the French knights were stupid enough to charge across a plowed field right after a rainstorm where, mired in the mud, the famous English yeomen could hardly miss picking them off with their bows and arrows. Henry was in the process of swallowing France—not a very sensible thing to want to do—when he died. Henry VI (1422-1461) was a combination of Henry III and Edward III. Another gentle man, he had excellent taste in art, built a beautiful college at Cambridge, and went mad. As Henry's insanity became apparent, the English were expelled from nearly all of their French territories, while the crown went up for grabs—and for twenty years the Lancastrian and Yorkist factions in the aristocracy hacked away at each other to get it. No one knows exactly what this meant to society. Certainly there were great disturbances, at least among the landed class, and these exacerbated the breakdown of government and law, which had barely functioned for a long time anyway. Grim and unequivocal records of violence confront us at every hand. A petition to the king inscribed on the Parliament rolls for 1459 says that complaints are universal throughout the realm "of robberies, ravishments, extortions, oppressions, riots, unlawful assemblies, wrongful imprisonments." Even worse, the "misdoers be so favored and assisted by persons of great might, which in riotous and forcible manner disturb and hinder . . . your Justices of Assize and Peace in every part of this your realm, that no execution of your law may be had." And there was no redress "as your said true subjects . . . for fear and doubt of their lives, neither complain to your Highness, nor sue for remedy after the course of your laws, but rather . . . suffer such wrongs without remedy."

Finally, in 1461, the Yorkist leader Edward IV gained the throne. Edward represented a healthy change from the rulers of the previous 150 years. He was tough and austere, and he believed in the dignity of kingship. He was so little shackled to the idea of chivalry that he married a commoner—for which he was never forgiven by the aristocracy. It was not until 1471 that Edward was able to put down his Lancastrian enemies and devote himself fully to the reconstruction of royal government and law. From this year we can date the beginning of the resurgence of English monarchy. But it was a reconstruction that had to cope with the ravages left by the upheavals of the previous century and a half and to build upon the institutional changes that were coming about during the late medieval period.

II. The Institutional Legacy of
the Late Middle Ages

THE RAMBLINGS of Sir John Fortescue, chief justice of the king's bench who died in 1476, have given him a grand reputation. His celebrated treatises on English government and law have been carefully studied for centuries; in our own they have been hailed as examples of Renaissance political thought. This is a curious judgment, since Fortescue was not exactly the brightest or most subtle theorist ever to write a disquisition on law and politics. Still, he does deserve serious attention. Fortescue's writings are interesting, not because he is particularly brilliant or profound (rather he tends to be superficial and unreflective), but because he epitomizes, almost to perfection, the attitude of the well-educated gentleman who also happens to hold an important legal place in fifteenth-century England. What is finally most intriguing about Fortescue's work is the ambivalence—never quite resolved—that lies at the core of his thought.

There are two things Fortescue says, and he is compelled to say them over and over again. The first is that English institutions and customs are the best in the world. In their prosperity, felicity and virtue, the English put everyone else, particularly the benighted French, to shame and, as far as Fortescue is concerned, this happy English condition is a direct consequence of the superior quality of English political and legal institutions. His writing is sustained throughout by a smug and blatant nationalism. The second theme is his definition of the nature of the constitution. Here Fortescue owes, as do all serious political theorists, a large debt to Aristotle. There are two kinds of government, he tells us, regal government (*dominium regale*) and political government (*dominium politicum et regale*). By regal government he means absolutist, irresponsible monarchy, something more or less on the order of what the unfortunate French boors have to suffer. By political government, he means government by consent, government that takes account of the community, government in which the king cannot alter the laws without the consent of his subjects. As a Lancastrian supporter, Fortescue staunchly believes in the idea of consent (the Lancastrians were, admittedly, not powerful enough to rule without Parliament, hence they had little choice). At bottom, however, he is not irrevocably committed to government by consent. At times of crisis the king, he allows, must take the law into his own hands and rule by his own will. Even in England, the monarchy does at times rule, and ought to rule, without the consent of the political nation. These two ideas are worth pursuing. They will lead us to compare government in England and the continent during the fifteenth century and to analyze the tension between responsible and irresponsible monarchy that will set the pattern for English political history through the seventeenth century.

Nineteenth-century historians were too prone to make sweeping and less than tactful generalizations about national character. They expounded national stereotypes, were inclined to rhapsodize over mystical aspects of *Volksgeist*, and generally engage in the kind of ethnic history that modern scholars (who usually prefer to use some other jargon) mercilessly sneer at. Nevertheless, there is something to be said for the nineteenth-century treatment of nationality and national characteristics. Once we admit that the areas of western Europe do exhibit national peculiarities, we can see that these have, to a large degree, pretty much jelled by the end of the fifteenth century. Perhaps the best way to make sense of national character is to inquire what are the various pastimes, concerns and attitudes of fifteenth-century European peoples.

The French concern themselves with monarchy, *gloire*, and sport a flamboyant, noisy, but ineffective aristocracy. This persisted in French history down to 1789 and to some degree to the present. France, as a nation is, we must recall, the creation of the monarchy; kings shaped and unified it and in medieval Europe France was a "continental" country, rather like the United States. One government embraces, often uncomfortably, areas that are vastly divergent. Northern France is little like southern France, and the two parts have scarcely any natural relation to one another. As a country, France was one huge political construction. Frenchmen are apparently happy only when a strong monarchy gives them an aura of glory and a sense of national purpose; otherwise they sulk, relinquish their external notion of nationality, and go back to regional differences.

Germany, by the end of the fifteenth century, had also fulfilled its national character, though it is hard to say in what this consists. It appears to be an odd combination of childish enthusiasm and very high seriousness—an amalgam that leads to hard work, clean streets, and the pursuit of devils. It is an important clue to German history to recognize that since the middle ages the German soul has been haunted by devils —spiritual and political ones. The Italians, by 1500, had sunk into their characteristic attitude of privatism. Underneath a surface fire and idealism, Italians are the coolest, most realistic people in Europe. Italians believe in nothing but family, which is why they can afford to be so flowery when they speak about the state. Politics for them is merely a game, a luxury, an amoral sport; the only things that really count are family, sex and food. We can hardly blame them for cultivating an attitude of disengagement. Since the fifth century, Italy has been the battleground for everyone else in Europe; for a millennium foreign troops have been marching up and down the peninsula. Spain is the most mysterious country, and Spaniards the most mysterious people in Europe. They seem to be great activists, but all they really believe in is the moment. Thus they are the great existentialists of Europe. This is why

they are able to be so pious—they never stop to contemplate the significance of their piety. Spain has produced thousands of saints, but not
one theologian. The kind of world view that exalts the significance of
the moment produces great saints, street-fighters, dancers and artists,
but no great statesmen or thinkers.

The great national characteristic of the English is a devotion to government, law, and evangelical religion, traits that are already very clear
in the late fifteenth century. In spite of the myth issuing from England's lead in the Industrial Revolution, Englishmen were never notable
European businessmen. The coming of the Industrial Revolution to
England before any other country was an accident, a lucky combination
of factors necessary for industrial take-off, as historians and economists
are just beginning to fully understand. Today it is commonly acknowledged that the English are not effective as businessmen. Their economic
triumph was short-lived. Now that the temporary supremacy enjoyed
by Englishmen because the Industrial Revolution happened to take
place first in their country has vanished, we can see how the whole
business adventure was a transient thing. Dramatic events often lead
historians badly astray, and nothing has lured them down the garden
path more thoroughly than the eighteenth-century Industrial Revolution. Historiographically, everything has been organized around the rise
of the English bourgeoisie and the empire, but this has only served to
cramp our thinking about what forces really make English history go. In
law, government, and religion the English have excelled, and in these
areas the great tensions of English history are generated; here will be
found the spring that makes English history run. One of the most important themes in English history is the tension between central government, law and religion and local law, government and religion. (To
describe this as conflict between king and community is just a fancy way
of saying the same thing.) At any rate, this tension already existed in the
fourteenth and fifteenth centuries; by then the problems and issues of
the next two hundred years are formulated, though they are still obscure. Once we apprehend this, it becomes obvious that 1485 is a meaningless date, 1471 not much more significant, and that the four centuries
after 1300 must be seen as a distinct middle period of English history.

As usual, it is more sensible to begin at the local level, and we will ask
how political authority is wielded in the English countryside.

The familiar figure of the justice of the peace goes back to the middle
of the thirteenth century. During the barons' war of the 1260's a local

official called the keeper of the peace appeared. He was a prominent country gentleman appointed, in disturbed times, to assist the sheriff in maintaining law and order in the county. Between the four yearly appearances of the justices in eyre, the sheriff was the only local embodiment of royal authority, and it was plain that he could not cope with things by himself. The justices of the peace relished their tasks; it was a way to win social recognition, as well as legal and political influence. About one hundred years later, in the 1360's, their office was formalized and enhanced when they took over many of the administrative chores that had previously been the responsibility of the royal justices. As local society becomes more hostile to the activities of the justices in eyre, the office of the justice of the peace grows more important. The general eyre had become very unpopular; it was the scene of too many embarrassing revelations, and the inquisitiveness of the king's judicial representatives met with more and more obstinacy on the part of the country gentry. During the reign of Edward I we see the general eyre passing out of existence. After 1330 there were no justices in eyre at all. By the fifteenth century, all the administrative functions, as well as many of the judicial functions, of the itinerant justices are in the hands of the J.P.'s. In each county, the J.P.'s meet in quarter session; they sit in judgment on the greater share of the legal business of the shire; they are now the men who implement the day-to-day workings of the common law.

The justices of assize only pass through the county once or twice a year. They have time only to deal with the most difficult problems; with cases of great legal complications, or with felonies involving men of substance and influence. But all ordinary cases are tried at the quarter sessions, where the J.P.'s preside, a practice that will continue until the nineteenth century. What were the administrative tasks of the J.P.'s? They conducted investigations into property belonging to the crown, they assessed taxes and collected them. They were, for all practical purposes, the government. This was a tremendous legal and, in some ways, a social revolution, though it was accomplished without any fireworks. Historians who are set quivering by the rise of the gentry in the sixteenth century should take another hard look at the fourteenth and fifteenth centuries. The first statute of the game law system dates from 1390—and the game laws were the institutional guarantee that the gentry class could indulge in its favorite pastime without interference from those who were merely hungry. It was laid down in 1390 that only men whose income from land was at least 40 shillings per annum could keep hunting dogs, and kill deer and rabbits. By 1400 the country gentry had already absorbed much of the royal authority. Government was sloughing off more and more of its work on the community of the shire. It always had sought to use the community of the shire in the interests of royal power and authority, and it still does, but now there is a significant difference. Never before had government had to hand over any real power to the gentry. The local gentlemen served on juries, but juries were instruments of the royal judges who controlled them. Now the gentry do the work *and* have the power; in law and administration, the community of the shire virtually governs itself. The power of the local gentry has become enormous.

Why should this have happened? The gentry had always exerted pressure for substantial rewards; they had long been bent on seizing power as well as responsibility, but under a strong monarchy they had been frustrated. What makes the difference is abdication, derationalization, and decentralization on the part of royal government. What happened in the Angevin period has been checked and reversed. A slack and incompetent royal government finds governing the shires too difficult and expensive, and so it lets them govern themselves. The new pattern of authority and jurisdiction is tenacious; it will be maintained until the second half of the nineteenth century. We must remember, though, that while the authority of the central government has receded, the government itself has by no means vanished. Rather we should think of English administration in the fifteenth century in terms of duality, and recognize two forces at work. They are bound to operate in different directions and they will inevitably lead to tensions and contradictions in government—tensions that could, however, be glossed over for several hundred years.

While there were innovations outside the established administrative structure, a new legal procedure that operated outside the traditional framework of the common law was appearing. The idea of equity, which is the justification for the judicial proceedings in the king's chancery, is the principle out of which the conciliar courts will develop. The common law contains no idea of equity. The aim of the common law is to give every man his due, to maintain society as it exists, to preserve whatever belongs to a man in law, what he owns as the member of a group which has certain established privileges. But Roman law, which is structured around principles of abstract justice, says that the law should control society in conformity with the law of nature, with some sort of abstract, higher law. It equates law with justice. The notion of equity was not completely new in England. Henry II's clerics could be quite eloquent on the subject; still, the common law acknowledged no procedure for arriving at equitable decisions. In equity, a judge must be able to go above the law, to bypass due process, to appeal to a higher, sovereign authority. Henry II's justices may have been fully cognizant of the idea, but it is not until we come to the petitions of the mid-fourteenth century, addressed to the chancellor, that we see the beginnings of equity procedure.

The petitions are informed by a conviction that the common law—at least in a particular case—does not give justice. Why do men put their troubles before the chancellor? They are really appealing directly to the king, to the highest authority in the land, to the fount of justice, and the chancellor is the administrative embodiment of the conscience of the king. Technically, a writ out of chancery can redress the inequitable outcome of a case that either cannot be dealt with in the common law courts, or has been treated in a manifestly unjust manner. When it becomes apparent in a specific case that a particular common law rule needs to be broken, equity procedure is the way to do it. But equity also contains a threat; equity procedure can be used as an authoritarian tool by the crown. Later this would be seen as a serious problem. For who can dispute the chancellor's view of the moral law? "Equity is a roguish thing," complains the seventeenth-century common lawyer John Selden. "For Law we have a measure, know what to trust to; Equity is according to the conscience of the Chancellor, and as that is larger or narrower, so is Equity. 'Tis all one as if they should make the standard for the measure we call a 'foot' a Chancellor's foot; what an uncertain measure would this be!" But in the fifteenth century equity procedure represented a vast improvement over the common law, and men were not yet ready to worry that it might, in the hands of a despotically inclined ruler, be used to subvert and destroy the common law itself. Rather, equity is a safety valve that allows the rigid and ponderous common law to keep functioning while its general structure remains unchanged. For the common law is even slower and more cumbersome than it had ever been. There is a certain irony about this. Under Henry II English law worked in an extremely quick and efficient manner in contrast to Roman law where, because everything must be put in writing and then studied, a case is likely to drag on for more time. Justice under Henry II was, no doubt, sometimes rough and ready; it was not very probing or subtle, but it was speedy. The most notable characteristic of the common law in the four-

teenth century, however, was sluggishness—a quality that is still fundamental in the eighteenth century. Why was law so slow and unwieldy?

First, it was uncodified. In many cases it was hard even to know what
the law prescribed. Obscurity did not discourage chicanery on the part of
fee-hungry attorneys, and it did lead to much fumbling and uncertainty.
It fostered the development of devious schemes to circumvent the obstacles that were impossible to remove. The major function of an attorney in the common law is to see that a case never comes to trial, and the
English attorney was, by the fourteenth century, extremely skilled at this
aspect of his work. In civil cases the defendant was entitled to three
excuses (called *essoins*) before he was forced to come into court; thus at
least a year and a half would go by before a case even came to trial. At
this point, a special plea, which turned on the validity of the writ, could
be invoked. This sort of prevarication could go on for years. The very
nature of the law was slow and unwieldy, and the qualities built into the
common law structure were compounded by the greed and selfishness of
the legal profession.

The other thing that undermined the law was violence. The technical
words for this form of subversion are livery and maintenance and,
though the words have far-reaching implications, they may be strictly
defined. Livery means to wear a uniform, like a liveried servant. But it
was not necessary to put on the whole uniform; a badge would suffice to
show that you belonged to a group that enjoyed the patronage of a powerful lord. To wear livery means to belong to a gang; it means you are a
client of a great patron who retains you; it means that in return for your
loyalty he will bring pressure to bear on your behalf. Great lords were not
likely to be very delicate about making their power felt, nor were their
retainers apt to be squeamish about the kind of services they were
asked to perform. It was not unusual for a local lord to appear at the
assizes with a great force of retainers at his back. A show of force like this
was quite effective in serving its purpose, which was to overawe the
court. Livery, in short, is gangsterism in the guise of aristocratic affiliation. Great lords did not hesitate to practice what we immediately recognize as lynch law. We have a description in a fifteenth-century source
of the behavior of the Earl of Oxford concerning a certain Piers, a man
imprisoned in the bishop's jail at Lynn, an important town in Norfolk.
"My Lord pulled him out of the . . . gaol, and made to put him upon a
horse, and tied halter to his arm and so led him forth," we are told.
"Forthwith, the . . . Bishop, the Mayor, and others of their fellowship

met with my said Lord . . . and . . . Piers tied by an halter, the Bishop having these words unto my Lord with his hat in his hands. 'My Lord, this is a prisoner, as you may know. . . . What will you do with him?' Thereto my Lord said, 'He is my prisoner now.' Whereto the Bishop said, 'Where is your warrant or commission thereto?' My Lord said, 'I have warrant sufficient for me.' And thus they departed, the Mayor and all the Commonalty of Lynn keeping their silence."

Maintenance means something beyond mere payment. It too has a very precise technical definition. The legal sense of maintenance is any action of wrongfully aiding and abetting litigation; it means to subvert juries and judges, to bribe, to pay in court. And maintenance, in its larger connotation, means the destruction of the common law. According to Lambarde, a sixteenth-century writer, a broad definition of maintenance is "to disturb the course of the common law." Livery and maintenance go together. A man wears the livery of a great lord, who maintains him. They are ominous words, and they represent a sinister alliance. Together they helped to ruin the common law.

We can see how it was done clearly enough in the Paston letters. The Pastons were country gentry, an intelligent, substantial gentry family who lived in fifteenth-century Norfolk. Their letters are taken up to a large extent with the favorite activity of the gentry—securing their property. But for the Pastons this occupation was particularly wearisome and unrewarding, for they invariably had a very hard time of it in the courts. It seemed that the great lord in Norfolk was against them, and they at odds with him. There was little they could do. Dismay runs through their letters and a bitter, melancholy plaint. The letters between the Pastons and their friends are full of stories of bribery, perjury, the corrupting of judges as well as juries, and the intimidation of witnesses. The sheriff was a key official in the operation of local justice, for he was the one who empaneled the jury, yet the complicity of sheriffs in judicial corruption was widespread. Justice Yelverton prays that "we may have a good shereve and a good undershereve that neythir for good favore no fere, wol returne for the King, ne betwix partie and partie, none othir men but such as ar good and trewe, and in no wyse will be forsworne; for the pepil here is loth to compleyne til thei here tydinges of a good shereve." The judge's hopes, we can readily imagine, did not soon come true. John Paston, at one point, is rash enough to indict the local lord who had attacked his manor of Gresham. The sheriff receives a letter from the king in which he is instructed to empanel a jury that will acquit, a practice that was apparently not unusual, for Paston notes that six or eight shillings would buy such a royal letter. Thus we can easily understand why William Paston, the lawyer, advises a client to drop his suit because his opponent is befriended by the Duke of Norfolk. There was simply no point in trying to go against a man like the duke who, when he seized the Paston's castle of Caister, was able to send a force of three thousand men to surround it. The common law, which the gentry had loved and supported, seems to be turning against them. The intervention of their aristocratic enemies is effective. The law, which had long been slow and cumbersome, is now malevolent as well.

In a situation like this the only recourse is to amend procedure. Since the reign of Edward III in the mid-fourteenth century, a means of improvement had been required; by the fifteenth century, particularly in the 1460's and 1470's, the need is imperative. In the Yorkist period the procedure by which the common law may be supplemented expands at an astonishing rate. The new system works out of the king's prerogative power to maintain justice and provide peace. Before the Star Chamber Act of 1487 the new courts had no statutory basis, and the procedural details were pragmatically delineated. But the new judicial form obviously issues from the royal prerogative, hence the term prerogative court. The chancellor, in the name of the king, bestows justice; he protects people from fraud and violence; he issues extraordinary writs to secure property. In the 1470's the procedure was probably rather casual. The king and his ministers meet to hear petitions and give justice in cases of fraud for which there is no other remedy. Star chamber was simply a branch of the king's council that happened to meet and deal with riots in a room with stars painted on the ceiling, whence the evocative name. The operative word for a star chamber case was riot; the key word that bestirred the court of chancery was fraud. The men who sit in these courts—chancery and what will become star chamber—are members of the king's council. Though in theory the law works out of the king's personal prerogative, it is universally understood that the prerogative is exercised by his ministers who, as they examine the petitions and hand down justice, are exercising power on behalf of their master.

The procedure stands at the opposite extreme of what the justices of the peace do. As the office of the J.P. develops, the common law is surrendered to the gentry, to the influential men in the county. Yet at the same time, the king is acting in a more arbitrary and immediate way. He is operating outside the old, established writ system and jury system. He is encouraged to exercise an important public function directly out of his prerogative, to correct the law, to go beyond it. It might be hard to reconcile this with the deeply held notion that the king must be below the law. Here is an important ground of potential conflict. King and J.P. represent contrasting principles and forces. The J.P. stands for decentralization; his new powers proclaim how far in fact decentralization has gone, but at the same time the new prerogative courts stand for a high degree of centralization; they embody a new form of royal intervention and control. It is easy to see how the contradictions between the two are creating a great tension within the law itself. Striking as it is, this tension is not unique. Similar strains exist in government and, to some extent, in religion as well.

In government, there were two important late medieval developments and, as in law, they point in opposite directions. First is the entrenchment of Parliament. The bill procedure is worked out and systemized. During the fourteenth century the House of Commons had begun to assume a distinct character; now it has a speaker; it sports all the appurtenances we are familiar with today. Men are beginning to take Parliament for granted. There is a feeling that for important things, like new taxes, parliamentary legislation is necessary. Parliament is recognized as a place, an occasion, and an institution where important matters concerning the nation are to be decided. Thus during the fourteenth- and fifteenth-century struggles over control of the crown, Parliament was used to give an aura of legality to whichever aristocratic faction had the upper hand at a particular time. This is not to say that Parliament decided the fate of England; rather it was a rubber stamp employed by aristocratic gangs. Still, for unglorious purposes Parliament itself was glorified. The appearance of strict legality was required, and nothing was more legal than a clear-cut and entrenched procedure, and so by the end of the fifteenth century, all the fundamental parliamentary procedures were worked out. This means that the parliamentarians of the seventeenth century will be able to appeal to precedent, although their interpretations may be somewhat specious. The House of Commons in the fifteenth century may not actually be deciding anything, but its formal procedures are clearly established. By the middle of the fourteenth century the separation between Lords and Commons was evident; by 1376 the House of Commons is meeting in its own place—the chapter house of the abbot of Westminster. (The room is not very large, and the members are forced to sit in two groups facing one another. Thus it may not be completely frivolous to suggest that an architectural accident has influenced the traditional two-party nature of the English parliamentary system.) In 1376 we see that the Commons chooses one of its members, Sir Peter de la Mare, to "assume the duty of expressing their will in the great parliament before the . . . lords." Sir Peter happens to be a flunkey of a great lord—the Earl of March—but he is also the first Speaker of the House. By 1399, Parliament has become so confident, and its use of procedure so sophisticated, that, under the leadership of Henry of Lancaster, it undertakes to depose Richard II.

The second great development, though it stands at the opposite pole from parliamentary power, is the entrenchment of the king's council. From the late fourteenth century the council takes on a new complexion. The council comprises a group of men privy to the king's secrets and desires who issue writs under the king's privy seal, not the great seal of the realm. The privy seal is small, it is portable, personal; the king always has it with him; it is, somehow, less official. This is a personal kind of government. Under conciliar government taxes are collected and funneled through the household chamber instead of the more cumbersome public institution of the exchequer. The council works quietly and secretly and, by the middle of the fifteenth century, we can see that it is irresponsible. Mystery and irresponsibility are the essential qualities of conciliar and household administration. The council is very much the king's—it is not responsible to Parliament. In the thirteenth and fourteenth centuries there were vociferous demands that the king's ministers should be responsive to Parliament, that they should be appointed with consent of Parliament, impeached if necessary, that at least they should make reports. There was a sense, however obscure, of the idea of responsibility. Faced with these demands, the king relies more and more on his private administration; he extends the activity of the royal council. It is significant that its members take an oath of secrecy.

Edward IV was a master of household administration, and in his reign we encounter a new officer called the king's secretary. At first it is hard to know what his function is. In the late fifteenth century he is, primarily, the king's hatchet man—an obscure, rather unsavory character who schemes and pulls strings. Though his operations are devious and elusive, he is a central figure, he plays a key role in the new form of government that allows the king to extricate himself from a royal alliance with Parliament. Edward IV, who does this very skillfully, is thus setting a pattern we will see more clearly in the early Tudor government. Royal government carefully husbands the resources of the crown; it cagily exploits old taxes, it makes no new ones. It makes its will known by proclamation, not statute, and, when Parliament is called, the House of Commons is sure to be packed with dependents of the royal council. Though it requires intelligence and much effort to make them work in practice, the rules are simple. Do not provoke great issues of state, do not present reform legislation, do not suggest new taxes to Parliament. But manipulate the old taxes, administer affairs efficiently, pinch pennies, and issue proclamations that are ambiguous enough to be interpreted as merely declaring or clarifying what the law already is. To make sure the judicial system operates to fit the purposes of government, send *sub rosa* letters of instruction to the judges. Expand the scope and jurisdiction of the prerogative courts, so that they may be instituted quietly and effectively without stirring up Parliament or the lawyers. Again we note an important contradiction. Conciliar and household administration undermines ministerial responsibility. A new breed of ministers manages things so that Parliament need seldom be called. Parliament may be uneasy, but it is not given a chance. Nevertheless, the presence of Parliament alongside the conciliar government is bound to generate the kind of tension we have already seen in law.

It was a tension that found a counterpart in religion. In the twelfth and thirteenth centuries, England was the most orthodox and devout country in Europe. England was moved, as no other country was, by the coming of the friars. The friars gave self-consciousness to the burgesses and the intelligent peasants; they inculcated the idea that men can communicate directly with God, an idea that led, rapidly enough, to the proliferation of heresy. The fourteenth and fifteenth centuries saw the rise of religious individualism in England, a movement that surged on toward the outright heresy of Lollardry and eventually culminated in radical Protestantism. At the heart of popular piety was the belief in the validity of the religious experience of the common man. The contradiction here is that in no other country in Europe was the church more under the control of royal government. After the papacy came under the control of the French monarchy early in the fourteenth century, and then suffered the further indignity of a schism in 1378, there was nothing to withstand the crown. At any rate, the crown since 1066 had always run the church in England, except for a relatively brief interval extending from the first decade of the twelfth century to the first decade of the thirteenth when the king had to pay some attention to papal demands.

England had an ecclesiastical organization that was very much like a state church. Church appointments were directed by the crown, and the king made great use of the financial and intellectual resources of the church. But at the same time a very different kind of Christianity was flourishing. It is as though two streams flow past each other. At one level we find traditional sacerdotalism, exemplified by the power of the bishops. Bishops and kings both rule, though bishops serve the monarch. At the other extreme, under the influence of the friars, we have incipient heresy, religion based on personal experience and communication, a Christianity that rejects hierarchy, a religion that is not embodied in an institution, but is charged with piety and feeling. Though they have not yet clashed directly, their incompatibility is obvious.

We can begin to see the outlines of the fundamental problems of the sixteenth and seventeenth centuries taking shape while Edward IV sits on the throne in the 1470's. The issues that will bedevil the Tudors and Stuarts can already be discerned. There is the question of law: does the law operate to serve the interest of the gentry—or the crown? What shall be the balance between the legal power of the gentry as exercised through the office of the J.P., and the legal power and influence of the crown? Next is the question of the relationship between Parliament and the king and his council. This problem is much more familiar, and it will be a great political issue in the reign of Elizabeth Tudor. Can the king rule without Parliament? To what degree are his ministers responsible; what are the limits of the crown; what is the role of Parliament in levying taxes, in assenting to legislation? These are the issues that will confront Elizabeth, James I, and will finally be settled by the men of 1688. Then, what is the nature of Christianity in England? Will it be a formal religion established by the episcopate and the crown, or will the standard be set by religious experience and the men, whoever they are, who are truly godly? This is, of course, inseparable from the political question, as James I (whose cry "No Bishop, no King," was much more than a petulant outburst) understood very well. The religious tension we can observe in the fifteenth century finally appears full-blown in the confrontation of the Stuarts and the Puritans. The fundamental religious issues of the sixteenth and seventeenth centuries, as well as the fundamental problems of law and government, are spawned by the critical tensions that develop in the late Middle Ages.

Why were these issues left unresolved until the sixteenth century and, really, until the seventeenth? We must remember that even in 1600 England was a relatively underdeveloped society with bad communications; inertia alone keeps an issue from becoming crucial. Before things reach the level of "crisis" (the label historians apply promiscuously to seventeenth-century events), strong personalities must intervene. It is perfectly possible, as we all know, for a society to live and function and survive despite the presence of contradictory principles. Issues may exist, but until someone bothers to raise them, to worry, to search out solutions, to agonize about them, they may lie dormant. Radical leadership, the one thing wanting in fifteenth-century England, appears late in the sixteenth century. Then a new generation of men want to resolve the tensions. They are agitated, and—most important—they do not keep their concern to themselves. They make the loudest complaint about religion which, in the seventeenth century, is ostensibly the one issue they mean to settle. Rather it is the problem they tackle first, not realizing at the outset how far the thread they grasp will unravel. Before the 1580's no generation clearly perceived the tensions and bothered to attack them. Fortescue sees them, but either he does not really care, or he does not care enough. He chooses to bury them, to obscure the contradictions in English government and society. But by the late sixteenth century this was no longer possible, and men are even more determined to have things out. The problems had been building up for two hundred years, but for two hundred years men had been distracted. First the aristocratic domination clouded all the issues. Men could hardly see that tensions were pulling at the law when the gentry and the king's court had a common enemy in the overmighty subject. By the end of the fifteenth century, the aristocratic dust was beginning to settle, and in the 1530's Henry VIII, with the aid of his great minister Thomas Cromwell, intended to make great changes in government and religion. There seemed to be a new rationality working in the world, and it seemed to be working through men of concern, perception, and capability. But the reckoning was forestalled by prosperity. As soon as the aristocracy finished beclouding the landscape, the economic boom was launched that would last for nearly a century. It is no accident that when prosperity fades toward the end of the sixteenth century, men grow more upset, more rational, and grave. In the sixteenth century men did not have to organize society, only enjoy it; in the seventeenth they were forced to ponder, to evaluate, and to try to reshape a world in which they could find no comfort. The tensions in government, law, and religion that were already prevalent in the fifteenth century finally became critical after 1600.

As the government and society of late medieval England begin to be closely studied at last, it becomes apparent that the fourteenth and fifteenth centuries do not only represent the waning of the medieval order. They also constitute the era that inaugurates the central issues which Englishmen will have to contend with in the following two hundred years.

By 1307, when Edward I died, the problems of the early Middle Ages had been resolved through the rise of centralized government and law; yet even in Edward's later years a new set of problems and tensions was already forming. Given the effects of Angevin government, the institutionalization of Parliament and law in the thirteenth century, combined with the dual strands of authoritarianism and decentralization that mark the later Middle Ages, a whole new set of problems was bound to arise.

CHAPTER SEVEN

FROM THE MEDIEVAL TO

THE MODERN WORLD

I. *The Interpretation of Modern*
English History

THE INTERPRETATION of medieval English history has been molded by the genius of F. W. Maitland, but our understanding of the course of the history of English government and society since the late fifteenth century has not had the benefit of an historical mind of equivalent magisterial authority. It would not be wrong to say, in fact, that since the death of Maitland in 1906 England has not produced an historian of monumental greatness. While in France in the 1930's there were at least two scholars, Marc Bloch and Lucien Febvre, who brought to the study of the French past that extremely rare but necessary combination of knowledge and insight which is able to effect a revolution in historiography, the study of English history has not been shaped by scholars of this highest quality. This puzzling deficiency in English historiography is part of a much larger problem of English educational and intellectual development in the twentieth century.

If the study of modern English history is still waiting for a Maitland, it has nevertheless benefited from the labor and insight of several scholars, all but one of them native or nationalized Englishmen, who while falling short of genius have yet made outstanding contributions and fun-

278

damentally conditioned our comprehension of the course of political and social change in England since the late fifteenth century. While the process of labelling historians is bound to be over-categorical and lacking in subtlety, it is nevertheless useful to group the historians of modern England into schools according to their basic assumptions. Historians of modern England can be divided into four distinct groups, and at least three of these are sufficiently self-conscious and consistent in their assumptions and methods to warrant the label of an historical school. The first of these is the Whig-liberal school, whose most brilliant twentieth-century representatives have been G. M. Trevelyan and the French scholar Élie Halévy. The second school of modern English history is one which relies upon a socialist, basically Marxist class conflict interpretation and whose most important spokesman has been R. H. Tawney. At the other end of the political spectrum is the school whose assumptions can apparently be identified as Tory or conservative and whose most famous protagonist has been L. B. Namier. The members of this group of historians sometimes claim the title of the School of Social Politics, although its critics would say that this is a euphemistic and question-begging term. The last group of interpreters of modern English history might be described as the political functionalists, among whom G. R. Elton and J. H. Plumb are pre-eminent; they are not yet sufficiently self-conscious and cohesive to be regarded as a school of historical interpretation.

The most deeply rooted, consistent, holistic—and in terms of a total pattern—the most meaningful and comprehensible view of English history is the one presented by the Whig-liberal school. The long and resplendent tradition of this school goes back beyond Sir Edward Coke in the early seventeenth century to the thirteenth-century church historian Matthew Paris. The exponents of this view—whether like Coke writing in the seventeenth century or like Stubbs and Macaulay in the nineteenth—see all of English history as unfolding one grand theme: the struggle between the king and the community over individual liberty and the rule of law. We have seen how historians of this school have portrayed the medieval period, how they saw in it the development of English government and society to the point where the king was bound to rule with the consent of the community and to maintain the law. This was the essence of English constitutionalism as it was glimpsed in the thirteenth century and then elaborated and articulated by Coke shortly after 1600. It was Coke who firmly enunciated that the grand theme of English history was the sovereignty of king in Parliament and the due process of the common law. This interpretation was widely accepted through the seventeenth and eighteenth centuries, and in the mid-nineteenth century it received its most magisterial exposition in the work of Thomas Macaulay, whose narrative of English history in the later seventeenth century became the historical bestseller of all times. Macaulay saw King James II as a betrayer of the historical constitution, a wrong-headed man who tried to introduce continental absolutism into England and was justly overthrown by the Whig aristocrats who saved English free institutions. Macaulay was unblushingly moralistic and xenophobic; the Glorious Revolution of 1688 meant to him the salvation of England from a terrible French fate. As seen by Macaulay, the English nation in 1688 had the wisdom to avoid the revolutionary mistake of the 1640's and the good sense to leave the business of leadership to the great lords who were the upholders of the constitution and the founders of what was to become nineteenth-century liberalism. There is much to recommend Macaulay's interpretation, and no other account of these great events has been able to provide another interpretation as consistent and significant as this one. Yet there are obviously defects in Macaulay's view of 1688 as the determining turning point in English history. Undoubtedly Macaulay softened and romanticized his Whig aristocrats; they were in fact tough, uncouth, selfish, unsentimental men whose ambiance was actually quite far from that of Macaulay and his gentle humanitarian, liberal friends of early Victorian England. It may also be questioned whether the nature of the English constitution was as fixed in 1688 and its principles as universally comprehended as Macaulay assumed.

Whatever its defects, the Whig-liberal view is the fundamental canonical interpretation of modern English history against which all other schools have to contend and must be measured. The Whig-liberal view is also the most constitutional: for the writers of this school there really is a constitution and they focus their histories upon the constitution as a thing, a discernible entity. Furthermore the Whig-liberal historians deeply believe in the English constitution as a moral force. They think that there is a higher law governing English polity, and woe to him who violates it—a belief that gives their accounts a quality of smoothness and consistency that none of the historians of other schools can match, at least when they have to view English history as a whole. Historians of other schools of interpretation have perhaps provided more convincing analyses of brief periods, but when it comes to viewing the whole scope of modern English history since the fifteenth century only the Whig-liberals can provide a framework for the whole sweep of political and social change and yet not ignore economic and intellectual factors. The Whig-liberal historians tell us that the constitution was established during the Middle Ages and that it meant the rule of law and the consent of the community. In the seventeenth century the Puritans were the first who valiantly defended the constitution against Stuart usurpation, but the Puritans discredited themselves by resorting to radical and extremist political experiments, and it was left to the great Whig aristocrats in the last decade of the seventeenth century to restore the balance of the constitution, founded on the principle of the sovereignty of the king in Parliament and the rule of the executive with the consent of the national community. The final stage in the development of the constitution was its democratization through the broadening of the franchise in the nineteenth century. The Whig-liberal historians believed that the constitutional adjustments after 1689 required to make the system work properly came about with a minimum of difficulty and certainly without the revolutionary upheaval that marked the history of continental states. There were of course important disputes and debates and a couple of critical moments when the political consensus was threatened. George III in the 1760's tried to turn the clock back and undo the settlement of 1688, and in 1832 the landed classes had to be pressured into sharing their power with the urban middle class. But these crises were weathered without the need for a revolution. In marked contrast to French violence and cataclysms, in the two centuries after 1688 the English constitution was peacefully adjusted to serve the needs of modern industry, empire, and democracy. As seen by the Whig-liberal historian, the eighteenth century produced the cabinet system by a kind of natural institutional childbirth, and in the nineteenth century the constitution was supple enough to allow for democracy. Yet fundamentally it was the same old medieval constitution, steadily adapted to meet the changing needs of modern society.

The Whig-liberal interpretation can be dreadfully dull, bland, smug, and unsubtle, but in the hands of its best protagonists it is intelligent and highly convincing. The Whig-liberal historians have remained unmatched for the quality of their narrative art, and this is not surprising since their interpretation offers a view of English history which best provides a coherent framework for a compelling and consistent account of a long period. The finest twentieth-century exemplar of the Whig-liberal tradition was a scion of the comfortable pre-World War I upper middle class, George Macaulay Trevelyan, great-nephew of Thomas Macaulay. Trevelyan wrote several books on various eras of English history from the fourteenth to the twentieth centuries; all have been bestsellers, and justifiably so because of the humanity, literary skill, and breadth of view which distinguishes all of this historian's work. Perhaps Trevelyan's outstanding book is *England under the Stuarts*, which remains after sixty years the most readable and on the whole the most convincing political history of seventeenth-century England. We can easily criticize his tendency to foreshorten and simplify, to assume there was a liberal rule of law in the Middle Ages, that the Stuarts were betrayers of the constitution, that the whole issue was neatly resolved in 1689, and we cannot believe that the late seventeenth-century aristocrats were really as humane and sensitive as Trevelyan depicts them. But we still must agree with Trevelyan that liberty was the fundamental issue behind the seventeenth-century conflict, and although he may have romanticized the people about whom he writes, he makes them real and alive for us in a quite personal and unforgettable way. Among the legion of writers on seventeenth-century English history no one has succeeded as well as Trevelyan in making us care about the issues of the period.

For the Whig-liberal school the only significant problem of English history after 1689 is to determine how the people were brought specifically within the constitution so that political democracy was finally achieved in an industrial society. The French scholar Élie Halévy, writing in the second and third decades of the twentieth century provided a full-scale account of the democratization of the eighteenth-century constitution. Halévy was ideologically committed to liberalism and had the romantic passion for English institutions of which perhaps only a foreigner is capable; he was a product of a tradition of admiring Frenchmen going back to Voltaire and Montesquieu. An unkind critic would say that Halévy understood nineteenth-century England not much better than Montesquieu understood the realities of the eighteenth-century constitution. Halévy intended to write the *History of the English People* from 1815 to 1914; in several volumes he dealt with the period from 1815 to about 1850 and from 1895 to 1914, but he never lived to give his account of the intervening era. Although Halévy worked only from published sources, his learning was prodigious and at his best he is a grand and impressive scholar; he can also be very tedious, and the later volumes he wrote, dealing with the 1830's and 1840's, are both dull and confused.

The first volume of his work, *England in 1815*, in which he tried to show the forces in English society which made possible the movement from Whiggery to liberalism, from aristocracy to democracy, is generally regarded as a masterpiece and is certainly the most persuasive and influential of his many volumes. Halévy enriched but did not substantially alter the Whig-liberal interpretation. He tells us that the ramshackle eighteenth-century oligarchic political and social system was rationalized and democratized through the impact of two great ideas—utilitarian philosophy and evangelical religion. Many historians have been convinced by Halévy that these two strands of thought are indeed the dominant themes of nineteenth-century English history. But subsequent research and consideration have raised doubts about how clear-cut and effective was the impact of utilitarianism and evangelicalism on nineteenth-century English government and society. Historians have come to question Halévy's optimistic conclusion that the leaders of English society in the nineteenth century came to be overwhelmingly inspired by these liberal and humane ideals. But no other writer has been able to present such a grand account of the process of political, social, and intellectual change in England between 1815 and 1914, and it can be said that Halévy concluded the Whig-liberal interpretation of English history with a final inspiring chapter.

In the 1930's it was fashionable to sneer at the Whig-liberal school of historians but the more work that is done on English history, and the more other schools attempt to undermine the views of Macaulay, Trevelyan, and Halévy, the more imposing and permanent does their achievement appear. Naïve in some ways, these historians possessed and controlled a total vision of the English past and they presented it in a glowing and eloquent manner. Whether any particular historical theory is ultimately true is something very hard to know, and no general view of the whole history of a society can fit all the data and be impervious to criticism. But any interpretation that is unified, generally applicable, sane, consistent, and morally persuasive will always have a great deal of merit in use, and this can be confidently asserted about the work of Macaulay and his twentieth-century disciples.

Although the Whig-liberal historians have been assaulted from both the left and the right, their critics have not been able to put forth any really viable and holistic interpretation to supplant it. The socialist and Tory attempts at the demolition of the Whig theory of English history were roughly contemporaneous, and they were the special occupation of

the generation of scholars working between about 1910 and 1940. The
first to arouse the imagination of readers, and not just academic ones,
was the socialist critique, whose originator and most convincing spokesman was Richard Henry Tawney. It could be argued that Tawney had
more influence on twentieth-century England than any other member of
his generation, Winston Churchill notwithstanding. We can say this in
all seriousness because Tawney's influence was for change, and for
change in the direction of the welfare state, which was finally effected in
England in the late 1940's. R. H. Tawney was a doctrinaire Christian
socialist, a Fabian, and something of a Marxist as well, who drew heavily
upon the great Protestant lower middle class traditions of righteous indignation. He was an important leader in the establishment of adult
education in England before the First World War and became the most
universally respected Labor Party intellectual. Tawney held the chair of
economic history at the London School of Economics for three decades,
and with his immense learning and elegant style he devoted himself to
the systematic undermining of the Whig-liberal interpretation. It cannot
be said that he succeeded in demolishing that interpretation but he
made it at least seem one-sided and tendentious, and induced not only
professional historians but also the general educated reader to question
the validity of its assumptions. Tawney's general view of English history
is already evident in his first book, *The Agrarian Problem in the Sixteenth Century,* which was published before the First World War. It is
a broadly conceived, beautifully written, fascinating work, although the
effectiveness of its argument has been somewhat vitiated by later research which has cast doubt upon the validity of the pertinent statistical
information on changes in rural society which Tawney worked out and
from which he drew his conclusions. Tawney's second historical book,
Religion and the Rise of Capitalism, published in the late 1920's, offers a
general interpretation of English history in the late sixteenth and seventeenth centuries; it had an astonishing influence on the historical outlook
of a whole generation and it remains, although no longer as widely read
or seriously regarded, a profound and important work.

Tawney's view of English history is based on economic determinism.
He accounted for historical change since 1500 in terms of the rise, development, and impact of capitalism. He believed that the capitalist spirit
definitely predominated in sixteenth- and seventeenth-century England,
and discusses it with the same angry and bitter tones he uses to de-
nounce the "acquisitive society" of modern industrial capitalism. For

Tawney, the sixteenth- and seventeenth-century gentry are as exploitative, greedy, and class-conscious as the meanest nineteenth-century coal and cotton barons. Like the Whig-liberal historians, Tawney also had a vision of what things were like in medieval England. He begins by positing medieval society as a kind of proto-socialist paradise, a paternalistic world where guilds sheltered the worker while monks dispensed charity and ecclesiastical authority inhibited usurers. Socialist theorists always have to set up a golden age in the past in order to show that the nature of man is basically good, and that it is only an irrationally organized society which produces evil and corruption in the world. In Tawney's view, what broke up this happy medieval community was the rise of capitalist agriculture at the beginning of the sixteenth century. The Stuart kings represent for Tawney the last ineffective vestiges of medieval paternalism, which was why the rising capitalists had to destroy them. In the earlier sixteenth century, Tawney tells us, the new capitalist landlords and the crown formed an uneasy alliance in opposition to the old feudal aristocracy, and both the monarchy and the gentry grew rich while the position of the aristocracy was undermined, the monasteries were obliterated, and the peasants were ground under. By the seventeenth century this alliance was no longer tenable because the insatiable capitalists of rural England and the rising merchant class were clamoring for an uncontrolled economic system so they could pursue their economic interests in a rational and untrammeled manner. Thus the civil war of the 1640's, in Tawney's view, is essentially the consequence of the capitalist class's ambition to break the last inhibiting shackles of the medieval community. In *Religion and the Rise of Capitalism* Tawney tried to show how the capitalists transformed Protestantism into their ideological vehicle and made Calvinism their special social ethic. In the 1930's this book was hailed by all sorts of people eager to prove that religion was a bad thing, despite the fact that Tawney had not said this at all. Rather, he contended that Protestantism was corrupted and made to serve the interests of capitalist exploitation, and it would be impossible to deny that there is some truth in this view.

There has been a long train of Tawney disciples working on Tudor-Stuart history—Christopher Hill and Lawrence Stone are the most prominent ones writing today. Hill's earlier work was little more than crass undergraduate Marxism but his more recent work has provided valuable insights into the course of social and intellectual change in the seventeenth century. He is not as enamored as his master of early Stuart paternalism and is not much more favorably disposed toward these kings than the Whig-liberal historians. But generally Hill continues to portray the sixteenth and seventeenth centuries as the initial stage of modern capitalism whose first great triumph in the overthrow of the Stuart monarchy in the 1640's was only part of the general destruction of the framework of medieval culture and society and the groundswell of the wave that swept on to the Industrial Revolution. Stone, a brilliant and omnivorously learned Oxford scholar who now holds a distinguished chair at Princeton, followed Tawney's interpretation closely in his early work. But his later studies in Tudor-Stuart history demonstrate a remarkable broadening of vision. Stone's most recent analysis of late sixteenth and early seventeenth century English development is strongly under the influence of the great historian of the French Revolution, Georges Lefebvre, who qualified his Marxist paradigm of social change with a complex causality drawn from twentieth-century sociological theory. Indeed, there are some strong parallels between Stone's view of social change in Elizabethan and early Stuart England and Lefebvre's explanation of the coming of the French Revolution. In both instances, the weakening of aristocratic leadership in society and the aborting of an aristocratic revival are made central themes. In his recent work, Stone has qualified Tawney's view of the central role of class struggle in English history with the theme of social mobility—the tendency of people of middling and lower status in pre-industrial society not to seek the emancipation and power of their own class, but rather to move upward into the class above. This view gives primacy to class relationships, but not class conflicts. The same sociological theme prevails in Peter Laslett's illuminating study of English society in 1700, *The World We Have Lost.*

Oddly enough, at least until very recently, the socialist historians have not been able to provide satisfactory accounts of the Industrial Revolution itself; their eyes are so filled with tears for the sufferings of the proletariat that they cannot critically examine the rise of modern industrial economy and society. Between the world wars a Fabian husband-and-wife team, J. L. and Barbara Hammond, ground out book after book, each one more breathless and grief-riven than the previous one, about the miserable fate of the English workers in the late eighteenth and early nineteenth centuries. It was not hard for more clear-sighted and less sentimental economic historians of a conservative inclination, John Clapham and T. S. Ashton, to present statistical evidence showing that real wages rose during the Industrial Revolution and that most workers were probably better off than they had ever been before. Eric Hobsbawm has revived the socialist indictment of the Industrial Revolution and claims that his assessment of the evidence confirms the earlier socialist view of the Industrial Revolution as a hellish era for the English workingman. It is obvious that different assumptions about what is or is not a good society will lead to very different conclusions on the moral significance of the Industrial Revolution. But this endless debate seems irrelevant in the context of the broader and fundamental problem of how and why eighteenth-century England experienced rapid industrialization and urbanization, and what these changes meant for English government, education, religion, and culture.

It is curious that in the 1920's and 30's no Tawney disciple appeared with insight and learning approximating his own, to apply the socialist view of English history to the period after 1700. This important work is at last under way in the 1960's. During the late 1950's, after a hiatus of a generation, a new group of important neo-Marxist scholars and critics has appeared in Britain. And in this group, Hobsbawm, George Rudé, and Edward Thompson stand out as historians of the age of transition from pre-industrial to modern society, from the mid-eighteenth to the mid-nineteenth centuries. Their studies are contributions toward a definitive left-wing interpretation of the emergence of industrialization and urbanization and the forming of working-class consciousness in England.

In the decade before the First World War, when Tawney was inaugurating the socialist onslaught on the Whig-liberal interpretation of modern English history, certain Roman Catholic writers made the first attempts to enunciate a view of the English past from a right-wing position. But this Catholic historiography never achieved respectability among academic historians; it immediately was bogged down by a lachrymose yearning for a medieval golden age that never existed and absurd apologetics for the Stuart kings. A truly conservative or Tory view of English history was almost entirely the result of the impact of one scholar, Lewis Bernstein Namier. The following that Namier eventually gained in academic circles throughout the English-speaking world was even greater than that enjoyed by Tawney in the 1930's; therefore, it would probably be true to conclude that Namier was the most influential of all twentieth-century historians of modern Britain. Although his own work on English history was confined largely to studies of the nature of politics in the 1760's, Namier's interpretations and methods were taken up and applied also to sixteenth-, seventeenth-, and nineteenth-century English history. Namier published his most important work in the late 1920's and 1930's, but it was not until the late 1940's and 1950's that he came to play the leading role in English historiography, to the point that Namierism was regarded by many academic scholars as synonymous with scholarship itself. Namier's influence and popularity were the result not only of the persuasiveness of his learning but also of the disillusionment with socialism experienced by the younger generation of English historical scholars. After the New Jerusalem of the Labor government of 1945-1951 had proved to be no more glorious than the free false teeth provided by the National Health Service, scholars who had become disenchanted with Tawney's class struggle and yet did not subscribe to faith in Trevelyan's liberal humanism rallied to Namier's Tory-conservative interpretation of the English past. During the 1950's Namier's work was if anything more vehemently acclaimed in the United States than in England. It is hard to know whether this was an index of American appreciation of Namier's self-conscious realism or rather of the peculiar fact that so many American historians of England are at heart romantic adulators of the English aristocracy.

There are obvious parallels between L. B. Namier and the nineteenth-century Tory statesman-theorist Benjamin Disraeli. Namier was the scion of a wealthy converted Polish-Jewish family which had envied the Polish nobility from whose ranks it was excluded. Sent to study at Oxford before the First World War, young Namier developed an intense admiration for the British aristocracy, a rather bizarre passion to indulge during the twentieth century. This went hand in hand with Namier's detestation of liberal ideology and indeed of all ideological formulations. It was not until 1931 when he had already published his first important work that Namier was able to obtain an academic post, and throughout his life he was chagrined by his failure to secure a place at Oxbridge. Until he became a professor Namier was a successful business executive, and this experience confirmed his deep-rooted belief that the only important thing in history is power, the only people who count are the "political nation," the men who control power, and the most interesting problem confronting the historian is analysis of the social bases of power.

Namier was the first English historian to take account of Freudian psychology, which he used, as was fashionable in the 1930's and 1940's, to undermine liberal ideology. Namier believed that hardly anyone ever grows up, particularly people inclined to radical political programs. He was himself obsessed with neuroses and insecurity, and this encouraged him to search for the fears that dominate men and to explain politics in terms of neurotic behavior. Without actually using Freudian terminology in his historical writings, Namier understood Freud's doctrines to confirm his anti-intellectual and anti-ideological bias. Anyone who enunciated a liberal or radical idea was for Namier *ipso facto* maladjusted and compensating for an unhappy childhood. In Namier's view the distinguishing characteristic of human thought and action is "senseless irrelevancy."

Namier's initial research on the 1760's was inspired by the work of some American historians of the American Revolution who, he realized, were not blindly following the Whig-liberal view of eighteenth-century British politics. His own great book, *The Structure of Politics at the Accession of George III*, aimed to show that the apparent moral and ideological struggles of George III's reign were meaningless smoke screens. Namier was a very careful researcher and his thesis is supported by an overwhelming mass of evidence. Yet he only studied closely two to three years of English history, and these happen to be the three years when there really were no distinctive parties, when party labels were only masks, and when the only things that made political life go were aristocratic interests, patronage, and clientage. But "Namierism" became inflated into a doctrine, a general statement about the nature of all British politics: all that matters in politics is social power, the top people in the county, great families and their interests, and high-sounding liberal ideologies are just a façade. The Marquis of Rockingham may hire a brilliant theorist like Edmund Burke to make fancy noises, but this is just another clever political move. There is much skill and practicality, no profound, idealistic commitment in English politics. As far as the early 1760's are concerned, Namier happened to be right, but this was one of the most miserable of all eras in English history. But once Namierism was expanded into a general principle, as it was in the late 1940's and 1950's, it was easy to make facile judgments that all liberals were either clever self-seekers or dupes and that all socialists were cranks overcompensating for bad upbringing. Namier's assumptions fitted in neatly with the neoconservative attitude of the younger generation of English historical scholars and intellectuals who were experiencing a long withdrawal from the radicalism of the 1930's. Namier allowed the left-wingers to shift ground without abandoning their contempt for Macaulay and Trevelyan. Clinging to their old disdain for the traditional Whig interpretation, they merely adjusted their conclusions and rushed to apply a Namierite interpretation to all the eras of modern British history.

Both Tawney and Namier dissented from Whig-liberal constitutionalism. Both saw English history as a struggle for power and working out of class interest. Both believed that the great constitutional issues morally exalted for centuries by the Whig-liberal school were only veils, that the real motivating forces in history are class interests and the struggle for power. Where these seminal minds of twentieth-century historiography diverge more than in any other aspect of their work is in their final evaluation. Tawney tells us that all of English history from the sixteenth to the twentieth centuries was deplorable; Namier finds in it a peculiar kind of glory. And although Namier claims to be a realist and although on the surface he does seem to be cool, dry, and extremely realistic, he too was captivated by an ideology—a rather archaic kind of romantic nationalism. In the 1920's Namier was a fervent supporter of Zionism; his view of English history was conditioned by the same kind of political romanticism. For Namier, nothing ever changed in modern English history; the top people in the counties were always on top, they deserved to be, and through the dominance of the Conservative party they always should be. Namier sounds very much like the eighteenth-century founder of romantic conservatism, Edmund Burke, but it is Burke at his worst—sentimental, snobbish, and blinded by a dizzying adulation of dukes.

While the high tide of Namierism was already beginning to recede in the 1960's, this scholar's impress upon the understanding of the English past is both permanent and profound. What Namier did succeed in showing is that we should not blithely take moral slogans and political ideology at face value; the historian must analyze all the available sources and must attempt biographical studies not only of great men but even of obscure politicians. We must look for the underlying personal motivations of political actions; we must not believe everything—possibly not anything—that politicians proclaim. Namier contributed an aspect of hard reality to English politics. He taught us that to read theorists like Burke is not enough; we must also study the papers of political organizers like the Duke of Newcastle; we must see the day-to-day manipulations of practical men working behind the ideologues' oratorical screens. Even those historians who cannot agree that the Whig-liberal ideology is mainly propaganda henceforth have to examine the hard social and political realities behind the traditional ideals.

What was particularly valuable in Namier's work was the method he employed—the extensive use of the most minute, probing kind of political biography. In the last stage of his career Namier conceived and inaugurated a vast project for publishing the biography of every member of Parliament since the time of Edward I. The only volumes of this project that have appeared are those on which Namier himself worked, dealing with the second half of the eighteenth century; they have not yielded any startling revelations but they will be a mine for future researchers. Namier also fostered a new interest in local and family history, not for antiquarian purposes but rather with the aim of establishing the social bases of English politics. While Trevelyan envisioned the persistence of a central constitutional ideal and Tawney the permanence of class struggle, Namier communicated a feeling for the continuity of English country life. He made us realize that whatever the upheavals at the center, the social structure of rural England and its way of life changed little from the sixteenth to the later nineteenth centuries. Thereby he allowed us to place many of the constitutional struggles which had so exercised the imagination of the Whig-liberal historians in a broader and more realistic framework. The major criticism that can be brought against Namier's devotion to country and family history is that he was too exclusively concerned with one stratum of society. The working classes are ignored in Namier's view of the English past, and the shopkeepers even pass unnoticed. Namier does not seem to know or care, although certainly many of his beloved dukes both knew and cared, about what was happening in the streets of London and Manchester. We also find missing in Namier what is so compelling in the best kind of twentieth-century French local historiography—a sense of the land itself, of the peasants, the fields, the crops, the agricultural tools, and the weather. It never rains in Namier-land.

Although Namier raised a whole generation of young scholarly disciples to apply his theses and methods to various aspects of eighteenth-century history, none of these has achieved the stature of his master. The two most important twentieth-century historians of eighteenth-century England after Namier are Herbert Butterfield, a neo-Whig and a fierce critic of Namierism, and George Rudé, an extremely subtle neo-Marxist. The most distinguished member of the Namier school is J. E. Neale, who has done for the sixteenth century what Namier did for the eighteenth, although with a much higher degree of literary skill. Neale's *Elizabethan House of Commons*, published in 1953, interprets sixteenth-century English politics in terms of county social structure. Politics, Parliament, and election all appear as routine aspects of the life of the ruling families in county society. Everything depends on patronage and clientage; ideas are insignificant and the Elizabethan House of Commons itself is only a reflection of the framework of power and wealth in the county. Neale's study is the most eloquent and persuasive exposition of the Namierite interpretation. Yet in his later work, *Elizabeth I and Her Parliaments,* Neale appears to depart from Namierism and to take ideology and religious disputes very seriously. Passionate speeches in Parliament about liberty become significant after all. The fulcrum of politics is now a small articulate Puritan group, and Parliament is caught up in the great European ideological struggle focusing on religion. Social interests, though present and important, are not the actual forces of change, and the account of sixteenth-century politics in Neale's later study would gladden the heart of a Macaulay or a Trevelyan. The ideological conflicts arising out of the Cold War of the 1950's appear to have powerfully influenced Neale's outlook, and he suddenly seems to have realized that political and religious slogans could signify deep beliefs and become powerful agents of social change.

Several historians, of whom Norman Gash and H. J. Hanham are perhaps the most important, have applied the Namierite interpretation to nineteenth-century English politics. They have succeeded in demonstrating the hard reality of the continuity of oligarchic, aristocratic leadership in the midst of all the famous conflicts about reform bills and all the utilitarian and evangelical doctrines that Halévy found so central. But every reader of Disraeli's novels knows that the great country houses still commanded enormous influence in the face of a rising industrial society, and the general significance of the work of the Namierite school on nineteenth-century English politics still remains to be assessed.

Weariness with both socialist and conservative history is reflected in the work of the new men of English historiography who came to the fore in the 1950's. Neither sentimental liberals, self-satisfied Tories, nor outraged Marxists, they are realistic men with few illusions. They tend to be from the middle or lower middle class, and they are intensely professional in attitude. Blinded by no slogans, they subscribe, but not in any naïve or sentimental way, to liberal constitutionalism. They will not melt at the sight of a duke, nor do they bleed for the working class; rather, they try to show the eras of English history in the round. Rejecting categories and dialectic, they are tough-minded rational men with excellent scholarly training behind them, whose alert minds are prepared to examine any kind of evidence in order to build up a total picture of the development of English government and society. G. R. Elton and J. H. Plumb best exemplify this new generation of English historical scholars, who, having absorbed the criticism which socialists and Namierites directed at the Whig notions of constitutional history, are going beyond the interpretations of the three traditional schools.

The independent judgment that Elton and Plumb exhibit in their work is partly a reflection of their provenance, which is outside the middle class from which most English historians of the nineteenth and twentieth centuries have stemmed. Elton is the son of a German emigré classical scholar, and although he came to England as a child he has retained a certain detachment in his studies of sixteenth-century government. He is awesomely industrious; no one for half a century has so completely mastered the sources of Tudor history. From the work he has done thus far, of which the most important is a magnificent general history of sixteenth-century England, it is quite clear that Elton possesses the most powerful critical mind at work on English history since Tawney, and indeed perhaps since Maitland. Elton is not without his own passionate interests. His admiration is reserved for bureaucracy, for technical, administrative, and legal competence, for governmental rationalism. As far as he is concerned, a government that can function well, even if it somewhat bruises individual liberty in the process, is good government. Elton has more tolerance than perhaps any other important writer on English history for authoritarian tendencies, though of course he too is glad that England became an enlightened and open society. What is important for Elton is getting the job done, and the important people are the men who can deal with the complex and exhausting problems of administration and law in an effective and rational manner. It scarcely matters who they are or from which class. The intelligent successful administrators, not aristocrats or theorists or saints, are the men who count. These are the men, Elton tells us, who made England, at least England in the sixteenth century, and he has an unmatched ability for showing them to us and allowing us to see political and social problems through their eyes.

J. H. Plumb has a working class origin; as a graduate of the University of Leicester, he was one of C. P. Snow's original "new men." Plumb studied at Cambridge under G. M. Trevelyan, whom he greatly admires, but at the same time in his own work on early eighteenth-century English politics and government he has clearly absorbed the best of what

Namier and Neale have to teach. The tone of Plumb's work is more liberal, personal, and humanitarian than Elton's; he has gone further than any scholar toward achieving a union of Whiggery and Namierism. His biography of Sir Robert Walpole, the eighteenth-century politician, is informed by a perpetuation of the old Whig-liberal feeling, but it is expounded in a much more realistic way and incorporates more social and economic history than the older Whig-liberal historians ever dreamed existed.

After having provoked a debate lasting for half a century, the Whig-liberal view still remains the only sensible, full interpretation of English history, but it has had to yield to the strong demands from both left and right for greater realism. The rising generation of English historians applauds the beneficent outcome of centuries of political and social change. But they want to find out, without being blinded by previous commitment to sentimental illusions, how the outcome was reached. The answers are found in many ways and places, some of them rather bizarre and unexpected and not always pretty or gentle. It is this open-mindedness which marks the technique of Elton, Plumb, and the new group of English historians, and it is the key to what may be termed their hard-headed political functionalism. They are willing to consider a great variety of explanations of what made modern English government, however inconsistent or incongruous. They recognize and even admire the grand constitutional theme set forth by the Whig-liberal historians, but they no longer feel bound explicitly either to justify or to attack it.

II. The Pursuit of the Modern

THE ACCESSION of Henry Tudor in 1485 is one of the select group of dates every English schoolboy and American college history student can identify, and it has come to be regarded as marking a great turning point in English history. How did 1485 come to be fundamental in English historiography, and is the beginning of the reign of Henry VII really of basic significance in the history of English government and society? It is often said by historians who hate to worry over vexing problems of periodization that dates like 1485 that are used to set off neatly one era from another are only conventions and handy devices, and that no one need believe they represent anything important. But periodization, much as we may rail against it, does matter very much to the historian. Once he chooses a set of dates as marking a period—no matter how random and arbitrary the original choice—this chronological fixing of an era inevitably conditions how the historian looks at the events, which have now been given a certain clarity and shape, and a date once established as beginning a new era will linger on in historical thought long after it has been proven unjustified and has outlived its usefulness. The trouble with dates is that people who bother to learn them hate to unlearn them and trouble themselves with new ones. The question of whether 1485 is a decisive turning point in English history is part of the larger problem of whether we should view the reigns of the Tudor monarchs from 1485 to 1603 as comprising a distinct and identifiable era in English history, and if so, what common qualities we should attribute to this era. G. R. Elton tells us that he is not entirely comfortable with the distinct periodization implied by the title of his book, *England under the Tudors,* but he can justify it by reflecting that England from 1485 to 1603 was after all ruled by a single dynasty. Some degree of unity was of course imposed on these decades by this dynastic fact, but it is necessary to go beyond this (as Elton in fact does) and consider whether the term Tudor period implies an identifiable era in the history of English society, government, and culture.

The first nineteenth-century writer who called attention to the Tudors and their special place in the whole scheme of English history was J. A. Froude in his *History of England from the Fall of Wolsey to the Defeat of the Spanish Armada* (1529-1588). Froude was a vehement Protestant nationalist, a violent anti-Catholic, an extremely effective writer in the romantic style, and the first masterly historian to study closely sixteenth-century England. He was something of an English Michelet but he also suffered unfortunately from a malady that came to be called "Froude's disease," of which the chief symptom is an inability to get anything exactly straight. Froude's Tudor history was written as a tract against popery and continental despotism; everything sweeps on to the grand climax of the defeat of the Armada in 1588, which Froude depicts as the most dramatic event in human history since Moses received the tablets. Soon after Froude came the Victorian publicist J. R. Green who coined the bright phrase "new monarchy," an admirable phenomenon that seemed to appear suddenly in England in 1485. The new Tudor monarchy,

Green believed, was a novel kind of government thoroughly distinctive from what had gone before—and much better. This attractive term, applied not only to English but also to continental political developments, has become embedded in historical rhetoric, where it has stuck so firmly that it has not been possible to pry it out in spite of cautions and animadversions by many twentieth-century scholars. It may still be permissible to use the term but it is also useful to ask what specifically was new about the Tudor monarchs, beyond their Welsh blood.

What is most surprising about the attitude of the Victorian historians toward the Tudors is their unabashed admiration for these dynasts who believed so unequivocally in the divine right of kings. At first sight it seems strange that the nineteenth-century historians, all of them sincerely committed to liberal ideals, could be enthusiastic about the tough-minded, despotically inclined people who ran Tudor government—so enthusiastic that they were quick to apologize for and either overlook or explain away some of the Tudors' more unsavory authoritarian qualities. Obviously there were important factors conditioning the nineteenth-century response to sixteenth-century monarchy, and the first of these is the nature of the sources themselves. The sources for fifteenth-century English history are extremely difficult to read and understand; most of the administrative and legal documents are written in depressingly poor handwriting and almost incomprehensible legal French, and even when in the latter half of the century English generally becomes the language of the sources, they are still difficult, frustrating, and uninspiring. But in a burst of style and clarity after 1485 come the beautifully drafted Tudor statutes and proclamations. Starting with the documents of Henry VII, the royal government exhibits an astonishing facility in its command of language, and with the statutes of Henry VIII, particularly those of the 1530's, we find the rolling preambles and gorgeous phrases that still have power to overcome the will and work like poetry on the imagination. The historian is always strongly tempted to believe that the rhetorical medium is equivalent to the message about the past. In studying Tudor history, it is almost impossible to separate style from content, very difficult to extrapolate the full implications of the statutes from their subtle phrasing; and we are never quite sure whether the magnificent language represents humanist rhetoric or a significant political doctrine. But no matter what they really mean, the Tudor documents are always exciting to read. The best of them have a felicitous Shakespearean ring, and in fact this excellence of language appears in sixteenth-century political documents before it is found in belletristic literature. No legislation in English history is so eloquently persuasive as the statutes of the Reformation Parliament of the 1530's.

In studying the Lancastrian and Yorkist periods, modern scholars flounder among muddled and dreary manuscripts, and then after 1485 they seem to emerge from darkness into light, and it is hard to resist the conclusion that this rhetorical Renaissance reflects the reality of political and social change. The chief means which the historian has to apprehend the nature of a society, particularly one for which there is no substantial and reliable statistical information, is through its language, and the very confidence and skill of Tudor English predisposes the historian to see 1485 as a great turning point. Any sensitive and highly literate scholar who peruses the legislation of Henry VIII can hardly keep from feeling in his heart something of momentous consequence has happened.

Another reason why the hundred and fifty years before 1485 remain confused and murky is that the printed sources for the fourteenth and fifteenth centuries are so scanty and defective; much more documentation has in fact been published for the reign of Henry II than for the reign of Edward IV. On the other hand, the late nineteenth-century Tudor revival prompted the publication under crown auspices of the Calendar of State Papers, a voluminous collection of summaries of governmental, administrative, and legal documents. The Calendar comprises not only domestic papers, such as the records of the Tudor Privy Council, but also extensive extracts from continental archives, of which the Spanish and Venetian have turned out to be particularly valuable—perhaps too valuable. The Spanish and Venetian ambassadors at the Tudor court provided long and elaborate accounts of what they found there. These accounts are indeed fascinating and informative, but it is often hard to know how far to rely on them. Certainly there is a great deal of wishful thinking in the Spanish correspondence's attempt to play down the rise of Protestant attitudes in England, and the learned Italians were so charmed by the classical learning they found at the Tudor court that they did not see much else that was happening in England. In addition to the vast collection of documents available in the Calendar of State Papers, the historian of sixteenth-century England can utilize a great variety of contemporaneously printed books and pamphlets, particularly on religious questions, with the result that he can gain a much clearer sense of public opinion than would be possible for any time during the medieval period. We are now familiar with the thesis propounded by

Marshall McLuhan: in the intellectual and social history of Western civilization the technological medium is the message itself, that is, the means of communication of ideas have tremendous significance for the way in which these ideas are received and understood. Not only was the new use of the printing press to communicate ideas of the greatest significance for sixteenth-century English society and culture; it also inevitably has affected the way in which we comprehend the sixteenth century. A society which can speak to us directly through printed books expounding opinions on all manner of political and religious subjects will tend to appear more like our own than one whose ideas have to be painfully extrapolated from a small group of awkward manuscripts. For the Tudor period it is possible to work so comfortably with published material that it is easy to ignore the masses of documents that still remain unpublished. Until the 1950's historians relied much too exclusively on the published sources which, in spite of the richness of their information on matters of high politics, have some very important gaps. The printed material is particularly weak in legal records, so that our knowledge of how the statutes and royal proclamations were actually enforced is frequently based on a rather hazardous guess. While the Court of Star Chamber is an institution that looms large on the Tudor scene, historians have built whole theories about the operation of this court from a very small body of published material, and reliable conclusions on sixteenth-century legal process would require difficult and painstaking research in manuscript sources.

Not only a visceral response to Tudor rhetoric, but other feelings as well, conditioned the image of sixteenth-century England that historians constructed. Victorian writers shared general historiographical assumptions resting on deep-seated nationalist and Protestant sentiments. Nationalism had already prompted nineteenth-century historians to look for the origins of beneficent English institutions in the medieval past, and it was also national fervor that induced them to discover the beginnings of English power, economic supremacy, and imperial expansion in the Tudor era. Not surprisingly, during the last two decades of the nineteenth century, when imperial attitudes were most aggressive and strident in Britain, the achievements of the Tudor dynasty were most vehemently celebrated. It was only natural to perceive in the dashing exploits of the intrepid "Elizabethan seadogs" the starting point of invincible English sea power and to transmute, by some kind of patriotic alchemy, slave traders like Sir John Hawkins and pirates like Sir Francis Drake into patriotic admirals and heroic Protestant gentlemen. This kind of myth-making declined somewhat after 1914 with the general deflation of imperialist attitudes, but after the Second World War, when English feelings of pride and power needed boosting, historians once more tried to evoke the heroic glories of the first Elizabethan age.

Along with untrammeled nationalism, strong Protestant sentiment contributed to the making of the Tudor image. A deep-rooted, at times hysterical, anti-Catholic feeling prevailed well into the later decades of the nineteenth century; as late as the 1850's there were anti-Catholic riots in the streets of London. Under these conditions it was again natural to look back fondly to the era when England broke out of popish bondage, supposedly vanquished superstition, replaced the cloister with the hearth, and established a sound and truly national religion. Until the very end of the nineteenth century no English historian who commanded an audience doubted that the Reformation was one of the very best and most wholesome things in all of English history. By 1900 Catholic publicists like G. K. Chesterton and Hilaire Belloc had inaugurated a vociferous reply to this traditional view of the Reformation. In their counteroffensive they went so far as to suggest that the English Reformation was cruel, crooked, and nasty both in its motives and its consequences. But they could not undermine the general consensus that the coming of Protestantism had a beneficent effect on English society, that it contributed to a more profound sense of individual liberty, and that it was one of the great legacies of the Tudor monarchy.

A third factor contributing to the late nineteenth-century Tudor revival was the whole concept of modernity, the notion that around the year 1500 Western civilization suddenly passed from its medieval to its modern phase. This advance to modernity is held to have taken place contemporaneously in all important aspects of political, social, and intellectual life: the modern state transcended medieval feudalism, Renaissance humanism flourished in the place of scholastic obscurantism, Protestantism triumphed over popery, science conquered superstition, and a capitalist economy rose to supplant a backward agrarian system. Historians went in search of anything modern in sixteenth-century England; they came up with an extensive assortment of items and were able to demonstrate that a great transformation in civilization occurred under the Tudor aegis. Although vehemently criticized by many scholars in the past half century, the concept of modernity has proved to be the most impregnable aspect of the image of sixteenth-century England which the Victorian writers initially established.

The first great Tudor historian of the twentieth century was A. F. Pollard, who published several important studies in the two decades after 1910. Although he was not himself a prolific editor of archival material, Pollard achieved a mastery of the sources of Tudor history. He was extremely learned in the political history of the first half of the sixteenth century, and was also a firm, clear, and convincing writer. It is symptomatic of the intellectual and moral climate of Edwardian England that a scholar of Pollard's stature had a very hard time securing a university chair; in bad old imperial Germany Pollard would early in his career have become a full professor with the rank and salary of a cabinet minister. After a lengthy stint writing articles for the Dictionary of National Biography, Pollard was finally given a chair at the University of London, but at first the post was purely honorary and carried no stipend. This happened, we may recall, while British wealth and prestige stood rather high in the world. The reasons behind Pollard's professional ill-fortune are to be found in the malaise that blighted English society in the early decades of the twentieth century. Yet Pollard never allowed these personal troubles to dissuade him from his full commitment to historical scholarship; he founded the Institute for Historical Research at the University of London, the first English parallel to the great German and French graduate schools.

Pollard wrote at a time when fortunately it was still assumed that the historian's proper audience was the general public, and his studies of early Tudor history are still important, relevant, and compelling. His favorite approach was biographical; through biographies of the outstanding leaders of English government and religion in the first half of the sixteenth century he succeeded in presenting an interpretation of the whole period. Although Pollard's ideas about the formation of character were pre-Freudian, Pollard was not at all insensitive to psychological problems. His biography of Wolsey, Henry VIII's chief minister in the 1520's, is still the only study of this important and complex man that is worth reading, and his Henry VIII is the best account we have, although he attributed to the king some achievements which later writers believe were mainly the work of Henry's ministers. Pollard did attempt a general history of the early Tudor period but he is not as impressive a narrative historian as he is a biographer. Pollard's bent for strictly political history and his inability to place statecraft within a social and economic framework make his general history rather arid reading today. Nevertheless Pollard's interpretation of the reigns of Henry VII and VIII (1485-1547) rapidly became the standard view, the classic picture for which all subsequent interpretations are corrections, adjustments, and revisions. Pollard's work outlined the basic structure of the new age; the Tudor era saw the onset of statism, nationalism, and modernity, the beginning of modern England. Pollard described a new national monarchy, highly competent, aggressive, and—not least important—enormously popular. He believed that in the sixteenth century the monarchy was at last leading the English people in the direction they wanted to go. The Tudor rulers created a strong centralized state, fostered industrial and commercial expansion, and cemented the spiritual unity of the nation by establishing a sensible Protestantism, which turned out to be a kind of easygoing low Anglicanism. Thus the Tudors were seen as the engineers of the breakaway from the disorganized feudal world of the fifteenth century. From aristocratic, chaotic, ineffective government England moved with startling swiftness to a national, modern, dynamic state. Not only did the Tudors lead and inspire the national spirit; in their own persons they were also its embodiment. This is an attractive picture and one that still prevails in all the textbooks. It would be wrong to say categorically that it has been fundamentally undermined by later scholarship, but it has been severely questioned and rudely challenged.

The first dissenters from Pollard's interpretation approached the problem in what now appears to be a somewhat bizarre fashion. Before the First World War, a group of neo-Catholic historians launched a vehement attack on the assumption that the Reformation was an unmitigated blessing. Was the Reformation beneficent in any way, they asked, or was it only the diabolical work of a selfish, power-mad ruler pursuing his private immoral interests? They went on to portray the Tudors not as agents of the will of the nation but as ruthless and irresponsible destroyers of all that was best and most beautiful in English society. The leader in this neo-Catholic offensive was Cardinal Gasquet, an angry and noisy controversialist who published a fiery book abut Henry VIII's dissolution of the monasteries. The Reformation, he said, was a brutal, shocking, and needless transition from the benevolent medieval community to a mean, grotesque, and immoral society. His thesis created a grand furor and provoked a good deal of teeth-baring among scholars over the proper reading of certain sources. In the 1930's Gasquet's interpretation was

revived in more subtle and persuasive form by R. W. Chambers, a professor of English literature at the University of London. Chambers' biography of Sir Thomas More, the chancellor of Henry VIII who preferred martyrdom to breaking with Rome, is the most skillful presentation of the Catholic dissent from the Protestant view of Tudor history.
Chambers contends that something rare and wonderful was taking shape
in early sixteenth-century England before the disasters of the Reformation. Although not exactly the modern world, what was coming into
existence was a high and rich culture based on the noblest ideals of
Christian humanism. A group of intelligent, learned, and devout men,
of whom More was the most sensitive and far-seeing, were working to
reconstruct the sagging fabric of medieval unity. These men were in the
act of transforming a noble vision of an ideal society into reality. For
Chambers, More is the tragic hero of sixteenth-century England: man of
letters and also of action, chancellor and Christian humanist, statesman
and elite reformer, More epitomizes the effort to revive and preserve all
that was best in the medieval world. In this light Henry VIII appears as
a coarse and blundering villain whose destruction of More ended the
possibility of attaining a good society and plunged England into an era
of greed and violence. Chambers' brilliant study of More has been widely
applauded as a sensitive apology but his general utopian interpretation of
what More could have done for his country has not been accepted.

The second attack on the glorification of Tudor England came from
Tawney and the socialist historians. They readily agree that the sixteenth
century saw the sudden dawning of the modern world, but they also
perceive it as the modern world complete with all its horrors, a capitalist
society whose modernity signified exploitation of the working classes.
Here Catholics and socialists share a vision: both presuppose a serene
medieval community and bewail its destruction by greedy capitalists and
ruthless landlords. The underlying thesis in Tawney's work is that if the
Tudors played a role in creating something new, this new and modern
society was a social structure built on the backs of the exploited masses.
While Pollard assumed an amiable, wholehearted alliance between the
crown and landed society, Tawney saw a brief and superficial marriage
of convenience which was never based on deep-rooted nationalist feelings. Crafty and aggressive gentry were happy to support the crown as
long as the Tudors petted and protected them. From the work of Tawney and his disciples we come away with the disturbing idea that the
Tudor monarchy was little more than a flashy façade, that all the royal

glitter and rhetoric masked a sordid social process, that under the nose of a largely impotent government a great economic and social upheaval was taking place and that the monarchy was really out of touch with the men who counted in society and commanded no deep-rooted or permanent loyalty from the gentry. We know that this thesis is presented in order to make the English civil war of the 1640's appear as the inevitable bourgeois revolution: the flimsy sixteenth-century alliance disintegrated into a war for the control of society between traditional royal paternalism and the aggressive forces of rising capitalism. Yet there is much in Tawney's view of Tudor history that makes any subsequent historian of the period stop and re-examine the facile assumption about the existence of a fundamental national union in the sixteenth century. At least we may conclude that the socialist interpretation provides something more provocative and penetrating than the Catholic mourning for a lost golden age that never was.

The work of G. R. Elton published in the 1950's encounters Pollard on his own political grounds and decisively rejects the whole notion that 1485 marked a modern revolution in government. Elton argues most persuasively that the administrative and legal structure set up by Henry VII was not only the same as that used by Edward IV, but was not even fundamentally different in kind from the government of Edward I at the beginning of the fourteenth century. Elton believes that the government of England in the first and second decades of the sixteenth century may have been operated by a very shrewd and intelligent ruler at a level of efficiency that his predecessors could not quite achieve, but there was nothing really new about it in the way of either institutions or political ideas. There was, however, according to Elton, a revolution in government in the early Tudor period and a start of political modernity. He posits an essential change in political institutions and ideals in the 1530's, although the revolution that he describes is not entirely congenial to everyone's concept of a revolution. Elton accepts the old Pollard thesis on Tudor modernity but gives it a disconcerting and startling new twist by moving the date of the revolution from 1485 to 1536 and by making the architect of the revolution not one of the Tudor kings but Henry VIII's chief minister, Thomas Cromwell. At this point we have the real beginning of modernity: the idea of sovereignty is clearly conceptualized by Cromwell, and an effective bureaucracy along modern lines is for the first time established. Elton attaches such great significance to the events of the 1530's that he sees the ministry of Thomas Cromwell as the most important dividing point in English political history between Edward I and the coming of the welfare state in the nineteenth century. Elton's interpretation and his exposition are very bold and learned, and he is so fully in control of the sources that all his critics—and they have not been reticent—look rather feeble in comparison. But his thesis is still not particularly captivating; it is not very inspiring to think of Thomas Cromwell, hitherto regarded as a social-climbing royal hatchet-man, as the greatest statesman England ever produced, and although scholars have been forced to treat Elton's work with respect, they are not inclined to accept wholeheartedly the validity of his thesis. His interpretation of Tudor history has gained a widespread but rather reluctant intellectual assent, but it has not been able to win the emotional acceptance from historians necessary for a new interpretation to become the basic assumption on which all future work is predicated.

In attempting a reappraisal of Pollard's view of Tudor history we have to begin by asking if there were any vast and stunning differences between fifteenth- and sixteenth-century English political, religious, and intellectual life. We are still appallingly ignorant about fifteenth-century England, but we do know enough at this point to see that many supposedly sixteenth-century innovations in politics, religion, and culture were not new at all. Historians have always emphasized that the Tudors had spectacular success with conciliar administration and law in central government, such as the use of the Privy Council and the Court of Star Chamber and with the institution of the justices of peace at the county level. But we know that these famous Tudor institutions were in fact already characteristic of fifteenth-century government. They were used with a high degree of skill by the Yorkist kings in the 1470's and 1480's, and even the earlier Lancastrian administration, infamous for its slovenly and ineffective operation, had essentially the same machinery. In terms of the institutional framework there does not seem to be any appreciable difference between the government of 1480 and that of 1520, and we still see much of the same framework even in 1600. In examining the financial institutions of the Tudor monarchy, the ironic persistence and even conscious revival of medieval traditions becomes even more apparent. The dynasty hailed as modern, anti-medieval, and breaking with the feudal past, has been shown by J. Hurstfield and other scholars to have relied more upon the feudal prerogatives of the crown for royal income than any government since the reign of King John. The Tudors resurrected with a vengeance the archaic institution of feudal wardship and also sought assiduously to increase the size of the crown lands, thereby freeing the monarchy from financial dependence on the House of Commons. It would be hard to find two royal institutions more distinctively medieval and less characteristic of modern bureaucracy than feudal wardship and the royal demesne. We might plausibly argue that the Tudors managed to infuse new life into the old forms, that they revitalized the old institutions with new vision and purpose, and that the robust Tudor wine poured into frail old bottles finally worked the destruction of the bottles themselves. But the use of such metaphors indicates how hard it is to maintain unblemished the Tudor reputation for political modernity. A government which did not develop the institutions of public credit upon which the finances of all modern states depend, which even far less than the rulers of the fourteenth and fifteenth centuries relied upon national taxation by consent of Parliament but instead desperately resorted to the expedient of recovering half-forgotten medieval royal prerogatives, at best existed in a kind of twilight world between medieval and modern political life.

The close examination of other aspects of life in Tudor England similarly weakens and undermines and occasionally explicitly contradicts the traditional attribute of modernity. There was nothing particularly novel about the Protestant religious doctrines prevalent in sixteenth-century England; they can be viewed as merely variants and extensions of medieval heresies which finally broke through the surface restraints of the old religion and the old authority. It is more useful to ask why this breakthrough did not begin before the 1520's than to expound its radical newness. What aspects of English government and society kept anti-papal, and anti-sacramental, and anti-sacerdotal ideas under control in the fourteenth century and what allowed them to come to the fore after 1520? Until recently this question has scarcely been formulated, but A. G. Dickens' *The English Reformation,* by far the best book ever written on the subject, has greatly changed the way historians will henceforth have to think about the origins and significance of Tudor Protestantism. For the first time a well-informed scholar has seriously devoted the early chapters of a study on the English Reformation to finding and explicating Protestant ideas in medieval heresy. Oddly enough this is really a rediscovery—only four hundred years belated. It is the way many knowledgeable people were thinking in the 1520's. The bishops at that time remarked that the new doctrines sounded suspiciously like those of Wyclif and recognized in them a resurgence of Lollardry, an acute perception that historians ought to have respected.

The first sentence of F. M. Powicke's interpretive book on the Reformation, published in the 1930's, confidently announces that "the English Reformation was an act of the state." We can no longer see it so simply and unequivocally. There were two Reformations in sixteenth-century England which, entirely different in origin and character, became inextricably intertwined with one another. The more obvious and easier to study is statist, political, and diplomatic; it forms the dramatic story of Henry VIII's break with Rome. But Henry VIII was no more Protestant than the Pope. At the same time there was occurring a popular Reformation, now strengthened and somewhat enriched by continental doctrine, which perpetuated the ideas that had been the stuff of medieval heresy. Nothing about the English Reformation is very clear except that it was not a sharp break with a discarded past but an infinitely complex and entangled upheaval which to a significant degree marked the triumph of ideas with deep roots in the fourteenth and fifteenth centuries.

It has been the common practice for historians to attribute to a small circle of humanist scholars in early sixteenth-century England—the native Englishmen John Colet and Thomas More, and Erasmus, the famous visiting scholar from the Low Countries—the formulation of certain ideas which are held to have had a great impact on their contemporaries. Thus the Renaissance is said to have come to England and introduced a new set of intellectual assumptions and attitudes. The ideas popular in the circle of these humanist reformers—the rejection of Aristotelian in favor of Platonic philosophy, a more personal and emotional manner of approaching religious experience, and severe criticism of the failings of the clergy—appear indeed to have inaugurated intellectual currents of far-reaching importance. But historians have ignored the lesson which they should have learned from their discovery that some of the adherents and preachers of radical religious doctrines in the 1520's and 1530's had been Franciscan friars. What has been attributed to the new wave of Renaissance humanism is, in fact, attitudes and doctrines which the Franciscans had been preaching in England for 250 years. This is a problem that still requires intensive study. Perhaps Erasmus and his humanist colleagues developed independently the same ideas which had been circulating in English Franciscan circles since the days of Duns Scotus and William of Ockham; it is more likely, however, that the Renaissance humanists merely contributed the influence of their eloquence and high social status to anti-clerical, devotional, and quasi-mystical doctrines that had long been indigenous to the radical wing of the English church itself. Perhaps we shall eventually see the explosive ideas at work in sixteenth-century England not so much as the result of humanist rhetoric or even of the impact of Lutheranism, but rather as the fruit of two centuries of Franciscan teaching. It is at least plausible to maintain that the ever-increasing concern through the Tudor period with an intensely personal religious experience again marks a perpetuation and accentuation of one strand of medieval life and thought.

The perpetuation of the medieval thought-world is readily apparent in sixteenth-century belletristic literature. In his brilliant and sensitive study *The Elizabethan World Picture* E. M. W. Tillyard makes us question the long-held assumption that the higher thought of Tudor England can be considered as inaugurating the modern world, and a somewhat similar thesis is presented in C. S. Lewis' *English Literature in the Sixteenth Century* and in Douglas Bush's *The Renaissance and English Humanism*. Tillyard, who was strongly under the influence of R. W. Chambers, shows us that the cosmology revealed in Elizabethan literature is still based on the medieval concept of hierarchy. The ideas which the writers of the period express about God, man, and the world, are still presented in terms of the traditional ordered structure, and the prevailing image of the cosmos is still that of the great chain of being. People continue to take these medieval ideas for granted as everyday, commonplace assumptions, and when men come to think and speak about any aspect of life—about human nature, religion, the state, society, and the universe—they frame their ideas in terms of a fixed, ordained hierarchy. They continue to think along these lines and to justify their conduct by hierarchic doctrine even though what they may actually be doing is contradicting and undermining the medieval world order. Even though sixteenth-century men may at times act in a new and individualistic way, when they explain themselves in the world around them they use the old concepts and the same familiar language. Tillyard's view of the thought-world of Elizabethan literature is readily confirmed by the concepts which prevail in the writings of practical men. The leaders of Tudor society, no matter how revolutionary their practice, strive to justify their conduct in terms of divine providence, natural law, and a sharply stratified world order. These are the ideas that spring most readily to their minds, and the theoretical allusions which still carry the heaviest weight of meaning.

Another way of questioning the arrival of the modern world in the sixteenth-century is to examine the commonplace aspects of human life and everyday environment, the daily occurrences and mode of existence that men take for granted. We can see quickly enough that just because Henry VII or even Elizabeth I is seated on the throne, the style of common life is not much different from that which had prevailed for several centuries. What constantly impresses us in reading the sixteenth-century sources—whether legal records or literature—is the continued prevalence of violence. This is not the grand violence of the Wars of the Roses, but it is violence nevertheless. Mayhem, manslaughter, and riots are still constant conditions of everyday life; rioting is so common that it is used as the judicial pretext for getting cases into Star Chamber, and it was a pretext so ready at hand that lawsuits on almost every possible subject could be impleaded in Star Chamber. In Tudor England everything— whether a disputed election, a disagreement over landholding, a question of enclosures, or, not least, religious controversies—seems to end in disturbance of the peace. Everywhere we may look we see fences being ripped down, knives being pulled out, and heads being smashed. Life and property are in constant jeopardy. Violence is still the basic style of life for sixteenth-century people; in some ways they are not very far from Anglo-Saxon society. And how do people respond and cope with violence and insecurity? With a deep attachment to order, to political and social conservatism, to the divinely ordained king, to the stable hierarchic view of the world inherited from the medieval period. This feeling is everywhere; we can see it not only in the political pamphlets and sermons of the period but also clearly enough in Shakespeare's dramas. Terrible things happen to Shakespeare's people when they go against the organized structure of the world; because they destroy order and shatter control they themselves are destroyed. We cannot ignore the violent temper of Shakespeare's tragedies though he is gentle in comparison to the unrelieved gore and psychotic terror of the early seventeenth-century dramatists. The blood feud is still one of the most common themes in literature, and it can be resolved only by the crudest kind of violence, as in *Macbeth* and *Hamlet*.

Sixteenth-century England remained primarily a pre-industrial, elitist, and underdeveloped country; at least eighty-five percent of the population still lived on the land. Its only metropolis was London, which in 1600 had probably 300,000 people, and no other city in the realm had even one sixth as many. The total population of England in 1600 could have been very little in excess of three million, only three times greater than the population of England when William the Conqueror invaded the country. In spite of the celebrated woolen industry and expanding overseas commerce, there was no factory system and nothing to compare with the industrial masses of modern society. The royal administration and all local government and law were still overwhelmingly under the control of landed society. The concepts which men used to explain the world to themselves were largely the same ones that had been used in 1300. In addition a streak of violence ran like a dark thread through everyday life as it had from time immemorial. There is therefore much to be said for the conclusion that Tudor culture and society were still medieval in tone.

The attributes of modernity which several generations of historians so hastily awarded to Tudor England have been shown by recent scholarship to be, in many instances, at best highly dubious and at worst totally invalid. Nevertheless, from the time that Edward IV securely gained the throne in 1471 to the death of Elizabeth in 1603, fundamental and lasting changes in English government and society undoubtedly occurred. The revival of royal power and the restoration of the effective functioning of central government and law are the overriding conditions of these decades. It is necessary, however, to probe more deeply to determine whether this revival of monarchy merely re-established royal power to the point it had reached at the death of Edward I in 1307 or whether there were innovations in political and social institutions and ideas which mark a break with the inherited medieval traditions and provide the conditioning framework of the following two centuries.

Many of the celebrated deeds of the captains and kings of late fifteenth- and sixteenth-century England, however dramatic and interesting to behold in themselves, were of no serious consequence for the general history of English government and society. But amid all the confusions and upheavals of the period it is possible to ascertain seven general patterns of change looking forward to the following centuries:

(1) There was a shift in the social basis of politics. Aristocratic political leadership, such as had prevailed in the fourteenth and first three quarters of the fifteenth century, greatly declined, and gentlemen who had neither noble titles nor even unusually great wealth became very important in the royal administration and national politics.

(2) The sovereignty of the national state was established in theory and to some degree in practice as well. Those areas and institutions—the

frontier marches and the church—which had hitherto been at least partly immune from effective royal control were now subjected, in a sweeping attempt at political rationalization, to the leveling authority of the central government. To put it another way, medieval pluralism began to be subordinated to the aspiration of a sovereign national state, although the effectiveness of this proposed centralization was greatly inhibited by the severe practical limitations of backward communications and the small size of the royal bureaucracy.

(3) A strenuous effort, which had only a qualified success, was made to improve upon the awkward late medieval household system of royal government by substituting a more public kind of bureaucracy managed by a great minister of the crown under delegated and immediately revocable royal authority.

(4) There was a confused, hesitant, largely pragmatic, and never clearly conceptualized shift from the medieval to the modern idea of legislation, from the assumption that king in Parliament declared, confirmed, and registered prevailing law to the belief that king in Parliament had sovereign authority to make new law for the enhancement of common welfare.

(5) In a half-hearted manner the central government added to its traditional functions of defense and peace the regulation of economic and social life so as to further the interests of the commonweal and to make sure that the poor and unfortunate were given some outside assistance toward attaining a basic sustenance.

(6) In the second half of the sixteenth century the House of Commons becomes not merely a part of the high court of Parliament or even a mere branch of a sovereign legislature, but a theater for debate on high matters of government and statecraft.

(7) Finally, what is most elusive of all, we glimpse an enhanced sense of the dignity and both moral and rational potentiality of human nature, contributing to greater self-confidence among the leaders of society to make decisions on institutional innovations in both church and state.

CHAPTER EIGHT

THE
RECONSTRUCTION OF
GOVERNMENT AND
SOCIETY
from 1471 to 1603

I. Inflation's Wake

I T IS NOT SURPRISING that socialist historians like Tawney should have been attracted to sixteenth-century English history because this is one of the eras when economic change vitally affected politics and society, and therefore the Marxist historian's commitment to economic determinism takes on some degree of plausibility. From the late thirteenth century to the middle of the fifteenth century, the English economy, both rural and urban, had stagnated, and even in 1480 it was only slowly emerging from the long late-medieval depression. This fundamental fact does not, of course, imply that during these two centuries life was uniformly harsh for all members of society, and in fact a chronic labor shortage aided the manorial peasants in their eventually successful attempts to gain manumission from serfdom, but the later Middle Ages were in general a period of price deflation and population decline. The market for both agricultural and industrial goods was shrinking, trade was poor, and land steadily went out of cultivation. The most obvious difference between Lancastrian and Tudor England was a change in economic conditions. The economic hardships of the fifteenth century, which had plagued landed society and worried the merchant class, began to clear away in the reign of Edward IV, and from about 1500 until the last twenty years of the sixteenth century Englishmen enjoyed the happy experience of a general economic boom, which seemed all the more beneficent because of its stark contrast with life in the Lancastrian period. Prosperity, like depression, was not experienced in an equal degree by all classes in society or even by men and families within the same social group. The entrepreneurs engaged in commerce and industry suffered severely in the sixteenth century from rapid market fluctuations, and by and large the condition of the agricultural worker became worse instead of better. But for about one hundred years there were unprecedented opportunities for ambitious men, particularly if they were landlords, to become rich, and the consequent soaring prosperity profoundly affected both the social structure and the policies of the royal government.

The fundamental fact of late fifteenth- and sixteenth-century economic life in England as in the rest of western Europe was a steady and, at times, runaway inflation, and one thing that the mysterious science of economics teaches us is that inflation and prosperity usually go hand in hand. At no previous time in European history was there such a precipitous rise in the inflationary curve; during the first half of the sixteenth century prices in England more than doubled and in 1600 prices were five and a half times what they had been in 1500. This phenomenal inflation was contemporaneous with a population growth of no more than thirty percent, so that it was not primarily the natural consequence of market expansion. The causes of the price rise in fact bewildered contemporaries, to whom economic change appeared almost as irrational as changes in the weather, and it was not until the second half of the century that even learned, intelligent, and well-informed men attained a hazy understanding of the factors which had induced this economic revolution. We now know that prices began to rise very slowly in the late fifteenth century in response to population growth and the opening up of new silver mines in Germany, which put a little more money into circulation. But the explosive inflation of the sixteenth century was induced by two other factors, one of them indigenous and the other foreign in origin to the English economy.

The first was the misguided and ultimately disastrous debasement of the coinage by the royal government in the 1520's, 1540's, and early 1550's. The second and more important cause of inflation, particularly during the second half of the century, was a flood of specie into Europe from Spanish America via the Hapsburg territories. The Spanish Hapsburgs used most of their treasure to underwrite their huge mercenary military machine, and thus American gold and silver spread all over western Europe and drove prices up at a fantastic rate. Since Antwerp, in the Hapsburg-controlled Low Countries, became during the first half of the sixteenth century the prime English export market, the English economy was immediately affected by price fluctuations at Antwerp as Spanish specie was funneled directly from the Low Countries across the channel.

Some economic historians, like J. U. Nef, view the English price rise as a symptom of something more important than these accidental and tangential factors. Citing such changes as the rise of the Lancashire coal industry and an increase in production of the English woolen industry, they see the price rise as part of a so-called first Industrial Revolution in the later sixteenth century. Careful consideration, however, has led to the prosaic conclusion that neither the quality nor the quantity of English industrial production in the sixteenth century gives evidence of any revolutionary or even highly significant change, certainly not enough change, at any rate, to have been a primary cause of the business boom during the period. Some new industries did develop in Tudor England, but the expansion of the most promising of these, namely coal production, was greatly limited by a failure to find a satisfactory way of using coal to smelt iron. Coal in the sixteenth century was carried by sea from Newcastle to London and the south, principally for heating use, to compensate for the steady diminution of the once vast English forests, but the process of making coal into the usable form of coke for steel production was not discovered until the eighteenth century. There was an appreciable increase in woolen production but the machinery used was still simple and primitive, and the improvements made in the sixteenth century were not of great importance. In 1600, unfinished woolen cloth remained as it had been since the later fourteenth century, the chief English export. The cloth industry continued to be organized according to the domestic or "putting out" cottage system of production, and if one entrepreneur possibly did construct something resembling the modern factory, his ingenious experiment was not imitated, and again English industry had to await eighteenth-century improvements. It is naïve to portray a domestic system of production, no matter how well-organized and widespread, as an incipient industrial revolution. If the latter term means anything, it signifies the factory system and the transforming of the industrial workers into an urban proletariat. The woolen workers of the sixteenth and seventeenth centuries were dispersed in country villages, maintained gardens and small farms, were only part-time employees of the merchant entrepreneurs who controlled the woolen industry, and were not completely dependent on their income from industrial production. This certainly does not look like the Industrial Revolution.

The sixteenth-century English wool magnates failed to use the factory system not because it was unknown or because they were too conservative or obtuse to effect an industrial revolution, but rather because they had no desire for greatly increased productivity. Since the nineteenth century the challenge faced by the capitalist entrepreneur has been to increase production; if he can produce more, better, and cheaper goods than his competitors, he will outsell them because, given the circumstances created by modern technology, distribution is no problem and is equally available to all producers. The critical problem faced by all capitalist industrial entrepreneurs before the transportation revolution of the later eighteenth and nineteenth centuries was just the opposite of that of their modern counterparts, and England's insular position made this a particularly difficult matter for the men who controlled the Tudor woolen industry. There was no point in expanding production when transportation technology remained so primitive and precarious, and international distribution of goods therefore so expensive that despite the price inflation the size of the foreign market was severely limited. The decade-by-decade increase of the English population during the sixteenth century sufficed to absorb only a modest increase at home in woolen production, and the built-in defects of the export system across the channel similarly allowed only a small expansion of the Flemish market. It is not surprising that under these conditions the Tudor entrepreneurs were far from eager to allow uncontrolled production and market competition; they were in fact monopolistic and protection-minded, in marked contrast to their nineteenth-century laissez-faire counterparts. The Tudor wool magnates could have produced more but they could not profitably distribute and sell the surplus abroad. Hence they constantly urged the crown to give them a corporate monopoly which would keep out new producers and protect the limited market. It is painfully evident that the whole European economy, the English included, suffered from a crippling distribution problem from the fourteenth to the eighteenth centuries, and until this was overcome there could be no Industrial Revolution. It is also apparent that economic stagnation was a constant threat to this defective economic system. The hundred years' spurt between the late fifteenth and late sixteenth centuries was not the dawn of modern capitalism. Rather, it was an anomalous and short-lived economic situation. When the magic effect of American specie wore off in the last decade of the century, deflation again set in, the endemic depression reappeared, and after 1600 we again hear bitter complaints from both landlords and merchants.

The inflationary boom of the late fifteenth and sixteenth centuries was, therefore, a peculiar interlude in the chronically difficult conditions of the English economy between the late thirteenth and early eighteenth centuries. Its uniqueness makes it all the more important. This era of prosperity provided unusual opportunities for entrepreneurial endeavor, especially in agriculture, an activity that in turn stimulated far-reaching social changes to which the royal government was forced to adjust.

The new prosperity of the late fifteenth century engendered an expanding market for agricultural produce. The small farmers and peasants were apparently first to take advantage of this situation. Prices for grain and wool rose steadily and men who owned their own farms or held land on fixed rents were making impressive profits, even if their holdings were small. By the 1480's, however, the landlords themselves, particularly if they were enterprising and rational, were cognizant of the new opportunities, and for the next hundred years propertied men in search of profit did everything they could to capitalize on the steady demand for grain, meat, and wool in an inflationary market. The movement toward capitalist agriculture took two forms: first, the landlords set out to rationalize the use of their resources, and second, they eagerly sought to acquire more land.

The first step in the rationalization of prevailing resources was the attempt to transform traditional fixed rents paid by copyholders and other kinds of tenant farmers into short-term leases so that rents could be raised to keep pace with rising prices. Goaded by the demand for meat and wool, which was insatiable in the first half of the sixteenth century, more enterprising and aggressive landlords went further. They sought to enclose the old open fields and common pasturages, which were vestiges of the medieval manorial economy, and to turn their estates into vast sheep-runs whose wool and mutton fetched huge profits in the inflationary market. This late fifteenth- and sixteenth-century enclosure movement was partly inhibited by the desperate resistance of the threatened tenant farmers. The royal government, always spurred by fears that extensive dispossession of the peasantry would lead to social disorder and thus inspire rebellion against the crown, also hindered the enclosure movement, though with intermittent and usually half-hearted prohibitions. The dearth of statistical evidence has made it difficult for historians to establish the extent of enclosure in the sixteenth century. It is now generally believed that not more than five percent of the agricultural land of England was enclosed before 1600, but in a few counties where the land was particularly suitable for sheep-raising, the figure may be as high as twenty-five percent. Enclosure certainly created grave social problems which forced the royal government for the first time in English history to regard the relief of the poor and unemployed as one of its functions.

The prosperity enjoyed by those landlords who were willing and able to practice the new capitalist agriculture provoked an insatiable demand for more land among the rural entrepreneurs. Their greed and energy drove them to look longingly upon the vast estates held by the monasteries. Some landlords had long drawn substantial income as secular managers of monastic estates, but they too were caught up in the inflationary hysteria of the sixteenth century and, just as they raged against the fixed rents and dues of their tenants, so the landlords were no longer satisfied with a limited profit even when it took the form of a sinecure. In these circumstances the dissolution of the monasteries by the Tudor crown in the 1530's was bound to be vehemently approved by nearly all the leaders of rural society. The sale of monastic lands by the crown from the 1540's to the end of the century became, therefore, the chief means of appeasing the land-hunger in rural society. The monasteries had held perhaps half of the best agricultural land in England, which was now subject to exploitation for the market, and yielded immense profits to those who had successfully bid for these prized estates.

The combined effect of enclosure and secularization of monastic property was the inauguration of a radical change in the face of rural England; in the extensively enclosed areas it assumed an appearance which it retained at least until the nineteenth century, and which it still has in many rural counties of south-central and eastern England at the present day. The unfenced open fields and commons were now encircled by the green hedges of merry England, and the new dominant position of the entrepreneurial landlords was symbolized by the erection of their stately homes, many of which were, in fact, refurbished monastic houses.

Novel economic conditions provided unprecedented opportunities for men of middling and even modest provenance to rise high in county society. Not again until the Industrial Revolution of the late eighteenth century would the qualities of energy and daring combined with rational allocation of resources and the absence of moral scruples—in other words, the qualities we associate with the capitalist entrepreneur—bring such immediate reward in England. Some of those who did well in this expanding economy were younger sons of the nobility, who had the initial advantages of family wealth and prominence; others were men who were given preference by the crown because they were faithful servants or court favorites. But many who rose to great wealth and at least provincial importance during the late fifteenth and sixteenth centuries were men who made their own way in the world and triumphed in a society that was relatively open and freely competitive in comparison with the rural England of the later Middle Ages. Yet it would be a grave error to suppose that the Tudor countryside was exclusively the scene for the exercise of rational planning and greed by upwardly mobile capitalist gentry; this mistake has frequently been made by Marxist historians. The term "gentry" in the sixteenth century simply meant the gentlemen, and it may be applied to a very large and heterogeneous group that includes as much as twenty percent of the population of England. "Gentry" is a very supple word, and it stretches all the way from a flamboyant younger son of the nobility to a petty landlord domiciled in a very modest manor house eking out a living from the rents of three or four tenants. "As for gentlemen, they be made good cheap in England," writes the commentator Sir Thomas Smith in 1551. "For whosoever studieth the laws of the realm, who studieth in the universities, who professeth liberal sciences and, to be short, who can live idly and without manual labour, and will bear the port, charge and countenance of a gentleman . . . shall be taken for a gentleman."

The fortunes of the people called gentry varied greatly with the circumstances of the sixteenth-century boom, and those able to take full advantage of the new economic conditions formed a small minority. Certainly there were as many among the landlords of Tudor England who failed to adjust to the new conditions and whose status and income remained static, or even deteriorated, as there were those who possessed the necessary qualities to rise high in the county society. Nevertheless the fact remains that by the second half of the sixteenth century every county of England had a group of newly important gentry stemming from families that only one hundred years before had been impoverished knights, simple yeoman farmers, or urban merchants or lawyers. One of

the fundamental conditions of Tudor history was the prominent place in
the county enjoyed by men who gained their superior status neither from
aristocratic descent nor through royal favor, but rather from their economic success, a social fact attested to by the scramble to hold the coveted and prestigious offices of county life—sheriff, justice of the peace,
member of Parliament.

Historians have not yet fully unraveled the intricate and often obscure
relationship between politics and social change in the late fifteenth and
sixteenth centuries, although this is obviously a subject of the greatest
importance. The surface manifestations of late fifteenth- and sixteenth-
century social politics are easy enough to describe. From the reign of
Edward II to that of Edward IV—that is, from 1307 to 1471—politics
and government were dominated by the aristocracy. Dukes and earls who
owned vast estates also maintained huge private armies and swarms of dependents and retainers. The aristocrats were the most important people
in military life and in politics; it was only natural that they should also
control the House of Commons and use it in their maneuvers to gain
leverage against the royal council, and from there to carry out their designs on the crown itself. But in the later years of Edward IV's reign
aristocratic leadership in politics was rapidly disappearing, and certainly
for 175 years from the time that Henry Tudor gains the throne in 1485,
the aristocracy does not loom large on the political scene of England.
During these two centuries people with high titles of nobility, inex-
haustible resources, and an aristocratic style of life and habit of mind
cease to dominate political life. Only at a few exceptional moments do
aristocrats meddle in politics, and even then, while they momentarily
become the center of controversy, they achieve very little aside from notoriety. During the fourteenth and most of the fifteenth centuries the
House of Commons was the tool of aristocratic factions, but in the course
of the two centuries after 1471 the hold of great lords over the M.P.'s
is no longer an important aspect of the political scene. The very
few peers who do wield any influence during this period owe their power
to a personal relationship with the king or queen and to prominence at
court. They no longer have, in their own right, any real control of the
House of Commons.

From the late fifteenth century the House of Commons was dominated by independent gentlemen who were rarely allied with great families. In the fourteenth- and early fifteenth-century House of Commons
such men of middling status were capable of creating a certain amount

of noise, but it is perfectly obvious that they were dependents of great lords. The sixteenth-century House of Commons looks as though it were under the sway of new men, gentry of means and reputation who have already gained prominence in their counties as J.P.'s and sheriffs and who, while they may have done well in capitalist agriculture, cannot call upon the unending resources of the old aristocracy. The new and central role of these men on the parliamentary stage has led historians to see clearly—perhaps too clearly—the political rise of the gentry.

Perhaps ten or twenty percent of the sixteenth-century M.P.'s owed their allegiance to certain members of the Privy Council and constituted a court faction or steering group in the Commons; the rest were genuinely independent gentlemen, and factions committed to one or another great aristocratic family no longer appear in the House of Commons. The problem for the crown and the Privy Council was to win over the independent majority of the M.P.'s, something they found easy to do until the later decades of the sixteenth century. The king and his ministers no longer had to worry that groups in the Commons were manipulated by dukes and earls bent on seizing control of the royal government and usurping the crown itself. Not only has the aristocracy withdrawn from the leadership of the House of Commons, but the political importance of their stronghold, the House of Lords itself, has markedly declined as well. No Tudor monarch found it hard to get legislation through the upper house, nor did the Commons, except in moments of greatest crisis, pay the lords much heed. For about sixty years, from 1471 to 1529, Parliament was not often summoned by the crown, and political decision-making was the province of the royal council. After 1529, when it seemed necessary to obtain statutory confirmation for religious and ecclesiastical changes, Parliament again became central to political life and henceforth the decisions of the lower house are the crucial ones. The Privy Council took pains to secure the Commons' assent to its policies; the House of Lords also readily bowed to royal leadership.

In the wider context of English history the political decline of the aristocracy was only temporary, for in the late seventeenth century aristocratic leadership came back with a vengeance, and from then until the end of the nineteenth century the great noble families did not relinquish their hold on government, nor have they entirely relaxed their grip in the twentieth century. Nevertheless the general abdication of aristocratic leadership for almost two centuries is an astonishing historical phenomenon which inevitably had ramifications on the social framework of politics from the late fifteenth to the late seventeenth century. Tawney and his disciples have claimed that the price revolution and the expansion of the market which gave the gentry such great opportunities also made life irremediably difficult for the aristocracy. In the face of the rapidly changing economy, their thesis runs, only men with the canny bourgeois temperament that insured success in capitalist agriculture could survive and prosper. Only the group of alert middle class landowners adjusted to the new conditions while the careless aristocrats, accustomed to economic drift and caught up in their old, courtly, extravagant ways, were left far behind. The undermining of the aristocracy went hand in hand with the rise of a group of entrepreneurs who, having stunningly applied reason to economics, proceeded with equal success to apply rationality to politics. Tawney's thesis has been found rigid, simplistic, and inaccurate by later scholars who cannot accept his Marxian class categories. Elton has refused to acknowledge that any problem of aristocratic decline exists. It is just not possible, he believes, to separate the gentry from the high aristocracy. Titles are misleading and very insignificant in the sixteenth century; it only mattered to be a gentleman, and the gentry formed a vast and amorphous group. There were so many landowners, and their resources were as varied and divergent as the extent of their political involvement, that it is wrong to think of them in terms of an identifiable, self-conscious, or cohesive class. Even an earldom may not denote any particular mark of distinction that can serve to separate the aristocracy from the gentry, for the possession of an aristocratic title in the sixteenth century frequently means only that the holder of the title has been a loyal Privy councillor or a court favorite. Neale's interpretation is similar. Society and politics were dominated by one ubiquitous landowning class. Some gentry were very important politically; others, although they resembled this elite group in almost all aspects, were lesser men. In every county political and judicial leadership was exercised by two or three families who, by virtue of wealth, crown favor, tradition, or simply extraordinary energy, filled up the county offices. Titles were a minor index of power-holding, and many men who were simply knights dominated their counties as much or more than holders of aristocratic titles. In Neale's view, the fundamental fact of Tudor social politics was an alliance and basic agreement between the crown and the great county families, and the community of interest and political consensus that prevailed among these families.

It is true that in the sixteenth century we cannot make an absolute

ANNO · ETATIS ·   · SVÆ · XLIX ·

King Henry VIII (1509–1547)

Thomas Cromwell (1485?–1540)

Queen Elizabeth I as Diana seated in judgment upon the Pope, in an engraving of 1558. Elizabeth in the guise of Diana is represented as the Virgin Queen; each of her attendant nymphs holds a shield bearing the arms of the Protestant allies. The Pope, in the act of hatching his monstrous eggs, is being stripped by Time and Truth.

The South Prospect of HATFIELD HOUSE.

Hatfield House, home of the Cecil family, built by Robert Cecil between 1608 and 1611. It now belongs to the Marquess of Salisbury, a direct descendant of the sixteenth-century Cecils, and may be toured for the fee of a few shillings. This engraving was done in 1707.

Nationalist historiography—1614: Fusion of Races. This is the frontispiece of John Speed's Atlas, which was first printed in 1611.

Sir Edward Coke (1552–1634)

Charles Warburton James, Chief Justice Coke, *published by Country Life Ltd.,* London, 1929

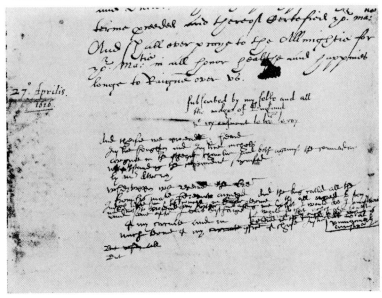

Coke's "Answer to the King" in the case of Commendams, 1626. Coke had been instructed to stay action in the case until the royal pleasure was known, an order that Coke advised the other judges to disregard as illegal. He then wrote a letter "subscribed by my selfe and all the judges of England," which the King refused to accept. Coke's description of the proceedings is scrawled at the bottom of his draft of the letter. His handwriting, usually very clear, is here almost indecipherable.

"And therefore we proceeded and heard Justice Haughton and Justice Nichols in the Exc. Chamber, and both against the commendams, notwithstanding the commandment signified by Mr. Attorney [Bacon].

"Whereupon we received the lre. from his maj. . . . and the Kinge called all the Judges before him and the Councell in Easter terme, and they all agreed to stay and not proceed any further, and asking me what I would doe, I answered I would do that which an honest Judge ought to doe which is entred in the Councell book as an unmannerly answer, and soon after I was discharged of my circuit and in Michelmas terme of my office as cheafe Justice."

John Hampden
(1594–1643)

John Pym
(1583?–1643)

Lord Clarendon on Hampden

"In the beginning of the Parliament he was not without ambition to be of power in the Court, but finding that satisfaction quickly, he changed it into another ambition of reigning over the Court, and was deepest in all the designs to destroy it, yet dissembled that design so well that he had too much credit with men most moderate and sober in their purpose. . . . In a word . . . he had the head to contrive and a tongue to persuade, and a hand to execute any mischief, and his death appeared to be a great deliverance to the nation."

Lord Clarendon on Pym

"No man had more to answer for the miseries of the kingdom, or had his hand or head deeper in this contrivance; and yet I believe they grew much higher even in his life than he designed . . . [he] understood the temper and affections of the kingdom as well as any man, and had observed the errors and mistakes in government, and knew well how to make them appear greater than they were."

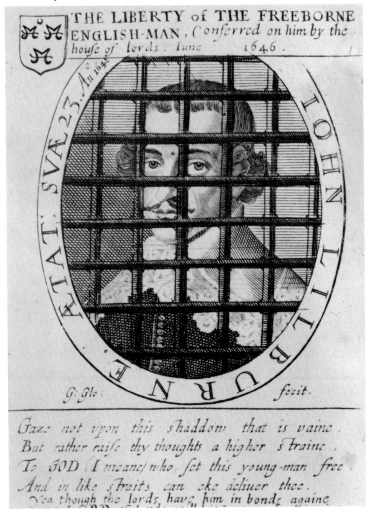

THE LIBERTY of THE FREEBORNE
ENGLISH-MAN, *Conferred on him by the*
houfe of lords. Iune 1646.

Gaze not vpon this shaddow that is vaine,
But rather raife thy thoughts a higher ftraine,
To GOD (I meane) who fet this young-man free,
And in like ftraits can eke deliuer thee,
Yea though the lords, have him in bonds againe.

FRONTISPIECE TO A LEVELLER TRACT, 1646

"Free-born John" Lilburne (1614–1657) was a political agitator, Leveller polemicist, and popular hero.

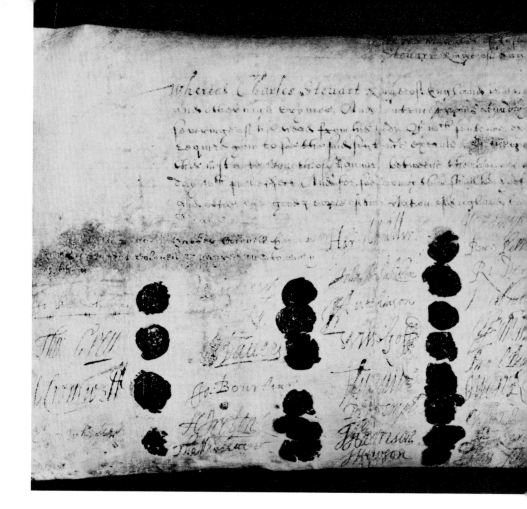

DEATH WARRANT OF CHARLES I, 1648

At the bottom are the signatures of the members of the tribunal that judged the king. (A notary's seal appears next to each.) These were the men who were later declared regicides. Cromwell's signature is prominent in the left-hand column.

Courtesy House of Lords Record Office

The House of Commons in 1651—Seal of the Commonwealth

Courtesy New York Public Library

Oliver Cromwell as the savior of England—
a Puritan view of 1658

THE COMMONWEALTH AS DRAGON

"Arbitrary Government displayed in the Tyrannick Usurpation of the Rump . . . and Oliver Cromwell." Frontispiece to a tract in support of Charles II, 1683.

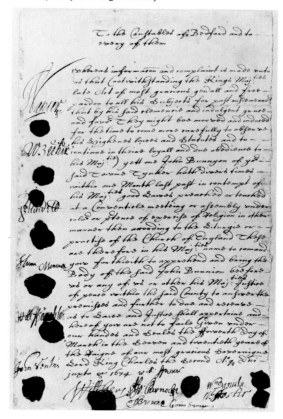

Restoration religious settlement. Writ of arrest of John Bunyan for holding an unlicensed conventicle. It was during this six months' imprisonment that Bunyan wrote *Pilgrim's Progress*. The text of the writ is:

Whereas information and complaint is made unto us that (notwithstanding the Kings Maj^ties late Act of most gracious generall and free pardon to all his subjects for past misdemeanours, that by his said clemencie and indulgent grace and favour they might be mooved and induced for the time to come more carefully to observe his Highenes laws and statutes, and to continue in theire loyall and due obedience to his Maj^tie), yet one John Bunnyon of your said towne, Tynker, hath divers times within one month last past in contempt of his Maj^ties good laws preached or teached at a Conventicle meeteing or assembly under colour or pretence of exercise of Religion in other manner than according to the Liturgie of Practice of the Church of England. These are therefore in his Maj^ties name to comand you forthwith to apprehend and bring the Body of the said John Bunnion before us or any of us or other his Maj^ties Justice of Peace within the said country to answer the premises and further to doe and receave as to Law and Justice shall appertaine, and hereof you are not to faile. . . .

"The Lawyer's Arms," a satire of 1692

An election won by bribery, 1727

distinction between gentry and aristocracy; important gentlemen are sometimes younger sons of the nobility, and a sonorous title may represent nothing more important than a wave of the king's sword or a wink of the queen's eye. But there is something conspicuously absent for two centuries in the framework of English social politics—the high aristocracy that played a main role in the history of government in the later Middle Ages and that will do so again in the late seventeenth and eighteenth centuries. The great nobles are oddly missing from the familiar political landscape. Great dukes in control of several counties are no longer exerting a commanding influence on national political life, nor does the high aristocracy still control the counties. The place of the great lord is now occupied by the substantial gentleman, Sir so-and-so, with his flourishing but not enormous estates, his strenuous role as J.P., his sharp eye for the main chance, and his ties by blood and marriage with his counterparts in the nearby counties. This is the kind of man who normally exerts ordinary day-to-day local leadership, who provides ninety percent of the membership of the House of Commons, and who occasionally rises to greater prominence in the Privy Council and on the bench. The high aristocratic leadership with its peculiar style of life, its vast resources, its self-conscious ethos, its sweep and confidence, is missing from the center of the scene. The great aristocrats stay quietly in their great homes or illuminate the royal court, but they rarely assume an important role in political life. The aristocratic lapse opened up grand opportunities for middling men, the gentry who had rarely achieved political prominence in the previous two centuries. Now they appear to be catapulted into the limelight. Some of them were indeed younger sons of peers or enormously wealthy entrepreneurs, but others were genuine middling men who were not necessarily wealthy or particularly well-connected at the beginning of their careers, and occasionally they were of quite modest provenance. The gentry who rise in politics in the late fifteenth and sixteenth centuries are always restless and ambitious men; they are avid—and not infrequently unscrupulous—pursuers of wealth and power. As often as not they are men who have had to make their own way in the world. One of the most trusted ministers of Henry VII was the son of a man barely above the yeoman class and another rose from the ranks of the petty bourgeoisie. Thomas Cromwell, the greatest statesman of early sixteenth-century England, was the son of an obscure wool manufacturer, and the Cecil family, which played the leading role in royal administration during the second half of the century, began as ordinary country squires. The social texture of political life had become looser, and there were unprecedented opportunities for ordinary gentlemen to make their mark.

The Marxist economic explanation for the aristocratic abdication does not stand up to close scrutiny; it is not plausible that men of grandeur and wealth suffered so severely from the impact of the price revolution that they became politically impotent. It is likely enough that a sixteenth-century earl was too busy with court revels and military parades to take full advantage of market conditions, but there is no reason to suppose that a noble courtier could not rack up rents and squeeze his tenants as severely as an ordinary squire. In any case, a great lord's estates were so substantial that he could still maintain his position among the wealthier men in the kingdom. It is nonsense to suppose that English lords were at any time reduced to penury in the manner of destitute Italian nobles. Even if a sixteenth- or seventeenth-century aristocrat was totally lacking in entrepreneurial competence, he still had enough income to strike a handsome figure at court and he was never reduced to becoming a robber baron, which was the fate of some of his German and French counterparts during the same centuries.

The political retreat of the English nobility must first of all be explained by the fact of aristocratic genocide. In the fifteenth and early sixteenth centuries many great lords were slaughtered either by fighting amongst themselves or by judicial murder in the form of a bill of attainder whereby their aristocratic lineage ceased and their lands escheated to the crown. According to statistics provided by Lawrence Stone, there were in 1487 among a total of fifty-seven lay peers, only twenty great lords—dukes, marquises, or earls. In 1603, among fifty-five lay peers, only seventeen held great titles—sixteen earls and one marquis. Anyone with a great title and any kind of Plantagenet affiliation, no matter how remote, was threatened by the Tudor monarchy. The Tudors were extremely—but, on the basis of past experience, not unduly—sensitive about the ambitions of lords who had even a speck of royal blood. Those who tried to imitate their freewheeling fifteenth-century forebears soon found themselves in unpleasant circumstances. Thus a combination of extermination and fear made the remnant of the old aristocracy quiescent. Cautiously in the first half of the century, scarcely at all in the later decades, and recklessly in the early seventeenth century, ennoblement of royal servants and court favorites by the crown gives rise to a new aristocracy. But these new lords are either too loyal or too timid to give the crown any trouble; they do not try to strike out on their own or attempt to establish factions in the House of Commons. It is during the sixteenth and early seventeenth centuries that English court life most closely conforms to the French model. The court is a brilliant place, the center of art and literature, the theater for spectacular drama, and it is to these commendable but politically insignificant pursuits that the sixteenth-century aristocracy was principally devoted. The Tudor aristocracy functioned in a way remarkably similar to that of the French nobility in the reign of Louis XIV.

There are a few moments in the sixteenth century, principally during its middle years and its last two decades, when dukes and earls momentarily try to assume an important role in government and politics. These attempts at aristocratic political revival were invariably ephemeral and frequently resulted in the special court revel of a highly ceremonial execution that also served as a timely warning to the other peers to stick to their literary pursuits. But these fitful moments of aristocratic political activity serve to remind us that we ought not to attribute the perplexing aristocratic lapse exclusively to general causes. An historical change is often determined by a series of accidents which in retrospect are hypostatized and congealed into far-ranging social and political changes. The fact is that those few nobles of the sixteenth century who did meddle in politics were singularly inept; one man as clever and bold as Henry Bolingbroke or Henry Tudor himself would have made a world of difference, and it was precisely because the Tudor monarchs realized how easy it was for one great duke or earl to turn the clock back to the fifteenth century that they kept such a close watch on the aristocracy and treated them so severely when they fell out of line. In the late seventeenth and early eighteenth century, on the other hand, there was a succession of some half dozen intelligent peers who played important, and at times brilliant roles in politics. Therefore we must be careful not to turn several plausible accidents into a sweeping generalization. Perhaps it is only necessary to say that in the sixteenth and early seventeenth centuries aristocrats in politics were unsuccessful because no lord appeared with the requisite personal qualities, and that during this period, therefore, the aristocracy happens to be politically unimportant. This interpretation is a somewhat crude oversimplification but it is worth setting against the more general explanations for the decline of the aristocracy.

The recent study by Lawrence Stone, *The Crisis of the Aristocracy*, contends that the decline of aristocratic power was related to a real shift in social values. In the reign of Elizabeth, Stone finds, there still prevailed the traditional habit of obsequious deference to great lords on the part of the ordinary gentry. But by 1600 a process of erosion had already set in. Stone concludes that the "attitude of respectful subservience was breaking down," and that there was "a general weakening of the hierarchical framework of upper class society." After the aristocracy had lost its political importance, it still retained the deferential respect of ordinary gentlemen. By 1600 it was also losing the traditional support that a hierarchic social value system had given it for centuries.

We can cite several plausible reasons—economic change, decimation of noble blood, the courtier's propensity to lead an innocuous life, simple poverty of mind, a subtle shift in social attitudes—without being able to single out one as the critical cause for aristocratic decline. The fact remains that for almost two centuries the aristocracy was effectively neutralized as an important force in English political life. This meant that the fortunes of monarchy in the sixteenth and early seventeenth centuries were largely determined by the relations between the crown and the gentry. The Tudors were fortunate enough to rule precisely during the hundred years when the more ambitious and aggressive gentry families enjoyed the greatest prosperity they had ever known, and the economic boom, along with its concomitant softening of the traditional social structure, created conditions singularly favorable for the stability and continuity of royal government. In sixteenth-century England it was hard for a government to lose the approval and support of the group of men who counted most in political life. The glory of the Tudor dynasty was ready-made. It is a truism that when people are thriving governments can do virtually no wrong, and that when men are distressed and worried about their economic circumstances governments are subjected to enormous pressure and scrutiny. As long as the important gentry families were kept busy overhauling their resources to tap the soaring market, as long as they had the money and leisure to build great houses and to cultivate sport, art, and literature, and as long as their social horizons seemed unlimited, they were not going to examine very closely the politics or religion of the king and his ministers.

II. The Resurgence of Monarchy

THE POLITICS of the mid-fifteenth century, in England as throughout western Europe, was the politics of despair. Kings had lost their dignity; they had adopted the style of life of the high aristocracy and had become its captives. Monarchy itself had been submerged in the turmoil of aristocratic life, and kings had abdicated their responsibilities to society. By the sixth decade of the fifteenth century, politics was only an aristocratic game; it was not conditioned by social concern nor by ideology nor by intense feeling of any sort. To the families of gentry, merchants, and other intelligent and perceptive people, it was only natural that family life and personal religion were more worthy of attention than the question of which incompetent Lancastrian or Yorkist aristocrat should be seated on the throne. But by the end of the 1460's, the dislocation of royal government and the breakdown of judicial process had gone so far that a reaction was inevitable. A stable royal administration and an effective national legal system were required. The wealthy gentry and the urban oligarchs, eager to take advantage of the return of prosperity, could no longer endure the breakdown of royal government which aristocratic factionalism had engendered. They could see no particular merit in the claims of either the Yorkists or Lancastrians, and they were willing to give their loyalty to any ruler who would rise above the aristocratic style of life and seriously devote himself to the maintenance of peace and order.

The first fifteenth-century king to perceive that the revival of royal administration and law could inspire a new devotion to the crown was Edward IV of the house of York (1461-1483). But not until he had decisively defeated the Lancastrian faction in 1471 and effectively secured the throne, could Edward fully put into practice his program for the reconstruction of the monarchy. The two kings who succeeded Edward, his brother Richard III (1483-1485) and Henry VII Tudor (1485-1509), who belonged to the Lancastrian faction, continued to implement the main lines of Edward's program. Thus the year 1471 marks an important turning point in the history of royal government.

The primary accomplishment of late fifteenth-century monarchy was its escape from engulfment in aristocratic life. Kings recovered their sense of dignity; they realized they were something more than jumped-up, glorified dukes. The late fifteenth century saw an enhancement of the secrecy of monarchy, of the mystery and majesty of the state. This was a reaction to the long era in which the business of royal government had been invaded and debased by aristocratic factionalism. Kings bent on restoring their tarnished prestige will naturally tend to withdraw the management of their governments from public scrutiny. Edward IV, Richard III, and Henry VII all exhibited an almost pathological concern to avoid public examination of their conduct of government. During the previous century and a half royal dependence upon parliamentary taxation had given the entering wedge to the aristocratic factions whose dependents in the House of Commons attacked the royal administration. Consequently, the three late fifteenth-century kings resorted to all sorts of peculiar financial expedients in order to evade calling upon Parliament for a subsidy. They conducted all the affairs of government through a small council whose members were carefully chosen for their loyalty, discretion, and energy. Nobles and bishops continued to play their traditional roles as chief ministers of the king, but the royal councillors of the late fifteenth century also included men of middling or even obscure families who could be counted upon to devote themselves zealously to the problems of royal administration and law and to avoid totally any involvement in conspiratorial high politics. Edward IV, Richard III, and Henry VII aimed to recover the dignity of monarchy by lifting the crown above the common gaze, and at the same time they strove to avoid curiosity about the inner workings of the royal administration by making it an effective engine for peace, order, and prosperity in the realm. We may say that the characteristics of this late fifteenth-century royal government were self-consciousness, secrecy, efficiency, and a fair measure of cynicism. These are indeed the necessary qualities for princely rule advocated by the Florentine diplomat Machiavelli in the early sixteenth century. As so often happens in the history of political theory, Machiavelli was simply rationalizing a system of government already in existence. Machiavelli experienced it at first hand as an ambassador at the French royal court. After 1471 this same spirit was operative in the English monarchy.

Edward IV and his immediate successors were confronted by the question whether to become involved in continental wars. War at any time is a tremendous expense for a national government, and two factors made this especially true in the fifteenth and sixteenth centuries. In the first place, wars were fought by mercenaries whose salaries were always a severe drain on the royal treasury. Secondly, the late fifteenth century is significant in the history of warfare; gunpowder was coming to be used effectively for the first time in western Europe, and the result was an arms race extremely costly for any king who wished to put into the field a fighting force that was technologically up-to-date. Under these conditions a monarch who could put his hands on a lavish supply of specie could become a great warrior almost overnight. It was not because they ruled a wealthy European domain, operated a particularly skillful administration, or were renowned as statesmen of genius that the Spanish kings became, around 1520, the most powerful rulers in Europe; they were simply fortunate enough to gain control of American gold. The French Valois kings did not have such singular luck, but in general they were shrewd and forceful rulers, and they drew upon the resources of a country whose population was three or four times greater than England's and whose gross national product in 1500, if it could be established statistically, would undoubtedly be found to be at least three times greater than that of England. Edward IV and his immediate successors were at a great disadvantage. England lacked transatlantic resources and was far poorer than Valois France; furthermore, the English kings had also found it necessary to avoid asking for those parliamentary subsidies that could most effectively have taxed the wealth of the realm. It was expedient for the late fifteenth-century English monarch to live frugally on nonparliamentary revenues and to avoid the difficult confrontations with Parliament that had so disturbed the continuity of royal government in the previous 150 years. Edward IV, Richard III, and Henry VII got along well enough as long as they were at peace with the other European monarchs, but they knew that they would be in trouble if they had to put an army into the field. They were, therefore, exceedingly wary of involvement in war, but at the same time they could not afford to appear cowardly. Thus beginning with Edward IV, continuing through the reign of Henry VII and by and large until the end of the sixteenth century, it was royal policy to make rumblings of war but never actually to commit more than a token force to continental conflict. The rules of this diplomatic game were simple, but it was a difficult and strenuous exercise requiring great skill: always make a ferocious roar, seem to be poised on the brink of war, occasionally even declare war and announce an invasion of France or the Low Countries, occasionally mount a small expedition, but never become so seriously engaged in conflict that the painfully limited royal resources must be committed to the building of a great mercenary army. This policy of brinkmanship was worked very well by Edward IV and Henry VII. They impressed the continental rulers so much that they were willing to grant the English financial compensations and favorable trade concessions; simultaneously the English kings convinced their own people of their important stature on the European scene while forbearing to demand new national taxes to underwrite this prestige.

Because he kept aloof from protracted continental conflict, Edward IV was able to stabilize royal finances for the first time since 1300. In the one instance in which he asked for a heavy parliamentary subsidy, he encountered bitter opposition in the Commons, and he generally preferred to avoid such embarrassing confrontations by obtaining royal income from nonparliamentary sources. He announced that his policy was in accordance with the medieval ideal that had so often been violated by rulers during the previous 150 years—"to live of his own and to spare the Commons." The three chief sources of income for Edward's government were customs, crown lands, and "benevolences," or gifts to the crown extorted from wealthy people. The increase of English exports and imports due to a general melioration of international trade was aided by commercial concessions which Edward obtained from continental rulers on behalf of English merchants. In addition, the general restoration of royal government and law led to improved customs administration, and this increased royal income from tonnage and poundage, as the customs' levies were called. The overthrow of Edward's Lancastrian enemies resulted in the escheating to the crown of enormous estates, among them the lands of the Duchy of Lancaster. During Edward's reign the income from the royal demesne increased seven-fold and provided a more important source of royal revenue than at any time since the twelfth century. The forcing of benevolences from the landed classes evoked vociferous complaints, but there was no way of resisting the royal demands. In any case, the benevolences were not too high a price to pay for the return of peace and law in the realm.

Edward's government was very quiet, so quiet that nineteenth-century historians did not understand that its policy was identical with that of early Tudor government. The Yorkist king rarely summoned Parliament, and in the last five years of his reign the Lords and Commons did not meet at all. In law and administration everything important was done by the royal household and council. Financial management was taken from the cumbersome and debt-ridden exchequer and placed in the

hands of the household clerks in the chamber, which was to remain until the 1530's the prime institution of royal finance.

The "Sovereign Lord's Council" met in the Star Chamber at Westminster to consider all cases involving the peace and order of the realm
and devoted itself particularly to rendering judgment against anyone
who might upset the Yorkist hold on the throne. What was slowly to
develop into the new conciliar court of Star Chamber received its legal
sanction from the king's duty to maintain the peace. The members of
the council sitting in Star Chamber directly examined the defendants
brought before them and convicted and rendered judgment without recourse to a jury. The Star Chamber was, in terms of its sanction and its
procedure, a Roman law, rather than a common law, court. But this
fundamental change in English legal procedure was the pragmatic result
of the necessity for the council to attend to pleas having political overtones, and did not develop from any ideological devotion to Roman law.
In civil pleas, for several decades, the court of chancery had likewise
rendered judgment on abstract equity grounds of "reason and conscience," on the basis of the king's obligation through his chancellor to
provide justice where the traditional common law courts were unable to
function. In Star Chamber jurisdiction, which began to take shape in
the last decade of Edward IV's reign, the procedure and process already
operative in civil pleas in chancery was applied to criminal cases. It certainly did not appear, in the late fifteenth century, to be an instrument
of Roman tyranny. On the contrary, it signified the much needed use of
the royal prerogative for securing peace and justice in the realm after the
breakdown of the common law courts under the impact of aristocratic
factionalism and stress of civil war. The Yorkist government restored
and revived the common law both in the form of the central courts of
King's Bench and Common Pleas at Westminster as well as the assizes
and J.P.'s quarter sessions in the counties. But the new conciliar courts
of chancery and Star Chamber now took their place alongside the older
tribunals at the head of the judicial system to render judgment in those
civil and criminal pleas which were of greatest importance to the king and
the top stratum of landed society.

The Yorkist administration was fecund in institutional innovations
that became the hallmark of Tudor conciliar government. A new royal
official, entitled the king's secretary, appeared in the 1470's and early
1480's with the power to issue letters under the king's signet. The secretary, who was usually a member of the royal council, was a confidential

agent of the king who was called upon to deal with pressing and politically sensitive matters and to give special assistance on difficult administrative matters. It is furthermore evident that the Yorkist government wanted to reconstruct law and administration not only within the traditional geographical boundaries of effective royal power but also to bring under control at last the gray frontier areas of Wales and the North Country. Both Edward IV and Richard III experimented with special adjuncts to the royal council in Wales and "the northern parts," and the Council of the North, which was established by Richard III, at least laid the foundation on which royal authority would eventually be established in these wild, still tribal counties whose names —Lancashire, York, Westmorland, Northumberland, Cumberland, Durham—still remind us of the great lords who virtually owned them. Before these conciliar agencies could be fully developed, however, a series of dynastic crises again undermined the stability of royal government.

Edward IV deserves to rank very high among the kings of late fifteenth-century Europe who generally exhibited a new sense of the dignity and interests of the state in marked contrast to the courtier and warlord kings of the previous century and a half. The Yorkist ruler's only weakness as a statesman, which eventually brought about the downfall of the dynasty, was his amorous proclivity. His personal life was sordid and he had difficulty restraining himself from the seduction of any woman who caught his eye. As was the case with King John, who had the same problem, this conduct ultimately brought him into trouble. Edward's love match with Elizabeth Woodville was politically disastrous. Not only were her family commoners, but they were a group of particularly greedy gentry who aroused the hostility of the great nobles and the envy of people from their own class. Therefore, when Edward IV died in 1483 leaving as his heir a twelve-year-old son, only the Woodville family was willing to preserve the crown for Edward V against the ambitions of Edward IV's hunchbacked brother, the shrewd and energetic Richard, Duke of Gloucester. Richard moved immediately to gain the throne by placing Edward V and his younger brother in the Tower and disseminating the plausible story that Edward IV's marriage to Elizabeth Woodville had been uncanonical, and that therefore the offspring of the marriage was barred from the throne by the taint of bastardy. Edward V and his brother never emerged from the Tower, and all evidence indicated that the Duke of Gloucester, who easily claimed the throne as Richard III, had them quietly murdered, as Shakespeare and all sixteenth-century writers believed. Certain misguided twentieth-century writers have tried to vindicate Richard III by claiming that the princes in the Tower were actually done away with by Henry VII. But this is to rehabilitate Richard III on anachronistic moral grounds that neither he nor any other late fifteenth-century statesman would have applauded. Richard's murder of his nephews, seen in the context of late fifteenth-century political thought and action, was not a villainous deed but a necessary act of state, a sensible and inevitable attempt to rationalize the blood line. This was exactly the way a Machiavellian king concerned for the stability and continuity of royal government was supposed to act. For a century there had been intermittent civil war in England, and the claims to the throne had been made along dynastic lines. Richard knew that in order to avoid renewed conflict he had to remove a minor from the throne and confine the royal blood line to his own family. The lesson of the chaotic Wars of the Roses was that princes of the blood carried portents of civil war in their persons; they were a clear and present danger to be eliminated as promptly and efficiently as possible. All the Tudors worried about this kind of dynastic threat, and they were no more gentle than Richard III in dealing with their rivals.

Richard was in every way worthy of continuing the Yorkist government that his brother had inaugurated; he was an experienced and wise administrator and an excellent general, and there is no reason to doubt that if fortune had not turned against him he would have been in every way as effective a ruler as Edward IV and Henry VII. Richard's problems arose not from his murder of the princes in the Tower, which bestirred no one except the Woodvilles, but rather from the premature death of his own heir and subsequent death of his wife. As a result, there was no prominent male in the Yorkist line left to succeed him by 1485. These misfortunes alone provided an opportunity for a rather obscure and penniless offspring of a junior branch of the Lancastrian house, the half-Welsh Henry Tudor, to rouse himself from his French refuge and claim the throne. Even then, it seemed improbable that Henry's invasion of England would be successful, for his army was decidedly inferior to the royal forces he encountered at Bosworth Field. But Richard was so concerned about the loyalty of some of his lieutenants that he pressed the attack too rashly, and he died on the field of the Battle of Bosworth, leaving Henry Tudor in possession of the crown.

In 1485, and for a good fifteen years thereafter, there was no certainty that Henry VII would succeed in founding a new royal dynasty. His dynastic claim to the throne was not very impressive, and in fact the Act of Succession passed by a hastily called Parliament in 1485 evaded this embarrassing question by merely confirming the fact that the crown does "be, rest, remain, and abide in the most royal person of our now sovereign lord King Henry VII, and in the heirs of his body lawfully coming." As a matter of fact the crown was to rest on Henry VII and his heirs to the present day, but even in 1495 this outcome was doubtful. A Statute of Treason of that year sought to instill loyalty to the Tudor ruler by stating that whoever gave allegiance to the "king for the time being" could not later be attainted for high treason, ironically implying that the overthrow of the Tudor dynasty was a prospect lying well within the bounds of possibility. Henry sought to placate his Yorkist enemies by marrying the daughter of Edward IV, but this act did not prevent the hatching of several conspiracies against him during the first decade of his reign. Two of these were particularly dangerous; the Yorkists were strongly entrenched in Ireland and from there sought to overthrow the Tudor dynasty by twice putting up impostors claiming to be Yorkist princes of the royal line. The retention of the throne was a difficult task for Henry Tudor during the first dozen years of his reign, and it was only the skillful discovery and crushing of conspiracies and the lavish use of attainders against people of royal blood, combined with his efficient management of royal administration that firmly entrenched him in his possession of the throne by 1500.

From Sir Francis Bacon, who wrote the first important history of the reign of Henry VII at the end of the sixteenth century, to A. F. Pollard in the early twentieth century, Henry Tudor was acclaimed as the founder of a new national monarchy. Recent writers, among them S. B. Chrimes and G. R. Elton, have established that in every important respect Henry VII was following lines in administration and law already set down by Edward IV and Richard III. Before he gained the throne, Henry appeared to be merely a clever and desperate plotter; as king he exhibited the rational, cautious, and parsimonious soul of a successful wool merchant. He ran a very tight, successful royal business, rather like a semi-private, semi-public corporation and moved with extreme caution, doing his best not to stir up trouble either at home or abroad. He never spent two shillings where one would do, and he went to great lengths not to be beholden to Parliament, for which he had a strong antipathy. Like Edward IV, he conducted his government primarily through the royal council and household. The older, more public organs of government were de-emphasized; the exchequer was allowed to fall into disuse and the chamber became the only effective royal financial institution. Parliament was summoned only once in the last twelve years of his reign, and the activity of the Star Chamber and chancery was greatly increased, particularly in pleas between private parties. Henry VII never did anything whose import was not carefully calculated beforehand; he was an austere and even dim figure who had no taste for the glory and drama of monarchy, yet he gave England peace, order, and the best government the country had enjoyed since Edward I. This policy satisfied the gentry and the merchants, greatly enriched the crown, and ultimately gained for the Tudor dynasty the reluctant respect and admiration of the more flamboyant continental rulers.

One of Henry VII's early statutes clearly proclaimed the ideals of Tudor government: "to the king nothing is more joyous than to know [that] his subjects live peaceably under his laws and increase in wealth and prosperity." The purpose of the king's law and administration was to advance "the politic weal, peace, and good rule . . . and [the] perfect security and restful living of his subjects." This statement set the tone for all the Tudor statutes and state papers down to 1603. Tudor government always shrouded its acts in rhetoric stressing the king's devotion to the welfare of his subjects and his concern for improving the conditions of life in the realm. The humanist term "politic weal" or later, "the commonwealth," becomes the stock phrase for the public spirit and altruistic obligation which, the Tudor monarchy claimed, inspired all its acts. Undoubtedly this tone of morality represents a high degree of political subterfuge, but it is significant that the role of kingship was discussed in terms that emphasized the king's public responsibility rather than his divine ordination. The Tudors withdrew the administration of royal government from public gaze and managed to reduce parliamentary scrutiny of the conduct of royal government that had proved so troublesome to the monarchs of the later Middle Ages. But they also wished to appear as rulers selflessly devoted to the security and prosperity of the landed and mercantile classes—without whose good will, of course, they could not long have held the throne. What they rejected was any institutional means by which the community of the realm could exercise control over the crown.

The late fifteenth and sixteenth centuries in Europe were the heyday of royal legitimacy (the so-called divine right of kings), the doctrine that God, through the sacred medium of legitimate blood lines, designated rulers for Christian people. There was nothing—in theory at least—that any political community could do to modify or negate the divine dispensation. The Tudor dynasts believed in this doctrine no less vehemently than the kings of France and Spain; their view of government was fundamentally authoritarian and despotic. Henry VII and his successors, like their continental contemporaries, did not doubt that the kingship had been given them by God and that government was their possession through divine grace. The great difference between the Tudors and the Hapsburg and the Valois kings arose from practical rather than theoretical considerations. The Tudors had no standing army, no national police force, and no local paid bureaucracy. Henry VII's bureaucratic resources consisted of himself, a dozen or so royal councillors, permanently attendant on the king, and perhaps forty or fifty other centrally located administrators. Government and law in the counties were operated almost entirely by the prominent families of gentry holding the office of justice of the peace. However authoritarian the spirit, however keen the king and his councillors might be to use Parliament solely as a legislative tool and prevent the reassertion of partial parliamentary control over royal government, Henry VII and his successors had perforce to rule with the consent of the elite groups in rural and urban society which comprised the political nation. Therefore whatever the king wanted had to be presented as though his only purpose was to answer the needs of the commonwealth. But cant phrases alone could not have sufficed to gain the Tudors the support of the political nation, and the Tudor monarchy actually did further peace, good rule, and prosperity, thereby fulfilling Henry VII's promises. It could not have endured otherwise.

For Henry VII and his councillors Parliament had an important but clearly limited function. It could be sparingly used to grant subsidies to the crown, since Henry VII drew his revenue almost entirely from nonparliamentary sources. Parliament, in the eyes of early Tudor government, was certainly not intended to serve as the institutional means by which the community could criticize and control the king's ministers. The function of Parliament, as seen by Henry VII, was simply to confirm and register the law by means of statute so that the judicial validity of certain important and possibly controversial public regulations would be unquestionable. The early Tudor idea of law was still medieval; it was identical with the legislative doctrines of the fourteenth or even the twelfth century. There was in existence a "due order of the law"; legislation did not mean the formulation of new law, but only the clarification, refinement, and amplification of a legal order that was already in existence. The law could be made known by royal proclamation, and such proclamations, drawn up by the king in council, were used extensively all through the Tudor period and considered to have the force of legislative enactments. Certain matters, however, were so fundamental to the commonwealth that it seemed expedient, although not legally necessary, to cast them in the traditional statutory form of king-in-Parliament as well as by the less magisterial method of proclamation issued by the king in council.

The early Tudor theory of legislation can be seen in its purest form in Henry VII's first statute, the Act of Succession of 1485. The act did not purport to make Henry Tudor king of England, for the function of statute was only to declare and perhaps clarify what the law already was. Henry was king by the grace of God. God's grace was apparent in the royal blood line (and Henry did have a legitimate dynastic claim to the throne), but it was also made manifest by the providential victory at Bosworth Field. The Act of Succession, therefore, was aimed only at "avoiding . . . all ambiguities and questions." The kingship already resided in Henry, "our now sovereign lord . . . and in the heirs of his body lawfully coming . . . and in none other." Yet this statement of fact was also "enacted by authority of this present parliament." Theoretically, the sole function of all Tudor legislation—at least before the middle of the sixteenth century—is to remove doubts and clarify ambiguity. Statute lends to any particular aspect of the legal order a special force and authority, and it is usually reserved for those matters—such as the legitimacy of the royal succession—about which any political question would be intolerable. Statute enhances and enshrines law; it dictates immediate and universal acceptance of a specific legislative provision. The existence of the statute means that anyone who dissents or doubts, either by speech or conduct, is liable to the full punitive force of law. After 1485, anyone who might question Henry VII's right to the throne was subject to prosecution for high treason.

For Henry VII Parliament was a subservient body which could reinforce whatever the king in council decided was the legal order of the realm; thus it was only logical that when Parliament was summoned, its membership and proceedings should be carefully scrutinized and controlled by the royal council. The freewheeling character of the late fourteenth- and earlier fifteenth-century House of Commons was anathema to the early Tudor government, which soon took steps to insure that independence on the part of the M.P.'s was not perpetuated. All legislation of public or general significance was initiated by the royal council, and during the early Tudor period the first drafts of what sometimes became parliamentary statute took the form of royal proclamations. A group of privy councillors and their dependents sat in the House of Commons, and it was their job to serve as a kind of steering committee for the House, to make sure that any obstreperous M.P.'s were silenced and that the Commons devoted itself only to the business for which it was summoned. This was simply to implement the king's legislative plans. In addition to these precautions, Henry VII and his councillors did not hesitate to write letters to sheriffs and borough corporations in which they discreetly suggested that certain gentlemen who were dependents of privy council members or who were personal favorites of the king be returned from the county and borough seats. Intervention by the crown in the election of M.P.'s had in 1399 been condemned as one of Richard II's nefarious acts, in punishment of which Parliament had declared him rightly deposed. Early Tudor government, as it manipulated elections to and proceedings in the House of Commons, was simply adopting the characteristic tactics of the leaders of aristocratic factions in the Lancastrian period. But the Tudors used these methods to further the interest of the crown. During the first half of the fifteenth century, M.P.'s had been returned as the dependents of one or another great duke, and the Lancastrian and Yorkist factions had striven to use the Commons for the furtherance of their political ambitions. The selfsame techniques were now to be used not by aristocratic factions but by the royal council on behalf of the king. Until the second half of the sixteenth century there was only one cohesive steering group in the House of Commons—the dependents of the crown.

In practice Henry VII was able to restrict Parliament to such an extent that his view of it as a very limited institution was amply borne out. During the first decade of his reign the function of Parliament was narrowly defined. Henry used Parliament to give the key aspects of his administrative and legal program a statutory basis. But once the necessary statutes were secured, it was rarely summoned. Legislation prohibited the keeping of indentured and liveried retainers. This, it was hoped, would put an end to "unlawful maintenances," the practice by which great lords had corrupted and suborned judges and juries on behalf of their dependents and thus undermined the judicial process. Parliament was also used to give formal legislative sanction to the institution and procedure of the conciliar court of Star Chamber. Another of Henry VII's statutes confirmed the leading role in county administration and law which the justices of the peace had steadily grown into since the late fourteenth century. The quarter sessions of the J.P.'s were, by act of Parliament, now made the ordinary court of jurisdiction in the counties; the justices of assize were only to go out on circuit once or twice a year and to deal with felonious indictments which—because they dealt with serious crimes, complex cases, defendants of high social status—the J.P.'s preferred not to act upon.

The institutions of Tudor administration and law that existed in 1500 were not to undergo any significant changes until the 1530's. All the essential ingredients of this system—the almost exclusive role of the council in central administration and law, the designation of the household chamber as the prime royal financial institution, the tremendous responsibilities placed on the J.P.'s in the county, and the elimination of private armies—were present in the reign of Edward IV and can be seen evolving in the fourteenth century, and in some instances they go back beyond 1300. The workings of Tudor government are covered by a facade of moral purpose; the Tudors are careful to cultivate an image of themselves as highly sensitive and responsive to the social and economic welfare of the political nation. But the chief characteristics of the Tudor system are its authoritarian spirit and its constant search for policies that involve minimal expense to the crown.

The king, as the preserver of peace and order in the land, had always had the prerogative power to summon before him and to examine personally or through his chancellor anyone he suspected of subverting the stability and harmony of the realm. From time to time a momentary crisis demanded that the king and a few councillors whom he happened to have with him should indict and judge a defendant, but this kind of summary action had raised doubts as to whether the king had followed due process of law. Kings who habitually acted outside the customary forms of the common law invariably antagonized the leaders of society who claimed to speak for the community and to preserve the law of the land. Antagonism had often inspired rebellion. But what in previous centuries had been either extraordinary or highhanded conduct on the part of the king was now given full judicial sanction by the Star Chamber Act of 1487 and the Statute of Liveries of 1504. By these statutes anyone whom the council in Star Chamber knew by "information" to be endangering peace and order by practicing livery and maintenance was to be summoned before the court "by writ, subpoena, privy seal, or otherwise." "Otherwise" covered a lot of ground where no rules or traditions obtained. The councillors in Star Chamber were to have the power to "examine all . . . defendants . . . as well by oath as otherwise," which means that—contrary to common law procedure—the defendant could be forced to testify against himself and to convict himself by confession. Since the Statute of Liveries provided for their "reasonable reward," informers were not only allowed but actively encouraged. There was no provision for the defendant to face and cross-examine his accusers. The Statute of 1504 specifically stated that defendants might be found guilty by "confession, examination, proofs, or otherwise, . . . as though they were condemned therein after the course of the common law." The Liveries Act was allowed to lapse in 1509, but the terms of the act do reveal the ultimate judicial principles adhered to by the royal councillors who presided in Star Chamber.

These principles flagrantly contradicted both the spirit and the well-known institutions of the common law. Yet all evidence shows that Star Chamber jurisdiction was enthusiastically applauded by the dominant groups in county and urban society, and that the enabling statutes were passed by the Commons without dissent. The reasons for this are readily apparent: common law procedure, during the fourteenth and fifteenth centuries, had not served to give the gentry the peace and security they needed, and the traditional judicial processes which were ineffective and socially useless had become widely discredited. Secondly, the Statute of Liveries was specifically aimed against the great lords who, with private armies, had made life miserable for ordinary gentlemen during the fourteenth and fifteenth centuries. Thirdly, the surviving fragmentary records of the Council in Star Chamber in Henry VII's reign indicate that in practice this tribunal was judicious and fair in its procedure and mild and generous in its judgments—much more so than the provisions of the 1487 and 1504 acts seem to promise.

In the reigns of Henry VII and VIII the council greatly widened the actual scope of Star Chamber jurisdiction. The initial purpose of the court was to curb the aristocracy, but it became desirable to use the court for all sorts of matters. If, by almost any stretch of the imagination, a case could be said to involve "riot," it was deemed to imply the forming of an armed conspiracy. Whether in fact this was true or not, the case was therefore actionable in the court of Star Chamber. "Riot is called in our English term of speech, where any number is assembled with force to do anything," we are told by the sixteenth-century writer, Sir Thomas Smith, who goes on to describe how "the party is sent for, and he must appear in this Star Chamber, where seeing (except the presence of the prince only) . . . the majesty of the whole realm before him . . . he will be abased. . . . For that is the effect of this court, to bridle such stout noblemen or gentlemen which would offer wrong by force to any manner of men and cannot be content to demand . . . by order of law." It is not hard to see why the legal departure of Star Chamber was accepted with equanimity by the gentry. The problem facing the late fifteenth and early sixteenth centuries was the achievement of good government and effective judicial process. The question of choosing between good government and free government was not something that bothered men in the late fifteenth and early sixteenth centuries. In this violent society liberty was not a pressing concern. Liberty only implied aristocratic license, the destruction of peace and order, and the ruination of good husbandry. The vast majority of the political nation wanted to be saved from anarchy not despotism, and anyone who protested against the Tudor disregard for common law principles would have been scorned as a devotee of the old aristocracy. Yet the fact remains that the Tudors, following lines already set down by Edward IV, had constructed a legal system which resembled to a significant degree the institutional forms of continental Roman law.

In view of the judicial doctrines expressed in the 1487 and 1504 acts, the devotion of Henry VII and his heirs to the divine right of the royal blood line, and the royal government's view of Parliament as the convenient legislative tool of the king's council, it is by no means implausible or invalid to speak of "Tudor despotism." In several important respects, early Tudor government parallels the absolutist French and Spanish monarchies of the period, a comparison borne out by Henry VII's envy and admiration for the Valois and Hapsburg rulers. It is significant that in the latter part of his reign he worked assiduously to marry off his elder son to a Spanish princess and believed that he had achieved a great moral and diplomatic victory when he at last gained this concession from the Hapsburgs. Yet the term "Tudor despotism," while plausible, is also misleading, because in some critical areas, both ideological and institutional, the early Tudor monarchy lacked many of the elements—in style as well as substance—that characterized continental absolutism.

The early Tudor monarchy solidified and amplified the Yorkist program and succeeded in integrating the prerogative conciliar court of

Star Chamber within the old common law judicial system. But this was done on grounds of expediency rather than because of any ideological devotion to the Roman law, whose doctrines of judicial absolutism were an indispensable aid to the rulers of the sixteenth-century continental states. There were also limitations on the authoritarian tendencies of the Tudors built into the institutional framework of administration and law. No sixteenth-century European government, however absolutist it might be in spirit and ideology, could approach modern totalitarian regimes in the degree of control exercised over the conduct and thought of the populace. Totalitarianism was feasible only after the enormous improvements in transportation and communication of the Industrial Revolution of the eighteenth century. The Tudor monarchy, like every sixteenth-century despotism, suffered from a general feebleness. There was simply no way to overcome the technological weaknesses of an underdeveloped communications network. But in the case of the Tudors, an authoritarian disposition was further neutralized by a parsimonious reluctance to employ the forms of state control that were available. In spirit and in central institutions, the early Tudor monarchy was authoritarian, but the king and his councillors were unwilling to put up the money necessary to achieve the degree of central control over society exercised by continental rulers. A government which had no standing army and no police force and whose local agents were not professional bureaucrats, but unsalaried country gentlemen, could not really be despotic in practice. This is the clue to the paradoxes of Tudor rule. Those men whom royal scrutiny found standing in the way of advancing royal power were always treated severely, sometimes quite ruthlessly. But the vast majority of the population of sixteenth-century England, including wealthy country gentlemen and merchants, lived out their lives, pursued their personal and family ends, and thought, and even spoke, their thoughts without ever arousing the wrath, or even the curiosity, of the king and his councillors.

The structure of early Tudor government contains a fundamental ambiguity: the central administrative and legal system, authoritarian in spirit and to a degree also in institutional form, depends on the local agency in the counties of the justices of the peace—voluntary, nonprofessional civil servants drawn from the top stratum of county society. The late sixteenth and early seventeenth centuries will reveal the conflicts inherent in this ambiguous situation. But the relationship between central and local administration was not a problem for early Tudor monarchy, and the underlying flaw in the institutional nexus of government went unrecognized by Henry VII and his councillors. The royal council carefully supervised the J.P.'s, who received annual commissions from the king and could be dismissed from office by royal writ. But even without close royal control, the confluence of interests between the monarchy and the political nation was so great, and the gentry so eager to give loyal service to any government intent on establishing peace and order, that the gentlemen who were appointed as justices of the peace had no reason to question the policies of Henry VII. The many acts of attainder passed during Henry VII's reign were directed against members of the aristocracy or chronic disturbers of the peace in the countryside, and the gentry who dominated the House of Commons and comprised the ranks of the J.P.'s never balked at passing the bills of attainder proposed to them by the royal council. By the same token, the judicial work of the council only appeared to the J.P.'s as a beneficent effort to bring peace and order to county society; Star Chamber greatly assisted the J.P.'s in quarter sessions by dealing with the cases which they found difficult or impossible to handle. The long record of petitions to the conciliar courts in the reign of Henry VII that involve pleas between private individuals or corporations is itself a testimony to the high regard in which the prerogative courts were held by the gentlemen of county society.

The successful royal reconstruction of government and law within England allowed the king and his councillors to turn their attention to the frontier areas. Here Henry VII's policies again perpetuated and amplified the work of the Yorkist monarchy. A distinct royal council for Wales destroyed for all time the power of the western marcher lords who had caused so much trouble since the thirteenth century. Henry VII's attempt to establish similar conciliar government in the north was less successful. The problems of carrying viable royal government into the North Country were particularly difficult, although it was, as Sir Thomas Smith tells, "marvellous necessary . . . to repress the insolency of the noblemen and gentlemen of the north parts . . . who being far from the king and the seat of justice made almost as it were an ordinary war among themselves and made their force their law." In the fifteenth century the justices of assize had rarely penetrated as far as Yorkshire. Royal justice, once it was available, soon became very popular among the smaller gentry; it was not so welcomed, however, by the old local authorities, and the separatist currents endemic in Yorkshire society—which retained its tribal and patrimonial character well into the sixteenth century—were too strong for the government of Henry VII. Henry IV had begun to reabsorb the long established local rights of private jurisdiction when he appointed his son and his brother-in-law as the justices of the peace in the North, and Henry VII tried to use the procedures of the prerogative courts to curb the great northern lords, but it was not until the end of the reign of Henry VIII that private liberties and franchises were finally abolished and royal authority thoroughly imposed on the North Country.

In regard to northern England, Henry VII's diplomacy created the basis for later far-reaching changes which he and his councillors were as yet not able to carry out by administrative arrangement. Skillfully pursuing the dynastic diplomacy characteristic of his age, Henry married his daughter to the king of Scotland, thereby paving the way for a long peace between the two realms and cutting into the military influence of the northern magnates. The removal of Scottish pressure on the northern border rendered the northern lords obsolete as frontier defenders, and the royal government could finally begin to treat them with the severity it applied to other overmighty subjects.

The use of Ireland as a base for Yorkist conspiracies against the Tudor crown in the first decade of Henry VII's reign forced the king and his councillors to work out a tight control over this long-neglected and chaotic frontier area. Their solution involved no consideration for the peasantry of eastern Ireland, who since the twelfth century had been subjected to ruthless exploitation by the Anglo-Irish baronial overlords. Henry VII's interest in Ireland was entirely negative; he only wanted to prevent his enemies from using the country as a bastion for insurrectionary activity. He appointed one of his ablest councillors, Sir Edward Poynings, as lord lieutenant, and gave him the job of enforcing the same kind of conciliar control over the Anglo-Irish barons that the council for Wales was imposing on the Welsh marcher lords. In order to augment the strength of conciliar government in Ireland a statute, called Poynings Law, was forced through the Irish Parliament in 1494. It provided that all legislation proposed to the Irish Parliament had first to be certified by the lord lieutenant and his council and then affirmed by the English king and council "to be good and expedient for that land." Henry VII's Irish policy did not begin to deal with the fundamental problems of Irish government and society; it consisted only of short-term expedients, but it did effectively reassert the authority of the crown over this most disorganized and dissident of the frontier regions.

342

For Henry VII a prime desideratum of government was that it be cheap. The king went to great lengths to avoid any extraordinary expenditures for war which would place a heavy burden on the royal treasury. To this end he was willing to forego military glory and, like Edward IV, his diplomacy consisted of making loud roars and perhaps mounting a token expedition, and then greedily accepting payments from continental rulers in return for a peace treaty. Parsimony was also why Henry was willing to take the risks involved in leaving local administration and law to the J.P.'s. It would have been prohibitively expensive to establish a salaried provincial bureaucracy. At the end of Henry's reign, the crown was in a sounder financial position than at any time since the early thirteenth century, an achievement due not only to stinginess, but also to a great increase in the annual income of the crown. Between the first and the last year of Henry's reign, the royal revenue had tripled.

The first years of Tudor financial administration were marked by a bold plan for reforming parliamentary taxation. The subsidy of tenth and fifteenth had become formalized during the fourteenth and fifteenth centuries, so that it brought in 30,000 pounds every time it was levied. There was no longer any attempt to make a realistic assessment or to adjust the income of the parliamentary subsidy to keep pace with the economic changes of the fourteenth and fifteenth centuries. Henry's government was acutely aware of the new prosperity; in 1487, after obtaining a parliamentary subsidy, it sent out commissioners who undertook a genuine assessment of individual incomes for the first time since the early fourteenth century and imposed a real tax of ten percent. This program of financial rationalization was bitterly resisted, however, and the government reverted to the Yorkist policy of drawing royal income from nonparliamentary sources—customs, crown lands, judicial fees, and revenue from the feudal prerogatives of the crown.

Royal customs revenue substantially increased in Henry VII's reign, partly because of improved administration and partly because of the upward turn in foreign trade, which in turn made the English merchants more willing to cooperate with the royal government in customs collection. Commercial growth was partly the consequence of the general improvement in economic conditions, but it was also aided by the king's adroit diplomacy—his negotiation of favorable commercial treaties with continental rulers that opened up new markets for English merchants. In spite of the improvement in the customs yield, it is nevertheless true that the early Tudor monarchy did not attempt a complete reorganization of the tariff system; customs revenue did not keep pace with economic growth. It was not in the spirit of Henry VII's government to undertake the kind of financial rationalization that would engender bitter resistance or require any sweeping administrative change. Henry wanted to improve upon the old sources of crown revenue, but only in a piecemeal way; he was unwilling to cope with the problems involved in any fundamental departures from medieval financial techniques.

The same cautious and pragmatic policy is reflected in Henry's use of the crown lands, which were a prime source of royal revenue. In his own right or through his Yorkist wife, Henry inherited a huge portion of the estates of the fifteenth-century aristocracy, and additional land came to him through the attainders and other escheats of the early part of his reign. Consequently, by 1509 the English crown possessed the largest demesne it had held since the reign of Henry II, and the annual income from the crown lands was not much less than that of the customs revenue. Henry's assiduous pursuit of aristocratic wealth did not differ, however, in a fundamental way from the stratagems of Edward IV. Henry and his ministers never even considered taking the drastic step of incorporating landed possessions of the church—which comprised at least a third of the rural wealth of England—into the royal demesne. As for the confiscation of aristocratic estates, Henry VII followed a cagey, *ad hoc* policy; he was always alert to the main chance, but never formulated a new program aimed at harnessing every available national resource for the benefit of the monarchy.

A royal official early in Henry VIII's reign referred to the ordinary income from the courts, the judicial writs and fines, as "a sheet anchor of the crown revenues," and legal fees were an important steady source of wealth for the royal treasury. The chaotic conditions of the fifteenth century left many questions of landholding to be decided in pleas among individuals and corporations, and the volume of litigation was increased by new activity on the part of Tudor gentry, who looked upon lawsuits as a major hobby and diversion. The strict enforcement of laws against retainers and the business of the newer conciliar courts also contributed to the swelling profits of justice. Henry VII's inclination to fine rebels and rioters rather than to hang them whenever he and his councillors believed them incapable of seriously troubling the crown also increased the royal judicial revenue.

In keeping with its generally pragmatic and conservative outlook, the early Tudor monarchy did not attempt to rationalize and codify the ramshackle medieval land law, which was already a maze of writs, precedents, and legal fictions. Henry VII's government carefully studied the medieval land law, but only in order to define and revivify the old feudal prerogatives of the crown, so that eventually they were able to make greater use of this source of revenue than at any time since the twelfth century. They shrewdly perceived that, after two centuries, the statute of *Quia emptores* and other land-law changes of Edward I's reign had altered the feudal relationship between the crown and landed society so that all landholding families were now direct tenants-in-chief of the king. This meant that the incidents of feudal taxation, which had once fallen only on the great barons, could now be imposed equally upon all members of landed society. Henry VII did not shrink from demanding an archaic regular feudal aid at the knighting of his eldest son and the marriage of his daughter. But much more important as a continuous source of royal revenue was the feudal prerogative of wardship, by which the crown could exploit the lands of an under-age heir and could marry off heiresses to the highest bidder. The early Tudor revival of feudal wardship was a very hard burden for the gentry to bear, involving as it did the intermittent siphoning off of the wealth of their estates to the royal treasury and occasional arbitrary royal control of their personal lives and family ambitions. The effects of prerogative wardship were only slightly mitigated by constant attempts to conceal the existence of minor heirs. Yet this draconic taxation scheme, while extremely unpopular, was accepted by the gentry as an inevitable condition of political and legal life. It was a hazard of landed fortune that had to be tolerated in view of the general benefits provided by a revived monarchy, the steady increase in the incomes of landed families, and the government's retreat in the face of opposition to the proposed increase in the yield of the parliamentary subsidy.

In escaping from the chronic indebtedness and intermittent bankruptcy that had crippled the English monarchy since the thirteenth century, Henry VII achieved his greatest triumph, but it was a triumph marred by severe defects in financial policy which would plague his successors. Henry and his ministers chose to avoid the challenge of obtaining an annual parliamentary subsidy collected on the basis of a real assesment of national wealth, a radical policy which would have been the only way for the crown constantly to increase royal revenue in accordance with the nation's economic growth. By squeezing nonparliamentary sources of income for all they were worth, by carefully avoiding war, and by his unrelenting concern with bureaucratic parsimony, Henry amassed a surplus in the royal treasury. But it was money that represented only a victory of expediency and not that rational reconstruction of royal taxa-tion which could put the crown permanently on a sound financial basis and provide the means for new ventures in war and administration.

The general character of early Tudor financial policy is revealed in the fact that Henry VII made no effort to secure the general auditing of royal income and expenditure. He actually took most of the financial business of the crown away from the exchequer, which alone could have provided more or less accurate audits, and instead placed the administra-tion of the greater part of crown revenue in the hands of the chamber officials of his household. These men, who could have no general view of the conditions of crown wealth, were personally accountable to the king. Thus Henry was in effect his own financial minister and literally kept the audit of royal revenue in his own head. From the standpoint of rational accounting, the royal financial system was no more advanced in 1509 than it had been in the reign of Edward III. The distribution of respon-sibility for royal finances among several officials of the chamber and ex-chequer, which had been the bane of the English treasury for two centu-ries, was not altered in any decisive way by Henry VII, and this confused and incoherent system was to prove a disaster to his successor.

Both Edward IV and Henry VII had attempted early in their reigns to exploit the institution of the parliamentary subsidy as a primary source of royal revenue, and the early Tudor administration had been so radical as to transform the traditional medieval tenth and fifteenth into a genuinely assessed tax on the wealth of landed society. In both in-stances, opposition had been so severe that the royal government had sensed the danger of reviving the political conflicts with the Commons that had been the scourge of the Lancastrian monarchy. Both kings, therefore, adopted the more expedient and—in the short run—effective method of resorting to nonparliamentary sources of income. Although Henry VII and his councillors may have initially envisioned a financial system that departed decisively from the traditions of the previous two centuries, they quickly came round—in taxation as in other aspects of government—to the policy of refining the various institutions of concil-iar government which had been imperfectly and intermittently employed since the early fourteenth century. Henry VII, like Edward IV, did not feel sufficiently secure on the throne to attempt a far-reaching revolution in royal administration, and his cautious and parsimonious temperament only confirmed him in his preference for expedient and *ad hoc* methods.

The framework of English government at the death of Henry VII in 1509 was destined to undergo fundamental alterations in the following hundred years. In the 1520's the immediate direction of the central government was delegated to a great minister of the crown. In the 1530's, a radical, although ultimately inconclusive, nationalization and rationalization of royal administration would be projected on ambitious lines far beyond anything Henry and his ministers could have conceived in even their boldest moments. The breakdown of religious consensus, within Europe as a whole and among the English people themselves, and the pressure of economic and social changes, would force the Tudor monarchy to make difficult decisions in areas of social life where royal legislation had hitherto not been required. But the basic characteristics of royal government established by Edward IV and Henry VII to meet the challenge of the chaotic conditions of the late medieval world would, in a very fundamental way, inform the course of sixteenth- and early seventeenth-century politics. The underlying ambiguity and tension implicit in the administrative and legal institutions familiar to Henry VII would, by the end of the sixteenth century, become the source of profound constitutional conflict. A regime with a self-consciously despotic ideology and clearly authoritarian tendencies in its central institutions had found it possible to rule without the service on the local level of a professional bureaucracy. Late Yorkist and early Tudor monarchy in effect depended, as had medieval English government, on the enthusiastic cooperation of the county communities, now under the leadership of the chief families of the gentry. When in the later sixteenth century the decisions of royal government on critical religious and economic questions induced disaffection among important groups in the political nation, when the Tudor legal system and tax methods lost their beneficent images, the national consensus upon which Henry VII's monarchy had been founded would be destroyed by an acute political crisis.

III. The King's Great Minister

I N THE YEAR 1547, a few months after the end of the thirty-eight year reign of Henry VIII—the most powerful personality to occupy the English throne since the twelfth century—a minister of the newly defined Church of England delivered a homily on the necessity of obedience to kings and the virtue of nonresistance to monarchs even when they violated God's commandments. This homily may be taken as a summary of the most common assumptions of political and social thought in England after all the upheavals and changes of the Henrician era. The fundamental principle to which men at all social and educational levels still subscribed was the medieval doctrine of the hierarchic and ordered universe: "Almighty God hath created and appointed all things in heaven, earth and waters in a most excellent and perfect order. . . . In the earth he has assigned kings, princes, with other governors under them all in good and necessary order. . . . Every degree of people, in their vocation, calling and office, has appointed to them their duty and order." The power of monarchy, in the common opinion of the times as enunciated by the homilist of 1547, is justified in the first instance by the need for social order; otherwise there can be no peace, security or the possibility of a good and happy life for individuals and family. "Take away kings, princes, rulers, magistrates, judges and such states of God's order, no man shall ride or go by the highway unrobbed, no man shall sleep in his own house or bed unkilled, no man shall keep his wife, children and possessions in quietness." In these and similar eloquent statements the homilist vividly reflects the ineradicable conviction of all men in sixteenth-century England that only the power and glory of monarchy stood between them and violent anarchy. This constant, visceral response to all political and social problems in itself goes a long way to explain how Henry VIII and his ministers could effect, with scarcely any organized opposition, changes of great consequence precisely in that form of religious life which was still at the core of the common experience of English society.

The homilist of 1547 goes on to refer to the medieval tradition of sacred monarchy which had enjoyed a fashionable revival among the courtiers of Henry VIII. "We may not resist, nor anywise hurt, an anointed king which is God's lieutenant, vice-gerent and highest minister in that country where he is king." The theocratic nature of royal office, which was accentuated by the Byzantine-like adulation of Henry VIII by his courtiers, was certainly one dimension of political thought during his reign, but as a reinforcement of the glory of royal majesty it was much less important than the deep-seated fear of disturbing the necessary and apparently fragile order of the universe. The doctrine of theocratic monarchy had not stood in the way of insurrection and civil war in the fourteenth and fifteenth centuries.

The political thought of the four tumultuous decades after the second Tudor came to the throne in 1509 still perpetuated the medieval belief in hierarchic order and sacred kingship, but we can also perceive two new ideas. They may not be entirely new as abstract intellectual concepts, but for the first time their real political significance is exploited; they are used as programmatic guides to action, and elaborated so that they enhance the authority, majesty, and unity of the state. In examining these ideas, we should begin with the terms in which sixteenth-century men described them—"imperial realm and crown" and "commonwealth."

"This realm of England is an empire, and so hath been accepted in the world, governed by one supreme head and king having the dignity and royal estate of the imperial crown of the same." So proclaims the preamble to the 1533 Act in Restraint of Appeals, which legally removed the English church from the jurisdiction of the Roman Pope and is, therefore, the single most important legislative act of the English Reformation. The act talks about a sovereign territorial state, not simply a supreme king; the personal claim of the king has become identified with something that is greater than princely rule; thus the phrase about the imperial crown of the realm really is equivalent, in the political and legal language of the early sixteenth century, to an enunciation of a doctrine of sovereignty. The preamble goes on to declare that the king is instituted "with plenary, whole, and entire power, pre-eminence, authority, prerogative, and jurisdiction . . . within this his realm, in all causes, matters, debates and contentions . . . without restraint . . . [by] . . . any foreign princes or potentates." Foreign princes, of course, included the Pope, and the king of England—who held a sovereign power—was in no way subject to any external jurisdiction; nor could his subjects appeal to any foreign or international authority since, in all cases whatsoever, the king was empowered "to render and yield justice and final determination."

This imposing and redundant phraseology was designed to express the idea of the absolute sovereignty of the state, a doctrine that would be elaborated later in the sixteenth century by the French theorist Jean Bodin. But in 1533 the principle of sovereignty had not yet been given a theoretical formulation; indeed the term "sovereign lord" still had ambiguous feudal connotations, which was why Thomas Cromwell, who drafted the revolutionary Act in Restraint of Appeals, resorted to the vocabulary of the Justinian Code of Roman law and the way in which it had been interpreted by late-medieval civil lawyers. In the fourteenth century, officials of the French king trained in Roman law had contended "that every king is an emperor in his own kingdom." This meant that every king—and the French ruler in particular, of course—possessed the *imperium*, that sovereign power attributed by the Justinian Code to the Roman emperor, which had been claimed by the medieval Holy Roman emperors of Germany. Thus, in later parlance the phrase "imperial crown of this realm" was really a way of talking about the sovereign crown of England. While Henry VIII's predecessors as far back as William the Conqueror himself had often in practice acted independently of Rome, it was also true that since 1174, when Henry II was forced to make a settlement with the Pope, after Becket's martyrdom, the Roman *curia* had been the ultimate court of appeals for the English church. Therefore, the fourteenth century statutes of præmunire notwithstanding, in legal doctrine and from time to time in practice as well, it was possible for English clergy to go over the head of the king and seek the decision of a superior international authority. This avenue was abruptly closed in 1533 and the sovereign legal authority of the English crown decisively and clearly established by act of king-in-Parliament.

The statute of 1533 was only the beginning. It declared the papal authority in England null and void; it was essentially a piece of negative legislation; it remained to settle, beyond any question, what positive jurisdiction would be established in the place of Rome. The Act in Restraint of Appeals declared that all disputes involving the church came under royal jurisdiction. The next year, another statute specified that the king's court of chancery was to be the highest court dealing with matters concerning the English church. Also in 1534 an act put an end, logically enough, to the payment of Peter's pence, the small ecclesiastical dues which England had been sending to Rome ever since Anglo-Saxon times. This statute also contains an exalted definition of the absolute legislative supremacy of the king-in-Parliament. "Your royal majesty and your lords spiritual and temporal and commons, representing the whole state of your realm in this your most high court of parliament, have full power and authority . . . to dispense . . . [and] . . . also to authorize some . . . persons to dispense with those and all other human laws of . . . your realm and with every one of them." This has a distinctive tone, it expresses a new idea. The power of the king-in-Parliament to make law, to change law, and even to abrogate law made by previous Parliaments, could not be stated with more force or clarity.

The statutes of the Reformation Parliament did not, however, resolve all the ambiguities involved in superimposing a doctrine of sovereignty upon the patchy operations of English government and law. It was easy enough to say that the English crown was imperial and sovereign as set against the Pope in Rome, but the Henrician statutes do not begin to define the relationship between a sovereign king and what medieval writers called the community of the realm, a corporate body represented by Parliament itself. This was not an issue which anyone in the reign of Henry VIII cared to raise, nor was anyone called upon to do so. Parliament was the willing servant of the king and his ministers and it was enough to know that the king-in-Parliament had the sovereign authority to effect fundamental changes in church-state relationships and the inner life of the church itself. The great statute of 1533 envisioned "a body politic, compact all sorts and degrees of people divided in turn and by names of spirituality and temporalty" who toward the imperial crown are "bounden and owe to bear next to God a natural and humble obedience." This happy image was reinforced by a legal imperative, for upon those who resisted or challenged the sovereign legislative authority of the Henrician state fell the penalties of treason.

There was no need for Thomas Cromwell to worry about the question, which had been clearly perceived as long ago as the mid-thirteenth century, of whether a distinction could be made between the institutional crown and the person of Henry Tudor. Sixteenth-century lawyers well knew the medieval doctrine of the king's two bodies, political and natural, but this potentially volatile idea played no part in the political thought of the Henrician era. Without any qualms the king could flatter the House of Commons in 1543 with tinseled rhetoric. "We be informed by our judges that we at no time stand so highly in our estate royal as in the time of parliament, wherein we as head and you as members are conjoined and knit together into one body politic." This statement is always cited to show that Henry recognized, emphasized, and even enhanced the importance of Parliament. In a sense he did; behind his remarks lies the inviolable, incontrovertible character of parliamentary statute law, which was especially necessary when the royal government embarked on a course so drastic as the break with the Roman church. But the real emphasis in the king's statement is on monarchy, on "the estate royal," not on Parliament. The meeting of a Parliament implements the will of the royal government and causes the king to stand out all the more gloriously in his royal estate by dramatizing his headship of the body politic. But does his headship depend on Parliament's assent? Is the estate royal something members of Parliament are competent to discuss; can the king's actions and decisions concerning the management of the royal estate be considered—perhaps even criticized? These embarrassing questions are ignored by the king, as well they might be. They had, however, been the critical questions of English political life from the thirteenth to the mid-fifteenth centuries and would again occupy a central position in a fierce national debate that begins in the later years of the sixteenth century. As long as the House of Commons was the ready instrument of the privy council all the constitutional ambiguities, tensions, and conflicts so easily glossed over by Henry VIII's phrase-mongering could be ignored. Thus, for the time being, explications of the doctrine of sovereignty took the innocuous form of continual affirmation of the sovereign authority of the English state against foreign potentates and international agencies.

The second novel aspect of Henrician political thought centers on the idea of the "common weal" or "commonwealth." The term originated among humanist intellectual circles where a kind of sentimentalized Platonism was fashionable and had already reached court circles in the later years of Henry VII. It grew steadily more prominent in the first two decades of Henry VIII's reign and came to stand for a vision—it was too vague to be a program—of a paternalistic monarchy turning its sovereign power toward the good of the community of the realm as a whole. For the humanists, royal benevolence particularly took the form of the advancement of education and the protection of the defenseless poor against the ravages of a harsh society, exemplified in this case by greediness of the men who were profiting by enclosing land. Thomas More, then a rising London lawyer in close touch with the Platonic humanists at Cambridge, denounced in his *Utopia* the "conspiracy of rich men procuring their own commodities under the name and title of a Commonwealth." More is perhaps the first to enunciate a theme which is to have a long history in English social thought: a harmonious beneficent community, which supposedly existed in a devout medieval past, has been destroyed by the depredations of selfish capitalists, and was now to be recreated—in an improved form of course—with the aid of modern knowledge. "You must not leave and forsake the Commonwealth," More tells his readers, and what he wrote in 1516 is the heart of the message preached by nineteenth- and twentieth-century advocates of moralistic, paternalistic statism. As chancellor under Henry VIII, More was not to do much more for the Commonwealth than burn a few heretics but perhaps he did not hold the office long enough to build Plato's ideal republic in England's green and pleasant (but in his eyes, increasingly sordid and corrupt) land. Yet in the 1530's there was to be another chance for the creation of the paternalistic Commonwealth. For Thomas Cromwell, who came to hold greater power than Sir Thomas More in Henry VIII's government, was also an early convert to the ideal. As early as 1523, when he was still a somewhat obscure M.P., we find Cromwell writing to a friend that one of Parliament's functions was to determine "how a commonwealth might be edified and also continued within our realm." The idea of Commonwealth is secondary in importance to sovereignty, but it glimmers constantly in the speculative writings of the royal circle in the 1520's and 1530's.

Given the foundations of political thought of royal government in the reign of Henry VIII—hierarchic order, sacred kingship, more significantly the sovereignty of king-in-Parliament and the sovereignty of the realm against Rome, and finally the paternalistic attitudes implicit in the Commonwealth ideal—the thirty-eight years after 1509 and particularly the crucial decade of the 1530's can be regarded as a decisive advance to the modern state. In support of this thesis, so brilliantly propounded by G. R. Elton, it is possible to point to institutional innovations within the royal administration effected by Thomas Cromwell, innovations which are inspired by a radical spirit of nationalization and rationalization, marking (it may be claimed) a break with the confusions and drift of the later medieval period and signaling the beginnings of modern bureaucracy. This interpretation of the Henrician state is a plausible one and in the long-range perspective of English history it is on the whole a valid one, but it is rather abstract and one-sided and does not do justice to the fundamental character of government in Henry VIII's reign, the motives and operating procedures of the prominent royal administrators, the inner dynamic of Henrician government.

If modern political thought and modern bureaucracy dawned in England in the 1530's, we are hard put to explain the confusions and doubts and ambiguities of royal policy in the six decades of the Tudor dynasty that followed Cromwell's fall in 1540 and the dislocation and wrecking of much of the structure of royal administration that this great minister of the crown had erected. Actually it is not the modern state that we perceive from Elton's *Tudor Revolution in Government* and A. G. Dickens' biography of Cromwell, and these doubts are reinforced by the marvelous insights into the day-to-day working of Henrician administration and law provided by Elton's *Star Chamber Stories*, a work far more important than at first appears from its deceptively simple storytelling format, for it casts more light than any other work on the diurnal methods and attitudes of the king's officials. We find that the administrative departments which Cromwell has reformed or newly created are personally dependent on him and not likely to survive his fall without undergoing great changes or experiencing complete destruction. We find Cromwell, the king's chief minister, yet not in firm control of the privy council, so that a successful conspiracy to overthrow him is within the reach of courtiers and disgruntled officials. We find Cromwell keeping in touch with the counties and towns of the realm through a wide variety of personal agents and informers, many of them obscure, or even (at least in one instance) psychotic characters. We find Cromwell holding daily court for all sorts of favor-seekers. Indeed he is the man to see about almost any kind of personal or family difficulty, for with the host of royal offices he holds Cromwell can at least inaugurate the settlement of just about any legal or financial problem that might come up in the life of a man who belongs to the landed or mercantile class. This does not sound like the modern bureaucrat, at least not in the English-speaking world: we recognize the type, however—Cromwell was much like Cardinal Richelieu and other great ministers of the French monarchy in the seventeenth and eighteenth centuries.

The comparative history of European political and social institutions tells us that there is a pre-history to modern bureaucracy, an intermediate stage between medieval and modern government, that of ministerial monarchy. The king hands over the management of his government to one great minister who completely controls—and often transforms—the administrative and financial structure. The great minister exerts his control by gathering offices into his own hand, building up new departments, and by bringing his own creatures into the royal administration. This was the way that Thomas Cromwell acted when he was in fact vice-regent of England for half a dozen years in the 1530's. In the system of ministerial monarchy, the king pays very little attention to the day-to-day administrative, financial, and legal work of his minister. As long as the minister can produce the required results, the king is content to let him operate the government. But it is still entirely the king's government; it belongs to him: and the minister himself, no matter how grandly he may loom in the affairs of the realm, is nothing but a royal creature, who can be instantly dismissed at the king's whim. When the minister goes, the administrative structure that has depended on his personal abilities and supervision is likely to collapse, and his subordinates will lose their offices unless they can attach themselves to the new royal favorite who becomes the great minister of the crown. The new minister may choose to preserve some of his predecessor's institutional innovations, but the king has no particular interest in the perpetuation of departments and techniques. He simply wants his new minister to get the results he orders and leaves it to him to work out the institutional details. When a king dismisses his great minister he may choose not to replace him; the monarch may temporarily leave off his courtly and personal pursuits and rouse himself—with the help of a council of senior officials and courtiers—to preside over the operation of the crown administration. This sort of reaction against ministerial monarchy and the return to a kind of medieval household government usually results, during the sixteenth and seventeenth centuries, in chaotic confusion and a great decrease in the effectiveness of royal administration.

These alternative forms of state management in this twilight world between medieval and modern government are readily apparent in the reign of Henry VIII. The first of the great ministers of the English crown was the royal chancellor Cardinal Wolsey (1515-1529), and he was succeeded after a three-year hiatus by Thomas Cromwell, who had originally risen to prominence as one of Wolsey's creatures. During the seven years of Henry VIII's reign that remained after Cromwell's fall in 1540 the king tried to manage his administration himself. The result was the collapse of a great part of the administrative structure that Cromwell had so skillfully erected. It is possible to interpret the subsequent 150 years of English government in terms of the development of ministerial monarchy, so that the historian's evaluation of effective royal rule depends upon how successful the king is in finding a great minister of the Cromwellian stamp. Henry VIII's daughter, Elizabeth I (1558-1603), was lucky enough to have the services of William and Robert Cecil. It might be said that the most crucial failing of the early Stuart rulers of the first half of the seventeenth century was their poor judgment in choosing ministers, so that invariably they trusted the incompetent and quickly dismissed those who belonged to the tradition of crown servants whose caliber we associate with Thomas Cromwell and William Cecil.

The system of ministerial monarchy makes its first appearance in western Europe in France at the end of the thirteenth century and appears to revive, after the disintegration of the French kingdom during the Hundred Years War, in the early sixteenth century. But in the second half of the sixteenth century France again experienced internal collapse during the civil Wars of Religion, so that it was not until the rise of Richelieu in the second decade of the seventeenth century that a French royal administrative system centered on the great minister is firmly established. It is, then, the Tudor dynasty beginning with Henry VIII that has the first clear success with ministerial monarchy. This certainly does represent a "Tudor revolution in government" but still cannot be designated as the beginning of modern bureaucracy. The distinctive character of a bureaucracy is its impersonality, its ability to function no matter who heads the administration. Perhaps Cromwell would have reached this stage, but he never had the chance, and thus the Henrician state represents the transition between medieval and modern techniques of government, between household administration and the evolution of bureaucracy.

The entrenchment of statism, as reflected in the ideology of sovereignty and paternalism and the attempts to nationalize and rationalize royal government, does signify an important change in the reign of Henry VIII. At the same time, it should be seen that the character of the Henrician state was generated as much or more by personal and individualistic inclinations than by ideological and institutional concerns. J. G. A. Pocock has shown how deeply the political thought and action of seventeenth-century England was rooted in historiographical consciousness, that is, a real devotion to what men thought were the traditions of the past combined with a strong belief that contemporary events could be judged in the light of what they assumed to be valid interpretations of English history. In Tudor England, too, we can also see how men's thinking about history informed their attitudes toward their own political world.

It is generally recognized that Renaissance humanist culture began to have a strong influence in England in the reign of Henry VIII, with the royal court and Cambridge University serving as the centers of humanism. Humanist influence had some impact on taste in art, literature, and music, but these departures are of small consequence for the history of government and society. Humanism was significant, however, in subtly altering the way certain important leaders of society, including the king and his chief ministers, thought of themselves in relation to historical change.

The most radical aspect of Renaissance humanist thought was its break with medieval historiography. Medieval men had seen the history of the world as the working out of God's providential plan for mankind, leading toward the Last Judgment. The actors on the stage of history— kings and magnates—were therefore God's instruments and their personal qualities of no significance. The humanist thinkers, without categorically denying this view of human history, greatly changed the focus of historical thought, and with it the way the leaders of society thought about themselves and their role in the world. The humanists made government, society, and economy merely the painted backdrop of historical change. They were interested mainly in the actors themselves, who now appeared to have freedom to pursue their own ambitions and achieve great stature—or *virtù*. History thus became a theater in which the motivations and sensibilities of the actors were the matters of greatest moment. The destiny of mankind was ignored: it was the experience of great men which counted, and the only thing that counts in humanist historical literature is the rise, triumph, or fall of great men.

This transformation in historiographical thinking was bound to have a strong influence on Henry VIII and the other leading personalities of his reign. They could not fully convince themselves that they were advancing the cause of the heavenly city in the world, as medieval leaders of society had believed. This traditional assumption was now severely weakened by humanist teaching. Hence the Henricians could not give themselves fully to any ideology or institution: ideas and governments were no longer as important as the lives of great men who used the theater of state and society for the fulfillment of their personal destinies. There is therefore a certain hesitation and lack of commitment about the men of the Henrician era even when they are making great innovations in ideology and institutions: it is really themselves they care most about, and a sensitivity to their own experiences always blunts their consciousness of the import of great social and political upheavals going on outside themselves.

The Henricians are really very private men, and their motivation is always conditioned by a compulsion to stand out as great personages against the backdrop of history. The Henricians effected a revolution; they made a breakaway toward the modern state; but they had no firm realization of the significance of these great upheavals. Because the only idea to catch their imagination was the fulfillment of personal destiny, they failed to grasp the significance of the implications of the upheavals they caused. They saw the king strike poses in the great theater of European politics, they witnessed the fall of the mighty Wolsey and the rise of Cromwell from obscurity to enormous power—and these were the things they could understand. But as for the practical formulation of the concept of sovereignty, the explication of the doctrine of statism, the sense of nationalism, even the Reformation itself—things so important to us, who have returned part way to the medieval belief that men are only the tools of vast impersonal forces—these political and social upheavals were for them little more than the backdrop which threw into high relief the feelings and the fate of great men.

When we try to describe the patterns of change during the four decades of Henry VIII's reign, we must take into account the intensely personal and self-conscious outlook that was held by most of the men who comprised the educated elite of Henrician society, because this shared attitude represents an innovation in ideology perhaps as significant as the institutional innovations of the early sixteenth century. It was important because it prevented these men, who in many ways were shaping a new society, from apprehending the significance of political and social change, and it is just their own lack of realization that may provide the clues to the contradictions, confusions and—finally—may explain why the revolution of the 1530's was only partial. The Henricians could have brought about a vast transformation in government in society; they had the talent, and they were given the opportunities. But in their hearts they could not believe in the value, or even the reality, of this kind of change; they believed only in themselves. Whatever changes and innovations they did accomplish were directly inspired by their private ambitions and informed by their inner sensibilities, and thus their achievements—though at times substantial—are more often unfinished, lopsided, and inconsistent. Once the high tide of humanism had receded, it was apparent that the ideological and institutional pieces did not really fit together, and the erratic achievements of the Henricians provided an ambiguous legacy—one that has been a source of endless debate and conflict for later generations who have tried to interpret this brilliant, but insubstantial era.

The self-consciousness of the Henricians was confirmed and intensified by the political and economic environment in the second and third decades of the sixteenth century. The governments of Edward IV and Henry VII, out of necessity, had been intensely private and secretive, and these set a tone that the new generation, under the sway of the humanist ethos, found quite congenial. Politics was concerned only with the king, his court, and his ministers; the vision of the government went no further, and since 1471 its scope had extended very little outside this narrow circle. No one conceived of the community of the realm as a separate or independent force; Parliament was only that lower part of the body politic conjoined to the crown, a pliant group to be summoned at moments of crisis—and then not to make decisions, but mainly to illuminate the majesty of the king, to make him stand higher in his royal estate.

As long as prosperity lasted in town and country—as long as the Antwerp market for wool continued to expand, and the demand for the agricultural produce of enclosing landlords remained strong—no one among the landed and mercantile classes minded very much. The gentry served in their role as spectators—now thrilled, now grieved, occasionally puzzled—by the high drama of the royal court, a splendid show highlighted by royal divorces, executions, marriages and a new cast of actors every half dozen years, except of course for the long-running and indispensable leading actor-director-producer himself, that grand impresario Henry Tudor. No one objected that the stage of royal government had a narrow proscenium.

London was also gaining in prestige; as the only real metropolis of England, it now assumed the overwhelming importance in commerce and industry it had always played in government and law, and this intensified the self-absorption of the king and his ministers. The court was in London, the only political theater in the only city in the realm worth thinking about. When rebellions broke out in the north and west Henry VIII and, after his death, the men who ruled in the name of his young son, Edward VI, were not so much angered as bewildered. It was astonishing to find there was some leadership, no matter how inept, outside the royal court and administration. It was as if a company of London actors were made to realize that a few obscure people were putting on good plays in York or Bristol, of all uncouth places! All great men appeared to be at the royal court, and humanist thought did not recognize the existence of other than great men. A court conspiracy was easy to understand, almost to be expected as part of the royal drama, but rebellions like the Pilgrimage of Grace in 1536 were led by gentlemen without a drop of royal blood in their veins; their goal, however dimly conceived, was political and social justice, and their motive was to preserve traditional religion, not to seize the throne. This kind of thinking was startling and incomprehensible to the king and his ministers. The hesitancy, awkwardness, and dumb lethargy with which Henry VIII's government initially met the rising of northern gentlemen and yeomanry in 1536 reveals how insulated the king and his ministers could be from the real issues of English life.

Henry VIII presided, at least nominally, over great changes in government, religion, and society and at times he took a direct hand in them. Yet the life and career of the second and greatest Tudor cannot be discussed in terms of his devotion to any particular public end but rather must be explained through a consideration of his personal ambitions. Henry VIII did not want to create the modern state: he was driven by his compulsion to satisfy certain intense psychological and physical needs.

As Henry grew to manhood in the last decade of Henry VII's reign, he exhibited qualities not uncommon in second sons of European princely families, although he was far better educated and more intellectually alive than most princes. His ambition to be a great man in the eyes of his peers in Europe was fed by his awareness of his superior talents and by the realization that grandeur would come more easily to his elder brother, the heir apparent to the English throne. But Prince Arthur died; shortly afterward the old, shrewd Henry VII died, and Henry—at the age of nineteen—found himself ruler of England. One of his first acts was to imitate his dead brother by marrying, after much hesitation, Arthur's widow, the pious and inhibited Spanish princess, Catherine of Aragon. He made a great show of courting Catherine, but the marriage was a disaster, and the mistake would dog Henry the rest of his life. Henry was a young and eager voluptuary, and his wooden Spanish bride soon bored him. He was handsome and energetic; what he demanded was a strong and vivacious woman, and he could never have been satisfied by Catherine, who was frighteningly serious about her religion, and was forever praying and confessing. She was also dreadfully serious about diplomacy, and was also always conferring with sour Spanish ambassadors. Besides, she was older than Henry, and rather plain. It was not long before Henry strayed from the Queen's dull bed and found the first of what seemed to be an infinite string of royal mistresses.

Nothing in this would have been unusual among reigning European families, except that Henry was deeply sensitive and rather intelligent (he was, in fact, the last male of spectacular qualities to sit on the English throne) and he had sincerely expected to fulfill himself in love. Now he pursued the vision of himself as an exalted personage in the great world of politics; he needed a dazzling success in war and diplomacy. The scholars and litterateurs who decorated his court during the early, sunny years encouraged Henry to cultivate himself, to write poems and songs, to dress well, to be a great lover; now the humanist exaltation of the individual inspired him again, and this time he felt he would realize his political yearnings, his fantasies of European greatness.

It is intriguing to imagine what would have happened to the Tudor monarchy if Henry VII had been succeeded by a cautious, careful, man like himself, a king who parsimoniously avoided luxury and extraordinary expenses, who studiously avoided involvement in the ruinously expensive game of war and high diplomacy, a ruler whose commitment was only to be bought out at a good price. His son was different in every conceivable way. Henry VIII was an emotional man, a flamboyant and exuberant personality; eventually he was frustrated and disillusioned. Henry VIII really was a humanist, but as a king it did not help him, nor did it make him happy as a man. He longed to be a monumental figure on the European scene, he yearned to lead huge armies, to preside in splendor over international conferences. The young king announced his break with his father's miserly practices by the first significant act of his reign; he sent his father's two ablest servants to the Tower and had them executed on trumped-up charges of treason. It was also an act of flagrant ingratitude, but it was designed to court popularity with the gentry, since it purported to signify the end of forced loans which the gentry found oppressive. At the same time Henry embarked on an extravagant foreign policy which steadily exhausted the largess his father had so carefully built up in the royal treasury.

Henry VIII had the qualities necessary for the highly stylized ritual of war and diplomacy. He had brains, learning, and flair, and he cut a handsome and dramatic figure on the European horizon, but he never got the chance to exploit these qualities on the international scene. The old, cramping problem frustrated him at every turn. England was a comparatively poor and backward country. Henry's competitors were also men of superior parts and they had at their disposal the great wealth which, in an age fully committed to mercenary armies, was the prime requirement for military success. Charles V ran his far-flung Hapsburg empire with American gold, and Francis I, the Valois king of France, also had great financial assets drawn from a realm with a population at least three times greater than England's and much more widely involved in profitable mercantile and manufacturing enterprise. Henry was no match for Charles or Francis. He could compete with them on a personal level, and when he encountered the French king at a conference he momentarily outshone him, but Henry VIII simply could not raise the stakes needed to play the cash-and-carry game of sixteenth-century international politics.

Toward the end of the first decade of his reign, Henry turned over the management of his government to his chancellor, Thomas Wolsey, who assured him he would win the triumphs which, for the king, had become compulsive needs. In return Wolsey intended to enjoy his exalted and powerful role as the great minister of the crown. Wolsey was himself one of those self-regarding magnificent potentates whom humanist literature loved to contemplate. The son of a wealthy butcher, Wolsey had been given the education necessary for a bourgeois who intended to use the ecclesiastical ladder to climb in society. He proved himself a loyal and able servant of the Tudor monarchy and managed at the same time to accumulate the offices of Archbishop of York, cardinal of the Roman church, and papal legate. A way of life that was flagrantly luxurious even in that ostentatious age, overbearing manners, and an unabashed accumulation of wealth and power for himself and his bastard son made Wolsey an object of hatred for the landed and mercantile groups—a feeling scarcely soothed by his much publicized crusade as chancellor to protect the weak and the poor by trying to slow down the pace of enclosure.

Wolsey was the first great minister of the English crown, but his appetite was insatiable, and he sought even greater prizes. He hoped to become the primate of the English church upon the death of the timid, aging Archbishop of Canterbury, and even beyond that was the lure of the Throne of Peter itself. None of these prizes, however, would be his unless he retained the favor of the king, and this in turn depended on his ability to bring home the foreign triumphs that Henry dreamed of. Wolsey was a corrupt and self-indulgent man, but he was alert to the brutal fact that all his plans would be jeopardized if he could not make Charles V and Francis I defer to Henry as the arbiter of the European power struggle and acknowledge the English king as the model of a glorious Renaissance prince. Nor did Wolsey delude himself about the magnitude of his task. England clearly lacked the military resources necessary to tip the scales of European power, and Wolsey was shrewd enough to see that only by playing a daring but reckless game did he have any chance to win. Charles and Francis had gone to war; whoever won would be in a position to dominate Italy, and thus control the papacy and determine the balance of power on the continent. Wolsey's plan was to support first one king, now the other, with the intention of being on the winning side at the finish. For a decade he seemed to be ahead of the game, though it is doubtful that Charles and Francis were ever completely taken in by the English maneuvers, no matter how self-confident and aggressive. But for Wolsey the game of shifting alliances was infinitely complex and exhausting, and in the middle of the 1520's he made, as he was bound to, a fatal mistake; he came out unequivocally for France just when Charles broke through to a decisive victory. By this time Henry VII's surplus had long vanished, and Henry VIII found himself humbled in Europe only to confront the bleak prospect of a half-empty treasury at home. Wolsey's policy was bold, but ultimately futile. He had dissipated the resources of the monarchy and had failed to make his king a master warrior or diplomat. So in 1529 Wolsey was exiled to the archdiocese which he had previously never once bothered to visit, and a timely death spared him from the final blow; only this kept the king from allowing the cardinal's long-suffering enemies to take their bitter revenge. In the end, Henry had let his great minister fall, for Wolsey had also faltered in the great matter of the king's divorce.

The king, at any rate, had developed a new interest. Four years earlier, about the time that Wolsey's diplomatic plans had been shattered by Hapsburg victory in Italy, Henry had begun to relinquish his ambition of astounding the rulers of Europe; he was captivated by a new obsession—to possess an intriguing and recalcitrant woman. Anne Boleyn was a court lady of high gentry lineage; she also happened to be the sister of the king's favorite mistress. She was not particularly beautiful, but she was adept at keeping the king off balance and clever enough to convince Henry that she would surrender to him only in the marriage bed, or at least hold out until she had a real prospect of sharing the throne.

"The gospel light which dawned from Bullen's eyes" gave Henry a dazzling new project. How, indeed, could he marry her? He now remembered, with shudders of guilt and remorse, that his marriage to his brother's wife violated the divine word which was found in Leviticus and confirmed by canon law. Before he could marry Catherine of Aragon, had not a papal dispensation been necessary? Thus the marriage to Catherine was a sinful union; and their failure to produce a son to inherit the throne was only a sign and a judgment. The king now dwelt on the welfare of the Commonwealth, and it became increasingly clear that he must renounce Catherine, and he demanded a papal annulment of his invalid marriage. But his victorious Hapsburg rival, Charles V, was in a position to intimidate the Pope; furthermore he was the queen's nephew, and Catherine bombarded him with letters and requests. The Pope was in rather an awkward position; Henry wanted him to dispense with the dispensation (thus incidentally bastardizing the princess Mary, his only legitimate child)—and this while Hapsburg armies occupied Rome. The Pope was a frightened, unassertive man, and the complex and difficult situation even bewildered Wolsey, confused another legate sent from Rome, and dizzied all the learned European scholars whose opinion was canvassed on the legal and theological snarl. Perhaps Henry was pleased by the ramifications of the issue revolving about him; probably all the furor was deliciously gratifying. Anne Boleyn was a worthy prize, it seemed, and soon she would have a child—a son, of course, whom it was imperative to legitimize by marriage. But the son turned out to be a daughter; Henry was soon disillusioned and quickly bored, and he eagerly believed malicious reports of Anne's infidelity so that she, too, could be removed as swiftly as possible, this time via the block.

The divorce from Catherine had been accomplished through a drastic expedient; England was separated from the Church of Rome, and a new Archbishop of Canterbury, Thomas Cranmer, was installed to promulgate the necessary ecclesiastical decrees. The plan had been engineered by one of Wolsey's most talented creatures—Thomas Cromwell. Like his mentor Wolsey, Cromwell was of modest provenance; he too worked to become the king's great minister and rose to exalted status in the world. But Cromwell was fundamentally different from the other colossi who strutted on the Henrician stage. Simply to reign was not his ambition; he was inspired by ideals and his vision of a rationalized government. He had a firm grasp of the concept of sovereignty, and he truly believed in the role of the state and the uses of paternalism in creating a better society. He had a grand plan to nationalize and rationalize royal government, a plan in which Henry acquiesced. The king was frustrated in his schemes for continental aggrandizement, his love-fevers were now somewhat moderated and he needed another stage on which to enact his greatness. He was willing therefore to take on—at least for the moment —the role of Justinian. It was Cromwell, of course, who would create the political and legal settings. Cromwell actually drafted the statutes. This momentary shift in royal concentration was very important in the history of English government and society, although for Henry it was only a third choice and one to which he never surrendered himself with complete enthusiasm. But the crown was bankrupt and he could not invade France, and his later, often ludicrous, affairs of the heart could not be transmuted into the great and noble pageant which had dramatized his pursuit of Anne Boleyn; Henry was ready to be beguiled by political matters and to let the genius of Cromwell exalt his authority in church, law, and society. It was temporarily entertaining to contemplate gravely the question of church-state relations; to advance the common weal, and to pontificate to the humdrum gentlemen of the Commons on how the estate royal never stood so high as in Parliament.

Not since the reign of Henry II had there been such a bold and far-ranging effort to rationalize and nationalize royal government as was undertaken by Thomas Cromwell in the 1530's. After the break with Rome allowed the king to become the final court of appeal for the English church, and provided the opportunity for diverting ecclesiastical taxes hitherto paid to Rome to the royal treasury, Cromwell addressed himself to a final solution of the monastic question. For three centuries, the monastic order, which held at least a third of the agricultural land of England, had contributed little to society. The monks, with very few exceptions, were not corrupt and depraved; they were simply bored with their socially useless routine. Already in the 1520's Wolsey had dissolved some of the smaller religious houses, with the intention of applying their resources to educational purposes. What Cromwell aimed at, however, was the complete extinction of monasticism and the incorporation of all the monastic lands into the royal demesne. To justify this revolutionary measure, he dispatched agents through the country to investigate religious and moral conditions in each religious house; he wanted to acquire evidence that the monastic life was lax and corrupt so that the king could be regarded as a defender of the faith in dissolving the houses. It is a tribute to the institutional strength of the religious orders that the royal investigators had to dig very deep to come up with even the few scandalous instances that could serve as the pretext for nationalization of the religious houses. In some instances, when the hard-pressed Cromwellian agents could find no salacious stories to report, they soberly informed the crown that monks had confessed to practicing masturbation. Here is the sovereign state of the Tudors at its meanest; the fascist big lie was not absent from Cromwell's arsenal.

Parliament was called in, not to extinguish the monasteries, but merely to confirm the abbots' surrender, with "their own free and voluntary minds," of their houses and property to the crown. And well the heads of religious houses might voluntarily surrender to royal nationalization: they were given generous financial settlements and forthwith emerged as prosperous gentry. The ordinary monks were also well treated by Cromwell; they were awarded quite liberal pensions and allowed to marry, although subsequent rapid inflation left some in a condition of genteel poverty. The nuns received the harshest treatment, and here the mores of the age, rather than the crown's malevolence was largely to blame. The nuns were also pensioned, but they were not freed from their vows of chastity. The double standard in sexual relations condemned the nuns to the ignominy of becoming superfluous maiden aunts returned to the unwelcome family hearth.

Cromwell set up new branches of the royal council to handle this "augmentation" of the royal revenue. And he frenetically set to work to rationalize other parts of the royal government, both central and local. The question of whether a landed gentleman held his property of the crown, and was thereby subject to feudal taxation, was brilliantly settled by a statute declaring that whoever had use of the land, no matter by what intricacy of feudal law it had come into his possession, was the party responsible to the crown. Wales was at long last united with England; its gentry was given representation in the House of Commons and its people given the same law and liberties as Englishmen. At the same time, Cromwell was not above the practice of cultural genocide; anyone using the Welsh language could henceforth hold no office under the crown. The great minister even made a stab at dealing with the question of the unemployed—the first time the English king and Parliament had taken questions of social welfare under their purview. The fundamental principle of the Elizabethan Poor Law, that was to remain in force until 1834, was already adumbrated in Cromwell's Beggar Act of 1536: the crown decreed that the unemployed and unemployable had to be dealt with in a systematic way—by providing charity for the latter and forced labor for the former—but it was local agencies which had to concern themselves with the actual implementation of this policy.

By the late 1530's, after a half dozen years of this game of statecraft, Henry had a treasury newly filled with revenue from ecclesiastical sources, and Cromwell was in the midst of reorganizing the royal government and at the height of his power. But the king had never been seriously committed to the plan to overhaul administration, or even to the idea of Commonwealth. He allowed Cromwell to fall to his enemies; these included men who were personal rivals as well as some whose conservative ideas about religion ran counter to the great minister's Lutheran inclinations. The king resumed the government in his own hands and, with the financial resources that Cromwell had built up, Henry decided to renew Wolsey's European schemes. Yet another diplomatic revolution led to an alliance with Charles V and an invasion of France. But this again resulted only in ruinous expense and military stalemate. The last years of Henry's reign, after Cromwell's execution in 1540, are grim and disappointing. Then the aging king becomes indeed the fat, boorish, sensualist of modern legend. The 1540's are the letting-go of the Henrician monarchy. After Cromwell there is drift, confusion, and ineptitude in everything. At his death Henry VIII left behind a bankrupt treasury, a disorganized administrative system, and a people deeply divided on critical religious questions. For one hundred years his successors on the English throne would have to contend with this legacy, until the institution of kingship itself would crack and splinter under the strain.

IV. The English Reformation in the Context of European History

THREE TIMES in the past ten centuries faith has broken free of the shackles of institutionalized tradition and confounded the mighty and the learned by claiming to preach anew the gospel of apostolic Christianity. Three times in the second Christian millennium religious controversy has powerfully shaped the course of social change. The first of these great upheavals was the Gregorian reform in the second half of the eleventh century, the second was the reformation of the sixteenth century, and the third is only now emerging and bids fair to be one of the critical intellectual and social movements of the later twentieth century. The contemporary reformation had its roots in the Pauline and Augustinian revival, in Protestant theology of the 1920's, and in the existential mysticism of Martin Buber's variant of Judaism. But it is only with the reform of the Catholic church proclaimed by John XXIII in the late 1950's, the new ecumenical spirit in both Catholic and Protestant churches, and the prominent role of religious leaders in the social revolutionary so-called civil rights agitation in the United States, that a spiritual and social upheaval equivalent in dimension to the Gregorian reform and the reformation of the sixteenth century has begun to loom on the historical horizon of the later twentieth century.

The experience of our own day has at long last allowed us to understand the nature of the sixteenth century reformation. From the second decade of that century some of its very best minds constantly addressed themselves to one set of questions to the exclusion of all others: What is man's relationship to God and what kind of church and society does this kind of relationship demand? Out of this reconsideration of the meaning of Christianity came the new Protestant churches and sects and the reformed Catholicism engendered by the Council of Trent. Not since the eleventh century had the intellectual and emotional capacities of European society been so exhaustively devoted to religious debates, and not again until the late 1950's and 1960's would ecclesiastical and secular institutions be again so critically examined by a reforming spirit which found a sanction against established authority in its consciousness of the recovery of the power and the spirit of apostolic Christianity.

Historians have in general been a little embarrassed by the unrestrained intensity of sixteenth-century faith. It did not quite fit into the standard picture of the dawn of the modern world, an era which in contrast to the medieval age of faith that preceded it was supposedly characterized by secularism and materialism, by the sovereignty of the state and the proliferation and intensification of the capitalist mentality and new forms of business enterprise. Therefore for a hundred years historians of the sixteenth century have desperately tried to establish a positive relationship between Protestantism on the one side and statism and capitalism on the other, so that reforming faith could be viewed as working together with royal sovereignty and entrepreneurial commerce and industry to give birth to the modern world. Liberal historians have consistently emphasized that Protestant teaching induced subjection of the church to the authority of the state and also valued the rights of individual conscience, in both these qualities standing in stark contrast to universalist and intolerant medieval Catholicism. Close examination shows that this interpretation is founded upon an anachronistic romanticization of sixteenth-century Protestantism, which was no more hospitable than medieval Catholicism to liberal ideals of an open society and freedom of conscience. The obscure voices on the extreme left wing of Protestant sectarianism which proposed respect for individual conscience of whatever religious persuasion were ignored or regarded as conducive to dangerous social subversion. At least 99½ percent of sixteenth-century Protestants firmly believed that it was both just and necessary to use force to suppress intellectual error and propagate doctrinal truth. There were plenty of martyrs in the sixteenth century for one or another kind of theological proposition; there were no martyrs for freedom of conscience. In its Lutheran and Anglican forms, sixteenth-century Protestant thought did support and enhance royal authority but in its Calvinist and radical Anabaptist varieties, Protestantism marked the revival of the doctrine of a purified Christian society under the absolute rule of a saintly theocracy, a doctrine which had been propounded by the Gregorian reformers in the eleventh century and Donatist heretics in the twelfth and thirteenth centuries, and which had been rejected by the consensus of the medieval church.

In the past half-century, several eminent scholars have found it necessary to establish a causal relationship between Protestantism and capitalism. In retrospect it now appears that they were agitated to undertake this difficult task by a fundamental misunderstanding of the pattern of economic growth in sixteenth-century Europe. They were fascinated by what appeared to be the rapid upsurge of commercial and industrial capitalism in Protestant Holland, England, and northern Germany while Catholic southern Europe was held to have slid into a precipitous economic decline marked by the Italian cities' failure to maintain their leadership in finance and trade, and by the catastrophic inability of the Spaniards to take advantage of their imperial American wealth.

Subsequent research has severely weakened the clear-cut contrast between the aggressive northern Protestants advancing into the modern world with bourgeois thrift and enterprise and the Mediterranean peoples sinking into stagnation and poverty under the dead weight of medieval Catholicism. This interpretation of sixteenth-century economic history was a favorite liberal Victorian myth but does not quite fit the facts, and twentieth-century scholars who felt impelled to establish a direct relationship between Protestantism and capitalism accepted the Victorian assumptions too easily at face value. The weight of empirical evidence strongly supports those astute critics, such as Winthrop S. Hudson and Sidney Burrell, who have dissented from the facile association of Protestantism and capitalism. The Flemish cities remained loyal to traditional Catholicism while continuing to enjoy substantial commercial and financial prosperity, and the supposedly steep economic decline of Spain and Italy in the sixteenth century has been disproven by F. Braudel and other scholars. At the end of the sixteenth century the Mediterranean world, for all its devotion to the Council of Trent, the Inquisition, and the Jesuit order, was still a thriving economic unit. The economic decline of Spain and Italy is largely a seventeenth-century phenomenon to which strictly political problems made important contributions.

Nor is it so clear that Protestant fervor necessarily implied capitalist enterprise. Fanatically Calvinist Scotland remained an intensely rural and backward economic area until the eighteenth century, while the Scandinavian countries, after their acceptance of Lutheranism, slowly retreated from their medieval involvement in international commerce, and by the end of the seventeenth century had, at least in the case of Norway and Sweden, become the underdeveloped areas they were to remain, for all their Protestant piety, until the twentieth century. Nor does the economic development of even Holland or England in the sixteenth and seventeenth centuries represent the steady and unmitigated advancement of capitalistic enterprise. The Dutch burghers flourished in commerce and banking in the late sixteenth and first three quarters of the seventeenth century but they proved totally incapable of effecting the industrialization which would have allowed them to maintain their leading place in European economic life; the hegemony of the merchant oligarchy of Holland proved as transient a phenomenon as the prominence in international finance and trade once enjoyed by the Florentines and Venetians. Nor did the break with Rome and even the spread of Calvinism in England prevent severe difficulties for English commerce and industry, periodic depressions, and a great slowing down of the pace of economic growth in the later sixteenth and earlier seventeenth centuries, as shown in the careful studies made by F. J. Fisher and B. E. Supple.

The great debate which has waged among historians for four decades about the validity of the theses propounded by Max Weber and R. H. Tawney on the causal relationship between Protestantism and capitalism has therefore to some extent been a needless and vain one since it has been based on false assumptions about the actual course of economic change in sixteenth- and seventeenth-century Europe. When Weber tells us the Protestant ethic of asceticism-in-the-world (self-restraint, hard work in one's calling, frugality) fostered modern capitalism, we can admit that there may just be some merit in this psychological proposition. But our general reaction must be the skeptical comment that the capitalist spirit, defined as viewing business success as the primary motive in life, was painfully prominent in medieval urban society, and that the Protestant ethic by no means of itself furthered entrepreneurial enterprise in the sixteenth century. When Tawney, with the righteous and commendable indignation of a Christian socialist, argues in his justly celebrated *Religion and the Rise of Capitalism* that capitalist greed corrupted Protestantism into a conformist social ethic, and that there was a potential inherent defect in the Calvinist mentality from the beginning which made it susceptible to becoming soft on capitalism, we again have to express grave doubts as to the validity of this thesis. Our initial response is to point to the violently anti-capitalist character of sixteenth-century Protestant teaching and to the fact that in Scotland and Scandinavia Protestantism became ossified and stultified into social conformity by 1700 without the debilitating impact of capitalist greed. That later seventeenth- and eighteenth-century Protestant divines were sometimes apologetic for the accumulation of wealth is true enough, but then they were generally easygoing and conformist toward the world. As Winthrop Hudson has said, it was "the waning of Protestant faith," rather than the nature of the faith itself, which made possible this blessing of business success. Finally it is necessary to reiterate that the advance of Protestantism in England was by no means concomitant with a steady rise of capitalist enterprise; the evidence perhaps reads more the other way. The period 1560-1640, which marks the rise and apotheosis of English Puritanism, was a very difficult time for English merchants who were severely bothered by chronic trade depressions of a severe nature. They did far better in the first three decades of the sixteenth century, when they were still papists. The sermons of Puritan divines did not seem to have given the London merchants the inspiration to overcome some very fundamental obstacles which every capitalist entrepreneur must face, in the way of solving the problems of supply and demand. It would not be too farfetched to draw from recent scholarship the ironic conclusion that the more devoutly Protestant the English became from 1560 to 1640, the less successful were they in business. Following Tawney's reasoning, the time is ripe for one of his many devoted disciples to write a book on "Religion and the Decline of Capitalism."

No other great movement in history has been as afflicted as the reformation of the sixteenth century by sober nonsense flowing from historians' pens. During the first half of the twentieth century, historians have tried to ascribe the origins of the reformation to almost every conceivable cause and motive except religious ones. In particular, Marxist historians made an unholy alliance with partisan Catholic writers to discredit the profound religious experience of the sixteenth century and to vilify the spiritual quest of the reformers as either conscious or unconcious subterfuges for materialist or secularist ambitions. It is only the great Christian revival of the mid-twentieth century that has allowed the emergence of a new historiography of the reformation era. Out of this background both Catholic scholars like Hubert Jedin, who has given us an extremely perceptive account of the Council of Trent and its background, and Protestant historians like Gerhard Ritter, E. G. Schwiebert, G. H. Williams, and A. G. Dickens, have emerged to interpret with a high seriousness the complex religious quest of sixteenth-century European society. The great upheaval in twentieth-century Christianity engendered by neo-Pauline Protestantism, the ecumenical movement, Pope John XXIII and the Second Vatican Council have impelled scholars to turn back to the sixteenth century and to find therein the similar impress of charismatic leadership, a similar manifestation of evangelical revolt against traditional authority, and a similar power of the Gospels to reach across the institutional barriers of centuries' duration and to raise up a whole generation of missionary teachers brave enough to take on and transform the world. Once again the message of the present has allowed historians to comprehend the meaning of the past. They have at long last begun to examine the religious history of the sixteenth century from within and not merely as the appendage of statism and secularism.

The history of the Christian faith has a life and integrity of its own. Until the latter part of the seventeenth century there is no reason to doubt that spiritual calling was as fundamental a cause of social change and a motive of individual action as political ambition and business profit-seeking. The reformation was by no means simply or even mainly a stalking-horse for statism, capitalism, or liberalism although it ultimately contributed in one way or another, often very tenuously and indirectly, to the making of these conditions of modern society. At heart Protestantism was not modern or progressive; it was self-consciously reactionary. It was founded in attempts to rediscover the temperament and doctrine of apostolic Christianity and to apply them in personal and social life. It may be that these efforts to rediscover and revaluate the pristine message of the church were foolish and troublesome, naïve and imprudent, that the result was liable to be anarchic and confused, so that a variety of new churches and sects would be the inevitable consequence. It may be that the reformers were recklessly rejecting the institutional wisdom derived from fifteen centuries of ecclesiastical development and undermining the stability of the social order. But the fact remains that the significance of the reformation can only be understood when we view it as a movement arising out of the depths of man's spiritual experience.

The more closely the religious history of the sixteenth century is investigated the more evident does it become that there were two reformations. One was a re-forming of institutions, whether it involved the assertion of royal sovereignty over the church or the reconstruction and revitalization of existing ecclesiastical organization. The other reformation was a genuine *reformatio*, a reconsideration of the nature of Christianity. The first kind of reformation was an external phenomenon, the latter reformation looked inward in trying to discover how corrupt and impotent humanity could be made righteous by faith.

The two reformations loomed on the European horizon at roughly the same time, for while a professor of theology named Martin Luther, who taught in a new and second-rate German university, was struggling to understand the meaning of Pauline doctrine, monarchy throughout western Europe was asserting an ever-stronger control over the territorial churches, and church scholars were searching for ways to improve ecclesiastical government, religious education, and clerical discipline. The two reformations went along together, interacting with each other, now cooperating and now entering into conflicts which showed the underlying disparity, even contradiction of the two movements. The two reformations overlapped not only in the same era and in the same country but within one individual, so that the young Luther was the greatest spokesman for spiritual reformation, while the older Luther, saddened and frightened by the apparent social anarchy his teaching had induced in the shape of the rebellion of the German peasantry, valued the external reconstruction of ecclesiastical institutions. And John Calvin was at all times a bifurcated religious teacher, who cemented together by the unsurpassed synthetic power of his towering intellect a radical theology and a conservative ecclesiology.

The resulting pattern of religious settlement in Europe was infinitely complex and markedly varied from country to country; it was a pattern that neither the institutional re-formers nor the spiritual reformers had envisaged, but was the consequence of the confluence and interaction of their efforts, as well as of regional political, social, and economic peculiarities. Left to itself, the re-forming of the church would have brought about a result conservative in the best sense of the word—a reconstruction or updating of medieval Catholicism to meet the circumstances of sixteenth-century civilization, only a little more bold than the actual decrees of the Council of Trent. Left to itself, it is hard to imagine what would have been the result of the unchallenged running of the course of spiritual reformation—perhaps the apocalyptic triumph of apostolic Christianity over the forces of greed and power in society; perhaps the achievement of a puritan world-order in which the saints would guide men to living the life which Jesus had advocated, a life of love and humility; perhaps social upheaval and political anarchy; perhaps the turning of the world into a monastery, in Max Weber's phrase, beside which the demands made upon people by the sovereign state would appear moderate indeed. But neither the conservatives nor radicals were to have their own way in the sixteenth century. We must remember that the upshot of all the yearning, controversy, ardor, hatred, and bloodshed was no man's plan, but the legacy of the interlacing and clash of the two reformations operating within the context of royal government and landed and mercantile society.

Both of the sixteenth-century reformations had a common starting point in widespread disaffection with the ossified and decadent late medieval church. They also had a common enemy in the familiar type of aristocratic Italian canon lawyer who made of the church a corporate jurisdiction and denounced anyone as a heretic who said this was an empty, unspiritual thing; therefore, the fundamental difference in the direction of the two reformations was easily obscured. Sixteenth-century religious leaders had a marvelous penchant for ambiguity and inconsistency, for talking at cross-purposes, for misunderstanding the drift of each other's doctrinal pronouncements, and for subtly shifting their own ground, sometimes without realizing it. They were constantly groping around the central issue of the struggle between institutionalized Christianity, more or less enlightened, learned, and benign, on the one side, and evangelical, personal faith on the other.

The young Luther of the period 1517-1525 clearly defined the issue at the start and in so doing shook European civilization to its foundations. His teaching was remarkable, as J. S. Whale has said, for "heartbreaking simplicity." Luther held that men are made righteous by God alone and not by institutions. "True faith is a work of God alone in us which transforms and regenerates us by the Power of God. . . . Oh, it is a living, energizing, active, powerful thing, this Faith." This obscure German friar had recaptured the central message of the Christian faith. St. Paul had understood it, but could not make it compatible with his concern to keep order in the church; St. Augustine had powerfully expressed this doctrine, but he was too much a Roman to escape from the traditional acceptance of institutionalized authority. St. Bernard of Clairvaux had glimpsed it, but he was too much a French aristocrat to fathom its social implications. Above all, the twelfth-century Donatist heretics had understood it, and from them it passed to William of Ockham and the radical Franciscans, and in muted form to the fifteenth-century German mystics and the "modern devotion" movement in the Low Countries. These last three communicants of evangelical Christianity had a strong influence on the young Luther. But the old Luther mitigated his own doctrine; its social implications were found to be too radical—it put faith above not only bishops but also kings and princes. The sixteenth century's morbid fear of anarchy closed in upon the evangelical spirit and tried to make it a less radical doctrine, one compatible with the world. In later Lutheranism and orthodox Calvinism, the evangelical reformation was muted and weakened, but in Anabaptism and left-wing English Puritanism it found an outlet which continued the struggle between the two reformations down to the second half of the seventeenth century.

Thus sixteenth- and early seventeenth-century Protestantism was divided into conservative and radical, institutional and evangelical forms. The young Luther, with his absolute faith in the immediacy of man's experience of God's love, was the founder of the radical movement in Protestantism; the older Luther with his pettifogging replacement of transubstantiation by consubstantiation, his hierarchic social doctrine, his acceptance of princely authority over the church, was a leading advocate of the conservative institutional reformation. Catholicism which in the medieval period offered the alternatives of institutional (orthodox) and evangelical (heretical) Christianity elected at the Council of Trent to extirpate all vestiges of the evangelical tradition from its midst, a choice which some of the more sensitive minds of the mid-twentieth-century Catholic church now find to have been mistaken. It is possible that in the late twentieth century Catholicism will foster a radical evangelical movement which was the historical role of left-wing Protestantism in the sixteenth and seventeenth centuries.

The course of the reformation of the late 1950's and 1960's allows us to understand the nature of the sixteenth-century reformation. The role which Pope John XXIII has played in our day was taken by Erasmus of Rotterdam, the universally respected Christian humanist, in the two decades after 1500. Both Pope John and Erasmus called for a modernization of the church, the common-sense adaptation of its increasingly outmoded institutions and teachings to the circumstances of the contemporary world. Both gave release to long pent-up dissent from the overly legalistic attitudes and rigid doctrines of the canon lawyers who controlled the papal *curia*. Both wanted the church to become more of a religious institution which could move the hearts of men, and rely less on its legal authority over the church members; they wanted more love and spirituality and less business and politics on the part of the hierarchy. In a way they could only vaguely define, John and Erasmus wanted the priesthood to take as its model the earliest, apostolic church which had to win men's hearts and could not yet possibly subject them to judicial and political authority, which only became available to ecclesiastical leaders when the first Christian Roman emperor, Constantine, ascended the imperial throne in 313 A.D. This reforming program gained a chorus of approval throughout the church, and particularly from laymen. But the Erasmian program, and it appears the Johnine as well, opened the way for a radical, evangelical movement which did not simply wish to humanize and soften the church's institutional authority—it aimed to substitute the power of individual faith for the authority of ecclesiastical institutions.

The young Luther who contrasted *fiducia* with *assensus*, inner faith as against external, formal assent, was the spokesman for the evangelical reformation. Who the twentieth-century Luther will be is not yet apparent, but several candidates have made their appearance. For a century historians have tried to determine the roots of the Lutheran gospel, and to account for the fantastically quick and profound response he stirred among so many of the best minds of western Europe in the 1520's. So many of these explanations of Luther's rise have been vitiated by a failure to distinguish between the institutional and evangelical reformations, thereby completely missing the significance of Luther's teaching, and by searching for the causes of reformation in every form of human endeavor except the obvious one of religious experience. The demands for a higher standard of clerical learning and conduct coming from humanist circles, the new facility in communicating ideas through the printing press, the use which princes could make of anticlericalism to strengthen their authority over the territorial churches, the transmission of reform ideas and the patronage of reformers by great merchants— these common explanations reveal the occasion but not the cause of Lutheranism.

Here again the course of the reformation of the 1950's and 1960's illuminates the religious change of five centuries ago. A world without reason, a world where traditional leadership has failed to provide for human happiness, a world where all traditions and institutions have become corroded with absurdity, has left only individual feelings, personal commitment, and immediate experience to claim the sanctions of goodness and common sense. The bankruptcy of authority and tradition, and the categorical imperative of personal relations and private morality— this is the dogma of the new generation of the 1960's. But the best theologians have been thinking along these lines for four decades. The sickness of Western society after the First World War forced the more sensitive religious thinkers to confront the primary facts of human existence—the weakness of man and the omnipotence and goodness of God: all else is dung and dross. The existential "decision" of full commitment to God propounded by Karl Barth and the neo-Lutherans in the 1920's has now a very wide currency in Protestant thought and has been taken up by the radical wing of the Catholic church; the latter too see faith in God's love as the only thing in the world not tinged with rottenness and absurdity.

This was the way it was too for many of the generation which came to maturity around the year 1500—Luther's generation. It was a peculiar generation, with little or no faith in institutions and traditions, whether of monarchy, aristocracy, church, or business because for several decades

377

all these social and political agencies had failed to achieve anything good or rational. For close to two centuries there had been chaos and decay in government, society, church, and economy. The traditional institutions of monarchy, aristocracy, and hierarchy seemed to have nothing to offer but corruption, anarchy, and misery. For the generation of 1500 the only fixed points left in the universe, the only things which did not carry the stamp of rottenness and absurdity were personal experience and the God of love. God alone could give meaning and hope to human life—not the kings, not the lords, not the bishops, not the guilds.

Luther's generation was astonishing for the extent of its cynicism and vulgarity, and at the same time for the irresistible intensity of its religious and moral commitments, and for its compulsive exultation of noncomformity in the face of traditional authority—the contemporary parallel does not escape us. The generation of 1500 was that rare thing in European history, an existential generation, one which had no consciousness of anything good in the world except humanity transformed by faith in God's majesty and love. So many of the very best of this generation, many of enormous talent and energy, sacrificed their careers and even their lives, to give themselves immediately to God, to be filled with energizing, living faith. To "have" God, Luther said, "is to go down on your knees," to commit your existence entirely to Him. There is no other meaningful and rational starting-point in life, there is no other authority for conduct that is not a snare and a delusion, a sick joke. The only categorical imperative is an inner one; as Luther's contemporary and disciple, the first great English Protestant writer William Tyndale expressed it, "As a man feeleth God in himself so is he to his neighbor. . . . Deeds are the fruit of love, and love is the fruit of faith."

Luther probably came to his existential doctrine by way of realizing that his father, who represented for him the best the world had to offer, was a hollow man. But in one way or another, hundreds of the best of his generation had similarly lost faith in the best the world had to offer, and instantly recognized their own convictions when the young German professor defined the primary fact of human existence: all righteousness is God's grace, not human merit. Justice is God's redemption of men, not the ordering of society. For Catholicism (and again, later for Calvin) the world can be transformed into a holy community. Luther thought this a ridiculous and dangerous delusion. The world, he said, has no goodness in it; it is and remains "refractory to the Holy Spirit." There can be no salvation in institutions. Faith for the young Luther is a total personal commitment, an "active" thing which consumes the whole of our existence and leaves no room for the absurd demands of institutionalized tradition and the false claims for the goodness of societies. Social justice is the reflection of personal righteousness, not the other way around. "We become divine through love," says Luther, "which causes us to do good to our neighbor."

It was not so much the printing press which gave such wide currency to Luther's writings in the 1520's; it was more his ability to articulate the deepest anxieties and yearnings of the better minds of his generation. But for those who came to maturity in the 1530's, Luther's teaching no longer induced a spontaneous shock of recognition. By the time this next generation appeared the political, social, and economic failures of the world seemed to have been reversed. Leviathan had a new birth and Mammon found new ways to satisfy human greed. The redemptive righteousness of God had to face the challenge of the institutional righteousness of royal government and capitalist business. And John Calvin who could so eloquently express Luther's evangelical idea—"We are not our own. . . . We belong to God"—was impelled by his legalistic cast of mind to expound a Protestant variant of the Catholic institutionalist doctrine, so that old priest now became new presbyter.

Only in England in the late sixteenth and early seventeenth centuries, in a society again made pessimistic by the indecisiveness of government and the bewildering decline of prosperity, did the left-wing Puritans perpetuate the evangelical reformation of the young Luther, with momentous consequences for the religious and political development of the English-speaking world. It is true the advance of Calvinism in later Tudor England committed Puritanism to the neo-medieval, institutionalist ideal of the authority of the holy community. But William Haller's *Rise of Puritanism* reveals the subtle transition by which Calvinist institutionalism was undermined by the Puritan leaders' need to emphasize the primacy of personal religious experience and the claims of individual conscience—the "trying of the spirit"—against the sanctions of an Erastian national church. The current of evangelical reformation, emerging in England with William Tyndale and the first generation of Protestants in the 1520's, welled up again in late sixteenth-century Puritanism.

The reformation in England is an integral part of the general European reformation of the sixteenth century and follows the same broad pattern as the movement of religious events and ideas on the continent. It is necessary to emphasize this obvious fact because so many nineteenth- and twentieth-century historians of the English reformation, although not the majority of either Protestant or Catholic writers in the sixteenth century, have for partisan purposes of their own, whether national or denominational, interpreted the English development as a peculiar phenomenon, distinct from the course of religious change on the continent. The extensive historical literature on the English reformation produced in the second half of the nineteenth century and shortly after 1900 is so strongly inspired by Roman, high and low Anglican, and sectarian Protestant commitments as to be mainly of value for the student of religious controversy in the Victorian era. The same judgment can be made of F. M. Powicke's general interpretive essay published in 1936, because it views the English reformation in a grossly tendentious and one-sided way as simply "an act of the state."

In the vast literature of the English reformation only two works of synthesis meet high standards of historical scholarship and these are products of the 1950's and 1960's. The three-volume work by Father Philip Hughes (1950-1954) is the most careful account of the English reformation written by a Roman Catholic. Its minutely detailed, almost day-by-day narrative is apparently designed to demonstrate the selfishness, confusions, and doubts that were involved in the process of reformation in England. Father Hughes convinces us of the accidents and injustices that marked the course of religious change in Tudor England, and we are left with the indelible impression that there was nothing inevitable and predetermined about the actual course of events. There were plenty of social pressures, mixed motives, personal failings, and awkward misunderstandings and fumblings involved in the English reformation, and the religious settlement that finally emerged was by no means the only one within the realm of possibility. These lessons are salutary but they are presented at the price of underrating the force and deep current of evangelical feeling, which while it did not determine, certainly gave a logic and thrust to the course of events. Father Hughes' penchant for minute detail heightens the reader's impression of the confused, inconsistent, and at times senseless character of the course of events in sixteenth-century English religious change; at times Hughes' work attains the level of history of the absurd, which is certainly not unintentional, but instead represents a most subtle kind of Catholic apologetic.

Both the qualities and defects of Father Hughes' imposing study stand in marked contrast to the even more recent synthetic interpretation offered by A. G. Dickens (1964). The long polemic against six-teenth-century English Protestantism conducted by socialist and Catholic writers was challenged by E. G. Rupp's *Studies in the Making of the English Protestant Tradition* (1947), which asserted that the English reformation of the 1530's was partly inspired by an evangelical tradition arising out of late medieval Lollardry. It is only as a result of Dickens' researches, however, that sufficient evidence has been adduced to sustain the thesis that Protestantism in England represented a continuous current of evangelical religion flowing from fourteenth-century heretical Lollardry into the 1520's, when it was widened and deepened by Lutheran and Anabaptist ideas coming across the channel. Dickens' one-volume account of *The English Reformation* is the best book by far ever written on the subject; it is learned, eloquent, and persuasive in its general thesis. The defects of this work are a somewhat deterministic and dialectical tendency to assume the inevitable triumph of Protestantism in England, a too easy acquiescence in the liberal Protestant assumption that the decrepitude of the early sixteenth-century church directly induced and somehow morally justifies the schisms and upheavals that followed, the playing down of the dumb disinterest or bewilderment of large masses of landed society with respect to the dramatic events at the center, and the cursory and inadequate treatment of the second wave of evangelical upheaval in the last four decades of the century. Rupp's and Dickens' claim that the Henrician reformation was not only an act of the state but also involved a widespread popular Protestantism very different from the outlook of Henry VIII, represents the historiographical rehabilitation of John Foxe, who in the 1560's and 1570's produced detailed accounts of the religious history of the 1520's and 1530's precisely along these lines. Through most of the nineteenth century and down to 1940 Foxe was regarded as a liar and fabricator but in the latter year J. F. Mozley argued that Foxe's work should be taken as generally reliable. Dickens' interpretation of the English reformation has done just this, and Foxe's veracity has recently been further confirmed in a study made by William Haller, the great American historian of Tudor Puritanism.

Amid all the twists and turns, fumblings, confusions, false starts, inconsistencies, and absurdities of the religious history of Tudor England, a recognizable pattern of meaningful change is provided as on the continent, by two fundamental movements, that of institutional and evangelical reformations. The institutional reformation had its conservative side —improvement in church discipline and learning while retaining loyalty to Rome—and its radical side—royal headship of the church, schism with Rome, the sovereignty of king-in-Parliament, and extensive nationalization of church property. This separated Roman Catholics from Anglo-Catholics, papists from Anglicans—the conservative side of the English institutional reformation is depicted for us in R. W. Chambers' biography of Sir Thomas More and the radical side in G. R. Elton's studies of Henrician government—but it had little or nothing to do with religious experience, and it was by no means an irrevocable split. In most countries which remained loyal to the Roman church in the sixteenth century there was an increase of royal control over church government and some expropriation of ecclesiastical property for use by royal treasuries. The extent of institutional reformation in England was disputed between conservative and radical institutional reformers largely as a matter of how the world-order should be organized. It was the evangelical reformation, drawing its inspiration from Lollardry, early Lutheranism, and Anabaptism which pressed for profound and irrevocable religious change.

The English evangelical reformers, at least in the 1520's and 1530's, were not primarily interested in world-order; they wanted to set man right with God, and this involved far more than royal or papal headship of the church or extent of nationalization of ecclesiastical property. It involved the nature of the sacraments, the means of salvation, the privilege of reading and interpreting the Bible, the forms and efficacy of prayer, and the content of the liturgy. The radical institutionalists and evangelicals had some common ground for temporary alliance against the conservative institutionalists. The radical institutionalists conveniently separated from Rome while the evangelicals violently hated the papacy as anti-Christ, the Whore of Babylon: on this single point the two groups were in agreement and anti-papal evangelical polemic could be useful to the statists. Furthermore, the specter of anarchic evangelical upheaval could be employed to frighten conservative clergy and laymen into accepting royal headship and nationalization as the far lesser of two evils. The English evangelicals of first generation, on their part, vehemently extolled the power of monarchy because the king was their only protection against heresy-hunting conservative bishops and because their belief in the self-evident truth of their doctrines was so great that they expected to be able to win the king and the royal court to undertake a full-scale religious reformation. This hope would prove vain for the most part before 1547 because while Henry VIII's great minister in the 1530's,

Thomas Cromwell, may have been a crypto-Lutheran, and the Archbishop of Canterbury, Thomas Cranmer, was somewhat under the influence of the radical Swiss reformer Ulrich Zwingli, the king himself never swerved from loyalty to the theological and sacramental traditions of medieval Catholicism. But it was of momentous consequence for the subsequent history of the English reformation that the royal government in the 1520's and 1530's had allowed the spread and entrenchment of Protestantism in England. No subsequent reaction, not even the momentary return of the monarchy to the Roman church, could extirpate it, or even greatly diminish its force and in the century after Henry VIII's death the shape of religious change in England would be mainly determined by the waxing and waning of the movement for evangelical "reformation without tarrying."

In the later decades of the sixteenth century, the continual frustrations experienced by the radical reformers in trying to win the Tudor monarchy to its side would slowly wear thin the Protestants' enthusiasm for royal authority. In the first half of the seventeenth century the alliance between the monarchy and the evangelical reform movement would break down altogether and out of radical English Puritanism would come a host of novel doctrines which we associate with the modern world: the liberal ideal of freedom of conscience, political democracy, republicanism, and on the extreme left the advocacy of communism. Thus in the end the sixteenth-century reformation was a harbinger of the modern world. But it was not liberalism, capitalism, and statism which produced the reformation. Rather it was the evangelical side of the reformation which was forced to turn against established order in England and in so doing gave vent to political and social doctrines which sounded the death knell of monarchical, aristocratic, and hierarchic European society.

If historians insist on isolating one aspect of human experience as the primary determinant of social change in the sixteenth and seventeenth centuries, they could make the most plausible case for the overwhelming thrust of evangelical faith, which, finding no satisfaction within prevailing social and political forms, eventually tried to supersede them by advocating a brave new world. When Luther in the 1520's discovered that evangelical reformation threatened the stability of society and aroused fear and hatred in princes and lords, he mitigated the radical tendencies of his teaching. The left-wing English Puritans did just the opposite: they tried to overthrow the prevailing social order. Although defeated by the landed oligarchy, the Puritans inaugurated a new era in European history when they announced first, that "it is conscience, not the power of man, that will drive us to seek the Lord's kingdom," and then that "the poorest he that is in England has a life to live as the greatest he."

The first great upheaval in post-apostolic Christianity, the Gregorian reform of the eleventh century, followed a similarly revolutionary and surprising course. There is no good reason to doubt that the ultimate effects of the twentieth-century reformation will be as shattering and as unanticipated by the first generation of reformers as the outcome of the Gregorian reform and the Protestant reformation.

V. The Precarious Balance

HISTORIANS have too often tended to depict the Elizabethans as ten feet tall. Sometimes they appear oversized models of wickedness, although they are more usually presented as virtuous supermen who were first in war, first in peace, great statesmen, shrewd entrepreneurs, valiant soldiers and dashing sailors. The truth is that except in literature the Elizabethans were terribly inept. They were miserable soldiers (the only efficient armies in sixteenth-century Europe were composed of mercenaries, which the English government could ill afford) and the royal treasury was so bare that the crown itself stooped to underwrite piratical raids. Nor was the Elizabethan navy worthy of the name. Historians who propagated the stories about great Elizabethan sea-dogs were never able to explain why the Stuart navy was virtually nonexistent and why Oliver Cromwell had to establish the British fleet in the 1650's. Not every failure of seventeenth-century England can be attributed to Stuart stupidity. It is easy to forget, amid all the furor, that the Elizabethan government employed the farfetched and desperate expedient of ship-money, though it lacked the initiative or strength to take it very far. Those who would glorify the Elizabethans can account for few of the agonies that gripped Stuart England. Swayed at first by the most blatant nationalist myths and then by the neo-nationalism and conservative ideology fashionable in the late 1940's and 1950's, historians have dwelt lovingly on Elizabethan achievements. Also, the commonplace notion —seductive but meretricious—that people who can write great poems must be great at everything, has caused historians to view all aspects of Elizabethan life with undiluted admiration. But one of the most striking qualities of Elizabethan literature is its tone of nervousness and tension. Marlowe and Shakespeare do not exude a sense of calm and success; their plays hardly convey a happy security that life is being lived in the best of all Englands. The relish of violence characteristic of Elizabethan drama shows clearly enough that something is very wrong in the society that produced it.

At the outset we should disabuse ourselves of the myth of Tudor military might. Not one of the Tudor rulers was a great warrior. Henry VIII never really frightened the Germans or the French; only fitfully did he loom very large on the European stage, but the Tudors who followed made the Hapsburgs and Valois even less apprehensive. In general, the late Tudor period is marked by corruption and mismanagement. In the 1570's and 1580's royal finances were always on the edge of catastrophe, and without cash a sixteenth-century government was bound to be in serious military trouble. Thus in the second half of the sixteenth century English might was probably on the decline. A haze of glory has surrounded the defeat of the Spanish Armada in 1588, a battle which supposedly set the pattern of English naval superiority. But there was, as Garrett Mattingly has shown, a crucial element of luck involved in the battle, which was more a Spanish defeat than an English triumph. Against the slovenly Elizabethan government Mattingly depicts the over-rationalized, overbureaucratized government of Philip II. The defeat of the Armada was the consequence of English good fortune and Spanish incompetence as much as anything else. Nor did the English deceive themselves into believing they had scored a decisive victory. A Spanish invasion was still a very real threat in the early 1590's and, though it is easy now to talk about incipient empire, Spanish decline, and British ascendancy, the English in the 1590's did not have this consoling insight. Nor can we blame them. In the sixteenth century Spain was engaged in some grand imperial activities; she conquered a huge continent, and though the Spanish empire may not be morally attractive, the conquest and exploitation of Central and South America remains one of the impressive achievements in human government. Aside from attempting to grab what Spain had already amassed, England did not contribute very much to this process. First England tried to lure trade away and, when that scheme failed, then turned to piracy. The most ruthless sixteenth-century slave traders were Englishmen; at least some Spaniards were vehemently against the slave trade on moral and religious grounds. We need not naively expect sixteenth-century adventurers to be sweet liberals, but it is necessary to point out that Drake and Hawkins, long hailed as knights of Protestantism, were no more enlightened than the men they were trying to steal from. Lord Acton has told us that the historian's function is not to devalue the moral currency—thus we must be careful about whitewashing these men who were, in most respects, nothing but successful pirates. Without an inflated belief in Tudor military prowess, we can better understand the problems that beset Elizabethan government and society and the methods devised for dealing with them.

Most recent works of Tudor history have not been sufficiently realistic about the achievements and shortcomings of the Tudors. One of the most popular and persuasive accounts, A. L. Rowse's *The England of Elizabeth*, portrays the age as one of unadulterated splendor. Rowse, whose ability to convey his enthusiasm for his subject is outstanding, is a man of many gifts, but his book, which presents the strongest possible case for the Elizabethans, simply ignores many things that did not happen to enhance the beauty of Elizabethan life. He refuses to discuss the Puritans seriously because he finds them repulsive, noisy cranks out to destroy the Elizabethan world. Though this view is understandable, it might be said that the Puritans—exactly because they were the bearers of change—were the most important people in Elizabethan England; that though less attractive than Rowse's favorite scholar-poet-geographer-esthetes, they are far more significant. Thus Rowse's personal quirk—an inability to attribute historical significance to people he detests—severely mars his work. J. B. Black, in his volume on *The Reign of Elizabeth* in the Oxford History of England, is not so taken in by the charms of life under Elizabeth, but neither does this view of England by a dour Scotsman provide a stimulating account. Among the surfeit of books about the queen herself only two are really enlightening—Neale's *Queen Elizabeth I* and Joel Hurstfield's biography, *Elizabeth I and the Unity of England*. The studies of Elizabethan government are not as many or profound as we might expect. The American scholar Conyers Read published several massive volumes purporting to be a study of Tudor administration. They consist mainly of undigested material and are so unfocused that it would be preferable to have only the documents themselves. The most perceptive study of Tudor administration is Hurstfield's *The Queen's Wards*, the only book, in fact, that manages to capture the spirit of Elizabethan administration; it shows the people involved, how they worked and thought, and tells us what kind of government it really was. On Protestantism, the best book—also one of the finest books ever produced by an American scholar—is William Haller's *Rise of Puritanism*. Here Haller illuminates the various strands of Puritan thought and feeling; he is brilliantly able to account for the changes in Protestantism that eventually led to political and religious radicalism, a tendency he traces back to the 1580's and 1590's rather than to the early seventeenth century.

Certainly the Elizabethans were great at literature, though we should not forget that much of it was court literature, written for a very specialized and highly cultivated audience. Nevertheless there is a new and expanded vision in the Elizabethan world, a sense of space and verve. It is the discovery of the world and of man. It represents the renaissance (if we believe in the phenomenon) which took place (if it ever did) to a greater degree in the second half of the sixteenth century than in the reign of Henry VIII. There is a new sense of topology, and intense love of the land; along with the entrenchment of the gentry goes a celebration of the land, its fruits, the country house, the organization of rural society itself. There is an excellent chapter on this discovery of England in Rowse's book. Of course people had made maps before, but never with such care and concentration. This love of the English countryside is accompanied by a new sensitivity to human experience, to the worth, fragility, and possibilities of human life—all the things, after all, that humanism is about.

What is the special characteristic of Elizabethan government? Upon first impression, after the previous twenty years of chaos, it seems to be very good, stable government. The reign of Edward VI (1547-1553) nearly brought a return of the aristocratic government of the fifteenth century, and with it, catastrophic struggles for control of the king among great lords and the menace of the overmighty subject. Edward's reign was the only time during the sixteenth century when the aristocracy seriously tried to get hold of government; fortunately it was a brief and unsuccessful attempt, and luckily Edward died before fighting within the royal family ruined England. The reign of Mary (1553-1558) was hardly an improvement. It is hard to rehabilitate Mary, though she probably does not deserve the harsh treatment she has received from nationalist Protestant historians. She was not necessarily stupid and inept just because she was a Roman Catholic. As a matter of fact Mary did have some wit, she was well-educated, and certainly she was irreproachably pious. But she was extremely rigid and unimaginative, and she complicated matters by setting herself the impossible task of bringing England back into the arms of Rome. Mary probably would have been a good abbess—she had the soul of a fanatical Spaniard—but as a queen she was hopeless. Her domestic problem was insurmountable; too many churchmen were opposed to her, and they had either to be converted or exiled. Most of them chose to go into exile, but this made things even worse for Mary. Most people in England were probably not particularly stirred by religion, nor did they mind what religion the crown required them to observe, but the hard core—perhaps 5 percent—who did care were able to stir up a tremendous response to the Protestant martyrs that Mary and her chief minister, Cardinal Reginald Pole created. A few Protestant leaders, like Thomas Cranmer, went to the stake; most chose to flee to the continent. The exodus of the "Marian exiles" to Geneva also revealed how ineffective the Tudor police powers were. Mary was not really despotic; probably she was not despotic enough. A hard-headed historian could make a fairly good case that she should have burned more people. Mary's birds eventually came home to roost; the Marian exiles were red-hot Calvinists when they came back from Geneva in Elizabeth's reign.

The return to Rome also raised embarrassing questions about the monastic lands, which the leading families of England were happily incorporating into their estates, and Mary was forced to compromise. They kept their lands, but even this sop to the gentry did not make her popular. One of the few significant aspects of Mary's reign is that it ended the era of good feeling between landed society and the crown. It showed that even though Parliament had confirmed the seizure of monastic lands, other conflicts of interest could break down the consensus. The crown could not rule without the good will and consent of landed society, and the gentry were not soothed by Mary's marriage to Philip II, a Catholic and a Hapsburg. The political ramifications of the alliance probably upset most Englishmen more than the popish aspect. If there were an heir, it seemed to them that England would be swallowed up by the Hapsburg empire. This was more than a hysterical fantasy; if there had been a child the danger would have been real enough. Mary's great contribution to her realm was to provoke Englishmen into worrying about the future and independence of their country.

After twenty years of drift and anxiety almost anything would have been welcome, and aside from her other considerable assets Elizabeth I

(1558-1603) was no Catholic nor was she the kind to prod her people about monastic lands. She was a mature woman and—it was soon clear —she was eminently intelligent and sensible. Nevertheless her reign too was characterized by drift and hesitancy. There was, of course, a fine style, but much of it was a slick charade, a court masque. The Elizabethan government was engaged in a balancing act. There were some brilliant people doing it—particularly William Cecil (later Lord Burghley) and Sir Francis Walsingham—and they did not often miss their tricks, but we cannot get around the fact that the important decisions of Elizabeth's reign were taken for her and her government. She and her ministers took little initiative. They waited. They carved whole careers out of waiting, and the queen herself developed the expedient of doing nothing gracefully to something of a high art. People have struggled to explain Elizabeth—how much of her performance was clever duplicity, diplomacy and insight, how much of it was temper, hysteria, or a pathological inability to come to a decision. We still cannot say for sure. Nor can we say it was the wrong policy to follow.

Elizabeth's government faced vast problems. Europe was split into two ideological camps, and the Catholic camp, which controlled far greater military resources, was successfully carrying out a counterattack. The organization of government had deteriorated since the death of Thomas Cromwell in 1540 and there was slackness in every area of administration. The crown no longer had much money, certainly not nearly enough to justify involvement in a real continental war. And English society was itself divided along ideological lines. It was hard to exercise leadership, either in international affairs or domestic matters. Elizabethan government managed to function at all only through creative caution and canny uncommitment. This entailed endless diplomatic negotiations; marriages that never quite came off, threats that were never really unveiled. Government had to keep religious and political dissidents under control, but it could not afford brutally to suppress them. Open rebellion had to be avoided at all cost, and sleight of hand had to take the place of any real program. It was government by precarious balance.

In a vast and complicated world, Elizabeth's government was a small, personal thing. The queen had had a hard life; she was lucky to be on the throne and she had the sense to surround herself with good advisors and reward them as they deserved. They were a small, hardheaded group of realistic people. They knew they could not embark on great schemes without running tremendous risks. So they did not try to do very much; their ambitions were small. In many ways it was a political interlude, a kind of marking time. If, at times, important events seem to happen, it turns out that they happen in spite of, not because of, government. In comparison with Henry VIII's government of the 1530's we can see little leadership exerted under Elizabeth. Probably it was wise for Elizabethan government to function in the way it did. Considering the power structure of county society, the absence of any effective police force, and the creaking administrative structure, the only feasible course of action was inaction. The central government was pitifully small and exposed; it consisted only of the queen, her court, a few courtiers, fewer competent officials. They could only deal with a few problems and make decisions on a small scale. That they left such a reputation is one of their most amazing achievements and a tribute to their abilities. In terms of their limited resources this was probably wisdom, but it should not be mistaken for creative leadership.

How did they manage? By thrusting the basic responsibilities and everyday tasks of government on to local administration, but at the same time making it appear that policy was actually being set by the central government. Desperate measures to keep the peace were given a cloak of fine rhetoric, so that legislation that was politically expedient looked as though it were prompted by motives of social welfare and a desire to further the common good. The late sixteenth century was a time of great depression; the enclosure movement was causing a vast dislocation in rural society—certainly not as widespread and ominous as many people perceived it, but it was nevertheless a source of considerable apprehension among men of peace and property. The hordes of vagabonds and sturdy beggars who terrified the countryside did constitute a real political problem, and thus the peace function of the famous Elizabethan poor laws was much more signficant than their pretensions to be welfare legislation. Social disturbance bred rebellion, and the Elizabethans understood this very well. Royal government was right to be concerned and alarmed. It wanted to cope with the problem, and it passed a whole series of statutes purporting to deal with poverty and ease the state of the poor. There was no choice, however, but to delegate the authority to administer the statutes to local men. There was really nothing unprecedented about the Elizabethan social legislation. Most of the statutes simply laid down procedures that had always been carried out, often on an *ad hoc* basis by local authorities—either municipal or manorial courts, for instance. Only now they were given parliamentary sanction; they were carried out at the behest of the central government; they applied to the whole country; and their administration was entrusted to local men who were also royal officials. For the justices of the peace were appointed by the crown.

An impressive stream of what we think of as social and economic legislation courses through the Elizabethan period. It deals with agriculture, the regulation of industry and manufacturing, apprentices, poor relief, beggars. But these were matters that always were handled locally, either by the parish, by municipalities, or by guilds. Two things, however, seem to be new. These regulations are made uniformly for the whole country and they are set down, at least on the statute book, as compulsory obligations imposed on the rich in order to provide for the poor. It is during the early years of Elizabeth that the J.P.'s are given statutory authority to levy a compulsory poor rate. But exactly because this was all done locally by a small group of country gentlemen, because the men who set the rate were also the ones who paid, the statutes were loosely enforced. Had they really been implemented, the burden would have been staggering. Of course, in some places the poor might receive good treatment, but on the whole the Elizabethan statutes represent welfare legislation of the meanest and toughest sort.

How extensive and absolute was the power of the J.P. over the lives of the lower order of society may be seen in the case of vagabonds, or sturdy beggars. A contemporary writer, William Harrison, describes how the problem was dealt with. "The rogue" is apprehended, "committed to prison, and tried in the next assizes (whether . . . gaol delivery or sessions of the peace). If he happens to be convicted . . . either by inquest . . . or the testimony of two honest and credible witnesses . . . he is then immediately adjudged to be greviously whipped and burned through the gristle of the right ear with an hot iron of the compass of an inch about, as a manifestation of his wicked life, and due punishment received for the same. And this judgement is to be executed upon him [unless] some honest person worth five pounds in the Queen's book, or twenty shillings in lands, or some rich householder to be allowed by the justices, will be bound in recognizance to retain him in his service for one whole year. If he be taken the second time . . . he shall then be whipped again, bored likewise through the other ear, and set to service. . . . If he depart before a year . . . he is condemned to suffer pains of death as a felon . . . as by the statute doth appear." The "impotent poor" (the sick, blind and aged) and their children (who were bound out as apprentices) were treated somewhat less harshly. Still, none of this "welfare" legislation was a real attempt to deal with poverty, but simply an expedient to check the social disruptions that went hand in hand with severe unemployment.

Because the crown was desperate, stingy and hard-pressed, the role of the justice of the peace becomes more and more important and as the century wears on these officials wield their power with more and more assurance. Relatively free from aristocratic interference, they had the scope to be independent and free-wheeling, and the crown, which needed their cooperation, was forced to let them do pretty much as they pleased. The gentleman who was appointed a J.P. took an impressive oath: he swore to do "equal right to the poor and to the rich after your cunning, wit, and power, and after the laws and customs of the realm and the statutes . . . and ye shall not be of counsel with any quarrel hanging before you"—a series of promises that were not always followed. The J.P. was appointed because he was an important man in the locality; he was bound to have lands in the vicinity, and servants, and hangers-on and enemies; often he really could not help but be involved in the cases he adjudged. But even if he tried to be impartial and unprejudiced, he had deep interests in the neighborhood. It is impossible to believe that the typical J.P. could have been anything like the unbiased administrator and law-officer the crown needed to carry out its laws. The matters which the J.P.'s dealt with in quarter sessions (and the quarter session records provide a fascinating, though relatively untapped source for the routine matters of local jurisdiction) are minor. Illegal entry, misdemeanor, petty thievery, brawling, drunken pranks, nuisances, absurd personal feuds, are the common cases. But in dealing with them, the J.P. is supreme. This is the kind of law most people encountered most of the time, and thus the law in Tudor England is represented in the person of the J.P.; it is not shaped by any royal government and controlled from the center.

The queen did what she could, but the execution of the laws was firmly in the hands of these men—local gentry who owned fair amounts of property and had acquired a smattering of legal knowledge. It is not her fault, protests the Lord Keeper in his closing speech in Parliament in 1571, if the laws are badly executed. The negligence is on the part of the J.P.'s. The queen proclaims the law and she grants her commission to supposedly good men. At least once a year she brings some of them to the Court of Star Chamber to be exhorted on their duties. But that was exactly the problem. The queen could only exhort, not coerce. Her government could be creative only when it came to phrase-mongering. The queen's ministers could implore or preach—but they were finally helpless if they had to impose their will.

Decision-making came, always, from outside the government. The two most critical dates for Elizabethan political history are 1570 and 1588. Both were decisions imposed from outside. After Elizabeth's excommunication by the Pope in 1570 she had to be a positive monarch. Elizabeth had been made a Protestant by the Pope. The Pope had denounced the queen as the archenemy of international Catholicism, a role she never asked for and one she always played reluctantly, with more feinting than aggression. Although Elizabeth now had to be firmly in the Protestant camp, she did not do much for the cause. She sent some dilapidated soldiers and a trickle of money to the Dutch in the Low Countries, but it did not really help. At home, however, her position meant that government had to be more tolerant of Protestant dissent, and the articulate Marian exiles were allowed a freer rein. After 1570 Elizabeth became tremendously popular—one of the few things Englishmen could agree on was their dislike of the Pope, and her excommunication reinforced the unity of the nation, it rallied the landed classes, and it also strengthened English Protestantism itself.

The Armada year, 1588, was, to some degree, a release. The English were still afraid of Spain, but they were no longer totally paralyzed by terror, they no longer shivered waiting for the blow to fall. Government now had an opportunity to deal with pressing domestic matters. As the danger receded, the pressure was somewhat reduced, but the decline of the Hapsburg menace also helped to dissolve the unity of England. The dissidence that had always been present now came out in the open; the consensus of fear fell apart. Ideas that would be so troublesome to the early Stuarts were quite evident in the 1590's, and government could no longer keep the lid on. The brilliant people were no longer so resilient; the queen was older, so were her ministers—it was as though their reflexes were dulled. The House of Commons could be more critical of the government; its members were no longer apprehensive of expressing their worries about the succession, about economic policy and, particularly about trade monopolies awarded to court favorites. It was the anger over monopolies that provoked Sir Robert Cecil to exclaim in 1601 that he had never seen the house in such great confusion—"more fit for a grammar school than a court of parliament." And even worse, parliamentary matters were becoming ordinary talk in the street; Cecil himself had heard words about the prerogative from persons (obviously dangerous) who "would be glad that all sovereignty were converted into popularity." The Hapsburg failure gave Elizabethans the freedom to engage in debate on fundamental issues; by the last decade of the reign they were becoming more articulate in Parliament and outside. Disagreement about grave issues is no longer hidden. It will be harder and harder for governments to avoid making decisions; the balancing act will be more tricky to sustain. And eventually no monarch will be able to govern this way.

For a while James Stuart, Elizabeth's Scottish cousin who succeeded the old Queen in 1603, was refreshing. He took stands on issues, he tended to be rational, he planned to move government along certain lines. So did Charles I. And yet, the first two Stuarts were a disaster for the monarchy. They believed in firm and direct action; they tried to be despotic enough to get things done. The early Stuart kings were the opposite of Elizabeth, whose favorite tactic was the velvet fist in the iron glove. We need only compare the case of Peter Wentworth with the more overt treatment of hostile parliamentarians by James and Charles. Wentworth, who sat for a Cornish pocket borough, stemmed from the Puritan stronghold in East Anglia; he stirred up uncomfortable debates over the freedom of speech enjoyed by members of the House of Commons. Parliament could discuss any matter at all, claimed Wentworth. "There is nothing so necessary for the preservation of the prince and state as free speech," he argued. "And without, it is a scorn and mockery to call it a parliament house; for in truth it is none, but a very school of flattery and dissimulation, and so a fit place to serve the devil and his angels in, and not to glorify God and benefit the commonwealth." As if this were not reckless enough, Wentworth went on to cite Bracton's maxim and announce that the ruler ought to be under the law, so that the embarrassed members, "out of a reverend regard of her majesty's honour" had Wentworth sent before the Star Chamber. But his punishment was very mild. He was, of course, sent to the Tower, but almost immediately, "by the queen's special favour," he was released and restored to his seat. A few years later Wentworth again found himself in trouble when he made a speech exalting the liberties and privileges of Parliament—a speech that implied Parliament was supreme in the land. For this Wentworth earned another sojourn in the Tower. The point, however, is that he was never really persecuted or treated at all meanly. He was given no opportunity to become a martyr, to stir up a following of outraged parliamentarians. When stung by the barbs of a Wentworth, or annoyed by a fierce radical Protestant speech in the House of Commons, Elizabethan government would make a great show of force, but no one was ever really hurt. Elizabeth knew how to sound menacing, but never did anything her people would brood about. Stern words, but no irrevocable action; threats were seldom translated into action men would remember. James and Charles would fly into rages no one could forget.

Though Elizabethan government successfully dodged them, the issues that appeared late in the sixteenth century burst out in the seventeenth century. The main problem was crown finance—the great problem of English government throughout the sixteenth and seventeenth centuries was how to pay its own way. The early Tudors had been exceptional in their wealth. Henry VII's was the result of intense frugality; Henry VIII's was due to the seizure of monastic lands. But by the second half of Elizabeth's reign the wealth had melted away, partly as a result of the runaway inflation, and her government was reduced to cheese-paring of the most undignified kind. One of Elizabeth's favorite tricks was to go traveling about her realm, honoring the homes of rich subjects with her presence. A royal visit could ruin a man. Cecil's official salary was four hundred pounds a year, not enough, he said, to pay for his stable. Hence the queen's favorite ministers were rewarded by lavish gifts and wardships, perhaps a generous but not an efficient way to run an administration. Judges were expected to take gifts from both parties; when he was impeached, it was in an attempt to bolster his defense that Sir Frances Bacon later asserted he had accepted bribes with utter impartiality. Government descended to mean, petty, and dangerous expedients in order to scrape along. Real reform was out of the question. An overhaul of the whole financial structure was required in order to tap the growing wealth of the country, but government was frightened. Reform would have meant dealing with the House of Commons; it would have led to scrutiny of royal policy and required concessions to the vociferous Puritan faction. So the queen and her ministers continued to engage in side ventures, in intricate schemes and wasteful methods which, each year, were less effective.

By the second half of the century the great boom was over; in the 1580's it was becoming harder to make money. Until then it had been hard not to make money, but now a gentleman had to be tough and alert in order to prosper. Many of the landed gentry did go under. We can subscribe to Trevor-Roper's distinction between court and county factions. Many county families found themselves in serious trouble and, since the surest way to wealth was through serving the crown, there was a growing disparity between gentry who had friends at court, and those who had to rely on the yield from their estates. The lesser gentry fought for jobs and sinecures in the household and the exchequer. It was now the best way to make money, to achieve power and influence. The new reliance on court influence led to an increasing jealousy among the gentry; it introduced the theme that will prove to be of greatest significance in the seventeenth century, when the gentry class forms itself into two opposing factions—the court and country party. In the late Elizabethan period we can no longer say that the gentry class is united. It is a gross oversimplification to think of the gentry as one cohesive group straining to throw off the restrictions of a paternalistic monarchy. There are all kinds of gentry; the term includes a wide range of people and—except for a few London merchants—the gentry constitutes the only important class in society. Any split in the ranks of the gentry will inevitably make itself felt in the whole of society. Some gentry have access to court privileges while others, eager to share the patronage and booty, are increasingly anxious to obtain wardships and monopolies. In a mercantilist economy it is a normal way to make money.

Mercantilism—that loaded word—simply means crown control of the economy, particularly control of international trade. During the sixteenth century mercantilism is commonplace all over Europe. Economic flow had never been unrestricted; there had always been monopolies, tight restrictions, oligarchic corporations. The emergence of stronger national monarchies meant only that control passed from town corporation to crown corporation. International relations, diplomatic strategy, and economic suasion were now matters of crown policy. The crown granted charters and monopolies to certain groups of merchants—the East India Company was a chartered crown corporation. Monopolies were another method of rewarding crown service and, as we know from irate speeches in Parliament, monopolies have become the single most aggravating issue by the end of the sixteenth century. They were a wedge that widened the split between the court and the country gentry. A few men were lapping up all the profits, while the majority could only watch and complain. As the economic situation worsened it became even more painful to see a few court favorites prosper while the majority of the honest hardworking gentry had to strain to make ends meet. This situation was bound to foster deep and bitter feeling. Discontented businessmen invariably become hostile to government, and in the late sixteenth century we find these disgruntled men supporting Puritan preachers, angry common lawyers, and parliamentary dissidents. While Elizabeth is still queen, there is no alliance among these men; they form an unorganized group whose ideas, nevertheless, are disquieting. What they have in common so far is a chip on the shoulder, but they already constitute a threat to the stability of government. They represent a strain in the social and political structure—one that is critical by the end of the Elizabethan period, and that becomes strikingly clear in the seventeenth century when the smoldering hostility in landed society bursts out into civil war.

The queen managed to maintain her control. She was careful not to provoke; she usually knew when to soothe. In her way, she was a great leader and though they were sometimes afraid of her, her people loved her too. "I count the glory of my crown," she told the House of Commons at the very end of her life, "that I have reigned with your loves." She also reigned with the indispensable aid of a few devoted royal officials, who included some of the cleverest and most conscientious men in the kingdom; these she elected to the privy council. Certain privy councillors and their dependents (the nucleus of the court party) are the central, organized steering group in the Commons. Through the council they are linked to the crown by the bounty of patronage. The privy council manages everything; somehow this small group of men binds together an unwieldy conglomeration of autonomous parts and disparate interests. All these men need in order to control the House of Commons is a court party that comprises about twenty percent of the members. The privy councillors are themselves powerful in Parliament, and they have in their hands several "nominated" boroughs. They will be careful to nominate M.P.'s whom they can readily control. The queen may be the resplendent symbol of the Commonwealth, but it is the tireless activity and skill of her servants who belong to the council that gives England its unity.

How are most of the members of the House of Commons chosen? They are an accurate reflection of the structure of county society, and they represent the dominance of a few prominent families in each shire. County members—the prestigious knights of the shire—are almost invariably members or dependents of these leading families, and they hold their seats by right of their natural superiority. From time to time there may be a real election in a county, but usually there is agreement among the leading families of the shire as to who shall be returned as M.P. An election is usually the symptom of an unsettled feud between great families, or the final gambit of one family ready to oust another. Election procedures have not changed since the thirteenth century; knights of the shire are chosen by a consensus in the county court. But there has been a great change since the thirteenth century in borough representation. Throughout the Tudor period the number of boroughs underwent a steady expansion, and some of the newest were never anything but rotten boroughs. Obscure Cornish fishing villages and sleepy midland market towns were sending two burgesses to London. The number of boroughs increased because the county families called for them, and at a rate that is truly astounding. At the beginning of Henry VIII's reign there were 298 seats in the House of Commons; by the end of the century there were 467. The new "nominated" boroughs were not created by fiat of an authoritarian government, but rather at the behest of landed society who wanted more opportunities for the offspring and dependents of the great families that already controlled the shires. The rising bourgeois, that elusive animal, had nothing to do with the increase of borough representation or the multiplication of pocket boroughs. The men who represented the boroughs in the Elizabethan House of Commons could rarely be considered burgesses; they were gentlemen, full-fledged members of landed society, who had obtained their seats through the support of great families. The procedure so familiar in the eighteenth century was then two centuries old.

No longer is it an onerous duty to serve in the House of Commons, rather it is a prestigious assignment. Parliament is gaining in confidence; the House of Commons is growing more conscious of itself as a corporate group; it has absorbed—and at times even goes beyond—the ethos fostered under Henry VIII. Parliament had been called upon to establish forms of religion, to legitimize the royal succession as well as to set down ambitious programs affecting social and economic life. "The most high and absolute power in the realm consisteth in the Parliament," writes Sir Thomas Smith in the 1560's. He was expressing a commonly held opinion. "For every Englishman is intended to be there present," he goes on, "either in person or by procuration and attorney . . . from the Prince . . . to the lowest person in England. And the consent of the Parliament is taken to be every man's consent." It would be correct to agree that every interest—at least those among the ruling elite—was present in Parliament. But the interests did not always harmonize as in theory they were supposed to, and as the early-Tudor consensus disintegrates, conflicts appear in Parliament.

It is painfully obvious that there are sharp differences of opinion in the Elizabethan House of Commons on crucial issues. Enough gentlemen of weight and importance are disgruntled. There is enough independence on the part of some M.P.'s to assert their opinions, and unhappy, dissident men are likely to express their hostility in moral and ideological terms. It is not enough to demand a share in the spoils; the way to change things is by raising political issues along with economic grievances. Indeed, the two were inseparable. The ideological issues that appear in the late-Elizabethan House of Commons have probably been exaggerated by Neale. Nevertheless, a small, articulate group is busily raising political and religious questions of great import; they are thinking very hard about law, government, and religion. Who are these other gentry, the ones who snipe at the government? We must believe that some county families are actively unhappy—the parliamentary dissidents are not just cranks, nor was the support they gained from the other M.P.'s ephemeral. They make noise in the House of Commons because they want to embarrass the queen and the privy council; they raise issues they know are difficult for the government to fend off. Some of these vociferous M.P.'s are genuinely committed to ideas and programs, particularly where their religion is concerned. They want the crown to cease its equivocation, they try to force the queen to take a firm stand in the direction of making the Church of England more clearly Protestant. They are motivated by more than envy and greed—real religious convictions drive them on, and resolution of religious issues is their most urgent demand. This persistent cry for "reformation without tarrying" signals the undermining of the precarious political balance of the later sixteenth century.

CHAPTER NINE

THE STRUGGLE FOR
LIBERTY
from 1603 to 1660

I. *The Gentry in Power*

L ATE IN THE SIXTEENTH and early in the seventeenth century, long suppressed issues emerge and whittle away the consensus among the
men who run the country. The House of Commons continues to represent an accurate image of the landed classes, but the loosely defined,
heterogeneous group of men that comprise the gentry is no longer
united, particularly over matters on which they had previously spoken
with one voice—politics and religion. While on the continent, and particularly across the channel in France, government became ever more
firmly the possession of king, court, and bureaucracy, in England during
the first of the seventeenth century a group of gentry tried to place ever
stronger and broader limitations on the power of the crown; they ended,
in the 1640's, by taking up arms against the king, condemning him as a
traitor, and sending him to the execution block. These violent and
revolutionary acts seemed to continental people as improbable as the
proposition that men can spread their arms and fly. The dissident English gentry had gone against the ordained order of the universe; they had
violated what God, nature, and history had provided for mankind. And
indeed the opposition group among the gentry did finally break through

to a new way of human government, and a new sense of human dignity.

The men who made the revolution against the Stuarts, from 1603 to the final split in 1642, have no consistent economic and social background, aside from their belonging to the large, amorphous group called gentry. A very few of the rebels had aristocratic affiliation; a few more were genuinely wealthy men with extensive commercial as well as landed interests. But the majority of the important leaders of the House of Commons in the early Stuart period were in their background ordinary landed gentlemen of the middling sort and several were quite modest in their income and property. These men do not fit into any Marxist category. Their economic interests do not provide the mainspring of their existence. Certainly they care about profiting from whatever they engage in, whether agriculture or commerce; but they are not hard-faced capitalist entrepreneurs, busy driving peasants off the land. Gentry engaged in that kind of activity are much too busy to worry about the liberties of the House of Commons and the condition of the English church. Certainly the parliamentarian radicals were seeking power and wealth, but they were, above all, seeking a constitutional settlement without which, they believed, no man's life, liberty, and property were safe from arbitrary despotism. Capitalist fatcats and selfish men seeking only their personal advantage would not have endangered their careers and social status by standing up against the king; they would have simply joined the mob of sycophants and homosexuals that congregated at the court of James Stuart and gained titles and monopolies from a king who had an appreciative ear for flattery and a sharp eye for a well-turned (particularly masculine) leg.

Peter Wentworth and the few other M.P.'s who criticized the queen in the 1580's were the first of this new breed of Parliament men. They were courageous, impassioned, and articulate men, many of whom sacrificed their wealth and security for their beliefs. And if, from one point of view, the king had precedent, theology, and even common sense on his side, and the rebellious gentry appear often narrow-minded, querulous, and unreasonable, we still cannot afford to disparage or denigrate these parliamentarians. Against absolutism and hierarchy, they raised the banner that we recognize as juristic and political liberalism—the principles that governmental authority is subject to the due process of law, that every citizen is entitled to the protection of the law, and that government cannot change the law without the consent of the governed.

Out of respect for the glorious and aged queen, the country party in the House of Commons had confined themselves to occasional critical speeches. When James Stuart came to the throne in 1603 and called his first Parliament, the discontented gentry—if not a majority of the House of Commons, then at least a large minority among the M.P.'s—organized themselves as a cohesive group and greeted the new king with *The Apology of the Commons,* a long and clear statement of their constitutional doctrine. The main issues of the next four decades appear full-blown in the programmatic statement of the radical gentry: "The prerogatives of princes may easily and do daily grow; the privileges of the subject are for the most part at an everlasting stand. They may be by good providence and care preserved; but, being once lost, are not recovered but with much disquiet." And these privileges of the subject are identical with the liberties of the House of Commons: freedom to decide on disputed elections of M.P.'s, freedom of speech, and freedom from arrest while the House is in session. These are "the ancient right of the subjects of this realm," and not a matter of royal grace. In addition the M.P.'s in 1604 called for the continuation of the English Reformation, "that the land might be furnished with a learned, religious, and godly ministry."

James would have none of this. All over western Europe in the early seventeenth century the modernization and rationalization of government was effectively carried out by absolutist monarchs. Why should England be different? Besides, James had a grandiose view of the power of the royal prerogative and he feared the radical political implications of Calvinist doctrine. The result was continual political deadlock: the summoning of Parliaments, repeated quarrels between the king and the country party, and James's angry and contemptuous dissolution of Parliaments. There could be no compromise between a king who fancied himself an expert on the theory of royal absolutism and those whom James called the "fiery and popular spirits in the House of Commons." Without recognition of the privileges of the House of Commons, James could not obtain parliamentary approval for taxation subsidies. In an effort to augment the income from nonparliamentary sources of royal revenue, he resorted to increasing the customs rates. The consequence was only further bickering and quarreling. Judicial decisions made by judges whom the king and his ministers regarded as "lions under the throne," whose duty it was to uphold the royal prerogative, supported the king's tax schemes. But these judicial expedients only intensified public debate and alienated more and more of the gentry from the crown. The situation became even more aggravated and intense in the early years of Charles I's reign. By 1629 matters had reached such a pass that the M.P.'s held the Speaker of the House in the chair while they passed resolutions declaring that whoever sought to change religion or increase the customs tax without consent of Parliament was "a capital enemy of the kingdom and commonwealth" and "a betrayer of the liberties of England."

Sir Edward Coke must be considered the most important parliamentary leader of the first three decades of the century, if only because he gave cohesion to the unchanneled feelings of discontent that suffused the gentry in the House of Commons. Certainly Coke was driven by greed and ambition, but he was a grasping lawyer, not a greedy capitalist. During the Elizabethan period we see him as a brilliant, self-seeking lawyer—an unabashed careerist, whose mastery of the common law was unmatched. Coke rose to become chief justice of the King's Bench, where he propounded a doctrine of the supremacy of the law over king as well as Parliament, and he claimed for the judges an overriding power to interpret what the law was in any particular instance. Drawing entirely upon common law tradition which, as later critics have never ceased to point out, he often distorted to serve his own needs, he developed a full-scale constitutional theory that also happened to exalt the position of the bench. Whether Coke's ideas can be put quite so explicitly is a matter of some controversy; he was not a systematic thinker and his statements about the constitution are often obscure and convoluted, but his arguments do tend to set forth the primacy of the common law and the judges, even over the king himself. In 1607 Coke even had the audacity to inform James directly that he stood clearly below the law. The king, of course, was appalled as well as furious, but "it was answered by me," Coke reports, "that the law was the golden metwand and measure to try the causes of the subjects; and which protected his majesty in safety and peace." At this, we are told, "the king was greatly offended, and said then [that] he should be under the law . . . was treason to affirm. . . . To which I said that Bracton saith, 'Quod rex non debet esse sub homine, sed sub Deo et lege.' " Coke was, if anything, inspired further by the opposition of the king, and by the second decade of the seventeenth century he envisioned the judiciary as a kind of supreme court; the royal judges were the arbiters and guardians of the common law which, in turn, enshrined the constitutional law of the land.

Coke's claims were intolerable to the king, and it was inevitable that he be expelled from the bench. Thereupon, Coke becomes an M.P. and soon emerges as a leader of the House of Commons. At this point Coke drops his notions about judicial supremacy; rather he exalts the power and authority of Parliament and moves toward the doctrine that will assert the sovereignty of king-in-Parliament. And since the doctrine formulated under Coke's direction in the 1620's clearly states that the king cannot make any changes in law, religion, or taxation without the consent of the House of Commons, it really means the supremacy of the House of Commons. "The power and jurisdiction of the Parliament, for making of laws in proceedings by Bill," Coke said, "is so transcendent and absolute, as it cannot be confined either for persons or causes within any bounds."

When Coke assumed the leadership of the parliamentary opposition, he was taking the second great stride forward in the formation of what modern historians have called the country party, whose organization, even inside the House of Commons, had hitherto been diffuse and fragmentary. In the early Stuart period its members did constitute a parliamentary party, although this was not anything like a national party in the modern sense. From isolated factions in the Elizabethan period a cohesive parliamentary party slowly evolved. It consisted of independent M.P.'s, men whose interests were widely divergent, who sought to control the privy council, who wanted to take over the operations and supervise the decisions of government. Coke's function was to bring together the dissidents: the common lawyers, the radical Protestants, and the disgruntled members of the House of Commons. The people who lead the House of Commons are lawyers or Puritans—often they are both—and it is remarkable how the Stuarts unerringly chose a course of action that was bound equally to antagonize men who took their law or their religion with the utmost seriousness. In his *Institutes* Coke goes to extraordinary lengths to show that the common law is in conformity with the Bible—an enterprise scarcely ascribable to his own devotion, which was minimal. Still his loyalty to the common law was as intense as any Puritan's to the word of God, and where the Puritan sought the light of revelation, what dazzled Coke throughout his life was what he called "the gladsome light of jurisprudence." What Coke did, with the aid of men like John Eliot and, later, John Pym, was to put every issue on a legal basis, to give every grievance a constitutional focus. Thus he brought together the common lawyers and the Protestant dissenters in one grand alliance, until they were eventually so united in Parliament that they were in a position to assert successfully the legislative authority of the House of Commons.

Coke is a very complicated and difficult man, and his own motivations have never been satisfactorily explored. In his early life he was a rank careerist, and even on the bench his constitutional and legal views were inspired by a desire for personal aggrandizement. And when he leads the House of Commons in the 1620's it is easy to say he is only repeating the procedure—that he again tailors constitutional theory to enhance his own importance. It is, nevertheless, not entirely fair, or wise, to interpret Coke's thought purely in terms of personal motivation. What he did was really dangerous for himself. He was a rich man, a landowner, and the admired head of the English legal profession, yet he jeopardized all these achievements. In 1628, when he inspired the House of Commons to force the Petition of Right on the king, he was an old man, with nothing to gain from ambition. We must attribute to Coke a sincere belief in what he said. We can only assume that he did believe the common law was in danger, that the principles of trial by jury, due process, and taxation with consent of Parliament were threatened by the Stuart monarchy. These were the tenets of the "Ancient Constitution" which the king was made to confirm in the Petition of Right. Coke's fears may have been exaggerated, but they were shared by a sizable body of men whom he led in the House of Commons.

The last important act of Sir Edward Coke's long, and in many ways incomparable, career as lawyer, judge, and parliamentary leader, was the carrying of the Petition of Right through Parliament in 1628. He was already an old and sick man and in the stormy Parliament of the following year the leading figure in the rebellious Commons was Sir John Eliot. But Eliot died shortly after being sent to the Tower, and in 1634 Coke also died. Their places were taken by a new generation of gentry leaders, who dominate the political scene in the 1630's and 1640's. One of the ablest of these, Thomas Wentworth, went over to the king's side, and served Charles I as Earl of Strafford. Between 1629 and 1640 no Parliament was summoned, and with the advice of Strafford and Archbishop Laud, the king experimented with a nonparliamentary, purely conciliar government. The new leaders of the opposition group among the gentry, Coke's disciples John Pym, John Selden, and Sir John Hampden, found it difficult to bring pressure on the crown in the absence of the meeting of the House of Commons, but they were in no way placated.

By the mid-1630's the royal government was in deep financial trouble and was resorting to ever more bizarre and desperate expedients in taxation. One of these expedients, the levying of ship money over the whole kingdom, engendered a new crisis in the relations between the Stuart government and the discontented gentry. Since the fourteenth century, certain port towns had occasionally been required to outfit ships for the protection of the English coasts, and the Elizabethan government had used this prerogative tax on the coastal towns rather extensively. But in 1637 Charles' government applied the ship-money tax to the whole realm, first getting the bench to justify this expedient as being necessary for the safety of the kingdom. Hampden, a wealthy landowner of the inland county of Buckinghamshire, refused along with several other gentlemen to pay the tax, and *The King versus John Hampden* became a test case for the validity of ship money and the whole policy of nonparliamentary taxation. The judges decided in favor of the king, but by a surprisingly narrow vote of seven to five, and it was becoming evident that a crisis stage in the political conflicts of the previous three decades was at hand.

The crisis was not long delayed. In 1637 Laud's attempts to impose the Anglican prayer book on Scotland brought about rebellion in the north, and by 1640 the crown was so short of cash with which to raise an army to put down the rebellion that, after eleven years, Parliament was again summoned. It was immediately evident that the country party, under Pym's leadership, was completely in control of the Commons, and Pym's men refused to vote supply until a long list of demands for the virtual extinction of prerogative and conciliar government were met. Charles angrily dissolved Parliament once again. But as the Scottish rebellion got completely out of hand, he had to summon a new Parliament almost immediately, and give in completely to its assertion of sweeping constitutional and religious reform and its impeachment of the king's two chief ministers. It was this Parliament which was to take the name of the Long Parliament, because the House of Commons elected in 1640 was to sit continuously until 1653, although by then less than a fifth of the original members remained, the others having left or been purged or having died. It was the Long Parliament which in 1642 went to war against Charles I and in 1648 set up a special court that tried and executed the king for high treason.

Until his death in 1643, Pym was the leader of the Long Parliament. He was a middling landholder with extensive commercial interests, passionately devoted to the traditions of the common law as Coke had defined them. Pym was a very skilled parliamentarian, adept at controlling the House, and steering legislation through it. There was little of the hysterical hothead in Pym; he was a grave, restrained man, who, as J. H. Hexter has shown, kept the more unbridled members of the Long Parliament firmly under control. After Pym's removal from the political scene in 1643, the Commons came much more under the influence of ideologues who were not content to aim at specific constitutional and legal reforms but rather sought to abolish the monarchy and achieve a perfect moral order in England. Pym was immoderate only in one thing —his hatred of the king's ministers, Laud and Strafford, whom he despised as betrayers of English liberty and of English society.

After Pym's death, the dominant political role among the gentry was taken by the leader of the parliamentary army, Oliver Cromwell, who exerted an influence that spilled far beyond the confines of Parliament and the gentlemen who sat there. He formed and led the New Model Army that defeated and captured Charles I; he put through and carried out the trial and execution of the king in 1649—an absolutely astonishing event in the Europe of the Old Regime; he then parted company with his former allies on the democractic left and prevented a democratic revolution; and he ruled England as Lord Protector until his death in 1658.

Cromwell only slowly came to prominence among the Protestant gentry and radical M.P.'s in the 1630's. His background was humble; he came from modest circumstances, and had a hard time making much of a living even though he was a descendant of Thomas Cromwell's brother. Oliver's relatively humble origins perhaps account for his drift into radical religion as well as his ability to recruit men from the lower social groups into his New Model Army. Out in the dank swamps of East Anglia Cromwell was barely a gentleman, and it is more realistic to think of him as a frontier farmer than a rising capitalist. He actually fought against progress and rational development, by opposing the land companies which were trying to drain the fens, and the early Cromwell was more like a seventeenth-century populist than an opulent landlord. Nor, for all his qualities of leadership and organization, was Cromwell a rational man. The central experience of his life was emotional commitment to God; the most striking aspect of Cromwell's character was his religious hysteria, the rough fervor of a Bible-thumping backwoodsman. Nor was he a typical Parliament man. In his early career in the House of Commons he delivered just one speech—a long-winded complaint about the archbishop's persecution of a Puritan divine who had been Cromwell's old schoolteacher—that was barely coherent and most embarrassing to other members. Yet Cromwell was to be the greatest leader the English gentry ever produced.

The years 1646 to 1660 (from the defeat of Charles I to the restoration of Charles II), frame a very odd period of English history. For a short time the gentry were in power, but they could not seem to accomplish anything in the way of a permanent constitutional or religious settlement. Macaulay was the first to tell how the gentry failed so thoroughly that they had to bring back the Stuarts and start all over again. Why did these earnest men, with their fierce sense of the common law, of parliamentary sovereignty, of Protestantism, blunder so irrevocably; why should they have had to retreat so far? Why were they unable to shape the kind of policy they so badly wanted and so fervently believed in? All sorts of explanations have been offered. Current jargon would describe the debacle as a failure of decision-making; once in power, the gentry simply could not decide what to do. It is only too clear how the country party rapidly disintegrated after the death of Pym in 1643, but under the collapse of organization there must have been a deeper flaw.

The Parliament men had begun as an anti-royal party. They knew very well what was wrong, and all their energies had been devoted to attacking the government; their force was a negative one. But once in power they could not agree on what, specifically, they really wanted to do. The revolutionary Long Parliament of the 1640's failed to reach any decision on religion. This was their first problem and the greatest; their failure to solve it marked the beginning of their downfall. For years they had fumed and raged about the Whore of Babylon, about Catholics, and about Laud's anti-Calvinist Arminianism. They had called for reformation without tarrying, for the establishment of the godly religion, but they could not agree on what was godly, or what reformation should comprise. Should it be low Anglicanism, Episcopalianism without Laud's fancy liturgy, Presbyterianism, or Independent Congregationalism? What about the Quakers, the Fifth Monarchy Men, the furthest fringe groups of experiential religious mysticism? The House of Commons itself was dominated by Presbyterians, the army by Independents (Congregationalists) and other religious democrats. The House of Commons could not reach any conclusion that would satisfy the army. It was a disastrous failure of decision-making, and before they knew it the M.P.'s found themselves in an inescapable trap. They were dependent on the one hand on a Scots Presbyterian army, their northern allies, and also on Cromwell and his Congregationalists in the New Model Army in the south.

Nor could the gentry agree on the kind of government they wanted. They had fought the executive, but they could not decide how the executive should be constituted, or what powers it should have. It is an understandable failure. They had never done anything except snipe and complain, their only program had been to reiterate that present policy was no good. They had never stated—or probably thought much about —what *was* good. James, who was a shrewd man, had at one point challenged the Commons and asked for advice on the taxation problem, but the M.P.'s had only responded with waspish questions about what James meant to do about the suffering Bohemians. Once the gentry were in power, it was only too apparent that the government's financial problem was not the sinister invention of a despotic ministry, and the new methods of taxation inaugurated by the Long Parliament would never have been accepted under James or Charles.

Since the Long Parliament could not decide, Cromwell did, from 1648 to his death ten years later. There is no point in glossing over his role; he was a dictator. A plausible case can be made that Cromwell was the first modern dictator, that he grasped all power in the state and ruled by the army. He established a military system, he did rule by the sword. In the 1650's Cromwell placed county government under the para-military rule of "major generals"; this was probably the most efficient government England had ever had. Under the Cromwellian Protectorate there were even some attempts at reform. There were efforts to rationalize archaic legal procedures. By the mid-seventeenth century the court of chancery was already in the state of advanced atrophy that would be described by Dickens. It was said that there was a backlog of 20,000 cases, and some of the more optimistic members of Cromwell's Parliament of Puritan "saints" wanted the court to be abolished out of hand. It was suggested that the judges of the high courts be given fixed salaries rather than be supported by fees; it was even resolved that trials should not be delayed by special pleadings, and an act of 1650 ordered all court proceedings to be in English. These reforms were all long overdue, but they did not survive Cromwell. Nor did some others whose necessity was less apparent—the act of 1650, for instance, that made adultery a capital offense. The new tax system, however, was very effective. There was an excise, as well as something called the monthly assessment—a strict property tax which was levied, by counties, under military supervision. Under the rule of Cromwell's major-generals, royalists were also subjected to the aptly named "decimation."

Cromwell did not shrink from his role as dictator. He held power and, at times, assumed the requisite ideological stance, but still he lacked the temperament. He knew he was good, he knew he possessed to an astonishing degree what we call leadership capacity, and he must, at times, have reveled in his powers. But often he did not want them—or at least he doubted the wisdom and rightness of what he did. Often he exerted leadership brilliantly and with much force. His speech dissolving what remained of the Long Parliament in 1653 could still strike sparks in 1940, when it was used to get rid of Neville Chamberlain: "You have sat here too long for the good that you have done. In the name of God, go!" But at other times Cromwell was embarrassed and hesitant. He found it easy to make decisions about war, about imperial policy, about the army and navy, but excruciatingly difficult to know what to do about domestic matters. Cromwell, not Elizabeth, was the first British imperialist; it was he who first envisaged the "Western design" which resulted in the taking of Jamaica. He took a general, sat him down on a quarter-deck, told him he was an admiral, and—under Blake—the British navy swept the seas and defeated the Dutch. But when it came to domestic and constitutional matters, Cromwell was almost ludicrously ineffective. He sincerely depended on guidance from the divine spirit, but it sometimes happened that God neglected to tell him what to do, as the Puritan poet Andrew Marvell implies in his great eulogy of Cromwell:

> But a thick cloud about that morning lies,
> And intercepts the beams of mortal eyes,
> That 'tis the most which we determine can
> If these the Times, then this must be the Man.

Cromwell truly believed that God had taken him out of the swamps and had led him by the hand through the darkness. God's presence always seemed to be handy enough on the battlefield, where Cromwell became so fired with divine inspiration that he became absolutely hysterical.

> And well he therefore does, and well has guessed,
> Who in his age has always forward pressed:

> And knowing not where Heaven's choice may light,
> Girds yet his sword, and ready stands to fight;

On imperial policy, too, the word was forthcoming; the Spanish problem was easy—the Dutch question (they were, after all, Protestants) somewhat more taxing, but worst of all, God kept quiet about the English constitution:

> But men alas, as if they nothing cared,
> Look on, all unconcerned, or unprepared;
> And stars still fall, and still the Dragon's tail,
> Swings the volumes of its horrid flail.

The questions were agonizing. Should Cromwell govern with the old structure of society, the old propertied classes? But they were now just as terrified of radical Protestantism as of Catholicism and were returning to the Anglican church in droves. Cromwell was torn apart by his own problem. A radical in religion, the protector of the godly people, he was at the same time a conservative in politics, where he found himself naturally allied with the old parliamentary country party. He tried to conquer this difficulty by calling a nominated Parliament of godly people. A council of the army picked 140 names from a list of men nominated by the Congregational churches; most of them were small gentry, tradesmen, schoolmasters. These were the men who were to legislate and direct the government. Cromwell brought them together and made a rousing opening speech in which he informed them they were to do great things, whereupon they immediately fell to quarreling. They may have been true godly men, but it was soon apparent that they were also utopian visionaries who could not begin to grasp the elements of parliamentary procedure. Now Cromwell himself was trapped. On constitutional, legal, and social issues he stood with county society; on religion he was one with the lower middle class and even working-class radicals who supported the democratic doctrines propounded by the Levellers. Thus he had no party of his own; there were hardly any other men like him. Nor did he want to rule as a military dictator. Cromwell made no attempt to set up a self-perpetuating military republic. In this light he does not look like a modern dictator. He never said that the godly people would rule for a thousand years; he shrugged his shoulders, he resigned himself to darkness unilluminated by God's word, he was willing to let the others take over when the time came. In 1660, two years after Cromwell's death, the new head of the army, an ex-butcher named General Monk, summoned back Charles I's son from his French exile and the restoration of the Stuart dynasty was effected.

The main theme in the political history of the following three decades is the struggle for power between the restored monarchy and a rejuvenated and increasingly aggressive aristocracy. After 1660 the political leadership which the gentry had exercised in the previous six or seven decades steadily declines as the familiar pattern of aristocratic domination is reimposed on English society.

II. The Causes of the Civil War

THE ENGLISH CIVIL WAR was the first upheaval to show all the characteristics of a modern revolution. Not simply an aristocratic maneuver or a sectional uprising, it turned out to be a full-scale revolution. It grew out of the collapse of a consensus in society, and it generated an ideology that challenged the dominance of the traditional ruling classes. It led to the first clearly democratic movement in European society, at least one whose ideals were based on secular political formulations as well as on religious beliefs. Thus the English revolution must be taken to mark a clear turning point in modern European history.

Though many things about the Civil War conform to the now familiar structure of revolution, many things about it are also puzzling, provocative and, perhaps, unique. That an upheaval like this should have taken place in a backward, pre-industrial society is astonishing. Revolutions are supposedly bred in urban society, but seventeenth-century England had virtually no urbanization. There was only one important city; the great majority of the population—at least 85 percent—lived in the country. A traditional landed elite dominated the nation, and it was among this small group that the revolution was made. The stresses caused by a dramatic polarization within a fundamentally conservative ruling class led to upheaval, civil war and, finally, allowed the advancement of radical democratic ideas. The whole process, at times, seems to take on an air of unreality and aberration. We feel that things ought not to have happened this way. It is much easier to account for the democratic movement of the eighteenth and nineteenth centuries than for the phenomenon that contemporaries accurately called the "Great Rebellion." The prevailing attitude among nineteenth-century liberal historians was that the rebellion, although tremendously interesting, had little lasting effect on English life, that Cromwell's government was unworkable—and un-English to boot. It was generally agreed that a chagrined nation was forced to make its way back to 1641. The slightly mad events of the next nineteen years were a series of hazy episodes that it was only proper to forget. On the surface the rebellion may seem inconsequential, or even ridiculous, but it was, nevertheless, of long-range significance. First, it caused the English landed classes to become even more conservative in the late seventeenth and early eighteenth centuries than they might otherwise have been. It was a nasty lesson that taught them to fear even the vaguest threat of social upheaval as well as any thorough rationalization in government and society. The Civil War became a collective nightmare that had been shared by the landed classes, a trauma that accounts for their extreme reluctance over the next hundred years to contemplate any fundamental reform or change along democratic lines in government and law. The war made radical expedients—or even rational endeavors—profoundly distasteful to the gentry. Secondly, we cannot be at all certain that the ideas of the democratic Levellers were forgotten. Historians who are now studying the material can perhaps see some continuity—an underground but tenacious streak of democratic thought in England that comes to the surface again late in the eighteenth century. These eighteenth-century ideas sound very like the doctrines enunciated in the 1640's, and it is possible that there was a real continuity of democratic thought.

The first historian seriously to deal with the Civil War was the Earl of Clarendon, who wrote his account three decades after the event. As Sir Edward Hyde, he had been a kind of junior minister in the Stuart government that failed. Like many officials turned historian, Clarendon has the tremendous advantage of personally knowing the men he wrote about. His account is essentially his war memoirs—a reminiscence that is obviously modeled on that of Thucydides. At the heart of Clarendon's interpretation is a conviction that the Civil War came about through a series of blunders. Clarendon is not much concerned with ideology; rather he takes the pragmatic view of the government man, the insider who believes upheaval is always senseless, and considers chaos and turmoil as simply the inevitable price of bad administration and muddy policy-making. Clarendon's account is filled with human error, laxity,

and confusion, and the most crucial factors are the incompetence of the
king and his courtiers, and the errors of imprudent and faltering ministers. Government collapsed, Clarendon tells us, because the men at the
top were weak and muddle-headed, and gave unprecedented opportunities to ideologues and schemers. This is a plausible account. Revolutions
are seldom inevitable; they can be averted by eliminating the right people at the right moment. Oliver Cromwell proved this when, by a small
but highly strategic show of force in 1649-50, he aborted what might well
have been a second revolution. If Cromwell had faltered, if he had not
shot or exiled a few Levellers, the Great Rebellion might have resulted in
a democratic victory. Clarendon also tells us that Charles I's government
was phenomenally unlucky; the Scots war that precipitated the Civil War
was merely the final event in a long series of mischances that brought
about Charles's downfall, though Clarendon makes it clear that even this
can be traced to Stuart incompetence. Clarendon is considered too personally involved to give us a dispassionate account, but it is refreshing to
have the realistic opinion of a government man.

Until the nineteenth century, Englishmen found the Rebellion too
painful an experience to recall. That the gentry could have become so
overwrought was to be deplored, and eighteenth-century historians, always ready to exalt 1688, often seemed to forget that the Civil War ever
took place. This reticence lingered on to color the nineteenth-century
Whig-liberal view. Macaulay, who never questioned the virtue and up-
rightness of the parliamentarians, and believed that almost anything
done to a Stuart was justified, had to admit that in the 1640's they had
gone too far. Extremism could not be condoned—much less investigated. Cromwellian government was shockingly authoritarian and un-
English and bound to be doomed from the start. There was not much
more to say about it. The interregnum was an unpleasant interlude after
which Englishmen had to find their way back to the sane and traditional
concept of the king-in-Parliament. It was the Glorious Revolution, Macaulay believed, that marked the turning point in English history—not
the 1640's.

It required extremists to appreciate the peculiar quality of the events
of the 1640's, and in the early nineteenth century one appeared. Carlyle
is sometimes labelled a proto-fascist, but he happened to be one of the
most influential writers in nineteenth-century England. In his search for
heroes in history it was almost inevitable that Carlyle be attracted to
Cromwell: the combination of moral fervor, religious nonconformity

and physical strength was irresistible to him. Carlyle's Cromwell is a
great, bold man who refuses to conform to slack bourgeois standards,
who rejects the easy life for a warrior's austere existence. Carlyle's raving
account of Cromwell (which did at least portray him as a human being,
albeit a kind of superman) revived interest in the Civil War, and soon
the subject was taken up by other writers.

The first, and perhaps the last, systematic study of the war was the
work of S. R. Gardiner who in the late 1860's began a full-scale, multi-
volume history of seventeenth-century England. Gardiner, who belonged
to an obscure evangelical sect, treated history like a personal calling
(which for him it was), and managed to turn out volume after volume
without the support of an academic post or any personal fortune while
maintaining himself, and a large family, on the meager salary of a
schoolmaster. His embarrassing career is another example of how shab-
bily Victorian England treated its greatest scholars. Gardiner literally
learned his history on the job. His early volumes make painful reading;
the first ones are almost completely unreadable, but as his great task
developed, so did his skill—though to read him is always a chore. His
gifts as a researcher were always awesome; he seemed to have an instinc-
tive mastery of archives, and Gardiner's work provides material available
nowhere else. Every subsequent historian of the early Stuarts has pillaged Gardiner remorselessly, which is perhaps why all subsequent accounts—aside from any superimposed theoretical viewpoint—have a
similarity which, considering how divergent are the interpretations of
the period, can be very disconcerting. There is, at least, general agreement about what actually happened during this period, a consensus rare
among historians—and one that in this case can be traced to the work of
one man. Gardiner's account begins in 1603 and closes in 1658. He
meant it to be a complete narrative; what he dreamed of was a great
popular success like Macaulay's. But Gardiner was no Macaulay, and his
first volume sold about one hundred copies. Gardiner was devoted to
two things, and literary excellence was unfortunately not one of them.
But he cared desperately about assimilating all the sources, and to make
sure nothing escaped him he ransacked the European archives at his own
expense. His other inspiration was the bizarre notion that history should
be written as it actually happened day to day (a misreading of a famous
dictum by the German historian Leopold von Ranke), and so Gardiner
wrote his chronological account while he was still in the process of doing
research. He seems to have believed that Ranke's injunction meant "as it

actually happened" to the historian. This may have been a noble vision, but when actually practiced, it becomes history of the absurd; it produces disastrous history, simply because the pattern of history more often than not unfolds in the most absurd ways, and great history, which requires reflection as well as industry, simply cannot be written on a day-to-day basis. Ranke certainly never intended the historians to render events more impenetrable than they seemed at the time to contemporaries, but unfortunately this is what Gardiner often does. The result is very strange, a dismaying kind of proto-impressionism, but without any particular esthetic justification. Gardiner's early account is a confusing mélange of random facts and episodes. After he moved into the latter part of James I's reign, however, he realized that some conscious organization was required and he soon turned into a first-class historian. He continued to get better and better—it was only a pity that he could not begin his work all over again. His lectures on Cromwell, produced toward the very end of his career, provide what is still the best book on the subject. No one without a special craving for self-torture would want to sit down and read Gardiner through, but students and scholars who want to know all the the details about the Petition of Right, or the Grand Remonstrance, or the murder of the Duke of Buckingham, will find them buried somewhere in Gardiner's work, which is really a massive collection of research reports. And even a scholar as remote from Gardiner's point of view as the Marxist historian Christopher Hill tells us (in a note to his *Century of Revolution*) that any serious student of the seventeenth century must become familiar with Gardiner's work.

As far as he allows himself to propound any general interpretation, Gardiner too falls within the Whig-liberal tradition. He believes that Stuart government is not just ineffective, but malicious as well, and he persists in his beliefs in the face of his own evidence. If read closely, Gardiner conveys an inescapable impression that the Parliament men were a bunch of cranks, but he still pours blame on the Stuarts. And though it is clear that the Presbyterians are no more the friends of religious liberty than the Anglo-Catholic Archbishop Laud, Gardiner is warmly sympathetic to them, since he believes they are at least on the side of light and righteousness. Gardiner died before his work was completed, and it was finished by his disciple, C. H. Firth.

Firth, another pioneering historian often brushed aside, but always pillaged, by recent scholars, was the first historian to do a careful, systematic study of the composition of Cromwell's army and to consider the significance of its makeup. He also published the Clarke papers—a gold mine which includes, among other things, the "Putney debates," a stenographic record of a debate in 1648 among the officers of the army about the future of English government which dramatically preserves the democratic ideas of the Levellers and the more conservative views of Cromwell and his son-in-law, Henry Ireton. Firth's general account of the Civil War, *Cromwell and the Rule of the Puritans in England,* though more than seventy years old, is still one of the best books on the subject. Before Firth, historians had interpreted the Civil War largely in terms of politics, and Firth's great contribution was to show the important role played by religion and social factors.

By the First World War Macaulay's facile interpretation, though essentially unchallenged, had been considerably expanded and enriched. The House of Commons still fought to preserve the traditional rights of Englishmen against Stuart usurpation; the Puritans, heroic of soul, stood for religious freedom against Catholic reaction; the causes and the main issues of the Revolution were religious and constitutional. The 1920's and 1930's saw the rejection of this view and the establishment of a sweeping revisionist interpretation that persists in some degree to the present day. The attack was launched by Tawney and his disciples, who had no disagreement with Gardiner's reconstruction of events, but who drew rather different conclusions from the same material. For Tawney, the English Civil War was the first bourgeois revolution; it represented an overt seizure by the rising capitalist class of control over the whole of government and society. To sustain this view Tawney assumes that the gentry—particularly the more substantial gentry—possess a capitalist mentality, that they are rational about the use of economic resources, and that they are greedy. The great landed capitalists, along with the merchants of London and Bristol, are only acting according to their basic style and mode of thought when they attempt to rationalize politics as well. Like the copyholder, the Stuart king is merely another annoying obstacle that must be swept away. In *Religion and the Rise of Capitalism* Tawney clearly says that Laud and Strafford, Charles I's ablest ministers, are hostile to the capitalists, and he describes the economic issues of the early seventeenth century in terms of an ideological struggle. For Tawney, Stuart administration is not just a decrepit old regime ready to collapse at the first tentative push; rather it includes a group of intelligent men morally committed to the tenets of medieval paternalism, who are quite capable of fighting back. Tawney's view was almost universally accepted in the 1930's and his themes, though modified, are perpetuated in many recent scholarly accounts. Tawney disciples like Christopher Hill, reluctant to concede any virtues to Stuart administration, have subdued the moral tone that informs all of Tawney's work. But Hill does emphasize that Laud's sincere but doomed attempt to reform the abuses in the Church of England and reinstill a sense of corporate cohesion, aroused the hostility of the gentry who were bent on retaining every bit of church income they had appropriated in the late sixteenth and early seventeenth centuries.

Tawney posited a real and meaningful, though not necessarily causal, connection between capitalism and Protestantism. The sociologist Max Weber, writing before the First World War, had described some aspects of Protestantism that seemed specifically to encourage capitalistic activity—a theory Tawney seized upon only to stand on its head. In Tawney's view it was capitalism that worked upon Protestantism and transformed it into an ethos that lauded the capitalist virtues. He never said that Protestantism provided a ready-made rationale for capitalism; he did say, however, that seventeenth-century Calvinism was forced to yield an apologia for competitive enterprise. Wistful but timid entrepreneurs were not transmuted into thriving capitalists by any Circean magic in Protestantism; rather a vigorous, aggressive, and already triumphant capitalism made Protestantism its own tool. The Weber-Tawney thesis, as it is inaccurately called, has been tremendously controversial, and many facts that Tawney blithely overlooked have been cited in order to discredit his book, *Religion and the Rise of Capitalism*. Scotland, where capitalism never developed, is the favorite example of a country where undiluted Calvinism seemed to have no effect whatever on economic life. Tawney would reply that this is not really a fair criticism, since he never claimed that Protestantism produces capitalism. Where there was not capitalism—and there was none in Scotland to begin with—Calvinism alone could not become its ideological vehicle. Tawney did, however, tend to apply his theory too indiscriminately. Even in England some preachers welcomed capitalism, others rejected it. We can see now that the ambiguities inherent in Protestant thought itself made a consistent attitude toward social problems difficult to formulate, and that the seventeenth-century failure to develop an idea of social justice cannot be ascribed to the insidious influence of capitalism. For Catholics the rules of conduct had been laid down, but it was hard for Protestantism to move from religious tenets, many of which were hazy and obscure anyway, to a social doctrine. By the eighteenth century English Protestantism had become rigidly conservative. That strange bundle of thoughts and beliefs that is English Protestantism is capable of producing a wide range of social doctrine. Tawney was too reckless in generalizing about seventeenth-century Protestantism, and though there are many insights in his description of capitalism and Protestantism, he still does not explain what they really had to do with politics. Even if we grant that Protestantism became a convenient adjunct of middle class ideology, we are still uncertain about the grand significance of this interraction, and unsure if it had any real influence on the course of political life.

Tawney's description of the rising gentry (which he set forth in a famous article in the *Economic History Review* in 1940) inaugurated an extended controversy which, a quarter of a century later, is still raging sporadically. During the late sixteenth century, Tawney tells us, the upper stratum of gentry, along with the merchants, was growing enormously rich. Tied together by the bonds of mutual self-interest, they constituted a newly rich, confident, and self-conscious class. Thus the upheavals of the early Stuart period are due to the machinations of an aggressive new class, anxious to assert its will in political life as it had before in economics. Tawney's critics have been thorough and dedicated, and certainly it has not been hard to attack his oversimplified use of class terminology. All sorts of men owned land; all men wanted to own land; the fact and the desire are much too common to justify any class label. There is little evidence to show that these men thought of themselves as a new phenomenon in society. The significance of their role as a new group seemed to elude them completely; rather they tended to think of themselves within the traditional framework of county and family. At any rate, it is only sensible to eschew the sloppy label "middle class" which, as J. H. Hexter has emphasized, is really a misnomer before the nineteenth century. Only in the nineteenth century will there be an idea and the self-consciousness to go along with the phrase; only then will it signify an idea understood by all members of society and, perhaps most important, only in the nineteenth century will the middle class itself develop the self-awareness that makes it permissible to use the term seriously. The seventeenth century was innocent of the phrase. In so far as men thought of themselves at all in relation to society, they were bound to think in terms of local groups—of family, of county.

A second, and more devastating criticism, has been put forth by H. R. Trevor-Roper, who charges that Tawney's economic statistics are misleading, and claims that accurate statistics (such as they are) show that in the seventeenth century the gentry are actually falling. The flagrant and unlimited economic expansion of the sixteenth century was over. Beginning late in Elizabeth's reign, landed society found itself in serious trouble and by the early Stuart period economic problems were so severe that prosperity was only a nostalgic memory. In this kind of environment, the men who do well will need connections at court and with the crown. For Trevor-Roper the origins of the Civil War are to be found in the polarization within the gentry class itself. By the reign of Charles I there are two distinct groups. They are the same kind of men in every way—only some are in at court, and some are out. The outs, disaffected and frustrated, are susceptible to political and religious suasion. Politics and religion merely serve to urge them on; they become concerned, then angry, finally rebellious. Trevor-Roper's thesis is plausible, and even has a certain ironic appeal. But it is always dangerous to generalize from a few known cases (and for the seventeenth century there are really not very many). Also, the seventeenth-century statistics, always unreliable, are frail props on which to build a whole theory. Nevertheless it is true that the literature of the 1620's is filled with complaints about scarce money and hard times. We do not see Tawney's fat, sleek middle class; these are frightened, insecure men. If forced to take sides in the gentry controversy, we would have to agree that the Civil War grew out of fear, insecurity, and, finally, panic. It was a violent and irrational outburst, not a cool and calculated takeover by a group of self-assured capitalists.

Accounts of the events of the Civil War are many and varied. One of the most popular and readable views has been presented by C. V. Wedgwood. A prolific writer on many aspects of the seventeenth century, Miss Wedgwood has undertaken a multi-volume history of the Civil War, of which three books have so far appeared. The series began propitiously, but as the fortunes of the Stuarts deteriorate, so does the quality of Miss Wedgwood's work. Her first volume, *The King's Peace*, was a perceptive, well-wrought and enlightening book which conveyed a real feeling of what it must have been like to live in England in 1637. It was a happy blend of Clarendon's insight into men and places with Gardiner's learning. In the second volume, curiously titled *The King's War*, Miss Wedgwood indulges a bit too much in schoolgirl crushes. Here the Earl of Strafford (who at least is an interesting and problematic man) is replaced as a central character by Charles's foolish nephew Prince Rupert, and this book seems to have as its main concern Prince Rupert's not very mysterious failure to win the war. The account does reveal, albeit incidentally, that both sides were confused, blundering, and ludicrously ignorant in military matters. This is plausible enough—Miss Wedgwood's disjointed and episodic narrative may well be an accurate reflection of the way the war really was fought. Englishmen had not been involved in a land war since the fifteenth century, and after two hundred years of peace they were pathetically amateurish. There was terrible ineptitude and stupidity on both sides and, as is probably true of most military encounters, victory went to the side that happened to make the fewest mistakes. Miss Wedgwood may do justice to the geographical and meteorological history of the war (she never fails to tell us how the land lay and whether it rained), but there was much more going on in these years than she likes to admit. In her account the Long Parliament is somewhere offstage, though it might be argued that the most exciting events were taking place in the House of Commons. In her most recent book Miss Wedgwood's royalist sympathies are most apparent. This superficial account is appropriately titled *A Coffin for King Charles*. The fundamental political and constitutional issues are slighted, particularly the most interesting question about the king's trial—what made men regicides? Miss Wedgwood is entitled to her particular view, and in this case she appears to lean to the king and the royalist cause. Her favorite literary reservoir is the Cavalier poets, and her books (particularly *The King's War*) are strewn with pretty lyrics dipped out of it. One would not guess that the two most important mid-century poets, Milton and Marvell, were Puritans.

Recent studies of Stuart finance and administration have yielded some useful information and provocative ideas. Tawney's last book, *Business and Politics under James I*, published in 1951, is a detailed and sympathetic study of the rise and fall of Lionel Cranfield, James's most talented minister during the 1620's. Cranfield was a wealthy London merchant who was given the opportunity to organize the treasury on an efficient, rational basis. He was about to do the job, but his reforms annoyed the courtiers and the king allowed him to be impeached by Parliament. Here Tawney restates his thesis that the bourgeois mind is rational (Cranfield's incisiveness is set against Stuart stupidity and inertia), but he seems to have subdued his ideas about the rising gentry, and it is quite clear that in this case Tawney's feelings lie with the intelligent reformer, cagey capitalist though he may be.

Robert Ashton's *The Crown and the Money Market* is essential to understand the financial problems of the early Stuarts. Ashton shows conclusively that the most desperate of all Stuart problems was the inability to raise extraordinary funds or impose new taxes. Their credit rating became so weak that they were reduced to pitiful schemes and, after an eleven-year experiment with nonparliamentary government, which included such bizarre measures as ship money, were finally forced into summoning the House of Commons. The development of institutions of public credit is an important key to the complexities of seventeenth-century constitutional history. The emergence of a viable system of public credit in the 1690's was to be a critical factor in the achievement of political stability in England.

Gerald Aylmer's painstaking study of *The King's Servants* raises more questions than it answers. Aylmer may have been overwhelmed by his material, or perhaps he could not organize it in a satisfactorily coherent fashion. He does succeed in showing that early Stuart government worked more or less smoothly in its routine operations, but that it was a bureaucracy that depended on the guidance of a great minister for anything beyond this. Stuart government was a continuation of the technique initiated by Thomas Cromwell and perfected by Burghley. At its best it worked very well indeed, but the Stuarts had no great minister. To function with any more than minimal effect, to do more than mark time and stumble along in the wake of events it cannot anticipate or control, seventeenth-century government required definite aims and, above all, creative and intelligent leadership. The Stuarts never kept a great minister. Whenever one appeared he frightened them. James got rid of Cranfield and Charles betrayed Strafford, who might have been the man strong and intelligent enough to pull back the Stuart monarchy from the brink of the precipice.

Perhaps the most interesting of all the recent works on the Civil War is the detailed analysis by Brunton and Pennington of the members of the Long Parliament. This is a successful use of the Namier technique of wholesale biography to elucidate the structure of politics. Who were the men who made the revolution, what was their background, their class interest, their wealth, their religion? It was hoped that this kind of basic statistical data would reveal what specifically in their background and beliefs turned men into either radicals or supporters of the king. Though predicated on deterministic assumptions, the book's conclusions were depressing for Tawneyites. It is conclusively proved only that we cannot account for the Civil War in terms of class interest. (There is one clear exception in the case of the London merchants and bankers, who almost invariably were against the king, but this is not particularly surprising.) The only significant variable was a marked difference in age between parliamentarians and royalists. In May, 1642, the members of the House of Commons, hitherto almost united, split apart into revolutionary and royalist groups. Those who took up arms against Charles I were, on the average, eleven years older than the two-fifths of the M.P.'s who became royalists. On the basis of this elaborate study, therefore, we may conclude that young people can be more conservative than their parents or elder brothers, an observation that is not particularly startling, but one which is often overlooked. The trend of the statistical evidence in this case opens up all sorts of speculation. It tends to bear out Marc Bloch's instruction that the only meaningful periodization in history follows generations, that the most significant unit in time consists of men who belong to the same generation. The motivations for men's actions and beliefs are not developed overnight. The men who came to maturity in the 1620's had grown up in a bitter time; their era was marked by turmoil, debate, and suspicion of the crown, and as they grew older suspicion turned to hostility. There was a slackening of confidence in the very institutions of the crown. At first the attack focused on the prerogative courts; it led, finally, to a repudiation of the monarchy itself. The tone of the procedings surrounding the Petition of Right in 1628 reached a peak of bitterness and ferocity that is hardly surpassed even in the 1640's.

On the other side were men who had come to the fore in the 1630's, once the crisis was past. We must remember that Parliament did not meet once during the thirties. The conflicts between king and commons were still unsolved, but they were somewhat subdued and hidden from view. 1628-29 had been a kind of turning point; never again would the parliamentarians feel quite so desperate. The Protestant cause was being beaten back on the continent, the king's actions at home seemed more and more irresponsible and authoritarian. In 1629 there was a punitive campaign against the activists in the House of Commons. Selden and Eliot were sent to the Tower, others—established men of repute who were known to have Puritan tendencies—were deprived of jobs and offices. (The Puritan John Humphrey, for example, lost his position as attorney in the Court of Wards.) Things looked so gloomy and hopeless that some men who belonged to the parliamentary opposition seriously considered leaving England. They were not in the least hotheaded revolutionaries. Rather they were solid, successful men with deep roots in traditional English society; many were Puritan sympathizers, but they were not religious radicals. They had little in common with the more marginal, frantically devout men of the *Mayflower*.

In the 1630's, however, the atmosphere was less charged. Royal government made a strenuous effort to pull itself together; the country did not topple into complete despotism. The grievances of the 1620's were not removed, but they were not inflamed either. In spite of the fears of the Parliament men of 1628, England had not yet become an intolerable place in which to live. Thus the formative years of the younger generation were not shaped by the same tensions; bitterness and suspicion did not play so great a role in their youth and they were untouched by the feelings that had left an indelible impression on their elders. People born a few years apart will see the world rather differently, and these younger men were less disturbed, more secure, and more complacent than the preceding generation. We are led to speculate that there was only one truly revolutionary generation, the one schooled in the struggles of the 1620's. The men of this generation, hostile and aggrieved for twenty years, got their own back in the Long Parliament. We may think of them as something like Old Bolsheviks, as rapidly aging men with long and bitter memories. In 1628, Coke was seventy-six; he had been fighting the king for two decades. In 1634 Coke was dead; by 1640 the men who had followed his lead in the twenties had been angry for two decades. While they had been obsessed by their grievances and their hope of redress, their brothers, nephews, and sons had turned to other concerns. The men who had missed this moment were more like their grandfathers—traditional and conservative. They were not enslaved by theology, nor were they in general even interested in ideas. When the ideological struggle became fiercer and, finally, overwhelming, they were the first to withdraw from it. For a while they were carried along, but when, in 1642, they saw they were about to participate in the overturning of traditional society, that radical change was upon them, they could not retreat fast enough. Once the older generation that had led the fight against the king was no longer on the scene (and it is remarkable how fast the old parliamentarians like Pym and Hampden vanish in the 1640's), the revolution collapsed and the course of English history lapsed back into its old patterns. The next generation was, if anything, even more conservative than their grandfathers.

This theory assumes that a whole generation was caught up by hysteria. Something gnawed at the men who made the revolution, and they had to have it out. Whether they finally were satisfied is a matter of some debate, but they did find an outlet for their pent-up passions. Their fears and concerns about government and religion were probably the most important thing in their lives, and the intensity of these feelings is exactly what their younger brothers and sons were unable to understand.

The Civil War did become a revolution; it was an attempt to change society, to wrest power and leadership from the crown and deliver it, through the House of Commons, into the hands of the leaders of landed society. How revolutionary these men really meant to be is also a debatable point. It is easy to say they were forced into extremism they had never contemplated. But, by the early 1620's, and perhaps even earlier, we can discern a group of men who already take an extreme view of political life. They want to abolish the conciliar courts and assert control by the House of Commons over royal government. The important question to answer is why they came to hold this view. Several things bothered them, particularly finance and religion. Religion was probably more important than is generally acknowledged. Men do not engage in revolution just because of money; even greed must be impelled by some kind of ideology. The Civil War was only partly a result of declining prosperity. Opportunities were not as lush as they had been, but men were still required to pay taxes. In fact new taxes were being imposed, and the crown was trying to force greater yields out of old taxes. A hard-pressed government was attempting to achieve a workable tax system while the gentry were floundering in economic difficulties of their own. This was bound to create an uneasy situation. But railing against taxation and officialdom does not cause a revolution. High taxes are not enough; the means by which they are levied must seem to be illegal. It is not sufficient that the men who operate the government be nasty and stupid; they must appear as devils incarnate. Neither discontent, however grievous, nor subversive leadership, however effective, nor governmental ineptitude, however gross, will make a revolution. An element of emotion is required; so are profound convictions, and a great —though unreasoned—fear of the men who hold power and represent constituted authority. Hysteria and irrationality are necessary catalysts for revolution, and in three important aspects of life Englishmen of the early seventeenth century were highly susceptible to emotion. These were foreign affairs, religion, and law.

The impact of foreign affairs on the English Civil War has not usually been given the importance it warrants. Under the pressures of the international situation, the sound, conservative gentlemen of England were turned into fanatics. Concern over foreign policy may be the deepest motive for their intransigence and their increasingly bitter criticism of the crown. Men eager only for money would have held their tongues and tended their business; rational capitalists would not have been so quick to endanger their wealth, land, and social position. But these intelligent and well-educated men were not rational. They were on the verge of hysteria; they lived with a terrible fear and in daily terror of a Catholic triumph in Europe. This was a threat that had loomed over the Protestant cause since the 1560's, and by the reign of James I (1603-1625) it had, if anything, increased. The reaction of these men to international tension should not be incomprehensible to us. They believed that Europe was divided into two camps—the power of light and that of darkness—and until well into the 1630's it looks as though the force of evil, the Hapsburg counterreformation, was winning. England slept while the continent was being inundated by a satanic, authoritarian movement. Even if their own deep feelings of religion had not prompted them, Coke and his successors would have been worried. They looked on the Stuarts in a way not very different from that in which Winston Churchill viewed Neville Chamberlain. The forces of darkness were afoot in Europe—and it looked as though England were bent on appeasing the aggressors.

The king was allied with what was known as the Spanish party. In terms of international political realities this group of courtiers and officials was eminently practical. They were soberingly aware that the financial situation of the crown was unsteady, and thus they advocated a policy of peace and conciliation. They were also very unpopular. On the other side was the strongly Protestant group, violently antipathetic to Spain, in favor of the "French" policy in the Thirty Years War, and hot for engagement on the continent. The men who opposed the foreign policy of the court would merge, eventually, with the parliamentary opposition, and with the men who were fighting the crown over religious issues.

Of course the opposition group tended to oversimplify the problem. Still, their prophecies of doom were plausible, and we cannot with any certainty say that their fears were unfounded. In any case, the pressures of the Thirty Years War (which was their equivalent of the Cold War) drove them into the necessary frenzy. A substantial number of concerned men wanted England to be more active, but James I was a dove rather than a hawk, and Charles was even more reluctant to become a Protestant champion. As early as 1603—during the treason trial of Sir Walter Raleigh—Coke had raved hysterically about the Spanish menace. And this was just the beginning. In what appeared to be England's most dangerous hour, the government, under James's desultory leadership, stood idly by. In the first decade of the reign of Charles I (1625-1649) the situation seemed to grow steadily more grave. The king had a Catholic wife whom he adored; it was hard to tell where William Laud, the Archbishop of Canterbury, left off, and the Pope began, and in Europe Protestants were being massacred by Hapsburg mercenaries in the Thirty Years War. By 1630 it looked as though the forces of the counter-reformation were winning, and during the thirties the goverment under Charles seemed to be selling out. All the tensions Englishmen could not release on the continent poured out into the Civil War.

They could not force the king into war—everyone knew that war belonged to the royal prerogative. But they could attack the crown. They became troublemakers. Often they were sly and unfair; at times they were downright malevolent; their constitutional arguments, always learned and elaborate, were often specious. They were desperate men willing to do whatever they could to needle, to harass, to undermine the government. Nor were they, even at their most gentle, squeamish men. By the 1630's they had become really hateful and completely unyielding; their rage had carried them so far that they no longer wanted this Stuart king or his ministers.

Particularly his bishops. It is impossible to believe that without the religious question, which mined a deep vein of emotion, the rebellion could have happened. Like all the issues that helped cause the Civil War, the roots of the religious problem are readily traced to the Tudor period. The general assumption in sixteenth-century Europe was that the ruler decided the religion of his subjects. But Elizabeth never really decided. Starting with the Anglican apologist, Richard Hooker, at the end of the sixteenth-century, this indecisiveness has been praised and defended as a course of wisdom. But like the other unresolved questions left over from the Tudor period—concerning Parliament, the prerogative—it plagued the Stuarts. Elizabethan government never really told men what to believe. They were allowed to debate, and naturally a wide variety of views were expressed and flourished. Thus, when the Stuarts did decide what English religion should be, the divergent Protestant movement for church reform turned all its religious fervor against one devil—Archbishop William Laud. Laud intended to direct the Church of England toward Anglo-Catholicism, and he managed to antagonize a wide spectrum of Protestant opinion that ranged from low Anglicanism to Congregationalism. Although the anti-Laudians had very little in common, the government of Charles I provided a devil they could all hate together. Milton's icy phrase about the bishops—"blind mouths"—tells us very well how they must have felt. Later they would find that they hated each other as much as they did Laud, but the threat of a neo-Catholic revival in the 1630's brought a temporary cohesion to the unstable Protestant movement.

Laud's campaign to tighten church organization and impose a uniformity of ritual also stirred up fears that the common law was endangered. It seemed to many of the gentry that a Catholic victory would mean the establishment of an inquisition in England. Nor were they entirely wrong here; the unwieldy process of the common law did stand in the way of Laud's program, and he was constantly seeking new ways to encroach on the authority of the common law courts and even to bypass them altogether. Under Laud the ecclesiastical Court of High Commission (which had been established under Elizabeth) was busier than it had ever been. And the court was like an inquisition. Elizabeth had said she desired to open no windows into men's souls. But this court pried into men's beliefs, and it had at its disposal some very effective levers. Like Star Chamber, the court followed the procedures of Roman civil law. There was no need to obtain an indictment, nor was there a jury. The court could force men to answer questions under oath (and thus incriminate themselves); it imposed humiliating punishments. At the mercurial will of the judges (who included bishops as well as civil— rather than common—lawyers), it fined men sums that seemed absurdly high for religious eccentricity. As long as the Court of High Commission victimized unknown, insignificant men there was little outcry against it. But under Laud the court moved against men of substance and position —it no longer confined itself to badgering obscure sectarian Protestants who mostly came from the lower middle class, or even from the apprentice group. In 1637 Laud got an order from the king that forbade the common law courts to intervene in the ecclesiastical courts without the permission of the archbishop. This direct and undisguised attack on the common law was as important a factor in alienating country opinion as the imposition of ship money, which happened that same year. It is no coincidence that in 1638 the Puritan leaders in Parliament again contemplate emigration.

Stuart blunders had a great part in making the revolution. There is no doubt that James and Charles were incompetent in the arts of government though it is questionable whether they were fiends or malicious. James I was learned and intelligent in some ways—he could write long treatises on kingship, and his advocacy of peace and Sunday sports and his advanced idea that tobacco was bad for health must draw a favorable response from the modern student of the period. But James was a terrible politician, and his mistakes were to prove fatal. Soon after he took the throne he managed to lose control of the House of Commons, which the crown had maintained for the past 120 years. By 1620 the privy council was virtually impotent in Parliament; and by 1629 at least 70 percent of the members of the House of Commons, although they reflected all sorts of disgruntled opinion, had become well organized into the oppositional "country party." Charles was even worse. He was slow-witted, although he did have excellent taste in art and was truly devoted to the Anglican church and its rituals. Still, the story of these two kings shows that good intentions alone do not take a ruler very far, and that ineptitude can be just as effective as severity or despotism in making men villains in history. When he is on trial for his life in 1648 Charles even emerges as a figure of great dignity and some pathos; and it is quite clear that his legal arguments have more validity than those of his tribunal.

> Though Justice against Fate complain,
> And plead the ancient rights in vain:
> But these do hold or break
> As men are strong or weak.

Charles was nothing more than a frail man. In his great poem, Marvell sees him not as a king, but as an impostor, merely a "Royal Actor." The fact is that due to the first two Stuarts, kingship itself had lost its sanctity and authority in England; Elizabeth was the last monarch to illuminate the luster of the crown. There was a very significant shift in attitude during the first part of the seventeenth century, which is summed up pungently by John Selden, the common lawyer and Parliament man. "A King is a thing men have made for their own sakes, for quietness' sake," he writes, "just as in a Family one man is appointed to buy the meat."

Without the exertion of a few highly talented and dedicated leaders, the Civil War could never have come about. These were the common lawyers who, as soon as they began to identify their own interests with those of certain dissident groups in the House of Commons, naturally assumed the direction of the opposition movement to the crown. Men like Coke, Selden, and John Pym may well have had private family and economic grievances; certainly they shared the discontents that agitated the country. No one could deny that they were ambitious men with a craving for power, or that as common lawyers they were motivated by a jealous desire to preserve the security of their professional positions. But they were more complicated than this. They believed that the rights of Englishmen were identified with the due process of the common law, and that the central place of the common law in English life was threatened by the Stuart kings. For wherever the Stuarts antagonized their subjects—whether in finance or religion—they also managed to touch this excruciatingly sensitive legal nerve. It became clearer and clearer that a government that could not be trusted to observe the common law traditions that were fundamental to the life of the gentry class could not be trusted to govern at all. The pronouncements of the judges on the bench contributed powerfully to the development of the conviction that the common law was in danger of subversion. Because of the deadlock between king and commons in the early Stuart period, these decades comprise one of the few periods in English history when judicial review became important. Matters that could not be settled by legislation were left to be decided by the bench. The king called upon the judges to uphold his prerogative taxation powers. The precedents were ambiguous on such matters, and the judges had plausible grounds for deciding in favor of the crown. But many of the judges could not leave well enough alone; as is the wont of the bench when given the power of judicial review, they inclined to judicial overkill. They warmed to their task of protecting the royal prerogative, and uttered such sweeping and judicially unnecessary statements as that "it is common and most true that Rex is Lex, for he [the king] is . . . a living, a speaking, an acting law." This statement, delivered from the bench in the ship money case in 1638, gave credence to those who claimed that the royal government had no respect for the traditions of the common law. Perhaps it was farfetched and fantastic to believe that the Stuarts were laboring to introduce continental despotism into England, but this is the way things began to look to the lawyers and gentlemen of the House of Commons.

We can see how their hostility developed by considering the change in their attitude to the court of Star Chamber. For most of the sixteenth century the gentry welcomed the proceedings of Star Chamber, even though the essential characteristic of the court was its power to overrule the operations of the common law. Star Chamber mitigated the abuses of the common law—it attempted to correct corrupt juries, for instance —and it was very popular among the gentry. Star Chamber was something men could rely on; it was seen as a haven of redress. "I will make a Star Chamber matter of it," Justice Shallow boasts when he is abused by Falstaff. "The council shall hear it; it is a riot." But by the end of the sixteenth century the gentry are coming to resent the court and to grow increasingly suspicious of what seems a wrong and dangerous intervention by the prerogative of the crown into the operations of the common law. It can be argued that Star Chamber itself did not change, but there is no question about the shift in attitude toward it.

Somewhere between 1570 and 1610 sentiment changes drastically. This is very hard to study, but it might be instructive to consider how the opinion of Coke himself changes. When he was a successful royal official, Coke wrote that Star Chamber "is the most honourable court (our Parliament excepted) that is in the Christian world, both in respect of the judges and of their honourable proceeding." And he went on to praise its role: "This Court, the right institution and ancient orders thereof being observed, doth keep all England in quiet." Yet shortly after the accession of James we find Coke challenging the jurisdiction of the conciliar courts, a crusade he undertakes with such ferocity that it contributes to his dismissal from the bench.

The common law was a bulwark against the authoritarian tendencies of the Stuarts—this was acknowledged even by Charles's ministers, Laud and Strafford, who strenuously attempted to circumvent the common law as they implemented their policy of "thorough." Strafford had been instrumental in pushing through the Petition of Right, but a few months later he accepted the post of Lord President of the Council of the North, where his work for the crown appears as authoritarian paternalism at its best. Perhaps for Strafford, good government was more desirable than free government. At any rate, the common law held no particular sanctity for him. The Articles of Impeachment brought against him by the Long Parliament include the charge that he had tried to intimidate the local gentry in the north by declaring that the "King's little finger was heavier than the loins of the law." Strafford claimed that he had said exactly the opposite, but by 1642 he was so despised as a betrayer of English liberty that no one thought to believe him.

By 1641 the hysteria had reached its peak, and a very substantial part of landed society was no longer able rationally to assess the situation. They really believed in the imminence of an Irish invasion, which Strafford was presumably about to lead against the Protestant gentry at home. When men are sure their enemy is the devil, when they are fearful that their way of life is about to be destroyed, when they feel they must fight *now* for survival and dignity, then revolution is possible. And in the 1640's the gentry engaged in revolution with a vengeance. They forced Charles to acquiesce in the destruction of Strafford via a procedure that was nothing more than judicial murder; they abolished the temporal power of the clergy; they abolished the hated prerogative courts of Star Chamber and High Commission. In the Act Abolishing the Court of High Commission of 1641, the revolutionary Long Parliament asserted, for all time in England, the principle that no "person whatsoever," whether rich or poor, should henceforth be required or forced "to confess or accuse him or herself of any crime, offence, delinquency, or misdemeanor, or any neglect . . . or thing whereby, or by reason whereof, he or she shall or may be liable or exposed to any censure, pain, penalty, or punishment whatsoever." The Long Parliament further declared—by statute—that no tax could be levied without parliamentary consent, and they declared—also by statute—that Parliament could not be dissolved except with its own consent.

They went even further. In 1642 the House of Commons asserts the right to call out the county militias, a power that had unequivocally belonged to the prerogative of the crown. This was truly a revolutionary act. It was followed on May 27, 1642, by a supporting declaration, a theoretical statement proclaiming the sovereignty of the king-in-Parliament over the king himself. This declaration is the most important constitutional document since Magna Carta. It makes vividly clear the distinction between the king as a person and the king as a part of the state. "The king is the fountain of justice and protection," it says, "but the acts of justice and protection are not exercised in his own person, . . . but by his courts and his ministers, who must do their duty . . . though the king in his own person should forbid them." Parliament is the highest court of all. "What they do herein hath the stamp of the royal authority although his majesty, seduced by evil counsel, do in his own person oppose or interrupt the same." This was the moment at which the king was forced to take up arms.

It was irrational for the gentry to precipitate the Civil War; they were going counter to all their experience and the weight of tradition; they were betraying their idea of an ordained, hierarchic world order, and it was soon apparent that they were carried further than they had intended to go. They soon realized that what they had done was entirely out of character. Revolutions rarely occur, and they are hardly ever made by a large group of substantial men who belong to an established and privileged class. But it happened in England in the 1640's.

III. The Idea of Liberty in England

T HE SEVENTEENTH-CENTURY constitutional struggles are really a series of conflicts fought around the idea of liberty. From this tangled cluster one idea ultimately triumphed in England—an idea of such astonishing simplicity that it is sometimes hard to know why all the controversy should have been necessary. In England, liberty is what the law gives to a man; the law is whatever the king-in-Parliament says it is. But beyond this conclusion lies a whole complex of ideas of what liberty is and ought to be—a web of different strands rooted in several distinct sources and traditions. It was the conflict among the diverse strands of liberty that generated the great seventeenth-century debate. All of them emerge directly from the medieval background. Historians have had inordinate difficulty in straightening out these ideas, mainly because they fail to understand medieval ideas or appreciate their lasting influence. In spite of all the ink that has been spilled about the impact of humanism and the dawning of the modern world, the great debates of the sixteenth and seventeenth centuries (in which politics and religion are inextricably twined) can be seen as a working out of various strands of medieval thought. In order to understand the important ideas of seventeenth-century England—the most radical and "modern" doctrines as well as the conservative and old-fashioned ones—we must trace them back to their medieval sources and, specifically, to two significant foundations, the common law and religious ideals.

The idea of liberty in political thought can, in a sense, be taken back to Socrates, though in the terms we shall be using, the Platonic concept of the state does not contain much of an idea of liberty. Nor does the Old Testament, where the idea of liberty is essentially authoritarian and leads, logically at any rate, to modern totalitarianism. This variety of authoritarianism is perfected in the Pauline and Augustinian doctrine of the freedom of Christian man. Here, liberty can be achieved only by the man who places himself in absolute subjection to the divine will as expressed in the world through the authority of the church. We are familiar enough with this construct—substitute other authorities for the church, and it becomes a very modern notion. In order to meet philosophic terms and psychological needs this may be a very neat and satisfying solution; in practice, however, it fosters authoritarianism. In the Augustinian scheme of things, liberty assumes a peculiar form. It is liberty voluntarily to accept absolute authority. It may be defined as positive liberty, a strange definition that points to the semantic problems raised by the very notion of "liberty." Liberty can be discussed in two ways—in terms of negative or positive liberty, but except for the most theoretical debates of philosophers and theologians, the notion of positive liberty is a clumsy, elusive and, finally, a self-defeating concept. Certainly it does not mean very much in terms of practical politics. In England when we speak of liberty, we almost always use the word in its negative sense; it is bound to have connotations of freedom *from* something—from coercion, from authority, from interference, from arbitrary forms of action.

The common law tradition of liberty—the most significant one in English history—is straightforward and unambiguous. The common law idea of liberty is, just as Coke said it was, enshrined in Magna Carta. Historians persist in sneering at him, but on this point Coke was right. Liberty in England is nothing more than the right to have what is due to you under the law. Magna Carta did not provide for any generic liberty; it only set forth—for all freemen—the right to enjoy what the law gives. The only universal right is the procedural one of due process, a protection available (in different forms, to be sure) to all men. What due process guards in any case may in fact be most unequal. Nevertheless, the fundamental idea of common law liberty is due process. "The law of the land" merely confirms to every man his own liberties and possessions. The common law envisages a hierarchic society in which every man carries with him certain privileges. The law protects these, but by

434

no means equalizes them. Specific liberties will belong to you according to your status in society, and they will be granted (or, more usually, confirmed) by a legal declaration of the king-in-Parliament. A great lord will possess vast liberties along with his acreage, but as far as a man of lesser status is concerned, the law of the land may say he has nothing— except, of course, freedom from arbitrary proceeding. Due process is simply a procedural technique enlarged into a principle; but it is a principle that acknowledges no theoretical limits; it is a principle concerned only with means, not ends. Due process can itself be the vehicle for depriving a man of his life and property, even if he is a duke. A parliamentary bill of attainder is a remorseless measure that could scarcely be more arbitrary. Yet it too is part of due process. Does due process, then, not know any constraints? Yes, in the sense that it contains a strong principle of self-preservation. The due process that the law affords must itself be changed by due process. This, of course, was the great problem, posited but unresolved, in early English constitutional history, and we can say that the Civil War and the Glorious Revolution were fought and won on the principle of changing the law by the king-in-Parliament. But even before this was finally worked out, it was a clear principle that the law can be changed only by a legal, constitutional process, whatever that might be.

The common law idea of liberty is antithetic to equality. In Magna Carta, where the idea is resoundingly enunciated, liberty and property are virtually synonymous. Liberty is what one possesses—tenure, or franchise; but even the man who owns nothing has the right to the due process suitable to his status in society—however unenviable that may be. Due process is a superb protection for what you already have, though it is innocent of any criteria for evaluating the justice by which possessions are divided. Dukes and peasants own quite different things, but each has some liberty. The common law assumes that the rights granted to men are very disparate, but among them there is one universal right— the right to have what belongs to you under the law. For seventeenth-century dukes, due process means trial by peers, for a peasant it means trial by the J.P.'s in the quarter session—and no one would claim that these tribunals hand down the same kind of justice. But that is English liberty. Under the common law every man has some civil and legal rights, but no economic or political rights. Political liberty in England is simply a variety of the legal rights an individual may or may not be entitled to. In England liberty under the law means the right to be free from arbitrary exaction, but not from exaction—and certainly not from exaction that may have the same result as the most arbitrary kind of proceeding. But so long as due process is observed, the results, no matter how brutal or unjust, cannot be questioned—there is nothing beyond due process to which one can appeal. This is the fundamental concept of English liberty; it is the only idea of liberty that appears in every century, the only one to survive unvanquished. It is simple, sturdy, and tenacious. It is the one continuous thread of an idea of liberty in England, though from time to time others are intertwined around it. But this is the basic strand, and the hardiest. Any challenges or modifications will come about through the impact of ideas coming out of medieval Christianity or, in the seventeenth century, from ideas of medieval Christianity that have been reworked into secular forms.

It is hard to reduce these ideas to a simple rubric. Though the common law tradition runs in one deep track, Christian ideas about liberty tended to veer off in several directions. Within the spectrum of Christian ideas, the views of churchmen (unlike the common lawyers) were not at all in harmony. Rarely could they present such a cohesive front as the common lawyers—and this, perhaps, helps to explain why the most significant and enduring ideas of liberty in the sixteenth and seventeenth centuries were the ones supported wholeheartedly by the legal profession. It also means that the ideas coming from Christianity are more elusive.

There are three distinct and identifiable ideas of liberty in medieval and early modern Christianity. First is the stern Pauline-Augustinian tradition of positive liberty we have already noted which, though fundamental to canon lawyers (and though it still prevails in the Roman *curia*) has had little importance in English history. Liberty defined as complete dedication to God through the church never caught hold in England, though it was a very influential notion in France and Germany. Here freedom is really subservience to the absolute will of a greater power—either the church or the Roman law. This idea is to some slight degree present in England at various times. Medieval bishops believed in it, so did medieval kings. Certainly Archbishop Laud subscribed to it. Laud was not the power-mad tyrant of parliamentarian myth. He was perfectly willing to give people liberty, but it was liberty to serve the king and the church. His problem was that Englishmen in the seventeenth century were rejecting that kind of liberty. (It is interesting that, unlike their French and German counterparts, Englishmen hardly ever found the greater power sufficiently attractive to outweigh their fierce devotion to a personal negative kind of liberty.) At any rate, in the seventeenth century they were more concerned about reasserting the traditional negative "freedom-from" brand of liberty they knew in the common law. And they were turning to the two other Christian sources that seemed more relevant to the English experience.

The doctrine propounded by St. Thomas Aquinas, the thirteenth-century philosopher, the first of these, is difficult to explicate, and it might plausibly be argued that it is an image of order more than a coherent idea of liberty. Thomism—which was eloquently restated around 1600 by the brilliant Anglican theologian, Richard Hooker—provides an elaborate theological and moral justification for the empirical doctrine of liberty embodied in the common law. To man's law is assigned a place within the grand structure of the universe. Due process is the reflection of natural law, which is itself a reflection of divine law. Though men may not be rational enough to attain heaven, implanted in their minds is a glimmer of reason which will suffice to let them create the good society on earth. A doctrine of social contract is, though inchoate, implicit in Thomism. The only aim of government is to serve man and the common good. The law of the state must reflect moral law, the law of God and the law of reason—and men are rational enough to shape a polity that satisfies these criteria. Thomist political thought, which identifies the secular government with the divine order, is basically conservative, but beneath the apparently seamless surface of the Thomist synthesis lies a potentially explosive ambiguity. Insofar as it tells men that the political order is ordained by God's will, it tends to support the status quo. But it can also lead to an attack on the law of the state. The important Thomist doctrine that positive law must conform to natural law inevitably opens up the kind of question that can cast doubt on the entire structure of the state and society. The question—are the laws of the state in accordance with divine law?—is likely to elicit some disturbing answers. Thus an unanswered and volatile question lies at the core of Thomist thought—it was never resolved by St. Thomas, nor by Richard Hooker, nor has any other natural law theorist managed to cope with it satisfactorily. The Thomist structure has been borrowed by radical and conservative political thinkers, and we will see how the central idea of Thomist doctrine is really a two-edged blade. The idea that the state is formed by reason, which can be used to rationalize any existing order, can also open up radical possibilities. The doctrine can be extrapolated that men, in order to form the kind of society suitable to reason, may choose their own government. This loose thread, the implications of which St. Thomas himself shrank from, makes Thomism potentially much more radical than the unequivocally conservative idea of liberty in the common law. Where Thomism can lead to action, the common law is purposely bent on maintaining the status quo; due process has a built-in sluggishness that defies action. The common law idea of liberty is ignorant of political rights, but Thomism contains the germ of the idea that men have the right to judge society, and sufficient reason to bring it into conformity with the law of nature. The snag is that Thomism is very vague about who shall judge and what their standards shall be. Common law doctrine suffers from no such confusion.

The other streak in medieval Christianity is thoroughly radical. In the millennial apocalyptic ideas of the twelfth and thirteenth centuries are to be found the roots of democracy, as distinct from liberalism. At the basis of medieval radical religion is an idea of real equality among men, of the innate dignity of every man. Through the Franciscan order, and later, through the English Lollards, these left-wing ideas spilled out of the church and became rooted in secular society. The illuminative nature of Christian knowledge was exalted and set forth against the authority of the church. The church hierarchy did not embody any absolute divine authority—the only mandate from God, said the radicals, is the one known in the individual mind and heart. Every good man, rich or poor, duke or peasant, can experience God in his own heart; every man can stand face to face with God and be in touch with the divine will. And if man knows God, he can know other things too. Compared to the experience of God, knowledge of law, or economics, or morality is neither abstruse nor privileged. The dignity of man in all his aspects is elevated. For the first time in Western civilization the doctrine that the poor man is as good as the rich man was widely diffused in the later Middle Ages. It is a doctrine which is bound to encourage activism. If the common man can speak directly with God, why should he be without a fitting share of worldly goods, why should he not participate in a life appropriate to the dignity of a man who knows God?

Ideas like this were seething in the urban society of medieval Europe. For a while England remained uncontaminated and aloof. But when these ideas finally did come to England in the late thirteenth century, they were not unheeded. They were the inspiration of the Peasant's Revolt, as well as the motive behind the panicky retreat of the gentry from

Lollardry. The upheaval of 1381 made the social significance of radical Christianity all too apparent; even the dullest duke could see that Lollardry did not stop short at attacking the authority of the church; it undermined the social and political order as well. The idea that God wants people who love him to have a share of the things of the world had terrifying implications. And the gentry were right to close ranks and turn away:

> When Adam delved and Eve span
> Who was then the gentleman?

This was a truly radical idea. Religious individualism, when it moved into the social sphere, ran absolutely counter to the conservative, stable tendencies of due process; it did portend revolution. And so in the last decade of the fourteenth century the aristocrats recoiled from their own dalliance with Lollardry and began to hunt down the heretics with a vengeance.

The radical wing of Christianity which again becomes prominent in left-wing Puritanism sheltered a real revolutionary movement. It is Norman Cohn's contention, excitingly presented but not conclusively proved, in his *Pursuit of the Millennium,* that modern versions of totalitarianism are merely secularized forms of the medieval belief in a holy brotherhood that is meant to rule the earth. This is a plausible theory, and no doubt there is an authoritarian strain in the radical Christian movement—one that will become very important in England in the 1640's and 1650's. Paradoxically, though, the kind of thinking that can lead to totalitarianism also provided, for the first time, a glimpse of the idea that men are equal in dignity. It was the first attempt to say that in the light of God all social and political distinctions are wiped away, that the only thing that matters is to experience God, that influence and power in society ought to derive from a man's standing with God and heaven, not from what he owns of the earth. This could hardly be more alien to the common law ideas which buttressed inequality. Radical Christianity finds nothing sacred or binding in the law simply because it is the law. Rather it admits that the law may be wrong in the eyes of God and, to go much further, it may claim that whatever does not conform to God's law is no law. Thus an ideal of religious equality was raised against the validity of the common law. It was no wonder that landed society developed a pathological fear of Lollardry and again in the seventeenth century of the radical Puritan sects.

439

In Tudor-Stuart England the most familiar arguments about liberty are conducted within the common law framework; the natural idiom of English polemicists is the vocabulary of the common law; the most recurrent metaphor is the linking of liberty and property. And the most important figure in the common law tradition is Sir Edward Coke. An historian's assessment of Coke will ultimately depend on his feelings about the merits of the common law idea of liberty which Coke epitomizes in his person, his career, and his lasting influence on English legal thought. If you subscribe unreservedly to egalitarian ideas, you are bound to find Coke a repellent figure. But the historian who believes due process is the most important guarantee of liberty in civil society will probably appreciate the canonical role of Coke in the elaboration of English common law thought.

There are three distinct stages in the development of the common law concept of liberty from the late sixteenth century to 1628. The first stage emphasized the liberties of the House of Commons, which in themselves were seen as the protection of the liberties of Englishmen and a bulwark against arbitrary power. The need to define and exalt the liberties of the House of Commons led men to examine and define the liberties of Englishmen. Some of these appeared to be more general than others and, beginning in the 1590's, there was an intelligent and conscious effort to claim more generally than ever before what these liberties were. In the Elizabethan House of Commons a concerned and articulate group of men stated that if the idea of due process was to be maintained, the law must only be changed with the consent of Parliament. If the House of Commons has no liberties, they said, the way is clear for arbitrary government and its inevitable perversion of power—arbitrary changes in the law. The liberties of Englishmen depend, finally, on nothing beyond the law itself; the men who best understood this were moved by an intense concern about how the law shall be changed and, at the same time, by a deep reluctance to entertain any notion of changing the law at all.

It became generally believed, then, that to prevent the assumption of arbitrary power by the crown, the liberties of the House of Commons must be secure and unthreatened. Hence the obsessive worry about the M.P.s' freedom of speech and freedom from arrest. A member of the House must be able to exercise his rights as the representative of his community. He must be independent, unfettered, and completely free from intimidation. Otherwise due process will be subverted—the procedure by which the community of the realm consents to changes in the law will deteriorate into a meaningless farce. Any breach of parliamentary privilege will be seen as the first frightening step on the road to arbitrary power. This belief is clear and widespread: unless the House of Commons is truly a free estate, the law of the land will be subverted, it will be nothing more than the king's law. The men in the Elizabethan Commons argued this point with great eloquence, and we cannot say they were wrong to believe that the only bulwark standing between Englishmen and arbitrary power was the independence of the House of Commons. It still is—though in the twentieth century the danger of arbitrary power is no longer embodied in the person of the king, but rather in an overweighty and irresponsible bureaucracy. It is easy to depict Peter Wentworth as a charming maverick and Coke as a self-seeking neurotic, but four centuries after their passionate assertions the House of Commons remains the only thing protecting the rights of Englishmen.

The common law concept was firmly stated in the 1628 Petition of Right, which does enunciate certain general rights. These are not, however, anything like natural rights; they are simply the rights that belong to men under due process. In theory they might be legally abrogated by legislation. It is always assumed, of course, that an alert Commons never would permit the king to violate them. Still, the only abstract principle on which they rest is the idea that due process must be maintained. The Petition of Right is not a theoretical document; nor is the Bill of Rights of 1689. Both enumerate the specific liberties that men possess—and these are the liberties that should be protected. There shall be no arbitrary taxation, there shall be no changes in religion by fiat of the crown, there shall be no quartering of soldiers, no cruel punishments. These could hardly be more specific. Certain rights are inherent in the law of the land. But they have not existed forever, from time immemorial; they were not granted by God, nor are they justified by any quality of human nature or the soul or the divine will. Rather they owe their existence and their sanction to the law itself—they exist because the law of the land bestows them upon certain specific people, the freemen of England or— as we might choose to define them—the political nation. This is the common law idea of liberty, and we might say that the revolutions of the 1640's and of 1688-1689 were fought to uphold it. The revolution of the 1640's was led by men who knew they were defending the common law idea, but as the revolution gathered momentum the common law idea of liberty itself came under attack from men (i.e., the Levellers) who drew

441

their justification from other ideas. But this did not happen until the Long Parliament had established and ratified the common law doctrine.

The Long Parliament removed the possibility of arbitrary action by the crown; it wiped out the conciliar courts and affirmed that no man should be forced to incriminate or give testimony against himself; it clarified all doubt about what the nature of due process is and what the law of the land gave to the gentlemen of England. And then the M.P.s' work was done, although in fact the revolution had barely begun. There was not much egalitarian feeling inspiring the men of the Long Parliament, and it is possible, if one's own ideological sentiments urge, to take the class conflict interpretation of what the Long Parliament accomplished. It can be said that their aim was to protect their property from the crown and from the landless, that for them liberty was just another freehold. And it is quite true that they were not concerned about the people of England (perhaps seventy or eighty percent of the whole) to whom the law had not granted anything to protect, who had no voice in the House of Commons, who were never asked to consent to changes in the law. It did not occur to them that for the copyholder and artisan due process meant only the right to class decision, that it might be an incongruous due process that included summary judgment by the J.P. in the quarter sessions alongside the right to trial by peers. But then no one had ever claimed they were the same. That was the kind of liberty granted to the lower order; there was really nothing more to say about it.

By the 1640's, however, people were saying a great deal about it. In the overheated climate of the 1640's, the other ideas of liberty were flourishing. By 1642 the common law doctrine had triumphed as the doctrine of parliamentary supremacy, but the new teachings of radical Puritanism could not be fitted so neatly into the constitutional structure. We must remember, however, that not all Protestants subscribed to the radical notions. Presbyterian thought was in fact rather like the medieval doctrine of authoritarianism. Society should be governed, Presbyterians said, by the elders of the church, by men of devotion and property. Presbyterianism was actually an oligarchic system—it only replaced the medieval hierarchy with a new order that was scarcely less rigid, and certainly no more libertarian than the old sacerdotalism the Calvinists found so repugnant. It is easy to overlook how much Calvin owed to the Pauline-Augustinian tradition of authority. Men of substance, piety, and authority are to control society in order to purify it—from the top. Historians have deluded themselves about how much in Protestantism was "new."

The split within the medieval church was merely perpetuated in the Protestant movement, which also had its conservative and radical wings. For a while all shades of Protestants united to fight against Catholicism and the schism, always present, was obscured. But by 1648, when the king was broken by Cromwell's army, the Protestant movement in England had begun to disintegrate. Once it appeared that the enemy was not winning, the alliance fell apart, and radical Puritanism, which was in many ways a perpetuation of medieval heretical illuminative religion, came—for a brief time—into its own.

Radical Puritanism turned against the conservative element in Protestantism—against Presbyterianism, against the authority of the Bible, the rule of elders and, finally, against every form of authority in society, the state, and the law. Only authority derived from direct religious experience was to be recognized, the authority of trying the spirit. The Christian man is the man who knows God. He may be a duke, but he may just as well be an obscure apprentice. He may even be a woman. Only salvation and God's light mattered, wherever they might appear. Any man could find salvation. The word of God was not necessarily given to those who sat in the seats of the mighty, who dominated the urban corporation or the county quarter sessions. By 1648 radical Puritanism had spawned political radicalism. (This inevitable development has been brilliantly explicated by Haller in *Liberty and Reformation in the Puritan Revolution*.) In many ways it was the fourteenth century all over again. Inner illumination was to hold precedence above the authority of the Bible and the social order; the only men ordained to govern other men were the saints.

Two important ideas emerged from radical Puritanism. The first proclaimed there are truly spiritual men who have a right to rule; it dreamed of government by the godly people on earth. This might have been little more than an eccentric ideal—but for a while the godly people did control the English polity. Cromwell's government was an attempt to establish the rule of the saints in England. The Major Generals were all devout men; their government, which fostered an authoritarian system, was at the same time egalitarian—or at least more egalitarian than anything that had yet been seen in England. Most of the Major Generals were ordinary people; in society they stood just below the gentry. Against the old tradition of class, land, property, the radical Puritans set up a new criterion and, for a while, observed it. Cromwell brought in new men, yet he did not mean to do much to bring in new law. But the

Levellers, whose members were generally lower middle class, went far beyond Cromwell to formulate a genuinely modern idea of democracy.

It is not clear how far they hoped to go, and there is no point in quibbling over just where they intended to draw their lines or to whom they were willing to extend the franchise. What they did was to take radical Puritan democracy and combine it with a concept that stems from St. Thomas and Hooker. For them liberty was an abstract right. Every free man, they said, was rational enough to take part in government and society—even though he was poor. Every man was sufficiently moral, good, and rational to make decisions; every man's voice should be heard. Thus the idea of reason we saw in Thomism is carried to its logical conclusion. Society is for the good of men, and men are sufficiently rational to organize and change society. From here it is not hard to arrive at a doctrine of legal and political reform. It makes reform appear possible, then desirable and, finally, mandatory. The Levellers sponsored the first English democratic reform movement; their constitutional drafts such as "The Agreement of the People" are the first attempts to overhaul the antiquated franchise, and reform government and law, and they are the first advocates of political rights. It is easy to see why the Levellers were feared and hated by the men of the Long Parliament.

The Putney debates, which were prompted by the draft constitution presented by the radical Levellers to Cromwell's Army Council in 1648, bear sharp witness to the confrontation between the traditional doctrine that liberty is property and the new natural rights idea that in some ways all men are equal. Only people who have a "permanent fixed interest in this kingdom" should participate in government, maintains Ireton, Cromwell's son-in-law, for if men without property are given a voice in making laws, "there may be a law enacted, that there shall be an equality of goods and estate"—a suggestion that Ireton, a member of the gentry class, finds repulsive. Certainly men are born with rights, Ireton admits, but this birthright entitles one only to the freedom of the highways, and the freedom to remain in the country—to what we would call civil rights. But to have a "share in power that shall dispose of the lands here, and of all things here, I do not think it a sufficient ground." Government should be in the hands that hold the land "and . . . in corporations in whom all trading lies. This is the most fundamental constitution of this kingdom." Ireton, who was historically quite correct, was baffled by the new idea that certain political, as well as civil, rights are inalienable—and that God and reason may not have ordained the prevailing

444

"fundamental constitution." God gave man reason in order that he use it, argues Rainborough, the impassioned and articulate Leveller spokesman. There is nothing in the law of God, or of Nature either, that says "a lord shall choose twenty burgesses, and a gentleman but two, or a poor man shall choose none." By birthright men are entitled to more than just their existence, than being subject to the sanctions of a law created by others, for "the poorest he that is in England hath a life to live, as the greatest he."

The Levellers called for a new democratic way in England. Rejecting the inert conservatism built into the due process of law, the Levellers invoked universal reason and abstract right in order to justify radical change. In the late 1640's a universalist natural rights doctrine of liberty challenges the limited civil rights tradition. The Levellers wanted to change the basis of the English franchise, they even wanted to reform the common law itself. They were moving, with terrifying haste, toward a moral theory of society very far removed from the doctrine enshrined in Magna Carta and propounded by Coke. But the Levellers were stopped when Cromwell remained loyal to the traditional order of landed society—their ideas were conclusively rejected and, as a political group, they were brutally suppressed.

Thus the common law doctrine of liberty prevailed in England; it continued to dominate English political thought for centuries. The traditional idea proved to be the sturdiest—and the most constitutional. But there had been flashes of radically different ideas. In the 1590's Hooker's notion of the social contract (a perpetuation of the Thomist idea of a natural order that informs men and action) revealed a flicker of thought antithetical to the common law tradition. And when radical Puritans seized upon the same ideas, they began to point toward liberal democracy. Later in the seventeenth century the Thomist and Leveller doctrines were shaped—by the work of Hobbes and Locke—into the foundations of our most familiar political theories.

Writing in the 1650's, Thomas Hobbes incorporated ideas taken from liberal theorists and managed to fashion them into a neo-authoritarian system. Though Laud might have applauded it, Hobbes's state was not based on religious grounds, and it was never intended to be Anglican or Presbyterian or Puritan. Hobbes took the abstract theory of society propounded by St. Thomas, Hooker and the Levellers, and transformed it; by turning it inside out, he exalted the secular authority of the state where they had mounted an attack. The men Hobbes learned from were all liberals—or at least they used their system to further what we consider liberal ends. Hobbes also belongs firmly within the natural law tradition, but the subtle twist he gave to natural law ideas made all the difference. Though he built upon the work of Aquinas and Hooker, Hobbes is finally much closer to Marsilio of Padua, the fourteenth-century Italian theorist, and *Leviathan* is really a new, updated edition of Marsilio's *Defensor Pacis*. Hobbes contended, with a terrifying simplicity, that the people had by the social contract irrevocably surrendered all rights to the state and that law was simply the sovereign will of the state, without any moral content whatever. These doctrines lead directly to modern totalitarianism but they were unpalatable to English landed society who much preferred John Locke's theories.

Locke, who wrote his *Treatise on Government* just before the Glorious Revolution, presents a subtle brew of practically all the contending ideas of the 1640's. Common law, natural rights, and social contract doctrines are all contained within the Lockean structure. What appeared to be a successful assimilation of the common law idea of liberty into a moral and theoretical framework was, however, an uneasy and ultimately an unsuccessful synthesis. Locke went further than the seventeenth-century common lawyers when he borrowed from Thomist thought (which he had absorbed through Hooker's writings) to proclaim the attractive doctrine that the purpose of the state is to protect liberty and property. Though Locke wrote to justify revolution, 1689 was revolution by the propertied men of England on behalf of the common law.

From Hooker, Locke took the idea that government is an artificial creation formed by rational men for the common good, that governments are established by a contract drawn up by men who sensibly delegate their individual power and authority for the good of all. But there are certain rights men can never alienate. Like certain estates that are never to be sold, life, liberty, and property (the rights that belong to people because they are men) cannot be given up or taken away. This is where Locke incorporates the Leveller doctrine of abstract human rights. The end of Lockean government is to secure property, to defend liberty, and allow men freedom from arbitrary acts. Though government is established via social contract, the end of all government is still the maintenance of due process, the protection of life, liberty and property under the common law. It was a tour de force. Locke included something to appeal to everyone—and there should be nothing mysterious about his immense popularity. On the surface Locke is neither radical nor conservative; his beautiful, though very precarious synthesis, presents a smooth and ingratiating front.

From 1689 until the 1760's Locke was interpreted in the most conservative fashion. Everyone knew that government existed to protect the liberty and property of the gentlemen of England—and his writings were used to give a sophisticated theoretical defense and presentation of the old common law idea of liberty. The Whig aristocrats who worshipped Locke were able to combine both strands of thought. The common law that had granted inalienable privileges was supported by a theory of the universe. At just the point where it had once been challenged, the old common law was now buttressed by the doctrine of natural law. The ideas that Locke borrowed from Hooker and the Levellers were used in a thoroughly conservative way.

But there is also a radical side to Locke. All the Thomist ambiguities were preserved intact in his work, though they were recast in an up-to-date, pseudo-scientific language from which the scholastic vocabulary has been expunged. The radical strand that Locke seemed to weave so neatly into his pattern could also be re-extrapolated—and then used to unravel the whole Lockean fabric. When traced back to its source, it was bound to expose a liberal democratic theory. Thus Locke also opens the door to an attack on the common law. If life, liberty, and property are the natural, inalienable rights of all men, why should these universal rights actually be enjoyed by only some men? And if the common law is a reflection of the natural law, why does it support privilege and manifest inequality? We are back to the fatal Thomist tension, to the place where a revival of Leveller ideas of liberty and democracy is possible, and we arrive, finally, at the Jeffersonian statement that men's rights are not given, but belong to them.

Locke's construct was too ambiguous to be sustained, and it was quite evident by the middle of the eighteenth century that, in the face of new pressures for reform, the Lockean synthesis could only be perpetuated by the kind of dubious rhetoric we are familiar with in Blackstone, who tried to accord to common law inequality a romanticized rationality. But Blackstone, who wrote in the 1760's, was the exponent of an outworn philosophy that no longer was viable. By the 1760's it was becoming clearer and clearer that the natural rights theory of liberty was incompatible with the common law doctrine.

The radical natural rights idea of liberty, submerged for a century, tentatively reappeared in England after 1760, reached a new peak in the propaganda of the American Revolution, and was subsequently pursued so vehemently in France that Englishmen developed a positive phobia toward the doctrine from then on. The concept of natural rights that had been so important in the 1640's flourished again in England from 1760 to 1793, when it became so tainted with uproarious French extremism that it was put away once more. Though the idea of natural rights was preserved in the working class movement, the gentlemen of England—the political nation—turned away from it and back to the kind of congenial thinking they had recognized in Locke. And they found a new Locke in Burke. Led by Burke, the gentry went back to a purely common law idea. Burke saw very clearly that there are two ideas to be sorted out and kept apart: the abstract political rights based on a universal justification, and the civil rights which are supported by the common law foundation. At the end of the eighteenth century the landed classes, embattled at home and abroad, shuddered, turned completely away from the natural rights idea, and welcomed Burke.

Thus we find a very odd system of thought in England during the first three quarters of the nineteenth century. A democratic movement triumphs and great political reform is accomplished—but without any recourse to natural rights theory. It was an amazing process. Without claims that any man had a right to it, the franchise was nevertheless widely extended. Throughout the rest of the world the democratic movement has rested on a natural rights doctrine, but English democratization proceeded along utilitarian lines. It was better, more useful, to reform; by providing for a more rational government men would manage to avoid revolution. Democracy in England was thus finally based not on natural rights, but on utilitarianism. The natural rights plea that vanished (or went underground) after 1793 did not appear in any influential way until it was re-introduced by the late nineteenth-century socialism. And even then the phrase "natural rights" was avoided. The socialists chose instead to rely on the vaguer but less repugnant concept of universal human dignity, the notion that all men have a right to dignity, to health, to a sufficiency of goods. But the idea itself came originally from the 1640's, and it is no wonder that several of the scholars who first discussed the significance of Leveller tracts were socialists, and that the first people to write the history of the Leveller movement were committed to the Labor party.

Thus the common law idea has triumphed over the whole span of English history. In England men have the right to vote only because

Parliament declares they have it. Parliament could refuse to grant the vote to anyone—to women, or to lefthanded men; it could also restrict the vote to them, it would all be part of the same process. The right is granted by the law of the land, and the law of the land is, in turn, whatever the king-in-Parliament chooses to say it is. This is the kind of classic example used to illustrate the doctrine of parliamentary sovereignty, but also may stand for the legacy, and the triumph, of the common law idea of liberty.

CHAPTER TEN

THE ERA OF
BENEVOLENT OLIGARCHY
from 1660 to 1760

I. The Aristocratic Century

THE REIGN of Charles II (1660-1685) represents a partially successful attempt to reconstruct royal political leadership. Charles himself has been treated unfairly by history. Clever, able, and thoughtful, he was also a desperate man in a very precarious position. Charles was capable of hard work and, in spite of all the racy narratives, he did not spend all his time in bed or playing with his spaniels. His reign set the foundations for the eighteenth-century party system and is thus not just a frivolous interlude in English political history; it marks the beginning of eighteenth-century politics.

It is possible to talk about the emergence of two distinct parties during the Restoration period, but we must think of parties in the late seventeenth and eighteenth centuries not in terms of formal organization, but in the much looser sense of involvement. A party is a faction in Parliament that also attempts to go beyond Parliament and make some sort of national appeal. By 1680 it is clear that there are two parties. The one that held power in Charles II's reign was the court and treasury party; it consists of men who support the king and his policy. Soon we will know it as the Tory party.

Charles was a master of patronage, and he judiciously distributed treasury funds (which were replenished secretly and regularly by Louis XIV) to maintain a pivotal group of placeholders in the House of Commons. Before long, this will be the routine method by which governments stay in power. All the old techniques are once again put in operation—the government tinkers with borough franchises to make sure that amenable men are returned to Parliament; it carefully awards patronage, and thus creates a hard core of reliable supporters in the House of Commons. Old tricks that go back to the sixteenth century are revived, though now they are practiced in a modern form by the court and administration group in the House of Commons. The leaders of the House of Commons are important members of the privy council, and they can count on the assistance of an administration group whose loyalty is made certain by patronage. These techniques, which have been meticulously described by the Namierite historians, persist throughout the eighteenth century. The court and treasury party does, however, have an element of popular support. On most issues, perhaps thirty or forty placemen in the Commons can be counted upon to unite with a large group of what was once known as the country party. The system works efficiently enough; the only puzzling aspect is the new willingness of the old country party to support the crown. The men who were once rebellious gentry are now Tories.

The events of the 1640's and 1650's have instilled in the gentry a pathological fear of change, and they have come to look upon the crown as the bulwark and protection of their way of life. They want security for their property and support for their religion; above all they want peace and stability. These are not the richest gentry. They are the sons and grandsons of the men who supported Pym, the same breed as the middling men who opposed James I and Charles I, the gentry who—for a brief time—surpassed their political expectations. The memories of this time were all too vivid. They had allowed themselves to be carried away into revolution in the 1640's, and now they are docile and penitent. The young Pepys, with a job at stake in the admiralty, happens to dine, shortly after the Restoration, with some country gentlemen, among them "Mr. Christmas, my old school-fellow. . . . He did remember that I was a great Roundhead when I was a boy, and I was much afraid that he would have remembered the words that I said the day the King was beheaded (that, were I to preach upon him, my text should be— 'The memory of the wicked shall rot')." It turned out, much to Pepys's relief, that Mr. Christmas had left school before this indiscretion, but it had been a bad moment—and one that must have been fairly common throughout the country in the first few years after Charles II's accession.

Ordinary gentry will no longer control the government or dictate foreign policy. They bear the brunt of taxation, are firmly antiwar, and will not blink if Charles plays a close game with Louis XIV. They are upstanding country gentlemen who are utterly loyal to the crown—and to the Church of England. Of course it is no longer Laud's church, nor is it a church that men like Milton could any longer hope to reform. It is a thoroughly sedate institution, from which the Presbyterians were expelled in the 1660's. In the 1640's the gentry thought they were only defending the church, but they had been swept much further than they had ever dreamed of going, and now they are anxious to embrace the established church which had made them so restless before. The events of the past twenty years which had put them off democracy also taught them to be afraid of Protestant dissent, with its overtones of political radicalism—a fear not unmixed with economic jealousy of the thriving merchant class where dissent was still strong. The squires cling to their own portion and position, they shun any kind of change out of principle, and because they feel the crown will protect them against the aggression of great lords on the one hand and encroachments from the lower orders on the other, they wholeheartedly support the Stuart king. Those unpolished, atavistic squires will not change much for the next hundred years, and they are the backbone of the Tory party. That Charles II was a rather different kind of man from these country bumpkins does not seem to have bothered them.

During Charles's reign another party is taking shape, which will be called Whig, though it is not yet cohesive or successful. Bitterly critical of the king and his ministers, it is very active during the period of the Exclusion Crisis (1677-1681), when a desperate and unsuccessful attempt was made to exclude Charles's Catholic brother and heir from succession to the throne. But the Whig party loses its bid for the support of the middling gentry and in the Restoration era plays a role that might be described as one of intermittent opposition. The main thing about this new party is that it is growing up under the leadership of the great aristocrats who now emerge from their long hibernation. For more than a century and a half the aristocracy had been politically quiescent; they had been dealt some very hard blows by the Tudors, and even in the early Stuart period, when the size of the peerage was increased by royal elevation of court favorites, most lords chose to maintain their political reticence. Although a few strongly Protestant lords supported the Long Parliament, most of the aristocracy were, as was only natural, royalists during the Civil War. But the new generation was showing a renewed political vigor in the Restoration period. In 1685 there were 145 lay peers; about half can be termed great lords in terms of title, wealth, and influence. They have tremendous resources, and they can rival even the crown when it comes to the use of patronage and coercion. Some of these great lords were unwilling to sit by and watch the king gather all political power into his hands. Like their fifteenth-century counterparts, they wanted a system where they controlled the House of Commons. Whiggery then, may be seen as a modern revival of the political interest of the aristocracy as it had operated in the fifteenth century. For the Whigs were not great Parliament men; rather they simply believed that government should be in their hands. As far as they were concerned the Stuarts were just discredited foreigners, and they viewed the House of Commons as a tool for prying power away from the crown, for restricting royal authority, and for delivering into their possession the great offices of the state. They too can muster parliamentary support. The wealthier gentry, who are frequently linked by kinship to the high aristocracy, are allied with them, and so are the wealthy townsmen and merchants, who are often dissenters. The Whig aristocrats were tolerant, and even those merchants who were not dissenters liked the Whigs because they were the party that stood for war, empire, and commercial expansion. "Tory" and "Whig" were originally terms of abuse: the Tories were Irish bandits; the Whigs, Scottish horse thieves—the implication, of course, being that the Tories were pro-Catholic and the Whigs friends of the dissenters.

In the first party clash, in the late 1670's, the Whigs—under their first leader, the Earl of Shaftesbury—found themselves at a disadvantage, although they almost overcame it by their skillful use of anti-Catholic hysteria. It was hard to match the patronage of the crown, as Shaftesbury discovered when he tried to use the House of Commons to bludgeon the government. It was at this point that the Whigs resorted to ideology, which will sometimes be important in eighteenth-century politics, along with royal patronage and aristocratic clientage. Ideology was a necessary political instrument in the late 1670's; the new aristocracy had to command allegiance not merely as Shaftesbury's men, but as Whigs. They had to stand for something, and so they preached liberty and property, cited Magna Carta, proclaimed toleration in religion, and hailed the sovereignty of Parliament as the defense against absolutism, tyranny, and the despotism of the crown. Although the Whigs did become more radical from expedience, these were also things that they did believe in to some extent.

The political leaders of the later Stuart era were not lacking in profession of—and even sincere dedication to—ideals, whether the Whig doctrine of constitutional monarchy or the Tory faith in royal prerogative. Where they were deficient was on the side of common sense, tactical skill, balance and moderation, and in many cases also, personal integrity and simple honesty. The debilitating malaise that commonly infects political life after a long war or some other profound social upheaval in the modern world was already operative in late seventeenth-century England. There is much to be said in favor of the harsh judgment that Andrew Browning has made on the political leaders of the Restoration period; he calls them "singularly inexpert practitioners of the baser arts of politics, who contrived to do their country the maximum amount of harm while doing themselves remarkably little good." Amid the welter of politicians in the reign of Charles II and the following three decades we search in vain for a man who combines high and clearly conceived ideals with administrative and political ability. The best was the Earl of Clarendon, Charles II's first chief minister. Clarendon was a relic of a nobler time, a moderate conservative who wanted to recapture the sanest spirit of the Long Parliament. But his attempt to turn the clock back to 1642 was hopeless, and Clarendon was soon impeached and driven into exile, where he wrote his memoirs, thereby establishing a tradition long followed by ousted English politicians. The leaders of the next half century were men from the landed elite whose lives are known to us in massive detail. All of them were prolific writers, and their papers have been preserved inviolate, but the long-winded and monumental biographies which modern historians have constructed cannot disguise their incompetence or their moral turpitude. The student of the period swims dizzily amid the stream of names as politician follows politician, and he is confused even more by the fact that at one time or another most of them bear different names and titles—witness to their climb up the ladder of place and preferment. There was not one real statesman among them. We can gaze at their portraits, which stare down from the walls of Oxford and Cambridge colleges and the stately homes of England (often still inhabited by their descendants), and find it easier to discern the gout and venereal disease that were their common afflictions than any striking marks of ability or idealism. Many of these men were quite intelligent, most were not fanatics, and a few were unusually perceptive, but their vision was confined to the narrow, petty world of Restoration politics, and none was able to rise above what was nothing more than gilded political squalor. Nor could they ever resist striking a clever pose, the characteristic stance of the Restoration man of affairs. A sparkling exchange between two typical politicians sums up a great deal of their activity and conveys the specific quality of their political style. "You, sir," says the first, "will either die on the scaffold or of the pox." "Then," retorts the other, "I must embrace either your principles or your mistress."

The shortcomings of late seventeenth-century leaders are painfully evident in the career of Anthony Ashley Cooper, the first Earl of Shaftesbury, and leader of the opposition to Charles II. Shaftesbury has been memorialized as the founder of the Whig party and hailed as the formulator of the principles of the Revolution Settlement—although in 1688 he had been in his grave for five years. Perhaps Shaftesbury did help to bring about the Glorious Revolution, but this achievement was only incidental to his main aim, which was to gain political power by whatever means came to hand. Shaftesbury was a cynic who happened to possess many talents. His main strength lay in a remarkable capacity for stirring up popular support by methods which, in twentieth-century America, are associated with the names of Tammany Hall and Senator McCarthy. Shaftesbury was not above lending his support to a psychotic liar named Titus Oates who created a panic by conjuring up the fantasy of a Jesuit conspiracy to take over the royal government. Shaftesbury was clever enough to cultivate his image as the great protector of Whig principles, but he deserves to be known as an unscrupulous demagogue who can claim the distinction of being the first ward boss in English history. The founder of the Whig party finally ruined himself by attempting to foment a rebellion that sought to gain the succession to the throne for the Duke of Monmouth, one of the king's Protestant bastards, in place of his Catholic brother James. Charles put down the rebellion easily, and Shaftesbury died in exile.

Shaftesbury is particularly unsavory, but none of the other important politicians of the period lend themselves to heroic treatment. Even the most talented among them are unglorious. John Churchill, who became the first Duke of Marlborough and the general who ultimately checked Louis XIV's expansionist aims, was a court favorite noted for his unpar-

alleled opportunism, and the sensitive and witty Earl of Halifax is best
known for his nickname of "Trimmer." Tom Wharton (later Lord
Wharton), one of the youngest but also the ablest of the Whig leaders
in 1688, achieved the high point of his political career by writing a popular song that depicted the Stuarts bringing over Irish Catholics to cut the
throats of English Protestants and gentlemen. Wharton also gained ce-
lebrity by urinating on the altar of a church while on a drunken spree.

Even William of Orange, the Dutch prince who became the hero of
1688 and reigned as William III until 1702, can hardly be glamorized.
His was not the fairy tale success often told by Whig historians. William
married his cousin Mary, who was James II's daughter, because she was
the closest Protestant to the throne; William himself was the second.
The Dutch prince saw himself as the last hope of Protestant Europe,
and his dream was not to save England, but to organize a grand Protestant alliance against Louis XIV. To this end William had been plotting
for years to gain the English throne, and amid the confusions of 1688, he
was the one who urged the English on and organized the revolution. We
can almost understand how Tory romantics hankered after the Stuart
monarchy. Nevertheless, by 1688 it was quite clear that William of Orange and the Whig aristocracy were preferable to James II (1685-1688)
and his ministers. Among them the king's favorite was the malevolent
Judge Jeffries of the notorious Bloody Assizes—the savage condemnation
and execution of three hundred peasants of the West Country on the
doubtful charge that they had all supported a second abortive rebellion
by the Duke of Monmouth. James's claim that he could suspend the
operation of statute law by royal prerogative and his efforts at reviving
the Court of High Commission reveal how incompetent he was as a king
and a statesman. James was hopeless; he was inept, impolitic, and wanted
the impossible. The end of his dreams had come in 1642, but this was
something he never even began to apprehend.

Every revolution has a slogan, and the war cry of the Glorious Revolution was "liberty and property." Of course, the two stood for the same
thing; they were the twin pillars that symbolized the traditional way of
life of the conservative gentlemen of England. For 1688 was an act of
conservation; the men who effected the revolution did not want to
change anything—rather they believed, as they explained in the Bill of
Rights, that they had found "the best means for the vindicating and
asserting their ancient rights and liberties." 1688 was depicted as a defensive necessity against a despotic ruler who was in the process of sub-

verting the law, religion, and constitution of the nation. Thus it was revolution in the name of the law, revolution whose essential quality is the insistence upon legality. The actual proceedings of 1688 were dubious, messy, and awkward, but they were also highly successful because they rested on a national consensus. Even high Tory enthusiasts for royal power were forced to agree with the Whigs that James II could no longer rule. After William of Orange landed in England, not only the Whig aristocracy but also John Churchill, the head of the royal army, affirmed their loyalty to him, and James had no alternative except to flee to France.

By alienating every important segment of the political nation James himself was the prime inspiration of the Glorious Revolution. The fear of Catholic power was so strong in England that it is doubtful whether any Catholic king who lacked the skill and cynicism of Charles II could have managed to keep the throne. In any case, the men of 1688 solved the problem for all time by statute. The Bill of Rights stipulates that any Catholic is forever excluded from the English throne. It goes on to state that if a Catholic should claim to rule, "the people of these realms shall be . . . absolved of their allegiance." Since the Bill of Rights is still law in England, this means that if Elizabeth II should convert, her citizens could depose her. As if his religion were not horrifying enough, James did not show the proper regard for the laws and institutions of his kingdom or any respect for the social order. What immediately precipitated the revolution was James's prosecution of the Archbishop of Canterbury and six bishops for seditious libel. James was usually obtuse and generally stupid, but this was one of his very worst ideas. The episcopate was itself a reflection of the social order, and the trial of the seven bishops inflamed even the most staid and conservative. Just about everything James did could be construed as an attack on liberty and property. We need only cite one striking example—the case of the president of Magdalen College, Oxford, who had been expelled from his office by James II's ecclesiastical commissioners. The learned president, who was not exactly a hotheaded radical, had only to state that the king had illegally deprived him of his freehold property, and the charge inevitably aroused the fears and anger of the men of his class who were basically as conservative as he.

The Bill of Rights, which may be described as a very sophisticated version of Magna Carta, is essentially a bill of particulars against the illegal actions of the king. It is a beautifully drafted statute. James had assumed the power to suspend laws and execute laws "without consent of parliament"; he had claimed to establish a new court and to levy money "by pretence of prerogative"; he had interfered in the due process of the common law by packing juries and inflicting cruel and unusual punishment, and demanding excessive bail. In short, the way he had manipulated the beloved legal system of the nation was "utterly and directly contrary to the known laws and statutes and freedom of this realm." And the Bill of Rights goes on to state that all these actions are henceforth illegal. There is nothing theoretical here, no profound statement of principle, but merely a constant reiteration of due process. Every grievance is specified, listed unequivocally, and henceforth banned by statute. "Illegal," "illegal and pernicious," "arbitrary and illegal courses," "against law," "illegal and void"—the negative phrases are repeated over and over, and their cumulative effect is nothing less than an enunciation of the fundamental rights of Englishmen.

1689 provided a definitive solution to the problem of sovereignty that had unsettled the constitution and disturbed the English polity for four hundred years, and the men who believed that English constitutional history culminated in 1689 were not entirely misguided. The Glorious Revolution established, beyond any doubt or question, the supremacy of the king-in-Parliament and the ultimate authority of parliamentary statute. Even the coronation oath was laid down according to statute and, in a sense, this may be seen as the end of a long story that goes back to the tenth century. In essence, the oath taken by the king is the same as it was in the Anglo-Saxon period; there is, however, one small but crucial adjustment. Not only does the king swear to uphold the established church and observe the laws and customs of his people; he promises to govern "according to the statutes in parliament agreed on." The problems that were formulated first in Magna Carta are finally resolved in 1689 by means of a conservative revolution.

Once it was effected, the revolutionary settlement was considered inviolable. Most Englishmen believed in the eighteenth century that 1689 marked the end of legal history and the highest point the law could hope to attain. There are many criticisms that can be made of the English common law which the Glorious Revolution aimed to preserve. It was harsh, it was cumbersome and slow, it was obscure, it was expensive and thus favored the rich, and it was not even very effective in preventing violence and disorder. Yet to the men of 1688 it was the most wonderful legal creation of the human mind. One thing the common law was not, in spite of its many drawbacks. It could not easily be used as an instrument of royal tyranny or governmental oppression. As James was cha-grined to learn, it was very difficult to make a jury bring in a verdict at the behest of the government. The common law admirably served the interests of the gentlemen freeholders of England; it was a bulwark against royal authority and the protection of their property. The last thing they wanted to do was change or reform the law.

Once the dust had settled, it was easy to see how conservative the men of 1689 really were. The abolition of the prerogative courts by the Long Parliament left gaps in legal procedure that the common law could not fill, and the reforms that were urgently put forward in the 1650's were not seriously considered until the nineteenth century. The legal system late in the seventeenth, and throughout the eighteenth century, was in-efficient, ramshackle, inequitable, and often unjust. But as long as the common law both symbolized and safeguarded the way of life of the gentry class, they were unwilling to change it. It provided a career for their younger sons who swarmed to London for their apprenticeship at the Inns of Court. In terms of legal learning, what they were taught was negligible. In the 1670's, Louis XIV had established regius professorships of law at the French universities, but the system of instruction at the Inns of Court was casual in the extreme. A young gentleman would eat his dinners and meet the right people; perhaps he would painfully make his way through a few volumes of Coke's reports; certainly he would read Locke on government and find him admirable. He would probably at-tend the courts at Westminster, but that was about the extent of his education. Again, there was little demand to reform this aspect of the system. Men who by birth had a natural place in it were happy, and those who aspired to become gentlemen were not eager to change a sys-tem which did provide substantial rewards for talent and industry. Men believed it was dangerous to tamper with the ancient structure of the common law (which had already been unwieldy in the fourteenth cen-tury), and perhaps they were wise to leave well enough alone. Tradition was all—and even the important Habeas Corpus Act of 1679 only made minor changes in a writ that goes back to the fourteenth century. There were a few procedural reforms under William and Mary, but in law 1689 means the closing of the lid on reform. It would not be lifted until the nineteenth century.

The period comprising the closing decade of the seventeenth century, and the first sixty years of the eighteenth has been called the Age of Whig Supremacy, the Age of Aristocratic Domination, as well as the

Age of Reason. But the labels—all of them superficially accurate—have been applied too haphazardly. It is a very difficult period to study, and the modern literature is on the whole scanty and unsatisfactory. On the surface the political history of the period seems unrelievedly dull and, to make matters even worse, terribly confusing as well. The first half of the eighteenth century is one of those rare periods in English history when politics and government seem to count for very little in national life. It is a situation not seen again until the 1920's and 1930's, when the proceedings of the House of Commons seem to have little relevance to the most exciting things that are happening in the nation. It was a bad day for the historical craft when the Namierites carved a whole field of scholarship out of the political desert of early eighteenth-century England. Probing studies of intellectual and religious change and the obscure course of the Industrial Revolution would be much more enlightening than the interminable measuring up of the Duke of Newcastle's patronage.

The two prevailing interpretations of the eighteenth century are still the Whig-liberal view and the Namierite statement. The Whig-liberal view was resoundingly set forth by Macaulay and perpetuated by Trevelyan in his engaging little book, *The English Revolution*. Trevelyan's account is still the most lucid, and his presentation of the Whig-liberal interpretation, though we are taught to sneer at it, remains more sensible than the fashionable Namierite analysis. Trevelyan firmly tells us that 1688 was *the* great turning point in English history; it marked the origin of English power and wealth, the empire, industry, and inaugurated the golden age of English thought.

Trevelyan is more right than wrong. After 1689 England does emerge as an important center of European civilization. During the eighteenth century English power and influence on the continent reached their peak, and English achievements—in economics, commerce, science, literature, philosophy—are enormous and impressive. For Trevelyan, England's relatively sudden flowering was not very hard to explain. The forces that made modern England were released by the Glorious Revolution. Now that the Whig aristocrats had sure control of government, their skill—informed by beneficence—rapidly and effectively guided the nation to greatness. What had they accomplished in 1689? According to Trevelyan, they clarified the question of sovereignty that had vexed the seventeenth century by preserving and ratifying, beyond any doubt, the supremacy of the House of Commons. From there they went on to establish cabinet government; henceforth, a healthy and combative national spirit inspired British expansion. England fought successfully against the Dutch and the French to secure her rightful position in the world and her just share of the world market. The Whigs, of course, never failed to encourage the commercial classes, thus proving to be men of astuteness and vision, but—best of all—they were tolerant and skeptical. Religious conflict was healed, and the nation as a whole could move forward under a confident and energetic consensus government. The only failing on the part of the great Whig statesmen, as far as Trevelyan is concerned, was an inability to appreciate the political potential of the lower middle and working classes—but eventually they cultivated even this sensibility. In short, the men of 1689 as the Whig-liberal school has traditionally portrayed them, just fell short of the standards set by nineteenth-century liberals. For Macaulay and Trevelyan, the only real difference between them was a greater awareness on the part of the nineteenth-century Whigs of the common people of England, although even the seventeenth-century Whigs were more responsive to the needs of "the people" than their Tory and Stuart opponents.

This is a rather grand interpretation but one too jovial and smooth for most tastes today. In the cold light of the twentieth century, the men who made the Revolution of 1689 do not appear especially glorious. Compared with Coke, Pym, Cromwell—even with Laud—they are narrow in vision and interest. One thing is clear; they are extremely selfish. Though its horizons would be extended during the eighteenth century, the world of the Whig aristocrats was very limited. They were men of rudimentary education; perhaps they had a few fun-filled years at the Inns of Court or the university, and some would have a year or two of the grand tour. But that was all. They were not cultivated men, not people who read or reflected very much. Lockean elegance notwithstanding, the Whig aristocracy subscribed to a very simple political philosophy—the country should be ruled by people like themselves. They put it that they were England's natural rulers, that they held the trust of the people, and in a sense this was true. Politics was a part of their lives; they were actively interested in political life, which they identified with themselves and their own interests. Along with their land, houses, and horses, politics was an intrinsic part of their style of life, part of an attitude of life of a rich, self-conscious, aggressive and tough aristocracy. The emphasis must be on the toughness, which was often sheer grossness. They were not at all devout. The term "deist" is accurate enough as a label, but it cannot convey their lack of involvement with all things spiritual. Religion is not something they worry about. These are the kind of men who will dominate political life well into the nineteenth century. Although they made a revolution of sorts, they are quite different from the liberal utilitarians and dissenters who carried through the reforms of the nineteenth century. The Whig-liberal historians would argue that the Whig oligarchy was the prerequisite of nineteenth-century liberal democracy. Perhaps this is true. There was a great deal of common sense in the Whig aristocrats. Because they were hardheaded and self-interested, they were always willing to compromise. Late in the seventeenth century they compromised with the dissenters, they collaborated with a shrewd Dutch ruler, and then with thick-witted Hanoverian princes. Later in the nineteenth century they compromised with liberals, and even met democrats half way. Thus they were still running the government in the 1860's— and even beyond.

Trevelyan does make everything about 1689 too neat. The Glorious Revolution was not nearly so well-groomed nor was it in itself responsible for subsequent British power, but nevertheless his account is not a bad explanation of what remains a puzzling phenomenon. Still, it has been savagely attacked. Although no one book presents a full-scale critique of the Macaulay-Trevelyan account, we can, however, extrapolate the opposing view propounded in various places by the Namier school.

It consists, first of all, of blunt denial. There was, we are told, no such thing as the Whig party—and certainly no Whig ideology that included admirable packaged concepts, like "toleration." Rather, the period 1689-1760 is characterized by the struggle for control of government and crown patronage among aristocratic factions, most of whom find it convenient—after 1714—to call themselves Whigs. But Whig is merely a label without a meaning. Who are these factions? They represent vast wealth, the supremacy of important families whose influence is so extensive that they dominate whole counties. It is like the sixteenth century all over again, but on a more lavish scale. Power and patronage has only one aim—new aggrandizement and the continued possession of power. It is a very different kind of politics from the dynamic patriotism described by Macaulay. Now the ingrained Namierite skepticism about ideology and public morality inevitably sets the tone. The happy, robust world of Macaulay and Trevelyan is virtually unrecognizable. Now the great Whig lords appear mean and narrow; we see them as small, insecure men frantically grasping after and then clinging to power. Where Trevelyan painted a great canvas, we now have needlepoint. The focus of history has sharpened, but narrowed too. We need to remind ourselves, after threading through the minute and painstakingly documented accounts of the Namier school, that during this time England was experiencing tremendous upheavals, that it was an era of unprecedented national expansion. No doubt the Whig-liberal historians were too naïve about the motivations and personalities of the Whigs; obviously they did attribute too much to the Whig way of life. But at least the Whig historians knew great things were going on, although they were wrong in ascribing them solely to political events. The Namierites, however, do not seem to know that anything at all was happening, outside of parliamentary politics. Namier loved to enmesh himself in the mechanics of politics; his meticulous studies are brilliant, and everything he says is accurate. But he never considered the role of politics in society or the influence of politics in national life. These are things the Namierite historian never talks about. As a consequence we have a very distorted general picture of English life during the first part of the eighteenth century. Even though Namier's teachings are true, to take Namierism seriously is to accept the view that politics is dissociated from culture and society, that political life may be studied in a vacuum.

Fortunately we have some specialized studies which do provide an insight into the broad complexities of early eighteenth-century England. The first volume of J. H. Plumb's biography of Sir Robert Walpole brilliantly places politics in a wide social and cultural context, although the second volume, which concerns Walpole in power, suffers from a much narrower vision. John Carswell's *The Old Cause* succeeds, as no other book has, in making us understand Whiggery as a way of life, and not simply as a system of patronage and pocket boroughs. Another work by Carswell, on the South Sea Bubble, provides an exciting picture of the commercial and financial boom of the early eighteenth century. John Clapham's detailed study of the rise of the Bank of England gives us some insight into the same subject, but the approach is too institutional; Clapham was interested in economic growth but not particularly concerned about the making of an economic mind. Norman Sykes's many studies of the eighteenth-century church, on the other hand, always probe deeper than the institutional framework, and allow us to see how changes in religious feeling profoundly affected the general pattern of culture and society.

Although on the surface they may seem to have little effect on the machinations of the great Whig families, new and important things were taking place in England in the early eighteenth century. The commercial and financial worlds were lively and prosperous, and intellectual life was more exciting for more people than ever before. It was, after all, the Age of Newton, with all the confidence and glory associated with the phrase. Perhaps the trouble is that early eighteenth-century English politics are pre-Newtonian. Political life often seems to be irrelevant. It hardly matters what the politicians do, because the nation's real vitality lies outside the political system. It is very hard to say what part politics played in the dynamic aspects of English life during this period. Here the Namier influence has been unfortunate. The really critical question —how politics was related to society—was never even posed. England in the late seventeenth and early eighteenth centuries was changing drastically, a whole new world was coming into existence. Perhaps politicians did not shape it, but still it must have impinged on political life. It was a world that even the shallowest office-seeker must have known and heeded, even if he tried to ignore it.

It was a world that in many ways was glorious. Only for a few brief periods have Englishmen been really important in European intellectual life. There were three English ages in European culture: the age of Bede, in the eighth century; the age of Ockham, in the fourteenth; and the age of Newton, in the late seventeenth and early eighteenth centuries. (The influence of Darwin was, in comparison, pale and fleeting.) It is astonishing that during the Restoration, when politics were so bitter and confusing, there should have been this achievement in science. Newton is only the most famous; if he did not tower over all of them, men like Hooke and Boyle would be remembered as giants today. The problem is intriguing and important, yet no historian has been able so far to account for this efflorescence during a period of political frustration and moral decay. In fact historians have tended to retreat from formulating the problem at all, and have been much too ready to march into dialectical traps. Christopher Hill, for instance, a scholar of great learning and intelligence, chooses to see Newton as a reactionary, as compared with Sir Francis Bacon.

Admirable as he is, Sir Francis Bacon, at the beginning of the century, cannot really be seen, nor can Harrington in the mid-1600's, as the founder of modern science. Bacon did, of course, strike some memorable phrases to describe the empirical method; certainly he wrote about it more elegantly than anyone has done since. Bacon told us to go and study nature; he wanted to collect masses of data, to accumulate more and more knowledge. Certainly he strove to understand nature, but for all the fine words and good intentions, Bacon did not grasp the notion of making nature explicit in mathematical terms and, since Newton, this is what science has been. "The Lord Bacon was not yet acquainted with Nature," Voltaire wrote, "but then he knew, and pointed out, the several paths that led to it." And it is quite true; Bacon may have anticipated the scientific method, but he did not create modern science.

Newton's whole apprehension of the world was expressed in terms of pure mathematics. This was a vision Bacon never approached—it is on a level different from massive data collecting, no matter how intelligent. Ockham and his disciples had had a glimpse of explicating nature in terms of number; perhaps Plato was vaguely groping for it, certainly Galileo was. But the consensus is that Sir Isaac Newton (d. 1727) was the first really to grasp the idea with absolute clarity. It transcended data collecting. "It is the art of numbering and measuring exactly a thing whose existence cannot be conceived": again Voltaire, discussing the differential calculus, which he describes as "this method of subjecting everywhere infinity to algebraical calculations." It might stand as a definition of the kind of new science Newton had made.

Why should this vision have crystallized in the mind of a Cambridge mathematics professor in the 1660's? If we considered only the political history of the Restoration era, neither the time nor the place would seem propitious for an intellectual revolution. But in the second half of the seventeenth century there was an intense appreciation of mathematics throughout Europe, and nowhere were its effects more striking than in England. The patterns and terms in which men thought were changing, and new modes of thought were being established. One was the understanding of nature in mathematical terms; the other was the understanding of society in similar terms. Late in the seventeenth century, along with the new physics and chemistry, we can see the beginnings of statistics and economics. Here were the first attempts to obtain statistics on population and to arrive at principles of economics that could be expressed in mathematical language. The collection of statistics was even undertaken by the state. Public revenue had to be estimated and projected. Under William III, the government used life annuities to repay loans, and it is not surprising that this period witnesses the rapid development of life insurance. Early in the eighteenth century the Bishop of Ely compiled a history of prices—the first important book of its kind in Europe. It was, in a very unsophisticated manner, the beginning of the empirical attitude toward social science with which we are familiar. These new methods represented a breakthrough in human thought, a step across what had been the frontiers of knowledge. One of the rarest events in human history is the formulation of a new view of the world; the first development in five hundred years came in the late seventeenth century, and it came primarily in England. Science, as we think of it now, is a way of expressing a statistical and mathematical understanding of nature; economics—and from it, the rest of the social sciences—is a way of applying the same method to an understanding of the nature of men and society.

It is hard to say what caused the new scientific development, and historians have not succeeded in explaining it satisfactorily. Sometimes they trace it back to the Renaissance and Baconian humanism, claiming to find its roots in a new and expanded concept of man. Pursue things germane to the human mind—this was, after all, the Baconian canon. This account is nice, plausible, and maddeningly vague. In a way, Renaissance humanism is antithetical to science. It is ultimately concerned with moral life, with teaching people how to live well, how to fulfill themselves. Renaissance humanist education was not aimed at producing men like Newton, or the demographer King and the economist Petty. Other historians have laid the whole phenomenon at the feet of the ubiquitous bourgeoisie, whose skeptical, rational attitude toward the world supposedly impelled them to cultivate nonreligious disciplines. But it is hard to find much that was rational about the seventeenth-century English bourgeoisie. They may have shown a certain deft skill and coolness in calculating their own interests, but they were otherwise intensely emotional and extravagantly religious. What they sought in religion was an escape from the world; they were much less interested in confronting it and converting nature into formulae.

Still other historians have turned to radical Puritanism—and this explanation is probably the most persuasive. The Puritans emphasized human experience; they were concerned above all with the human mind and its understanding of God. Beginning with the primacy of internal experience, they were led to a general concern with the mind and its powers. After 1660, the more radical varieties of religion were discouraged, religious emotionalism was neutralized, and the concern with inner experience was secularized. The end of religious wrangling did lead to the kind of complacency that Milton, writing in the heat of the 1640's had gloomily predicted. "Recreations and jolly pastimes . . . will fetch the day about from sun to sun, and rock the tedious year as in a delight-ful dream. . . . These are the fruits which a dull ease and cessation of our knowledge will bring forth among the people," he wrote in the *Areopagitica*. The intensity of mind, however, which Milton himself represents, persisted. No longer preoccupied with religious experience and knowing God, the Puritans now thought about nature, society, and the operations of the mind itself. During the great debates over religion and theology earlier in the seventeenth century, an intellectual concern had built up. People had applied their minds to the nature of the church and of government; they worried over them as hard as they could, and they established certain patterns of thought. After 1660 they were weary of politics and religion and their fervor died down, and after 1689 there was nothing much left to debate about forms of government. But the habit of hard thinking survived, and the men used it to attack other problems. The energy which had found an outlet in religion now focused on secular concerns. Instead of straining to know God and build His church on earth, men now exerted themselves to understand nature and society.

Although it is hard to single out the causes of the scientific revolution, it is readily apparent that the new kinds of inquiry were greatly facilitated and encouraged by the founding of the Royal Society in the early 1660's. The meetings of gentlemanly scholars under royal auspices to consider the work of Newton and his colleagues gave the new scientists an appreciative audience, public recognition, and the opportunity to criticize each other's work. In the later decades of the seventeenth century, the better minds in the country found the activities of the Royal Society much more attractive than the passionate and confused world of politics. To a degree, the scientific revolution was made possible by the dismal condition of the contemporary political world. It no longer seemed possible that men of intelligence and good will could do much in the public sphere of life. They were turned inward to intellectual pursuits, and they satisfied their ambition to contribute to social melioration by trying to understand the operation of natural laws.

The intellectual revolution was contemporaneous with unprecedented economic expansion. The single most important factor in England's new economic life was the development of institutions of credit without which modern capitalism is impossible. There were, after all, only two things that prevented capitalism from flourishing in the seventeenth century. One was the lack of a network of transportation and a viable method of distribution; the other was the persistence of primitive forms of credit—particularly of public credit. But during our period these limitations were overcome. Banking reached a new level of organization and the familiar modern methods of credit were established. The full commercial capitalist system was functioning; the public debt, a low interest rate, and joint stock companies are all important and commonplace aspects of English life in the age of the Whig aristocrats. The growth of a working system of public credit was in fact partly responsible for British military successes in the eighteenth century.

The discovery of credit mechanisms engendered feverish speculation in the first two decades of the eighteenth century and created a tremendous boom in joint stock projects to promote overseas trade. The boom inevitably got out of hand, and the collapse of the South Sea Company in the early 1720's ruined hundreds of investors and almost brought down the government. The frightened politicians proceeded to put through the Bubble Act, which prohibited limited liability and put a brake on investment and speculation. Yet there was a large reservoir of capital available in England in the first half of the eighteenth century, a great portion of which was derived from overseas commerce and empire, especially in India. Parliamentary statute inhibited reckless speculation, and in the middle years of the century this large surplus began to find an outlet in industrial growth.

Starting in the 1730's, the first improvements in transportation in seven hundred years take place—and these inevitably encouraged new forms of industry. There was some improvement of roads through the turnpike trusts, but far more significant was the growth of canals and the general development of the river system. Both of these—roads and canals—encouraged speculative ventures in commerce and industry. For more than two hundred years industrial expansion had been blocked by logistical problems. By the 1730's and 1740's we can see in England the beginning of the process by which science is converted into technology— the process that makes the modern world possible. By the end of the nineteenth century this process will mark the difference between western and oriental—or between industrial and underdeveloped—societies.

It is hazardous, certainly for the eighteenth century, to try to distinguish where science leaves off and technology begins. Scientific inquiry is, of course, the first requisite for a modern society, but perhaps how science is applied to society through technology is even more important. Or, in our own jargon, how is theory turned into hardware? We know this was being done in eighteenth-century England, though it is very difficult to say exactly how. At first, scientific knowledge was applied to agricultural production. Beginning in Charles II's reign—if not before—fertilizer was used intelligently. We are not sure why, but men began to take a new and important attitude toward farming. The distribution of crops, the allocation of land, the improvement of livestock—none of these were innovations, but now, for the first time, they were being applied by English landlords on a vast scale. Now technology matters. We can scarely call it science; rather it was the rational application of old knowledge to human needs.

The second stage of the process came in the eighteenth century. This was the application of new science—Newtonian mechanics—to industrial production. This too is a problematic phenomenon, and it is often hard to tell whether it really was new knowledge or merely the application of old knowledge and the extension of new techniques. The new machinery was often developed in a chancy and pragmatic way by craftsmen, some of whom were illiterate. James Watt was lucky to study at the one university in Britain (Edinburgh) where a man could be exposed to the new science, but in many other instances the relationship between science and invention is impossible to find. At least Watt's case provides one clear example of how the new science influenced industrial development.

We can outline two stages in the Industrial Revolution. The first, which occurred during the seventeenth century, saw the application of old methods on an extensive scale; this meant an increase in agricultural production. The second, much more dramatic stage, took place in the second half of the eighteenth century, and this was the application of physics to industrial production. It was haphazard and disorganized, it is hard to narrate systematically, but this vague process was what made the modern world. Why should it have happened in England? In 1700, the population of France was at least three times greater than England's, and French industry was much larger and more intense. Still, the Industrial Revolution did not occur first in France, and it was not until the last three decades of the nineteenth century that other countries caught up with the industrial lead established by England in the eighteenth.

Thus what was happening in the English countryside from 1680 to 1760 is highly significant—much more meaningful than the intrigues at Whitehall. The new agricultural methods produced an increased food supply, and now English agriculture could support a tremendous increase in population. This is another crucial, but puzzling, phenomenon. In

1300 there were probably two and a half to three million people in England, perhaps as many as four million. During the fourteenth century the population fell catastrophically, and began to rise slowly late in the fifteenth century. By 1600 it was probably just a little above the level of 1300—that is, three to four million. By the end of the seventeenth century there were about five million people in England. But in 1801—the year of the first census—there were approximately ten million. The population of England virtually doubled in one hundred years and, though there was some growth in the 1720's and 1730's, most of the increase came in the second half of the century. An increase on this scale is staggering—historians and demographers cannot easily account for it. The rise before 1750 (which is not overwhelming) can be ascribed mainly to the increased food supply and an increase in life expectancy brought about by a few elementary improvements in medicine. Hospitals were built (they were the result of charity and good works) and they did provide some care; primitive public health measures raised the standards of urban sanitation. People no longer die so commonly in the streets, and it is notable that the population rise is particularly marked in the cities. The really phenomenal rise in the population curve takes place in the latter part of the century however, and the demographers and economic historians are still debating its causes.

Eighteenth-century England was a society undergoing a tremendous transformation—in agriculture, in science, in experiments with the application of science to industry. The increased population and the appearance of new institutions of credit are simply the most obvious indicators of how society was changing. We now know the necessary ingredients for making an industrial revolution: a surplus food supply, a mobile labor force, reserves of capital, technological advances (not so much new inventions, but their application to old problems), and credit facilities. In addition, profitable markets, especially for textile goods, were available in the overseas colonies. Keeping these in mind, we can answer the question of why the first Industrial Revolution happened in England. The question might really be: given these conditions, how could the Industrial Revolution possibly have *not* occurred in England? All the necessary factors were present during the first half of the eighteenth century, and they were given free rein by the easy-going Whig oligarchs, who had no policy of economic planning.

Eighteenth-century England is the home not only of modern science and economics, but modern literature as well. Defoe, Richardson, Swift,

Fielding, and Sterne invented the technique of the modern novel; of those writers at least the last three also managed to write novels that may never be surpassed. The novel is the form of literature associated with bourgeois life; it deals with moral problems middling men have to grapple with in a mobile society, and ever since its inception, the English novel has been traditionally concerned with social problems and social institutions. The themes were—as Jane Austen put it—simply love and money, subjects that in conjunction were not, oddly enough, common literary subjects before the eighteenth century. These novelists had a narrow range of outlook; they knew about poverty—certainly Fielding, who was a magistrate, did—but they were not really concerned about the masses, or mass society. Society seen as a whole was not their province. They knew a little about science, but do not seem aware of the importance of technology to society. They operated within a clear framework of moral life and human values; although they were disinterested in theology, they supported Christian ethics; they describe and accept a mobile society in which the possibilities of going up and down, very far and very quickly, are real and gripping, and in their novels all the important events hinge on this one social phenomenon. This is the framework for the eighteenth-century, as well as the nineteenth-century novel. Its function was to deal with the social and moral problems of individuals. Yet, though we are engulfed in the problems of a technological mass society, we still read the eighteenth-century novels. At any rate, no literary form since has superseded them. Certainly our own writers are no more literate or sensitive, our range of literary culture is no wider, our exploration of human motivation no deeper. Eighteenth-century Englishmen invented a new form and they carried it as far as it could go—it is plausible to say that no subsequent novelist has ever transcended Swift or Sterne. To develop a new art form and carry it to its highest peak in one generation is a remarkable achievement, in its way as impressive as the work done in eighteenth-century science.

In philosophy, the achievements of the Age of Newton are also remarkable. Historians of ideas have more and more come to see John Locke's *Essay on Human Understanding* as the harbinger of the new cluster of views on man and society we call the Enlightenment. The dominant seventeenth-century Cartesian philosophy had claimed that man's ideas are innate. This psychology fitted in with the static, hierarchical assumptions of the Old Regime in Europe: men's concepts and ideas are what they are born with; human nature cannot be changed.

Locke, however, claimed that the human mind at birth is a clean slate
and men's ideas and attitudes are the consequence of the impress of
their environments. This Lockean psychology inaugurated a novel, optimistic view of human nature that lies behind the eighteenth-century
idea of progress. A better environment, more rational and enlightened
ways of organizing political and social institutions, a more salubrious
physical milieu, will make men more peaceful, intelligent, and generous.
Society no longer had to endure the vestiges of medievalism; man's future was unlimited; all that was required was better government and
social organization. In these assumptions, that slowly emerged out of
Locke's psychology, are heralded the progressive philosophy of the modern world, that stands in the starkest contrast to the hierarchic, authoritarian, and static beliefs of the older order.

In intellectual and economic aspects of life, early eighteenth-century
English society was astonishingly fertile and creative. In many ways it
appears modern; so much of what we see, so many of the responses, are
familiar and readily comprehensible. We can find our way easily in its
literature, its science, its economics, and its philosophy. Yet in politics
and government it is still an old regime. Here is a world that seems
untouched by modernity, the freshness and creativity seen in every other
aspect of life seems to have passed it by. Commerce was expanding, industry growing, England's best writers were catering to the middle class
and fashioning a new thought-world. Yet a strong case could be made
that England was probably never worse governed than during this period. It must be stressed that there were some real achievements in government during the long Whig tenure of power. The cabinet system was
slowly hatched, and the old forms of conflict between king and Commons were abolished forever. Yet in its day-to-day operations, as well as
in the formulation of long-term policy, early eighteenth-century English
government fully deserves its reputation for slackness and irresponsibility. The vast problems of society all required moral decisions; all involved
pressing social issues. But the issues were carefully ignored, and the
moral decisions were not taken. The prevalence of poverty, the question
of extending the franchise, the granting of full civil rights to dissenters
and Catholics, the development of public systems of police, health, and
education, and the reform of the common law—these were great issues,
but the Whigs never even considered them as susceptible to solution.
Perhaps they were right; perhaps a real attempt to tackle the problems
would have fractured society irrevocably. We cannot excuse the Whigs

on ground of incapacity. We know they were talented, energetic, and astute. Certainly they showed enough energy and brainpower in gaining and clinging to office, and in foreign affairs their skill and resourcefulness are impressive indeed. These men, who were so negligent about domestic policy, presided over the steady growth of English naval and military power and inflicted defeat after defeat on France, whose military strength had been far superior to England's in the second half of the seventeenth century.

Why did English government of the first half of the eighteenth century decline to attack the problems posed by their changing society? How are we to explain the puzzling gulf between a lethargic government on the one hand and unprecedented economic and intellectual growth on the other? A few suggestions may be made. First of all, the Whigs were afraid to meddle with anything that impinged on social problems. They had long memories, and they feared to reawaken the democratic monsters of the seventeenth century. The shadow of Cromwell and the Levellers still made them shudder, and to grapple with the problems of an expanding commercial and industrial society might again raise the specters of anarchy and dictatorship, both of which equally terrified the landed class. Secondly, they were not particularly alert to domestic problems. They were aware of them, of course, but their attention was riveted on overseas concerns. Foreign and colonial affairs were what captured their imagination. There were vast opportunities abroad, and much of the rational, organizing intelligence of the ruling elite focused on the problems of imperial government. To settle, control, and exploit Ireland, India, the West Indies, and the eastern seaboard of North America was a tremendous task that absorbed so much energy that little was left to rationalize society at home. The empire would always be the *damnosa hereditas* of the English elite. It is tempting to speculate on what might have happened if half the intelligence and industry exhibited by the political nation during periods of intensive imperial expansion had instead been devoted to the reform of society at home; modern England might have become the outstanding model of a planned, beneficent, and fruitful society in the history of the world.

Thirdly, in order even to contemplate reforms that might overturn society, men must be convinced of the urgency of change, they must be alienated from their society, or at least be at odds with it to some degree. And few eighteenth-century men—at least before the 1760's—questioned the structure of society as they knew it. Why should they have?

473

Although the order of society was rigidly defined, it was also very flexible. Of course a huge portion of the population existed at a level that was barely human, but they did not count in government. For the large number whose opinions could be expressed, however, the opportunity to rise in the world had never been better. If the doors to wealth, power, and fame had been closed to them, they would have demanded change. But wherever we look—in law, politics, finance, war—all the potential agents of reform are absorbed. In the late 1750's, for the first time in the eighteenth century, an authentic product of a high bourgeois family, William Pitt, becomes a minister of the crown. Pitt's grandfather was one of those merchant oligarchs who made a fortune in India. But like other such "nabobs" and merchant oligarchs in the first half of the eighteenth century, the prime aim of the Pitt family was to acquire a landed estate and to be absorbed into the aristocracy. The high bourgeoisie of England had as yet no sense of class consciousness, of achieving the political emancipation of the urban middle class, but only a sense of social mobility, of advancement into landed society. Thus the "great commoner," William Pitt, a statesman of enormous ability, becomes a minister of the crown as a member of one of the Whig factions and later takes the title of Lord Chatham. Unlike the other politicians of the 1750's, Chatham knows how to appeal to the bourgeoisie on moral and ideological grounds; he successfully cultivates popular support at a time when his Whig colleagues still regarded democratic politics with contempt and fear. But Chatham uses his popular appeal and ideological commitment only for foreign policy. He made the Seven Years War with France an emotional thing, a great crusade for the preservation and increase of the British Empire. Yet he makes no effort to apply this ideological commitment and popular enthusiasm to domestic questions. Fundamentally, Chatham remained a man of the old regime, a middle class *arriviste* who was content to be absorbed into the ruling oligarchy.

It is unrealistic to expect that men who know that possibilities are ripe for them will do anything but applaud the *status quo*—and seize their own chances. Thus the early eighteenth century is a paradoxical time. Men are bustling, creative, self-absorbed, and very content in the pursuit of their own ambitions. Society itself appears to be static and political life ultimately arid, yet the life of the individual in England had perhaps never been so rewarding for so many.

II. *The Triumph of the Old Order*

THE STABILITY of the Georgian era was due, in large measure, to the important changes in the structure of English government that were made between 1689 and 1722—the year in which Sir Robert Walpole and his Whig cronies secure power and thus bring to a close a period of turbulence. Almost any era can be described as a time of transition, but this particular period does, more than most, merit the label. On the surface, the politics of the reigns of William III (1689-1702) and Anne (1702-1714) appear as bewildering and bootless as those of the previous quarter-century. Ministries come and go; parties prosper, seem to triumph, but soon suffer defeats, which in turn are only temporary. The fluctuations of faction in the 1660's, 1670's and 1680's had little lasting effect on English politics. The leaders of the quarter-century following the Glorious Revolution, however, did take important steps toward a solution of the two most pressing problems that confronted the late seventeenth century. These were the questions left unresolved by the Civil War and the 1689 settlement: what would be the relationship between king and Commons, and what was the role of parties in political life? The politicians of the late seventeenth and early eighteenth centuries often seem to have stumbled unwittingly on the answers, but they did achieve a viable form of government which was sustained—with a minimum of tension and difficulty—through the reigns of the first two Georges. William III and Marlborough were turning back the armies of Louis XIV and laying the foundations for English leadership in Europe, while at home the politicians—unimpressive as they were as individual leaders—somehow managed among themselves to shape a stable framework of government out of the petty party strife that is characteristic of the early eighteenth-century political world.

The politicians of the 1690's finally solved the financial problem that had bedeviled the English monarchy ever since Edward I. Since Elizabeth it had been the most insidious hazard of the English government, and it had inflamed the constitutional crises of the seventeenth century, and persisted even into the early years of William III's reign. The old constitutional principle, that to the king belonged the government and to his subjects belonged property, had been made irrelevant by the requirements of the modern state, but it also seemed impossible to reconcile both sides of the theory. The solution, when it finally came about, was absurdly simple and obvious. Instead of the Commons keeping the money while the king kept the government, they made a trade. The king could have his money if Parliament approved what he did with it. William III was not happy about this, but he badly wanted to fight Louis XIV and he chose not to quibble. William did not have much sense of the sovereignty of Parliament, and in the first years of his reign his relations with it were not very amicable. Still, his main interest was in foreign affairs and, slowly and reluctantly, he had to give way. Thus the seventeenth-century deadlock was broken. The House of Commons had demanded to know where the Stuarts were spending the money granted to them, and the Stuarts had refused to say. William was willing to make concessions, and he let the Commons scrutinize expenses. At the same time the development of public credit made the financial operations of government smoother and more rational. The whole system of the public debt was developed pragmatically. The government, which needed money to go to war, found it expedient to borrow through the Bank of England, and gradually this practice achieved a working relationship whereby the House of Commons and the government shared the control of royal finances.

The Commons in William III's reign became more realistic about the king's financial needs; instead of re-echoing the traditional parliamentary cry that the "king should live of his own," they agreed to tailor the king's revenue relative to his potential expenditure; it was recognized that he needed money to implement the policy of the government. For the first time the crown was given the power to borrow specific amounts against revenue to be provided by parliamentary taxation. In other words, it was made easier for the king to borrow because Parliament provided a guarantee for his loans. This is the beginning of the national debt. What had been the personal financial obligations of the king were now assumed by the state. The hazy line between the king's two bodies, that had caused so much constitutional controversy, was now redefined. The crown truly had become a public corporation.

If the need for the king and Commons to get together and cooperate on financial matters in order to provide supply for the military and naval forces committed against Louis XIV was a powerful motive for fiscal rationalization, then the improved banking techniques and new statistical and economic knowledge available in the country helped to work out the means of modernization. In the reign of William III, the king's ministers began to present the estimates of their departments' needs for the year to the Commons, and the M.P.'s, in Committee of Supply, considered, and frequently reduced these estimates. But the government obtained most of what it wanted in the way of supply for the year, and the Commons was able to find out, and by specific designation in tax bills, assign the purposes to which the funds granted were to be put. In the second year of George I's reign (1715) another important step was taken in the management of crown revenue: if actual revenue available to the crown for the year turned out to fall short of the sum Parliament had estimated, the M.P.'s agreed to a supplementary appropriation.

Thus the old squabbles about the king's revenue are eliminated, and the chronic friction gives way to a relatively harmonious balance in which control over public expenditure is vested jointly in the king and the House of Commons. Because the Commons now has partial control over the king's revenue and because an increased proportion of the king's revenue comes via parliamentary grant, the period 1688-1714 shows a greater distinction than was ever before apparent between the king's private income and the crown's public revenue. And since the distinction was so clear, the area of conflict was virtually eliminated.

The other change was in the operation of the government itself. The "rise of the cabinet system" is an obscure but nevertheless fundamentally important development. Just precisely when it happened is hard to tell. The responsibility of the king's ministers to Parliament had been a critical question ever since the fourteenth century, but it was finally worked out—in a haphazard way—between the time of William III and George III. The cabinet system was the end product of a series of experiments whose course is difficult to chart with any accuracy, though too much dull history has been written with exactly this unedifying purpose in mind. We can tell how frustrating the problem is from the fact that not until the twentieth century does any statute actually mention the cabinet. Technically, the cabinet comprises a group of people within the privy council who hold ministries under the crown, but it is, of course, much more than this. In the seventeenth and eighteenth centuries it was an informal group of privy councillors who actually carried on the work of the government. They were Parliament men—from the Commons as well as the Lords—who made policy, secured the king's consent, and then put through the necessary legislation. Although the process is hard to delineate, it was not entirely subterranean—in the eighteenth century people knew changes were being made in the executive.

The men who formed the king's government were, at the same time, leaders of Parliament. The cabinet system depends on this elementary principle: the chief minister of the crown must also be the leader of Parliament—eventually he will have to be the leader of the House of Commons; he must be able to muster majority support in the House of Commons. (The trouble is that during much of the eighteenth century there was no cohesive majority party, and men groped their way to this principle only with a good deal of difficulty and hesitation.) In short, the king's ministers are leaders of the House of Commons as well as servants of the crown. Thus the classic friction between the executive and legislature was overcome by merging the two and eliminating the sensitive spot where the friction occurred. Bagehot, the nineteenth-century constitutional theorist, used the graphic image of a hinge between executive and legislature to describe how the cabinet functioned.

The problem was solved by a very narrow margin. For a long time there was great suspicion of the king's ministers in the House of Commons. They seemed to be dangerous; it was feared they would corrupt the members and compromise their independence. The original 1701 Act of Settlement, which legitimized the Hanoverian succession, stated that no one who held office under the crown could sit in Parliament. Had this gone into effect, the result would have been something like the American separation of powers. But a few years later the Commons had second thoughts—it seemed that when the officeholders were removed, leadership vanished too. So they decided that a minister could sit in the House, but that if an M.P. became a minister (or held an office) he would have to resign his seat and stand again for election. He had to go back to his electorate as an officeholder and stand again on that basis. This statute, the Place Act of 1707, is what makes the development of the cabinet system possible, though at the time there was not much farsighted constitutional theory involved. Rather, M.P.'s were exceedingly reluctant to give up their comfortable government sinecures. Nevertheless, this somewhat self-serving piece of legislation provides the key; it allows leadership to be exerted and it opens an avenue of communication between the king and the Commons. The cumbersome procedure they set forth actually worked fairly well. In the eighteenth century about fifteen percent of the members who took office and stood again were rejected, particularly in constituencies where the franchise was comparatively widespread. Thus men who were appointed to office—like Walpole—could sit in the House of Commons. There was also another effect. To stand for re-election was expensive and chancy—though the expense was usually more worrisome than the hazards of defeat—and hence ministries were staffed heavily from the peerage well into the nineteenth century. This was partly a natural reflection of the political power structure, but it was also an easy way to avoid the fuss and expense of a new election. To some extent, then, the Place Act did inhibit the role of the House of Commons.

Why did the politicians of the period abandon the separation between executive and legislature? Why was such a pivotal change made so rapidly and casually? They could see no other way to give cohesion to the House of Commons. Unless something was worked out, Parliament would disintegrate into squabbling factions; it would be constantly occupied in criticizing the executive, no government would be able to function, and any stability in government would be impossible. When we scoff at the dullness and sloth of Parliament in the eighteenth century, we should remember that stability was exactly what these politicians wanted, and that they had the great gift of being able to learn from past errors. They learned the lesson of the Stuarts who had not been able to lead the House of Commons. There was no reason why the eighteenth-century House of Commons would be any better. For three decades after the Glorious Revolution government remained shaky and unsure while factions fought among themselves. Since 1688 men had been tremendously stirred up over a few important issues; they expressed their concern in bitter debate, and they also indulged in extreme forms of action. The issues were not trivial. Questions of religious toleration and the real power of the monarchy were still open and unsettled. There were agonizing decisions to be taken about war and peace. There were doves and hawks in early eighteenth-century England, and they fiercely debated whether England should commit all her resources to a struggle with the Dutch and French; or should she renounce her overseas ambitions and conserve what she had? Should there be high taxes or low expenditures? These involved other problems—what we would call questions of policy and priority. Should government policy be dictated by the interests of groups who favored war and did not recoil at high taxes? Whig aristocrats, urban merchants, and dissenters constituted an active war party. The country gentry who constituted the peace party hated dissenters even worse than Catholics, felt that foreign commitments were treacherous, and knew that the high land tax was nothing but a plot among generals, great lords, merchants and profiteers to make the upstanding gentry of England pay for their wicked foreign schemes. It was a time of volatile politics—Anne's reign was not at all placid.

By the 1720's the prime aim of the political nation was tranquillity. And they got it—the new executive system worked. The men who controlled the treasury also controlled Parliament; the leaders of the House of Commons held positions of legitimate authority and responsibility. Of course the king's ministers were always chosen from a small group of Whig aristocrats and their allies in the Commons. In some ways it was a perpetuation of the old "court and treasury" party—a nucleus of men dependent on the crown played a central role in the day-to-day proceedings of the House of Commons. Compared to the 1620's and 1640's, this is a very special and limited world, yet the system they evolved allowed them to enjoy a period of remarkable stability. And meanwhile the system itself, which had at first been a casual and practical solution to an immediate problem, was becoming an institution.

Still, we must be wary of what we mean by a "cabinet" in the eighteenth century. Certainly it reveals none of its modern characteristics before 1780. The most significant characteristics of the modern cabinet are its prime minister (one man who has overriding power) and the notion of collective responsibility. Cabinet members cannot speak against each other; they are theoretically unanimous, they express one opinion. It would not be true to say that none of these aspects was present in the eighteenth century, but none of them was very marked. There was a first minister—the First Lord of the Treasury, the chief dispenser of patronage—but he was not a prime minister (prime minister was a pejorative term which had connotations of French ministerial despotism), and he had nothing like dictatorial power. Though the prime minister in the nineteenth century will speak to the king for the whole cabinet, in the eighteenth century the king speaks individually to his ministers as it suits him, and often they give him conflicting advice. The formulation of policy was also much looser in the eighteenth century. It is often apparent that the government is too divided among itself to function and often it does split. The eighteenth-century cabinet was very much the king's government; the ministers were still his ministers, and the royal prerogative was still active in picking them. It was not that the royal prerogative itself was particularly strong, but party lines were so vague it was often hard to determine who the leader of the majority party might be. Four-fifths of the House of Commons were nominally Whigs (which only meant they were against having a Catholic on the throne), and they belonged to one of several aristocratic factions. The king needs only to give his confidence to one group of Whig aristocrats. Once a particular politician is favored, he usually need only gather up the scattered bits of power and distribute patronage from the royal treasury in order to emerge as leader of Parliament. The House of Commons had 534 seats, and to maintain its control any ministry needed 300 supporters. These were never very hard to obtain—about 100 M.P.'s (Walpole's cohorts) were dependent on the Newcastle family, and another 100 were beholden to the court and treasury, which distributed offices, pensions, and sinecures. The government had only to win over another 100 M.P.'s or, if they insisted on a solid majority, another 150. Since they needed these uncommitted M.P.'s, the Whigs tried to keep them happy by doing favors, and by following a policy whose main goals were the maintenance of peace and quiet security.

Beneath the political confusion and lethargy, there has been a fundamental change in government and a significant constitutional development. The financial crisis is solved, and the centuries-old split between executive and legislature was healed by a neat graft.

A subsidiary but still important aspect of the institutional framework of the Whig Supremacy was a change in the duration of Parliaments. The Triennial Act of 1694, which established three years as the maximum length of time that could elapse between Parliaments, was directed against royal schemes of nonparliamentary government. By 1694, however, intervals of as much as three years between summoning of Parliaments were no longer feasible. Beginning with William III, the king's reliance on the Commons for financial supply implied that he would have to summon Parliament every year, and issue writs for the summoning of a new Parliament as soon as the old one was dissolved.

At the same time, it also seemed desirable to prescribe the maximum life of a Parliament. This idea, which developed over the next twenty years, had far-reaching consequences. The political history of the two decades following the Triennial Act of 1694 demonstrated some unfortunate consequences, in the eyes of the M.P.'s, of a relatively short duration for Parliaments. Frequent general elections were expensive for the politicians and in addition worked against political stability by inflaming public debate on important issues. The Septennial Act of 1716 set seven years as the period within which a Parliament must be dissolved. The Septennial Act did not rule that every Parliament should last seven years, but only prescribed a maximum parliamentary duration before a new election had to be called. As Betty Kemp has shown in her excellent study, *King and Commons,* in practice the Act of 1716 was interpreted as if it had set down the normal duration of a Parliament: every Parliament summoned between 1716 and 1783, with the exception of the one dissolved, as was the custom, by the king's death in 1727, lasted for at least five and a half years, and all but two endured as long as six years. These long lives of eighteenth-century Parliaments tended to give the M.P.'s a sense of corporate identity that encouraged parliamentary independence of the king. The long duration of the Commons before new elections were held also contributed to the stability of Georgian ministries; it was the very same group of M.P.'s that the king's ministers had to placate and control for stretches as long as six years.

The Septennial Act, however, had another effect. It not only lessened the dependence of the Commons on the crown, but also the dependence of the M.P.'s on the people, on the electorate. To a Georgian Whig, the notion that M.P.'s ought to consult their constituents or follow their instructions seemed shocking and irresponsible. Such restrictions would represent an infringement on the Commons' independence no less dangerous than interference by the king. An eighteeth-century political textbook, quoted by Miss Kemp, defines the commonly held idea of representation: "Although every Member of the Commons' House be chosen to serve for one particular county, city, or borough, yet he serves for the whole Kingdom. . . . [He has] power absolute to consent or dissent without ever acquainting those that sent him, or demanding their assent." Just as the Septennial Act greatly lessened royal interference with the Commons, so it also lessened popular control of the Commons. Once the members were elected they formed a sort of exclusive club which looked upon meddling from either king or electorate with equal scorn. No on could touch them for the seven years that Parliament lasted. Thus the eighteenth-century political stability was founded upon a constitutional arrangement which inhibited, as far as possible, popular as well as royal control over the decisions and proceedings of the elected M.P.'s.

There would come a time when this system would be criticized, but in the 1730's the Whig political leaders considered it the essence of wisdom. For they believed no more in democracy than in absolutism; what they aimed at was benevolent oligarchy. By and large it was rule by an enlightened aristocracy which used its grip on royal government not merely to further particular family interests; they also governed with an eye to the welfare of the mercantile class, and they turned their energies to further the military and imperial power of the nation. The Whig leaders had all been exposed to a classical education, and they readily identified the Georgian political system with Aristotle's ideal of "mixed government," a belief which was only reinforced when they read Montesquieu. Walpole defended the anti-democratic implications of the Septennial Act on the grounds that it was the great safeguard of mixed government. There "the monarchical, aristocratical and democratical forms of government are mixed and interwoven . . . so as to give us all the advantages of each, without subjecting us to the inconveniences of either." The constitution had at times been in danger "of running too much into that form of government which is properly called democratical." Parliaments of short duration are "as wavering and unsteady as the people usually are, [and] by such frequent elections there would be so much power thrown into the hands of the people, as would destroy the equal mixture, which is the beauty of our constitution. . . . Therefore, in order to preserve our constitution, in order to preserve [us from] our falling under tyranny and arbitrary power, we ought to preserve that law [the Septennial Act] which I really think brought our constitution to a more real mixture, and consequently to a greater perfection than it was ever in before that law took place." Walpole's constitutional views, as quoted by Miss Kemp, show that the Whig leaders were not hypocritical; they never pretended to subscribe to the notion that government should be responsible to the people.

The nature of political parties in the late seventeenth century and early eighteenth century has been a difficult and controversial issue among historians. In a brilliant essay published in the 1920's, G. M. Trevelyan claimed that "the party bond" greatly facilitated the emergence of the cabinet as a political institution. In his view, achievements of royal ministries in the later Stuart and early Georgian eras was due to the cohesiveness and unity imposed by party loyalty. Ministers committed to the Whig or Tory parties tended to join in a political union; thus they were able to form the cooperative group that was later to be given the institutional label of cabinet.

Trevelyan argued that "the habit of cooperation had to be very strong to counteract the selfishness and want of principle that characterized statesmen in the time of the later Stuarts." Ministers who had previously intrigued against each other were now brought into line by the party bonds. Trevelyan concludes that the great accomplishments of royal ministries in the last decade of the seventeenth century and the first two decades of the eighteenth owe much to party politics. The winning of the war against French expansionism under Anne, the 1707 union with Scotland, the diplomatic triumph of the Peace of Utrecht in 1713 that ended the long French War, and the viability of the Hanoverian Protestant succession in 1714 (which Trevelyan sees as fundamental to eighteenth-century prosperity and stability) are all the fruits of the growth of cabinet government, which, in turn, depended on party cohesiveness.

Trevelyan's synopsis of the political history of the 1689-1714 period has all his characteristic brilliance, but the work of Namier and his many disciples has shown how Trevelyan's view is vitiated by the too facile assumption that there was a real "party bond" at all. "Tory" and "Whig" are merely labels to cover certain social groupings, ideological leanings, and (perhaps most important of all) family factions. These bonds could usually instill a cohesion that led to the formation of ministries but was insufficient to ensure any long-term stability. From 1689 to the early 1720's no ministry was able to hold office for long precisely because loyalty to party took second place to individual—and often eccentric—political ideology or to the bitter and confused struggle for power among family factions. Still, from 1688 to 1714 parties—although they were little more than unstable fusion groups—were very important. They really did stand for something, they took sides on the crucial issues of the day. It is true that they represented factions of the landed class who were fighting among themselves for control of the government, but they also represented ideological positions. From the 1720's until the 1760's ideological issues, however, were not important in parliamentary life. They existed, but in an exceedingly muted fashion, although because they were sublimated and suppressed by the deceptive Georgian stability, we must not assume that they vanished altogether.

During the reign of Anne (1702-1714), the Tory party had a natural and substantial majority in the House of Commons. Fervent Anglicanism and innate conservatism—as well as jealousy of the Whig aristocracy —predisposed all but the most wealthy and prominent gentry to the Tory cause. Yet after 1714 the party disintegrated and drifted aimlessly in the political wilderness for the next half-century. There were two reasons for this collapse: the Tories lacked able and sensible leadership (the brilliant, but fanatical and unstable Lord Bolingbroke is just one example), and their inability to accept the Hanoverian succession shattered the unity of the party and turned the Tories into political outcasts.

A group of disgruntled M.P.'s comprising no more than twenty percent of the House of Commons was all that survived of this once-powerful group. From 1720 to 1760 there were about one hundred independent Tory gentry—back-benchers all—who were uncompromisingly opposed to war, taxes, and corruption in government. As a group they were too small and disorganized to be of much importance. They had no leadership, they were limited men, they had little wealth and not much native intelligence or political instinct. But they were forthright, honest, and goodhearted. Addison's Sir Roger de Coverley is the prototype of the Tory country squire. His most profound statements about politics are reflections "on the mischief that parties do in the country; how they spoil good neighbourhood, and make honest gentlemen hate one another; besides that they manifestly tend to the prejudice of the land tax, and the destruction of the game." The type does not change much during the eighteenth century. Their complaints were often true and always sincere. But they could never secure power, they never were able to take over and clean up the mess. All they could do was sit for their counties and complain. They made snide remarks, and sang ditties about Walpole and the Robinocracy, and sighed about what England was coming to, but that was all.

During the reigns of William III and Anne, the Whigs did not seem to be much more stable than the Tories. Their leaders had still not learned moderation; there was still a tendency to rely on Shaftesbury's tactics of extremism, and propaganda could backfire. In 1710 the Whig junto initiated a needless prosecution of a Jacobite clergyman named Sacheverell which only aroused popular resentment and brought down the ministry. Then, too, it was hard to prevent the aristocrats who were Whig leaders from quarreling among themselves. After two or three years in power the party tended to divide into various factions or groups. This had been true in Queen Anne's reign; it was true in the early years of George I's reign. After 1714 there was again a Whig ministry in power, though it consisted of two unfriendly factions. One was led by members of the old junto of the previous reign; the other by a Whig opposition group to which the Duke of Newcastle and his Pelham family supplied votes and money, while the intelligence came from a country gentleman and former junior minister, Robert Walpole. For a half-dozen years the Whig party was torn by the struggle between the two groups, until the Walpole-Pelham faction won out (partly because of the timely death of Walpole's rival, Sunderland). Walpole skillfully manipulated treasury patronage and proceeded to put together a combination of men from the old court party with the Whigs; he even secured some support from the gentry who had belonged to the old country party and were now back-benchers. This formidable combination kept Walpole in power for twenty years, and his allies, the Pelhams, continued to dominate the cabinet until 1760.

As leader of the House of Commons, of the Whig party, and as first minister of the crown, Walpole found his task made easier by the fact that in George I he had to contend with a rather slow-witted monarch who never learned to speak English well and whose time and energy were considerably taken up by the affairs of his native Hanoverian principality. But George was no cipher; Walpole had to justify his policy and retain the king's good will in order to hold onto the office of first lord of the treasury. And it was his judicious distribution of treasury patronage that allowed him to control the House of Commons. A constant stream of promises, jobs, favors, and sinecures secured the loyalty to the Pelham faction of Whig M.P.'s who were otherwise uncommitted. At least 25 percent of the members of the House were kept happy (or at least quiet) by their allotment of the patronage. The Walpole-Pelham Whigs were hard workers and some of them were very talented men indeed. They chose, however, to devote their energies mainly to one end—staying in office—and in this they were amazingly successful. They were so capable at manipulating an awkward and ramshackle system of government that they gave England a forty-year period of stability it had not known since the reign of Elizabeth I. It was a stability that contributed significantly to prosperity at home and imperial glory abroad. But it also demanded a certain price.

These men used their power mostly in a negative way. Walpole's favorite maxim, which he usually observed, was to "let sleeping dogs lie." Important problems were left untouched; even the most obvious question of removing the political disabilities of the Whigs' nonconformist allies was ignored. The more complex problems of colonial and economic planning were easy to overlook, but the question of what should be the government's role in social welfare and the political life of the great majority of its population was, by and large, also disregarded. There were some small efforts but, like the Gin Act of 1736, they were usually a response to a desperate situation. It can be argued, however, that the government had little choice, that any real attempts at reform —or even aggressive administration—were dangerous. In 1733 Walpole tried to rationalize the tax structure by introducing an excise bill; the reaction in London was so hostile, and revealed political sentiments of such explosive potential, that it would have been foolhardy to do anything but back away. Apparently peace and stability were the main things men wanted in the first part of the eighteenth century, and Walpole was able to satisfy them. He was able to boast, while the European powers were fighting the war of the Polish Succession, that there were "50,000 men killed in Europe this year, and not one British." Nor should it be overlooked that, in spite of their limited program, the long and sluggish reign of the Whigs allowed the salutary institutional changes made early in the eighteenth century to become entrenched in English political life. Thus the Whig rulers, in a haphazard and unplanned way, did profoundly affect the shape and style of the modern British constitution.

Visiting *philosophes* from France found it difficult to comprehend two of the most important aspects of English life in the reigns of George I (1714-1727) and George II (1727-1760)—politics and religion. The working of the parliamentary system and the peculiar nature of religious commitment in England was bewildering to men who believed human activities could be analyzed according to rational categories. Montesquieu was convinced that the most distinctive—and laudable—quality of English government was a very clear separation between executive and legislature, even though the cabinet system, ill-defined as it was in the early eighteenth century, had put an end to the separation of powers long before Montesquieu wrote. What astonished enlightened continental observers about English religion was its diversity. Hence Voltaire's famous remark that England was a country of a hundred religions and only one sauce.

For several hundred years, English political life had been gravitating toward the center, a tendency aided by geography and the centralizing work of royal government. By the eighteenth century it was clear that the heart of all English politics was Parliament and that the only way to participate in the mainstream of political life was to be a member of Parliament. Except for peers, the only way to get into Parliament was to stand for election to the House of Commons. In many instances, of course, this was merely a formality. Still, a seat in the Commons was the sole avenue to success in political life. "You will be of the House of

Commons as soon as you are of age," writes Lord Chesterfield to his son in 1749, "and you must first make a figure there if you would make a figure in your country." An admiral comments in 1780 that "to be out of Parliament is to be out of the world." Parliament was the world; for the small group of Englishmen who constituted the educated elite it represented their whole way of life. A seat in Parliament was the way to serve the country, and it was also the stepping stone to high political office and even private fortune. And for most of the men who sought to rise in this world, a seat was fairly accessible. In that very tightly knit society it was not difficult, if one persevered, to get into Parliament sooner or later. The number of people who actually voted was tiny, and the percentage of elections that were—according to our standards—truly contested, seems minute. A comparatively large number of seats were controlled absolutely by a wide range of individuals, from the king himself, to wholesale borough-mongers like the Duke of Newcastle, down to the men for whom politics was a hobby and who might be proprietors of one or two seats, just as they would keep a racehorse or two. And even without political connections or influence, of course, a seat was always available for hard cash. Namier, who knew more about the workings of Parliament in the eighteenth century than anyone has before or is likely to henceforth, has concluded that of all the men who really wanted a seat in Parliament, only a very few ultimately failed to get their heart's desire.

What kind of men occupied most of these seats; who were the people to use Parliament as a ladder leading to political power? We may consider George Bubb Dodington as typical of the middle range of Parliament man under the first two Georges. John Carswell's study of Dodington in *The Old Cause* is detailed and perceptive, and Dodington's political diary, which has been published recently, imparts a very palpable sense of the nature of political life in the mid-eighteenth century. Dodington's contemporaries thought of him as typical of a certain kind of parliamentary animal, and Hogarth chose him as the model for his mordant drawing, "Chairing the Member." Here the M.P. has a grossly corpulent body and an appropriately unattractive, unthinking face, and it would be easy to make Dodington symbolize all the fabled corruption and shoddiness of Georgian politics, to forget that Hogarth's fat, well-greased figure is, after all, a caricature and therefore an extreme view. For perhaps the most surprising quality to be gleaned from Dodington's diary is his own lack of extremism of any kind.

He is, certainly, not much of an idealist, but there are limits to his corruption. He is not wicked, though he is ambitious, and he is fairly bright. He is moderately rich, and moderately happy with his lot in the world. He is even moderately liberal—at one point he makes a moderately rousing speech against the extension of military law—and very moderately religious. (The day he loses an election he actually attends church twice, though it is not very clear if he goes to pray or to be seen.) He is fairly well connected, somewhat shrewd, and very conscientious at tending to his interests, yet he somehow never rises very far in the political world which is the only world he contemplates. Dodington devotes his life to the business of politics; he dashes back and forth between the country and the city, although he suffers from toothache and gout. He circulates through the parliamentary corridors, now conferring with Newcastle, now pleading with Walpole, now doing his best to disarm the Princess of Wales. His interests are not purely selfish; we see him looking after his friends, securing posts for his supporters, livings for his clergyman. After a disastrous fire, he obtains a grant of a market town for the people in his constituency; he begs pardons for criminals sentenced to transportation. For Dodington, politics is a business—and, like any businessman anxious for a great coup, he speculates—speculates and loses. Walpole does not seem to like him, and thus the prospect of the high office for which Dodington yearns seems to recede. Like many of his contemporaries, he proceeds to speculate in futures; the Prince of Wales is at odds with George II, and Dodington, planning for the day when the prince becomes king, identifies himself with the faction that supports the prince. Among this group, he seems to have some stature, but then the prince dies before his father, and Dodington, who is no longer a young man, loses his political future. He never becomes a great minister, but remains a rank-and-file party member, destined for immortality only because he is caricatured by Hogarth.

English political life in the first half of the eighteenth century is often paradoxical and confusing. There are many motives that send men into politics, and their methods are equally diverse. Walpole uses politics as the gateway to wealth and aristocratic life; Newcastle, the aristocratic borough-monger, borrows the means of the market place to keep the Whigs in power; Dodington, the political hack, just wants to make a small place for himself, and his approach is one that we would not be surprised to find in any area of life. The institutions and varied practices of the period form a sloppy and amoral system that men at the end of the century would find disgusting. Yet the first two Georges ruled during a period of steadily increasing prosperity and expanding empire. Perhaps it really is true that—at least for certain eras in a nation's history—that government is best which governs least, and it is quite clear that if the ramshackle government of the eighteenth century did little to aid the country's growth, it also did little to impede it.

One thing we can say with certainty; however we may disdain it, the political style was congenial to the men who counted. The small group of men who constituted the political nation found that the system satisfied their needs and, compared to the tensions of the seventeenth century, perhaps the very blandness of political life was itself salutary. The system of politics mirrored the social structure, and most men were not at odds with either. Together they presented tremendous opportunities —if not for dazzling ascents to power like Thomas and Oliver Cromwell's—at least for personal fulfillment and moderate achievement. Through Parliament, men could share the profits of power; they had an adequate share in deciding the course of the nation. Eighteenth-century politicians have been berated for sinking happily into their environment, like pigs at the trough, but these men were completely at ease with their society, and perhaps it would be demanding too much of human nature to expect them to criticize rather than enjoy their way of life. We should not be surprised to find that the typical M.P. in the reign of George II considered the English political system of his day the greatest achievement of political wisdom which mankind had ever known. Nor should we wonder that the legal scholar William Blackstone, who began writing his monumental paean to the common law in the 1750's, was able to perceive and describe an inner rationality behind the confused facade of English institutions.

The style of Georgian politics was perfectly congruent with the style of life known as Whiggery, although Whiggery encompasses much more than politics and government. Whiggery is a complete way of life, which was practiced in its purest form by two dozen or so aristocratic families of enormous wealth and influence. As a style, it flourished even in the changed milieu of nineteenth-century industrial society, nor did it entirely disappear even in the twentieth century. It was personified by Winston Churchill, and the prime minister in the latter years of the 1950's, Harold Macmillan, was the son-in-law of a duke whose ancestors were prominent members of the eighteenth-century oligarchy.

The most perceptive description of the nature of Whiggery is to be found in the first pages of Lord David Cecil's biography of the early nineteenth-century statesman Lord Melbourne. Cecil, an Oxford scholar who himself bears an illustrious aristocratic name, calls the Whig nobility "a unique product of English civilization," for there is nothing quite like them on the continent. The Whigs poured all their energies into perfecting their style of life. The right way to live meant an Eton and Oxford education (where the curriculum, such as it was, consisted almost exclusively of the classics), the grand tour (from which they returned with a smattering of French culture and an appreciation of Italian art), two or three great country houses, a London town house, vast retinues of servants, and amazing quantities of food and wine. They were men who prided themselves on their sense and taste, which meant they cultivated elegance, but had no desire to pursue any radically new forms of art or literature. They sported a healthy earthiness in sexual relations, were not disturbed by promiscuity, and yet accepted the formal teachings of the Church of England and the centuries-old Christian doctrines of hierarchy and ethics. Unlike their counterparts in France, the Whig aristocrats never became courtiers, nor was their life urbanized. They sank their roots into the soil of rural England, spent at least half the year on their country estates and, if they did come to London for the season, it was mainly to enjoy one another's company—not to fawn before the king. Some of the Whigs had hated the Stuarts, but for the Hanoverians they had only scorn and contempt. They were able to use government in their own interests. Certainly they never had anything to fear from the crown, and so the king was simply a necessary but rather inconsequential personage whom they could largely ignore.

The Whigs were intensely involved in government, and in a sense did consider themselves public servants—though very exalted ones indeed. The Whig aristocracy loved politics, but they had no taste for the day-to-day work of bureaucratic administration. They were eager to be leaders of the nation, makers of public policy, organizers of parliamentary parties, diplomats and ambassadors. They saw themselves as Roman proconsuls and delighted in the high style of political life. The tedious, diurnal tasks of administration seemed to them not only boring but beneath the dignity of their social order. Perhaps this attitude helps to explain why, in the end, the Whigs contributed so little to genuine social reform: they had no taste for the details of public administration; they were only capable of the grand gesture, the high political style, that government leaders are privileged to enjoy as long as they avoid the mean problems that affect the daily lives of ordinary people. Similarly, the Whig aristocracy had no taste for critical and original political theorizing. They were well satisfied with the general principles that went under the rubric of "liberty and property." In practical terms, this meant that royal despotism and democracy were equally bad, and a threat to their way of life. They sneered at the royal family and they feared the mob.

The early Hanoverian period left a dual legacy to the new industrial society of the late eighteenth and early nineteenth centuries. One side was the entrenchment of aristocratic leadership in political life and the habit of deference to benevolent oligarchy. Another side was the Anglican church and the peculiar religious settlement that had been worked out during the hundred years between the Restoration of 1660 and the accession of George III.

The Restoration church settlement, for better or worse, marks a decisive turning point in the religious history of modern England. In 1660 there was still a chance to reconstruct a national church that would fulfill the Elizabethan ideal of "comprehension." Such a church would not impose rigid standards of belief or behavior; uniformity and homogeneity would have to take second place before diversity and moderation. This was the kind of church that Elizabeth sought—from personal preference as well as political astuteness; Richard Hooker had glowingly described its virtues, and in 1660 a substantial number of men sincerely desired to establish a comprehensive church. For a while it looked as though it might be possible. A few changes in the Book of Common Prayer, and some adjustments in the institution of episcopacy and the role of bishops in church life could have served to unite Presbyterians and Episcopalians in one church. Independents, Baptists, and Quakers —who could not accept either Prayer Book or bishops on any terms— would, of course, still be excluded, but the reabsorption of the Presbyterians, who were strongly represented among the urban commercial classes, would lend a tremendous new strength to the Church of England. A church which comprised Anglicans and Presbyterians might have been powerful enough to force the radical sects out of existence—and thus the Elizabethan standard would eventually be attained.

But a very different solution to the religious problem was adopted. The religious decision was legally ratified by the cluster of statutes known as the "Clarendon Code" and by the amending Toleration Act of 1689. Between 1662 and 1689, as Norman Sykes has pointed out, the English religious tradition was severed. The Restoration period was a real parting of the ways. "We do declare a liberty to tender consciences," Charles II had said in 1660, but the bishops managed to outwit the Presbyterians, and the legislation that implemented the royal promise—the Act of Uniformity of 1662—was actually very tough. It was, however, a near thing; Parliament wrote into law all the suggestions put before it by convocation, but the majority in favor of the Act was a very small one. The Act of Uniformity effectively drove the Presbyterians outside the church and, since dissenters could not hold any office of the crown, kept them outside the political establishment as well. In 1662 almost two thousand out of about ten thousand parish clergy resigned their livings. They were ministers that the church—desperately short of educated and zealous men—could ill afford to lose. Considered merely from a practical point of view, the religious legislation of the early 1660's was unwise. The Anglican church did, of course, have the support of the majority of the people, but a strong and impassioned minority, particularly in the urban areas, remained outside the church. Since all were excluded, the Presbyterians now made common cause with the Independents and Baptists—an alliance that could only have come about through practical necessity. The Anglican church was still the national church—but at a price. The church suffered the loss of some of the most intelligent and industrious men of future generations; that this was a real deprivation becomes painfully apparent when we think of the mediocre talents of many eighteenth-century bishops.

The church settlement had a profound effect on the political and social life of modern England. The Toleration Act of 1689, which allowed dissenters to practice their religion, did not give them full political rights. They could not hold public office (in the case of municipal office, however, this law was often evaded), and they could not send their sons to Oxford and Cambridge. Dissenters could assume public office by practicing "occasional conformity," which meant taking the sacraments once or twice a year in the Anglican church in order to fulfill the letter of the law. But they were effectively excluded from playing an important role in national political life. The dissenters responded to their exclusion from the universities by developing their own schools, the dissenting academies. These, in fact, were far better than the old universities; they were the first to be aware of the new scientific achievements, and the first to teach history and economics. Although the dissenters actually had access to a much more modern and useful education than the Anglicans, their educational separation only increased the social distance between the

Anglican elite and even the wealthiest dissenters. Discriminated against in politics, separate in education, the dissenters were, in a real sense, segregated. They could not help but feel cut off and isolated. Down to the middle of the nineteenth century, when they finally achieved full rights, and even beyond, there was a deep social and intellectual gap between dissenters and Anglicans, a division that, since it outlived their theological and ecclesiastical differences, was far more difficult to bridge. Thus, along with the idea of toleration, the Restoration settlement also bequeathed to English society a long-term split between the Anglican majority and intelligent, well-educated, and extremely prosperous dissenting minority.

Of course the Restoration church settlement cut both ways. A great number of Presbyterians gave up the fight and accepted the Church of England, a process that also continued well into the nineteenth century. And though it would be hard to define what contribution the dissenters made to the Church of England, this is a fascinating problem of religious sociology—one that has not yet been properly studied. John Wesley's parents, for instance, grew up as non-conformists, but later changed their minds. His father had attended dissenting academies, and then Oxford. Thus Wesley was born, and always remained, a devoted Anglican.

Another remarkable change—and perhaps this is the most important ecclesiastical development in the first half of the eighteenth century—was the conversion of the Whigs from being the friends of dissenters to staunch supporters of the position of the established church. After all, the Whigs *were* the establishment and, because they appropriated the key roles in Parliament and politics, they absorbed to themselves the power and function of the national church. The church, like every other institution in eighteenth-century England, was pervaded by Whiggery. Indeed, even the theology of the Anglican church was congenial to the Whig style of thought. The intellectual revolution that was taking place in the latter decades of the seventeenth century is summed up by John Locke in his *Essay Concerning Human Understanding*. If we can believe in scientific laws, says Locke, we can believe in God. "It is plain to me we have a more certain knowledge of the existence of a God, than of anything our senses have not immediately discovered to us. Nay, I presume to say, that we more certainly know there is a God than there is anything else without us." Religious belief was now founded on rational science, and the laws of nature instead of revelation. This kind of religion was, therefore, called natural or rational religion, and its deity was the watchmaker God of the Newtonian natural order. Thus, by the second quarter of the eighteenth century, the Anglican church preaches a reasonable, optimistic religion which frowns equally on all forms of enthusiasm, self-sacrifice, and mystery. This religion was moderate and tolerant in attitude, but narrow in scope, and oblivious to human potentiality for both saintliness and depravity. It was an age of what the churchmen called practical Christianity; charity took precedence over theology, and comfort over self-examination and guilt. This social gospel is described perfectly in Pope's crystalline verse:

> For modes of faith let graceless zealots fight,
> His can't be wrong whose life is in the right.
> In Faith and Hope the world will disagree
> But all mankind's concern is charity.
> All must be false that thwart this one great end,
> And all of God that bless mankind or mend.

The Hanoverian church did not encourage a preoccupation with sin. The favorite text of eighteenth-century Anglican churchmen, from archbishop down to parish priests, was "And His commandments are not grievous." God's standards were not difficult or unrealistic. "The laws of God are reasonable," Tillotson said in his famous sermon, "that is, suited to our nature and advantageous to our interest." The advice to "depart from evil" was seen "to express the whole duty of man" and, Sykes tells us, the new religious temper was symbolized in the favorite eighteenth-century church decoration—whitewash—which was taken to stand for the light of reason, while it was cheap and clean at the same time.

We must not think that this attitude was cynical, or that it was designed as a subterfuge for laxity. It was not fanatical; it was eminently humane, though uninspiring, and it was well suited to most men, who did not want to be bothered by problems of religion. There is an upsurge of charitable endeavor in the eighteenth century and thus, in an age when the state did not regard it as a duty to provide for social welfare, practical Christianity did serve social needs. By the middle of the century, however, it was evident that this undemanding, easy-going Christianity—when judged by traditional religious standards, and even social needs—was not a complete success. The Church of England was very much on the defensive. Intelligent deists had launched an attack on the basic dogmas of Christianity—an attack which the church was unable to refute effectively. The church had also failed in its task of communicating religion to the mass of the people. To the farmer or artisan, Sykes concludes, the church was only an institution, not the visible expression of the Holy Spirit whose teachings were supposed to be the motivation of his thought and action. There appeared to be no distinction between clergy and laity. The church was rapidly losing its hold on society. No longer did it provide leadership or offer the kind of teaching that could inform men's lives. It was becoming an ossified institution, the propagator of comfortable platitudes designed to maintain the status quo and serve the interests of the ruling class. It is no wonder that so many nineteenth-century churchmen looked back at their eighteenth-century predecessors with disdain and contempt.

The decay of the Anglican church becomes all the more evident during the eighteenth century as the church proves itself unable to adjust to the needs of a new industrial society, though it is only fair to point out that the Industrial Revolution was a bewildering phenomenon to almost everyone at the time. For many decades the church, as well as other traditional institutions, failed to recognize the existence of the new England. The church, for instance, did nothing to adjust its parish system to serve the mushrooming cities, and thus the greater part of the industrial proletariat remained in effect heathens—much to the shock and outrage of the mid-Victorians who noticed this. This was not entirely the fault of the churchmen. For the Church of England, as it was the state church, suffered from all the problems of the state, and one of the main problems was legal decrepitude and governmental sloth. While the Methodists could respond to population shifts by building meeting houses wherever they liked, an act of Parliament was required to create a new parish within the Church of England.

The backwardness of the Anglican church was reinforced by intellectual as well as institutional factors. The rational, easygoing theology of the early eighteenth century was, later in the century, doing nothing but harm to the church. We tend to applaud latitudinarianism and the absence of fervor and fanaticism, but it is easy to forget that latitude too often means simply the path of least resistance, and there is no question but that the eighteenth-century church was quick to identify itself with the prevailing political and social order. The Anglican church of the eighteenth century had lost its self-consciousness and its sense of mission.

Just as Parliament was the world, the church was society. Instead of leading it, the church had become absorbed by society, and now conformed to the attitudes and interests of the landed class. The alliance between church and ruling elite was complete, and in fact it was hard to tell where the one left off and the other began. There were, of course, bishops of learning and ability in the eighteenth century, but they achieved their positions, even if they had these qualities, through their social and political connections. Birth, party, and political service, just as they smoothed the road to high administrative posts, also paved the way to high ecclesiastical office. Everyone recognized this, and Dr. Johnson's comment is not untypical: "No man can now be made a bishop for his learning and piety, his only chance of promotion is his being connected with somebody who has parliamentary interests." An eighteenth-century bishop frankly remarked, "I happened to please a party and they made me a bishop." The Duke of Newcastle, who could dispense vast church patronage, was thus a great ecclesiastical minister.

The Whig slogan "liberty and property" was also applied to the church, where it meant the enjoyment of the property attached to church offices (which was often large and lucrative) rather than any devotion to the duties of office. A church living was property; legally it was exactly the same as a freehold. As livings were held by tenants, they were also owned by landlords. None of this seemed to have much relation to religion and, in fact, Geoffrey Best has estimated that the patrons of over half the benefices in England were laymen. The aristocracy and the wealthier gentry were quick to obtain church livings for their younger sons —if not a bishopric, then a cathedral place, or at least a country vicarage. This represents a social change of some significance. In the seventeenth century the social position of the clergy had not been at all high; the church was not an attractive career for a member of the gentry class. In the eighteenth century the church is one of the few careers approved for gentlemen and, along with the posts in the army, the best church livings and sinecures are appropriated for the sons of the gentry. But between the best and the rest was a vast difference. Although the income of a bishop might allow him to live like a great lord, the parish clergy who were expected to do all the boring work were pitifully underpaid. There were about six thousand appointments worth less than fifty pounds per year.

The absorption of the church into the social structure was not intrinsically bad. The same thing happened to Parliament, yet the governments of Walpole and Newcastle, shot through with jobbery and corruption, led England to new greatness. But by this pragmatic test, the church was deficient. For its duties were seldom carried out by the landed class who appropriated its offices. Offices were often held in plurality, while the hard work of the parish priest, who brought to the great majority of the people the only religion they ever knew, was usually left to the underpaid, poverty-stricken, half-educated curate. Of course there were exceptions, but they were usually so rare that they called for special notice, like the worthy incumbent who served his small Derbyshire parish—with a small stipend—for more than thirty years, and when offered preferment wrote to his benefactor that "as . . . I am always at hand to perform divine offices, and to teach my little flock, by my constant example as well as doctrine, I may hope that God will accept of this discharge of duty from me. The general good of the Church is the principle by which every Clergyman ought to direct himself; and to enter upon a remote Benefice, advancing in years and less active in life, a Cure on which perhaps I should not chuse to reside long, would shew more of the lucrative mind than the Pastoral care, and therefore I think I ought to disclaim it." Absenteeism, pluralism, ambition, and general slackness were a more common story.

The decline of the great universities went hand in hand with the feebleness of the church. Oxford and Cambridge were ecclesiastical institutions which required religious tests for admission. In the first half of the century the appointment of dons (who were often chaplains or other dependents of great aristocrats) was more and more subject to government pressure. It is not surprising, therefore, that only one outstanding English scholar of the early eighteenth century held a university post and that he—the Greek scholar Richard Bentley—spent his career feuding with the other dons of his college. Nearly all the dons occupied themselves with petty politics and heavy drinking. The universities were nothing but playgrounds. The curriculum was sterile, the teaching virtually nonexistent; the students—as that disgruntled alumnus, Edward Gibbon, tells us in his autobiography—were left entirely free to drink and riot.

In religion and higher education the Whig supremacy shows its darkest side. There is no inherent reason that churchmen or professors appointed because of family or political connections should not fulfill the duties of office. It is not possible to explain the failure of the Hanoverian church on the grounds that the bishops were appointed by the government. By and large this was how it was done ever since the eleventh century. And it is probable that the abuses in the church, such as absenteeism, were no worse in the eighteenth century than they had been in the fifteenth. Still, a leading place in the medieval, Tudor, and early Stuart churches had been assumed by well-educated, zealous men who had a strong sense of mission and an abiding consciousness of the church's distinctive role in society. The permeation of every aspect of life by the Whig ethos helped to undermine the church; for the great Whig aristocrats who set the style were indifferent to religion. Religion was not something they needed, and it never occurred to them that there were deep religious demands in the nation that were going unanswered. Thus the dilapidated Anglican church will be ill prepared to cope with the problems of the new industrial society that was emerging after 1760.

England in 1760 exhibits all the qualities identified with the "old regime" of pre-industrial Europe. Government is dominated by an hereditary aristocracy which uses it as a vehicle to maintain the social order; institutions of church and education also are harnessed to support the status quo and at the same time serve the family interests of the ruling elite. A conservative social doctrine is cloaked in the language of philosophic and scientific rationalism; the ramshackle, haphazard institutions of government and society are accepted as part of the rational order of the universe, and the sanction of reason is used to perpetuate traditional privilege. But at its moment of greatest triumph and unchallenged serenity, the old regime fails to notice that outside the narrow centers of power, great economic and intellectual movements are taking place. In the later part of the eighteenth century they will shake the framework of the old order to its foundations. In 1760 the English political nation is still basking in the Indian summer of the Whig supremacy, unaware of the coming upheavals and conflicts that will announce the dawn of the industrial and democratic era.

SELECT
BIBLIOGRAPHY

Works marked with an asterisk (*) are *historical classics*.

For *collected source material*, see Douglas, D. C., ed., *English Historical Documents*, New York: Oxford University Press, 1953 — (in progress, several volumes).

A convenient one-volume collection of *sources* is Stephenson, Carl, and Marcham, Frederick G., *Sources of English Constitutional History*, New York: Harper and Row, 1937.

Important *studies and interpretations* selected from the work of 85 twentieth-century historians of England are anthologized in Cantor, N. F., and Werthman, M. S., *The English Tradition*, New York: Macmillan, 1967, 2 vols.

For an introduction to *literature as a background to English history*, see Daiches, David, *A Critical History of English Literature*, London: Secker and Warburg, 1960.

I. THE MIDDLE AGES (TO 1485)

A. GENERAL

Boase, T. S., ed., *Oxford History of English Art*, Vols. I–III. Oxford: Clarendon Press, 1949–50.

Cam, Helen M., *England before Elizabeth*. London: Hutchinson's University Library, 1950.

* Cantor, N. F., ed., *William Stubbs on the English Constitution*. New York: Thomas Y. Crowell, 1966.

Chrimes, S. B., *Introduction to the Administrative History of Medieval England*. Oxford: Blackwells, 1952.

Jolliffe, J. E. A., *Constitutional History of Medieval England: From the English Settlement to 1485*, 4th ed. Princeton: Van Nostrand, 1961.

Lyon, Bryce, *Constitutional and Legal History of Medieval England*. New York: Harper and Row, 1960.

* Pollock, F. and Maitland, F. W., *History of English Law before the Time of Edward I*, 2nd ed. Cambridge: University Press, 1899, 2 vols.

Sayles, G. O., *The Medieval Foundations of England*. Philadelphia: University of Pennsylvania Press, 1950.

Simpson, A. W. B., *An Introduction to the History of the Land Law*. Oxford: Blackwell, 1961.

* Stubbs, William, *Constitutional History of England*. Oxford: Clarendon Press, 1880, 3 vols.

Tout, T. F., *Chapters in the Administrative History of Medieval England*. New York: Longmans, Green, 1920–28, 6 vols.

B. ROMAN BRITAIN (TO 450 A.D.)

Collingwood, R. G., and Myres, J. N. L., *Roman Britain and the English Settlements*, 2nd ed. Oxford: Clarendon Press, 1937.

Richmond, I. A., *Roman Britain*, rev. ed. Baltimore: Penguin Books, 1962.

C. ANGLO-SAXON ERA (450–1066)

Blair, P. Hunter, *Introduction to Anglo-Saxon England*. Cambridge: University Press, 1956.

* Chadwick, H. M., *The Heroic Age*. Cambridge: University Press, 1912.

Darlington, R. R., "Ecclesiastical Reform in the Late Old English Period," *English Historical Review*, LI (1936), 385–429.

Hodgkin, R. H., *History of the Anglo-Saxons*, 3rd ed. New York: Oxford University Press, 1959, 2 vols.

Hollister, C. W., *Anglo-Saxon Military Institutions on the Eve of the Norman Conquest*. New York: Oxford University Press, 1962.

* Maitland, F. W., *Domesday Book and Beyond*. Cambridge: University Press, 1907.

Stenton, F. M. *Anglo-Saxon England*, 2nd ed. New York: Oxford University Press, 1947.

Whitelock, Dorothy, *The Beginnings of English Society*. Harmondsworth: Penguin Books, 1954.

D. NORMAN AND ANGEVIN ERA (1066–1216)

Caenegem, R. C. van, *Royal Writs in England from the Conquest to Glanville*. London: B. Quartich (Seldon Society Publications No. 77), 1959.

Cantor, N. F., *Church, Kingship, and Lay Investiture in England*. Princeton: Princeton University Press, 1958.

Douglas, D. C., *William the Conqueror: The Norman Impact upon England*. Berkeley: University of California Press, 1964.

Galbraith, V. H., *The Making of Domesday Book*. New York: Oxford University Press, 1961.

Holt, J. C., *The Northerners: A Study in the Reign of King John*. New York: Oxford University Press, 1961.

————, *Magna Carta*. Cambridge: University Press, 1965.

* Jolliffe, J. E. A., *Angevin Kingship*, 2nd ed. New York: Barnes and Noble, 1963.

* Knowles, M. D., *The Monastic Order in England, 943–1216*. Cambridge: University Press, 1940.

Lennard, Reginald, *Rural England, 1086–1135*. Oxford: Clarendon Press, 1959.

McKechnie, W. S., *Magna Carta: A Commentary on the Great Charter of King John*, 2nd ed. Glasgow: J. Maclehose, 1914.

Mitchell, Sidney K., *Taxation in Medieval England*. New Haven: Yale University Press, 1951.

Painter, Sidney, *Studies in the History of the English Feudal Barony*. Baltimore: Johns Hopkins Press, 1943.

* ————, *The Reign of King John*. Baltimore: Johns Hopkins Press, 1949.

Poole, A. L., *From Domesday Book to Magna Carta, 1087–1216*, 2nd ed. New York: Oxford University Press, 1955.

Prestwich, J. O., "War and Finance in the Anglo-Norman State," in *Transactions of the Royal Historical Society*, Series 5, IV (1954), pp. 19–44.

Sayles, G. O., and Richardson, H. G., *The Governance of Medieval England*. Edinburgh: Edinburgh University Press, 1963.

Southern, R. W., *St. Anselm and His Biographer*. Cambridge: University Press, 1963.

* Stenton, F. M., *The First Century of English Feudalism, 1066–1166*, 2nd ed. New York: Oxford University Press, 1961.

————, *William the Conqueror and the Rule of the Normans*. London: Putnam's, 1925.

Stephenson, Carl, *Borough and Town*. Cambridge, Mass: Mediaeval Academy of America, 1933.

Tait, James, *The Medieval English Borough*. Manchester: University Press, 1936.

E. THE THIRTEENTH CENTURY (1216–1307)

Cam, Helen M., *Liberties and Communities in Medieval England*. Cambridge: University Press, 1944.

Harrison, Frank L., *Music in Medieval Britain*. London: Routledge and Kegan Paul, 1958.

Homans, George C., *English Villagers of the Thirteenth Century*. Cambridge, Mass.: Harvard University Press, 1941.

Keen, Maurice, *The Outlaws of Medieval Legend*. Toronto: University of Toronto Press, 1961.

* Knowles, M. D., *The Religious Orders in England*, Vol. I. Cambridge: University Press, 1948.

Plucknett, T. F. T., *The Legislation of Edward I*. Oxford: Clarendon Press, 1949.

Postan, M. M., *Cambridge Economic History*, Vol. I, 2nd ed. Cambridge: University Press, 1966, I, 549–632.

Power, Eileen, *The Wool Trade in English Medieval History*. London: Oxford University Press, 1942.

Powicke, F. M., *The Thirteenth Century, 1216–1307*. New York: Oxford University Press, 1962.

* ———, *King Henry III and the Lord Edward: The Community of the Realm in the Thirteenth Century*. New York: Oxford University Press, 1947, 2 vols.

Wilkinson, B., *Constitutional History of Medieval England, 1216–1399*, Vol. I. New York: Barnes and Noble, 1948.

Willard, J. F., *Parliamentary Taxes on Personal Property, 1290–1334*. Cambridge, Mass.: Mediaeval Academy of America, 1934.

F. THE LATER MIDDLE AGES (1307–1485)

Bennett, H. S., *The Pastons and Their England*. Cambridge: University Press, 1922.

Bloomfield, Morton, *Piers Plowman as a Fourteenth-Century Apocalypse*. New Brunswick: Rutgers University Press, 1962.

Chrimes, S. B., *Lancastrians, Yorkists and Henry VII*. New York: St. Martin's Press, 1964.

———, *English Constitutional Ideas in the Fifteenth Century*. Cambridge: University Press, 1936.

Holmes, George, *The Later Middle Ages, 1272–1485*. Edinburgh: T. Nelson, 1962.

Jacob, E. F., *The Fifteenth Century*. New York: Oxford University Press, 1961.

Knowles, M. D., *The Religious Orders in England*, Vol. II. Cambridge: University Press, 1957.

Leff, Gordon, *Bradwardine and the Pelagians*. Cambridge: University Press, 1957.

McFarlane, K. B., *John Wycliffe and the Beginnings of English Non-Conformity*. London: English Universities Press, 1952.

McKisack, M., *The Fourteenth Century, 1307–1399*. New York: Oxford University Press, 1959.

Myers, A. R., *England in the Late Middle Ages*. London: Penguin Books, 1952.

Owst, G. R., *Literature and the Pulpit in Medieval England*, 2nd ed. New York: Barnes and Noble, 1961.

Pantin, W. A., *The English Church in the Fourteenth Century*. South Bend: University of Notre Dame Press, 1963.

Perroy, E., *The Hundred Years War*. New York: Oxford University Press, 1951.

Postan, M., "Some Economic Evidence of Declining Population in the Late Middle Ages," in *Economic History Review*, Ser. 2, II, No. 3 (1950), 221–246.

Roskell, J. S., *The Commons and Their Speakers in English Parliaments, 1376–1523*. New York: Barnes and Noble, 1964.

Steel, Anthony, *Richard II*. Cambridge: University Press, 1963.

Templeman, Geoffrey, "A History of Parliament to 1400 in the Light of Modern Research," *Birmingham Historical Journal*, I, No. 2 (1948), 203–230.

II. TUDOR ENGLAND (1485–1603)

A. GENERAL

* Elton, G. R., *England under the Tudors*. New York: Barnes and Noble, 1955.

———, *The Tudor Constitution: Documents and Commentary*. Cambridge: University Press, 1960.

Lockyer, Roger, *Tudor and Stuart Britain 1471–1714*. New York: St. Martin's Press, 1964.

Read, Conyers, *The Tudors*. New York: H. Holt, 1936.

B. 1485–1558

Baskerville, G., *The English Monks and the Suppression of the Monasteries*. New Haven: Yale University Press, 1937.

Baumer, F. L., *The Early Tudor Theory of Kingship*. New Haven: Yale University Press, 1940.

Chambers, R. W., *Thomas More*. London: J. Cape, 1935.

* Dickens, A. G., *The English Reformation*. New York: Schocken Books, 1964.

———, *Lollards and Protestants in the Diocese of York, 1509–1558*. New York: Oxford University Press, 1959.

———, *Thomas Cromwell and the English Reformation*. London: English Universities Press, 1959.

* Elton, G. R., *The Tudor Revolution in Government*. Cambridge: University Press, 1955.

———, *Star Chamber Stories*. London: Methuen, 1958.

Hughes, Philip, *The Reformation in England*. London: Hollis and Carter, 1954, 3 vols.

Knowles, M. D., *The Religious Orders in England*, Vol. III. Cambridge: University Press, 1959.

* Lewis, C. S., *English Literature in the Sixteenth Century*. Oxford: Clarendon Press, 1950.

Mattingly, G., *Catherine of Aragon*. New York: Viking, 1960.

Pickthorn, K. W. M., *Early Tudor Government: Henry VIII*. Cambridge: University Press, 1934, 2 vols.

* Pollard, A. F., *Henry VIII*. London: Longmans, Green, 1913.

* ———, *Wolsey*. London: Longmans, Green, 1929.

———, *Thomas Cranmer and the English Reformation*. New York: G. P. Putnam's, 1906.

Reid, Rachel, *The King's Council in the North*. London: Longmans, Green, 1921.

Richardson, W. C., *Tudor Chamber Administration, 1485–1547*. Baton Rouge: Louisiana State University Press, 1952.

* Tawney, R. H., *The Agrarian Problem in the Sixteenth Century*. New York: Longmans, Green, 1912.

C. REIGN OF ELIZABETH I (1558–1603)

Black, J. B., *The Reign of Elizabeth, 1558–1603*, 2nd ed. New York: Oxford University Press, 1959.

Burrell, S. A., "Calvinism, Capitalism and the Middle Classes," *Journal of Modern History*, XXXII (1960), 129–141.

Fisher, F. J., "Commercial Trends and Policy in Sixteenth-Century England," in *Economic History Review*, X, No. 1, (1940), 107–117.

* Froude, J. A., *History of England from the Fall of Wolsey to the Defeat of the Spanish Armada*. New York: Scribner's, 1872, 12 vols.

Graham, G. S., *The Empire of the North Atlantic*. Toronto: University of Toronto Press, 1950.

Haller, William, *Foxe's Book of Martyrs and the Elect Nation*. London: J. Cape, 1963.

Hexter, J. H., *Reappraisals in History*. Evanston: Northwestern University Press, 1961.

Hurstfield, J., *The Queen's Wards*. Cambridge, Mass.: Harvard University Press, 1958.

———, *Elizabeth I and the Unity of England*. London: English Universities Press, 1960.

Knappen, M. M., *Tudor Puritanism*. Gloucester, Mass.: P. Smith, 1963.

* Mattingly, G., *The Armada*. Boston: Houghton Mifflin, 1959.

* Neale, J. E., *The Elizabethan House of Commons*. New Haven: Yale University Press, 1961.

————, *Elizabeth I and Her Parliaments.* New York: St. Martin's Press, 1953–57, 2 vols.

————, *Queen Elizabeth I.* New York: St. Martin's Press, 1959.

————, *Essays in Elizabethan History.* New York: St. Martin's Press, 1959.

Nef, John U., *The Rise of the British Coal Industry.* London: Routledge, 1932.

Pearson, A. F. S., *Thomas Cartwright and Elizabethan Puritanism.* Cambridge: University Press, 1925.

Read, Conyers, *Lord Burghley and Queen Elizabeth.* New York: Knopf, 1960.

————, *Mr. Secretary Walsingham and the Policy of Queen Elizabeth.* Cambridge, Mass.: Harvard University Press, 1925.

————, *Mr. Secretary Cecil and Queen Elizabeth.* New York, Knopf, 1955.

Rowse, A. L., *The England of Elizabeth.* New York: Macmillan, 1950.

————, *The Expansion of Elizabethan England.* New York: St. Martin's Press, 1955.

Stone, Lawrence, *The Crisis of the Aristocracy, 1558–1641.* Oxford: Clarendon Press, 1965.

Tillyard, E. M. W., *The Elizabethan World Picture.* New York: Macmillan, 1961.

III. THE STRUGGLE FOR LIBERTY (1603–1660)

A. GENERAL

Davies, Godfrey, *The Early Stuarts, 1603–1660,* 2nd ed. Oxford: Clarendon Press, 1959.

* Gardiner, S. R., *History of England from the Accession of James I to the Outbreak of the Civil War.* New York: Longmans, Green, 1896–1900, 10 vols.

Hill, Christopher, *The Century of Revolution, 1603–1714.* Edinburgh: T. Nelson, 1961.

Kenyon, J. P., *The Stuarts.* London: Batsford, 1958.

* Trevelyan, G. M., *England under the Stuarts: 1603–1642.* London: Methuen, 1904.

B. EARLY STUART ERA (1603–1640)

Akrigg, G. P. W., *Jacobean Pageant.* Cambridge, Mass.: Harvard University Press, 1962.

Ashton, Robert, *The Crown and the Money Market.* Oxford: Clarendon Press, 1960.

Aylmer, G., *The King's Servants: The Civil Service of Charles I.* New York: Columbia University Press, 1961.

* Haller, William, *The Rise of Puritanism.* New York: Columbia University Press, 1938.

Hill, Christopher, *The Economic Problems of the Church: From Archbishop Whitgift to the Long Parliament*. Oxford: Clarendon Press, 1963.

———, *Intellectual Origins of the Puritan Revolution*. Oxford: Clarendon Press, 1964.

Judson, Margaret, *The Crisis of the Constitution*. New Brunswick: Rutgers University Press, 1949.

Notestein, Wallace, *The Winning of the Initiative by the House of Commons*. London: British Academy, 1926.

Pocock, J. G. A., *The Ancient Constitution and the Feudal Law*. Cambridge: University Press, 1957.

Simpson, Alan, *The Wealth of the Gentry*. Chicago: University of Chicago Press, 1961.

Supple, B. E., *Commercial Crisis and Change in England, 1600–1642*. Cambridge: University Press, 1959.

Tawney, R. H., *Business and Politics under James I*. Cambridge: University Press, 1958.

* ———, *Religion and the Rise of Capitalism*. New York: Harcourt Brace and Company, 1926.

Trevor-Roper, H. R., *The Gentry, 1540–1640*. London: Cambridge University Press, 1953.

Walzer, Michael, *The Revolution of the Saints*. Cambridge, Mass.: Harvard University Press, 1965.

Wedgwood, C. V., *The King's Peace*. New York: Macmillan, 1955.

Willson, D. H., *King James VI and I*. London: Cape, 1956.

C. THE CIVIL WAR AND COMMONWEALTH

Abbott, W. C., *Writings and Speeches of Oliver Cromwell*. Cambridge, Mass.: Harvard University Press, 1937–47, 4 vols.

Ashley, Maurice, *The Greatness of Oliver Cromwell*. New York: Macmillan, 1957.

Brailsford, H. N., *The Levellers and the English Revolution*. Stanford: Stanford University Press, 1961.

Brunton, D. and Pennington, D. H., *Members of the Long Parliament*. London: G. Allen and Unwin, 1954.

* Clarendon, Lord (Edward Hyde, First Earl of Clarendon), *History of the Rebellion and Civil Wars in England*. Oxford: Clarendon Press, 1888, 6 vols.

Firth, C. H., *Oliver Cromwell and the Rule of the Puritans in England*. New York: Oxford University Press, 1958.

* Gardiner, S. R., *Oliver Cromwell*. New York: Longmans, Green, 1925.

Haller, William, *Liberty and Reformation in the Puritan Revolution*. New York: Columbia University Press, 1955.

Hexter, J. H., *The Reign of King Pym*. Cambridge, Mass.: Harvard University Press, 1941.

Solt, Leo F., *Saints in Arms.* Stanford: Stanford University Press, 1959.

Wedgwood, C. V., *The King's War.* New York: Macmillan, 1959.

———, *A Coffin for King Charles.* New York: Macmillan, 1957.

Woodhouse, A. S. P., *Puritanism and Liberty.* Chicago: University of Chicago Press, 1951.

Yule G., *The Independents in the English Civil War.* Cambridge: University Press, 1950.

IV. THE ARISTOCRATIC CENTURY (1660–1760)

A. GENERAL

Clark, G. N., *Later Stuarts, 1660–1714,* 2nd ed. Oxford: Clarendon Press, 1955.

Marshall, Dorothy, *English People in the Eighteenth Century.* London: Longmans, Green, 1956.

Plumb, J. H., *England in the Eighteenth Century.* Harmondsworth: Penguin Books, 1950.

B. THE LATER STUARTS (1660–1714)

* Carswell, John, *The Old Cause: Three Biographical Studies in Whiggism.* London: Cresset Press, 1954.

Clapham, J. H., *The Bank of England, A History.* Cambridge: University Press, 1945, 2 vols.

Hall, A. R., *The Scientific Revolution.* Boston: Beacon Press, 1956.

Kemp, Betty, *King and Commons, 1660–1832.* New York: St. Martin's Press, 1957.

Laslett, Peter, *The World We Have Lost.* New York: Scribner's, 1965.

Macpherson, C. B., *Theory of Possessive Individualism: Hobbes to Locke.* Oxford: Clarendon Press, 1964.

Ogg, David, *England in the Reign of Charles II.* Oxford: Clarendon Press, 1956, 2 vols.

———, *England in the Reigns of James II and William III.* Oxford: Clarendon Press, 1963.

Pinkham, Lucile, *William III and the Respectable Revolution.* Cambridge, Mass.: Harvard University Press, 1954.

Trevelyan, G. M., *The English Revolution, 1688–1869.* New York: Oxford University Press, 1938.

———, *England under Queen Anne.* London: Longmans, Green, 1930–34, 3 vols.

Walcott, Robert, *English Politics in the Early Eighteenth Century.* Cambridge, Mass.: Harvard University Press, 1956.

Wilson, Charles, *England's Apprenticeship.* New York: St. Martin's Press, 1965.

C. THE WHIG SUPREMACY (1714–1760)

Ashton, T. S., *Economic History of England: The Eighteenth Century*. New York: Barnes and Noble, 1955.

Beckett, J. C., *The Making of Modern Ireland, 1603–1923*. London: Faber and Faber, 1966.

Best, G. F. A., *Temporal Pillars*. Cambridge: University Press, 1964.

Carswell, John, *The South Sea Bubble*. Stanford: Stanford University Press, 1960.

Humphreys, A. R., *The Augustan World*. London: Methuen, 1954.

Mackintosh, John P., *The British Cabinet*. Toronto: University of Toronto Press, 1962.

* Namier, L. B., *The Structure of Politics at the Accession of George III*, 2nd ed. New York: St. Martin's Press, 1957.

* ———, *Personalities and Powers*. London: H. Hamilton, 1955.

Owen, J. B., *The Rise of the Pelhams*. London: Methuen, 1957.

Pares, Richard, *A West-India Fortune*. London: Longmans, Green, 1950.

* Plumb, J. H., *Sir Robert Walpole*. London: Cresset Press, 1956–60, 2 vols.

Robbins, Caroline, *The Eighteenth-Century Commonwealthman*. Cambridge, Mass.: Harvard University Press, 1959.

Sutherland, L. S., *The East India Company in Eighteenth-Century Politics*. Oxford: Clarendon Press, 1952.

Sykes, Norman, *Church and State in Eighteenth-Century England*. Cambridge: University Press, 1934.

———, *From Sheldon to Secker*. Cambridge: University Press, 1959.

INDEX

Great Seal of Edward the Confessor (1042–1066)

Seal of Edward I (1272–1307)